Fodor's

ARGENTINA

6th Edition

Fodor's Travel Publications New York, Toronto, London, Sydney, Auckland
www.fodors.com

Be a Fodor's Correspondent

Our latest guidebook to Argentina—now in full color—owes its success to travelers like you. Throughout, you'll find photographs submitted by members of Fodors.com to our "Show Us Your ... Argentina" photo contest. Facing this page is one of our favorites, taken by contest runner-up Sara Nixon. The ornate tombs and mausoleums in La Recoleta Cemetery in Buenos Aires were "endlessly fascinating," she says; "I found myself returnnig to this part of town over and over again." The contest's grand-prize winner, Andrew Mirhej, captured a different kind of moody stillness in his photograph of a gaucho on horseback near Bariloche; you can see it on the opening pages of Chapter 1.

We are especially proud of this color edition. No other guide to Argentina is as up to date or has as much practical planning information, along with hundreds of color photographs and illustrated maps. We've also included "Word of Mouth" quotes from travelers who shared their experiences with others on our forums. If you're inspired and can plan a better trip because of this guide, we've done our job.

We invite you to join the travel conversation: your opinion matters to us and to your fellow travelers. Come to Fodors.com to plan your trip, share an experience, ask a question, submit a photograph, post a review, or write a trip report. Tell our editors about your trip. They want to know what went well and how we can make this guide even better. Share your opinions at our feedback center at fodors.com/feedback, or email us at editors@fodors.com with the subject line "Argentina Editor." You might find your comments published in a future Fodor's guide. We look forward to hearing from you.

¡Buen viaje!

Tim Jarrell, Publisher

FODOR'S ARGENTINA

Editors: Kelly Kealy (lead editor), Laura Kidder, Erica Duecy, Carolyn Galgano

Editorial Contributor: Astrid DeRidder

Writers: Eddy Ancinas, Brian Byrnes, Steve Dunn, Andy Footner, Nicholas Gill, Rick Hind, Victoria Patience, Tim Patterson, Margaret Shook, Jack Trout

Production Editor: Carrie Parker, Astrid DeRidder
Maps & Illustrations: David Lindroth; Mark Stroud and Henry Colomb, Moon Street Cartography, *cartographers;* Bob Blake, Rebecca Baer, *map editors;* William Wu, *information graphics*
Design: Fabrizio La Rocca, *creative director*; Guido Caroti, Siobhan O'Hare, *art directors*; Nora Rosansky, Tina Malaney, Chie Ushio, Ann McBride, Jessica Walsh, *designers*; Melanie Marin, *senior picture editor*
Cover Photo: (Tango lesson, Buenos Aires): Javier Pierini/Getty Images
Production Manager: Amanda Bullock

COPYRIGHT

6th Edition

ISBN 978-1-4000-0433-1

ISSN 1526–1360

SPECIAL SALES

This book is available at special discounts for bulk purchases for sales promotions or premiums. Special editions, including personalized covers, excerpts of existing books, and corporate imprints, can be created in large quantities for special needs. For more information, write to Special Markets/Premium Sales, 1745 Broadway, MD 6-2, New York, New York 10019, or e-mail specialmarkets@randomhouse.com.

AN IMPORTANT TIP & AN INVITATION

Although all prices, opening times, and other details in this book are based on information supplied to us at press time, changes occur all the time in the travel world, and Fodor's cannot accept responsibility for facts that become outdated or for inadvertent errors or omissions. So **always confirm information when it matters,** especially if you're making a detour to visit a specific place. Your experiences—positive and negative—matter to us. If we have missed or misstated something, **please write to us.** We follow up on all suggestions. Contact the Argentina editor at editors@fodors.com or c/o Fodor's at 1745 Broadway, New York, NY 10019.

PRINTED IN CHINA

10 9 8 7 6 5 4 3 2 1

CONTENTS

Fodor's Features

MAPS

ABOUT THIS BOOK

Our Ratings

Sometimes you find terrific travel experiences and sometimes they just find you. But usually the burden is on you to select the right combination of experiences. That's where our ratings come in.

As travelers we've all discovered a place so wonderful that its worthiness is obvious. And sometimes that place is so unique that superlatives don't do it justice: you just have to be there to know. These sights, properties, and experiences get our highest rating, **Fodor's Choice**, indicated by orange stars throughout this book.

Black stars highlight sights and properties we deem **Highly Recommended**, places that our writers, editors, and readers praise again and again for consistency and excellence.

By default, there's another category: any place we include in this book is by definition worth your time, unless we say otherwise. And we will.

Disagree with any of our choices? Care to nominate a place or suggest that we rate one more highly? Visit our feedback center at www.fodors.com/feedback.

Budget Well

Hotel and restaurant price categories from ¢ to $$$$ are defined in the opening pages of each chapter. For attractions, we always give standard adult admission fees; reductions are usually available for children, students, and senior citizens. Want to pay with plastic? **AE, DC, MC, V** following restaurant and hotel listings indicate whether American Express, Diners Club, MasterCard, and Visa are accepted.

Restaurants

Unless we state otherwise, restaurants are open for lunch and dinner daily. We mention dress only when there's a specific requirement and reservations only when they're essential or not accepted—it's always best to book ahead.

Hotels

Hotels have private bath, phone, TV, and air-conditioning and operate on the European Plan (aka EP, meaning without meals), unless we specify that they use the Continental Plan (CP, with a continental breakfast), Breakfast Plan (BP, with a full breakfast), or Modified American Plan (MAP, with breakfast and dinner), or are all-inclusive (AI, including all meals and most activities). We always list facilities but not whether you'll be charged an extra fee to use them, so when pricing accommodations, find out what's included.

Listings

- ★ Fodor's Choice
- ★ Highly recommended
- ✉ Physical address
- ✣ Directions or Map coordinates
- ✆ Mailing address
- ☎ Telephone
- 🖷 Fax
- 🌐 On the Web
- ✉ E-mail
- 🎟 Admission fee
- ⏲ Open/closed times
- Ⓜ Metro stations
- ▭ Credit cards

Hotels & Restaurants

- 🏨 Hotel
- 🛏 Number of rooms
- ♨ Facilities
- 🍽 Meal plans
- ✕ Restaurant
- ✍ Reservations
- 👔 Dress code
- 🚬 Smoking
- 🍷 BYOB

Outdoors

- ⛳ Golf
- ⛺ Camping

Other

- ☺ Family-friendly
- ⇨ See also
- ✉ Branch address
- ☞ Take note

Experience Argentina

WHAT'S WHERE

1 Buenos Aires. Elegant boulevards and quirky cobbled streets give the capital a European air, but the chaotic traffic and protest marches are distinctly Latin American. The home of the tango is *the* place to learn the dance or take in a show. Also visit world-class boutiques, restaurants, and museums.

2 Side Trips from Buenos Aires. Vastly varied scenery lies an hour's bus, plane, or ferry ride from Buenos Aires. Traditional estancias (ranches) dot the pampas near San Antonio de Areco, waterways replace roads in the semitropical Tigre delta, and windswept dunes line the Atlantic coast. Gorgeous colonial buildings are the pull at Colonia de Sacramento, Uruguay, but nature built the mind-blowing Iguazú Falls.

3 Córdoba and Environs. The nation's geographical heart is rich in history, and Córdoba city unites colonial buildings with great food and nightlife. To the north find rugged red sandstone formations, a pre-Colombian art site, Jesuit estancias (ranches), and Argentina's best golf courses. German and Austrian immigrant heritage characterizes the food and architecture of the southern mountain towns.

4 The Northwest. Lofty mountain passes, deep red gorges, peaceful valleys, subtropical jungles, Inca ruins, and the arid landscape of the Puna: the Northwest's backdrop changes constantly. Rich Andean traditions live on in the region's unique food and folk music, beautiful Salta city has a distinctly colonial feel, and wines from nearby high-altitude vineyards are the latest thing.

5 The Wine Regions. Argentina's vintners use desert sun, mountain snow, and extreme altitudes to craft distinctive wines—especially Malbec, the area's signature red. Mendoza's wineries enjoy the greatest reputation, those in the Valle de Uco grow their grapes incredibly high up, and family-owned wineries in tiny San Rafael focus on quality. The Pan-American Highway passes through Mendoza, heading west over spectacular Uspallata Pass to Chile. Along the way are hot springs, Inca ruins, and incomparable views of Aconcagua Mountain.

6 The Lake District. Alpine scenery on a gigantic scale is one way to describe this region's pine forests and snowcapped peaks, many protected in national parks. There are breathtaking views of its eponymous lakes on the Camino de los Siete Lagos (Seven Lakes Route), which connects the posh resort towns of San Martín de los Andes and Villa La Angostura. Like the region's hub, Bariloche, these are near some of Argentina's best ski spots. In summer, climb Lanín Volcano, hike or bike the Circuito Grande trail, or just indulge in the freshly caught trout, barbecued lamb, handmade chocolate, and artisanal beer the Lake District is also famous for.

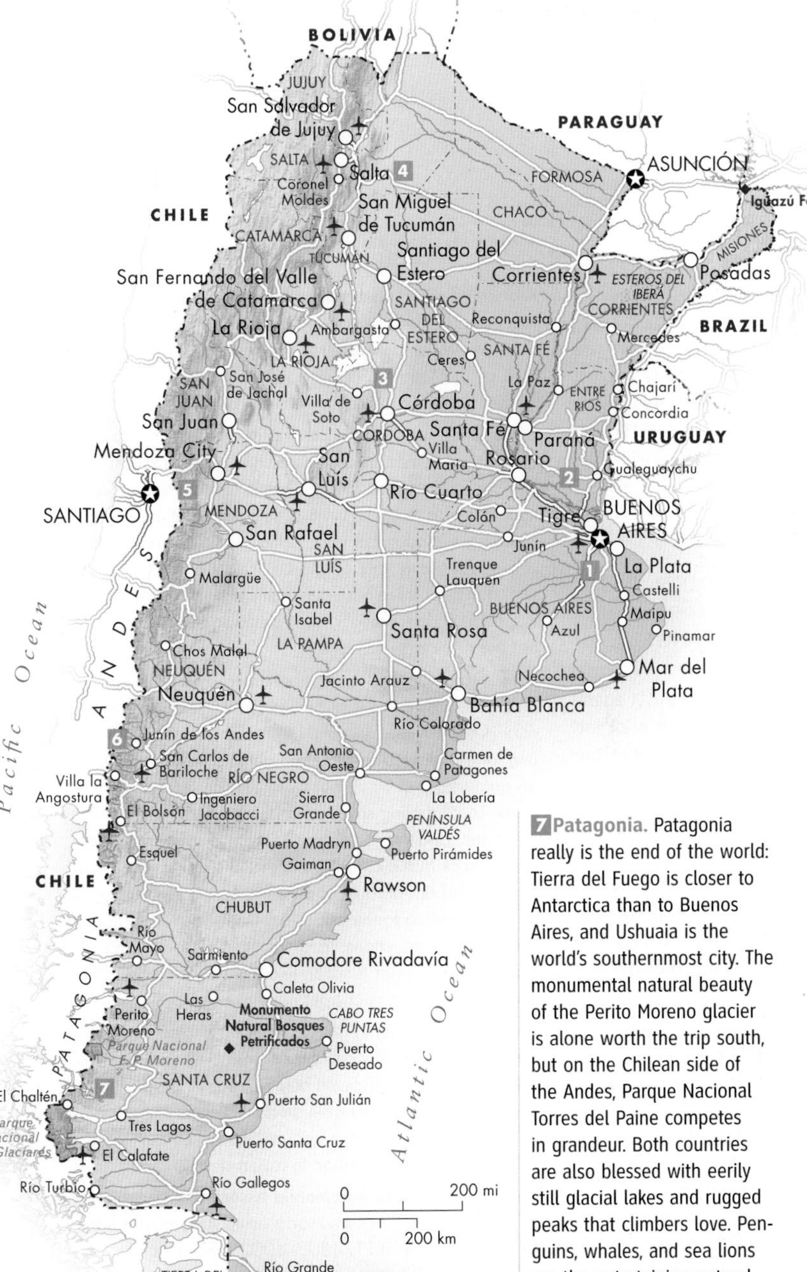

7 Patagonia. Patagonia really is the end of the world: Tierra del Fuego is closer to Antarctica than to Buenos Aires, and Ushuaia is the world's southernmost city. The monumental natural beauty of the Perito Moreno glacier is alone worth the trip south, but on the Chilean side of the Andes, Parque Nacional Torres del Paine competes in grandeur. Both countries are also blessed with eerily still glacial lakes and rugged peaks that climbers love. Penguins, whales, and sea lions are the entertaining natural attractions on the windswept, wave-battered Atlantic coast.

ARGENTINA PLANNER

Visitor Info

Travel advice, the lowdown on learning tango, tips on buying property, winery recommendations—you'll probably find it all on the government-run **Argentina** (🌐 *www.argentina.ar*) Web site. The umbrella organization for all regional tourist offices is the Secretaría de Turismo (*Secretariat of Tourism* 🌐 *www.turismo.gov.ar*).

Travel Agents

Argentina-based travel agents can help you pack a lot into a short trip. The 24-hour support many offer is particularly good when internal flights are delayed, a common occurrence. Argentina Escapes, Buenos Aires Tours, and Wow! Argentina are reliable local agencies. Limitless Argentina is a U.S.-based company with offices in Argentina.

Argentina Travel Agents
Argentina Escapes (☏ *11/5032–2938* 🌐 *www.argentinaescapes.com*). **Buenos Aires Tours** (🌐 *www.buenosaires-tours.com.ar*). **Limitless Argentina** (☏ *202/536–5812 in U.S., 11/4776–8870 in Buenos Aires* 🌐 *www.limitlessargentina.com*). **Wow! Argentina** (☏ *11/5239–3019* 🌐 *www.wowargentina.com*).

Driving

Argentina is a fantastic place for a road trip: the vast distances and unique windswept scenery are some of the most drive-worthy on the planet. If you're heading to the Lake District, or Mendoza or Córdoba province, for example, try to spend at least a little time driving around.

If you don't fancy dealing with driving yourself, you can also hire a *remis con chofer* (car and driver) in most cities. You can arrange this through hotels or local taxi companies. For trips to and from a specific destination, you pay a pre-agreed-upon flat fare. Otherwise most companies charge an hourly rate of around 50–70 pesos (sometimes with a two- or three-hour minimum) to have a driver at your disposal all day. Rental companies also offer this service, but are more expensive.

Some major highways are maintained by private companies, others by provincial governments; surface conditions vary greatly. Many national highways (*rutas*) have only one lane in each direction; you get two or three lanes on an *autopista* (freeway), but these only connect some major cities. Local driving styles range from erratic to downright psychotic, and the road mortality rate is shockingly high. Heavy truck traffic can also make some routes slow, frustrating, and dangerous for passing. Don't count on good signage leading to the estancias. Do as the locals do: pull over and ask directions. In towns, intersections without traffic lights or signs function like four-way stops: a car approaching from your right has right of way.

Your rental car agency should have an emergency help lin; the best is usually through the Automóvil Club Argentina (ACA), which can dispatch help to nearly anywhere in the country within a reasonable amount of time. In the event of an accident, stay by your car until the police come. Head to the nearest police station to report a stolen car.

Contacts **American Automobile Association** (*AAA* ☏ *800/564–6222* 🌐 *www.aaa.com*). **Automóvil Club Argentino** (*ACA* ☏ *11/4808–4000,* emergencies *800/777–2894* 🌐 *www.aca.org.ar*). **Police** (☏ *101*).

Information **Dirección Nacional de Vialidad** (☏ *11/4343–8520* 🌐 *www.vialidad.gov.ar*).

Safety

Argentina is safer than many Latin American countries. However, recent political and economic instability has caused an increase in street crime—mainly pickpocketing, bag-snatching, and occasionally mugging—especially in Buenos Aires. Taking a few precautions when traveling in the region is usually enough to avoid being a target.

Crime. Walk with purpose; if you don't look like a target, you'll likely be left alone. Avoid wearing jewelry, even nice-looking immitation items. Keep a grip on your purse or bag, and keep it in your lap if you're sitting (never leave it hanging on the back of a chair or on the floor). Make use of your hotel safe, consider carrying a dummy wallet, or keep your valuables in several different places on your person. Keep enough on hand to have something to hand over if you do get mugged. Nearly all physical attacks on tourists are the direct result of their resisting would-be pickpockets or muggers; comply with demands, hand over your stuff, and try to get the situation over with as quickly as possible—then let your travel insurance take care of it.

Piropos. Women can expect pointed looks, the occasional *piropo* (a flirtatious remark, usually alluding to some physical aspect), and some advances. These catcalls rarely escalate into actual physical harassment—the best reaction is to make like local girls and ignore it; reply only if you're really confident with Spanish curse words.

Protests. Argentines like to speak their minds, and there has been a huge increase in strikes and street protests since the economic crisis of 2001–02. Protesters frequently block streets in downtown Buenos Aires, causing traffic jams. Trigger-happy local police have historically proved themselves more of a worry than the demonstrators; though protests are usually peaceful, exercise caution.

Scams. Beware scams such as a kindly passer-by offering to help you clean the mustard/ketchup/cream that has somehow appeared on your clothes: while your attention is occupied, an accomplice picks your pocket or snatches your bag. When taking a taxi, hailing one during the day in big cities is usually safe, but be sure the driver turns the meter on. Have a good idea of where you're headed to avoid being taken on a circuitous route. Some salespeople, especially street vendors, take advantage of confused tourists by charging dollars for goods that are actually priced in pesos. If you're in doubt, ask.

Advisories and Other Information **Transportation Security Administration** (*TSA* 🌐 *www.tsa.gov*). **U.S. Department of State** (🌐 *www.travel.state.gov*).

When to Go

Just remember: when it's summer in the Northern Hemisphere, it's winter in Argentina.

Buenos Aires is least crowded in January and February, when locals beat the heat at resorts along the Atlantic and in Córdoba Province. City sightseeing is most pleasant during the temperate spring and fall. Try to visit Iguazú Falls in August through October, when temperatures are lower, the falls are fuller, and the spring coloring is at its brightest.

If you're heading to the Lake District or Patagonia, visit during the shoulder seasons of December and March. Southern seas batter the Patagonian coast year-round, and winds there often reach gale force. In Tierra del Fuego, fragments of glaciers cave into lakes with a rumble throughout the thaw from October to the end of April.

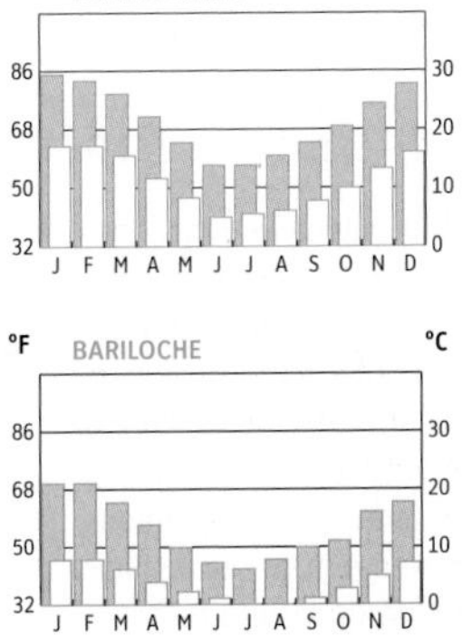

ARGENTINA TODAY

They say the only thing certain in life is change, and no one knows it like Argentinians do. A decade of political uncertainty and financial instability has left the country's inhabitants wondering what's next. For many, times are still very tough. But from the ashes of economic burnout, a vibrant, global Argentina is rising. The uncertainty can be both worrying and exciting.

Today's Argentina . . .

. . . is full of free speech. Forget writing to your representatives when you've got a gripe with the system—in Argentina, you take to the streets. Both city avenues and highways are regularly blocked by drum- and banner-toting crowds chanting in a tuneful unison that can come only from practice. Sometimes they're protesting low salaries or police repression; other times they're marking an event. It's not all on the streets, though. In 2009, independent journalists and media-watchers rejoiced when the congress and senate replaced the country's anachronistic TV and radio licensing laws, a legacy from the last military dictatorship. Previously, one media group controlled the majority of local TV and radio licenses, while the new law benefits educational, community, and non-profit programming.

. . . is going global. Locals can't get over the amount of out-of-towners flooding the country. And more and more of the 2.3 million annual foreign visitors are staying on. Tango enthusiasts are snapping up old apartments in Buenos Aires, wine aficionados are investing in vineyards, outdoors enthusiasts are buying chunks of Patagonia. The number of exchange students at universities in Buenos Aires and Córdoba has soared, and there's a thriving expat scene complete with how-to blogs and magazines. Comparatively low property prices and a favorable exchange rate mean many of these European and North American newcomers can afford not to work: would-be novelists, painters, musicians—and former investment bankers—abound. Quick to see the benefits of visitor dollars, the government is eager to improve Argentina's image. Popular tourist sites are getting the spit-and-polish treatment and tourist-friendly attitudes are being keenly promoted.

. . . is coming to terms with its past. The military juntas behind Argentina's 1976–83 dictatorship called their reign the National Reorganization Process, a grim euphemism for six years of state-run terror during which 30,000 people "disappeared" and countless more were brutally

WHAT'S HOT IN ARGENTINA NOW

- El Bicentenario. Argentineans have always been patriotic, but flags are flying higher and brighter than usual as the country's 2010 bicentenary of its independence approaches. Cultural events, competitions, and even a major new cultural center in Buenos Aires are being planned to mark the occasion.

- Electric music. Listening to *cumbia* (a local tropical-style rhythm) was once as trashy as it got. But now Argentina's hottest club nights spin around electronic cumbia remixes. Some call it "electrotropical" or "electrocumbia," others "cumbiatrónica"; whatever its name, its trademark "shh-chicki-shh" beat has clubbers hooked. Itinerant Club Night Zizek (🌐 *www.zzkclub.com*) is *the* place to go: it even toured the United States in early 2008.

tortured. Justice has been slow in coming: although some military officials were brought to trial in the 1980s, President Carlos Menem later pardoned them all. But after years of tireless campaigning by victims and human rights groups such as the Madres de Plaza de Mayo (Mothers of Plaza de Mayo), these pardons have been revoked and military officers are slowly going on trial for crimes against humanity. Former clandestine detention centers have been transformed into cultural centers, and the anniversary of the start of the dictatorship, March 24, has been made a public day of remembrance marked by thousands each year.

Another organization, Abuelas de Plaza de Mayo (Grandmothers of Plaza de Mayo), continues to search for their missing grandchildren, stolen at birth from kidnapped mothers and raised by the very people who killed the children's parents. The creation of a genetic information bank has meant that 97 children—now in their twenties and thirties—have been "found." It's not all progress, however. In 2006 Jorge Julio López, the 77-year-old key witness in the trial of a high-ranking former police officer, disappeared before he could testify and has never been found.

. . . is ever more divided. At first glance, Argentina seems to be on its feet. Largely thanks to soy and beef exports, the economy is growing; and unemployment and poverty levels have decreased. But it's a slow process and many people still live below the poverty line, and despite all those food exports, hunger remains a cruel reality in much of the country. The fact that Argentina had a middle class once made it unusual in Latin America. Today, however, Argentine society is beginning to polarize into very wealthy and very poor classes, like the rest of the region. The contrasting housing along the access roads to big cities is testimony to this widening gap: alongside exclusive country clubs and gated communities sit growing shantytowns.

■ Being out. Being out has never been this in. "Friendly" is the latest Spanish buzzword: Argentina is keen to become Latin America's gay capital. It's not just bars and clubs, either: we're talking travel agencies, tango schools, *milongas* (tango dance halls), and now Axel, a swish gay hotel in Buenos Aires. The local community has plenty to cheer about, too: same-sex civil unions have been legal in the capital since 2003, and the annual Marcha del Orgullo Gay (Gay Pride March) attracts tens of thousands of revelers each November.

■ Food Culture. Time was when all Argentine diners cared about was how big their steak was. But serious foodie culture has definitely arrived, and locals are beginning to value quality over quantity. A new generation of celebrity chefs is busy evangelizing enthralled TV audiences, and former table-wine drinkers now vigorously debate grape varietals and name-drop boutique vineyards.

ARGENTINA TOP ATTRACTIONS

A

B

C

D

Iguazú Falls

(A) On the Argentine–Brazilian border, some 1.7 million gallons of the Iguazú River plummet over a precipice each second, forming a 275-meter-wide (900-foot-wide) wall of water. Trails, metal catwalks, and Zodiacs all allow for spray-soaked close-ups.

La Quebrada de Humahuaca

(B) Dramatically colored, craggy rock faces overlook the traditional villages that nestle in this gorge. The most stunning section is the Camino de los Siete Colores (Seven Colors Trail), with its red, ocher, and mossy-green rock layers. Music pouring from area *peñas* (folk bars) is the perfect sound track.

Laguna de los Pozuelos

Thousands of Andean flamingos form a salmon-pink stain across this remote lake near Argentina's border with Bolivia. The harsh beauty of the Puna region's gritty slopes and scrubby high-altitude plains offsets the birds' extravagant plumage perfectly.

Mendoza Wineries

(C) Malbec is the grape that has made Argentina's name in the wine world, and Mendoza is where they do it best. But getting you tipsy isn't all the 20 or so area wineries do: informative tours, atmospheric accommodation, and top-notch dining are also on offer, all within spitting distance of the Andes.

Plaza de Mayo and San Telmo, Buenos Aires

(D) Revolution, mass protests, Evita's inflammatory speeches: never a dull moment for the square that is the historical heart of Buenos Aires. The past also lives on in the cobbled streets of the San Telmo neighborhood. Its elegant 19th-century mansions once housed brothels, tenements, and tango dens. The tango

remains, but these days it's antiques and hip designers drawing crowds.

Perito Moreno Glacier

(E) A translucent blue-green cliff of frosty majesty forms where this glacier reaches Lago Argentino in southern Patagonia. Blocks splinter off the ice face all the time, but they're ice cubes compared to the tons that come crashing down roughly every four years as a result of pressure building from behind.

Camino de los Siete Lagos (Seven Lakes Route)

(F) Between San Martín de los Andes and Villa La Angostura, the partly paved RN234 winds alongside seven beautiful bodies of water fringed by pine forests and overlooked by the Andes. You can do the trip in a day, or stay on at inns or campsites for the gorgeous sunsets and sunrises.

Península Valdés

(G) Graceful *ballenas francas* (southern right whales) are literally the largest attraction at this Atlantic coast nature reserve. They come for mating season, June through November. Sea lions, elephant seals, and vast penguin colonies keep the beach busy the rest of the year.

Salta

(H) Stately colonial buildings, hopping nightlife, and fabulous local food and wine make the city of Salta more than just a gateway to the Northwest. When you do decide to get out of town, hiking, rafting, and tours to wineries and salt lakes are all options.

QUINTESSENTIAL ARGENTINA

Beef

Argentina is cow country. The beef is so good that some Argentineans see little reason to eat anything else, though chicken and Patagonian lamb are tasty alternatives, as is *chivito* (kid). *Carne asado* (roasted cuts of beef) might be done on a grill over hot coals (*a la parrilla*), baked in an oven (*al horno*), or slowly roasted on a metal spit stuck in the ground aslant on a bed of hot coals (*al asador*). A family *asado* (barbecue), where men show off their barbecuing skills, is the classic way to spend a Sunday afternoon. The nearest restaurant experience is to order a *parrillada mixta* (mixed grill). Expect different cuts of beef—both on and off the bone and usually roasted in huge pieces—as well as chorizo sausage, roasted sweetbreads, and less bloodthirsty optional accompaniments like provolone cheese and bell peppers.

Vino

Given their high consumption of beef, Argentineans understandably drink a lot of *vino tinto* (red wine). Although much of the wine consumed here is nondescript table wine, in recent years the industry has boomed and Argentine vineyards (especially so-called boutique vineyards) are firmly on the map. The most popular grapes are Cabernet Sauvignon, Malbec, and Shiraz (known locally as Syrah), but Tempranillo, Tannat, and Merlot are also on the rise. If you prefer *vino blanco* (white wine), try a sauvignon blanc or chardonnay from Mendoza, or lesser-known wineries from farther north, such as La Rioja and Salta, where the Torrontés grape thrives. This varietal produces a dry white with a lovely floral bouquet.

It's easy to partake of Argentina's daily rituals. Among other things, you can enjoy some fancy footwork—on the field or in the ballroom—or savor the rich flavors (and conversation) of a leisurely meal.

Fútbol

In a country where Diego Maradona is revered as a god, nothing unites and divides Argentineans as much as their passion for soccer. Local teams are the subject of fiery dispute and serious rivalry; the national team brings the country together for displays of unrivaled passion and suicidal despair, especially during the World Cup. Argentina's blue-and-white-stripe jerseys have flashed across TV screens since it won the 1978 and 1986 World Cups, and nothing can lift—or crush—the spirits of the nation like the result of a soccer match. Every weekend, stadiums across the country fill to bursting with screaming fans toting drums and banners and filling the air with confetti and flares in their team's colors, which—together with the play on the field—make for a sporting spectacle second to none.

Tango

There's no question as to what the sound track of Buenos Aires is: the city and the tango are inseparable. From its beginnings in portside brothels at the turn of the 19th century, tango has marked and reflected the character of Buenos Aires and its inhabitants. Although visitors associate tango with dance, for locals it's more about the music and the lyrics, and you can't help but cross paths with both forms. You may hear strains of tango on the radio while sipping coffee in a boulevard café or see high-kicking sequined dancers in a glitzy dinner show or listen to musicians in a cabaret. Regardless, you'll experience the best of this broody, melancholic, but impassioned, art form.

IF YOU LIKE

The Wild, Wild World

Climates range from tropical to subantarctic, and altitudes descend from 22,000 feet to below sea level, so every conceivable environment on earth is represented. Plants, birds, and animals thrive undisturbed in their habitats. Along the south Atlantic coast, sea mammals mate and give birth on empty beaches and in protected bays. To the north, guanaco, rhea, and native deer travel miles over Andean trails and across windswept plains, while birds pass above in clouds of thousands or descend on lagoons like blankets of feathers.

Glaciar Perito Moreno, Patagonia. Tons of ice regularly peel off the 60-meter-tall, 4-kilometer-long front of this advancing glacier and crash into Lago Argentino.

Cataratas de Iguazú, Northeast. Iguazú Falls National Park protects 275 waterfalls and countless species of birds, mammals, insects, and amphibians. Trails disappear into a greenhouse of lianas, creepers, epiphytes, bamboo, orchids, and bromeliads.

Península Valdés, Patagonia. Small boats bring you alongside southern right whales as they feed, mate, give birth, and nurse their offspring.

Parque Nacional Nahuel Huapi, Bariloche. Rich forest surrounds the sapphire-blue waters of Lake Nahuel Huapi. Smaller bodies of water nearby make this Argentina's lake district.

Quebrada de Humahuaca. Vibrant pinks, yellows, and greens color the walls of this northwestern canyon like giant swaths of paint.

Reserva Faunistica Punta Tombo, Patagonia. It's home to the world's largest colony of Magellanic penguins.

Adrenaline Rushes

If an eyeful of natural beauty doesn't make your heart race in the way you'd like, why not try an adventure sport? Argentina is great for winter rushes—skiing, snowboarding, and dogsledding among them. When temperatures soar, you can cool down by white-water rafting or leaping (with a parachute) into the breeze.

Ice Trekking on the Perito Moreno Glacier. You can trek over the glacier's 1,000-year-old ice, then celebrate your ascent with cocktails served over cubes of it.

Hang gliding and paragliding at Cuchi Corral. Argentina's top jumping spot is a natural 1,320-foot-high parapet in northwest Córdoba Province with spectacular Río Pinto valley views.

White-water rafting in the Río Mendoza. This river's medium-to-difficult rapids course through Andean foothills. You can combine one- or two-day descents with horseback riding in the mountains.

Skiing and snowboarding at Las Leñas, Catedral, and Chapelco ski areas. Las Leñas near Mendoza, Catedral near Bariloche, and Chapelco near San Martín de los Andes offer groomed runs, open bowls, and trails that follow the fall line to cozy inns or luxurious hotels.

Tierra Mayor, Patagonia. This family-run Nordic center near Ushuaia has such novelties as dogsled rides, snowcat trips, and wind skiing.

Mountain climbing at Aconcagua, Mendoza Province. Close to the Chilean border, this 6,959-meter (22,831-foot) peak is the highest in the Western and Southern hemispheres and is surrounded by a host of other climbable mountains.

Culture and History

Buenos Aires is a city of Paris-inspired boulevards and historic neighborhoods. Beyond the city, gauchos work ranches that sprawl over every horizon, and old Jesuit estancias evoke Argentina's colonial days in Córdoba Province. The Andes tower above the age-old vineyards of Mendoza and San Juan, while Salta and Jujuy retain traditions that stretch back to before the arrival of Europeans. The windswept reaches of Patagonia roll on forever and a few miles more.

Museo de Arte Latinoamericana de Buenos Aires (MALBA). One of the world's few museums specializing in Latin American art is in a stunningly simple building.

Camino de la Historia, Córdoba. Five-hundred-year-old Jesuit estancias, reminders of Argentina's colonial past, dot the countryside around Córdoba City.

Festival de Tango, Buenos Aires. The world's most important tango festival is a nine-day extravaganza culminating in a huge *milonga* (dance session) along Corrientes Avenue.

Festival de la Vendimia, Mendoza. At the grape-harvest festival, during the first week of March, parades, folk dancing, and fireworks take place. The crowning of a queen marks the grand finale.

Museo de Arqueología de la Alta Montaña, Salta. The rich pre-Columbian heritage of Argentina's Northwest is explored at this modern museum.

Museo Marítimo, Ushuaia. A museum in Tierra del Fuego's penal colony sheds light on Patagonia's past.

Museo Paleontológico, Trelew. You can marvel at dinosaur bones and watch archaeologists at work at this impressive paleontology museum.

Shopping

Argentines love to shop. On weekends, town squares become *ferias* (open-air markets); street performers wind their way between stalls of handmade offerings. Big shopping malls stock local and international brands. Wine, chocolate, cookies, and preserves are some of the consumables.

Handmade jewelry and housewares, Buenos Aires. Artisans sell wares for you and your home in alpaca, wood, and leather.

Gaucho goods, San Antonio de Areco. Modern-day gauchos can stock up on saddles, bridles, asado knives, belts, and even handbags and jewelry in this town of leatherworkers and silversmiths.

Ceramics and weavings, Salta and Jujuy. Salta is famed for its rich red and black ponchos. Woven wall hangings and alpaca knitwear are ubiquitous in Jujuy. Red-clay figures and cookware abound.

Jams and cookies, Córdoba. If it grows on a tree, chances are that you'll find it made into a preserve. The province's *alfajores* (cookies) are delightful.

Wine, Mendoza and Salta. Tour the vineyards, sampling Malbecs, Cabernets, and Torrontéses at leisure, before stocking up on those you liked most.

Young designer clothing, Buenos Aires. In trendy Palermo Viejo and San Telmo, cobbled streets are lined with the boutiques of up-and-coming designers.

Chocolate, Bariloche. Many of Bariloche's original inhabitants were German, hence the thriving chocolate industry. The most famous is *en rama*, sticks of folded flaky chocolate.

GREAT ITINERARIES

PORTEÑOS AND PAMPAS

Day 1: Arrival

Arrive in Buenos Aires and pick up a city map from the tourist office right before you enter the main airport terminal. Ignore the drivers asking if you need a cab; head straight for the taxi booth, pay up front for your ticket (about 90 pesos) and let staffers assign you a driver, who will take you straight to a car. Spend the first afternoon in La Recoleta, whose famous cemetery contains Eva Perón's tomb. Make your first meal a memorable one at a grill with a *bife de chorizo* (sirloin strip steak).

Day 2: San Telmo and La Boca

Begin with a taxi ride to La Boca, the old tango neighborhood. The main strip is Caminito, which though colorful and iconic, is too touristy to merit more than an hour or two. Lunch at El Obrero is a classic. So is afternoon coffee (or a beer) at Bar Dorrego on San Telmo's Plaza Dorrego, a short taxi ride away. Spend the afternoon wandering through the antiques and clothes shops of this characteristic old neighborhood. Get up-close to its history with a visit to El Zanjón de Granados. Dinner at an innovative restaurant like La Vinería de Gualterio Bolívar might give you the fortitude to hit the bars. Ring the bell to be let into La Puerta Roja, a favorite late-night hangout for locals and expats.

Day 3: Palermo Viejo

Hop a cab to MALBA and spend the morning viewing Latin American art. Walk or take a short taxi ride to the Jardín Japonés or the Rosedal. From both it's a mere hop to the cutting-edge Palermo Hollywood neighborhood, where you can lunch on sushi, Vietnamese, or far-out fusion. Afterward, wander leisurely over to Palermo Soho, browsing the city's coolest clothing and shoe stores. When night falls, have coffee or a cocktail near Plaza Serrano, and finish with dinner at a modern restaurant, say Casa Cruz. If you're up for a nightcap, you're already where all the action is.

Day 4: El Centro and Puerto Madero

Have your morning coffee and croissants at ultra-traditional Gran Café Tortoni. Stroll down Avenida De Mayo to take in Plaza de Mayo and the nearby Museo Etnográfico. Cross over the old docks into Puerto Madero for a light deli lunch or a full-blown grill affair. Get back to nature only yards from the skyscrapers with a quick ramble in the Reserva Ecológica. Finish with an all-out evening wine experience at the Gran Bar Danzón in Retiro.

Day 5: Buenos Aires to the Pampas

After getting a sense of the city, hit the highway for gaucho country. The town of San Antonio de Areco, in the heart of the pampas, is home to several estancias, country houses where gauchos tend to the horses (and to the guests). Most estancias include three or even four meals per day in the room price. If you don't want to drive yourself, arrange ground transportation through estancias. If you drive, reserve a rental car downtown, not at the airport. After a late breakfast, take the Acceso Norte to the Panamericana (RN9) to Pilar and then RN8, a slower road, to San Antonio. Browse the silversmiths' and artisans' stores before having lunch at the Almacén de Ramos Generales. Then check out the gaucho museum, wander the sleepy streets, and finish with a beer or coffee at La Esquina de Mertí, an old-fashioned corner bar. Head to your estancia, where you'll have time to relax before dinner.

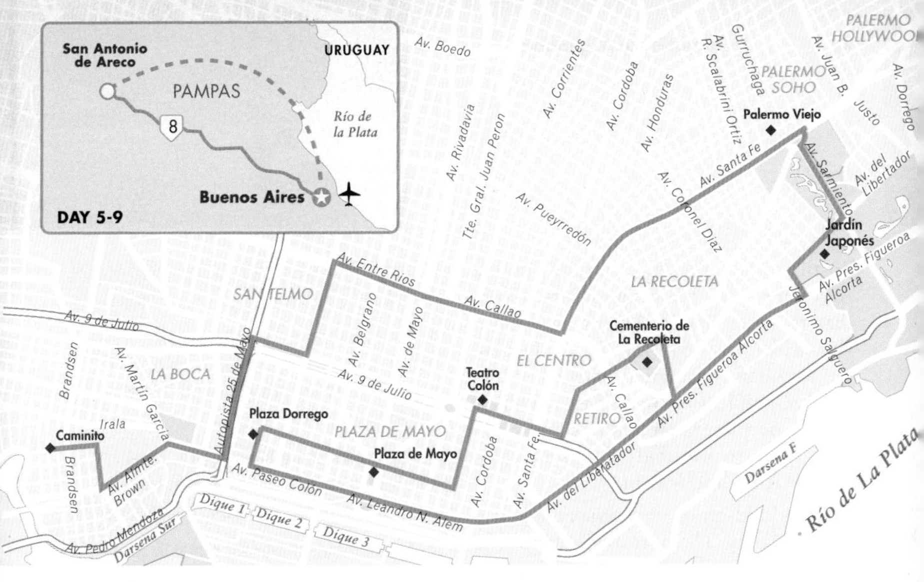

Day 6: San Antonio de Areco

Spend your morning in the pampas on horseback, roaming across the grassland with a resident gaucho. This, like other activities, should be included with the estancia price. Seasoned riders can gallop, while beginners walk, trot, or ride in a buggy. If there's a day-trip group coming in, the midday meal might be accompanied by a musical performance with whooping gauchos—cheesy, but fun. Take an afternoon swim in the pool, and then have dinner at the estancia, perhaps followed by a game of pool or cards with other guests, who by now may be good friends.

Days 7 and 8: To Buenos Aires and Home

Return to Buenos Aires after one last long estancia lunch. Spend the afternoon, revisiting your favorite neighborhood.

You could spend your last day catching up on culture at the Museo Nacional de Bellas Artes or history at the Museo Evita. Later, try out your footwork with a tango class and a visit to a milonga, or see the pros in action at an evening show.

Sportier alternatives include taking a bike tour with La Bicicleta Naranja or going for a long walk in Parque Tres de Febrero. If you're a soccer fan and Boca Juniors are playing during your stay in Buenos Aires, don't miss it. Getting tickets yourself can be complicated—consider booking with tour company **Tangol** (☎ *11/4312–7276* 🌐 *www.tangol.com*). A visit to the Museo de la Pasión Boquense is the next-best option. Local fans follow up with pizza at nearby Banchero.

If shopping is your idea of an extreme sport, divide your last day between the chain stores on Avenida Santa Fe, top-end mall Paseo Alcorta, and the boutiques in Palermo. Have a blowout final meal: good splurge restaurants are Tomo I, Le Mistral at the Four Seasons, and La Bourgogne.

On Day 8, allow at least an hour to get to Ezeiza for your flight home. If you kept your rental car so that you can drive yourself to the airport, make sure your hotel has a garage, and allow an extra half hour before your flight to return the car.

ALTERNATIVES

You can combine this eight-day itinerary with a trip to Iguazú Falls, in Argentina's northeast corner on the border with Brazil, or go there instead of San Antonio on days 5 and 6. Spend one day on the Argentine side of things, in the Parque Nacional Iguazú, then head into town for dinner at Aqva. Spend the second morning in the Parque Nacional Foz do Iguaçu,

Brazil's national park, then return to the Argentine park for a few hours. (Note that to enter Brazil, Americans need a visa, which costs $120. In Puerto Iguazú, the Brazilian consulate is open weekdays 8–12:30, and in Buenos Aires weekdays 10–1.) Aerolíneas Argentinas and LAN have three to five daily flights between Buenos Aires and Iguazú.

Another add-on or replacement side trip is to Uruguay. The port town of Colonia is easily accessible by Colonia Express, a fast ferry, which has connecting buses to Montevideo. In summer, the beach resort of Punta del Este is another option. Spending two or three days in Uruguay isn't just a fun way to get an extra passport stamp—it's a window into a country whose economic and cultural differences from Argentina (their heightened obsession with mate, for instance) are readily apparent.

IN PATAGONIA

Day 1: Arrival and on to Bariloche

Reaching Patagonia isn't easy. Your flight to Buenos Aires will be followed by a transfer from Ezeiza International to the downtown Aeroparque and a flight to Bariloche. Rent a car at the airport, and drive to your hotel (consider a place on the Circuito Chico outside town).

Day 2: Bariloche and Circuito Chico

Spend the day exploring the Circuito Chico and Peninsula Llao Llao. Start early so you have time for a boat excursion from the dock at Puerto Pañuelo on the peninsula's edge as well as for some late-afternoon shopping back in Bariloche. Spend the evening devouring Patagonian lamb *à la cruz* (spit-roasted over an open fire) wherever you can find it.

TIPS

1. The Porteños and Pampas itinerary works best if Day 1 (Arrival) is on a Friday and Day 8 (To Buenos Aires and Home) is the following Friday.

2. Stay in the same Buenos Aires hotel at the beginning and end of your trip so you can leave extra bags there while traveling.

3. An eight-day apartment rental in Buenos Aires, even if you aren't spending all your time there.

4. Flights to and from Iguazú use the Aeroparque in Palermo; international flights leave from Ezeiza. If you can't avoid same-day arrival and departure, allow at least four hours to get between the two airports.

Day 3: Circuito Grande to Villa La Angostura

Villa La Angostura is a tranquil lakeside retreat that marks the beginning of the legendary Circuito Grande. Getting there is a gorgeous experience, as you'll hug the shores of the Lago Nahuel Huapi on R237 and R231. Check into a hotel in Puerto Manzano, a little outside Villa La Angostura, whose hotels aren't as nice. The sparkling Puerto Sur is a good choice, with its endless water views.

Day 4: Villa La Angostura

You can spend your second day in Villa La Angostura skiing at Cerro Bayo, if it's winter and that's your thing; exploring the Parque Nacional los Arrayanes, the only forest of these myrtle trees in the world, or simply relaxing by the lake, which, if you're staying at Puerto Sur, might be the most appealing option.

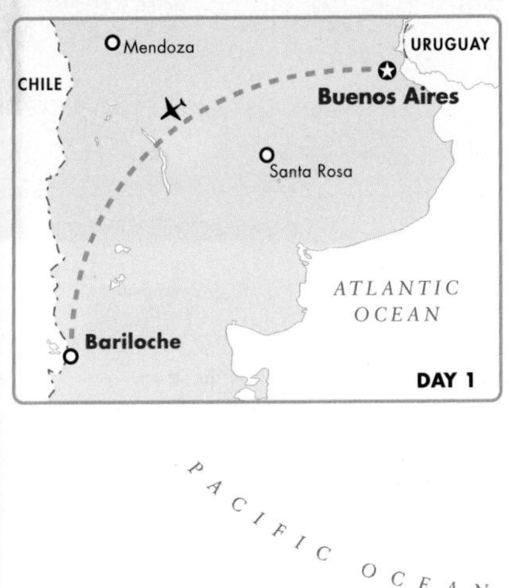

Day 5: Seven Lakes Route to San Martín de los Andes

Head out of Villa La Angostura onto the unbelievable Seven Lakes Route (R234), which branches right and along the way passes Lago Correntoso, Lago Espejo, Lago Villarino, Lago Falkner, and Lago Hermoso. If you leave early, add the hour-long detour to Lago Traful. The drive is today's main event; take the road all the way to San Martín, where you can spend the rest of the afternoon shopping, trying trout and other delicacies at the smoke shops, and enjoying an asado feast. Note that the Seven Lakes Route is closed in winter; you'll have to go through Junín de los Andes to get to San Martín.

Day 6: San Martín de los Andes

If you're here in winter and you're a skier, you will no doubt want to spend one full day in San Martín at Cerro Chapelco. Otherwise, spend the day relaxing on the beach, fishing, horseback riding, rafting, or otherwise outdoors.

Day 7: Flight to El Calafate

Get an extremely early start from San Martín de los Andes for the five-hour drive back to Bariloche, where you'll catch a flight to El Calafate. Be sure to take the longer but faster route through Junín from San Martín to Bariloche (RN234 and RN237). If you follow the only partly paved Seven Lakes Route, you'll have little chance of catching an early afternoon flight.

It's a mere 1¾ hours by plane from Bariloche to the Parque Nacional Los Glaciares. Grab a taxi to your hotel, have dinner, and get some sleep in preparation for glacier-viewing tomorrow. If you're on a no-holds-barred budget, stay at Los Notros, the only hotel within the park and in view of the glacier. It's also a place where all excursions will be taken care of for you. Otherwise, stay at a hotel in El Calafate and book your glacier visits through El Calafate tour operators—preferably before 7 PM today.

Day 8: El Calafate and Perito Moreno Glacier

Perito Moreno is one of the world's most impressive glaciers. Spend two days taking it in from different angles. Devote today either to the Upsala Glacier tour, which traverses the lakes in view of an impressive series of glaciers, or the hour-long "Safari Nautico" on a boat that sails as close as possible to the front of the glacier. Enjoy a well-deserved dinner back in El Calafate. Again, remember to arrange tomorrow's activities by 7 PM. Tonight, this means organizing an ice trek.

Day 9: El Calafate and Perito Moreno Glacier

It's all about one of Argentina's unique and most memorable activities: ice trekking. You'll don crampons and actually walk across Perito Moreno's surface. The trip is expensive, but worth every penny. (Note that ice treks are included in the rates if you stay at Los Notros.) You'll crawl through ice tunnels and hike across ice ridges that seem to glow bright blue. After all this, dinner—and everything else—will seem insignificant.

Day 10: Departure

Board a bus or taxi for El Calafate's gleaming new airport, and take a flight back through Buenos Aires and home. You'll be dreaming of glaciers for weeks to come. Note that if you are not connecting to another Aerolíneas flight home, you may have to spend an additional night in Buenos Aires on the way back.

ALTERNATIVES

Sports and outdoors enthusiasts can really customize this itinerary. Skiers, for example, can skip southern Patagonia, spending a day or two in Cerro Catedral, near Bariloche, and a day at Cerro Chapelco. Rafters can work with Bariloche operators to create trips that range from floats down the Río Manso—an eight-hour outing with easy rapids through a unique ecosystem—to 13-hour excursions to the Chilean border. Serious hikers can boat across Masacardi Lake to Pampa Linda, then hike to the black glaciers of Tronador, continuing up above timberline to Refugio Otto Meiling, spending the night, walking along the crest of the Andes with glacier views, then returning to Pampa Linda. Day hikes to the foot of Tronador leave more time for a mountain-bike or horseback ride in the same area.

The most adventurous travelers drive from Bariloche to El Calafate instead of flying. It adds, oh, about a week to the itinerary, but it involves an unforgettable trip down the largely unpaved RN40. Don't attempt this route without a four-wheel-drive vehicle that has two spares. And pack plenty of extra food and water as well as camping gear. Getting stuck in a place where cars and trucks pass only once every day or two is dangerous.

TIPS

1. In the dead of winter; limit yourself to the ski resorts in the Lake District. That said, Bariloche is teeming with kids on high-school vacation trips July through September.

2. Book your flight to Argentina and your round-trip ticket to Bariloche at the same time. Booking a separate flight with another carrier will mean you won't be able to check your luggage through, and you'll have to get the timing right to avoid missing your connection.

3. It's difficult to tour the Lake District without a rental car. If you don't want to drive, confine your visit to southern Patagonia, spending more time in El Calafate or extending into Tierra del Fuego.

ARGENTINA LODGING PRIMER

Booming visitor numbers have sparked dozens of new properties. There's plenty of variety, whether you're looking for a tried-and-tested international chain, a boutique property, the Old World charm of an estancia, local hospitality at a family-run B&B, or a cheap hostel that's not only clean but stylish, too. Nearly all hotels, and even many hostels, include breakfast in the room price.

Estancias

For a taste of how Argentina's landed elite live, book a few nights on an estancia (ranch). Most estancia accommodation is in grandiose, European-inspired, century-old country mansions. Rates usually include activities such as horseback riding and four generous daily meals, usually shared with your hosts and other guests.

Estancias vary greatly: some are still working cattle or sheep farms, but many have switched entirely to tourism. At traditional establishments you are hosted by the owners and stay in rooms that once belonged to family members. Accommodations are usually old-fashioned and tastefully furnished, but rarely luxurious: you might have to share a bathroom, and some rural locations don't have round-the-clock electricity.

Other estancias still belong to their original owners, but a private company runs the accommodation side of things. These properties are hit-and-miss: some are more luxurious and professional than traditional establishments, while others have become bland and generic. Some properties that advertise themselves as estancias are actually redevelopments of old rural houses which may not have originally been estancias. These emulate traditional estancia style but are generally more luxurious and have modern amenities.

Apartments and Cabins

Self-catering options are plentiful in Argentina and increasingly popular with visitors. The savings are especially significant if you're traveling as a family or group. In Buenos Aires and other big cities, you can rent furnished apartments (and sometimes houses) daily, although weekly and monthly rates are usually cheaper. Some properties are in new buildings with pools, gyms, and 24-hour concierges; others are in atmospheric, but less luxurious, older buildings.

Cabañas (cabins) often outnumber hotels in destinations popular with Argentine holiday-makers, such as the Atlantic coast, Córdoba province, or Bariloche. Some are independent holiday houses, while others form part of vacation complexes and include maid service and breakfast. Being outside busy town centers in natural surroundings is a boon, but you often need your own vehicle to reach properties comfortably.

Bed-and-breakfasts

In many smaller destinations, large mid-range hotels tend to be impersonal, institutional setups aimed at passing business travelers. If you're looking for local flavor, consider a smaller hotel or bed-and-breakfast. Some are simple family-run affairs, others are boutique properties; many are housed in recycled old buildings that pack plenty of charm. Friendly, personalized service is another major appeal. Although many now use the term "B&B," you may also find them labeled posada, petit hotel, or la casa de. . . . Hotels with fewer than 10 rooms are very common outside of Buenos Aires—as most hotels in Argentina include breakfast, these properties could be considered B&Bs, even if they don't actively advertise themselves as such.

FLAVORS OF ARGENTINA

Beef

Locals proudly boast that the grass-fed cattle of the pampas produce the world's tastiest beef. Sunday *asados* (barbecues) are a sacred national ritual. Whether they're grilling in the garden or ordering a *parrillada* (mixed grill) at a restaurant, Argentineans typically go for at least two cuts of beef, one on the bone and one off. *Tira de asado* (prime ribs) and *vacío* (flank steak) are the standard selections, and are usually slow-roasted in huge pieces weighing 5–10 lbs. Choicer cuts like *bife de chorizo* (rump) or *lomo* (tenderloin) are more likely to be cooked and ordered as individual steaks.

The preludes to the meat itself usually include chorizo and *morcilla* (blood sausage) and a selection of grilled offal: crispy curls of *chinchulines* (chitterlings) and rich *mollejas* (sweetbreads) are especially popular.

Andean Ingredients

Arguably the most unusual flavors in Argentina come from the pre-Columbian food traditions of Salta and Jujuy, in the northwest of Argentina.

Maize is the backbone of Andean fare and comes in an impressive range of sizes and colors. The most ubiquitous corn-based dishes are *humitas* and *tamales,* fist-sized balls of maize meal stuffed with cheese or ground beef, respectively, and steamed in corn husks.

Andean potato varieties (of which there are scores) are tiny, dense, and might be purple, crimson, green, or rich yellow. Traditionally, they're preserved by leaving them to freeze outside and then dehydrating them. The resulting starchy balls (or a flour ground from them) are known as *chuño* and are a common addition to soups and stews.

Llama steak is more fibrous than beef and has a sweet, gamey edge to it. *Charqui* (the local word for jerky or dried salted meat) is also commonplace in stews. At dessert, don't pass up a plate of *quesillo* (raw goat cheese or stringy fresh white cheese) with *dulce de cayote* (a sweet cactus preserve).

Patagonian Wild Foods

The star catch along the Atlantic coast is *centolla* or king crab, but mussels, clams, octopus, and shrimp are also regional specialties, as are freshly caught sole, salmon, hake, cod, or silverside. Fish is on the menu in Andean Patagonia, too, which is famous for its wild-river trout. Avoid the cheesy sauces local chefs favor and go for a something simple that lets you appreciate the star ingredient—*manteca negra* (browned butter) is a fail-safe choice.

If you're feeling game, *jabalí* (wild boar), *ciervo colorado* (red deer), and *liebre* (hare) are the land-lubbing southern specialties. They're usually served roasted or in stews, often accompanied by sauces made from berries or artisanal beer (or even berry-flavored beer), some of the other products Patagonia is famous for.

Dulce de leche

Milk, sugar, and not a whole lot else go into this gloopy brown milk caramel, which is practically a food group in Argentina. Get your first hit each day by spreading some on your toast at breakfast. Mid-morning you might encounter it sandwiched between two cookies to form an *alfajor,* the nation's favorite sweet snack.

Dulce de leche is a standard flavor for ice cream; you'll also find chocolate-chip dulce de leche, or dulce de leche with swirls of—you guessed it—extra dulce de leche.

A PASSIONATE HISTORY

by Victoria Patience

If there's one thing Argentines have learned from their history, it's that there's not a lot you can count on. Fierce—often violent—political, economic, and social instability have been the only constants in the story of a people who seem never to be able to escape that famous Chinese curse, "May you live in interesting times."

Although most accounts of Argentine history begin 500 years ago with the arrival of the conquistadors, humans have been living in what is now Argentina for around 13,000 years. They created the oldest recorded art in South America—a cave of handprints in Santa Cruz, Patagonia (c. 7500 BC)—and eventually became part of the Inca Empire.

Spanish and Portuguese sailors came in the early 16th century, including Ferdinand Magellan, who sailed along the country's coast. The Spanish were forced out 300 years later by colony-sick locals hungry for independence. Internal conflict and civil war wracked the early republic, which swung constantly back and forth between democratic governments intent on modernizing the country and corrupt feudal systems.

Spanish and Italian immigrants arrived in the 20th century, changing Argentina's population profile forever. Unstable politics characterized the rest of the century, which saw the rise and fall of Juan Perón and a series of increasingly bloody military dictatorships. Over 25 years of uninterrupted democracy have passed since the last junta fell, an achievement Argentines value hugely.

(left) Ferdinand Magellan (c. 1480–1521)
(right) Stamp featuring Evita

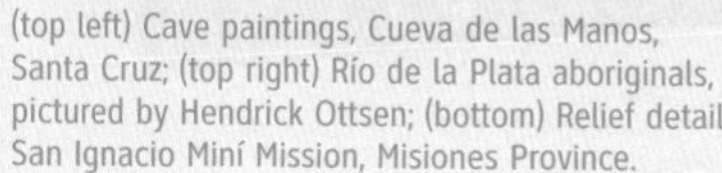

(top left) Cave paintings, Cueva de las Manos, Santa Cruz; (top right) Río de la Plata aboriginals, pictured by Hendrick Ottsen; (bottom) Relief detail, San Ignacio Miní Mission, Misiones Province.

PRE–1500

PRE-CONQUEST/INCA

Argentina's original inhabitants were a diverse group of indigenous peoples. Their surroundings defined their lifestyles: nomadic hunter-gatherers lived in Patagonia and the Pampas, while the inhabitants of the northeast and northwest were largely farming communities. The first foreign power to invade the region was the Inca Empire, in the 15th century. Its roads and tribute systems extended over the entire northwest, reaching as far south as some parts of modern-day Mendoza.

1500–1809

BIRTH OF THE COLONY

European explorers first began to arrive at the River Plate area in the early 1500s, and in 1520 Ferdinand Magellan sailed right down the coast of what is now Argentina and on into the Pacific. Buenos Aires was founded twice: Pedro de Mendoza's 1536 attempt led to starving colonists turning to cannibalism before running for Asunción; Juan de Garay's attempt in 1580 was successful. Conquistadors from Peru, Chile, Paraguay, and of course Spain, founded other cities. The whole area was part of the Viceroyalty of Peru until 1776, when the Spanish king Carlos III decreed present-day Argentina, Uruguay, Paraguay, and most of Bolivia to be the Viceroyalty of the Río de la Plata. Buenos Aires became the main port and the only legal exit point for silver from Potosí. Smuggling grew as fast as the city itself. In 1806–07 English forces tried twice to invade Argentina. Militia from Buenos Aires fought them off with no help from Spain, inciting ideas of independence among *criollos* (Argentine-born Spaniards, who had fewer rights than those born in Europe).

(left) Julio Roca
(right) Monument to General San Martín;

1810–1860s BIRTH OF THE NATION: INDEPENDENCE AND THE CONSTITUTION

Early-19th-century proto-Argentines were getting itchy for independence. The United States and France had provided inspiration with their revolutions, and when Napoleon defeated Spain, the time seemed ripe. On the May 25th, 1810, Buenos Aires' leading citizens, armed only with umbrellas against the rain, ousted the last Spanish viceroy. A series of elected juntas and triumvirates followed while military heroes José de San Martín and Manuel Belgrano won battles that allowed the Provincias Unidas de América del Sur to declare independence in Tucumán on July 9, 1816. San Martín went on to liberate Chile and Peru.

Political infighting marked the republic's first 40 years. The 1819 constitution established a centralist state run from Buenos Aires, a position known as *unitario*, but landowners and warlords in the provinces wanted a federal state. The issue was settled when dictator Juan Manuel de Rosas came to power: from 1829 to 1852 he killed or exiled opposition, censored the press, and made red lapel ribbons obligatory (sky-blue and white were unitario colors).

1860–1942 RISE OF THE MODERN STATE

Argentina staggered back and forth between political extremes on its rocky road to modern statehood. Relatively liberal leaders alternated with corrupt warlord types. The most infamous of these is Julio Roca, who effectively stopped proper voting and undertook a military campaign that killed off most of Argentina's remaining indigenous population. He also started the immigration drive that brought millions of Europeans to Argentina between 1870 and 1930.

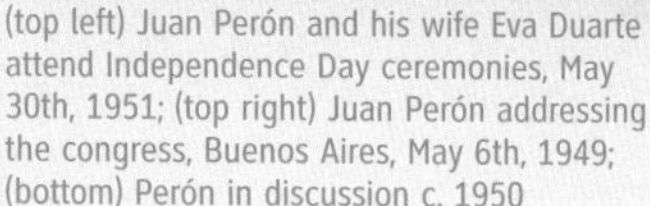

(top left) Juan Perón and his wife Eva Duarte attend Independence Day ceremonies, May 30th, 1951; (top right) Juan Perón addressing the congress, Buenos Aires, May 6th, 1949; (bottom) Perón in discussion c. 1950

1942–1973

THE RISE AND FALL OF PERONISM

A 1943 coup ended a decade of privatization that had caused the gap between rich and poor to grow exponentially. One of the soldiers involved was a little-known general named Juan Domingo Perón. He rose through the ranks of the government as quickly as he had through those of the army. Uneasy about his growing popularity, other members of the military government imprisoned him, provoking a wave of uprisings that led to Perón's release and swept him to the presidency as head of the newly formed labor party in 1946. In the middle of his campaign, he quietly married the young B-movie actress he'd been living with, Eva Duarte, soon to be known universally as "Evita." Their idiosyncratic, his-'n'-hers politics were socialism and fascism, and hinged on a massive personality cult. While he was busy improving worker's rights and trying to industrialize Argentina, she set about press-ganging Argentina's landed elite into funding her social aid program. Their tireless efforts to close the gap between rich and poor earned them the slavish devotion of Argentina's poor and the passionate hatred of the rich. But everything began to go wrong when Evita died of uterine cancer in 1952. By 1955, a dwindling economy was grounds for Perón being ousted by another coup. For the next 18 years, both he and his party were illegal in Argentina—even mentioning his name could land you in prison.

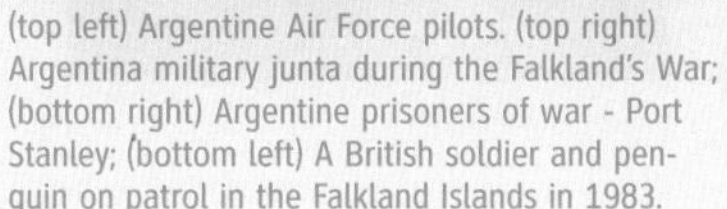

(top left) Argentine Air Force pilots. (top right) Argentina military junta during the Falkland's War; (bottom right) Argentine prisoners of war - Port Stanley; (bottom left) A British soldier and penguin on patrol in the Falkland Islands in 1983.

1973—1983

DICTATORSHIP, DIRTY WAR & THE FALKLANDS

The two civilian presidencies that followed both ended in fresh military coups until Perón was allowed to return in 1973. Despite turning his back on left-wing student and guerrilla groups who had campaigned for him in his absence, he still won another election by a landslide. However, one problematic year later, he died in office. His farcical successor was the vice-president, an ex-cabaret dancer known as Isabelita, who was also Perón's third wife. Her chaotic leadership was brought to an end in 1976 by yet another military coup. The succession of juntas that ruled the country called their bloody dictatorship a "process of national reorganization"; it would later become known as "the Dirty War."

Much of the world seemingly ignored the actions of the Argentine government during its six-year reign of terror. Throughout the country, students, activists, and any other undesirable element were kidnapped and tortured in clandestine detention centers. Many victims' children were stolen and given up for adoption by pro-military families after their parents' bodies had been dumped in the River Plate. More than 30,000 people "disappeared" and thousands more went into exile. Government ministries were handed over to private businessmen. Massive corruption took external debt from $7 million to $66 million. In 1982, desperate for something to distract people with, the junta started war with Britain over the Islas Malvinas or Falkland Islands. The disastrous campaign lasted just four months and led to the downfall of the dictatorship.

TIMELINE

Falkland's War	Menem made president	State of Emergency declared	Cristina Kirchner made president	
INFLATION REACHES 3,000%	1990	*ECONOMY IN TATTERS* 2000		2010

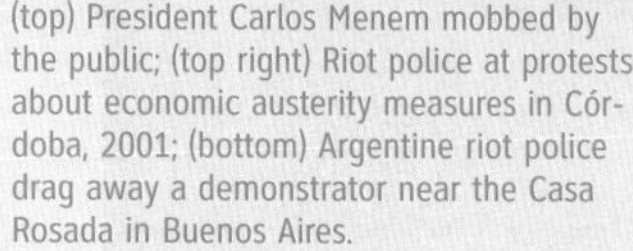

(top) President Carlos Menem mobbed by the public; (top right) Riot police at protests about economic austerity measures in Córdoba, 2001; (bottom) Argentine riot police drag away a demonstrator near the Casa Rosada in Buenos Aires.

1982—1999 RETURN OF DEMOCRACY

Celebrations marked the return to democracy. The main players in the dictatorship went on trial, but received relatively small sentences. Inflation reached a terrifying 3,000% in 1988 and only stabilized when Carlos Menem became president the following year. Menem pegged the peso to the dollar, privatized services and resources, and even changed the constitution to extend his mandate. But despite an initial illusion of economic well-being, by the time Menem left office in 1999 poverty had skyrocketed, and the economy was in tatters.

2000—PRESENT CRISIS & THE K YEARS

The longer-term results of Menem's policies came in December 2001, when the government tried to prevent a rush on funds by freezing all private savings accounts. Thousands of people took to the streets in protest; on December 20, the violent police response transformed the demonstrations into riots. President Fernando de la Rúa declared a state of emergency, then resigned, and was followed by four temporary presidents in almost as many days. When things finally settled, the peso had devaluated drastically, many people had lost their savings, and the future looked dark.

However, under the center-leftist government of Argentina's following president, Néstor Kirchner, the economy slowly reactivated. Unlike his predecessors, Kirchner openly expressed his abhorrence of the dictatorship and reopened trials of high-ranking military officials. In a rather bizarre turn of political events, he was succeeded by his wife, Cristina Fernandez. Her fiery speeches have inspired both devotion and derision. Times may be better than a few years ago, but Argentines have lived through so many political ups and downs that they never take anything for granted.

MADE IN ARGENTINA

There's no doubt that Argentinians are an inventive lot. And we're not talking about their skill in arguing their way out of parking tickets: several things you might not be able to imagine life without started out in Argentina.

Un *birome* (ballpoint pen)

BALLPOINT PEN

Although Laszlo Josef Biro was born in Hungary and first patented the ballpoint pen in Paris, it wasn't until he launched his company in Argentina in 1943 that his invention began to attract attention. As such, Argentinians claim the world's most useful writing instrument as their own.

BLOOD TRANSFUSION

Before ER there was Luis Agote, an Argentinean doctor who, in 1914, was one of the first to perform a blood transfusion using stored blood (rather than doing a patient-to-patient transfusion). The innovation that made the process possible was adding sodium citrate, an anticoagulant, to the blood.

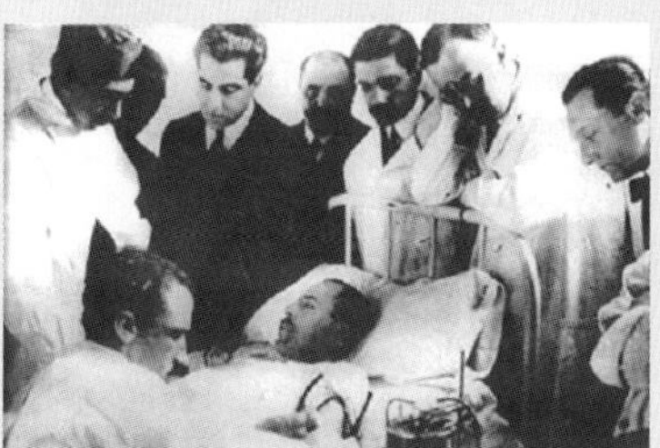

Luis Agote was one of the first to perform a nondirect blood transfusion, in Buenos Aires on November 9, 1914.

FINGERPRINTING

In 1891, Juan Vucetich, a Croatian-born officer of the Buenos Aires police force, came up with a system of classifying fingerprints. He went on to make the first-ever criminal arrest based on fingerprint evidence. Although his method has since been refined, it is still used throughout Latin America.

Huellas digitales (fingerprints)

- Other useful Argentinian claims to fame include the first working helicopter (1916); the first one-piece floor mop (1953); and the first one-use-only hypodermic syringe (1989).

DID YOU KNOW?

Galerias Pacifíco is one of Argentina's National Historic Monuments. Dating to 1889, this Beaux Arts building was modeled after Le Bon Marché in Paris; the first tenant was a store called Argentine Bon Marché.

Buenos Aires

WORD OF MOUTH

"Buenos Aires has a feeling all its own—edgy and pulsating, a blend of old and new . . . I'll forever have images etched in my mind of dilapidated elegance: of brilliant blue Boca graffiti on a crumbling old building, flowers draped over a trellis, unruly vines climbing up the blackened columns, faded symbols of melancholic grandeur."

—Magellan_5

WELCOME TO BUENOS AIRES

Feria de San Telmo

TOP REASONS TO GO

★ **Dance the Night Away:** This is the capital of tango, that most passionate of dances. But porteños also dance to samba, salsa, and DJ mixes until the wee hours.

★ **Shop 'Til You Drop:** High-quality silver and leather goods as well as fashionable clothing and accessories are available at world-class malls and boutiques. Open-air markets carry regional and European antiques and provincial handicrafts.

★ **Best of Both Worlds:** The architecture, wining-and-dining, and arts activities rival similar offerings in European capitals. But the lifestyle, low prices, and warm locals are more typical of Latin America.

★ **Meat-ing Your Destiny:** The capital of cow country has enough *parrillas* (traditional grill restaurants) to satisfy even the most bloodthirsty.

★ **The Beautiful Game:** Top matches play out in Buenos Aires's colorful stadiums, stuffed to bursting with screaming *futbol* (soccer) addicts.

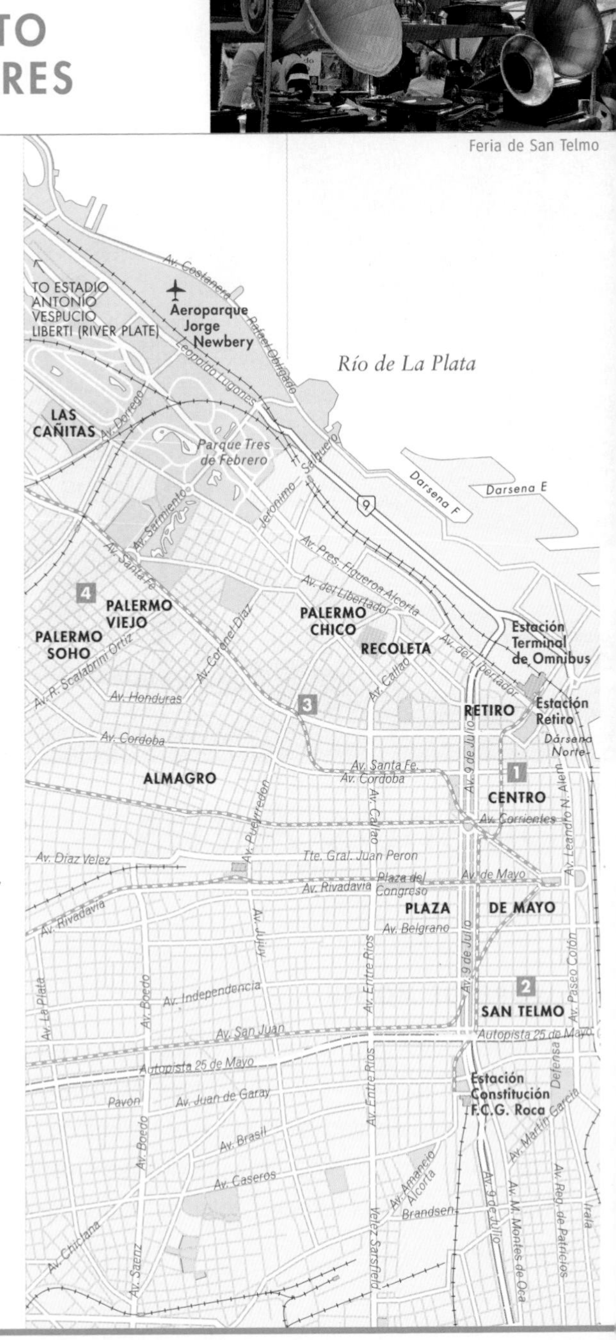

Showing La Boca love

GETTING ORIENTED

The world's ninth-largest city rises from the Río de la Plata and stretches more than 200 square km (75 square mi) to the surrounding pampas, Argentina's fertile plains. With more than one-third of the country's 39 million inhabitants living in or around Buenos Aires, it's clearly the country's hub as well as its main gateway. The city's identity lies in its 48 *barrios* (neighborhoods)—each with its own character and history. Several generations of many families have lived in the same barrio, and traditionally people feel more of an affinity to their neighborhood than to the city as a whole.

1 El Centro. Locals use "El Centro" as an umbrella term for several action-packed downtown districts. Microcentro, the city's heart, bursts with banks, offices, theaters, bars, cafés, bookstores, and crowds. The area around Plaza and Avenida de Mayo is the hub of political life. Posh hotels, gleaming skyscrapers, and an elegant boardwalk make up Puerto Madero.

2 San Telmo and La Boca. The tango was born in these southern barrios. These days antiques stores and chic boutiques compete for space along San Telmo's cobbled streets. Just to the south, La Boca was originally settled by Italian immigrants. Now people come from all over for a snapshot of colorful but tacky Caminito or for a soccer match in Boca Juniors stadium.

3 Recoleta and Almagro. Today's elite live, dine, and shop along Recoleta's Paris-inspired streets. They're also often buried in the sumptuous mausoleums of its cemetery. Art galleries and museums are also draws. Gritty, working-class Almagro is known for its fringe theater pickings and tango scene.

4 Palermo. Large Palermo has many subdistricts. If it's cool and happening, chances are it's in Palermo Viejo: boutiques, bars, restaurants, clubs, galleries, and hotels line the streets surrounding Plaza Serrano. The area across Avenida Juan B. Justo took the name Palermo Hollywood for the film and TV studios based here. There are two excellent museums (the MALBA and Museo Evita) in Palermo Chico, also home to parks and the zoo.

Floralis Generica

BUENOS AIRES PLANNER

No Time Like the Present

Fabulous wine, endless nightlife, friendly locals, the best steak, rock-bottom prices... shaking off a stereotype can be hard. But when yours reads like a shopping list for indulgence, why bother? Whether they're screaming for a soccer team or enjoying an endless barbecue with friends, porteños are always demonstrating that enjoying the here and the now is what life is all about.

Visitor Info

The Web site of the city tourist board, **Turismo Buenos Aires** (🌐 *www.bue.gov.ar*) has lively, downloadable MP3 walking tours in English. Bright orange info booths at the airports and seven other locations provide maps and have English-speaking personnel.

The **South American Explorer's Club** (✉ *Estados Unidos 577, San Telmo* ☎ *11/4307–9625* 🌐 *www.saexplorers.org*) is an American membership nonprofit that aims to help independent travelers in the region. The Buenos Aires clubhouse has a map library, a book exchange, and a bulletin board.

Get Around Just Fine

Intriguing architecture, an easy-to-navigate grid layout (a few diagonal transverses aside), and ample window-shopping make Buenos Aires a wonderful place to explore on foot. Street cafés abound for when your feet tire.

Public Transit. Service on the *subte* (subway) is quick, but trains are often packed and strikes are common. Four of the six underground lines (A, B, D, and E) fan out west from downtown; lines C and H (only partly open) connect them. Single-ride tickets cost a flat 90¢. The subte shuts down around 11 PM and reopens at 5 AM.

Colectivos (city buses) connect the city's barrios and the greater Buenos Aires area. Ticket machines on board only accept coins (fares within the city are a flat 90¢). Bus stops are roughly every other block, but you may have to hunt for the small metal route-number signs: they could be stuck on a shelter, lamppost, or even a tree. Stop at a news kiosk and buy the *Guía T,* a handy route guide.

Taxis. Black-and-yellow taxis fill the streets and take you anywhere in town and short distances into greater Buenos Aires. Fares start at 3.10 pesos with 31¢ per 650 feet. You can hail taxis on the street or ask hotel and restaurant staffers to call for them.

Safety

Although Buenos Aires is safer than most Latin American capitals, the country's unstable economy means crime is a concern. Pickpocketing and mugging are common, so avoid wearing flashy jewelry, be discreet with money and cameras, and be mindful of bags. Take taxis as much as possible after dark. Police patrol most areas where you're likely to go, but they have a reputation for corruption, so locals try to avoid contact with them.

Protest marches are a part of life in Buenos Aires: most are peaceful, but some end in confrontations with the police. They often take place in the Plaza de Mayo, in the square outside the Congreso, or along the Avenida de Mayo connecting the two.

Tours

Ghosts, crimes, and spooky urban legends are the focus of the Buenos Aires Misteriosa tours run by **Ayres Viajes** (☎ *11/4383–9188* 🌐 *www.ayresviajes.com.ar*). The super-personalized service—for tours in town and out—you get from Isabel at **Buenos Aires Tours** (🌐 *www.buenosaires-tours.com.ar*) is almost heroic. For a local's perspective, contact the **Cicerones de Buenos Aires** (☎ *11/4431–9892* 🌐 *www.cicerones.org.ar*), a free service that pairs you with a porteño to show you parts of town you might not see otherwise. Highly informed young historians from the University of Buenos Aires lead the cultural and historical tours at **Eternautas** (☎ *11/5031–9916* 🌐 *www.eternautas.com*). It offers orientation tours, neighborhood walks, themed outings (e.g., Evita, the literary city, Jewish Buenos Aires), and excursions outside town.

A dynamic way to see the city's sights is on two wheels through **La Bicicleta Naranja** (☎ *11/4362–1104* 🌐 *www.labicicletanaranja.com.ar*). See Buenos Aires from the river on a 2½-hour sailboat tour with **Smile on Sea** (☎ *11/15–5018–8662* 🌐 *www.smileonsea.com*). **Puro Remo** (☎ *11/15–6397–3545* 🌐 *www.puroremo.com.ar*) is a rowing club that offers guided kayaking and rowing tours (no experience needed) through the Tigre delta and Puerto Madero's docklands.

Large onboard screens make the posh minibuses used by **Opción Sur** (☎ *11/4777–9029* 🌐 *www.opcionsur.com.ar*) part transport and part cinema. Each stop on their city tour is introduced by relevant historical footage (e.g., Evita rallying the masses at Plaza de Mayo). You get serious insight into Buenos Aires's Jewish community on day tours run by Deb Miller's company, **Travel Jewish** (☎ *11/4106–0541* 🌐 *www.traveljewish.com*). For tailor-made city tours contact **Wow! Argentina** (☎ *11/5239–3019* 🌐 *www.wowargentina.com.ar*). Cintia Stella and her team can also arrange excursions all over Argentina.

WHAT IT COSTS IN ARGENTINE PESOS

	¢	$	$$	$$$	$$$$
Restaurants	under 15	15–20	21–30	31–40	over 40
Hotels	under 200	201–450	451–700	701–1,000	over 1,000

Restaurant prices are for a first course, second course, and dessert. Hotel prices are for two people in a standard double room in high season, including tax and service.

When to Go

Remember that when it's summer in the United States, it's winter in Argentina, and vice versa. Winters (July–September) are chilly, though temperatures never drop below freezing. Summer's muggy heat (December–March) can be taxing at midday but makes for wonderful, warm nights. During these months (as well as in July for school holidays), Argentines crowd resorts along the Atlantic. Meanwhile traffic-free Buenos Aires has a host of city-sponsored concerts that bring people out into the sun and moonlight.

Spring (September–December) and autumn (April–June), with their mild temperatures—and blossoms or changing leaves—are ideal for urban trekking. It's usually warm enough for just a light jacket, and it's right before or after the peak (and expensive) season. The best time for trips to Iguazú Falls is August–October, when temperatures are lower, the falls are fuller, and the spring coloring is at its brightest.

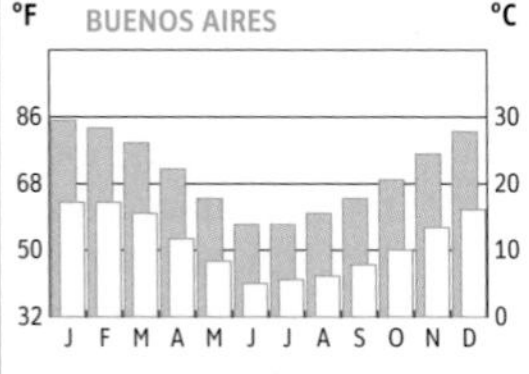

Updated by Brian Byrnes, Andy Footner, and Victoria Patience

Incredible food, fresh young designers, and a thriving cultural scene—all these Buenos Aires has. Yet less-tangible things are at the heart of the city's sizzle—for one, the spirit of its inhabitants. Here, a flirtatious glance can be as passionate as a tango; a heated sports discussion as important as a world-class soccer match. It's this zest for life that's making Buenos Aires one of Latin America's hottest destinations.

Of course, the devalued peso is a draw, too. There have never been so many foreign visitors on the streets. New boutiques—and boutique hotels—seem to open daily. World-renowned architects are designing luxury housing projects aimed at international customers who visit and then decide to stay. Old houses, it seems, are coveted by arty expats in search of inspiration for that novel they want to write.

A booming tango revival means dance floors are alive again. And camera crews are now a common sight on street corners: low production costs and "Old World generic" architecture—hinting at many far-off cities but resembling none—are an appealing backdrop for European commercials. Women are taking more-prominent social roles, not least in the form of the first female president, Cristina Kirchner, elected in 2007. (She's technically the second female president, though she's the first woman *elected* to the position. When Perón died, his third wife, Isabelita, took over for a disastrous couple of years.) Recognized civil partnerships and a thriving scene make Buenos Aires a prime gay destination. And the country is finally seeking to bring the torturers of the Dirty War (as the 1976–82 dictatorship is often known) to justice.

Sadly, there are increasing numbers of homeless people, and protests about the city government's health and education policies are commonplace. Some things stay the same, though. Food, family, and *fútbol* (or fashion) are still the holy trinity for most porteños. Philosophical discussions and psychoanalysis—Buenos Aires has more psychoanalysts per capita of any city in the world—remain popular pastimes. And in the face of so much change, *porteños* (as city residents are called) still approach life with as much dramatic intensity as ever.

EXPLORING BUENOS AIRES

Buenos Aires locals refer to themselves as porteños because many of their immigrant forebears arrived by ship to this port town. Known as thinkers, porteños launch readily into philosophical discussions and psychoanalysis (Buenos Aires has the largest number of psychoanalysts per capita of any city in the world). People here take their beliefs seriously, be they about politics, food, or sport, and passions (and voices) run high at dinner-table discussions. With 85% of the Argentine population of European origin, there's a blurred sense of national identity in Buenos Aires—South American or European? Residents are often concerned with how outsiders perceive them, and they also scrutinize one another—with casual, appreciative glances or curious stares—making many of them deeply image-conscious.

Unlike most other Latin American cities, where the architecture reveals a strong Spanish influence, little remains of Buenos Aires's colonial days. This is due in part to the short lifespan of the adobe (mud and straw) used to build the city's first houses, and also to the fact that Buenos Aires's elite have always followed Europe's architectural trends closely. The result is an arresting hotchpotch of building styles that hints at many far-off cities—Rome, Madrid, Paris, Budapest. With their boulevards lined with palatial mansions and spacious parks, Palermo, La Recoleta, and some parts of the downtown area are testament to days of urban planning on a grandiose scale (and budget), whereas San Telmo and La Boca have a distinctly working-class Italian feel.

CENTRO AND ENVIRONS

Office workers, shoppers, and sightseers fill the streets of Centro and its environs each day. Traffic noise and driving tactics also reach superlative levels. Locals profess to hate the chaos; unrushed visitors get a buzz out of the bustle. Either way, Centro provokes extreme reactions.

Plaza de Mayo is the original main square, and civic buildings both past and present are clustered between it and Plaza Congreso. Though you probably know Plaza de Mayo best from the balcony scene in the 1996 film *Evita,* many of Argentina's most historic events—including revolutions, demonstrations, and terrorist attacks—transpired around its axes. Bullet-marked facades, sidewalks embedded with plaques, and memorials where buildings once stood are reminders of all this history, and the protesters who fill the streets regularly are history in the making.

More-upbeat gatherings—open-air concerts, soccer victory celebrations, postelection reveling—take place around the Obelisco, a scaled-down Washington Monument look-alike that honors the founding of Buenos Aires. Inescapably phallic, it's the butt of local jokes about male insecurity in this oh-so-macho city. It's even dressed in a giant red condom each year on AIDS Awareness Day.

GETTING ORIENTED

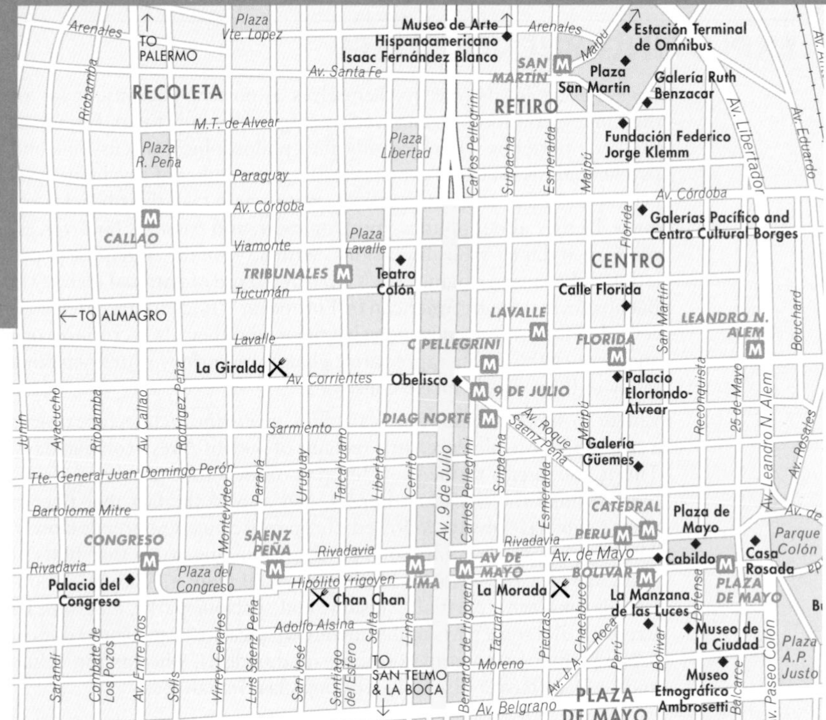

TOP EXPERIENCES

■ **Reflecting:** on Argentina's indigenous history at the Museo Etnográfico Juan B. Ambrosetti.

■ **Witnessing:** demonstrations in Plaza de Mayo, where Evita waved to crowds.

■ **Descending:** into the 17th-century tunnels the Jesuits built at La Manzana de las Luces.

■ **Wandering:** along Juana Manuela Gorriti and Pierina Dealessi to see Puerto Madero's "recycled" warehouses; Avenida de Mayo to visit 19th-century Europe; or Calle Florida for hustle, bustle, and souvenirs.

THE TERRITORY

The Microcentro (central business district) runs between Avenidas L. N. Alem and 9 de Julio and north of Avenida de Mayo. There are two axes: Avenida Corrientes (east–west) and pedestrian-only shopping street Calle Florida (north–south). Florida's northern end leads into Plaza San Martín in Retiro. South of the Microcentro lies Plaza de Mayo. From here Avenida de Mayo runs 12 blocks west to Plaza del Congreso. Puerto Madero borders the Centro to the east. Both it and its main thoroughfares, Avenida Alicia M. de Justo and Olga Cossentini, run parallel to the river.

SAFETY AND PRECAUTIONS

Be especially alert for "stain scammers" downtown: they squirt foul-smelling liquid on you surreptitiously, then "helpfully" offer to clean it off (as they pick your pocket). Use ATMs only during bank hours (weekdays 10–3); thieves target them after hours. Stay alert on Lavalle, a pedestrian street peppered with adult entertainment. At night wander with care.

2

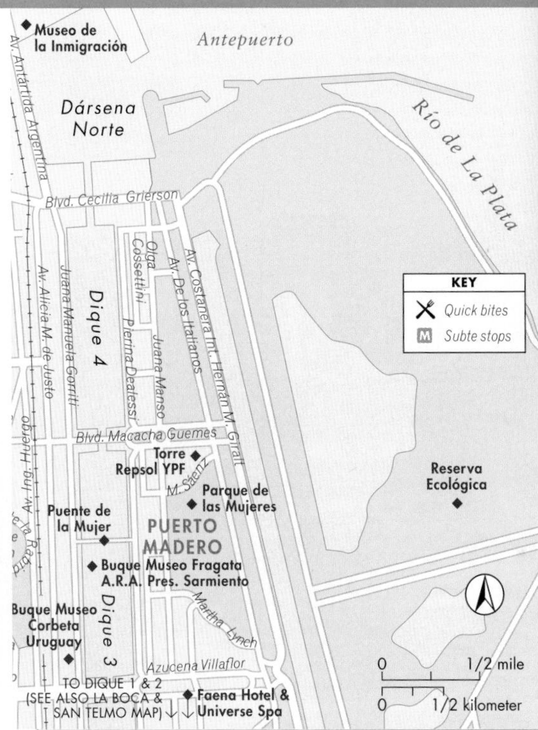

GETTING AROUND

The quickest way into Centro is by subte. For Microcentro, get off at Florida (Línea/Line B) or Lavalle (C). Retiro and Plaza San Martín have eponymous stations on Line C. Stations Avenida de Mayo (A), Catedral (D), and Bolívar (E) all serve Plaza de Mayo. Line A has stops along de Mayo, including at Congreso. Lines B, C, and D intersect at Carlos Pellegrini/Diagonal Norte/9 de Julio, one big, badly connected station under the Obelisco. Change lines here only if you're going more than one stop. Otherwise, walking is quicker, especially during rush hour. Puerto Madero is close to L. N. Alem on Line A, and is connected by the Tren del Este, a light-rail service running parallel to Avenida Alicia Moreau de Justo, between Córdoba and Independencia.

You can take a taxi or bus to the Microcentro, but, despite crowds and exhaust fumes, walking is the best way to move within it. Bus 17 connects Centro and Recoleta; so do buses 59 and 93, which continue to the Palermo parks. Bus 130 connects these areas with Puerto Madero. Buses 22 and 24 run between San Telmo and Microcentro.

QUICK BITES

Peruvian dishes at bargain prices have made a name for **Chan Chan** (✉ *Hipólito Yrigoyen 1390, Congreso* ☎ *11/4382–8492*). The spicy ceviches are ideal for stoking your sightseeing fires, and the deep-fried corn kernels they bring while you wait are almost a meal in themselves.

Local office workers know that the best empanadas in the Microcentro are made by **La Morada** (✉ *Hipólito Yrigoyen 778, Plaza de Mayo* ☎ *11/4343–3003*). Vintage adverts, 1960s LPs, and photos of late, great Argentinean celebrities are hung so close you can barely see the walls.

Beret-wearing intellectuals and perfumed theatergoers love the totally retro café **La Giralda** (✉ *Av. Corrientes 1453, Centro* ☎ *11/4371–3846*). Don't let the small tables or surly waiters put you off; its signature *chocolate con churros* (hot chocolate with crisp cigar-shaped donuts) are to die for. If it's savory you're after, try a *tostado mixto* (toasted ham-and-cheese sandwich).

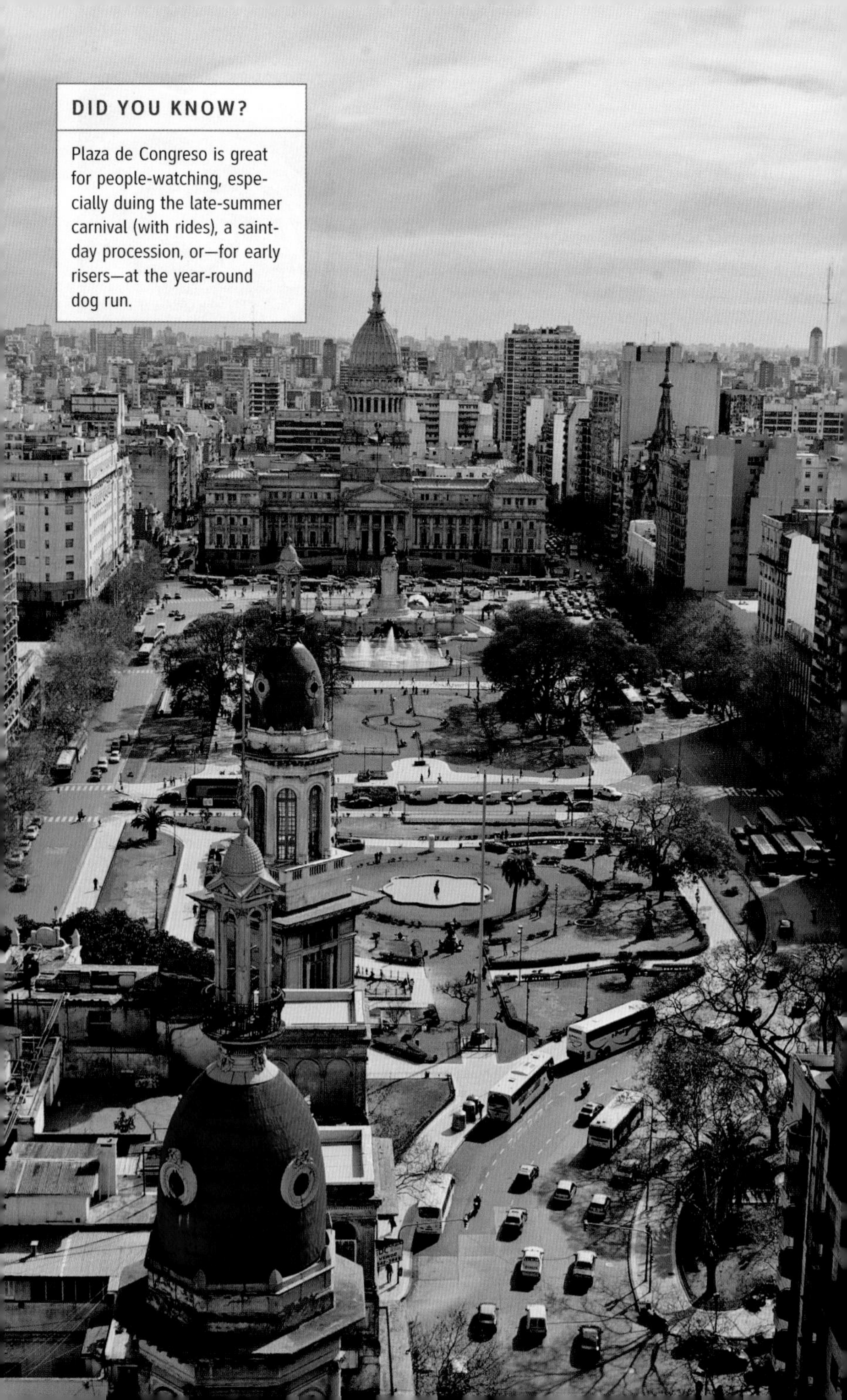

DID YOU KNOW?

Plaza de Congreso is great for people-watching, especially duing the late-summer carnival (with rides), a saint-day procession, or—for early risers—at the year-round dog run.

The town's most highbrow cultural events are hosted a few blocks away in the Teatro Colón, and the highest-grossing theatrical productions line Avenida Corrientes, whose sidewalks overflow on weekends with dolled-up locals. Argentina's biggest scandals center—the judicial district—is on nearby Tribunales.

Contemporary architecture by such world-renowned masters as Sir Norman Foster and local boy César Pelli are fast filling adjacent Puerto Madero. This onetime port area is now the city's swankiest district, with the most expensive real estate, hotels, and restaurants.

TAKING IT IN

Crowds and traffic can make touring draining: try to do a few short visits rather than one long marathon. You can see most of the sights in the Plaza de Mayo area over the course of a leisurely afternoon; a late-morning wander and lunch in Puerto Madero is one good way to precede this.

Half a day in the Microcentro is enough to take in the sights and have your fill of risky street-crossing, though you could spend a lot more time caught up in shops. Avoid the Microcentro midweek between noon and 2, or sit it out in a restaurant. If you're planning on hard-core shopping, come on a weekend. The area is quiet at night, and a little dangerous in its desolation.

HOW TO SPEND . . .

An Hour or Two: combine a visit to Plaza de Mayo with one nearby museum or some shopping on Calle Florida.

A Half-Day: start with a late-morning wander in Puerto Madero, then visit the Museo Etnográfico. Time lunch early enough to get to La Manzana de las Luces for the 3:30 tour. Finish your afternoon in the shops along Florida or walking along Avenida de Mayo to Plaza Congreso, refueling at Café Tortoni on the way.

TOP ATTRACTIONS

La Manzana de Las Luces *(The Block of Illumination).* More history is packed into this single block of buildings southwest of Plaza de Mayo than in scores of other city blocks put together. Among other things, it was the enclave for higher learning: the metaphorical *luces* (lights) of its name refer to the "illuminated" scholars who worked within.

The block's earliest occupant was the controversial Jesuit order, which began construction here in 1661. The only survivor from this first stage is the galleried **Procuraduría** (⊠ *Corner of Alsina and Perú*), the colonial administrative headquarters for the Jesuits' vast land holdings in northeastern Argentina and Paraguay (think: *The Mission*). Historic defense tunnels, still undergoing archaeological excavation, linked the Jesuit headquarters to churches in the area, the Cabildo, and the port. Visits here include a glimpse of a specially reinforced section. After the Jesuits' expulsion from Argentina in 1767 (the Spanish crown saw them as a threat), the simple brick-and-mud structure housed first the city's first school of medicine and then the University of Buenos Aires. Fully restored, it's now home to a school of luthiers and a rather tacky crafts market.

The Jesuits honored their patron saint at the **Iglesia de San Ignacio de Loyola** *(Saint Ignatius of Loyola Church)* (✉ *Corner of Alsina and Bolívar*). The first church on the site was built of adobe in 1675; within a few decades it was rebuilt in stone. Argentina's first congress convened within the **Casas Virreinales** *(Viceroyal Houses)* (✉ *Corner of Moreno and Perú*): ironic, given that it was built to house colonial civil servants. The remaining historic building on the block is the neoclassical **Colegio Nacional,** a top-notch public school and a hotbed of political activism that replaced a Jesuit-built structure. The president attends graduation ceremonies, and Einstein gave a lecture here in 1925.

The Iglesia de San Ignacio is open to the public, but you can only visit the rest of Manzana de las Luces on guided tours led by excellent professional historians. Regular departures are in Spanish, but they provide brochures with English summaries of each stage; groups of over 20 people can call ahead to arrange English-language visits. ✉ *Entrance and inquiries at Perú 272, Plaza de Mayo* ☎ *11/4342–6973 Ext. 129* 🌐 *www.manzanadelasluces.gov.ar* 🎟 *6 pesos* ⏲ *Visits by guided tour only; Spanish-language tours leave daily at 3 and at 4:30, and 6* PM *on weekends; call to arrange tours in English* Ⓜ *A to Plaza de Mayo, D to Catedral, E to Bolívar.*

Museo Etnográfico Juan B. Ambrosetti *(Ethnographic Museum).* Given that the 100-peso bill still honors General Roca, the man responsible for the massacre of most of Patagonia's indigenous population, it's unsurprising that information on Argentina's original inhabitants is sparse. This fascinating but little-visited museum is a welcome remedy.

The ground-floor galleries trace the history of human activity in Patagonia, with an emphasis on the tragic results of the European arrival. Dugout canoes, exquisite Mapuche silver jewelry, and scores of archive photos and illustrations are the main exhibits. In the upstairs northwestern Argentina gallery the focus is mainly archaeological. Displays briefly chronicle the evolution of Andean civilization, the heyday of the Inca empire, and postcolonial life. Artifacts include ceramics, textiles, jewelry, farming tools, and food: anyone for some 4,000-year-old corn?

The collection is now run by the liberal Philosophy and Letters Faculty of the University of Buenos Aires. Although their insightful labels and explanations are all in Spanish, you can ask for a photocopied sheet with English versions of the texts. It's a pleasure just to wander the quiet, light-filled 19th-century town house that houses both the collection and an anthropological library. The peaceful inner garden is the perfect place for some post-museum reflection when you're done. ✉ *Moreno 350, Plaza de Mayo* ☎ *11/4345–8196* 🌐 *museoetnografico.filo.uba.ar* 🎟 *3 pesos* ⏲ *Tues.–Fri. 1–7, weekends 3–7* Ⓜ *Line A to Plaza de Mayo; Line D to Catedral; Line E to Bolívar.*

★ **Plaza de Mayo.** Since its construction in 1580, this has been the setting for Argentina's most politically turbulent moments, including the uprising against Spanish colonial rule on May 25, 1810—hence its name. The square was once divided in two by a *recova* (gallery), but this reminder of colonial times was demolished in 1883, and the square's central monument, the Pirámide de Mayo, was later moved to its place. The pyramid you see is actually a 1911 extension of the original, erected in 1811 on the anniversary of the Revolution of May, which is hidden inside. The bronze equestrian statue of General Manuel Belgrano, designer of Argentina's flag, dates from 1873, and stands at the east end of the plaza. Here, too, you can witness the changing of the Grenadier Regiment guards; it takes place weekdays every two hours from 9 until 7, Saturday at 9 and 11, and Sunday at 9, 11, and 1.

The eclectic Casa de Gobierno, better known as the **Casa Rosada** (✉ *Hipólito Yrigoyen 219, Plaza de Mayo* ☎ *11/4344–3802* 🌐 *www.museo.gov.ar* 🎫 *Free* 🕐 *Weekends 10–6*) or Pink House, is at the plaza's eastern end, with its back to the river. The building houses the government's executive branch—the president works here but lives elsewhere—and was built in the late 19th century over the foundations of an earlier customhouse and fortress. Swedish, Italian, and French architects have since modified the structure, which accounts for the odd mix of styles. Its curious hue dates from the presidency of Domingo Sarmiento, who ordered it painted pink as a symbol of unification between two warring political factions, the *federales* (whose color was red) and the *unitarios* (represented by white). Local legend has it that the original paint was made by mixing whitewash with bull's blood.

The city council—now based in the ornate building over Avenida de Mayo—originally met in the **Cabildo** (✉ *Bolívar 65, Plaza de Mayo* ☎ *11/4334–1782* 🎫 *3 pesos* 🕐 *Wed.–Fri. 10:30–5, weekends 11:30–6*). It dates from 1765, and is the only colonial building on Plaza de Mayo. The epicenter of the May Revolution of 1810, where patriotic citizens gathered to vote against Spanish rule, the hall is one of Argentina's national shrines. However, this hasn't stopped successive renovations to its detriment, including the demolition of the whole right end of the structure to make way for the new Avenida de Mayo in 1894 and of the left end for Diagonal Julio Roca in 1931. Inside, a small museum exhibits artifacts and documents pertaining to the events of the May Revolution as well as a jail cell. Thursday and Friday from 11 to 6 an artisan fair takes place on the Patio del Cabildo. Ⓜ *Line A to Plaza de Mayo; Line D to Catedral; Line E to Bolívar.*

Teatro Colón. Its magnitude, magnificent acoustics, and opulence (grander than Milan's La Scala) position the Teatro Colón (Colón Theater) among the world's top five operas. An ever-changing stream of imported talent bolsters the well-regarded local lyric and ballet companies. After an eventful 18-year building process involving the death of one architect and the murder of another, the ornate Italianate structure was finally inaugurated in 1908 with Verdi's *Aïda.* It has hosted the likes of Maria Callas, Richard Strauss, Arturo Toscanini, Igor Stravinsky, Enrico Caruso, and Luciano Pavarotti, who said that the Colón has only one flaw: the acoustics are so good that every mistake can be heard.

The theater is currently dark owing to restoration work that's slated to end in 2010, but may go on for longer. Until then, tours of the theater—once very popular—are suspended, and the newly scrubbed stone facade is all you can see of it. Opera, ballet, and other performances normally held here are being held in other Buenos Aires theaters. ✉ *Main*

DID YOU KNOW?

La Puente de la Mujer, or "woman's bridge," connects Microcentro with Puerto Madero. The whole middle section of the bridge, including the skyward-reaching arm, swings like a door on a hinge to let boats pass.

entrance: Libertad between Tucumán and Viamonte; Box office: Pasaje Toscanini 1180, Centro ☎ 11/4378–7100 tickets, 11/4378–7132 tours 🌐 www.teatrocolon.org.ar Ⓜ *D to Tribunales.*

WORTH NOTING

Buque Museo Fragata A.R.A. Presidente Sarmiento (*President Sarmiento* Frigate Museum). The navy commissioned this frigate from England in 1898 to be used as an open-sea training vessel. The 280-foot boat used up to 33 sails and carried more than 300 crew members: the beautifully restored cabins afford a glimpse of what life onboard was like. Surprisingly luxurious officers' quarters include parquet floors, wood paneling, and leather armchairs; cadets had to make do with hammocks. ✉ *Dique 3, Alicia M. de Justo 900 block, Puerto Madero* ☎ *11/4334–9386* 🎫 *2 pesos* ⏲ *Daily 10–7.*

Museo de la Ciudad. "Whimsical" is one way to describe the City Museum, which focuses on random aspects of domestic and public life in Buenos Aires in times past. "Eccentric" is probably closer to the mark for the permanent collection: an array of typical porteño doors. Historical toys, embroidery, religion in Buenos Aires, and garden gnomes (yes, really) have been some of the focuses of temporary exhibitions. Still, the peaceful building—which was restored in 2009—is worth a 10-minute wander if you're in the neighborhood. Downstairs, the Farmacia La Estrella sells modern medicine and cosmetics from a perfectly preserved 19th-century shop. ✉ *Alsina 412, Plaza de Mayo* ☎ *11/4331–9855* 🌐 *www.museos.buenosaires.gov.ar/ciudad.htm* 🎫 *1 peso, free Mon. and Wed.* ⏲ *Daily 3–7* Ⓜ *A to Plaza de Mayo, D to Catedral, E to Bolívar.*

Puente de la Mujer. Tango dancers inspired the sweeping asymmetrical lines of Valencian architect Santiago Calatrava's design for the pedestrian-only Bridge of the Woman. Puerto Madero's street names pay homage to famous Argentine women, hence the bridge's name. (Ironically its most visible part—a soaring 128-foot arm—represents the man of a couple in mid-tango.) The $6 million structure was made in Spain and paid for by local businessmen Alberto L. González, one of the brains behind Puerto Madero's redevelopment; he also built the Hilton Hotel here. Twenty engines rotate the bridge to allow ships to pass through. ✉ *Dique 3, C. Lorenzini, at Alicia M. de Justo, Puerto Madero.*

Reserva Ecológica. The 865-acre Ecological Reserve was built over a landfill, and is home to more than 500 species of birds and a variety of flora and fauna. On weekends thousands of porteños vie for a spot on the grass, so come midweek if you want to bird-watch and sunbathe in peace or use the jogging and cycling tracks. A monthly guided "Walking under the Full Moon" tour in Spanish begins at 8:30 PM. Even if you don't speak Spanish it's still a great way to get back to nature at night; otherwise avoid the area after sunset. It's just a short walk from the south end of Puerto Madero. ✉ *Av. Tristán Achával Rodríguez 1550, Puerto Madero* ☎ *11/4315–1320, 11/4893–1588 tours* 🎫 *Free* ⏲ *Apr.–Oct., Tues.–Sun. 8–6; Nov.–Mar., Tues.–Sun. 8–7; guided visits in Spanish weekends at 10:30 and 3:30.*

LA BOCA AND SAN TELMO

"The south also exists," quip residents of bohemian neighborhoods like San Telmo and La Boca, which historically played second fiddle to posher northern barrios. No more. The hottest designers have boutiques here, new restaurants are booked out, and property prices are soaring. The south is also the linchpin of the city's tango revival, appropriate given that the dance was born in these quarters.

San Telmo, Buenos Aires's first suburb, was originally inhabited by sailors and takes its name from their wandering patron saint. All the same, the mariners main preoccupations were clearly less than spiritual, and San Telmo became famous for its brothels. That didn't stop the area's first experience of gentrification: wealthy Spaniards built ornate homes here in the early 19th century, but ran for Recoleta when a yellow-fever epidemic struck in 1871. Newly arrived immigrants crammed into their abandoned mansions, known as *conventillos* (tenement houses). Today these same houses are fought over by foreign buyers dying to ride the wave of urban renewal—the *reciclaje* (recycling), as porteños call it—that's sweeping the area.

Neighboring La Boca shares much of San Telmo's gritty history. It sits on the fiercely polluted Riachuelo River, where rusting ships and warehouses remind you that this was once the city's main port. The immigrants who first settled here built their houses from corrugated metal and brightly colored paint left over from the shipyards. Today, imitations of these vibrant buildings form one of Buenos Aires's most emblematic sights, the Caminito. Two quite different colors have made La Boca famous: the blue and gold of the Boca Juniors soccer team, whose massive home stadium is the barrio's unofficial heart.

TAKING IT IN

San Telmo thrives on Sunday, thanks to the art and antiques market in Plaza Dorrego. During the week a leisurely afternoon's visit is ideal. Start with lunch in a café at the northern or southern end of San Telmo, then spend an hour or two wandering the cobbled streets. You still have time for some shopping before winding up with a coffee or a drink. In La Boca, allow two or three hours to explore Caminito and do a museum or two. It's busy all week, but expect extra crowds on weekends.

HOW TO SPEND . . .

An hour or two: midweek, combine a brisk walk around San Telmo with a taxi-ride to La Boca for a visit to Fundación Proa and a cursory glance at Caminito. On Sunday, trawl the stalls at the market and do the shortened tour of Zanjón de Granados.

A full day: ground yourself in history at El Zanjón de Granados, then hit San Telmo's antiques shops before lunch. Do a gallery or some shopping, then catch Bus 53 or a cab to La Boca, where you can go arty at Caminito and Fundación Proa or sporty at the Museo de la Pasión Boquense. Finish back in San Telmo for drinks and dinner.

GETTING ORIENTED

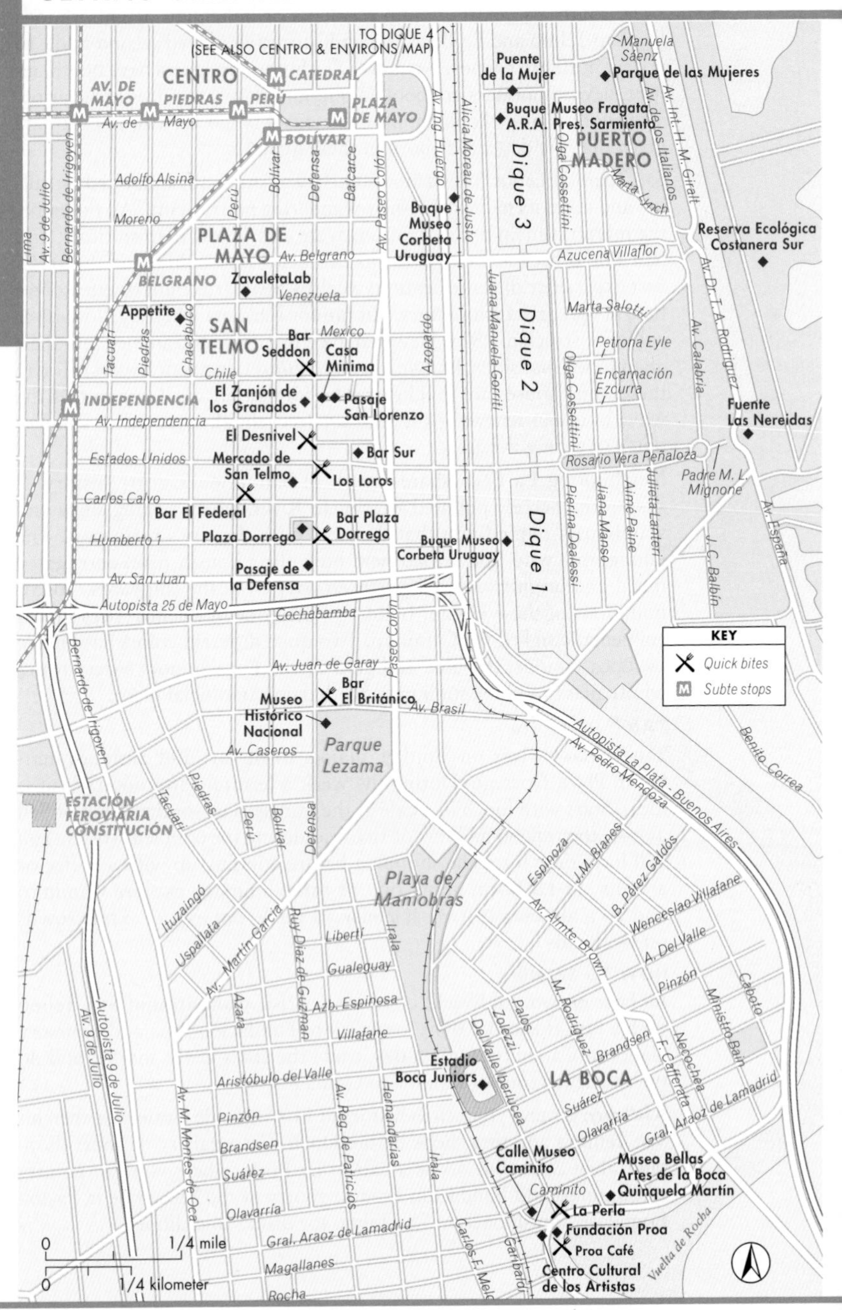

THE TERRITORY

San Telmo, south of the Centro, is bordered by Avenida Madero to the east, Avenidas Brasil and Caseros to the south, Piedras to the west, and—depending on who you ask—Chile or Belgrano to the north. The main drag is north–south Defensa, part of which is pedestrian-only. It forms one side of Plaza Dorrego, the area's tourist hub.

South of Avenida Brasil lies La Boca, whose westernmost edge is Avenida Patricios. The Riachuelo River forms a curving border; Avenida Don Pedro de Mendoza runs beside it.

GETTING AROUND

The subte takes you within nine blocks of San Telmo. The closest stations to the southern end are Independencia (Line C or E) and San Juan (Line C). Be prepared to walk nine blocks east along Avenidas Independencia, Estados Unidos, or San Juan to get to Defensa, the main street. To approach San Telmo from the north, get off at Bolívar (Line E) or Catedral (Line D) and walk eight blocks south along Bolívar. Buses 22, 24, 26, and 28 connect San Telmo to Centro. The same route by taxi costs 8–10 pesos.

There's no subte to La Boca, so taxi travel is a good bet, especially after dark: expect to pay 12–15 pesos to or from the Centro. Bus 29 runs between La Boca and the Centro; so do Buses 64 and 152, which continue to Palermo. Bus 53 connects La Boca and San Telmo.

SAFETY AND PRECAUTIONS

San Telmo's popularity with visitors has led to increased police presence in the busiest areas (especially near Defensa). Still, instances of petty crime are common. After dark, stick to busy, well-lighted streets close to Defensa.

La Boca is far sketchier, and you'd do best not to stray from the Caminito area. Avoid the neighborhood after dark, and take radio taxis if you must visit then.

TOP EXPERIENCES

- **Photographing:** cobbled streets, then comparing them with the pro's work at Appetite or ZavaletaLab galleries.
- **Descending:** into El Zanjón de Granados's restored tunnels for a different perspective.
- **Drinking:** in the atmosphere—and a *cortado* (coffee with a splash of milk)—at time-honored El Federal or La Perla cafés.
- **Watching:** the sun set from Fundación Proa's roof café.
- **Wandering:** Caminito (and adjacent Garibaldi and Magallanes), to tick the sightseeing boxes, or Defensa to cruise antiques stalls (on Sunday) and boutiques.

QUICK BITES

El Desnivel (✉ *Defensa 855, San Telmo* ☎ *11/4300–9081*) is a classic parrilla. Trimmings don't go beyond a mixed salad and fries, and surly waiters all but fling food at you. It's all part of the experience.

Gorgeous port views await at the rooftop **Proa Café** (✉ *Fundación Proa, Av. Pedro de Mendoza 1929, La Boca* ☎ *11/4104–1003*). Salads, quiches, and pastas cooked by local celebrity chefs the Petersen brothers.

Authentic **La Perla** (✉ *Av. Pedro de Mendoza 1899, La Boca* ☎ *11/4301–2985*) is *the* spot for a *licuado* (milk shake), or a tostado mixto (a local take on the croque monsieur).

TOP ATTRACTIONS

★ **Calle Museo Caminito.** Cobblestones, tango dancers, and haphazardly constructed, vividly painted conventillos have made Calle Museo Caminito the darling of Buenos Aires's postcard manufacturers since this pedestrian street and open-air museum/art market opened in 1959. Artists fill the block-long street with works depicting port life and tango, which is said to have been born in La Boca. It's all more commercial than cultural, but its embrace of all things tacky make it a fun outing.

Many of La Boca's tenements have been recycled into souvenir shops. The plastic Che Guevaras and dancing couples make the shops in the **Centro Cultural de los Artistas** (✉ *Magallanes 861* ⏲ *Mon.–Sat. 10:30–6*) as forgettable as all the others on the street, but the uneven stairs and wrought-iron balcony hint at what a conventillo interior was like. A sculptor artist owns the turquoise-and-tomato-red **Museo Conventillo de Marjan Grum** (✉ *Garibaldi 1429*). The opening hours of this gallery–cultural center are erratic, but even the facade is worth a look. ✉ *Caminito between Av. Pedro de Mendoza (La Vuelta de Rocha promenade) and Olivarría, La Boca* 🎫 *Free* ⏲ *Daily 10–6.*

★ **Estadio Boca Juniors.** Walls exploding with huge, vibrant murals of insurgent workers, famous inhabitants of La Boca, and fútbol greats splashed in blue and gold let you know that the Estadio Boca Juniors is at hand. The stadium that's also known as La Bombonera (meaning "candy box," supposedly because the fans' singing reverberates as it would inside a candy tin) is the home of Argentina's most popular club. Boca Juniors' history is completely tied to the port neighborhood. The nickname, *xeneizes,* is a mangling of *genovés* (Genovese), reflecting the origins of most immigrants to the Boca area. Blue and gold decks the stadium's fiercely banked seating.

The extensive stadium tour is worth the extra money. Lighthearted guides take you all over the stands as well as to press boxes, locker rooms, underground tunnels, and the emerald grass of the field itself. ✉ *Brandsen 805, at del Valle Iberlucea, La Boca* ☎ *11/4309–4700 stadium, 11/4362–1100 museum* 🌐 *www.museoboquense.com.ar* 🎫 *Museum: 14 pesos. Stadium: 14 pesos. Museum and stadium: 22 pesos* ⏲ *Museum daily 10–6 except when Boca plays at home; stadium tours hourly 11–5; English usually available, call ahead.*

Pasaje de la Defensa. Wandering through this well-preserved house affords a glimpse of life in San Telmo's golden era. Behind its elegant but narrow stone facade the house is built deep into the block around a series of internal courtyards. This type of long, narrow construction is typical of San Telmo, and is known as a *casa chorizo* (sausage house). Once the home of the well-to-do Ezeiza family, it became a *conventillo* (tenement), but is now a picturesque spot for antiques and curio shopping. The stores here are open daily 10 to 6. ✉ *Defensa 1179, San Telmo* ☎ *No phone.*

★ **Plaza Dorrego.** During the week a handful of craftspeople and a few scruffy pigeons are the only ones enjoying the shade from the stately trees in the city's second-oldest square. Sunday couldn't be more different: scores of stalls selling antiques, curios, and just plain old stuff

DID YOU KNOW?

If you're in La Boca at the right time, you might hear thousands of fans cheering from La Bombonera, the home stadium of the Boca Juniors *fútbol* team. Especially along El Caminito and other streets in this neighborhood, kids grow up dreaming of Boca Junior fame. Dreams are forever: 40% of Argentina's population supports Boca Juniors, the largest percentage for any Argentine team.

move in to form the Feria de San Pedro Telmo (San Pedro Telmo Fair). Tango dancers take to the cobbles, as do hundreds of shoppers (mostly tourists) browsing the tango memorabilia, antique silver, brass, crystal, and Argentine curios. Note that prices are high at stalls on the square and astronomical in the shops surrounding it, and vendors are immune to bargaining. More affordable offerings—mostly handicrafts and local artists' work—are on stalls along nearby streets like Defensa. ■ **TIP→ Be on the lookout for antique (or just plain old) glass soda siphons that once adorned every bar top in Buenos Aires. Classic colors are green and turquoise.** Be sure to look up as you wander Plaza Dorrego, as the surrounding architecture provides an overview of the influences—Spanish colonial, French classical, and ornate Italian masonry—that shaped the city in the 19th and 20th centuries.

★ **El Zanjón de Granados.** All 500 years of Buenos Aires's history are packed into this unusual house. The street it's on was once a small river—the *zanjón,* or gorge, of the property's name—where the first, unsuccessful attempt to found Buenos Aires took place in 1536. When the property's current owner—or custodian, as he prefers to be known—decided to develop what was then a run-down conventillo, he began to discover all sorts of things beneath the house: pottery and cutlery, the foundations of past constructions, and a 500-foot network of tunnels that has taken over 20 years to excavate. These were once used to channel water, but like the street itself, they were sealed after San Telmo's yellow-fever outbreaks. With the help of historians and architects, they've now been painstakingly restored, and the entire site has been transformed into a private museum, where the only exhibit is the redbrick building itself. Excellent hour-long guided tours in English and Spanish take you through low-lighted sections of the tunnels. The history lesson then continues aboveground, where you can see the surviving wall of a construction from 1740, the 19th-century mansion built around it, and traces of the conventillo it became. Expect few visitors and plenty of atmosphere on weekdays; cheaper, shorter tours on Sunday draw far more people. If you want to spend even more time here, you can rent the whole place (including an adjacent building reached via the tunnels) for functions. ✉ *Defensa 755, San Telmo* ☎ *11/4361–3002* 🌐 *www.elzanjon.com.ar* 🎫 *Guided tours 40 pesos (1 hr, weekdays only); $25 (30 min, Sun. only)* ⏲ *Tours weekdays 11–3 on the hr; Sun. 1–6 every 15 min. Closed Sat.*

WORTH NOTING

Museo de Bellas Artes de La Boca Quinquela Martín *(Quinquela Martín Fine Arts Museum of La Boca).* Vibrant port scenes were the trademark of artist and philanthropist Benito Quinquela Martín, the man who first put La Boca on the cultural map. His work and part of his studio are showcased on the third floor of this huge building, which he donated to the state for a cultural center in 1936. Don't be surprised to have to jostle your way in through kids filing into class: downstairs is an elementary school, something that the galleries' bland institutional architecture doesn't let you forget. Quinquela Martín set out to fill the second floor with Argentine art—on the condition that works were figurative and didn't belong to any "ism." Badly lighted rooms and lack of any visible organization make it hard to enjoy the minor paintings by Berni, Sívori, Soldi, and other local masters. Outside is a huge sculpture terrace with great views of the river and old port buildings on one side; and the Boca Juniors stadium and low-rise downtown skyline on the other. ✉ *Av. Pedro de Mendoza 1835, La Boca* ☎ *11/4301–1080* 🎫 *5 pesos* ⏲ *Tues.–Fri. 10–6, weekends 11–6. Also closed on days when Boca Juniors plays at home.*

Museo Histórico Nacional. What better place for the National History Museum than overlooking the spot where the city was supposedly founded? The beautiful chestnut-and-white Italianate mansion that houses the museum once belonged to entrepreneur and horticulturalist Gregorio Lezama. It became a quarantine station when cholera and yellow-fever epidemics raged in San Telmo, before opening as this museum in 1897. At this writing, the museum is closed for some much-needed renovations and is due to reopen in mid-2010.

The National History Museum sits in the shade of enormous magnolia, palm, cedar, and elm trees on the sloping hillside of **Parque Lezama.** Bronze statues of Greek heroes, stone urns, and an imposing fountain shipped from Paris hint at former glory. Patchy grass, cracked paths, and unpainted benches are a nod to more-recent times. A monument in the northwestern corner celebrates conquistador Pedro de Mendoza, said to have founded Buenos Aires on this spot. Watching over the park are the onion-shaped domes of the Catedral Santísima Trinidad Iglesia Ortodoxa Rusa (Holy Trinity Russian Orthodox Church) immortalized by Argentine writer Ernesto Sabato in his novel *Sobre Heroes y Tumbas* (*Of Heroes and Tombs*). ✉ *Calle Defensa 1600, San Telmo* ☎ *11/4307–1182* 🎫 *Free* ⏲ *Feb.–Dec., Wed.–Sun. 11–6.*

RECOLETA AND ALMAGRO

For the most-illustrious families, Recoleta's boundaries are the boundaries of the civilized world. The local equivalents of the Vanderbilts are baptized and married in the Basílica del Pilar, throw parties in the Alvear Palace Hotel, live in spacious 19th-century apartments, and wouldn't dream of shopping elsewhere. Ornate mausoleums in the Cementerio de la Recoleta promise an equally stylish afterlife.

Recoleta wasn't always synonymous with elegance. Colonists, including city founder Juan de Garay, farmed here. So did the Franciscan Recoleto friars, whose 1700s settlement here inspired the district's name. Their church, the Basílica del Pilar, was almost on the riverbank then: tanneries grew up around it, and Recoleta became famous for its *pulperías* (taverns) and brothels. Everything changed with the 1871 outbreak of yellow fever in the south of the city. The elite swarmed to Recoleta, building the *palacios* and stately Parisian-style apartment buildings that are now the neighborhood's trademark.

GETTING ORIENTED

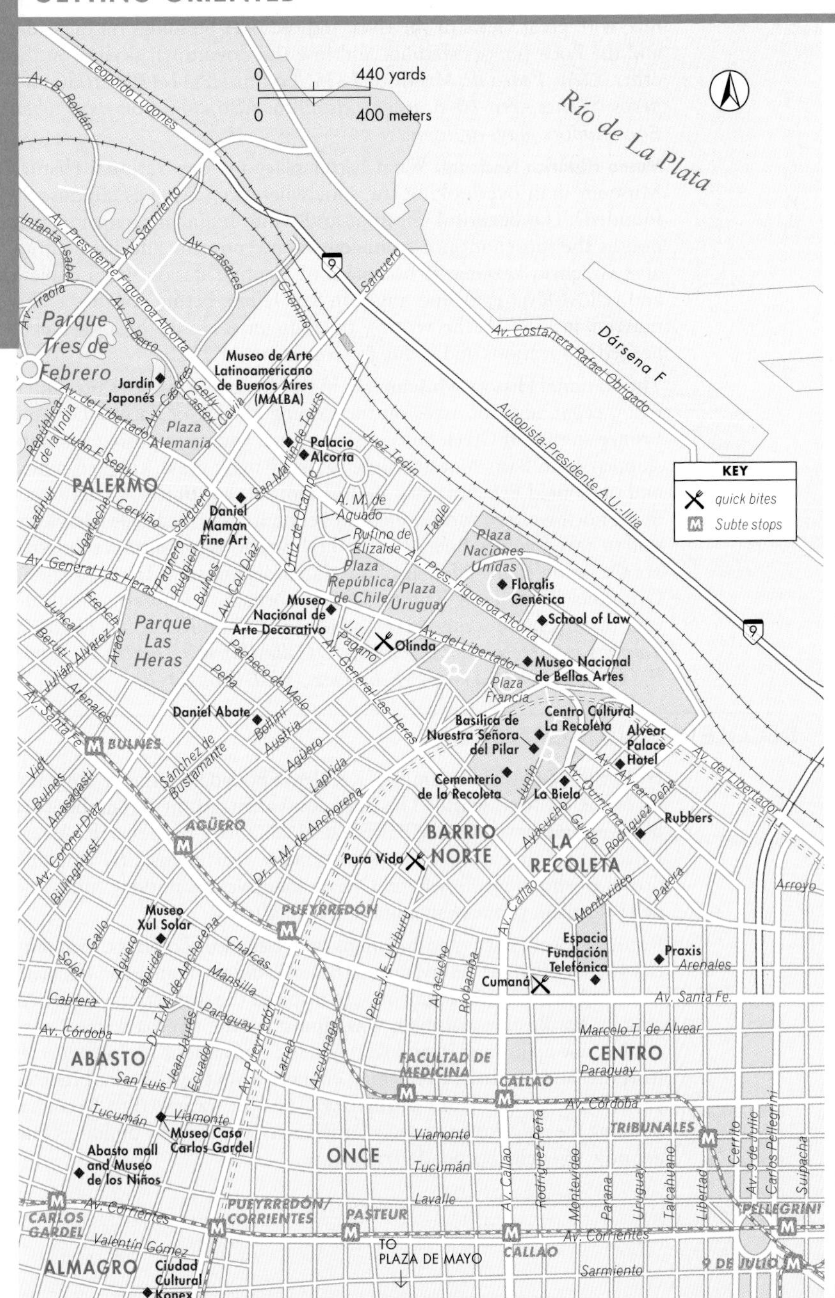

Río de La Plata
0 440 yards
0 400 meters
KEY
quick bites
Subte stops
Parque Tres de Febrero
Jardín Japonés
Plaza Alemania
Museo de Arte Latinoamericano de Buenos Aires (MALBA)
Palacio Alcorta
PALERMO
Daniel Maman Fine Art
Parque Las Heras
Plaza Naciones Unidas
Floralis Genérica
School of Law
Plaza República de Chile
Plaza Uruguay
Museo Nacional de Arte Decorativo
Olinda
Museo Nacional de Bellas Artes
Plaza Francia
Daniel Abate
Basílica de Nuestra Señora del Pilar
Centro Cultural La Recoleta
Alvear Palace Hotel
Cementerío de la Recoleta
La Biela
Rubbers
BULNES
AGÜERO
PUEYRREDÓN
BARRIO NORTE
LA RECOLETA
Pura Vida
Museo Xul Solar
Espacio Fundación Telefónica
Praxis
Cumaná
ABASTO
CENTRO
FACULTAD DE MEDICINA
CALLAO
TRIBUNALES
Museo Casa Carlos Gardel
Abasto mall and Museo de los Niños
ONCE
CARLOS GARDEL
PUEYRREDÓN/ CORRIENTES
PASTEUR
CALLAO
PELLEGRINI
9 DE JULIO
ALMAGRO
Ciudad Cultural Konex
TO PLAZA DE MAYO
Dársena F
Av. Costanera Rafael Obligado
Autopista-Presidente A.U. Illia
Av. del Libertador
Av. Presidente Figueroa Alcorta
Av. General Las Heras
Av. Santa Fe
Av. Callao
Av. Córdoba
Av. Corrientes
Av. Pueyrredón
Av. 9 de Julio

THE TERRITORY

The River Plate borders Recoleta to the north. Uruguay and Montevideo join to form the eastern border; the jagged western edge is made up of Mario Bravo, Coronel Díaz, and Tagle. The area between Juncal and Córdoba—Recoleta's southern boundary—is known as Barrio Norte, whose main thoroughfare is Santa Fe. In Recoleta proper, Avenidas Alvear and Quintana are the key streets.

Almagro is officially bordered by Avenidas Córdoba and Estado de Israel to the north, Río de Janeiro to the west, Independencia to the south, and Sánchez de Bustamente and Gallo to the east. The Abasto subdistrict, which centers on Gallo and Corrientes, stretches a few blocks farther east into neighboring Balvanera.

GETTING AROUND

True to its elite roots, Recoleta has no subway, so taxis are the best option. Expect to pay around 12 pesos from downtown or Palermo. Bus 17 runs from San Telmo and the Centro; the 92 connects Retiro and Recoleta, then continues to central Palermo and Almagro. Traffic can be slow within Recoleta and Barrio Norte—walking is fast and pleasant.

Heavy traffic means Almagro is best reached by subte. Line B runs along Avenida Corrientes through Almagro; Carlos Gardel station leads right into the Abasto mall. Bus 24 connects Almagro with Centro and San Telmo; the 168 goes west to Palermo Viejo.

SAFETY AND PRECAUTIONS

Recoleta and Barrio Norte are relatively safe in the day, but stick to well-lighted streets at night. Bag snatching is opportunist rather than systematic here: keep a firm grip on your purse in the crowded weekend market and in busy restaurants. Although Almagro is on the upswing, many streets near the Abasto mall are still run-down. Wander with caution.

TOP EXPERIENCES

■ **Seeking:** unusual statues in the spooky but stunning Cementerio de Recoleta.

■ **Window-shopping:** on Avenida Quintana for Argentine designs—Martín Churba, Celedonio Lohidoy, Min Agostini—but buying more affordable ones on Avendia Santa Fe or in the Abasto mall.

■ **Glimpsing:** the 19th-century on the first floor of the Museo Nacional de Bellas Artes.

■ **Wandering:** Avenida Alvear for the gorgeous late-19th- and early-20th-century mansions (many containing fancy clothing stores).

QUICK BITES

The stews and empanadas at chaotic **Cumaná** (✉ *Rodríguez Peña 1149, Barrio Norte* ☎ *11/4893–9207*) are a far cry from Recoleta's European pretensions. Skip dessert (nearby ice-creameries are better).

Expect super-fresh juices and smoothies at **Pura Vida** (✉ *Uriburu 1489, Recoleta* ☎ *11/4806–0017*). The sandwiches, salads, and wraps are just as healthy.

Offerings like mini lamb empanadas or quail eggs with Brie and sautéed mushrooms make for a perfect bistro lunch at **Olinda** (✉ *José León Pagano 2697, Recoleta* ☎ *11/4806–6343*). It's on a side street several blocks north of the cemetery and a block from the Museo Nacional de Arte Decorativo.

An unofficial subdistrict, Barrio Norte, is one step south of Recoleta proper and one step down the social ladder. Shopping is the draw: local chains, sportswear flagships, and mini-malls of vintage clothing and club wear line Avenida Santa Fe between 9 de Julio and Puerreydón.

Almagro lies southwest of Recoleta but is a world apart. Traditionally a gritty, working-class neighborhood, it spawned many tango greats, including the legendary Carlos Gardel. The Abasto subdistrict has long been the heart of the barrio: it centers on the massive art deco building (at Corrientes and Agüero) that was once the city's central market and is now a major mall.

TAKING IT IN

You can blitz Recoleta's main sights in half a day, though you could easily spend a full morning or afternoon in the cemetery or cultural centers alone. Come midweek for quiet exploring, or on the weekend to do the cemetery and Plaza Francia crafts market in one fell swoop.

In Almagro a couple of hours will suffice to see all things Carlos Gardel—tango's greatest hero—and get a feel for the district. The mall gets busier than most on weekends because of the Museo de los Niños (Children's Museum).

HOW TO SPEND . . .

An Hour or Two: after a quick walk around the cemetery, choose from great painting at the Museo Nacional de Bellas Artes, great furniture at the Museo Nacional de Arte Decorativo, or great clothes along Avenidas Alvear and Santa Fe.

A Half-Day: start with some coffee and people-watching at extortionate but strategic La Biela, then find Evita's grave at the cemetery and look in on the Basílica de Nuestra Señora del Pilar. Take your time over the Museo Nacional de Bellas Artes, then roll lunch and afternoon tea into one at Sirop Folie in Barrio Norte. If you've got a full day, add some shopping afterward.

TOP ATTRACTIONS

Basílica de Nuestra Señora del Pilar. This basilica beside the famous Cementerio de la Recoleta on Junín is where Buenos Aires's elite families hold weddings and other ceremonies. It was built by the Recoleto friars in 1732, and is considered a national treasure for its six German Baroque–style altars. The central one is overlaid with Peruvian engraved silver; another contains relics and was sent by Spain's King Carlos III. In the cloisters, which date from 1716, is the **Museo de los Claustros del Pilar** (*4 pesos Mon.–Sat. 10:30–6:15, Sun. 2:30–6:15*), a small museum of religious artifacts as well as pictures and photographs documenting Recoleta's evolution. There are excellent views of the cemetery from upstairs windows. *Junín 1904, Recoleta 11/4806–2209 www.basilicadelpilar.org.ar Free Daily 8 AM–9 PM.*

Fodor's Choice ★ **Cementerio de la Recoleta.**
See the highlighted listing in this chapter.

Centro Cultural La Recoleta. Former cloister patios of the Franciscan monks have been converted into a cultural center with exhibits, performances, and workshops. Kids love the **Museo Participativo de Ciencias**

(☎ *11/4807–3260* 🌐 *www.mpc.org.ar* 🎫 *12 pesos* ⏲ *Jan.–Feb., daily 3:30–7:30; Mar.–Dec., weekdays 10–5, weekends 3:30–7:30; winter school holidays (approx. mid-July–early Aug.), weekdays 12:30–7:30, weekends 3:30–7:30*), a mini science museum inside the complex whose motto, *Prohibido No Tocar* (Not Touching Is Forbidden), says it all. On weekends the area around the center and cemetery teems with shoppers and street performers in a large artisan fair: **La Feria de Plaza Francia.** At the end of a *veredita* (little sidewalk), you can find the Paseo del Pilar lined with expensive places to eat and the Buenos Aires Design Center, a mini-mall selling home wares and souvenirs. ✉ *Junín 1930, Recoleta,* ☎ *11/4803–1040* 🌐 *www.centroculturalrecoleta.org* ⏲ *Tues.–Fri. 2–9, weekends 10–9.*

★ **Floralis Genérica.** The gleaming steel and aluminum petals of this giant flower look very space age, perhaps because they were commissioned from the Lockheed airplane factory by architect Eduardo Catalano, who designed and paid for the monument. The 66-foot-high structure is supposed to open at dawn and close at dusk, when the setting sun turns its mirrored surfaces a glowing pink (sometimes the mechanism is out of order, however). The flower stands in the Plaza Naciones Unidas (behind El Museo Nacional de Bellas Artes over Avenida Figueroa Alcorta), which was remodeled to accommodate it. ✉ *Plaza Naciones Unidas at Av. Figueroa Alcorta and J.A. Biblioni, Recoleta* ⏲ *Dawn–dusk.*

Museo Nacional de Arte Decorativo. The harmonious, French neoclassical mansion that houses the National Museum of Decorative Art is as much a reason to visit as the period furnishings, porcelain, and silver within it. Ornate wooden paneling in the Regency ballroom, the imposing Louis XIV red-and-black-marble dining room, and a lofty Renaissance-style great hall are some of the highlights of the only house of its kind open to the public in Buenos Aires. There are excellent English descriptions of each room, and they include gossipy details about the house's original inhabitants, the well-to-do Errázuriz-Alvear family. The museum also contains some Chinese art. Guided tours include the Zubov Collection of miniatures from Imperial Russia. ✉ *Av. del Libertador 1902, Recoleta,* ☎ *11/4801–8248* 🌐 *www.mnad.org* 🎫 *2 pesos, free Tues. Guided tours in English 8 pesos* ⏲ *Tues.–Sun. 2–7; closed last wk of Dec. and 1st wk of Jan.; guided tours in English Tues.–Sun. at 2:30.*

Fodor's Choice ★ **Museo Nacional de Bellas Artes.**
See the highlighted listing in this chapter.

WORTH NOTING

Cementerio de Chacarita. This cemetery is home to Carlos Gardel's tomb, which features a dapper, Brylcreemed statue and dozens of tribute plaques. Rather than a monument, it's treated more like a shrine by hordes of faithful followers who honor their idol by inserting lighted cigarettes in his statue's hand. On June 24, the anniversary of his death, aging *tangueros* in suits and fedoras gather here to weep and sing. Fellow tango legends Aníbal Troilo and Osvaldo Pugliese are also buried in this cemetery, which is about equidistant from Palermo and Almagro. If you're heading from Almagro, hop subte Line B at the Carlos Gardel

CEMENTERIO DE LA RECOLETA

✉ *Junín 1760, Recoleta*
☎ *11/4803–1594* 🎫 *Free*
🕑 *Daily 8–6.*

TIPS

■ The city government runs free guided visits to the cemetery in English on Tuesday and Thursday at 11; visits in Spanish operate Tuesday through Sunday at 9, 10, 11, 2, 3, and 4. Gather at the entrance.

■ If you prefer an independent tour, the administrative offices at the entrance can usually provide a free photocopied map, and caretakers throughout the grounds can help you locate the more intriguing tombs. These are also labeled on a large map at the entrance.

■ It's easy to get lost in the cemetery, so start well before closing time.

■ Look out for intriguing statues such as the life-size likeness of boxer Luis Angel Firpo, who lost the world heavyweight title to Jack Dempsey in 1923. It stands on guard outside his tomb at the back of the cemetery, wearing a robe and boxing boots.

■ The cemetery had its blessing withdrawn by the Catholic Church in 1863, when president Bartolomé Mitre ordered that a suicide be buried there.

The ominous gates, Doric-columned portico, and labyrinthine paths of the city's oldest cemetery (1822) may leave you with a sense of foreboding. It's the final resting place for the nation's most illustrious figures, and covers 13.5 acres that are rumored to be the most expensive real estate in town. The cemetery has more than 6,400 elaborate vaulted tombs and majestic mausoleums, 70 of which have been declared historic monuments. The mausoleums resemble chapels, Greek temples, pyramids, and miniature mansions.

HIGHLIGHTS

Evita. The embalmed remains of Eva Duarte de Perón, who made it (almost intact) here after 17 years of posthumous wandering, are in the Duarte family vault. Around July 26, the anniversary of her death, flowers pile up here.

Late Greats. If the tomb of brutal *caudillo* (dictator) Facundo Quiroga looks small, it's because he's buried standing—a sign of valor—at his request. Prominent landowner Dorrego Ortíz Basualdo resides in Recoleta's most monumental sepulcher, complete with chandelier. The names of many key players in Argentina's history are chiseled over other sumptuous mausoleums: Alvear, Quintana, Sáenz Peña, Lavalle, Sarmiento.

Spooky Stories. Rufina Cambaceres is known as the girl who died twice. She was thought dead after suffering a cataleptic attack, and was entombed on her 19th birthday in 1902. Rufina awoke inside her casket and clawed the top open but died of a heart attack before she could be rescued. When Alfredo Gath heard of Rufina's story he was appalled and commissioned a special mechanical coffin with an opening device and alarm bell. Gath successfully tested the coffin in situ 12 times, but on the 13th the mechanism failed and he died inside.

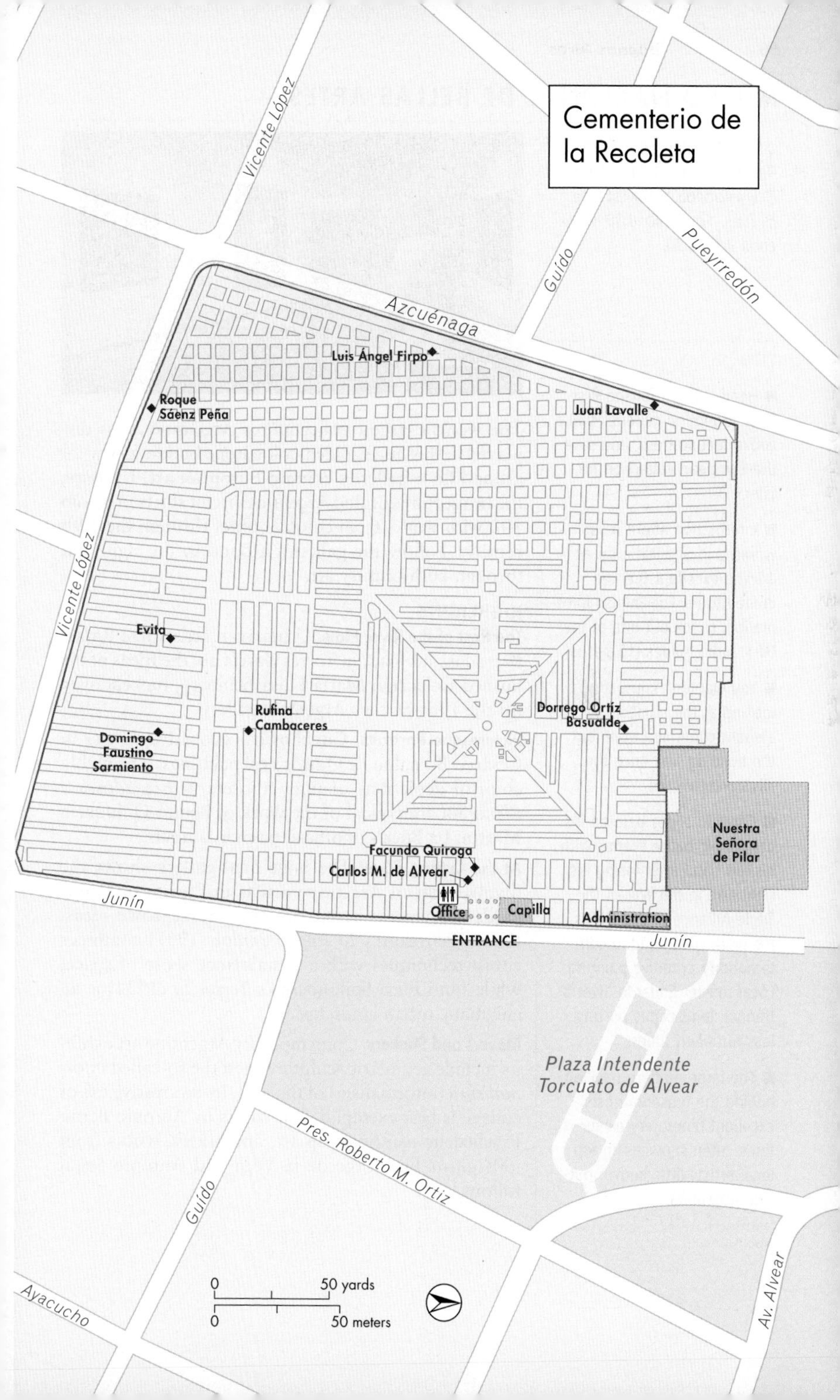
Cementerio de la Recoleta
Vicente López
Pueyrredón
Guído
Azcuénaga
Luis Ángel Firpo
Roque Sáenz Peña
Juan Lavalle
Vicente López
Evita
Rufina Cambaceres
Dorrego Ortíz Basualde
Domingo Faustino Sarmiento
Nuestra Señora de Pilar
Facundo Quiroga
Carlos M. de Alvear
Junín
Office
Capilla
Administration
ENTRANCE
Junín
Plaza Intendente Torcuato de Alvear
Pres. Roberto M. Ortiz
Guído
Ayacucho
0
50 yards
0
50 meters
Av. Alvear

MUSEO NACIONAL DE BELLAS ARTES

✉ *Av. del Libertador 1473, Recoleta* ☎ *11/5288–9900* 🌐 *www.mnba.org.ar* 🎫 *Free* 🕘 *Tues.–Fri. 12:30–8:30, weekends 9:30–8:30.*

TIPS

■ Head straight for the first-floor Argentine galleries while you're feeling fresh, and save the European collection for later.

■ Information about most works is in Spanish only, as are the excellent themed guided tours. For English information, check out one of the MP3 audio guides (15 pesos).

■ You wouldn't know it by looking at the museum's elegant columned front, but the building was once the city's waterworks.

■ Cándido López painted his panoramic battle scenes with his left hand after losing his right arm in the War of the Triple Alliance of the 1870s. His work spearheaded contemporary primitive painting. Local master Eduardo Sívori's tranquil landscapes portray less turbulent times.

■ The large modern pavilion behind the museum hosts excellent temporary exhibitions, often showcasing top local artists little known outside Argentina.

The world's largest collection of Argentine art is displayed in this huge golden-color stone building. The 24 ground-floor galleries contain European art. Upstairs, the beautifully curated Argentine circuit starts in Room 102 with works from colonial times through the 19th century. Follow the galleries around to the right and through 20th-century art.

HIGHLIGHTS

The Rest of the River Plate. Uruguayan artists like Rafael Barradas and Joaquín Torres García are the focus of the hushed Colección María Luisa Bemberg, tucked away off the 19th-century Argentine gallery.

Picturesque Portraits. Gauchos cut evocative figures in Cesáreo Bernaldo de Quirós's oil paintings. The highly colorful depictions of port laborers in *Elevadores a Pleno Sol* are typical of the work of Benito Quinquela Martín, La Boca's unofficial painter laureate.

At the Cutting Edge. The huge final gallery shows the involvement of Argentine artists in European avant-garde movements before adopting homegrown ideas. Emilio Pettorutti's *El Improvisador* (1937) combines cubist techniques with a Renaissance sense of space, while Lino Enea Spilimbergo's *Terracita* (1932) is an enigmatic urban landscape.

Movers and Shakers. Contemporary Argentine art exhibits include geometric sculptures and the so-called *informalismo* (informalism) of the '60s. Its innovative use of collage is best exemplified in works by Antonio Berni. Psychedelic paintings, op art, and kinetic works from '60s gurus like Jorge de la Vega and Antonio Seguí follow.

Museo Nacional de Bellas Artes

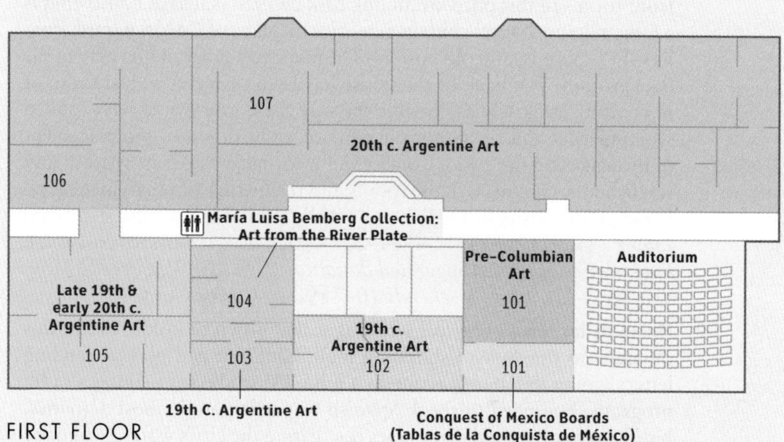
107
20th c. Argentine Art
106
María Luisa Bemberg Collection: Art from the River Plate
Pre-Columbian Art
101
Auditorium
Late 19th & early 20th c. Argentine Art
104
19th c. Argentine Art
105
103
102
101
19th C. Argentine Art
Conquest of Mexico Boards (Tablas de la Conquista de México)
FIRST FLOOR

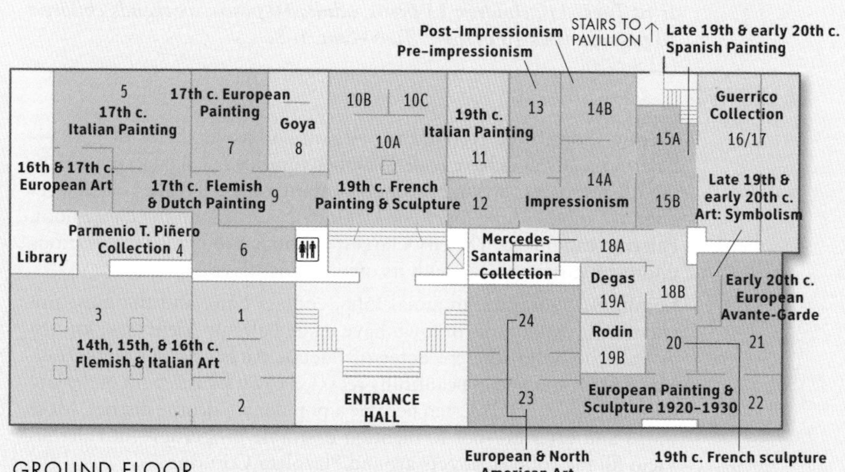
Post-Impressionism
Pre-impressionism
STAIRS TO PAVILLION
Late 19th & early 20th c. Spanish Painting
5
17th c. Italian Painting
17th c. European Painting
7
Goya
8
10B
10C
10A
19th c. Italian Painting
11
13
14B
15A
Guerrico Collection
16/17
16th & 17th c. European Art
17th c. Flemish & Dutch Painting
9
19th c. French Painting & Sculpture
12
14A
Impressionism
15B
Late 19th & early 20th c. Art: Symbolism
Parmenio T. Piñero Collection 4
Library
6
Mercedes Santamarina Collection
18A
Degas
19A
18B
Early 20th c. European Avante-Garde
3
1
14th, 15th, & 16th c. Flemish & Italian Art
24
Rodin
19B
20
21
2
ENTRANCE HALL
23
European Painting & Sculpture 1920–1930
22
European & North American Art
19th c. French sculpture
GROUND FLOOR

Station for a 10- to 15-minute ride west to the Federico Lacroze stop. Depending on where you are in Palermo, a cab here will cost you 10 to 20 pesos. ✉ *Guzmán 680, at Corrientes, Chacarita* ☎ *11/4553–9338* 🌐 *www.cementeriochacarita.com.ar* 🎫 *Free* 🕓 *Daily 7* AM*–6* PM Ⓜ *B to Federico Lacroze.*

Museo Casa Carlos Gardel. Hard-core tango fans shouldn't pass up a quick visit to the home of tango's greatest hero, Carlos Gardel. The front rooms of this once-crumbling *casa chorizo* (sausage house, that is a long, narrow house) contain extensive displays of Gardel paraphernalia—LPs, photos, and old posters. The maestro's greatest hits play in the background. The back of the house has been restored with the aim of re-creating as closely as possible the way the house would have looked when Gardel and his mother lived here, right down to the placement of birdcages on the patio. Concise but informative texts in Spanish and English talk you through the rooms and the history of tango in general. Short guided visits in English are usually available on request. ✉ *Jean Jaurés 735, Almagro* ☎ *11/4964–2015* 🌐 *www.museocasacarlosgardel.buenosaires.gov.ar* 🎫 *Suggested donation 10 pesos, Wed. free* 🕓 *Mon. and Wed.–Fri. 11–6, weekends 10–7* Ⓜ *B to Carlos Gardel.*

Museo de los Niños. The real world is scaled down to kiddie size at this museum in the Abasto shopping mall. Children can play at sending letters, going to a bank, acting in a mini-TV studio, or making a radio program. You need to speak Spanish to participate in most activities, but the play areas and giant pipes re-creating the city's water system are internationally comprehensible. ✉ *Abasto Shopping Center, Level 2, Av. Corrientes 3247, Almagro* ☎ *11/4861–2325* 🌐 *www.museoabasto.org.ar* 🎫 *Tues.–Fri. children 15 pesos, adults 10 pesos, weekends children 20 pesos, adults 10 pesos* 🕓 *Tues.–Sun. 1–8.*

PALERMO

Trendy shops, bold restaurants, elegant embassies, acres of parks—Palermo really does have it all. Whether your idea of sightseeing is ticking off museums, flicking through clothing racks, licking your fingers after yet another long lunch, or kicking up a storm on the dance floor, Palermo can oblige. The city's largest barrio is subdivided into various unofficial districts, each with its own distinct flavor.

Luminous boutiques, minimal lofts, endless bars, and the most fun and daring restaurants in town have made Palermo Viejo (also known as Palermo Soho) the epicenter of Buenos Aires's design revolution. Many are contained in beautifully recycled town houses built in the late 19th century, when Palermo became a popular residential district. Most shops and eateries—not to mention desirable properties—in Palermo Viejo fill the cobbled streets around Plazoleta Cortázar.

In neighboring Palermo Hollywood quiet barrio houses and the rambling flea market at Dorrego and Niceto Vega sit alongside sharp tapas bars filled with media types from the TV production centers that give the area its nickname.

Some say Palermo takes its name from the surname of a 16th-century Italian immigrant who bought lands in the area, others from the abbey honoring Saint Benedict of Palermo. Either way, the area was largely rural until the mid-19th century, when dictator Juan Manuel de Rosas built an estate here. After his defeat, these grounds were turned into the huge patchwork of parks north of Avenida del Libertador. Their official name, Parque Tres de Febrero, is a reference to February 3, 1852, the day Rosas was defeated in battle. The park, which is more commonly known as Los Bosques de Palermo (the Palermo Woods), provides a peaceful escape from the rush of downtown. The zoo and botanical gardens are at its southern end.

Palermo has two mainstream shopping areas. The streets around the intersection of Avenidas Santa Fe and Coronel Díaz are home to the mid-range Alto Palermo mall and many cheap clothing stores. There are more exclusive brands at El Solar de la Abadía mall and the nearby streets of Las Cañitas, Palermo's northwestern outpost. Its thriving, in-your-face bar-and-restaurant scene is the favorite of local models, TV starlets, and others dying to be seen. If a week away from your analyst is bringing on anxiety attacks, the quiet residential district around Plaza Güemes might bring some relief: it's nicknamed Villa Freud, for the high concentration of psychoanalysts who live and work here.

Plastic surgery and imported everything are the norm in Palermo Chico (between Avenidas Santa Fe and Libertador), whose Parisian-style mansions are shared out between embassies and rich local stars like diva Susana Giménez. Higher-brow culture is provided by the gleaming MALBA (Museo de Arte Latinoamericano de Buenos Aires or the Museum of Latin American Art of Buenos Aires), whose clean stone lines stand out on Avenida Figueroa Alcorta.

TAKING IT IN

Palermo is so big that it's best to tackle it in sections. An even-paced ramble through Parque Tres de Febrero should take no more than two hours, though you could easily spend an entire afternoon at the zoo, Japanese Garden, and Botanical Garden. In architectural and geographic terms, Palermo Chico and the MALBA tie in nicely with a visit to Recoleta: allow at least a couple of hours for such an experience.

HOW TO SPEND . . .

An Hour or Two: Palermo is too big to hedge your bets—you're best to pick one major museum (Museo Evita or MALBA) or park, and go for it.

A Full Day: start with a morning ramble through Parque Tres de Febrero then go arty at the MALBA and Museo Xul Solar, historical at Museo Evita, or back-to-nature at the zoo, Japanese Garden, and Botanical Garden. Shoppers have been known to spend their whole trip in Palermo Viejo, but a couple of hours and a meal are enough to get a feel for it.

GETTING ORIENTED

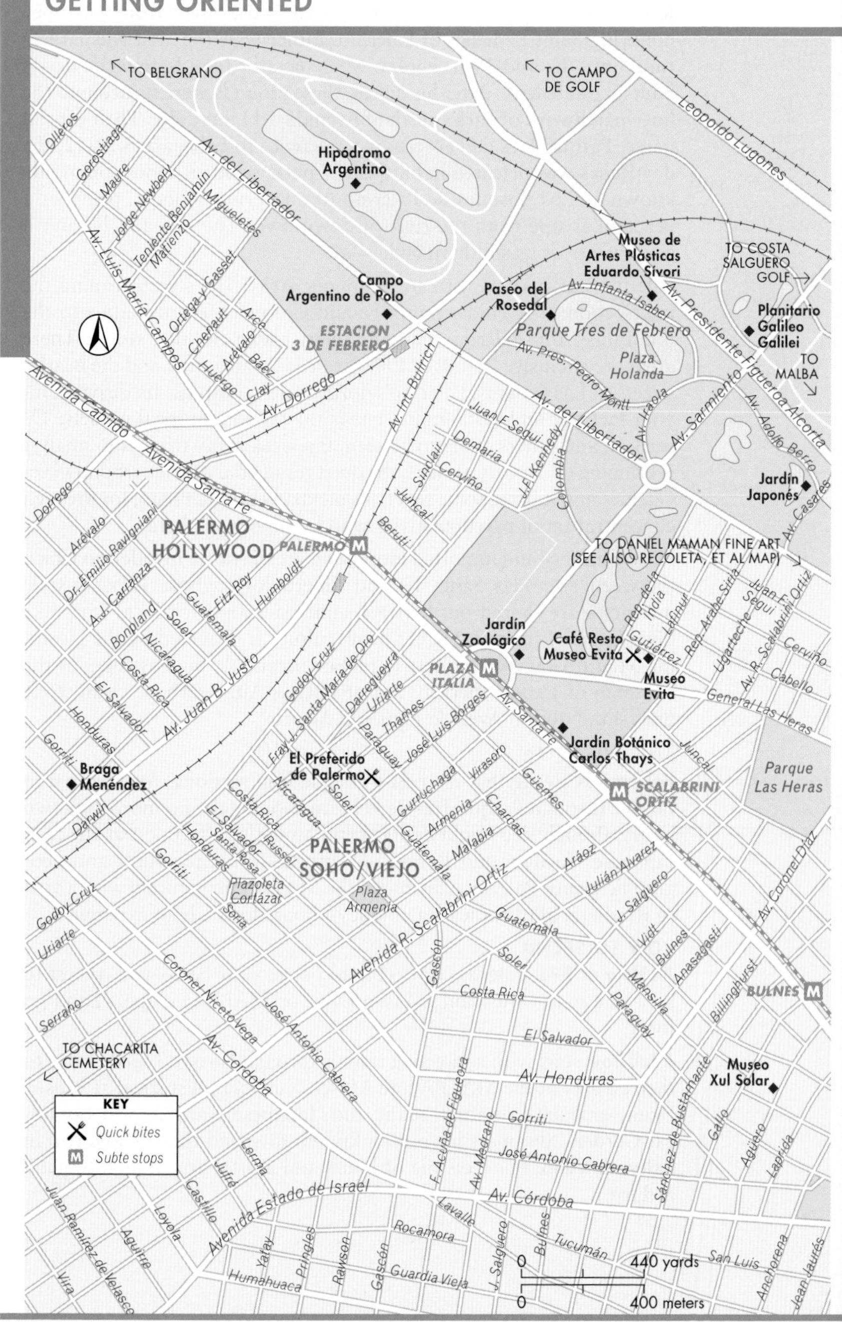
TO BELGRANO
TO CAMPO DE GOLF
Hipódromo Argentino
Campo Argentino de Polo
ESTACION 3 DE FEBRERO
Paseo del Rosedal
Museo de Artes Plásticas Eduardo Sívori
Parque Tres de Febrero
Plaza Holanda
TO COSTA SALGUERO GOLF
Planitario Galileo Galilei
TO MALBA
Jardín Japonés
TO DANIEL MAMAN FINE ART (SEE ALSO RECOLETA, ET AL MAP)
PALERMO HOLLYWOOD
PALERMO
Jardín Zoológico
Café Resto Museo Evita
Museo Evita
PLAZA ITALIA
Jardín Botánico Carlos Thays
SCALABRINI ORTIZ
Parque Las Heras
El Preferido de Palermo
Braga Menéndez
PALERMO SOHO/VIEJO
Plazoleta Cortázar
Plaza Armenia
BULNES
Museo Xul Solar
TO CHACARITA CEMETERY
Av. del Libertador
Avenida Cabildo
Avenida Santa Fe
Av. Dorrego
Av. Juan B. Justo
Avenida R. Scalabrini Ortiz
Av. Córdoba
Avenida Estado de Israel
Av. Honduras
Av. Sarmiento
Av. Presidente Figueroa Alcorta
Leopoldo Lugones
KEY
Quick bites
Subte stops
0 440 yards
0 400 meters

THE TERRITORY

The city's biggest barrio stretches from Avenida Costanera R. Obligado, along the river, to Avenida Córdoba in the south. Its other boundaries are jagged, but include Avenida Coronel Díaz to the east and La Pampa and Dorrego to the west. Avenida Santa Fe cuts the neighborhood roughly in half. Palermo's green spaces and Palermo Chico lie north of it. To the south are Palermo Viejo and Palermo Hollywood, east and west of Avenida Juan B. Justo, respectively.

GETTING AROUND

Subte Línea (Line) D runs along Avenida Santa Fe, but doesn't always brings you to the doorstep of Palermo's attractions, so you may need to combine it with a taxi or some walking. Indeed, weekday traffic makes this combination a better idea than coming all the way from Centro by cab (which costs 16–20 pesos). Get off the subte at Bulnes or Scalabrini Ortíz for Palermo Chico; Plaza Italia for Palermo Viejo and the parks; and Ministro Carranza for Palermo Hollywood.

A more scenic route to Palermo Viejo and Hollywood from Centro is Bus 39 (Route 3, usually with a windshield sign PALERMO VIEJO). It runs along Honduras on the way to Palermo and Gorriti on the way back, and it takes 30–60 minutes. Once you're in Palermo, walking is the best way to get around: much of the district is leafy, and there's little traffic on its smaller streets.

SAFETY AND PRECAUTIONS

Pickpocketing is the biggest threat, especially on crowded streets on weekends. Palermo Viejo's cobbled streets aren't well lighted at night, so avoid walking along any that look lonely. Although locals usually hail cabs on the street, it's safer to ask a restaurant or bar to call one for you. The usual caveats about parks apply to the Palermo woods: don't linger after dark, and avoid remote areas at any time if you're female and alone.

TOP EXPERIENCES

- **Betting:** on which up-and-coming artists at Daniel Maman or Braga Menéndez galleries will end up in MALBA.
- **Exercising:** your arms in Palermo Viejo carrying bags on a boutique crawl or lifting cocktails on a bar crawl.
- **Visiting:** with the Evita, getting to grips on the phenomenon that she was by taking in the footage (and the frocks) at the Museo Evita.
- **Wandering:** on the winding paths of Parque Tres de Febrero, to smell the roses, or along Honduras—east of Juan B. Justo for boutiques, west of it for bars and restaurants.

QUICK BITES

Trends come and go, but nothing changes the tall Formica tables of 1960s-general-store-meets-snackbar **El Preferido de Palermo** (✉ *Jorge L. Borges 2108, Palermo Viejo* ☎ *11/4774-6585* ⏲ *Closed Sun.*). A plate of cold cuts or basic (but delicious) sandwiches are the way to go.

The checkered floors and glossy black tables of **Cafe Resto Museo Evita** (✉ *J. M. Gutiérrez 3926, Palermo Botánico* ☎ *11/4800-1599*) are as stylish as the great lady herself. The Italian-Argentine dishes on the set-price lunch menu change daily.

TOP ATTRACTIONS

Jardín Japonés (Japanese Garden). Like the bonsais in the nursery within it, this park is small but perfectly formed. A slow wander along its arched wooden bridges and walkways is guaranteed to calm frazzled sightseeing nerves during the week; crowds on the weekend make for a less-than-zen experience. A variety of shrubs and flowers frame the ponds, which brim with friendly koi carp that let you pet them should you feel inclined (kids often do). The traditional teahouse, where you can enjoy sushi, adzuki-bean sweets, and tea, overlooks a zen garden. ✉ *Av. Casares at Av Adolfo Berro, Palermo* ☎ *11/4804–4922* 🌐 *www.jardinjapones.com.ar* 🎫 *Weekdays 5 pesos, weekends 8 pesos* 🕑 *Daily 10–6.*

★ **Museo Evita.**

See the highlighted listing in this chapter.

Fodor's Choice ★ **Museo de Arte de Latinoamericano de Buenos Aires** (MALBA, Museum of Latin American Art of Buenos Aires).

See the highlighted listing in this chapter.

Fodor's Choice ★ **Parque Tres de Febrero.** Known locally as Los Bosques de Palermo (Palermo Woods), this 200-acre green space is really a crazy quilt of smaller parks. Rich grass and shady trees make this an urban oasis, although the busy roads and horn-honking drivers that crisscross the park never quite let you forget what city you're in. South of Avenida Figueroa Alcorta you can take part in organized tai chi and exercise classes or impromptu soccer matches. You can also jog, bike, or in-line skate here, or take a boat out on the small lake.

If you're looking for a sedate activity, try the **Museo de Artes Plásticas Eduardo Sívori** (*Eduardo Sívori Art Museum* ✉ *Av. Infanta Isabel 555, Palermo* ☎ *11/4774–9452* 🌐 *www.museosivori.org* 🎫 *1 peso, Wed. and Sat. free* 🕑 *Tues.–Fri. noon–8, weekends 10–8*). The focus of this collection is 19th- and 20th-century Argentine art, including paintings by local masters like Lino Eneo Spilimbergo, Antonio Berni, and the museum's namesake Sívori. There are annual exhibitions of handmade textiles and weavings from all over the country, usually held in July. The shaded sculpture garden is the perfect combination of art and park. Close to the Museo de Artes Plásticas Eduardo Sívori is the **Paseo del Rosedal** (*Rose Garden* ✉ *Avs. Infanta Isabel and Iraola* 🎫 *Free* 🕑 *Apr.–Oct., daily 9–6; Nov.–Mar., daily 8–8*). About 12,000 rosebushes (more than 1,000 different species) bloom seasonally in this rose garden. A stroll along the paths takes you through the Jardín de los Poetas (Poets' Garden), dotted with statues of literary figures, and to the enchanting Patio Andaluz (Andalusian Patio), whose majolica tiles and Spanish mosaics sit under a vine-covered pergola.

The **Planetario Galileo Galilei** (*Galileo Galilei Planetarium* ✉ *Avs. Sarmiento and Figueroa Alcorta* ☎ *11/4771–6629* 🌐 *www.planetario.gov.ar* 🎫 *Free* 🕑 *Weekdays 9–5, weekends 3–8*) is a great orb positioned on a massive concrete tripod. It looks like something out of *Close Encounters of the Third Kind,* and it seems as though small green men could descend from its central staircase at any moment. Content inside is flimsy, but the authentic 3,373-pound asteroid at the entrance

MUSEO EVITA

✉ Lafinur 2988, 1 block north of Av. Las Heras, Palermo ☎ 11/4807–0306 🌐 www.museoevita.org 🎫 12 pesos, guided tours 18 pesos ⏲ Tues.–Sun. 11–7 Ⓜ D to Plaza Italia.

TIPS

- Laminated cards with just-understandable English translations of the exhibits are available in each room and at the ticket booth.
- Plan time for a post-museum coffee (or lunch) at the museum café's outside tables, shaded by classy black umbrellas. There's also a small gift shop.
- The gray-stone mansion dates from 1909. It was purchased in 1948 by the Fundación de Ayuda Social Eva Perón (Eva Perón Social Aid Foundation) and converted into a home for single mothers, to the horror of the rich, conservative families living nearby.
- The Evita myth can be baffling to the uninitiated. The museum's excellent guided visits shed light on the phenomenon and are available in English, but must be arranged by phone in advance.

Eva Duarte de Perón, known universally as Evita, was the wife of populist president Juan Domingo Perón. She was both revered by her working-class followers and despised by the Anglophile oligarchy of the time. The Museo Evita shies from pop culture clichés and conveys facts about Evita's life and works, particularly the social aid programs she instituted and her role in getting women the vote. Knowledgeable staffers answer questions enthusiastically.

Highlights

Photographic Evidence. The route through the collection begins in a darkened room screening footage of thousands of mourners lining up to see Evita's body. Family photos and magazine covers document Evita's humble origins and time as a B-list actress. Upstairs there's English-subtitled footage of Evita's incendiary speeches to screaming crowds: her impassioned delivery beats Madonna's hands down.

Death Becomes Her. The final rooms follow Evita's withdrawal from political life and her death from cancer at age 33. A video chronicles the fate of Evita's cadaver: embalmed by Perón, stolen by political opponents, and moved and hidden for 17 years before being returned to Argentina, where it now rests in the Recoleta Cemetery.

Fabulous Clothes. Evita's reputation as fashion plate is reflected in the many designer outfits on display, including her trademark working suits and some gorgeous ball gowns.

DID YOU KNOW?

Parque Tres de Febrero, in Palermo, is an oasis of calm. Leave the collectivo exhaust behind and come take a paddleboat ride, stroll through the woods, or just laze in the grass to people-watch with your mate in hand.

MUSEO DE ARTE DE LATINOAMERICANO

DE BUENOS AIRES

Av. Presidente Figueroa Alcorta 3415, Palermo 11/4808-6500 www. malba.org.ar 15 pesos, 5 pesos Wed. Thurs.–Mon. noon–8, Wed. noon–9.

The fabulous Museum of Latin American Art of Buenos Aires (MALBA) is one of the cornerstones of the city's cultural life. Its centerpiece is businessman and founder Eduardo Constantini's collection of more than 220 works of 19th- and 20th-century Latin-American art in the main first-floor gallery.

HIGHLIGHTS

Europe vs. Latin America. Early works in the permanent collection reflect the European avant-garde experiences of painters like Diego Rivera, Xul Solar, Roberto Matta, and Joaquín Torres García. Soon the Latin American experience gave rise to works like *Abaporu* (1928) by Tarsila do Amaral, a Brazilian involved in the "cannibalistic" Movimento Antropofágico (rather than eating white Europeans, proponents of the movement proposed devouring European culture and digesting it into something new). Geometric paintings and sculptures from the 1940s represent movements such as Arte Concreto, Constructivism, and Arte Madí.

Argentine Art. Argentina's undisputed modern master is Antonio Berni, represented by a poptastic collage called *The Great Temptation* (1962) and the bizarre sculpture *Voracity or Ramona's Nightmare* (1964), both featuring the eccentric prostitute Ramona, a character Berni created in this series of works criticizing consumer society. Works by living local greats Liliana Porter, Marta Minujín, Guillermo Kuitca, and Alejandro Kuropatwa form the end of the permanent collection.

Temporary Exhibitions. World-class temporary exhibitions are held on the second floor two or three times a year, and two small basement galleries show art by cutting-edge locals.

TIPS

- MALBA also has a great art cinema showing restored copies of classics, never-released features, and silent films with live music, as well as local films of note.
- Kids love hands-on kinetic works like Julio Le Parc's Seven Unexpected Movements, a sculpture with gleaming parts that move at the press of a button.
- Leave time to browse the art books and funky design objects of the museum's excellent gift shop.
- Young, enthusiastic guides give great tours in Spanish; you can call ahead to arrange group English-language tours.
- Give your feet—and eyes—a rest on the first-floor sculpture deck, with views over Belgrano and Barrio Norte.
- Córdoba-based studio AFT Arquitectos' triangular construction in creamy stone and steel is one of the museum's draws. The main galleries run along a four-story atrium, flooded in natural light from a wall of windows.

is a highlight. The pond with swans, geese, and ducks is a favorite. The park gets crowded on sunny weekends, as this is where families come for strolls or picnics. If you'd like to picnic, take advantage of the street vendors who sell refreshments and *choripan* (chorizo sausage in a bread roll) within the park. There are also many posh cafés lining the Paseo de la Infanta (running from Libertador toward Sarmiento in the park). ✉ *Bounded by Avs. del Libertador, Sarmiento, Leopoldo Lugones, and Dorrego, Palermo* Ⓜ *D to Plaza Italia.*

WORTH NOTING

Jardín Botánico Carlos Thays. With 18 acres of gardens and 5,500 varieties of exotic and local flora, the Carlos Thays Botanical Garden is an unexpected green haven wedged between three busy Palermo streets. Different sections re-create the environments of Asia, Africa, Oceania, Europe, and the Americas. Among the treasures is the Chinese "tree of gold," purportedly the only one of its kind. An organic vegetable garden aims to teach children healthy habits. Winding paths lead to hidden statues, a brook, and past the resident cats and dragonflies. The central area contains a beautiful greenhouse, brought from France in 1900, and the exposed-brick botanical school and library. ✉ *Av. Santa Fe 3951, Palermo* ☎ *11/4832–1552* 🎟 *Free* ⏲ *Sept.–Mar., daily 8–8; Apr.–Aug., daily 9–6.*

Jardín Zoológico. You enter through the quasi-Roman triumphal arch into the architecturally eclectic, 45-acre city zoo. The pens, mews, statuary, and fountains themselves—many dating from the zoo's opening in 1874—are well worth a look. Jorge Luis Borges said the recurring presence of tigers in his work was inspired by time spent here. Among the expected zoo community are a few surprises: a rare albino tiger; indigenous monkeys, known to perform lewd acts for their audiences; and llamas (watch out—they spit). South American animals you may not have seen before include the *aguará guazú* (a sort of fox), the *coatí* (a local raccoon), anteaters, and the black howler monkey. Some smaller animals roam freely, and there are play areas for children, a petting farm, and a seal show. *Mateos* (traditional, decorated horse-drawn carriages) stand poised at the entrance to whisk you around the nearby parks. ✉ *Avs. General Las Heras and Sarmiento, Palermo* ☎ *11/4806–7412* 🌐 *www.zoobuenosaires.com.ar* 🎟 *19.90 pesos* ⏲ *Tues.–Sun. 10–6.*

Museo Xul Solar. Avant-garde artist, linguist, esoteric philosopher, and close friend of Borges, Xul Solar is best known for his luminous, semi-abstract watercolors. They glow against the low-lighted concrete walls of this hushed museum. Solar's wacky but endearing beliefs in universalism led him to design a pan-language, pan-chess (a set is displayed here), and the Pan Klub, where these ideas were debated. One of its former members, architect Pablo Beitia, masterminded the transformation of the town house where Solar lived and worked. Open stairways crisscross the space, an homage to one of Solar's favorite motifs. ✉ *Laprida 1212, Palermo* ☎ *11/4824–3302* 🌐 *www.xulsolar.org.ar* 🎟 *10 pesos* ⏲ *Tues.–Fri. noon–8, Sat. noon–7.*

WHERE TO EAT

Buenos Aires isn't just the most cutting-edge food town in Argentina—it's the most cutting-edge food town in the Southern Hemisphere. Here, three things have come together to create a truly modern cuisine: diverse cultural influences, high culinary aspirations, and a relentless devotion to aesthetics, from plate garnishes to room decor.

And yet, at their core, even the most-modern international restaurants in Buenos Aires are fundamentally porteño, deeply informed by this city's aristocratic appreciation of the pleasure of a good bottle of wine, shared with friends and family, over a long and languid meal. People may eat dinner at 10 PM or 10:30 PM all over Argentina, but only in Buenos Aires are you likely to see a family, toddlers in tow, strolling into their local *parrilla* (steak house) at midnight.

Areas like Palermo Soho and Palermo Hollywood have emerged as the epicenters of Argentina's modern food movement. In these neighborhoods, sushi is all the rage, and you can find Patagonian lamb, trout, and king crab rubbing elbows with Asian curries and northern Argentine *locros* (stews).

But much of the old guard still stands strong. Most porteños have Italian ancestry, which is evident in the proliferation of pizzerias all over the city, from the simple shops to the trendy pizza-and-champagne joints. But don't miss the chance to try the deeper-dish Argentine-style pizza, the most classic of which is the *muzzarella* (cheese and tomato pizza) and the immortal combination of *jamón* (ham), *morrón* (roasted red pepper), and *aceitunas* (olives).

Cafés are also a big part of Buenos Aires culture: open long hours, they constantly brim with locals knocking back a quick *cafecito* (espresso) or taking their time over a *café con leche* (coffee with milk). And finally, there are the delicious *heladerías* (ice-cream shops) to finish it all off.

CENTRO AND ENVIRONS

Centro and its environs offer a bit of everything: old-school porteño hangouts, fast-paced lunch spots, and modern, tourist-friendly locales in Puerto Madero. Many restaurants serve truly excellent food, but expect more-traditional parrilla or pasta places, as opposed to the more-fusion-oriented options in neighborhoods like Palermo.

CENTRO

¢ CAFÉ ✕ **Confitería La Ideal.** Part of the charm of this spacious 1912 coffee shop–milonga is its sense of nostalgia: think fleur-de-lis motifs, time-worn European furnishings, and stained glass. No wonder they chose to film the 1998 movie *The Tango Lesson* here. La Ideal is famous for its *palmeritas* (glazed cookies) and tea service and for the scores of locals and foreigners who attend the milongas here. Tango lessons are offered Monday through Saturday at varying times throughout the day and night; evening concerts take place every night except Tuesday and Thursday. Its informality is its best trait; just show up at any hour and chances are you'll hear and see some great tango. ✉ *Suipacha 380, at*

Av. Corrientes, Centro ☎ *11/5265–8069* 🌐 *www.confiteriaideal.com* ▭ *No credit cards* Ⓜ *C to C. Pellegrini, D to 9 de Julio* ✣ *2:D4.*

WORD OF MOUTH

"Go to Café Tortoni for the atmosphere and the building itself. It is historic and elegant. Have coffee and dessert or a snack. It's not noted as a great place for dinner, but worth a visit more as part of your sightseeing and general Buenos Aires experience." —raquel_z

2

$$ SPANISH ✕ **El Globo.** Much like the neighborhood in which it resides, El Globo is touristy but good. Hearty *pucheros* (mixed boiled meat dinners), roast suckling pig, squid, and other Spanish-Argentine fare are served in a large dining area, as they have been since the restaurant opened in 1908. The *cazuela de mariscos* (seafood stew) is another specialty. ✉ *Hipólito Yrigoyen 1199, Centro* ☎ *11/4381–3926* ▭ *AE, DC, MC, V* Ⓜ *C to Av. de Mayo, A to Lima* ✣ *2:C5.*

$ CAFÉ ✕ **Gran Café Tortoni.** In the city's first confitería, established in 1858, art nouveau decor and high ceilings transport you back in time. Carlos Gardel, one of Argentina's most famous tango stars; writer Jorge Luis Borges; local and visiting dignitaries; and intellectuals have all eaten and sipped coffee here. Don't miss the *chocolate con churros* (thick hot chocolate with baton-shaped doughnuts for dipping). You must reserve ahead of time for the nightly tango shows, for which you'll pay a 50-peso cover. ✉ *Av. de Mayo 825, Centro* ☎ *11/4342–4328* 🌐 *www.cafetortoni.com.ar* ▭ *AE, MC, V* Ⓜ *A to Perú* ✣ *2:D4.*

$$ ITALIAN ✕ **La Parolaccia.** A polite waitstaff serves some of the city's better Italian fare in a warm, relaxing environment. Lasagna and other pasta dishes are well executed, as are the desserts like tiramisu. The real reason to go, though, is for the amazing-value three-course set lunch—including a complimentary lemon digestif—which will set you back 30 pesos. The company runs additional, equally good restaurants in Belgrano, Palermo, and Puerto Madero. ✉ *Riobamba 146, Centro* ☎ *11/4812–1053* 🌐 *www.laparolaccia.com* ▭ *AE, MC, V* Ⓜ *C to Congreso, B to Callao* ✣ *2:B4.*

$$$ ARGENTINE ✕ **Sabot.** You might consider Sabot a find if you're a tourist—but this dignified, timeless lunchroom is part of daily life to the scores of downtown businesspeople who have been coming here for ages to seal deals and be seen. Since the 1970s they've been doing the same things, day after (week)day. This means absolutely impeccable service, fresh *centolla* (crab), and a *puchero* that gets at the very essence of what boiled meat is all about, as well as classics like *bife de lomo* and impressive pasta dishes. ✉ *25 de Mayo 756, between Cordoba and Viamonte, Centro* ☎ *11/4313–6587* ✍ *Reservations essential* ▭ *AE, DC, MC, V* ⏲ *Closed weekends. No dinner* Ⓜ *B to L.N. Alem* ✣ *2:E3.*

$$$$ ARGENTINE ✕ **Tomo I.** For a truly sublime dining experience, visit the recently renovated Tomo I, the consistently superb restaurant that's been run by the Concaro sisters since 1971. The inviting beige burlap walls lead to a back-lighted bar fronted by a gorgeous wood table made from an Algarrobo tree. The two dining rooms can be both romantic and functional; perfect for closing a business deal or celebrating an anniversary. The food is extraordinary: chilled carrot soup with orange and ginger, fresh

Café Tortoni, on Avenida de Mayo, is as iconically Argentine as it gets.

Spanish octopus in pesto and garlic, and mouth-watering suckled pig are all top choices. This is food you won't soon forget. Reservations are recommended. ✉ *Carlos Pellegrini 521, Centro* ☎ *11/4326–6698* 🌐 *www.tomo1.com.ar* ▭ *AE, DC, MC, V* ⏲ *Closed Sun. No lunch Sat.* Ⓜ *B to Carlos Pellegrini, D to 9 de Julio* ✥ *2:C3.*

$$$ JAPANESE ✕ **Yuki.** Find your way through the unmarked door and you'll notice the Japanese clientele—no Palermo hipsters here. This is where foodies go to get great sushi. Even more impressive is the fresh fish, which includes interesting local white fishes like *lisi*, *reza*, and *pejerrey*. The fried fish is great, too. The *teishoku* dinners are interesting prix-fixe tasting menus, but if you just want raw fish, stick to a sushi combination platter or order à la carte. ✉ *Pasco 740, between Independencia and Chile, Centro* ☎ *11/4942–7510* ▭ *AE, MC, V* Ⓜ *E to Pichincha* ✥ *2:A6.*

PUERTO MADERO

$$$$ STEAK ✕ **Cabaña Las Lilas.** This place is a tourist trap, but a good one. It's probably the most famous steak house in all of Argentina, and has become wildly popular with foreigners. But although you'll definitely hear lots of English and German and French spoken here, if you look around, it's also populated with lots of locals, at least the ones who can afford it. Las Lilas is best known for its beef that comes directly from its own estancia in the Pampas. The best cuts are the *rib eye* and *bife de lomo*. Salads and desserts are fantastic, too. Bottom line: if you're pressed for time, and can't leave Puerto Madero, this is your place for steak, even though you'll pay dearly for it. Otherwise, venture out to some better, and cheaper, places outside downtown. ✉ *A. M. de Justo 515, Puerto Madero* ☎ *11/4313–1336* 🌐 *www.laslilas.com* ▭ *AE, MC, V* ✥ *2:E3.*

$$ **La Caballeriza.** People flock from all over the world to empty their
STEAK wallets at touristy Cabaña Las Lilas next door, but locals in the know (or those who can't get a table at Las Lilas) come instead to this big, lively, informal steak house, where you can pay much less for good, quality meat. Sip champagne at the friendly bar while you wait for a table. The parrilla is wood-fired, Uruguayan style, and the *asado de tira* (rack of beef short ribs) is a highlight, but you also can't go wrong with the classic *bife de chorizo* (bone-in sirloin or rump steak). There's another branch by the Recoleta mall next to the cemetery, but this one is superior. ✉ *A. M. de Justo 580, Puerto Madero* ☎ *11/4514–4444* 🌐 *www.lacaballerizapuertomadero.com* ▭ *AE, DC, MC, V* Ⓜ *B to L. N. Alem* ✣ *2:E4.*

RETIRO

$$ **DaDá.** Eclectic porteño '60s pop culture characterizes one of the city's
ARGENTINE best-kept secrets, where murals inspired by Dalí, Miró, Lichtenstein, and Mondrian are splashed across the walls and jazz fills the small intimate space. Seasonal specials are chalked up behind the cluttered bar. The short but inventive menu showcases local produce, with relentlessly modern flavor combinations, and the bar is a scene at night. This place looks like a movie set. ✉ *San Martín 941, Retiro* ☎ *11/4314–4787* ▭ *AE, MC, V* ⊗ *Closed Sun.* Ⓜ *C to San Martín* ✣ *2:D3.*

$$$ **Gran Bar Danzón.** Expansive wine lists have become all the rage in
ECLECTIC 21st-century Buenos Aires, but it will take more than just a rage to topple this king of wine bars from its lofty throne. The room is dark, loud, cramped, and filled with beautiful people; the menu is versatile, sometimes too much so—there's lamb ravioli with goat cheese and a pear sauce, steaks, and sushi. But skip the raw fish and focus on the simple small plates that serve as good accompaniments to one of the thousands of excellent red wines on offer. ✉ *Libertad 1161, Retiro* ☎ *11/4811–1108* 🌐 *www.granbardanzon.com.ar* ✍ *Reservations essential* ▭ *AE, DC, MC, V* ⊗ *No lunch* Ⓜ *C to San Martín* ✣ *2:C2.*

SAN TELMO AND LA BOCA

The most historic neighborhoods in the city may not be prime culinary destinations, but they do offer a few gems that are well worth visiting. Of the two, San Telmo has better and more varied options. Note that most of the eateries near the pedestrian-only El Caminito thoroughfare are cheesy tourist traps that offer basic pasta dishes for inflated prices.

SAN TELMO

¢ **Bar Dorrego.** Bar Dorrego probably hasn't changed much in the last
CAFÉ 100 years or so. Dark wood and politely aloof waiters set the stage; good coffee, *tragos* (alcoholic drinks), sangria, and snacks complete the scene. When the weather is warm, sit at a table outside, order a cold Quilmes beer and some salty peanuts, and soak in the scene of San Telmo's busiest hub. ✉ *Defensa 1098, at Humberto I, on Plaza Dorrego, San Telmo* ☎ *11/4361–0141* ▭ *No credit cards* Ⓜ *C or E to Independencia* ✣ *2:E6.*

$$$ FRENCH ✕ **Brasserie Petanque.** Upon entering this classic French brasserie you're greeted by a long and imposing bar, bookended by white pillars and backed by shelf after enticing shelf of liquor and wine. This festive San Telmo locale has scores of small white-linen tables where you can enjoy great onion soup and local interpretations of French classics, like steak tartare and beef bourguignonne. Surprisingly, the wine list is quite small, with only a few French wines, but they make up for it with an ample spirits selection and friendly bartenders. Get a table by the window to check out the people cruising by outside. Reservations are recommended. ✉ *Defensa 596, San Telmo* ☎ *11/4342–7930* 🌐 *www.brasseriepetanque.com* ▭ *AE, D, MC, V* ⊗ *Closed Mon. No lunch Sat.* ✣ *2:D5.*

WORD OF MOUTH

"Most restaurants are smoke-free, though you will encounter one or two that have closed off rooms where you can smoke or an upper mezzanine where smoking is permitted. In our five weeks in Buenos Aires we only came across two places that permitted smoking in designated areas."

—annetti

$$$ ARGENTINE Fodor's Choice ★ ✕ **La Vineria de Gualterio Bolivar.** A slow buzz has been building about the daring cuisine prepared by chef Alejandro Digilio in his small San Telmo wine bar. Digilio dabbles with foam and nitrogen-frozen toppings, while mixing extreme flavors for blissful tastes not normally found in Argentina—or anywhere for that matter. The ever-changing 11-course tasting menu is written on an elevated chalkboard and might feature salmon and sage sashimi with rabbit paté; scallops and lamb with pumpkin purée; and rib eye steak with an acidic Malbec sauce and turnip-stuffed ravioli. Some of the dishes work better than others, but you must applaud Digilio and his energetic young staff for their efforts. Each plate is expertly paired with hard-to-find Argentine whites and reds. Don't miss this place. ✉ *Bolivar 865, San Telmo* ☎ *11/4361–4709* 🌐 *www.lavineriadegualteriobolivar.com* ▭ *AE, MC, V* ⊗ *Closed Mon.* ✣ *2:D6.*

LA BOCA

$ STEAK ✕ **El Obrero.** When the rock band U2 played Buenos Aires and asked to be taken to a traditional Argentine restaurant, they were brought to this legendary hole-in-the-wall. For 50 years El Obrero has served juicy grilled steaks, sweetbreads, sausages, and chicken. The extensive blackboard menu includes *rabas* (fried calamari) and puchero. Try the *budín de pan* (Argentine version of bread pudding). This spot is popular with tourists and local workmen alike, so expect a short wait. This area of La Boca can be sketchy at any time of the day, so make sure to take a taxi there and call for another to take you back. ✉ *Augustín R. Caffarena 64, La Boca* ☎ *11/4363–9912* ▭ *No credit cards* ⊗ *Closed Sun.* ✣ *2:F6.*

$$$ ARGENTINE ✕ **Patagonia Sur.** Knowledgeable local foodies know to trust Argentina's most famous chef, even if he decided to put a restaurant in La Boca, a culinary no-man's land. Francis Mallman, the purveyor of all things Argentine, has created another great space in which to enjoy typical Argentine fare with a flair. The menu is fairly straightforward: beef, fish, and poultry prepared with hearty local vegetables, but what makes them

so good is that Mallman always uses the best cuts and ingredients available. The crab salad starter and *ojo de bife* are particularly good here. You'll feel as if you're eating at a friend's home: books and blankets are strewn about; antique furniture and glassware abound. ✉ *Rocha 801, La Boca* ☎ *11/4303–5917* 🌐 *www.restaurantepatagoniasur.com* 💳 *AE, D, MC, V* ⊗ *Closed Sun.–Mon.* ✣ *2:F6.*

RECOLETA

Recoleta is the toniest neighborhood in Buenos Aires, and as such, is home to some of the city's top hotels and restaurants. If your budget is more modest, head to Avenida Santa Fe or RM Ortiz, where there's an array of forgettable but family-friendly restaurants that offer Argentine staples like meat, pasta, and fish at good prices. More and more ethnic places are popping up all over.

$ AMERICAN

✕ **Buller Brewing Company.** The city's first microbrewery (the name is pronounced in the American way, not the Spanish double-L way) is more notable for its beer and its lively atmosphere than for its American-influenced brewpub food. But the brews really are impressive, and they're all made in a careful, German-inspired style. Don't miss the India Pale Ale or the unique honey beer. In Recoleta, which is full of cookie-cutter Irish pubs and sports bars, this is a nice break. ✉ *R. M. Ortíz 1827, Recoleta* ☎ *11/4808–9061* 🌐 *www.bullerpub.com* 💳 *AE, DC, MC, V* ✣ *2:B1.*

$$$$ MODERN ARGENTINE Fodor's Choice ★

✕ **Duhau Restaurante & Vinoteca.** Just as the Palacio Duhau Hotel changed the game of luxury in Buenos Aires, so has its eponymous restaurant. This wonderful spot serves some of the best food in the city, complemented with impeccable and friendly service. The menu is French-inspired, but with proud touches of Argentine cuisine: sweetbreads with Patagonian berries, king prawns from Tierra del Fuego, and trout from Bariloche. The beef is all certified Black Angus from the province of Santa Fe. The wine list reads like a book; more than 500 varieties are available on what must be the biggest wine list in the city. After dinner, visit the Cheese Room, which offers 45 different cheeses made from an Argentine dairy. ✉ *Av. Alvear 1661, Recoleta* ☎ *11/5171–1340* 🌐 *www.buenosaires.park.hyatt.com* 💳 *AE, D, MC, V* ⊗ *No lunch weekends* ✣ *2:C1.*

$$$$ FRENCH Fodor's Choice ★

✕ **La Bourgogne.** White tablecloths, fresh roses, and slick red-leather chairs emphasize the restaurant's innate elegance, and it is consistently considered to be one of the city's very best restaurants. A sophisticated waitstaff brings you complimentary hors d'oeuvres as you choose from chef Jean-Paul Bondoux's creations, which include foie gras, rabbit, lamb, chateaubriand, *côte de veau* (veal steak), and black hake. The loquacious chef is known to stroll through the vast room and sit down for a chat with patrons. The fixed-price tasting menu is more affordable and more adventurous than à la carte selections and features a different wine with each plate. Arrange to be seated in the mysterious wine cellar for a more-intimate experience. The wine list reads like a book, and offers the very best blends from France, Italy, and Argentina. ✉ *Alvear Palace Hotel, Ayacucho 2027, Recoleta* ☎ *11/4805–3857 or*

11/4808–2100 ✍ *Reservations essential* ▭ *AE, DC, MC, V* ⊙ *Closed Sun. No lunch Sat.* ✣ *2:B1.*

$$ STEAK ✕ **Juana M.** The minimalist chic decor of this hip basement restaurant stands in stark contrast to the menu: down-to-earth parrilla fare at good prices. Catch a glimpse of meats sizzling on the grill behind the bar, check out the impressive artwork on the walls, and then head to your table to devour your steak and *chorizo* (fat, spicy sausage). This place has the best salad bar in the city, hands down. The homemade pastas aren't bad, either. The staff is young and friendly. It's wildly popular with a lunchtime work crowd during the week and for birthday parties at night. ✉ *Carlos Pellegrini 1535, Recoleta* ☎ *11/4326–0462* ▭ *AE, MC, V* ⊙ *No lunch Sat.* Ⓜ *C to San Martín* ✣ *2:D2.*

$$$$ FRENCH ✕ **Nectarine.** This high-flying temple to nouvelle French cuisine consistently gets mixed reviews from local foodies. Every dish on the menu is delicious, though occasionally overambitious. The wine list is extraordinary. Set aside an entire evening for this gustatory trip, but expect to pay dearly for the experience, which is high-priced even by international standards. The feeling in the second-floor room is formal, except for the open kitchen—a concession, perhaps, to the trends of modern high-concept dining. Reservations are recommended. ✉ *Pasaje del Correo, Vicente López 1661, Recoleta* ☎ *11/4813–6993* ▭ *AE, DC, MC, V* ⊙ *Closed Sun. No lunch Sat.* ✣ *2:B2.*

$$$ ARGENTINE Fodor's Choice ★ ✕ **Republica.** This fabulous new upstairs restaurant opened in late 2007, and is run by two young and up-and-coming chefs, Maria Jose Moretti and Javier Hourquebie, who also happen to be a couple. Romantic lighting, hip mood music, and table seating in small alcoves create a dreamy atmosphere in which to try an impressive variety of fusion dishes made from such Argentine staples as beef, pork, and chicken. But the real reason to visit this place is the *costillar de ternera en dos cocciones,* a mind-blowingly flavorful rack of tender ribs that will literally melt in your mouth and leave you smiling for hours. ✉ *Vicente Lopez 1661, Local 6, Recoleta* ☎ *11/4816–7744* ▭ *AE, D, MC, V* ✣ *2:B1.*

PALERMO

If you want the tastiest, most cutting-edge, most traditional, most ethnic, most daring, and most fashionable food in Buenos Aires, then you head to Palermo. It's that simple. The sprawling neighborhood is home to the hip areas of Palermo Soho and Hollywood. Soho's main landmark is the artsy Plaza Serrano. But steer clear of the restaurants that line the plaza; they uniformly serve bland and overpriced food. Instead, wander a few blocks in any direction, and you're bound to come across a worthwhile dining spot. Across the train tracks and Avenida Juan B. Justo lies Palermo Hollywood, which does an admirable job of mixing old and new cuisines amid the TV production houses and studios.

PALERMO

$$$ PERUVIAN ✕ **Astrid & Gaston.** Its opening in early 2009 was marked by mass hysteria and hype by BA foodies, who had longed for famed Peruvian chef Gaston Acurio's cuisine in their city. As a whole, the food and atmosphere inside the beautifully recycled Palermo home is spirited, but

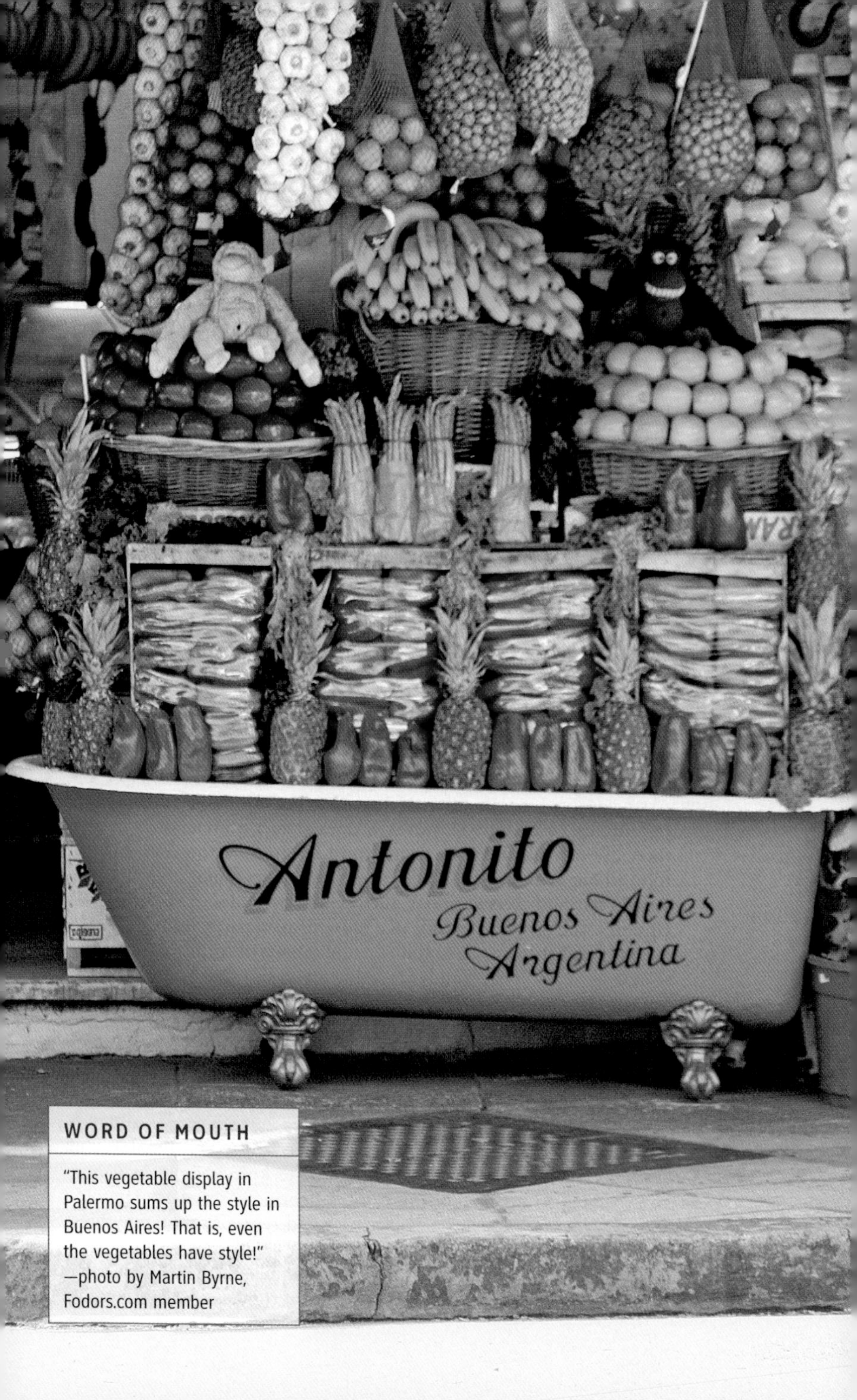

WORD OF MOUTH

"This vegetable display in Palermo sums up the style in Buenos Aires! That is, even the vegetables have style!" —photo by Martin Byrne, Fodors.com member in many cases style trumps service. The waitstaff look great in black suits and ties, but they don't offer consistent service, and non-Spanish speakers may have a hard time communicating with them. That said, the food is delicious and imaginative: marinated boneless pork with sweet potatoes and red onions; white salmon with peas and scallop risotto; *arroz con mariscos* (rice and shellfish), and *aji de gallina* (chili chicken) are all top choices. Not surprisingly, most of the food lacks the spice normally found in many Peruvian dishes, a regrettable trend that most ethnic restaurants in BA adhere to in order to cater to porteños' weak palates. ✉ *Lafinur 3222, Palermo* ☎ *11/4802–2991* ✍ *Reservations essential* ▭ *AE, MC, V* ⊙ *Closed Sun.* ✣ *1:H3.*

$$ JAPANESE ✕ **Jardín Japonés.** Easily the most impressive setting for sushi in Buenos Aires is inside the Japanese Garden on the northern edge of Palermo. Come for lunch, before or after touring the garden, or come for a romantic dinner. The sushi and sashimi are fresh, especially the salmon, but the hot dishes, such as pork with mushrooms, won't necessarily blow you away. ✉ *Av. Casares 2966, Jardín Japonés, Bosques de Palermo* ☎ *11/4800–1322* 🌐 *www.jardinjapones.org.ar* ▭ *No credit cards* ⊙ *Closed Tues.* ✣ *1:G4.*

$ ARGENTINE ✕ **Na Serapia.** Na Serapia, across from Parque Las Heras, is well known for its hearty authentic northern Argentine food. Creamy steamed *humitas,* made from cornmeal and fresh corn, are excellent, as are cheese-and-onion empanadas. Carafes of wine, like everything else, are a bargain. This is strictly no-frills—it's nothing but a basic room with a few little tables—but the food is consistently good. Don't miss the quirky wall art, which includes a portrait of the owner stabbed in the heart. ✉ *Av. Las Heras 3357, Palermo* ☎ *11/4801–5307* ▭ *No credit cards* ✣ *1:F4.*

$$$ JAPANESE/ PERUVIAN Fodor's Choice ★ ✕ **Osaka.** Osaka blends tradition with innovation, fusing Peruvian and Asian cuisines for truly lofty results, making it one of the most exciting restaurants in the city. However, it does attract a pretentious crowd: there are too many people trying too hard to look too cool, but the food all but makes up for it. The snug downstairs dining area has both a sushi bar and a cocktail bar, surrounded by tables of varying sizes. Upstairs, you can dine outside in a more relaxed patio setting. *Ceviche* is your best bet for starters, followed by rounds of fresh, delicious and imaginative (by local standards, anyway) sushi. Don't miss spot-on interpretations of Peruvian recipes that were imported directly from the chain's Lima location, like the *Misoudado*, an amazing red-curry grouper. ✉ *Soler 5608, Palermo* ☎ *11/4775–6964* 🌐 *www.osaka.com.pe* ▭ *AE, MC, V* ⊙ *Closed Sun.* ✣ *1:E3.*

$$ STEAK Fodor's Choice ★ ✕ **Rio Alba.** In terms of quality, price, and charm, this is the best parrilla in Buenos Aires. Period. It consistently serves the tastiest and tenderest cuts of beef. The *asado de tira* is particularly good, as is the flavorful *entrana*. Ask for a minigrill at your table to keep your meat warm; you're going to need time to finish the enormous servings. The old-school waiters wear vests and bow ties and refuse to write anything down, but they always get the order right. This place is packed every night of the week with businesspeople and families. If you arrive after 9:30 PM, expect to wait for a table. The front room is no-smoking; the

back room allows smoking. ✉ *Cervino 4499, Palermo* ☎ *11/4773–5748* ▭ *AE, D, MC, V* ✥ *1:G3.*

PALERMO HOLLYWOOD

$ INDIAN Fodor's Choice ★ **Bangalore.** This place does an admirable job of re-creating the atmosphere of a typical London pub, which probably explains its roaring popularity with Buenos Aires's booming expat population. Come here for fantastically spicy curries, microbrews, and the rowdy atmosphere. Seating is upstairs in a dark alcove. You won't be able to ignore the noise from the drinkers below, but who cares, you're not here for romance. This is a place for a quick Indian meal and jovial conversation. It's perfect for cheap food and a good beer before heading out to the many hot spots nearby. ✉ *Humboldt 1416, Palermo Hollywood* ☎ *11/4779–2621* ▭ *No credit cards* ✥ *1:D4.*

PALERMO SOHO

$$$$ ARGENTINE Fodor's Choice ★ **Casa Cruz.** Trendsetters come and go, but there are few whose food is truly sublime. With its imposing bronze-doored entrance, dim lighting, expanses of mahogany, and cozy banquettes, you'd have to be a bumbling fool not to impress your date here. And yet it's chef Germán Martitegui's kitchen that will really blow your mind, working rabbit medallions into a state of melting tenderness, and pairing delicately crisped *morcilla* (blood sausage) with jammy fruit. The wine list is expansive, and wildly overpriced. The cocktails served up by resident bar maiden Ines de los Santos are the best in the city. This is a place you won't soon forget. ✉ *Uriarte 1656, Palermo Soho* ☎ *11/4833–1112* 🌐 *www.casa-cruz.com* ✍ *Reservations essential* ▭ *AE, DC, MC, V* ⊗ *Closed Sun. No lunch* ✥ *1:E4.*

¢ ARGENTINE **Club Eros.** A basic dining room attached to an old soccer club, Club Eros has developed a cult following for its downscale charm. The excellent fare at rock-bottom prices have begun to draw young Palermo trendies as well as older customers who have been loyal to the club for decades. There's no menu, but you can confidently order a crispy *milanesa* (breaded meat cutlet), or, if available, a *bife de chorizo* and fries. Pasta sauces fall flat, but the *flan con dulce de leche* is one of the best (and biggest) in town. ✉ *Uriarte 1609, Palermo Soho* ☎ *11/4832–1313* ▭ *No credit cards* ✥ *1:E4.*

$$$ ARGENTINE **Desde El Alma.** It would be hard to create a cuter restaurant than this cozy little gem, which is nestled just to the Palermo Soho side of the train tracks. In front you can sit around an intimate fireplace, while the back room feels like an old Argentine family *comedor* (dining room). The menu is relatively short and simple; dishes like leek quiche and sesame-crusted salmon are tasty and thoughtful without overreaching. Reservations are recommended. ✉ *Honduras 5298, Palermo Soho* ☎ *11/4831–5812* ▭ *No credit cards* ⊗ *Closed Sun. No lunch* ✥ *1:B4.*

$ STEAK **Don Julio.** In a neighborhood where it's becoming increasingly hard to find a parrilla, this is an aberration, and a good one. As a result, it's almost always packed with locals, who come to sample the work of the distinguished *parrillero*, who can be seen tending to the glowing embers from the sidewalk. The room is simple and pleasant, with exposed brick walls, and the service is extremely polite. The creamy, spicy mor-

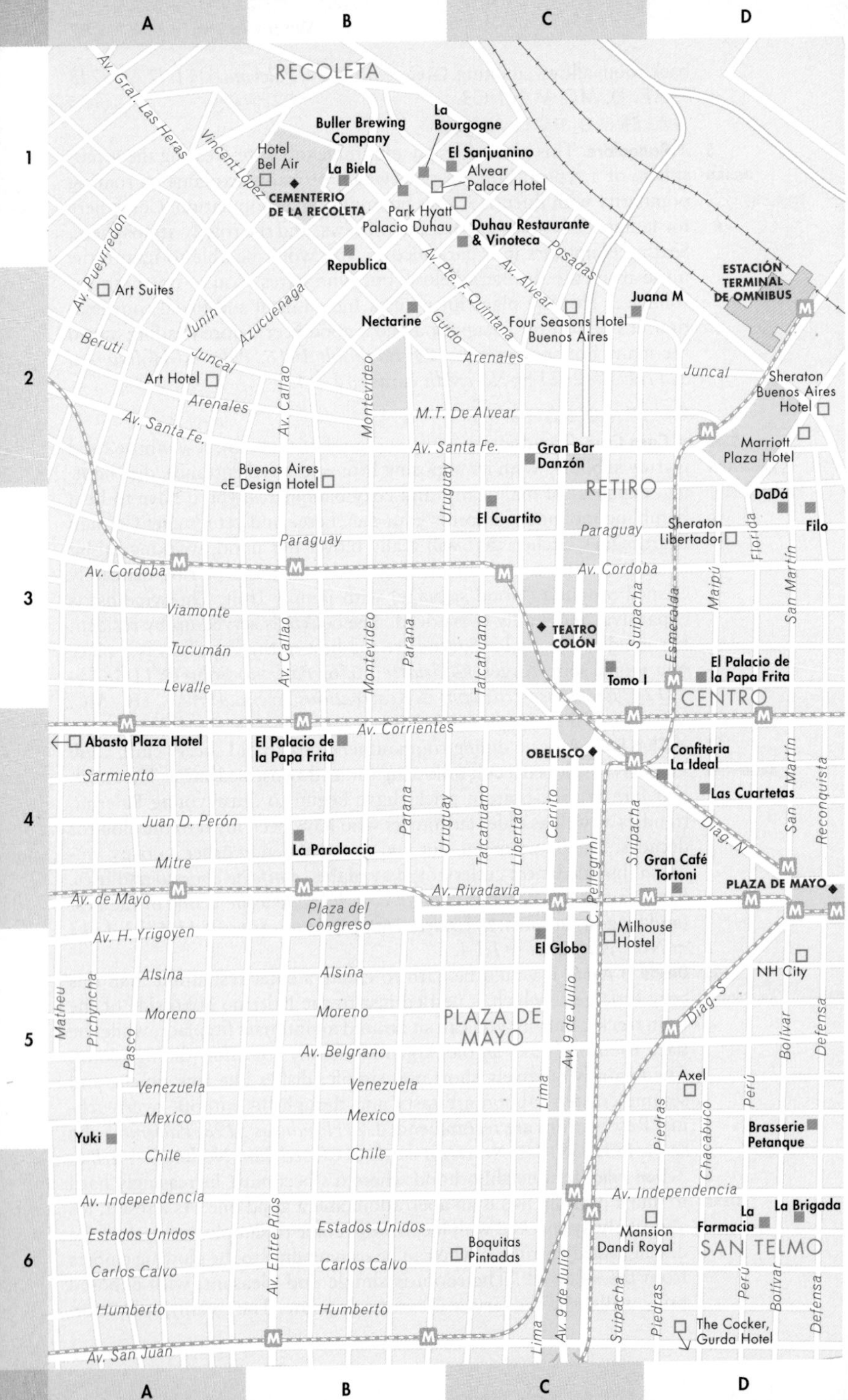

A
B
C
D
1
2
3
4
5
6
RECOLETA
Av. Gral. Las Heras
Vincent López
Hotel Bel Air
CEMENTERIO DE LA RECOLETA
La Biela
Buller Brewing Company
La Bourgogne
El Sanjuanino
Alvear Palace Hotel
Park Hyatt Palacio Duhau
Duhau Restaurante & Vinoteca
Republica
Av. Pueyrredon
Art Suites
Junín
Azucuenaga
Nectarine
Guido
Av. Pte. F. Quintana
Av. Alvear
Posadas
Four Seasons Hotel Buenos Aires
Juana M
ESTACIÓN TERMINAL DE OMNIBUS
Beruti
Juncal
Art Hotel
Arenales
Av. Callao
Montevideo
M.T. De Alvear
Sheraton Buenos Aires Hotel
Marriott Plaza Hotel
Av. Santa Fe.
Buenos Aires cE Design Hotel
Uruguay
Gran Bar Danzón
RETIRO
El Cuartito
DaDá
Filo
Sheraton Libertador
Florida
Paraguay
Av. Cordoba
Maipú
San Martín
Esmeralda
Suipacha
Viamonte
Tucumán
Levalle
Parana
Talcahuano
TEATRO COLÓN
Tomo I
El Palacio de la Papa Frita
CENTRO
Av. Corrientes
Abasto Plaza Hotel
OBELISCO
Confiteria La Ideal
Las Cuartetas
Sarmiento
Juan D. Perón
Libertad
Cerrito
C. Pellegrini
Diag. N
Reconquista
La Parolaccia
Mitre
Gran Café Tortoni
PLAZA DE MAYO
Av. de Mayo
Av. Rivadavia
Plaza del Congreso
Av. H. Yrigoyen
El Globo
Milhouse Hostel
NH City
Alsina
Moreno
Matheu
Pichyncha
Pasco
Av. 9 de Julio
Diag. S
Bolivar
Defensa
Av. Belgrano
Venezuela
Axel
Lima
Piedras
Chacabuco
Perú
Mexico
Yuki
Brasserie Petanque
Chile
Av. Independencia
La Farmacia
La Brigada
Av. Entre Rios
Estados Unidos
Mansion Dandi Royal
Boquitas Pintadas
SAN TELMO
Carlos Calvo
Humberto
The Cocker, Gurda Hotel
Av. San Juan

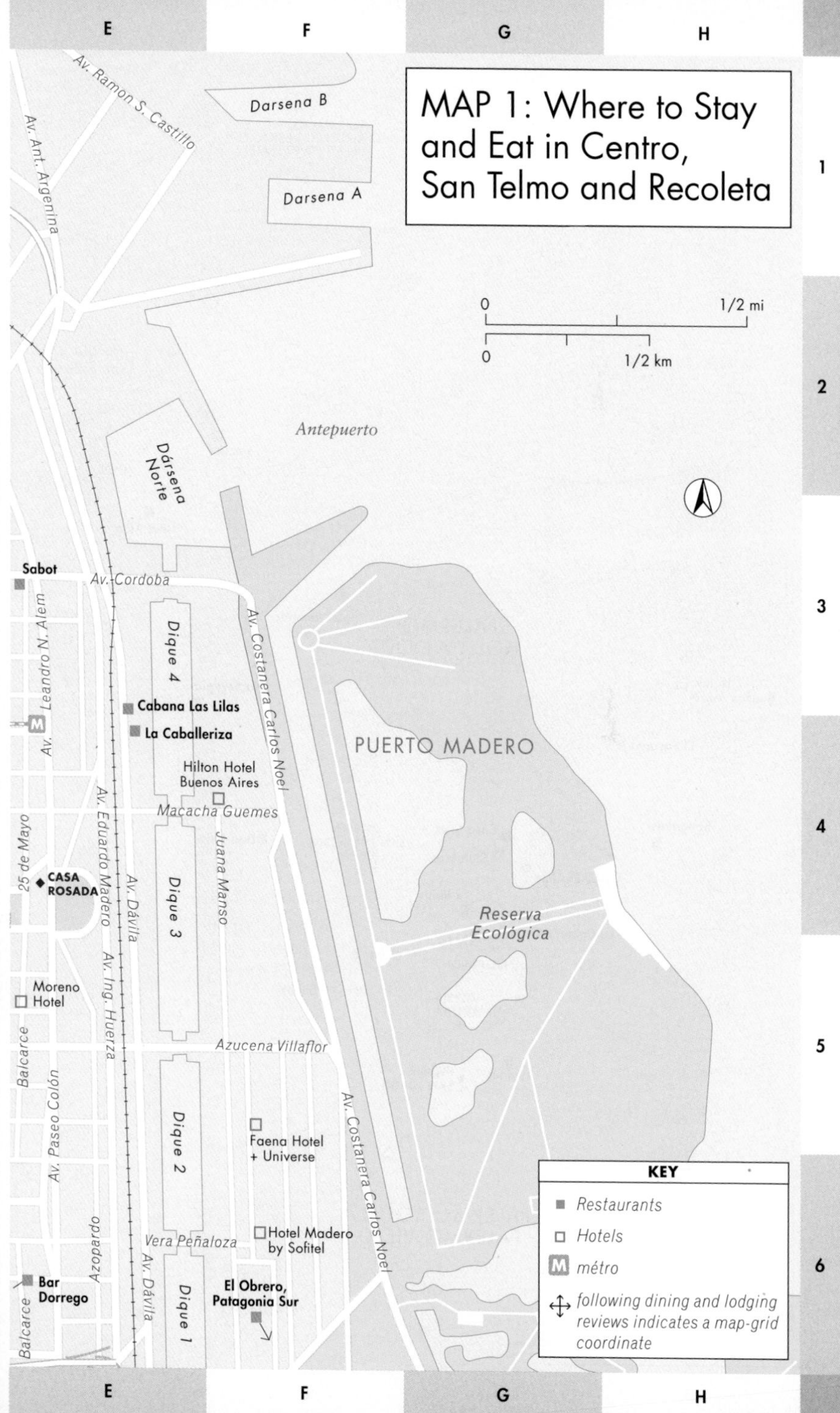

E
F
G
H
MAP 1: Where to Stay and Eat in Centro, San Telmo and Recoleta
1
2
3
4
5
6
Av. Ramon S. Castillo
Av. Ant. Argenina
Darsena B
Darsena A
0
1/2 mi
0
1/2 km
Antepuerto
Dársena Norte
Sabot
Av. Cordoba
Av. Leandro N. Alem
Dique 4
Av. Costanera Carlos Noel
Cabana Las Lilas
La Caballeriza
PUERTO MADERO
Hilton Hotel Buenos Aires
Macacha Guemes
Av. Eduardo Madero
25 de Mayo
CASA ROSADA
Av. Dávila
Dique 3
Juana Manso
Reserva Ecológica
Moreno Hotel
Av. Ing. Huerza
Azucena Villaflor
Balcarce
Av. Paseo Colón
Dique 2
Faena Hotel + Universe
Av. Costanera Carlos Noel
KEY
Restaurants
Hotels
métro
following dining and lodging reviews indicates a map-grid coordinate
Azopardo
Vera Peñaloza
Hotel Madero by Sofitel
Bar Dorrego
Av. Dávila
Dique 1
El Obrero, Patagonia Sur
Balcarce
E
F
G
H

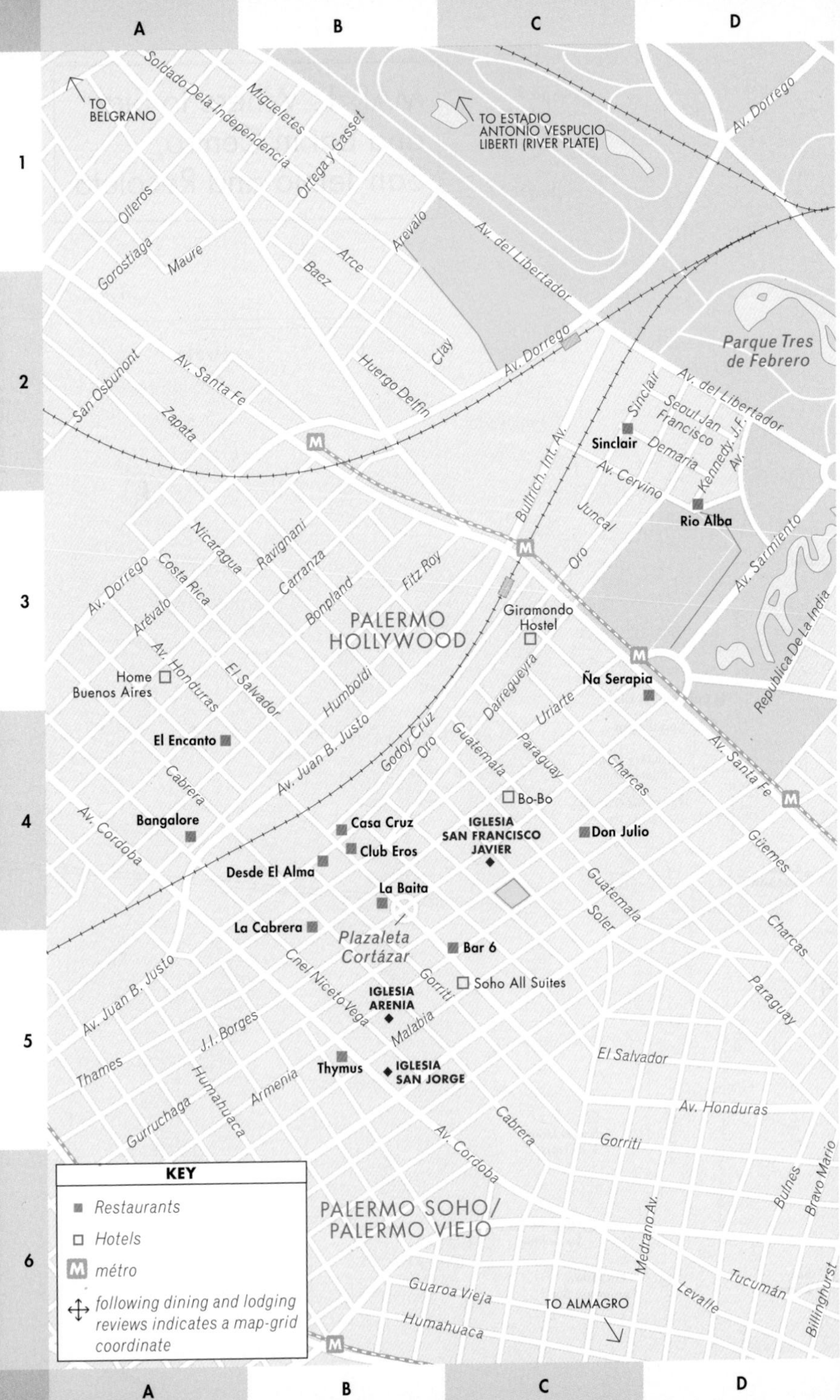

A
B
C
D
1
2
3
4
5
6
TO BELGRANO
TO ESTADIO ANTONIO VESPUCIO LIBERTI (RIVER PLATE)
Parque Tres de Febrero
PALERMO HOLLYWOOD
PALERMO SOHO/ PALERMO VIEJO
Plazaleta Cortázar
TO ALMAGRO
Sinclair
Rio Alba
Giramondo Hostel
Home Buenos Aires
Ña Serapia
El Encanto
Bo-Bo
Bangalore
Casa Cruz
Club Eros
Desde El Alma
IGLESIA SAN FRANCISCO JAVIER
Don Julio
La Baita
La Cabrera
Bar 6
Soho All Suites
IGLESIA ARENIA
Thymus
IGLESIA SAN JORGE
Soldado Dela Independencia
Migueletes
Ortega y Gasset
Olleros
Gorostiaga
Maure
Arce
Baez
Arevalo
Av. del Libertador
Clay
Huergo Delfin
Av. Dorrego
San Osbunont
Av. Santa Fe
Zapata
Sinclair
Seoul Jan Francisco
Demaria
Kennedy, J.F. Av.
Av. Cervino
Bullrich, Int. Av.
Juncal
Av. Sarmiento
Nicaragua
Ravignani
Carranza
Fitz Roy
Bonpland
Oro
Costa Rica
Arévalo
Av. Honduras
El Salvador
Humboldt
Av. Juan B. Justo
Godoy Cruz
Guatemala
Darregueyra
Uriarte
Paraguay
Charcas
Republica De La India
Cabrera
Av. Cordoba
Güemes
Soler
Cnel Niceto Vega
Gorriti
Malabia
J.I. Borges
Thames
Humahuaca
Armenia
Gurruchaga
El Salvador
Av. Honduras
Gorriti
Medrano Av.
Bulnes
Bravo Mario
Tucumán
Levalle
Billinghurst
Guaroa Vieja
Humahuaca
KEY
Restaurants
Hotels
métro
following dining and lodging reviews indicates a map-grid coordinate

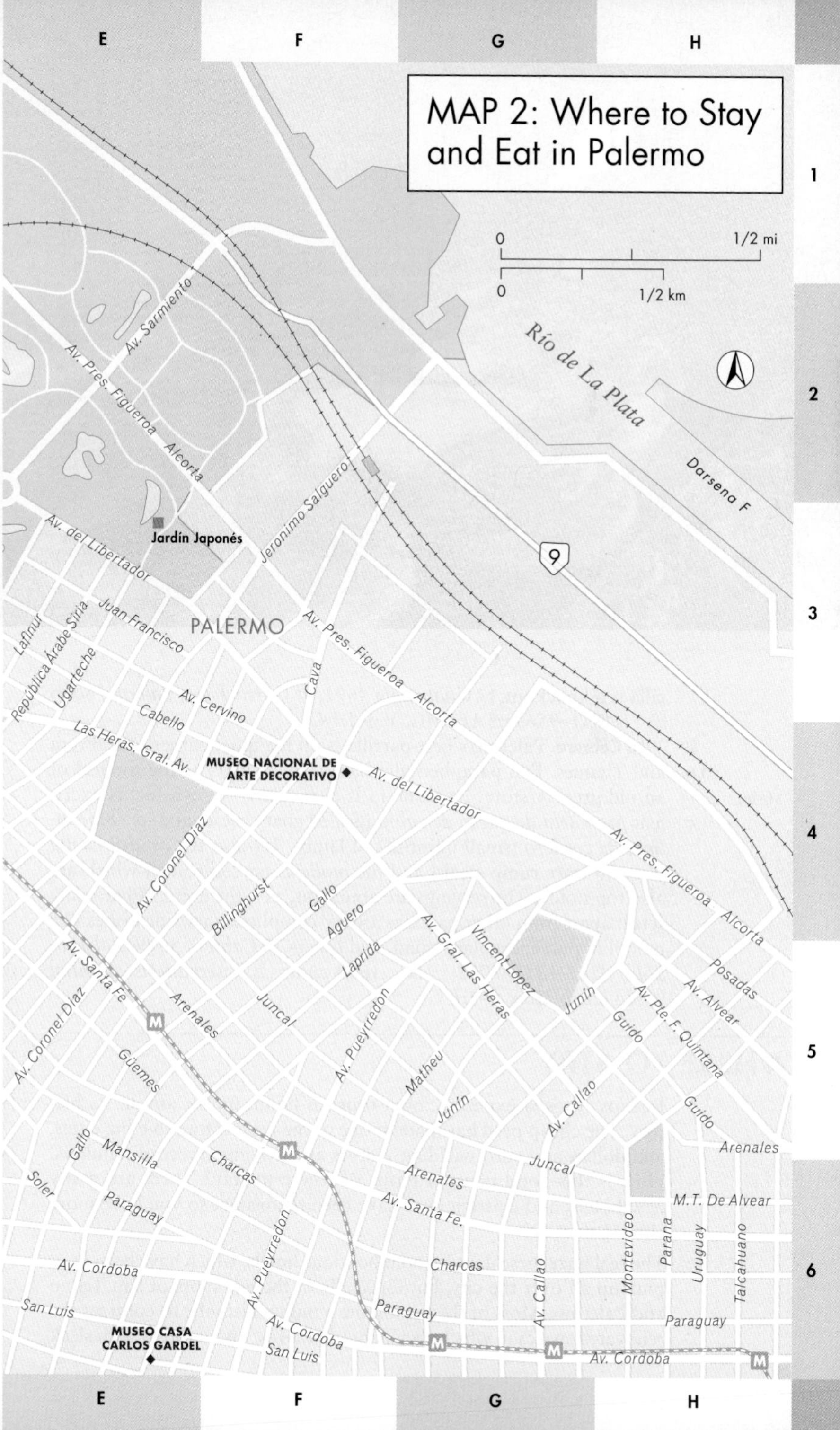

E
F
G
H
MAP 2: Where to Stay and Eat in Palermo
1
2
3
4
5
6
0
1/2 mi
0
1/2 km
Río de La Plata
Darsena F
9
Av. Sarmiento
Av. Pres. Figueroa Alcorta
Jardín Japonés
Jeronimo Salguero
Av. del Libertador
PALERMO
Lafinur
República Árabe Siria
Juan Francisco
Ugarteche
Av. Cervino
Cabello
Cava
Las Heras. Gral. Av.
MUSEO NACIONAL DE ARTE DECORATIVO
Av. Coronel Díaz
Billinghurst
Gallo
Aguero
Laprida
Av. Gral. Las Heras
Vincent López
Junín
Posadas
Av. Alvear
Av. Pte. F. Quintana
Guido
Av. Santa Fe
Arenales
Juncal
Av. Pueyrredon
Matheu
Av. Callao
Güemes
Mansilla
Charcas
Soler
Paraguay
Av. Cordoba
San Luis
Av. Santa Fe.
Arenales
M.T. De Alvear
Montevideo
Parana
Uruguay
Talcahuano
Av. Callao
MUSEO CASA CARLOS GARDEL
M
E
F
G
H

Restaurant parillas like this one offer everything from classic *bife de lomo* to all manner of offal.

cilla is a knockout. ✉ *Guatemala 4691, at Gurruchaga, Palermo Soho* ☎ *11/4831–9564* ▭ *AE, MC, V* ⊕ *1:F4.*

$$ STEAK Fodor's Choice ★ ✕ **La Cabrera.** Palermo's best parrilla is on the quiet corner of Cabrera and Thames. Fun paraphernalia hangs everywhere, giving the feel of an old grocery store. La Cabrera is particularly known for its excellent *provoleta de queso de cabra* (grilled goat cheese) and its *chinchulines de cordero* (small intestines of lamb). Try also the *cuadril vuelta y vuelta* (rare rump steak) and the *mollejas* (sweetbreads), which are also top-notch. The servings are abundant, as is the noise. What really sets it apart from other parrillas are the complimentary side dishes like pumpkin purée, eggplant salad, and others. ✉ *Cabrera 5099, Palermo Soho* ☎ *11/4831–7002* ▭ *No credit cards* ⚠ *Reservations essential* ⊗ *No lunch Mon.* ⊕ *1:E5.*

WHERE TO STAY

Buenos Aires is experiencing a tourism boom unlike any in its history. The cheap peso has made it one of the most affordable big cities, and dollar- and euro-wielding visitors are arriving in record numbers. How is this good news in terms of where to stay? There are many new hotels, and existing ones have been renovated, so you have more choices than ever.

The real buzz these days is about boutique hotels, which have been popping up all over the city, but especially in the hot spots of San Telmo and Palermo. Most of them combine a minimalist vibe to contrast the renovated spaces in which they're housed. Most are outfitted with sleek furniture, wood-paneled walls and floors, quaint outdoor gardens with reclining lounge chairs, bamboo and plants, and the requisite pool or *parrilla* (steak house). It's a style that has been perfected in Buenos Aires in recent years, and one the city can call all its own.

In San Telmo, hotels are primarily grand old mansions with soaring ceilings and impressive wooden doors. Tango is big in this neighborhood, and some hotels here cater to tango tourists.

Centro and Puerto Madero are teeming with international hotel chains, and most of them are well located. But as is the case in any Sheraton or Hilton or Marriott around the globe, once you close your door, it's easy to forget where you are.

Across town in Palermo, it's a hipper, more-urbane feel. These places are so new they haven't had time to develop their own character yet, but just like the city itself, this constant cyclical reinvention is what makes everything so enchanting here.

CENTRO AND ENVIRONS

CENTRO

$$ **Buenos Aires cE Design Hotel.** This hotel drips with coolness. The lobby's glass floor looks down to a small pool, just one example of the transparency theme that runs throughout. Floor-to-ceiling windows afford amazing views, and mirrors are placed for maximum effect. Rooms feel like pimped-out Tribeca lofts, with rotating flat-screen TVs that let you watch from bed or from one of the leather recliners. Mattresses are high and mighty and covered in shades of brown and orange. Kudos go to the architect, Ernesto Goransky, who also did the Design Suites next door. **Pros:** supermodern and spacious suites; great location; breakfast is served 24 hours a day. **Cons:** basement lounge feels like, well, a basement. ✉ *Marcelo T. Alvear 1695, Centro* ☎ *11/5237–3100* 🌐 *www.designce.com* *21 rooms, 7 suites* *In-room: safe, kitchen, Internet, Wi-Fi. In-hotel: bar, pool, gym, laundry service, public Wi-Fi* *AE, DC, MC, V* Ⓜ *D to Callao* ✢ *2:B2.*

$$ **Marriott Plaza Hotel.** This Buenos Aires landmark brims with old-school
Fodor's Choice ★
style. Built in 1909 and renovated in 2003, the hotel sits at the top of pedestrian-only Florida Street and overlooks the leafy Plaza San Martín. The elegant lobby, crystal chandeliers, and swanky cigar bar evoke Argentina's opulent, if distant, past. Rooms are comfortable and clean, if not particularly spacious. The hotel is next to both the Kavanagh Building, a 1930s art deco masterpiece that was once South America's tallest, and the Basilica Santísimo Sacramento, where renowned Argentines of all stripes, like Diego Maradona (former Argentine football player), have tied the knot. Exploring the myriad nooks and crannies of this grand old hotel is part of its timeless appeal. **Pros:** great prices; every area of the building offers a unique and fascinating view of the city. **Cons:** the main lobby is small and often gets crowded; check-in can be a lengthy process, especially now that it has become a popular stop for cruise-ship passengers. ✉ *Florida 1005, Centro* ☎ *11/4318–3000, 800/228–9290 in U.S.* 🌐 *www.marriott.com* *313 rooms, 12 suites* *In-room: safe, Internet (fee). In-hotel: 2 restaurants, room service,*

bar, pool, gym, laundry service, public Wi-Fi ▭ *AE, DC, MC, V* 🍽 *BP* Ⓜ *C to San Martín* ✥ *2:D2.*

¢ **Milhouse Hostel.** This lovely and lively hostel goes the extra mile to make backpackers feel welcome, with pool tables, televisions, and concierge services. The house, which dates from the late 1800s, has been tricked out with funky artwork and accessories. Its three floors overlook a beautiful tiled patio, and all lead out to a sunny terrace, which the hostel skillfully uses to entertain guests regardless of their interests. Morning yoga classes may well be followed by rowdy beer-swilling *asados* (barbecues). The dorm rooms are clean and big, and most have private bathrooms. At night the surrounding streets can be dodgy, so take precautions. **Pros:** fun and funky place; it's ideal for hooking up with travelers from around the world; close to all of San Telmo's nighttime offerings; there's a sister location nearby at Avenida de Mayo 1249. **Cons:** it's a hostel; hygiene standards are sometimes below par; no a/c. ✉ *Hipólito Irigoyen 959, Centro* ☎ *11/4345–9604 or 11/4343–5038* 🌐 *www.milhousehostel.com* 13 *private rooms, 150 beds total* *In-room: no phone, no TV, Internet, Wi-Fi. In-hotel: restaurant, bar, laundry facilities, parking (fee)* ▭ *No credit cards* 🍽 *CP* Ⓜ *A to Piedras, C to Av. de Mayo* ✥ *2:C5.*

$$$ Fodor's Choice ★ **NH City & Tower.** This enormous art deco hotel is a throwback to an earlier era. It would be the perfect image for a cover of Ayn Rand's *The Fountainhead*. Inside, molded pillars support a stained-glass ceiling, which filters sunlight onto white marble floors. Upstairs, the contemporary rooms have dark-wood floors and color schemes that include bold oranges, reds, and black. The rooftop pool and patio are beloved by producers of TV commercials, thanks to the view of the cupolas in nearby San Telmo. A new tower opened in 2006 and added 69 luxury rooms to the complex. **Pros:** old-school feel brings you back to another period in Buenos Aires's history; amazing views from the roof. **Cons:** despite its downtown location, feels isolated from other attractions; area can be sketchy at night. ✉ *Bolívar 160, Centro* ☎ *11/4121–6464* 🌐 *www.nh-hotels.com* *327 rooms, 42 suites* *In-room: safe, refrigerator, Internet, Wi-Fi (fee). In-hotel: restaurant, room service, bar, pool, gym, laundry service, public Wi-Fi* ▭ *AE, DC, MC, V* 🍽 *BP* Ⓜ *A to Perú, E to Bolívar* ✥ *2:D5.*

PUERTO MADERO

$$$$ Fodor's Choice ★ **Faena Hotel + Universe.** Argentine fashion impresario Alan Faena and famed French architect Philippe Starck set out to create a "universe" unto itself, and they have succeeded in spades. Entering the long, tall hall transforms you to another place and time; it's a space so truly unique that it's almost as if the air were different inside. Rooms are feng-shui perfect, with rich reds and crisp whites. Velvet curtains and Venetian blinds open electronically to river and city views; marble floors fill expansive baths; velvet couches, leather armchairs, flat-screen TVs, and surround-sound stereos lend more luxury. The "Experience Managers" are basically personal assistants, making reservations and tending to every whim. Other highlights are two excellent restaurants and an elaborate spa with a Turkish bath. In El Cabaret, a blood-red music box dotted with red-leather couches, you can swig champagne and

watch sensual tango shows. Next door in the Library Lounge you never know who might show up: Coldplay and local rock legend Charly Garcia once held an impromptu jam session around the piano, playing Beatles songs until the wee hours. **Pros:** quite simply, one of the most unusual hotels on the planet. **Cons:** an "are you cool enough?" vibe is ever-present. ✉ *Martha Salotti 445, Puerto Madero* ☎ *11/4010–9000* 🌐 *www.faenahotelanduniverse.com* *110 rooms, 16 suites* *In-room: safe, DVD, Internet, Wi-Fi. In-hotel: 2 restaurants, room service, 2 bars, pool, gym, laundry service, parking (fee), no-smoking rooms* ▭ *AE, DC, MC, V* ✥ *1:G5.*

$$$ **Hotel Madero.** This slick hotel is within walking distance of downtown as well as the riverside ecological reserve, and is a favorite for visiting British rock stars and fashion photographers. Culinary bad-boy and TV star Anthony Bourdain also slept here. The big, bright, modern rooms have wood accents and white color schemes. Many rooms also have fantastic views of the docks and city skyline. The restaurant, Red, serves great Argentine–French fusion cuisine in an intimate setting. The breakfast buffet features exotic fresh fruits and Argentine baked goods. The lobby bar attracts a cool after-office crowd and has some of the most original cocktails in the city. **Pros:** afternoon dance classes, where you can learn salsa, samba, and tango. **Cons:** the gym and pool are in cramped quarters. ✉ *Rosario Vera Penaloza 360, Dique 2, Puerto Madero* ☎ *11/5776–7777* 🌐 *www.hotelmadero.com* *165 rooms, 28 suites* *In-room: safe, Internet, Wi-Fi. In-hotel: restaurant, room service, bar, pool, gym, laundry service, public Wi-Fi* ▭ *AE, DC, MC, V* ✥ *2:F6.*

SAN TELMO

$$$ **Axel Hotel Buenos Aires.** Billed as Latin America's first gay hotel, the Axel Hotel Buenos Aires is modeled after the successful original hotel in Barcelona. The new building combines glass, wood, and water to an impressive effect, with lots of open spaces and fresh air. The floors of the common areas are lined with colorful mosaic tiling, a nod to the rainbow pride flag and Mac computers. The rooms are slick, modern, and bright, and equipped with hydro-massage tubs and leather-lined closets. The Axel also has what must be Buenos Aires's first transparent elevated pool, located on the top floor, and visible from all points below. Although the clientele and staff are predominantly homosexual men, the hotel vehemently promotes itself as "hetero-friendly." **Pros:** gigantic outside pool, bar, and deck area offer an upbeat and festive environment, a respite from the chaotic city streets. **Cons:** rooms are small and very close together; the doors and balconies practically sit on top of each other, therefore privacy is at a minimum. ✉ *Venezuela 649, San Telmo* ☎ *11/4136–9393* 🌐 *www.axelhotels.com* *48 rooms* *In-room: safe, Wi-Fi. In-hotel: restaurant, room service, bar, pools, gym, laundry service, parking (fee), no-smoking rooms* ▭ *AE, DC, MC, V* Ⓜ *E to Belgrano* ✥ *2:D5.*

¢ **Boquitas Pintadas.** The whimsically named "Little Painted Mouths" (a tribute to Manuel Puig's novel of the same name) is a self-proclaimed "pop hotel," and the German owner, Heike Thelen, goes out of her way to keep things weird and wild. World-famous "nude" photographer Spencer Tunick staged a shoot here and ended up spending the night, and other celebs have passed through over the years. Local artists, inspired by an array of provocative themes, redecorate and rename the five rooms every few months with names like "The Betrayal of Rita Hayworth." The restaurant serves dishes not often found in the city, including goulash. The hotel also hosts ever-changing art exhibitions and theme parties for an eclectic crowd. It is in the Constitución neighborhood, west of San Telmo, across Avenida 9 de Julio. **Pros:** a delightfully unique place that makes for an unforgettable stay. **Cons:** use caution at night: the surrounding area is dodgy. ✉ *Estados Unidos 1393, Constitución* ☎ *11/4381–6064* 🌐 *www.boquitas-pintadas.com.ar* *5 rooms* *In-room: Wi-Fi. In-hotel: restaurant, room service, bar, laundry service* ▭ *No credit cards* Ⓜ *E to San José* ✣ *2:C6.*

$ Fodor's Choice ★ **Gurda Hotel.** In the heart of San Telmo, the Gurda will give you a glimpse of what life was like at the turn of the 19th century. Seven rooms line the long, open-air hallway with exposed brick, green plants, and bamboo sticks. Each room is named after something or someone decidedly Argentine—Jorge Luis Borges, Malbec, Patagonia—and filled complete with decorations to match. (In the Borges room you find copies of his books and a colorful portrait.) The rooms are rustic and basic, but extremely charming. **Pros:** the young, friendly staff can organize wine tastings with local sommeliers and tango lessons. **Cons:** the entrance is right on a busy street full of buses; the restaurant and bar are noisy. ✉ *Defensa 1521, San Telmo* ☎ *11/4307–0646* 🌐 *www.gurdahotel.com* *7 rooms* *In-room: safe, Wi-Fi. In-hotel: restaurant, room service, bar, laundry service, parking (fee), no-smoking rooms* ▭ *AE, DC, MC, V* Ⓜ *C to Constitucion* ✣ *2:D6.*

$$ Fodor's Choice ★ **Moreno Hotel.** A gorgeous art deco building dating back to 1929, the Moreno's architects were posed with the challenge of restoring the 80-year-old site without disturbing its original elements, like mosaic tiling and stained-glassed windows. The seven-floor hotel has spacious and sexy rooms, each decorated in a color motif complete with chaise longues, Argentine cowhide rugs, and big fluffy beds. The "J-Loft" is decorated to the max, and has a big Jacuzzi inside. The top-floor terrace offers an outdoor fireplace, big wooden recliners, and amazing city views, including the enormous San Francisco Basilica directly across the street. **Pros:** there's a top-notch restaurant and 130-seat theater on-site. **Cons:** some rooms are just steps away from the main lobby and elevator. ✉ *Moreno 376, San Telmo* ☎ *11/6091–2000* 🌐 *www.morenobuenosaires.com* *39 rooms* *In-room: safe, refrigerator, Internet, Wi-Fi. In-hotel: restaurant, room service, bar, gym, parking (fee), no-smoking rooms* ▭ *AE, MC, V* Ⓜ *A to Plaza de Mayo* ✣ *2:E5.*

RECOLETA AND ALMAGRO

RECOLETA

$$$$ Fodor's Choice ★ **Alvear Palace Hotel.** The Alvear Palace has been the standard-bearer for upscale sophistication since 1932, and is undoubtedly the shining star of Buenos Aires's hotel offerings. Scores of dignitaries, celebrities, and VIPs have passed through its doors over the years, and they keep

Faena Hotel + Universe

Palacio Dohau–Park Hyatt

Moreno Hotel

coming back for the world-class service and atmosphere. Gorgeously decorated rooms feature silky-smooth carpets, thick curtains made from European fabrics, and featherbeds with Egyptian-cotton linens. Each room receives the services of a personal butler, who will unpack your bags, press your wrinkled clothes, and basically tend to your every need. The lunch buffet at L'Orangerie is out of this world, and the superchic French restaurant, La Bourgogne, is one of the city's best. **Pros:** the beautiful new spa features therapeutic wave pools, a sauna, and steam rooms. **Cons:** bathrooms are on the small side, owing to the building's age; one of the country's most expensive hotels. ✉ *Av. Alvear 1891, Recoleta* ☎ *11/4808–2100 or 11/4804–7777, 800/448–8355 in U.S.* 🌐 *www.alvearpalace.com* *100 rooms, 100 suites* *In-room: safe, Internet, Wi-Fi. In-hotel: 2 restaurants, room service, bar, pool, gym, laundry service, no-smoking rooms* *AE, DC, MC, V.* *BP* *2:C1.*

$ **Art Hotel.** The aptly named Art Hotel has an impressive ground-floor gallery where exhibits of paintings, photographs, and sculptures by acclaimed Argentine artists change monthly. You might even run into some fabulous art aficionados sipping Chardonnay and admiring the creations. Rooms are classified as "small and cozy," "queen," or "king," and many have wrought-iron bed frames with white canopies. The building's 100-year-old elevator will take you to the rooftop patio, where there's a hot tub and plenty of room to soak up some sun. **Pros:** its bohemian vibe will make you feel like you've joined an artists' colony. **Cons:** rooms are dark and somewhat antiquated. ✉ *Azcuenaga 1268, Recoleta* ☎ *11/4821–4744* 🌐 *www.arthotel.com.ar* *36 rooms* *In-room: safe, Internet. In-hotel: bar, laundry service, public Wi-Fi* *AE, MC, V* Ⓜ *D to Pueyrredón* *2:C4.*

$$$$ Fodor's Choice ★ **Park Hyatt Palacio Duhau.** This gorgeous new hotel has upped the ante for elegance in Buenos Aires. Its two buildings, a restored 1930s-era mansion and a 17-story tower, are connected by an underground art gallery and a leafy garden. The rooms are decorated in rich hues of wood, marble, and Argentine leather. Ask to stay in the mansion, where the rooms are larger and infinitely more charming. Be sure to sip a whiskey at the Oak Bar, constructed from 17th-century oak carvings from a Normandy castle, and visit the Ahin Spa (named after a Mapuche Indian welcoming ritual), which has five suites offering holistic and beauty treatments, next to the city's largest indoor pool. **Pros:** understated elegance; great restaurant; the 3,500 bottle Wine Library and "Cheese Room" are unique attractions. **Cons:** a long walk from one side of the hotel to the other; although elegantly decorated, some of the common areas lack warmth. ✉ *Av. Alvear 1661, Recoleta* ☎ *11/5171–1234* 🌐 *www.buenosaires.park.hyatt.com* *126 rooms, 39 suites* *In-room: safe, Internet, Wi-Fi, DVD. In-hotel: 2 restaurants, room service, bar, pool, gym, spa, laundry service* *AE, MC, V* *2:C1.*

ALMAGRO

$$ **Abasto Plaza Hotel.** This place is *all* about the tango. Photos and paintings of famous musicians line the walls that surround the checked-marble dance floor, which is next to a boutique where you can buy sequined skirts, stilettos, and fishnet stockings. Suites each have their

own dance floor for private lessons, or you can join other guests for nightly tango lessons and a live show. Rooms are large and elegant, with—surprise, surprise—a tango theme. The hotel is two blocks from an alleyway and theater dedicated to the godfather of tango, Carlos Gardel. The enormous Abasto Shopping Center is across the street. **Pros:** if you're in Buenos Aires to tango, this is your place. **Cons:** tango overload is a very real possibility; the furnishings and bedding are a bit tired. ✉ *Av. Corrientes 3190, Almagro* ☎ *11/6311–4466* 🌐 *www.abastoplaza.com* 120 *rooms, 6 suites* *In-room: Internet, Wi-Fi. In-hotel: restaurant, room service, bar, pool, gym* ▭ *AE, DC, MC, V* 🍴 *BP* Ⓜ *B to Carlos Gardel* ✣ *2:A4.*

PALERMO

¢ **Giramondo Hostel.** The funky Giramondo has all that a hostel needs: plenty of beds and bathrooms, a kitchen, a TV and computer lounge, and a patio, where backpackers from around the world grill up slabs of Argentine beef. The dark, dank underground bar serves up cheap drinks; it also has a small wine cellar. Giramondo is two blocks from buses and the subte on Avenida Santa Fe—an ideal locale for taking part in Palermo's pulsing nightlife while also being close to downtown. There's now a sister location with suites just down the street at Oro 2472. **Pros:** they have the budget traveler in mind, and cater to short-term and long-term stays. **Cons:** the surrounding streets are chaotic; loud buses buzz by all hours of the night; no a/c or elevator. ✉ *Guemes 4802, Palermo Soho* ☎ *11/4772–6740* 🌐 *www.hostelgiramondo.com.ar* *In-room: no phone, kitchen, no TV, Internet. In-hotel: bar, laundry facilities* ▭ *No credit cards* Ⓜ *D to Palermo* ✣ *1:F3.*

$$ **Home Buenos Aires.** It's run by Argentinean Patricia O'Shea and her British husband, Tom Rixton, a well-known music producer, and it oozes coolness and class. Each room is decorated with vintage French wallpaper and has a stereo, a laptop-friendly safe, and either a bathtub or a wet room. On-site there's a vast garden; a barbecue area; an infinity pool; a holistic spa; and a funky lounge bar where you can sip a cocktail and listen to mood music created especially for the hotel by famed record producer Flood (U2, Smashing Pumpkins, Nine Inch Nails), one of the hotel's investors. **Pros:** impossibly hip and fun; always interesting people staying here. **Cons:** lots of nonguests come here to hang out, reducing the intimacy factor. ✉ *Honduras 5860, Palermo Hollywood* ☎ *11/4778–1008* 🌐 *www.homebuenosaires.com* *14 rooms, 4 suites* *In-room: safe, Internet, Wi-Fi. In-hotel: restaurant, room service, bar, pool, spa* ▭ *AE, MC, V* Ⓜ *D to Ministro Carranza* ✣ *1:D3.*

$$ **Soho All Suites.** In the heart of Palermo Soho this smart hotel offers sneak peaks into the backyards of the neighborhood's many private homes, where some of Argentina's coolest artists reside. The big lobby area is great for informal business meetings and is chock-full of flyers and brochures that will help you seek out Soho's latest offerings. The amazing balconies in the front and back of the property are favored for local photo shoots and television commercials. The rooms all have kitchens, but the faux gray-marble tabletops and cheap porcelain toilets definitely take away from the charm. **Pros:** massage parlor on-site for

Don't forget your cowboy hat: dance clubs, like this one in Palermo, are a stylish affair.

those urgent post-shopping sores. **Cons:** not well maintained: walls need painting and wood floors need polishing. ✉ *Honduras 4762, Palermo Soho* ☎ *11/4832–3000* 🌐 *www.sohoallsuites.com* 21 *suites* *In-room: safe, Wi-Fi. In-hotel: public Wi-Fi, parking (fee), no-smoking rooms* ▭ *AE, DC, MC, V* Ⓜ *D to Plaza Italia* ✥ *1:E5.*

AFTER DARK

Porteños *love* to party. Many don't think twice about dancing until 6 AM and heading to work at 8 AM. And alcohol doesn't play a vital role in whether people enjoy themselves or not; porteños could have fun at an insurance convention, provided the conversation and music were good and everyone looked marvelous. Indeed, for many, it's better to *look* good than to *feel* good.

Nightlife these days is starting earlier. Lately, in an effort to drum up business during the post-work/pre-dinner window, many downtown bars are promoting "after-office" drink specials; it's a happy hour that often lasts until 9 or 10 PM. This recent phenomenon aside, timing in Buenos Aires nightlife is an exercise in patience. Get there too early and the bar will be empty, and you'll be tired when the atmosphere finally builds. When families with kids in strollers don't turn up for dinner until nearly midnight, you know it will take a bit of work to be fashionably late.

Hours are very fluid here but there are some general guidelines: theater performances start around 9 or 9:30 PM, and the last movie begins after midnight. Bars get busy in the small hours, and clubs, which attract crowds in the 18–35 age range, don't begin to fill up until 3 or 4 AM. If in doubt, turn up later than you think is reasonable. That said, the subte closes around 11 PM, so going out means taking a taxi home or staying out until 5 AM, when trains resume running.

COCKTAIL TIME

The late timing of porteño nightlife means even the busiest bars spend a good part of each evening empty. This has led to the rise of happy hours with half-price drink offers stretching for often three or four hours. This "after-office" trend is particularly noticeable in Centro. Most of the listings that follow offer some form of this; it's a good trend to take advantage of as you acclimate to a more Argentine schedule.

CENTRO

★ **Dada.** Dada is colorful and fun (a healthy contrast to its seedy neighbors), and well worth visiting for a meal, but it's the sociable bar that's the heart of the place—and of the neighborhood. It's cramped and serves very good drinks, meaning it gets livelier as the evening goes on. ✉ *San Martin 941, Centro* ☎ *11/4314–4787.*

Empire Thai. It's an "American bar" in a downtown Thai restaurant that treats its cosmopolitan after-work crowd to an extended happy hour until 9 PM weekdays and 11 PM weekends. The busiest nights are Thursday and Friday. ✉ *Tres Sargentos 427, Centro* ☎ *11/4312–5706* 🌐 *www.empirethai.net* Ⓜ *A to Piedras.*

The Kilkenny. A popular pub that spawned a whole street of imitators, the Kilkenny serves surprisingly good Irish food and has Guinness on draft. Celtic or rock bands play every night, entertaining the after-work crowd from nearby office buildings that comes for the 8 PM to 11 PM happy hour and stays into the small hours. ✉ *Marcelo T. De Alvear 399, Centro* ☎ *11/4312–7291* Ⓜ *C to San Martín.*

Le Bar. Le Bar is a stylish addition to the Centro drinking scene. Up the stairs from the cocktail lounge is a clever sunken seating arrangement; farther still is a smokers' terrace. Office workers get the evening started; DJs start a bit later and play until 2 AM. ✉ *Tucuman 422, Centro* ☎ *11/5219–8580.*

RECOLETA

Gran Bar Danzon. If Carrie, Samantha, Charlotte, and Miranda lived in Buenos Aires, they'd probably frequent this first-floor hot spot where local business sharks and chic internationals sip wine and eat sushi by candlelight. It's extremely popular for happy hour, but people stick around for dinner and the occasional live jazz shows, too. The wine list and the appetizers are superb, as is the flirting. ✉ *Libertad 1161, Recoleta* ☎ *11/4811–1108* 🌐 *www.granbardanzon.com.ar* Ⓜ *C to Retiro.*

★ **Milión.** At this beautiful mansion you can enjoy a cold Cosmopolitan or a nice Malbec at the upstairs bar while sophisticates chat around you. Be sure to explore all the hidden corners, including the back garden salon, which is illuminated with candles and soft, colorful lights. ✉ *Paraná 1048, Recoleta* ☎ *11/4815–9925* 🌐 *www.milion.com.ar* Ⓜ *D to Callao.*

PALERMO

Acabar. It's an offbeat bar that's become a big hit, and the lines to get in are only exacerbated by the abundance of board games inside. Those who do manage to get a table are quickly charmed by the buzz of the place and the easy-going atmosphere. ✉ *Honduras 5733, Palermo Hollywood* ☎ *11/4772–0845* 🌐 *www.acabarnet.com.ar* ⏲ *Sun.–Thurs. 8 PM–2 AM, Fri.–Sat. 8 PM–5 AM.*

Bar 6. Somewhat of a Palermo Soho institution, Bar 6 suffers from the indifferent, sometimes rude waitstaff that such a reputation demands. If you can get past that, it's a convenient Palermo meeting point (it opens at 8 AM), a stylish bar, and a decent restaurant. A DJ often plays good music in the evening. ✉ *Armenia 1676, Palermo* ☎ *11/4833–6807* 🌐 *www.barseis.com* ⏲ *Daily 8 AM–2 AM.*

Casa Rica. A very low-key cocktail bar, Casa Rica seems to consist of a series of little corners, each with a wooden table and most open to the stars. The atmosphere is relaxed and unpretentious, and patrons tend to arrive early and stay late. It's a good place go for conversation. ✉ *Nicaragua 4817, Palermo Soho* ☎ *11/4775–9861* 🌐 *www.casarica.com.ar* ⏲ *Daily from 7 PM.*

DANCE CLUBS

CENTRO

Fodor's Choice ★ **Bahrein.** Sheik—er, chic and super-stylish, this party palace is in a 100-year-old former bank. Eat upstairs at Crizia, or head straight to the main floor's Funky Room, where beautiful, tightly clothed youth groove to pop, rock, and funk. The downstairs Excess Room has electronic beats and dizzying wall visuals. Consistently good and popular with North American visitors is the Tuesday night drum and bass night. ✉ *Lavalle 345, Centro* ☎ *11/4315–2403* 🌐 *www.bahreinba.com* Ⓜ *B to Alem.*

Cocoliche. Cocoliche enjoys cultlike status in both the straight and gay communities. Upstairs is a diverse art gallery big on young locals; downstairs, underground house music drives one of the city's darkest dance floors. ✉ *Rivadavia 878, Centro* ☎ *11/4342–9485* 🌐 *www.cocoliche.net* Ⓜ *A to Piedras.*

SAN TELMO

Rey Castro. Just because this Cuban restaurant-bar gets a little wild on weekends doesn't mean things get out of hand: the bouncers look like NFL players. It's a popular spot for birthday parties and great mojitos. After the nightly live dance show, DJs crank up the Cuban rhythms; you're likely to learn some sexy new moves. ✉ *Perú 342, San Telmo* ☎ *11/4342–9998* 🌐 *www.reycastro.com* Ⓜ *C to San Juan.*

RECOLETA

The Basement. This rowdy nightspot downstairs at the Shamrock pub is owned by a couple of Irish guys and is popular with expats and young upwardly mobile porteño party people. Stop first for a Guinness at the bar upstairs, where you can yap away in English and easily forget you're in South America. Follow the techno beats to the downstairs dance club, where there's an enormous disco ball. ✉ *Rodríguez Peña 1220, Recoleta* ☎ *11/4812–3584* 🌐 *www.theshamrockbar.com* Ⓜ *D to Callao.*

PALERMO

Club Aráoz. It may be intimate, but it attracts a serious party crowd. Thursday is block-rocking hip-hop night; Friday and Saturday see DJs spinning rock music and electronic dance music for a relatively laid-back bunch of Buenos Aires youth. ✉ *Aráoz 2424, Palermo* ☎ *11/4833–7775* 🌐 *www.clubaraoz.com.ar.*

★ **Kika.** Right at the heart of Palermo and next door to the Congo bar, Kika is much bigger than you'd guess from the outside. Thanks to its funky musical orientation, though, its two dance floors fill up quickly. ✉ *Honduras 5339, Palermo Soho* ☎ *11/4137–5311* 🌐 *www.kikaclub.com.ar.*

Fodor's Choice ★ **Niceto.** One of the city's most interesting venues features everything from demure indie rock to the outrageous and legendary Club 69 (think under-dressed cross-dressers). The larger main room with a balcony has live shows and lots of dancing, and there's usually something contrasting and chill taking place in the back room, too. ✉ *Cnel. Niceto Vega 5510, Palermo Hollywood* ☎ *11/4779–9396* 🌐 *www.nicetoclub.com.*

GAY AND LESBIAN

CENTRO

Chueca Downtown. With a restaurant in Palermo Soho, a bar and yacht in Puerto Madero, and ownership of the Palacio Alsina, the Chueca group is rapidly getting bigger and better. Their famous cabaret show is now based here in the center of town, where the bar is open all day and serves as a "pre-dance" venue for the neighboring Palacio Alsina on Friday nights. ✉ *Alsina 975, Centro* ☎ *11/4331–5330* 🌐 *www.chueca-restobar.com.ar.*

Contramano. It's been around since 1984, when it was the city's most popular and pioneering gay disco. Today it operates more as a laid-back bar with an older, male-only clientele. Occasionally there's live music and male strippers. ✉ *Rodríguez Peña 1082* ☎ *No phone* 🌐 *www.contramano.com* Ⓜ *D to Callao.*

Palacio Alsina. This massive downtown club attracts a mixed-age crowd of gays and lesbians on Friday and Sunday nights for electronic music and pop tunes. On Saturday the club goes straight and changes its name to Big One for a night of hard-core techno. ✉ *Alsina 940, Centro* ☎ *11/4331–1277* 🌐 *www.alsinabuenosaires.com* Ⓜ *A to Piedras.*

RECOLETA

★ **Glam.** Young, hip, buff men come for smooth cruising in a classy setting: a fashionably restored home. Lesbians and straight women come for the festive atmosphere and raucous music. ✉ *Cabrera 3046, Recoleta* ☎ *11/4963–2521* 🌐 *www.glambsas.com.ar* Ⓜ *D to Pueyrredón.*

Zoom. It's a relatively new club half a block from the very cruisey section of Santa Fe, between Avenidas Callao and Coronel Díaz. Zoom has lots to offer, including a good bar, a maze, video cabins, and lots of dark corners. It can get pretty intense, but there's good security. ✉ *Uriburu*

DID YOU KNOW?

The uniquely porteño style of decorative sign art seen here is called *fileteado*. It's generally used in association with well-loved, nostalgia-inducing things, like tango halls, old *collectivos* (city buses), or a realy good *cortado* (coffee).

1018, Recoleta ☎ *11/4827–4828* 🌐 *www.zoombuenosaires.com* Ⓜ *D to Pueyrredón.*

PALERMO

Amerika. This big gay disco club has three floors of high-energy action and shows. Thursday and Sunday are quieter, with more emphasis on the music and cheaper drinks; Friday and Saturday are wild. ✉ *Gascon 1040 Palermo* ☎ *11/4865–4416* 🌐 *www.ameri-k.com.ar.*

LATE-NIGHT BARS

These bars—while late-night by all rational standards—aren't to be confused with the *late* late-night bars known as "afters." Spending the wee hours at one (or several) of these places is sort of like the evening's main course, so be sure to save some energy for it.

CENTRO

La Cigale. Sip cocktails at a large turquoise bar while smooth sounds and hipsters young and old spin around you. Some nights local indie bands squeeze themselves onto the small stage at the back of the venue, other nights DJs play reggae, rock, or electronica. Either way, it's a good place for a nightcap on the way home. ✉ *25 de Mayo 722, Centro* ☎ *11/4312–8275* Ⓜ *C to San Martín.*

SAN TELMO

Bar Britanico. This traditional corner bar opposite Parque Lezama is one of San Telmo's most iconic spots, and manages to find itself in the news for one thing or another every decade or so. Day and night it's full of characters and passionate discussions. ✉ *Brasil 399, San Telmo* ☎ *11/4361–2107.*

La Puerta Roja. Ring the bell at the Red Door and climb the stairs to a very cool-feeling bar free of the nostalgic trappings of much of the rest of San Telmo. The bar area is packed and serves cheap drinks, pool tables are in the back, and there's a sociable mix of locals and expats to get chatting with. ✉ *Chacabuco 733, San Telmo* ☎ *11/4362–5649.*

PUERTO MADERO

Asia de Cuba. Once *the* spot to be seen sipping champagne and eating sushi, Asia de Cuba still draws local celebrities, though it's lost some of its white-hot luster. The candlelight and red-and-black Asian decor set the mood for an exotic evening—by local standards. Sometimes there's live music. ✉ *Pierina Dealessi 750, Puerto Madero* ☎ *11/4894–1329* 🌐 *www.asiadecuba.com.ar.*

RECOLETA

Los Porteños. A traditional Buenos Aires bar with plenty of *fileteado* (colorful, swirly graphic embellishments) and wooden tables, Los Porteños serves coffee and snacks all day and stays open late into the night; it doesn't shut at all on Saturday. It's one block from Recoleta Cemetery and a good option when the dives on Vicente Lopez get to be too much. ✉ *Av. Las Heras 2101, Recoleta* ☎ *11/4809–3548.*

El Alamo Bar. From the outside, it's only the signs asking patrons to leave quietly that suggest this might not be the demure little bar it appears to be. The generous drinks promotions (ladies drink free until midnight every day) make sure that things get rowdy, and it turns into a proper little party zone on weekends. It also has nonstop sports on the TV and bikini competitions—just so you know. ✉ *Uruguay 1175, Recoleta* ☎ *11/4813–7324* 🌐 *www.elalamobar.com* ⏲ *24 hrs.*

PALERMO

★ **Antares.** New Antares brews seven of its own ales, all of which you can taste-test in shot-size glasses. It also attracts a cosmopolitan group of drinkers who keep the spacious bar open from after-office until the small hours. The service is friendly and efficient; the music's feel-good. ✉ *Armenia 1447, Palermo Soho* ☎ *11/4833–9611* 🌐 *www.cervezaantares.com.*

Bangalore. A pub and curry house in Buenos Aires? Well located, the Bangalore has it all—right down to a blazing log fire in winter. There's limited seating both at the bar and in the tiny restaurant upstairs, but somehow there's hardly ever too much of a wait at the bar. Service is friendly, and there's a wide range of draught beers. ✉ *Humboldt 1416, Palermo Hollywood* ☎ *11/4779–2621.*

★ **Congo.** A fashionable post-dinner, pre-club crowd—in faded fitted jeans, hipster sneakers, and leather jackets—frequents this hangout. The lines outside might seem a bit much, but it's all worthwhile once you get in. The back garden can get lively enough on warm nights to cause many would-be club goers to stick around for another gin and tonic. ✉ *Honduras 5329, Palermo Soho* ☎ *11/4833–5857.*

Kim y Novak Bar. On the edge of Palermo Soho, Kim y Novak is a kitschy cocktail bar that attracts both gay and straight lounge lizards. Upstairs, you can enjoy a mixed drink seated on vintage couches or outside on the pavement. Downstairs there's a trashy disco where lots of gay men and transvestites dance to heavy electronic beats. ✉ *Guemes 4900, Palermo Soho* ☎ *11/4773–7521* 🌐 *www.kimynovack.blogspot.com.*

Mundo Bizarro. They've been building their late-night crowd and perfecting their cocktails here since 1997, which is a long time in Palermo. Red lights, kitsch artwork, and rock and roll provide the backdrop; the rest gets improvised afresh every evening. ✉ *Serrano 1222, Palermo Soho* ☎ *11/4773–1967* 🌐 *www.mundobizarrobar.com.*

LIVE MUSIC

JAZZ

CENTRO

Clásica y Moderna. It's not just a jazz club but a restaurant and bookshop besides. An older, artsy crowd gathers here for dinner, drinks, philosophy, and live jazz. The program makes good use of their grand piano; singers take on bossa nova, tango, and bolero. ✉ *Av. Callao 892, Recoleta* ☎ *11/4812–8707* 🌐 *www.clasicaymoderna.com* Ⓜ *D to Callao.*

★ **Notorious.** It's a jazz bar, restaurant, and record shop rolled into one. Some of the area's best musicians, like Ricardo Cavalli and Adrian Iaies, play here often. You can also listen to the club's extensive music collection on the CD players at each table. ✉ *Av. Callao 966, Recoleta* ☎ *11/4813–6888* 🌐 *www.notorious.com.ar* Ⓜ *D to Callao.*

Continued on page 113

The Dance of Buenos Aires

by Victoria Patience

"THE TANGO IS MACHO, THE TANGO IS STRONG. IT SMELLS OF WINE AND TASTES LIKE DEATH."

So goes the famous tango "Why I Sing Like This," whose mix of nostalgia, violence, and sensuality sum up what is truly the dance of Buenos Aires. From its beginnings, tango and its two-four beat marked and reflected the character of Buenos Aires. You may hear strains of tango on the radio while sipping coffee in a café, see high-kicking sequined dancers in a glitzy dinner show, or listen to musicians in a darkened cabaret. But one of the most memorable ways to experience the best of this broody, melancholic, impassioned art form is through dancing it yourself.

DANCING THE TANGO

Many milongas now kick off with group dance classes which usually last an hour or two and cost 15–20 pesos; some lessons are free, though chaotic. These classes are great for getting over nerves and getting you in the mood. However, most *milongueros* (people who dance at *milongas*, or tango dance halls) take tango very seriously and don't look kindly on left-footed beginners crowding the floor. We recommend you take a few private classes first—they can make a huge difference to your technique.

English-speaking private teachers abound in Buenos Aires; classes generally last 1½ hours and prices can range from $20 to $80 a class. Complete beginners should plan on at least three or four classes before hitting a milonga. Many private instructors organize milonga outings with groups of their students (usually for a separate fee). Others even offer a so-called "taxi dance service": you pay for them to dance with you all night. See the end of this feature for a run-down of some of the best options for lessons and milongas.

DANCE STYLES

Tango milonguero, the style danced at milongas and taught in most classes in Buenos Aires, is quite different from the so-called salon or ballroom tango danced in Hollywood movies and in competitions outside Argentina. Ballroom tango is all fixed steps and staccato movements, and dancers' backs arch away from each other in a stiff embrace. Tango milonguero is a highly improvised style built around a variety of typical movements, not fixed steps. Dancers embrace closely, their chests touching. There are other, historical tango styles, but it's

less common to see them on milonga floors. (Confusingly, "milonga" refers both to traditional tango dancehalls and to a style of music and dance that predates the tango; though similar to tango, it has a more syncopated beat and faster, simpler steps.)

AT THE MILONGA

Dancers of all ages sit at tables that edge the floor, and men invite women to dance through *cabeceo* (subtle eye contact and head-nodding), a hard art to master. Note that women sitting with male partners won't be asked to the floor by other men.

Dances come in sets of three, four, or five, broken by a *cortina* (obvious divider of non-tango music), and it's common to stay with the same partner for a set. Being discarded in the middle is a sign that your dancing's not up to scratch, but staying for more than two sets with the same partner could be interpreted as a come on.

To fit in seamlessly, move around the floor counterclockwise without zigzagging, sticking to the inside layers of dancers if you're a beginner. Respect other dancers' space by avoiding collisions and keeping your movements small on crowded floors. Don't spend a long time doing showy moves on the spot: it holds up traffic. Finally, take time to sit some out, catch your breath, and watch the experts.

TANGO TALK

Abrazo: the embrace or stance dancers use; in tango, this varies from hip-touching and loose shoulders to close chests and more fluid hips, depending on style.

Abrazo

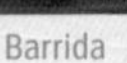
Barrida

Barrida: literally, "a sweep"; one partner sweeps the other's foot into a position.

Caminada: a walking step that is the basis of the tango.

Caminada

Canyengue: style of tango dancing with short and restricted steps; from the 1910s and '20s when tight hobble skirts were popular.

Ocho: eight; a criss-crossing walk.

Parada: literally a "stop"; the lead dancer stops the other's foot with his own.

Petitero: measured style of tango developed after the 1955 military coup, when large tango gatherings were banned and the dance relegated to small cafés.

MILONGA STYLE

Parada

Wearing a fedora hat or fishnet stockings is as good as a neon sign reading "beginner." Forget what on-stage tango dancers wear and follow a few basic rules.

Go for comfortable clothes that allow you to move freely; a sure bet are breathable, natural fabrics with a bit of stretch. Be sure it's something that makes you feel sexy. If in doubt, wear black. Avoid showy outfits: it's your footwork that should stand out. It's also smart to steer clear of big buckles, studs, stones, or anything that might catch on your partner. Try not to wear skirts that are too long or too tight. Also a bad idea are jeans or gymwear.

A good example of what to wear for men would be black dress pants and a black shirt; for women, two of many options are a simple halter-neck dress with a loose, calf-length skirt or palazzo pants with a fitted top.

As for your feet: look for dance shoes with flexible leather or suede soles that allow you to glide and pivot. The fit should be snug but comfortable. Note that rubber-soled street shoes or sneakers mark the dance floor and are often forbidden. High-heels are a must for women; the most popular style is an open-toed sandal with an ankle-strap (which stops them coming off). Black lace-ups are the favorite among men, so leave your two-tone spats at home.

TANGO THROUGH TIME

Carlos Gardel

The tango and modern Buenos Aires were born in the same place: the *conventillos* (tenement houses) of the port neighborhood of La Boca in the late 19th century, where River Plate culture collided with that of European immigrants. The dance eventually swept from the immigrant-quarter brothels and cabarets to the rest of the city; rich playboys took the tango to Paris on their grand tours, and by the 1920s the dance had become respectable enough to fill the salons and drawing rooms of the upper class in Argentina and abroad. In the 1930s, with the advent of singers like Carlos Gardel, tango music became popular in its own right. Accordingly, musical accompaniment started to come from larger bands known as *orquestas típicas*.

By the '40s and '50s, *porteños* (people from Buenos Aires) celebrated tango as the national music of the people, and tango artists lent Evita and Perón their support. The military coup that ousted Perón in 1955 forbade large tango dances, which it saw as potential political gatherings, and (bizarrely) encouraged rock 'n' roll instead. Young people listened, and tango fell out of popular favor.

The '90s saw a huge revival in both traditional *milongas* (dance halls) and a more improvised dance style. Musical offerings now include modern takes on classic tangos and electrotango or *tangofusión*. Even local rock stars are starting to include a tango or two in their repertory. And since 1998, thousands of people from around the world have attended the annual fortnight-long Festival de Tango in Buenos Aires (🌐 *www.festivaldetango.gob.ar*), held late winter or spring.

Whether you decide to take in a show or take up dancing yourself, sit down for a classic concert or groove at an electrotango night, there are more ways to experience tango in Buenos Aires than anywhere else on earth.

DID YOU KNOW?

- Tango so horrified Kaiser Wilhelm and Pope Pius X that they banned the dance.
- In 1915, before he was famous, Carlos Gardel was injured in a bar room brawl with Ernesto Guevara Lynch, Che's father.
- One of Gardel's most famous numbers, "Por Una Cabeza," is the tango featured in *Schindler's List*, *Scent of a Woman*, and *True Lies*.
- The coup of 1930 prompted composers like Enrique Santos Discépolo to write protest tangos.
- Finnish tango has been a distinct musical genre since at least mid-century and is still one of the most popular in Finland; there's even an annual *Tangomarkkinat* (tango festival) in Seinäjoki, complete with the crowning of a Tango King and Queen.

NEXT STEPS

TOURS & HOTELS

If you're serious about the dance of Buenos Aires, get in touch with the Web-based company **Argentina Tango** (🌐 www.argentinatango.com). Run by a British devotee, it offers highly organized, tailor-made tango tours.

SHOPS WITH TANGO GEAR

Head to shoe shop **Comme Il Faut,** for colorful, handcrafted high heels so gorgeous they're worth taking up tango for.

If you'd like high quality and classic designs, check out **Flabella.** At **Tango Brujo,** you'll find a variety of well-made footwear, clothing, how-to DVDs, and other tango merchandise.

Your best bet for milonga-worthy duds is regular casual clothing stores. (For more information, ⇨ *see* Shoes *and* Clothing *in* Shopping.)

SCHOOLS & INSTRUCTORS

Some schools we like are **La Escuela del Tango** (✉ San José 364, Constitución ☎ 11/4383–0466, 🌐 http://escueladeltango.blogspot.com), **La Academia de Tango Milonguero** (✉ Riobamba 416, Centro, 11/4373–2087 🌐 www.laacademiatango.com), and **Estudio DNI Tango** (✉ Av. Corrientes 2140, Centro ☎ 11/4952–1688 🌐 www.dni-tango.com.ar).

Private instructors **Ana Schapira** (☎ 11/4962–7922 🌐 www.anaschapira.com), **Claudia Bozzo** of La Escuela de Tango, and **Susana Miller** (🌐 www. susanamiller.com.ar) of La Academia de Tango Milonguero are worth their salt.

The **Academia Nacional de Tango** (🌐 www.anacdeltango.org.ar) runs high-brown seminars on tango culture and history.

MILONGAS

For a novice-friendly floor, try **La Ideal or La Viruta**. **La Nacional** and **Niño Bien** at El Centro Region Leonesa are popular with locals.

The hippest tangueros flock to **La Catedral** and **Parakultural at Salón Canning**.

For breaking the "he leads, she follows" rule, head to **La Marshall**. (For more information, ⇨ *see* Milongas *in* After Dark.)

For the latest list of milongas, and instructors, look for the English-language publication ***El Tangauta*** at newsstands (you can also download it for free at 🌐 www.eltangauta.com). The website 🌐 www.milmilongas.com has listings of most milongas in town.

(above) Milonga in Buenos Aries.

PALERMO

★ **Thelonious Bar.** The best porteño jazz bands (and occasional foreign imports) play at this intimate, upscale spot. Arrive early for a good seat, as it's a long narrow bar and not all the tables have good views; on weekends there are usually two shows per night. ✉ *Salguero 1884, Palermo* ☎ *11/4829–1562* 🌐 *www.theloniousclub.com.ar.*

★ **Virasoro Bar.** It's a smallish space for local jazz musicians and appreciative audiences. The names on the program won't be familiar to anyone outside the local jazz circuit, but don't let that put you off—they draw from a deep well of talent and cover a lot of ground, from improv to standards to experimental. ✉ *Guatemala 4328, Palermo* ☎ *11/4831–8918* 🌐 *www.virasorobar.com.ar* Ⓜ *D to Scalabrini Ortiz.*

TANGO

MILONGAS

La Catedral. Behind its unmarked doors is a hip club where the tango is somehow very rock. There are classes every evening, and casual milongas on Tuesday, Friday, and Saturday. It's a cool night out even if you're not planning to dance. ✉ *Sarmiento 4006, Almagro* ☎ *11/15–5325–1630* 🌐 *www.lacatedralclub.com.*

Fodor's Choice ★ **La Ideal.** Soaring columns, tarnished mirrors, and loose chandeliers are part of La Ideal's crumbling Old World glamour, along with rather pungent musty smell. The classic tearoom hosts milongas organized by different groups in its first-floor dance hall every day of the week—some are held during the afternoon and evening, others late at night. Many include live orchestras. ✉ *Suipacha 384, Plaza de Mayo* ☎ *11/4328–7750* 🌐 *www.confiteriaideal.com.*

Niño Bien. This belle epoque–style milonga's vast wooden dance floor is the place to go late on Thursday night. The mix of older couples and younger dancers means you see very different styles in one place; all respect traditional *cabeceo* (nonverbal invitation to dance) and partnership rules. ✉ *Humberto I 1462, Constitución* ☎ *11/4147–8687.*

Fodor's Choice ★ **Salón Canning.** Several milongas call this large dance hall home. The coolest is Parakultural, which takes place Monday, Wednesday, and Friday. Originally an alternative, "underground" milonga, it now attracts large numbers of locals (including longtime expats). ✉ *Av. Scalabrini Ortíz 1331, Palermo* ☎ *11/4832–6753* 🌐 *www.parakultural.com.ar.*

MUSICIANS

Centro Cultural Torcuato Tasso. Here, classic trios and quartets share the stage with young musicians performing hip sets. There are also milongas on weekends. ✉ *Defensa 1575, San Telmo* ☎ *11/4307–6506.*

Gran Café Tortoni. Excellent local musicians put on low-key performances of tango classics in the downstairs salon. These daily shows are some of the best for listening to tango music. There's jazz sometimes on weekends, too. ✉ *Av. de Mayo 829, Plaza de Mayo* ☎ *11/4342–4328* 🌐 *www.grancafetortoni.com.ar.*

ND Ateneo. This small, recycled theater has become a showcase for live music performances. Tango features heavily on the agenda. ✉ *Paraguay 918, Centro* ☎ *11/4328–2888* 🌐 *www.ndateneo.com.ar.*

La Trastienda. Catch new tango groups like the Orquesta Típica Fernández Fierro showcasing their very rock take on tango. ✉ *Balcarce 460, San Telmo* ☎ *11/4342–7650* 🌐 *www.latrastienda.com.*

SHOPPING

Whether you're looking for a unique handicraft, the latest boutique-vineyard Malbec, or jeans no one's got back home, you're sure to leave Buenos Aires with your bags full. An unstable economy's forced fashion-savvy porteños to abandon international brands and spend locally again. Couple this with bargain-hungry tourist hordes and you get an explosion of new design, a revival of classic brands, and a shopping scene that just keeps getting better.

If hustle and bustle are your thing, elbow your way to the stalls at the city's outdoor markets on weekends, or through the crowds of office workers that keep Centro buzzing on weekdays. In Recoleta, elegant old buildings that house hallowed brand names inspire a statelier pace (or maybe it's the price tags). Things are slower in Palermo and San Telmo, too: strolling their cobbled streets or people-watching in corner cafés are just as popular as buying.

CLOTHING: MEN'S AND WOMEN'S

CASUAL AND COOL

Antique Denim. Burberry meets Diesel at Antique Denim, where smart, dark jeans are worn with colorful tweed jackets with leather elbow patches. The denim cuts are sharp and tailored, made for cruising the town. ✉ *Gurruchaga 1692, Palermo Viejo* ☎ *11/4834–6829.*

Fábrica de Bananas. The entrance is small, but inside there's a vast warehouse filled with clothes by scores of young designers. Street wear predominates, but there's space for accessories, hats, underwear, art books, and even sex toys. On weekend nights the sofas in the middle of the store become Espacio Björk, a laid-back bar. ✉ *Arévalo 1445, Palermo Hollywood* ☎ *11/4777–6541* 🌐 *www.fabricadebananas.com.ar.*

Un Lugar en el Mundo. As a trailblazer of San Telmo cool, this hip little shop was showcasing young designer streetwear years before the fashion world got wise to the barrio. The eminently wearable togs on the racks include plain but garishly bright dresses by Muda, quirky print tees for guys and girls, and Manos del Uruguay's exquisite knits from the other side of the River Plate. Bolsas de Viaje's vinyl and canvas creations evoke the golden age of air travel, and Mir's satchels and totes in heavily stitched chestnut leather make you want to go back to school. ✉ *Defensa 891, San Telmo* ☎ *11/4362–3836* Ⓜ *C or E to Independencia (walk 6 blocks along Estados Unidos).*

Ona Saez. The ultrafitted jeans at Ona Saez are designed to be worn with sky-high heels and slinky tops for a sexy night out. The menswear is equally slick, mixing dressed-down denim with cool cotton shirts and tees. ✉ *Florida 789, Centro* ☎ *11/5555–5203* ✉ *Santa Fe 1609, Barrio Norte* ☎ *11/4815–0029* 🌐 *www.onasaez.com.*

HIGH DESIGN

Nadine Zlotogora. Bring your sense of humor to Nadine Zlotogora: her way-out designs are playful yet exquisitely put together. Sheer fabrics are embroidered with organic-looking designs, then worn alone or over thin cotton. Even the menswear gets the tulle treatment: military-look shirts come with a transparent top layer. ✉ *El Salvador 4638, Palermo Viejo* ☎ *11/4831–4203* 🌐 *www.nadinez.com.*

Fodor's Choice ★ **Pablo Ramírez.** His tiny shop front is unadorned except for "Ramírez" printed on the glass over the door—when you're this big, why say more? Pablo's couture doesn't come cheap, but these perfectly tailored numbers are worth every centavo. He favors black for both waspishly waisted women's wear and slick gent's suits, though a few other shades are creeping in. ✉ *Perú 587, San Telmo* ☎ *11/4342–7154* 🌐 *www.pabloramirez.com.ar* Ⓜ *E to Belgrano.*

★ **Varanasi.** The structural perfection of Varanasi's clothes is a clue that the brains behind them trained as architects. Equally telling is the minimal, cavernous shop, fronted by plate glass. Inside, A-line dresses built from silk patchwork and unadorned bias cuts are some of the night-out joys that local celebs shop for. ✉ *Libertad 1696, Recoleta* ☎ *11/4815–4326* 🌐 *www.varanasi-online.com.*

SPORTSWEAR

Stock Center. The official pale-blue-and-white shirts worn by the Argentine soccer team, the Pumas (the national rugby team), and the Leonas (women's hockey team) are some of the best sellers as this sporting megastore. The Nike, Adidas, and Puma clothing is all made in Brazil, and so is relatively cheap. Über-trendy Gola sneakers are another reason to come here. ✉ *Corrientes 590, Microcentro* ☎ *11/4326–2131* 🌐 *www.stockcenter.com.ar.*

Topper. The cuts of their tank tops and sweatpants aren't quite as spacey as Nike or Reebok, but then this classic Argentine brand's prices are more down-to-earth, too. Tennis clothing is a strong player, not surprising given that Topper sponsors '70s legend Guillermo Vilas as well as younger local stars like José Acasuso and Juan Ignacio Chela. There's off-court action, too: the black Converse-lookalike sneakers have been the foundation of the teenage concert-goer uniform for decades. ✉ *Av. Santa Fe 1570, Barrio Norte* ☎ *11/4816–6964* 🌐 *www.topper.com.ar.*

MEN ONLY

CASUAL AND COOL

Bolivia. Porteño dandies know that Bolivia is *the* place for metrosexual fashion. Expect floral prints on shirts, leather belts, even Filofaxes. Aged denim, top-quality silk-screen T-shirts, vintage military jackets, and hand-knit slippers are among the items that fill this converted Palermo town house to bursting. ✉ *Gurruchaga 1581, Palermo Viejo* ☎ *11/4832–6284* ✉ *Nicaragua 4908, Palermo* ☎ *11/4832–6409* 🌐 *www.boliviaonline.com.ar.*

★ **Hermanos Estebecorena.** The approach at this trendy street-wear store is 100% practical: all the flat-front shirts, pants, and rain jackets have pockets, seams, and buttons positioned for maximum utility. Everything

Stop in for a browse at Felix in Palermo Soho.

looks good, too, and the product range, including footwear and underwear, makes this a one-stop guy shop. ✉ *El Salvador 5960, Palermo Hollywood* ☎ *11/4772–2145* 🌐 *www.hermanosestebecorena.com.*

Tienda Rethink. Bored of drab utility-wear? Rethink has, well, rethought the issue. Grown-up skaters and sophisticated rockers love its well-made jeans, hoodies, and tees. They're simple in cut but come alive with lively, graffiti-inspired designs, which spill over onto the shop walls. ✉ *Marcelo T. de Alvear 1187, Barrio Norte* ☎ *11/4815–8916* Ⓜ *D to Tribunales (walk 4 blocks along Libertad)* ✉ *Jorge Luis Borges 1730, Palermo* ☎ *11/4833–5800* 🌐 *www.7rethink.com.*

HIGH DESIGN

★ **La Dolfina Polo Lifestyle.** Being the world's best polo player wasn't enough for Adolfo Cambiaso—he founded his own team in 1995, and then started a clothing line for which he does the modeling. And if you think polo is all about knee-high boots and preppy chinos, think again: Cambiaso sells some of the best urban menswear in town. The Italian-cotton shirts, sharp leather jackets, and to-die-for totes from the After Polo collection are perfect for after just about anything. ✉ *Av. Alvear 1315, Recoleta* ☎ *11/4815–2698* 🌐 *www.ladolfina.com.*

Spina. Traditional tailoring with lots of twists is one way to describe Spina's sharp menswear. Suit jackets might come with extra-cinched waists or with overlay work in different fabrics, and drainpipes are their favorite pant style. Add a lime-green shirt with pale-blue cuffs and a vermilion tie to really be seen. ✉ *Gorriti 5887, Palermo Hollywood* ☎ *11/4774–3574* 🌐 *www.grupospina.com.*

SPORTSWEAR

Gola. Other brands recycle Palermo buildings, but über-cool British sportswear label Gola has left this cavernous warehouse pretty much as is. Rust- and damp-stained walls somehow form a fitting backdrop for their ultra-utilitarian polo shirts, sweaters, and loose-cut trousers, all laid out on industrial cable bobbins. More incongruous is a small selection of posh Etiqueta Negra clothing, the brand responsible for making Gola clothing locally. ✉ *Pasaje Russel 4924, Palermo Viejo* ☎ *11/4833–2474* 🌐 *www.golaclassics.com.*

WOMEN ONLY

CASUAL AND COOL

Adorhada Guillermina. Local cinema and graphic-design students love Adorhada Guillermina's '80s-feel clothes. Box-pleated denim skirts are edgy but practical. More unusual materials such as metallic plush are also on hand. Dress things up or down with one of a hundred tops in fine, bias-cut T-shirt fabric. ✉ *El Salvador 4872, Palermo* ☎ *11/4832–9775* 🌐 *www.adorhadaguillermina.com.ar.*

Mäda. This store hails from posh Uruguayan beach resort Punta del Este, so it's no surprise that bikinis (think flower appliqués and glitter) are the main attraction. Slinky tank tops and T-shirts round out the collection. ✉ *El Salvador 4865, Palermo Viejo* ☎ *11/4833–9622* 🌐 *www.madastore.com.ar.*

Objeto. Creative use of fabrics and quirky crafting make the everyday clothes here something special. Their feminine T-shirts are textile collages combining silk screening and appliqué techniques; skirts and jackets often mix new materials with original '60s off-cuts. Check out the waterproof jackets cut from gingham-print tablecloths complete with photos of food. ✉ *Gurruchaga 1649, Palermo Viejo* ☎ *11/4834–6866.*

Vicki Otero. Her shop is barely wider than your average door, but Vicki Otero has managed to cram lots of goodies inside. Cotton is her favorite fabric and might take the form of a strapless A-line sundress or a long drapey top with built-in necktie. Some hems are edged with strips of another color—the only adornment you find here. The larger San Telmo branch stocks fellow palermitaños Mariana Dappiano and Hermanos Estebecorena as well as her own designs. ✉ *El Salvador 4719, Palermo Viejo* ☎ *11/4833–5424* ✉ *Carlos Calvo 600, San Telmo* ☎ *11/4300–8739* 🌐 *www.vickiotero.com.ar.*

HIGH DESIGN

★ **Cecilia Gadea.** The simple, almost stark, cuts Gadea favors are the perfect canvas for riotously pretty texture work. One dress might be adorned with hundreds of hand-embroidered petals, another made of an open, modern take on embroidery. Feast further on her skirts, suits, and well-cut cotton tops. High-heeled patent Mary Janes, designed specially for her by Belocca, are part girly, part sophisticated. ✉ *Ugarteche 3330, Palermo Botánico* ☎ *11/4801–4163* 🌐 *www.ceciliagadea.com.*

★ **Ffiocca.** Half of the store is stocked with posh frocks and smart streetwear by local designers like Benedit Bis and Cora Groppo, which you accessorize with Marina Massone's ultra-simple silver jewelry. The other half of the store has Ffiocca's own creations. Her asymmetrical tailoring and pleats might seem futuristic, but the dusky-rose and beige-and-black silk they come in hints of 1940s glamour. ✉ *Perú 559, San Telmo* ☎ *11/4331–4585* 🌐 *www.ffiocca.com* Ⓜ *E to Belgrano.*

Tramando, Martín Churba. This store's name means both "weaving" and "plotting": designer Martín Churba is doing plenty of both. Unique evening tops made of layers of draped and pleated sheer fabric adorned with circular beads and irregular embroidery look fit for an urban mermaid. Asymmetrical shrugs, screen-printed tees, and even vases are some of the other woven wonders in the hushed town-house store. ✉ *Rodríguez Peña 1973, Recoleta* ☎ *11/4811–0465* 🌐 *www.tramando.com.*

Vero Ivaldi. Unlike other heralded local designers, Vero Ivaldi sells gorgeous garments that flatter even less-than-perfect figures at scandalously accessible prices. Dresses and skirts come in bold tones like tomato-red or ocher, and are often built of different-textured panels and strips. ✉ *Gurruchaga 1585, Palermo Viejo* ☎ *11/4832–6334* 🌐 *www.veroivaldi.com.*

Zitta. It would be easy to pass by this unprepossessing Recoleta shop, but there's no way Fabián Zitta's evening dresses could go unnoticed. Local starlets love his bold designs, notable for their volume. Think balloon skirts, puffball sleeves, or organic-looking ruffled tubes snaking over severely tight bodices. Each collection includes black, white, and one other (usually blinding) color. ✉ *Av. Quintana 10, Recoleta* ☎ *11/4811–2094* 🌐 *www.zittacostura.com.*

HANDICRAFTS, SILVER, AND SOUVENIRS

Fundación Silataj. This small handicraft shop is run by a nonprofit organization that trades fairly with around 30 indigenous communities in Argentina. The shop smells like the aromatic palo santo wood used to make the trays, platters, cutting boards, and hair combs they carry. Other offerings include carnival masks, handwoven textiles, beaten tin ornaments, and alpaca jewelry. Prices, though higher than in markets, are reasonable; quality is excellent; and you know your money is going to the artisans. Note that the store closes for lunch. ✉ *Vuelta de Obligado 1933, Belgrano* ☎ *11/4785–8371* 🌐 *www.fundacionsilataj.org.ar* Ⓜ *D to José Hernández.*

Materia Urbana. The quirky, postmodern souvenirs this store specializes in are a welcome variation from all those matés and gaucho knives. The ubiquitous cow comes as a bright leather desk organizer, while the national icons Evita and Che adorn rolls of packing tape. Beautiful bags, jewelry, and housewares by a variety of designers as well as tango CDs, and prints by local artists are less ironic options. ✉ *Defensa 707, San Telmo* ☎ *11/4361–5265* 🌐 *www.materiaurbana.com.*

JEWELRY AND ACCESSORIES

Abraxas. "Yes" is guaranteed if you propose with one of the period engagement rings that dazzle in the window of this antique jewelers. If you're not planning on an "I do" anytime soon, how about some art deco earrings with the tiniest of diamonds or a gossamer-fine bracelet? ✉ *Defensa 1092, San Telmo* ☎ *11/4361–7512* Ⓜ *C to San Juan (walk 6 blocks along Humberto I).*

Fodor's Choice ★ **Celedonio.** Local boy Celedonio Lohidoy has designed pieces—often with frothy bunches of natural pearls—for Kenzo and Emanuel Ungaro; his work even appeared around Sarah Jessica Parker's neck on *Sex in the City.* He favors irregular semiprecious stones, set in asymmetrical, organic-looking designs. ✉ *Galería Promenade, Shop 39, Av. Alvear 1883* ☎ *11/4809–0046* 🌐 *www.celedonio.com.ar.*

Infinit. Infinit's signature thick acrylic frames are favored by graphic designers and models alike. If the classic black rectangular versions are too severe for you, the same shape comes in a range of candy colors and two-tones. Bug-eye shades and oversize '70s-inspired designs are other options. ✉ *Thames 1602, Palermo Viejo* ☎ *11/4831–7070* 🌐 *www.infinitnet.com.*

Metalistería. Seriously fun jewelry rules at this multidesigner boutique. As well as the silver, steel, and aluminum the store's name suggests, quirky pieces can include leather, wool, cotton, acrylic, laminated newspaper cuttings, or even colorful modeling clay. ✉ *Jorge Luis Borges 2021, Palermo Viejo* ☎ *11/4833–7877* 🌐 *www.metalisteria.com.ar.*

MALLS

★ **Paseo Alcorta.** If you're a serious shopper and only have time to visit one mall, make it this one. Local fashionistas favor it for its mix of high-end local chains and boutiques from some of the city's best designers. Trendsetters like Trosman, Jazmín Chebar, and María Vázquez do cool clothes for women, while for more classic chic there's María Cher and Chocolate. The men can hold their own up at Hermanos Estebecorena and Etiqueta Negra. Both girls and boys can break the bank at Tramando or save at Zara. Ultrahip accessories come as jewelery at the Perfecto Dragones stand, handbags at Jet, or as glasses at EXE. There's even a personal shopper service if it all gets too overwhelming. The international presence is strong, too, with stores from Armani Exchange, Hilfiger, Lacroix, and Cacharel, as well as the usual sports brands. Free transfers from hotels, a classy food hall, and Wi-Fi round off the reasons to come here. ✉ *Jerónimo Salguero 3172, at Av. Figueroa Alcorta, Palermo* ☎ *11/5777–6500* 🌐 *www.paseoalcorta.com.ar.*

Patio Bullrich. The city's most upscale mall was once the headquarters for the Bullrich family's meat-auction house. Inside, stone cow heads mounted on pillars still watch over the clientele. A colonnaded front, a domed-glass ceiling, and steel supports are other reminders of another age. Top local stores are relegated to the lowest level, making way for the likes of Lacroix, Cacharel, and Calvin Klein. Urban leatherware brand Uma has a shop here, as does Palermo fashion princess Jessica Trosman, whose spare women's clothes are decorated with unusual

TANGO TO GO

Need we remind you that Buenos Aires is the best place in the world to stock up on tango music, memorabilia, and serious dance wear? Some of the best tango shoes in town, including classic spats, 1920s T-bar designs, and glitzier numbers for men and women are all made to measure at **Flabella** (✉ *Suipacha 263, Microcentro* ☎ *11/4322–6036* 🌐 *www.flabella.com*). For foxier-than-thou footwear that's kicking up storms on milonga floors worldwide, head to **Comme Il Faut** (✉ *Arenales 1239, Apt. M, Barrio Norte* ☎ *11/4815–5690* 🌐 *www.commeilfaut.com.ar*); dedicated dancers love its combination of top-notch quality and gorgeous, show-stopping colors like teal or plum, usually with metallic trims. Animal-print suede, fake snakeskin, and glittering ruby take-me-home-to-Kansas numbers are some of the wilder options. **Tango Brujo** (✉ *Esmeralda 754, Microcentro* ☎ *11/4326–8264* 🌐 *www.tangobrujo.com*) is a one-stop tango shop selling shoes, clothes, and how-to videos. Recordings by every tango musician under the sun can be found at **Zivals** (✉ *Av. Callao 395, Congreso* ☎ *11/5128–7500* Ⓜ *B to Callao* ✉ *Serrano 1445, Palermo Viejo* ☎ *11/4833–7948* 🌐 *www.tangostore.com*). They stock CDs of classics, modern performers, and electro-tango as well as DVDs, sheet music, books, and even T-shirts.

heavy beadwork. The enfant terrible of Argentine footwear, Ricky Sarkany, sells dangerously pointed stilettos in colors that walk the line between exciting and kitsch. Edgy but elegant menswear line Etiqueta Negra has its first store outside the snooty northern suburbs here, and La Dolfina Polo Lifestyle is giving them fierce competition. When the bags begin to weigh you down, stop for cake at Nucha, on the Avenida del Libertador side of the building. ✉ *Enter at Posadas 1245 or Av. del Libertador 750, Recoleta* ☎ *11/4814–7400* 🌐 *www.shoppingbullrich.com.ar* Ⓜ *C to Retiro (walk 7 blocks up Av. del Libertador).*

MARKETS

Feria de Artesanías de la Plaza Vuelta de Rocha (Caminito). In the heart of colorful La Boca, Caminito showcases local artists all week long. You can find attractive port scenes in watercolors as well as stylish photographs of the neighborhood's old houses, though don't expect any budding Picassos. The market expands on weekends with stalls selling handicrafts and tacky souvenirs. As shoppers here are almost exclusively tourists, prices tend to be overambitious—sometimes irritatingly so. ✉ *Av. Pedro de Mendoza and Caminito, La Boca* ⏲ *Art market daily 10–6; crafts market weekends 10–6.*

Feria Artesanal de la Recoleta. It winds through several linked squares outside the Recoleta Cemetery. Artisans sell handmade clothes, jewelry, and housewares as well as traditional crafts. ✉ *Avs. Libertador and Pueyrredón, La Recoleta* ☎ *11/4343–0309* ⏲ *Weekends 10–dusk.*

Feria de Plaza Serrano. The business conducted in this hip Palermo Viejo market rivals that done in the neighborhood's trendy boutiques. In

Soda syphons for sale in the San Telmo flea market in Plaza Dorrego.

a small square—which is actually round—artisans sell wooden toys, ceramics, and funky jewelry made of stained glass or vintage buttons. This is also a great place to buy art: the railings around a playground here act as an open-air gallery for Palermo artists, and organizers control the quality of art on display. The feria continues unofficially at many nearby bars, which push their tables and chairs aside to make room for clothing and accessory designers: expect to find anything from cute cotton underwear and one-off T-shirts to clubbing dresses. Quality is often low, but so are prices. ✉ *Plazoleta Cortázar (Plaza Serrano) at Honduras and Serrano, Palermo Viejo* ⏲ *Weekends 11–dusk*.

SHOES

MEN'S AND WOMEN'S

Guido. In Argentina loafers means Guido, whose retro-looking logo has been the hallmark of quality footwear since 1952. Try on timeless handmade Oxfords and wing tips; there are also fun items like a tomato-red handbag or a cow-skin tote. ✉ *Av. Quintana 333, Recoleta* ☎ *11/4811–4567* 🌐 *www.guidomocasines.com.ar.*

28Sport. These leather bowling sneakers and boxing-style boots are the heart and, er, sole of retro. All the models are variations on a classic round-toed lace-up, but come with different-length legs. Plain black or chestnut uppers go with everything, but equally tempting are the two-tone numbers—in chocolate and orange, or black with curving white panels, for example. Even the store is a nod to the past, kitted out like a Buenos Aires living room from the 1950s. ✉ *Gurruchaga 1481, Palermo Viejo* ☎ *11/4833–4287* 🌐 *www.28sport.com.*

WOMEN ONLY

de María. María Conorti was one of the first young designers to set up shop in this area, and she's going strong. Wedge heels, satin ankle-ties, and abundant use of patent leather are the trademark touches of her quirky designs. Head to the basement at the back of the store for discounted past seasons. ✉ *Libertad 1661, Recoleta* ☎ *11/4815–5001* 🌐 *www.zapatosdemaria.com.ar.*

Divia. Step out in a pair of limited-edition Divias and it doesn't really matter what else you've got on. Designer Virginia Spagnuolo draws inspiration from travels to India, her own vintage shoe collection, and even her cat. The results are leather collages—suede, textured metallic, or patent leathers—in colors like teal, ruby, or plum. ✉ *Armenia 1489, Palermo Viejo* ☎ *11/4831–9090* 🌐 *www.diviashoes.com.*

★ **Lucila Iotti.** Two or three swaths of shockingly bright patent leather combined with thick tapering heels in another flashy color: these shoes are clearly meant to be showstoppers. *Sex and the City* stylists certainly agree: they ordered a dozen pairs. The open-toed but arch-covering sandals Iotti favors have a definite whiff of Carnaby Street about them. ✉ *Malabia 2212, Palermo* ☎ *11/4833–0206* 🌐 *www.lucilaiotti.com.*

WINE

Fodor's Choice ★ **Grand Cru.** Don't let the small shop front put you off: as with all the best wine shops, the action is underground. Incredibly savvy staffers will guide you through Grand Cru's peerless selection—high-end wines from small vineyards predominate—and they can FedEx up to 12 bottles anywhere in the world. ✉ *Av. Alvear 1718, Recoleta* ☎ *11/4816–3975* 🌐 *www.grandcru.com.ar.*

Ligier. Ligier has a string of shops across town and lots of experience guiding bewildered shoppers through their impressive selection. Although they stock some boutique-vineyard wines, they truly specialize in the big names like Rutini and Luigi Bosca, as well as more modest mass-produced wines. ✉ *Av. Santa Fe 800, Retiro* ☎ *11/4515–0126* 🌐 *www.ligier.com.ar* Ⓜ *C to San Martín.*

Fodor's Choice ★ **Terroir.** A wine-lover's heaven is tucked away in this white stone Palermo town house. Expert English-speaking staffers are on hand to help you make sense of the massive selection of Argentine wine, which includes collector's gems like the 1999 Angélica Zapata Cabernet Sauvignon. They even arrange private wine-tasting courses to get you up to speed on local vintages: call a week or two before you arrive. Terroir ships all over the world. ✉ *Buschiazzo 3040, Palermo* ☎ *11/4778–3443* 🌐 *www.terroir.com.ar.*

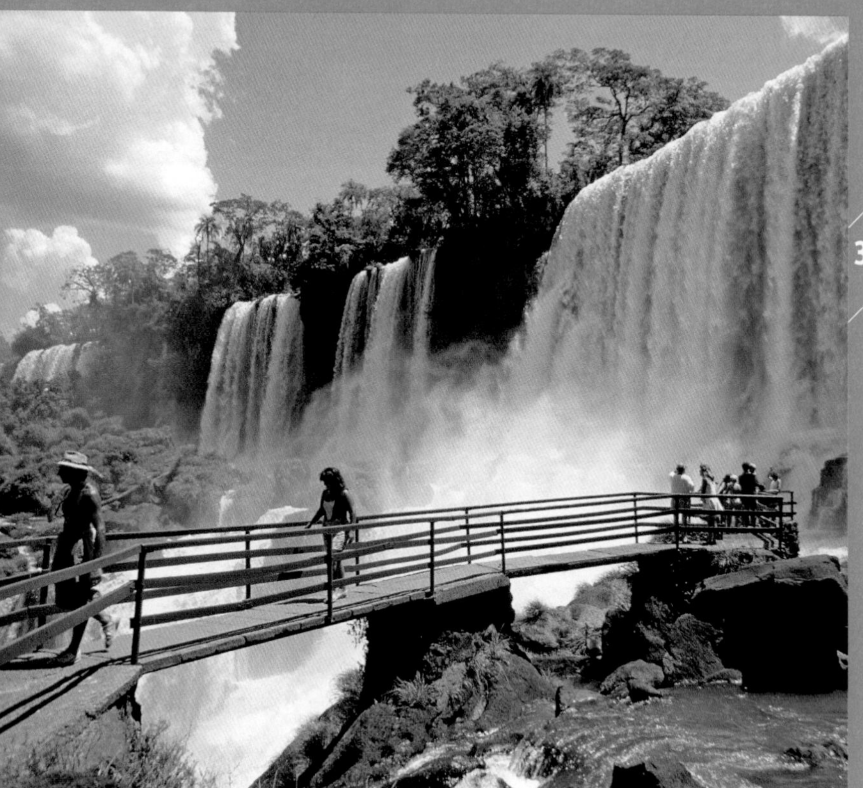

3

Side Trips

URUGUAY, BUENOS AIRES PROVINCE, THE COAST, AND IGUAZÚ FALLS

WORD OF MOUTH

"San Antonio is a great little town. . . . The folks at the Draghi Silver workshop visited with me for over an hour and shared their mate. It was a terrific day out."

—teach2travel

WELCOME TO BUENOS AIRES ENVIRONS

Iguazu Falls

TOP REASONS TO GO

★ **The Wall of Water:** Nothing can prepare you for the roaring, thunderous Cataratas del Iguazú (Iguazú Falls).

★ **Cowboy Culture:** No visit to the *pampas* (grasslands) is complete without a stay at an *estancia,* a stately ranch house, like those near San Antonio de Areco. Share meals with the owners for a true taste of the lifestyle.

★ **Wetland Wonders:** The Esteros del Iberá, an immense wetland reserve in Corrientes Province, is home to a bewildering variety of plants and animals, including howler monkeys and capybaras.

★ **Delta Dreaming:** Speeding through the Paraná River delta's thousands of kilometers of rivers and streams, we'll forgive you for humming "Ride of the Valkyries"—it does feel very Mekong.

★ **Colonial Days:** Gorgeous 18th- and 19th-century stone buildings line Colonia del Sacramento's cobbled streets. Many now contain the stylish bed-and-breakfasts favored by porteños escaping the city.

GETTING ORIENTED

Argentina's famous pampas begin in Buenos Aires Province—an unending sea of crops and cattle-studded grass that occupies nearly one-quarter of the country's landscapes. Here are the region's most traditional towns, including San Antonio de Areco. In southern Buenos Aires Province, the pampas stretch to the Atlantic coast, which is dotted with resort towns that spring to life in summer. From Buenos Aires ferries cross the massive River Plate estuary to the small Uruguayan town of Colonia del Sacramento. Suburban trains connect Buenos Aires to Tigre, close to the labyrinthine waterways of the Paraná delta, explorable only by boat. The delta feeds the Esteros del Iberá, an immense wetland reserve hundreds of kilometers north, in Corrientes Province. On Argentina's northeastern tip, readily accessible by plane, are the jaw-dropping Cataratas del Iguazú.

1 Colonia del Sacramento, Uruguay. It's hard not to fall in love with Colonia. The picturesque town has a six-by-six-block old city with wonderfully preserved architecture, rough cobblestone streets, and an easy grace. Tranquility reigns here—bicycles and golf carts outnumber cars.

2 Buenos Aires Province. An hour's drive from Buenos Aires leads to varied sights. The semitropical delta of the Paraná River lies to the north, near the town of Tigre. Elegant architecture and a quirky dinosaur museum stand out to the south in La Plata, the provincial capital. Northwest lies the gaucho town of San Antonio de Areco.

Colonia del Sacramento

3 The Atlantic Coast. Rolling dunes and coastal pine woods make windy Atlantic beaches peaceful places for some sea air in the low season; in summer, though, they're among Argentina's top party spots. Although they're a good escape from the city stifle, don't expect sugary sand or crystal-clear waters.

4 Los Esteros del Iberá. Few people have heard of these vast wetlands, halfway between Buenos Aires and Iguazú. Thousands of acres of still lakes, hordes of unusual animals—which you see up close—and a huge variety of birds are the attractions.

5 Iguazú Falls. The grandeur of this vast sheet of white water cascading in constant cymbal-banging cacophony makes Niagara Falls and Victoria Falls seem sedate. Allow at least two full days to take in this magnificent sight, and be sure to see it from both the Argentine and Brazilian sides.

Capybara

SIDE TRIPS PLANNER

When to Go

Temperatures in Buenos Aires Province rarely reach extremes. Note that some hotels and restaurants here open *only* on weekends outside of peak season—this coincides with school holidays in summer (January and February), winter (July), and the Easter weekend. You'll get great discounts at those that open midweek in winter.

November's a good time to visit San Antonio de Areco, which holds its annual gaucho festival then. Like Buenos Aires, it feels curiously empty in January, when everyone decamps to the coast. December through March is seaside peak season, and beach town establishments are usually booked up; make advance reservations. Beaches get cold and windy in winter (June–September).

Visit the Esteros del Iberá and Iguazú Falls April through October to avoid the heat and humidity. Argentineans usually go in July, when hotels book up (and prices soar). Though the falls are thrilling year-round, seasonal rainfall and upstream Brazilian barrages (minidams) can affect the falls' water volume. If you visit between November and March, booking a hotel with air-conditioning and a swimming pool is as essential as taking mosquito repellent.

Border Crossings

U.S., Canadian, and British citizens need only a valid passport for stays of up to 90 days in Uruguay. Crossing into Brazil at Iguazú is a thorny issue. In theory, *all* U.S. citizens need a visa to enter Brazil. Visas are issued in about three hours from the Brazilian consulate in Puerto Iguazú (as opposed to the three days they take in Buenos Aires) and cost $120. The Buenos Aires consulate also has a reputation for refusing visas to travelers who don't have onward tickets from Brazil.

If you stay in Foz do Iguaçu, travel on to other Brazilian cities, or do a day trip to Brazil by public bus or through an Argentinean company, you'll need a visa. There have been reports of getting around this by using a Brazilian travel agent or by using local taxis (both Argentine and Brazilian) that have "arrangements" with border control. Though the practice is well established (most hotels and travel agents in Puerto Iguazú have deals with Brazilian companies and can arrange a visa-less visit), it *is* illegal. Reinforcement of the law is generally lax but sudden crackdowns and on-the-spot fines of hundreds of dollars have been reported.

Brazilian Consulates

In Buenos Aires (✉ *Carlos Pellegrini 1363, 5th fl., Buenos Aires* ☎ *11/4515–6500* 🌐 *www.conbrasil.org.ar*).

In Puerto Iguazú (✉ *Av. Córdoba 264, Puerto Iguazú* ☎ *3757/421–348*).

Money Matters

Argentine money is accepted everywhere in Colonia, Uruguay—have an idea of the exchange rate to avoid overcharging. Not changing money? Use Argentine pesos for small transactions; hotels give better rates for dollars. Avoid exchanging at the ferry terminal as the commission's often high.

Uruguayan bills come in denominations of 20, 50, 100, 200, 500, 1,000, and 2,000 pesos uruguayos. Coins are available in 50 centésimo pieces (half a peso), 1, 2, 5, and 10 pesos. Coins for 5 and 10 pesos have replaced banknotes. At this writing, there are 6 Uruguayan pesos to the Argentine peso, and 22 Uruguayan pesos to the U.S. dollar.

Brazil's currency is the real (R$; plural: *reais* or *reals*). One real is 100 centavos. There are 1, 5, 10, 20, 50, and 100 real notes and 1, 5, 10, 25, and 50 centavo and 1 real coins. At this writing, there are 0.46 reais to the Argentine peso, and 1.78 reais to the U.S. dollar.

Hotel and Restaurant Costs

Hotels and restaurants in Colonia list prices in U.S. dollars.

PRICE CATEGORIES IN U.S. DOLLARS					
	¢	$	$$	$$$	$$$$
Restaurants	under $5	$5–$8	$8–$12	$12–$16	over $16
Hotels	under $50	$50–$80	$80–$130	$130–$200	over $200

PRICE CATEGORIES IN BRAZILIAN REAIS					
	¢	$	$$	$$$	$$$$
Restaurants	under R$15	R$15–R$25	R$25–R$38	R$38–R$50	over R$50
Hotels	under R$100	R$100–R$150	R$150–R$220	R$220–R$350	over R$350

PRICE CATEGORIES IN ARGENTINA PESOS					
	¢	$	$$	$$$	$$$$
Restaurants	under 15	15–25	25–38	38–50	over 50
Hotels	under 150	150–280	280–400	400–600	over 600

Restaurant prices are based on the median main course price at dinner. Hotel prices are for two people in a standard double room in high season.

Safety

Provincial towns like Tigre, San Antonio de Areco, and Colonia de Sacramento in Uruguay are usually extremely safe, and the areas visited by tourists are well patrolled.

Puerto Iguazú is fairly quiet in itself, but mugging and theft are common in nearby Foz do Iguaçu in Brazil, especially at night, when its streets are deserted. Worse yet is neighboring Ciudad del Este in Paragüay, where gun crime is a problem. Avoid the area near the border.

Taxi drivers are usually very honest, and are less likely to rip you off than the transport services arranged by top hotels. All the same, locals recommend unaccompanied women phone for taxis late at night, rather than hailing them on the street. The police in the provinces have an iffy reputation: at worst, horribly corrupt, and at best, rather inefficient. Don't count on support, sympathy, or much else from them if you're the victim of a crime.

Argentina Emergency Services: **Ambulance** (☎ *107*). **Fire** (☎ *100*). **Police** (☎ *101*).

Brazil Emergency Services: **General Emergencies** (☎ *199*). **Ambulance** (☎ *192*). **Fire** (☎ *193*). **Police** (☎ *194*).

Uruguay Emergency Services: **General Emergencies** (☎ *911*). **Ambulance** (☎ *105*). **Fire** (☎ *104*). **Police** (☎ *109*). **Policía Caminera (Highway Patrol)** (☎ *108*).

3

SIDE TRIPS PLANNER

Phone Home

To call Uruguay from Argentina, you dial the international access code 00, the country code of 598, the area code without the initial zero, and the local number. To call locally, dial the digits (Colonia's numbers have five digits) without any prefix (the prefix in Colonia is 052).

To call Brazil from Argentina, dial the international access code 00, the country code of 55, the area code without the initial zero, and the eight-digit local number. To call locally, dial the eight-digit numbers without any prefix. The area code for Foz do Iguaçu is 45.

Head Out on the Highway

Driving is the most convenient—though rarely cheap—option for getting around the province. Avis, Dollar, and Hertz have branches in many large towns and cities. At this writing, gas—known as *nafta*—costs around 2.60 pesos a liter, and if you plan to drive extensively, it's worth looking into renting a vehicle running on diesel, which will reduce fuel costs significantly. There are plenty of gas stations in cities and on major highways, but they can be few and far between on rural roads. A useful Web site when planning road trips is 🌐 *www.ruta0.com*, which calculates distances and tolls between two places and offers several route options.

Be careful. Argentina has one of the world's worst records for traffic accidents, and the busy highways of Buenos Aires Province are often where they happen. January and February are the worst times, when drivers anxious to get to and from their holiday destination speed, tailgate, and exercise illegal maneuvers even more alarmingly than usual. If you're driving, do so very defensively and avoid traveling on Friday and Sunday, when traffic is worst.

Expressways and interprovincial routes tend to be atrociously signposted, so take a map, and privately owned, which means frequent tolls. There are sometimes alternative roads to use, but they're generally smaller, slower, and in poor condition. On main roads the speed limit is 80 KPH (50 MPH), while on highways it's 130 KPH (80 MPH), though Argentinean drivers rarely pay heed to this.

Cabbing It

If you're in a major city, take a taxi. Generally inexpensive (the fare is based on the number of blocks traveled), they can be hailed just about anywhere, though it's generally easier to get your hotel or restaurant to call you one. In smaller towns, numerous minicab firms (*remises*) replace taxis. These can be hailed on the street or called. In many touristy towns, you can book remises to ferry you around for several days. With a group of three or four, you may find this a more-economical and convenient way to get around.

Updated by Victoria Patience

To hear *porteños* (inhabitants of Buenos Aires) talk of their city, you'd think Argentina stops where Buenos Aires ends. Not far beyond it, however, the skies open up and the pampas—Argentina's huge flat grasslands—begin. Pampean traditions are alive and well in farming communities that still dot the plains that make up Buenos Aires Province.

The best known is San Antonio de Areco, a well-preserved provincial town that's making a name for itself as gaucho central. You can ride across the pampas and get a taste of country life (and lots of grass-fed beef) by visiting—or staying at—a traditional estancia (ranch). Elegant architecture and a quirky dinosaur museum stand out to the south in La Plata, the provincial capital.

Ranchland gives way to watery wonders. The quiet suburban town of Tigre is the gateway to the network of rivers and tributaries that form the delta of the Paraná River, lined with luscious tropical vegetation. Low wooden launches speed along its waterways to the houses, restaurants, and lodges that are built on stilts along the river banks.

The waters are eerily still at the Esteros del Iberá, an immense wetland reserve almost a 1,000 km (600 mi) north of Buenos Aires. One of Argentina's least visited areas, it's home to thousands of native plant and animal species, including the *yacaré* (Argentine alligator) and the capybara, a huge water-loving rodent.

If you like your natural wonders supersized, take a short flight or a long bus-ride to Iguazú Falls, northeast of Buenos Aires in semitropical Misiones Province. Here, straddling the border between Argentina and Brazil, two natural parks contain and protect hundreds of roaring falls and a delicate jungle ecosystem. The spectacle caused Eleanor Roosevelt to exclaim "Poor Niagara!", but most people are simply left speechless by the sheer size and force of the Garganta del Diablo, the grandest falls of them all.

The sand and sea of the Atlantic coast begin just a few hours south from the capital. It might not be the Caribbean, but there's something charmingly retro about resorts like Mar del Plata and Pinamar. In the summer months, when temperatures in Buenos Aires soar, hordes of porteños seek relief here, and the capital's music and theater scene decamps with them, making these *the* places to see and be seen.

One of South America's most beautiful towns, Colonia del Sacramento, Uruguay, juts out on a small peninsula into the Río de la Plata and is only an hour from Buenos Aires. Here, sleepy cobbled streets and colonial buildings are a reminder of days gone by.

COLONIA DEL SACRAMENTO

The peaceful cobbled streets of Colonia are just over the Río de la Plata from Buenos Aires, but they seem a world away. Founded in 1680, the city was subject to a long series of wars and pacts between Spain and Portugal, which eventually gave up its claim. Its many small museums are dedicated to the story of its tumultuous history.

The best activity in Colonia, however, is walking through its *Barrio Histórico* (Old Town), a UNESCO World Heritage Site. Porteños come to Colonia for romantic getaways or a break from the city. It makes sense to follow their example: you don't get enough time here on a day trip to relax or see the city at its own pace. A night in one of its many colonial-style bed-and-breakfasts offsets travel costs and time and makes a visit here far more rewarding.

GETTING HERE AND AROUND

Hydrofoils and ferries cross the Río de la Plata between Buenos Aires and Uruguay several times a day. Boats often sell out, particularly on summer weekends, so book tickets at least a few days ahead. The two competing companies that operate services—Buquebus and Colonia Express—often wage a reduced rates war in the low season.

Buquebus provides two kinds of service for passengers and cars: the quickest crossing takes an hour by hydrofoil or catamaran (135.50 pesos one-way, four daily services in each direction), and the slower ferry takes around three hours (95 pesos, two daily services). The Buquebus terminal is at the northern end of Puerto Madero at the intersection of Avenida Alicia M. de Justo and Avnida Córdoba (which changes its name here to Bulevar Cecilia Grierson). It's accessible by taxi or by walking seven blocks from Leandro N. Alem subte station along Trinidad Guevara.

Colonia Express operates the cheapest and fastest services to Colonia but has only two daily services in each direction. The 50-minute catamaran trip costs 124 pesos one-way or 248 pesos for a same-day return, but there are discounts of up to 80% if you buy tickets several weeks in advance. The Colonia Express terminal is south of Puerto Madero on Av. Pedro de Mendoza, the extension of Avenida Huergo. It's best reached by taxi, but Bus 130 from Avenidas Libertador and L.M. Alem stop outside it.

At this writing, Colonia's ferry port is being renovated; work is slated to continue until 2010, so the port will be rather chaotic until then. The shortest way to the Barrio Histórico is to turn left out of the port parking lot onto Florida—it's a six-block walk. Walking is the perfect way

Cobblestones abound in the Old Town section of Colonia del Sacramento, Uruguay.

to get around this part of town; equally practical—and lots of fun—are golf carts and sand buggies that you can rent from Thrifty.

ESSENTIALS

Bank Banco República (✉ *Av. Gral. Flores 151*).

Ferry Contacts Buquebus (✉ *Av. Antartida Argentina 821, Puerto Madero* ✉ *Av. Córdoba 867, Centro* ☎ *11/4316–6500* 🌐 *www.buquebus.com*). **Colonia Express** (✉ *Av. Pedro de Mendoza 330, La Boca* ✉ *Av. Córdoba 753, Microcentro* ☎ *11/4313–5100 in Buenos Aires, 52/29676 in Colonia* 🌐 *www.coloniaexpress.com*).

Medical Assistance Hospital de Colonia (✉ *18 de Julio 462* ☎ *52/22994*).

Rental Cars Thrifty (✉ *Av. Gral. Flores 172* ☎ *52/22939* 🌐 *www.thrifty.com.uy*).

Taxi Taxis Colonia (☎ *52/22920*).

Visitor Info Colonia del Sacramento Tourist Board (✉ *General Flores and Rivera* ✉ *Manuel Lobo between Ituzaingó and Paseo San Antonio* ☎ *52/23700* 🌐 *www.coloniaturismo.com* 🕐 *Daily 9 AM–7 PM*).

EXPLORING

Begin your tour at the reconstructed Portón de Campo or city gate, where remnants of the old bastion walls lead to the river. A block farther is Calle de los Suspiros, the aptly named Street of Sighs, a cobblestone stretch of one-story colonials that can rival any street in Latin America for sheer romantic effect. It runs between a lookout point on the river, called the Bastión de San Miguel, and the Plaza Mayor, a lovely square filled with Spanish moss, palms, and spiky, flowering *palo borracho* trees. The many cafés around the square are an ideal place to take it all in. Clusters of bougainvillea flow over the walls here and in the other quiet streets of the Barrio Histórico, many of which are lined with art galleries and antiques shops.

Another great place to watch daily life is the Plaza de Armas Manoel Lobo, where you can find the Iglesia Matriz, the oldest church in Uruguay. The square itself is crisscrossed with wooden catwalks over the ruins of a house dating to the founding of the town. The tables from the square's small eateries spill from the sidewalk right onto the cobblestones: they're all rather touristy, but give you an excellent view of the drum-toting *candombe* (a style of music from Uruguay) squads that beat their way around the old town each afternoon.

You can visit all of Colonia's museums with the same ticket, which you buy from the Museo Portugués or the Museo Municipal for $2.10. Most take only a few minutes to visit, but you can use the ticket on two consecutive days.

❸ **Casa Nacarello.** A colonial Portuguese residence has been lovingly recreated inside this 17th-century structure. The simple bedroom and kitchen furnishings are period pieces, but the real attraction is the house itself, with its thick whitewashed walls and low ceilings. ⊠ *Plaza Mayor at Henríquez de la Peña* ⊙ *Wed.–Mon. 11:15–4:45.*

❹ **Faro.** Towering above the Plaza Mayor is the lighthouse, which was built in 1857 on top of a tower that was part of the ruined San Xavier convent. The whole structure was engulfed in flames in 1873 after a lighthouse keeper had an accident with the oil used in the lamp at the time. Your reward for climbing it are great views over the Barrio Histórico and the River Plate. ⊠ *Plaza Mayor* 🎫 *$0.60* ⊙ *Daily noon–7.*

❶ **Museo del Azulejo.** A small collection of the beautiful handmade French majolica tiles that adorn fountains all over Colonia are on display at the tile museum, housed in a small 18th-century building near the river. ⊠ *Misiones de los Tapies at Paseo San Gabriel* ⊙ *Fri.–Wed. 11:15–4:45*

❷ **Museo Municipal.** A sundry collection of objects related to the city's history is housed here. ⊠ *Plaza Mayor at Misiones de los Tapies* ⊙ *Wed.–Mon. 11:15–4:45.*

❺ **Museo Portugués.** The museum that's most worth a visit is this one, which documents the city's ties to Portugal. It's most notable for its collection of old map reproductions based on Portuguese naval expeditions. A small selection of period furnishings, clothes, and jewelry from Colonia's days as a Portuguese colony complete the offerings. Exhibits are well labeled, but in Spanish only. ⊠ *Plaza Mayor between Calle de los Suspiros and De Solís* ⊙ *Thurs.–Tues. 11:15–4:45.*

WHERE TO EAT

In Colonia, prices are displayed in dollars at all hotels and many restaurants. Uruguayan food is as beef-based as Argentine fare and also has a notable Italian influence. The standout national dish is *chivito*, a well-stuffed steak sandwich that typically contains bacon, fried egg,

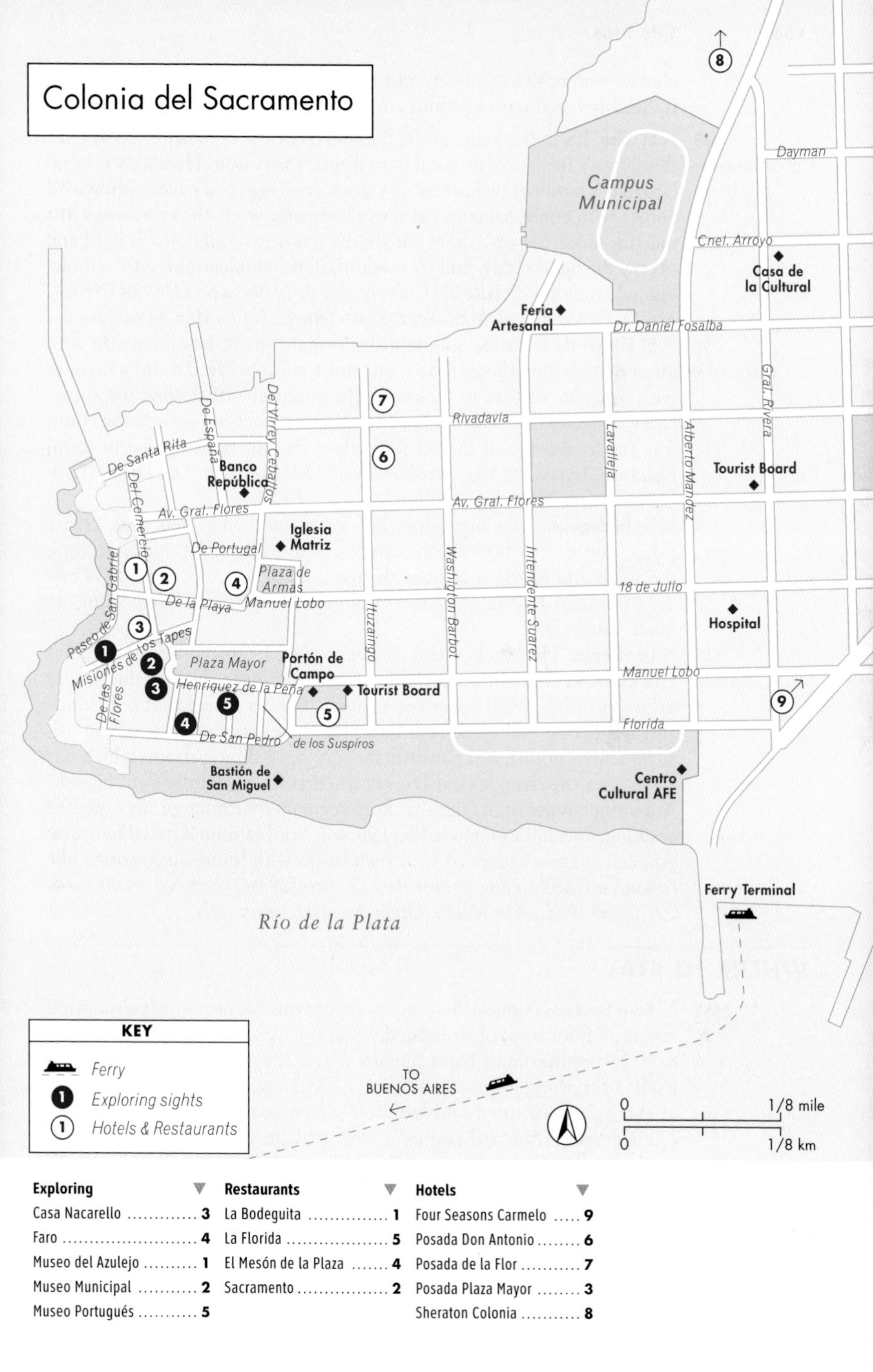

Exploring		Restaurants		Hotels	
Casa Nacarello	3	La Bodeguita	1	Four Seasons Carmelo	9
Faro	4	La Florida	5	Posada Don Antonio	6
Museo del Azulejo	1	El Mesón de la Plaza	4	Posada de la Flor	7
Museo Municipal	2	Sacramento	2	Posada Plaza Mayor	3
Museo Portugués	5			Sheraton Colonia	8

cheese, onion, salad, olives, and anything else you care to throw into it, heavily laced with ketchup and mayonnaise.

$$ CONTEMPORARY ★ **El Lobo.** It's in the heart of the Barrio Histórico, but chef Nicolás Díaz Ibarguren's fresh take on local ingredients is very now. His classy take on Uruguay's national dish, chivito (a steak, fried egg, and bacon sandwich), comes with confit tomatoes and smoked corn, while the cod swims in a martini sauce. Set on a quiet corner, the renovated old house is light and breezy during the day, and its modern, dark wooden tables are candle-lighted at night. ✉ *Calle del Comercio at de la Playa* ☎ *52/29245* ▭ *AE, MC, V* ⊙ *No dinner Mar.–Sept. Sun.–Thurs., Sept.–Mar. Mon.–Tues.*

$$ URUGUAYAN **El Mesón de la Plaza.** Simple dishes—many steak-based—made with good-quality ingredients have made this traditional restaurant a favorite with porteño visitors to Colonia. The comprehensive wine list showcases Uruguayan vineyards hard to sample anywhere outside the country. Try to get one of the outside tables that sit right on the peaceful Plaza de Armas. ✉ *Vasconcellos 153* ☎ *52/24807* ▭ *AE, DC, MC, V* ⊙ *No dinner Mon.*

¢ PIZZA **La Bodeguita.** This hip restaurant serves incredibly delicious, crispy pizza, sliced into bite-size rectangles. The backyard tables overlook the river, and inside is cozy, with rust- and ocher-color walls. ✉ *Calle del Comercio 167* ☎ *52/25329* ▭ *No credit cards* ⊙ *Closed Mon., no lunch Tues.–Fri.*

$$$ ECLECTIC **La Florida.** The black-and-white photos, lace tablecloths, and quaint knickknacks that clutter this long, low house belie the fact that it was once a brothel. It still has private rooms, but it's dining that politicians and the occasional celeb rent them for these days. You, too, can ask to be seated in one, but consider the airy back dining room, which has views over the river. It's hard to say whether it's the flamboyant French-Argentine owner's tall tales that keep regulars returning, or his excellent cooking. Specialties include kingfish, sole, and salmon cooked to order: you can suggest sauces of your own or go with house suggestions like orange-infused cream. ✉ *Florida 215* ☎ *94/293–036* ▭ *No credit cards* ⊙ *Closed Wed., Apr.–Nov. dinner by reservation only.*

WHERE TO STAY

$$$$ ★ **Four Seasons Carmelo.** Serenity pervades this harmoniously decorated resort an hour west of Colonia del Sacramento, reachable by car, boat, or a 25-minute flight from Buenos Aires. It's a destination in and of itself. Everything is done in a fusion of Asian styles—from yoga classes at the incense-scented and bamboo-screen health club to bungalows (considered "standard rooms") with private Japanese gardens (and marvelous outdoor showers). In the evening, torches illuminate the paths, which meander through sand dunes. **Pros:** all rooms are spacious bungalows; fabulous, personalized service; on-site activities compensate for distance to sights and restaurants. **Cons:** despite copious netting and bug spray, the mosquitoes can get out of hand; food quality is erratic; noisy Argentine families can infringe on romantic getaways. ✉ *Ruta 21, Km 262, Carmelo* ☎ *54/29000* ⊕ *www.fourseasons.com/carmelo* ⇨ *20 bungalows, 24 duplex suites* ◌ *In-room: dial-up, safe,*

refrigerator, VCR. In-hotel: 2 restaurants, room service, golf course, tennis courts, pools, gym, spa, bicycles, children's programs (ages 5–12), laundry service, airport shuttle, executive floor, public Internet, no-smoking rooms ▭ AE, DC, MC, V 🍽 CP.

$ **Posada Don Antonio.** Rooms open onto long galleries that overlook an enormous split-level courtyard at Posada Don Antonio, the latest incarnation of a large, elegant building which has housed one hotel or another for over a century. With their plain white walls and drab green carpets, the rooms lack the character promised by the architecture outside, but they're clean and functional, have comfy beds with wrought-iron bedsteads, and there's free Wi-Fi throughout the building. **Pros:** sparkling turquoise pool, surrounded by loungers; two blocks from the Barrio Histórico; rates are low but there are proper hotel perks like poolside snacks. **Cons:** staff are sometimes indifferent; plain, characterless rooms; ill-fitting doors let in courtyard noise. ✉ *Ituzaingó 232* ☎ *52/25344* 🌐 *www.posadadonantonio.com* *38 rooms* *In-room: refrigerator, Wi-Fi. In-hotel: room service, pool, laundry facilities, Internet terminal* ▭ *AE, MC, V* 🍽 *CP.*

$ ★ **Posada de la Flor.** This colonial-style hotel is on a quiet street leading to the river and is arranged around a sunny courtyard. Quilts and old china decorating the walls of the bright dining room announce a country-cottage vibe. You feel even more at home after attacking the large breakfast spreads or gazing at the river over a glass of wine on the roof terrace—the owner's happy for you to bring your own. The simple, clean rooms have cheery quilts and are named after flowers: it's worth paying a few dollars extra for the more-spacious ones, like Nomeolvides or "Forget-Me-Not. There's free Wi-Fi in the reception area. The posada is a pleasant five-minute walk from Plaza Mayor. **Pros:** peaceful location near river and the Barrio Histórico; gorgeous breakfast area and roof terrace; great value. **Cons:** standard rooms are cramped; damp spots on some ceilings; ground-floor rooms open onto the courtyard and can be noisy. ✉ *Calle Ituzaingó 268* ☎ *52/30794* 🌐 *www.posada-delaflor.com* *14 rooms* *In-room: safe, no phone. In-hotel: laundry service* ▭ *No credit cards* 🍽 *CP.*

$$ **Posada Plaza Mayor.** A faint scent of jasmine fills the air at this lovely old hotel. All the rooms open onto a large, plant-filled courtyard complete with a bubbling fountain. The main building dates to 1840 (a part at the back is even older) and the original stone walls are visible in most rooms, which also have gloriously high ceilings. There are river views from the first-floor dining room and from the garden tucked behind the building, whose deck chairs rival those in the courtyard. **Pros:** beautiful green spaces; on a quiet street of the Barrio Histórico; cheerful, accommodating staff. **Cons:** cramped bathrooms; the three cheapest rooms are small and lack the atmosphere of the regular standard rooms; high price of deluxe rooms isn't justified by the amenities. ✉ *Calle del Comercio 111* ☎ *52/23193* 🌐 *www.posadaplazamayor.com* *14 rooms* *In-room: Wi-Fi. In-hotel: room service, laundry service* ▭ *AE, DC, MC, V* 🍽 *CP.*

$$$$ ★ **Sheraton Colonia.** This riverside hotel and spa is a favorite with porteños on weekend escapes. It's easy to see why. Materials like copper,

terracotta, and golden-color stone add warm touches to the airy, light-filled atrium. So does the massive wood-fronted fireplace, which is always lighted in winter. Rooms are just as inviting, with handmade woolen bed throws that take the edge off the elegant, but rather generic, furniture. You can walk out straight onto the golf course and the sandy river beaches—who cares about the muddy water when you've got two gorgeous pools (one heated) to play in? Plan your visit midweek, when the rooms and spa packages are heavily discounted. **Pros:** rooms are often discounted mid-week; peaceful location with river views from many rooms; great spa. **Cons:** it's a 15-minute drive or taxi ride north of the Barrio Histórico; lots of noisy kids on weekends; staff are slow and sometimes unhelpful. ✉ *Cont. Rambla de las Américas s/n* ☎ *54/29000* 🌐 *www.sheraton.com* *88 rooms, 4 suites* *In-room: safe, Internet. In-hotel: 2 restaurants, room service, bar, golf course, pools, gym, spa, laundry service, no-smoking rooms* *AE, DC, MC, V* *CP.*

AFTER DARK

Much of Colonia's nightlife centers on its restaurants, which become default drinking and bar-snacking spots after 11 or midnight. In summer, outdoor tables on the Plaza Mayor, which is often lighted with torches, are particularly atmospheric. Locals in their twenties and thirties rub shoulders with visitors at **Colonia Rock** (✉ *Misiones de los Tapies 157* ☎ *52/28189*), a popular, laid-back bar on the Plaza Mayor. There's live music and even karaoke on Friday and Saturday.

BUENOS AIRES PROVINCE

Plains fan out where the city of Buenos Aires ends: this is the beginning of the pampas, which derive their name from the native Quechua word for "flat field." All over this fertile earth are signs of active ranch life, from the grazing cattle to the modern-day gauchos. The region is also noted for its crops—alfalfa, sunflowers, wheat, corn, and soy.

While Argentina was still a Spanish colony, settlers gradually began to force indigenous tribes away from the pampas near Buenos Aires, making extensive agriculture and cattle breeding possible. (In 1880, during the bloody Campaign of the Desert, the southern pampas were also "cleared" of indigenous tribes.) By the latter half of the 19th century the region had become known as the grain supplier for the world. From 1850 to 1950 more than 400 important estancias were built in Buenos Aires Province alone. Some of these have been modified for use as guest ranches and provide the best glimpse of the fabled Pampean lifestyle.

TIGRE AND THE PARANÁ DELTA

Tigre is 30 km (19 mi) northwest of Buenos Aires on the Ruta Panamericana, 35 km (22 mi) northwest of Buenos Aires on Avenida Libertador.

A coastal train ride or a drive through the shady riverside suburbs of Buenos Aires takes you to the river-port town of Tigre, the embarkation

point for boats that ply the Delta del Paraná. Half a day is plenty of time to visit the town itself from Buenos Aires; allow a whole day if you also plan to explore the delta—a vast maze of canals, tributaries, and river expanding out like the veins of a leaf. Heavy vegetation and rich birdlife (as well as clouds of mosquitoes) make the network of rivers feel tropical. The delta's many islands hide peaceful luxury getaways and cozy riverside restaurants accessible only by boat.

The waterways and close-packed islands that stretch northwest of Tigre are the most accessible part of the 14,000 square km (5,400 square mi) that make up the delta, where roads are replaced by rivers. Churning brown waters and heavy vegetation are vaguely reminiscent of Southeast Asia, though the chichi houses and manicured gardens that line the rivers of the *Primera Sección* (the First Section, closest to Tigre) are a far cry from Mekong River settlements.

If you want to take in more of the delta than a short boat trip allows, do as the porteños do and combine it with a day's wining and dining at an island restaurant or a weekend at one of the hotels or luxury lodges a little farther afield. Many offer private transport; otherwise inquire about which boat services take you there. The delta gets very hot and humid in summer, and the mosquitoes are ferocious; bring insect repellent.

A freighter seems small against the breadth of the Rio Paraná delta.

GETTING HERE AND AROUND

The cheapest way of getting to Tigre by train is on the suburban commuter train from Estación Retiro to the central Estación Tigre. There are about four departures an hour on the Ramal Tigre (Tigre Branch) of the Línea Mitre; round-trip tickets costs 2.70 pesos. Alternatively, take the slick, tourist-oriented Tren de la Costa. It meanders through some of Buenos Aires's most-fashionable northern suburbs and along the riverbank, stopping at nine stations before arriving at Estación Delta, near the Río Luján and Puerto de Frutos market. It starts halfway between Buenos Aires and Tigre, so you'll have to first take Línea Mitre, Ramal Mitre from Retiro to Estación Mitre, where you can change to the Tren de la Costa's Maipú Station. Round-trip fare is 24 pesos. The center of Tigre is small enough to walk around easily, but there are taxis outside both train stations.

The most comfortable—though touristy—way to travel the delta's waterways is aboard the two-story catamarans that leave from docks on the Luján River, inside the Puerto de Frutos market. Rio Tur does two-hour round-trips, which cost 40 pesos and leave weekends on the hour 11–7 December through March and 11–5 April through November and on weekdays at noon, 1, 2, and 4 PM year-round. ■ **TIP→ The last boat of the day usually catches the sunset.**

The low-slung wooden *lanchas colectivas* (boat buses) are the cheaper and more authentic way to explore the waterways; locals use them to get around the delta. These leave from the Estación Fluvial (Boat Station), on the other side of the roundabout from Estación Tigre, the main train station. The main transport company for the delta is

Interisleña, which serves all of the Primera Sección, the closest islands to the Tigre. One-way tickets start at 17 pesos. Líneas Delta Argentino uses similar boats but is tourism-oriented—one- and three-hour trips cost 20 and 30 pesos. Vessels leave every hour or two on weekends, but usually don't operate midweek. Buy tickets from Booth 6, opposite the jetty. Touts offering private boat trips loiter outside the Tigre tourist board offices at the train and boat stations, but it's best to stick with recognized companies. As the boats leave the delta, they pass the magnificent turn-of-the-20th-century buildings of Tigre's heyday and colorfully painted houses built on stilts to protect them from floods.

WORD OF MOUTH

"My brother-in-law had heard such great things about Tigre that he made us go there. It was a really a good choice. After a surprisingly easy train ride out, we took a day-long boat tour with Bonanza Deltaventura. It was a beautiful day, and the islands were peaceful and nice to look at." —Messifan

3

ESSENTIALS

Bank Banco de la Nación (✉ *Av. Cazón 1600* 🌐 *www.bna.com.ar*).

Boat Contacts Interisleña (☎ *11/4749–0900*). **Líneas Delta Argentino** (☎ *11/4731–1236* 🌐 *www.lineasdelta.com.ar*).

Medical Assistance Hospital de Tigre (✉ *Casaretto 118* ☎ *11/4749–0876*).

Train Contacts Trenes de Buenos Aires (Línea Mitre) (☎ *800/3333-822* 🌐 *www.tbanet.com.ar*). **Tren de la Costa** (☎ *11/4002–6000* 🌐 *www.trendelacosta.com.ar*).

Visitor and Tour Info Rio Tur (✉ *Sarmiento at Buenos Aires* ☎ *11/4731–0280* 🌐 *www.rioturcatamaranes.com.ar*). **Tigre Tourist Board** (✉ *Estación Fluvial, Mitre 305, Tigre* ✉ *Estación Tigre, Av. Naciones Unidas, Tigre* ☎ *11/4512–4497* 🌐 *www.vivitigre.gov.ar* 🕓 *Daily 8–6*).

EXPLORING

Museo de Arte de Tigre. An arcade of Doric columns leads from the Luján River to this gleaming white building with ornate moldings, built by in 1909 to house a social club and casino. It contains a modest collection of Argentine paintings by artists like Quirós, Castagnino, Soldi, and Quinquela Martín, as well as works portraying life in the delta. The real showstopper, however, is the beautifully restored architecture: a sweeping marble staircase, stained-glass windows, gilt-inlaid columns, and soaring ceilings conspire to form a microcosm of the fin-de-siècle European style adored by the porteño elite. A trim, flower-filled park surrounds the museum, which is best reached by walking along Paseo Victorica. ✉ *Paseo Victorica 972* ☎ *11/4512–4528* 🌐 *www.mat.gov.ar* 🎫 *5 pesos* 🕓 *Wed.–Fri. 9–7, weekends noon–7.*

Parque de la Costa. The devaluation of the peso has forced rich porteños to abandon their annual Disney World expeditions. Instead, they come here, to Argentina's largest, most-modern amusement park. Its main attractions are the two side-by-side roller coasters, *El Boomerang* and *El Desafío*. There's also a splashy river ride, swinging inverter ship, and a host of milder thrills, including a petting zoo. Entrance prices are often heavily discounted in winter. ✉ *Vivanco 1509* ☎ *11/4002–6000* 🌐 *www.parquedelacosta.com.ar* 🎫 *48 pesos* ⏲ *Jan. and Feb., Tues.–Sun. 11–8; Mar.–Nov., weekends 11–7.*

Paseo Victorica. Italianate mansions, restaurants, and several rowing clubs dot the this paved walkway that curves alongside the Río Luján for about 10 blocks. To reach it, cross the bridge next to the roundabout immediately north of Estación Tigre, then turn right and walk five blocks along Avenida Lavalle, which runs along the Río Tigre. ✉ *Along Río Luján between Río Tigre and Río Reconquista.*

Puerto de Frutos. The center of the action at Tigre is its picturesque market. Hundreds of stalls selling furniture, home ware, and handicrafts fill the area around the docks along the River Luján, about eight blocks from the stations. It's a good place to find reasonably priced souvenirs and is particularly busy on weekends (indeed, many stalls are closed midweek). You can grab a quick lunch from stands selling steak and chorizo sandwiches. ✉ *Sarmiento at Buenos Aires* ☎ *No phone* 🌐 *www.puertodefrutos-arg.com.ar* ⏲ *Weekdays 10–6, weekends 10–7.*

WHERE TO EAT

TIGRE

$$$ ARGENTINE ✕ **Il Novo María del Luján.** An expansive terrace overlooking the river is the appropriate backdrop for Tigre's best fish dishes. The kitchen favors elaborate preparations: some are so packed with unlikely ingredients that the fish gets lost; others, such as the sole in lemon-infused cream, are spot-on. Land-based offerings like pork belly braised in beer are equally well executed. Both the terrace and the sunny, peach-colored inside room fill up on weekends, when harried waitstaff often take a long time to bring your orders or even the check. ✉ *Paseo Victorica 611* ☎ *11/4731–9613* ✍ *Reservations essential* 💳 *AE, MC, V.*

WHERE TO STAY

PARANÁ DELTA

The city of Tigre is so close to Buenos Aires that there's no reason to stay overnight there—a night or two in the Paraná Delta is a much more rewarding experiences. The following places offer all-inclusive packages.

$$$$ 🏨 **Bonanza Deltaventura.** Thick vegetation surrounds the tomato-red 19th-century country house that's the center of the eco-action at Bonanza Deltaventura. The idea behind the establishment is to share the natural wonders of the area with visitors through organized walks, kayak expeditions, and horseback rides. Ten-foot ceilings, rustic furniture, and nothing but green outside the huge windows are among the simple pleasures. Hearty barbecues and drawn-out *mateadas* (maté tea and cake) are also highlights. Day packages are offered. **Pros:** very back-to-nature; great home cooking; lots of sports. **Cons:** rooms get hot in summer; no pool; minimal luxury. ✉ *Arroyo Rama Negra* ☎ *11/4728–1674* 🌐 *www.deltaventura.com* 🛏 *4 rooms, 3 guesthouses* 👍 *In-room: no a/c, no phone, no TV, Wi-Fi. In-hotel: beachfront, bicycles, Internet terminal* 💳 *No credit cards* 🍽 *AI.*

$$$$ ★ **La Becasina Delta Lodge.** Wooden walkways connect the luxurious bungalows—each with a private riverside deck. Rooms have hardwood walls, jute rugs, and feather pillows in thick cotton cases as well as such comforts as CD players, mosquito netting on the balconies, and reading lights over the bathtubs. You can explore the delta by in boats or kayaks, soak up the jungle atmosphere by the lagoonlike pool, take a yoga class, or have a massage. As well as a dining room and a grill, nighttime entertainment options include a living-room-style bar serving top cocktails and a well-stocked library. The lodge is a bit out of the way to justify a night's visit: inquire about the two- and three-day all-inclusive packages. **Pros:** total peace and quiet; lots of creature comforts; wild delta surroundings. **Cons:** the private boat is expensive; the public service is long and complicated; there's nothing else nearby so you're bound to the lodge; lots of mosquitoes. ✉ *Arroyo las Cañas* ☎ *11/4328–2687* 🌐 *www.labecasina.com* *15 bungalows* *In-room: no phone, no TV. In-hotel: 2 restaurants, pool, bar, Internet terminal, no kids under 14* ▭ *No credit cards* *AI.*

3

LA PLATA

55 km (35 mi) southeast of Buenos Aires via Autopista La Plata.

At the famous 1889 Paris Exposition (think Eiffel Tower), Jules Verne honored La Plata with a gold medal, citing the newly built city as a symbol of resplendent modernity. Accepting the medal was Dardo Rocha, the Buenos Aires governor who a few years prior assembled a team of architects and planners and created the provincial capital from the dust of semi-arid desert.

La Plata succeeds today from that creative genesis, a beautiful city of palatial estates on an ordered grid intersected by wide, diagonal boulevards and a rational scheme of parks and plazas every six blocks. The core of the city's planning is the "monumental axis" between 51st and 53rd streets, which contains most of the attractive churches and government and cultural buildings. A stroll around the city and a visit to the *Museo de Ciencias Naturales* (Natural Science Museum) make a pleasant day trip from Buenos Aires. Streets have numbers instead of names, and though the city's perfect geometry makes it seem like a cinch to get your bearings, the diagonals can be disorienting, so keep a map at hand.

GETTING HERE AND AROUND

The Autopista La Plata connects Buenos Aires with La Plata (tolls of 4 pesos). Plaza and Costera Metropolitana run comfortable commuter buses between the two cities every 10 to 15 minutes. Both services leave from opposite Retiro station: Plaza stops on the south side of Plaza Canadá and Costera Metropolitana on the west. Plaza also has stops (usually marked "129") at major intersections along Avenida 9 de Julio, and you can catch the Costera Metropolitana along Avenida Alem and Avenida Paseo Colón. Tickets for the 1¼-hour trip, which you need to buy from a vendor before getting on the bus, cost 9 pesos. Take the buses labeled LA PLATA X AUTOPISTA, which are the quickest.

Suburban trains run several times an hour on the Línea Roca from Buenos Aires's Constitución station to La Plata. It's slower than traveling by bus, and both the station and the ride itself can be dangerous, especially at night when muggers hang out around the station.

La Plata's city bus service is highly chaotic, and seems to baffle even locals. Thankfully, walking around the city center is both easy and pleasant. But, if you do get tired, flag down a black-and-white metered city taxi; note that there's a taxi stand outside the bus terminal.

ESSENTIALS

Bank Banco de la Nación Argentina (✉ *Calle 7 No. 842, at Calle 48* 🌐 *www.bna.com.ar*).

Bus Contacts Costera Metropolitana (☎ *800/222-6798* 🌐 *www.metropol.com.ar*). **Plaza** (☎ *800/333-1970* 🌐 *www.grupoplaza.com.ar*).

Medical Assistance Hospital Italiano (✉ *Calle 51 No. 1725* ☎ *221/453-5000*).

Taxi Tele Taxi La Plata (☎ *221/452-0648*).

Train Contact Estacíon de Trenes Plaza Constitución (✉ *General Hornos 11, Plaza Constitución, Buenos Aires*). **Estacíon de Trenes La Plata** (✉ *Av. 1 at Calle 44*).

Visitor Info La Plata Tourist Board (✉ *Palacio Campodónico, Diagonal 79 between Calles 5 and 56* ☎ *221/422-9764* 🌐 *www.laplata.gov.ar* ⏲ *Weekdays 9-5*). **Tourist Information Center** (✉ *Pasaje Dardo Rocha, Calle 50 between Calles 6 and 7* ☎ *221/427-1535* ⏲ *Daily 10-8*).

EXPLORING

Casa Curutchet. One of La Plata's architectural highlights is the only building designed by Le Corbusier in Latin America. The ultrageometric structure embodies all the modernist architectural principals for which the French master was famous. Appropriately, it now houses the official architect's association of Buenos Aires Province, which offers 45-minute, guided, Spanish-language tours of the interior Tuesday through Thursday. ✉ *Calle 53 No. 320, between Av. 1 and Calle 2* ☎ *221/482-2631* 🌐 *www.capba.org.ar/curutchet/casa-curutchet-presentacion.htm* 🎫 *40 pesos (includes guided tour)* ⏲ *Feb.-Dec., weekdays 10-2:30.*

Catedral de la Inmaculada Concepción. The graceful, pink-brick Cathedral of the Immaculate Conception stands at the south end of Plaza Moreno, the geographic center of the city and where the Piedra Fundacional (La Plata's Founding Stone) was laid in 1882. The neo-Gothic structure was inspired by cathedrals in Amiens and Cologne but includes local touches like gargoyles in the shape of condors and jabalíes (a kind of wild boar). Construction began in 1884, but the cathedral was still lacking its soaring twin spires at its 1932 inauguration. They were eventually completed in 1999, as part of a major restoration, along with the monumental stained-glass rosette window and a museum, located in the crypt, documenting the cathedral's history. From the museum, guides escort you (in an elevator) to two lookouts in the eastern tower for fabulous views over La Plata, the western tower (which contains a carillon of 25 bronze bells), and the cathedral's spindly buttresses. Many guides will add brief explanations in English to these Spanish-language tours; large English-language posters in the tower contain similar information. ✉ *Calle 14 between Calles 51 and 53* ☎ *221/423–3931* 🌐 *www.catedraldelaplata.com* 🎫 *Museum and tower 6 pesos* ⏲ *Museum daily 9–7:30; tours leave approximately every 20 mins.*

Centro Cultural Pasaje Dardo Rocha. The equestrian statue of South American liberator José de San Martín stands in the center of Plaza San Martín. On the squares north side is the black slate roof of the French neoclassical Legislatura (provincial legislature) building. Nearby is the Pasaje Dardo Rocha Cultural Center, housed in a massive Parisian-style building. Once the city's main train station, it's now home to a small art-house movie theater, temporary exhibition and performance spaces, and several small art museums including the Museum of Contemporary Latin American Art (MACLA), a small collection of artworks by Argentinean masters. It occasionally hosts small-scale international exhibitions: Dalí and Goya shows are two recent examples. ✉ *Calle 50 between Calles 6 and 7* ☎ *221/427–1843* ⏲ *Tues.–Fri. 10–8, weekends 10–10.*

3

★ **Museo de Ciencias Naturales.** In the northern portion of the city, the eucalyptus-shaded Paseo del Bosque is La Plata's biggest green space and a good place to relax. Recreational options include a small zoo, a lake with paddleboat rentals, an outdoor amphitheater, botanical gardens, an observatory, and an equestrian center. But the biggest attraction is in the very middle of the park. The Natural Science Museum, whose entrance is flanked by two lounging, stone, saber-tooth tigers, is Argentina's biggest such institution and is the apple of La Plata's eye. Both the museum and the rambling building housing it date from 1889, and despite ongoing renovations it still seems eccentrically Edwardian. On the ground floor, dusty glass cases display a host of bones, including a substantial dinosaur collection and fossilized Argentine megafauna (think rodents the size of elephants). The freakishly large collection of taxidermic animals, many rather moth-eaten, is eerie. Upstairs is a small but strong display of Latin American archaeological finds and two excellent displays on human evolution and indigenous cultures. ✉ *Paseo del Bosque* ☎ *221/425–7744* 🌐 *www.fcnym.unlp.edu.ar/museo* 🎫 *6 pesos, free Tues.* ⏲ *Tues.–Sun. 10–6; guided tours, in Spanish, Tues.–Fri. 3* PM*, weekends 11* AM*, 1, 2 and 4* PM.

Palacio Municipal. At the north end of Plaza Moreno is the 1883 German neoclassical City Hall, which is recognizable by its central clock tower. The sumptuous interior is worth a quick wander, especially the Salón Dorado (Golden Salon) on the first floor, with its painted ceilings, mosaic tile floors, and huge chandelier, reached by a marble staircase. ✉ *Plaza Moreno, Calle 12, 1066* ⏲ *Weekdays 10–5.*

WHERE TO EAT AND STAY

La Plata is so close to Buenos Aires and so well connected to it that most people make their visit here a day trip. Another option is to continue on from La Plata to Estancia Juan Gerónimo (⇨ *Ranch Stays box, below*) 120 km (75 mi; 2 hours) south.

$$ JAPANESE ✕ **Akari.** If sushi isn't your first culinary association with La Plata, think again: the city is home to one of Argentina's largest Japanese

communities. Second-generation chef Karen Yonashiro's quiet restaurant has become a favorite for its reasonably priced sushi and sashimi—salmon is the favored fish here. Wasabi ice-cream makes a punchy finish. ✉ *Calle 50 No. 836* ☎ *221/422–7549* ⏲ *No lunch weekends.*

$$ CONTEMPORARY ★ ✕ **Barra del Bosque.** When the Paseo del Bosque, La Plata's biggest green space, was designed in 1885, this diminutive stone building was the men's changing room for the now-defunct public pools. Two or three trim booths are squeezed into the cozy space, but the best seats are at the outdoor tables under the trees. The *rabas a la provenzal* (calamari rings sprinkled with garlic and parsley) come in deep white-china bowls, and the steak sandwiches are juicy and well stuffed. A blackboard displaying the four daily main courses is tilted in your direction when you sit down. Dishes like glazed *lomo* (filet mignon) with wild mushroom sauce are a welcome addition to La Plata's more classic offerings. The Museo de Ciencias Naturales is a five-minute walk away. ✉ *Calle 57 at Calle 115, inside Paseo del Bosque* ☎ *221/489–3115* ▭ *MC, V* ⏲ *No dinner Apr.–Oct.*

$ ARGENTINE ✕ **Cervecería Modelo.** This alehouse restaurant opened its doors in 1892—10 years after the city was founded—and maintains quirky traditions like tossing empty peanut shells to the floor. Pigeons, who have cleverly found a way inside, peck at them. The menu runs to several pages but no-nonsense basics like milanesas, stews, or boards of cold cuts are what they do best. ✉ *Calle 54 No. 496 at Calle 5* ☎ *221/421–1321* ▭ *No credit cards.*

SAN ANTONIO DE ARECO

110 km (68 mi) west of Buenos Aires.

There's no better place to experience traditional provincial life in the pampas than this well-to-do farming town off RN 8. Grand *estancias* (ranches) dot the land in and around San Antonio. Many of the families that own them, which form a sort of local aristocracy, mix lucrative soy farming with estancia tourism. The gauchos who were once ranch hands now cook up huge asados (barbecues) and lead horseback expeditions for the ever-growing numbers of foreign tourists. You can visit one for a day—*un día de campo*—or immerse yourself with an overnight visit.

Porteño visitors tend to base themselves in the town itself, which is becoming known for its B&Bs. The fiercely conservative inhabitants have done a good job of preserving the turn-of-the-20th-century Italianate buildings that fill the sleepy *casco histórico* (historic center). Many contain bars and general stores, which maintain their original fittings; others are the workshops of some of the best craftspeople in the country.

In summer, the banks of the Río Areco (Areco River), which runs through town, are teeming with picnickers—especially near the center of town, at the Puente Viejo (Old Bridge), which is overlooked by the open-air tables of various riverside parrillas. Nearby is the Museo Gauchesco y Parque Criollo Ricardo Güiraldes, which celebrates historical gaucho life. During the week surrounding November 10, the *Día de la Tradición* (Day of Tradition) celebrates the gaucho with shows, community barbecues, riding competitions, and a huge crafts fair. It's more fun to visit San Antonio on weekends, as many restaurants are closed Monday–Thursday.

GETTING HERE AND AROUND

To drive to San Antonio de Areco, leave Buenos Aires on RN 9, crossing to RN 8 when it intersects at Km 35 (total tolls of 10.6 pesos). There are more than 20 daily buses from Buenos Aires's Retiro station to San Antonio; most are run by Chevallier, and some by Pullman General Belgrano. Each company operates from its own bus stop in San Antonio. Once you've arrived, the best way to get around is on foot, but you'll need a *remis* (radio taxi) to get to most estancias, though some have their own shuttle service.

ESSENTIALS

Bank Banco de la Nación Argentina (✉ *Alsina 250, at San Martín* ☎ *2326/42591* 🌐 *www.bna.com.ar*).

Bus Contacts Chevallier (☎ *2326/453-904 in San Antonio de Areco, 11/4311-0033 in Buenos Aires* 🌐 *www.nuevachevallier.com*). **Pullman General Belgrano** (☎ *2326/454-059 in San Antonio de Areco, 11/4315-6522 in Buenos Aires* 🌐 *www.gralbelgrano.com.ar*). **Terminal de Ómnibus Retiro** (☎ *11/4310-0700* 🌐 *www.tebasa.com.ar*).

Medical Assistance Farmacia Risolino (✉ *Arellano at San Martín* ☎ *2326/455-200*). **Hospital Emilio Zerboni** (✉ *Moreno at Lavalle* ☎ *2326/452-759*).

Taxi Remis Centro (☎ *2326/456-225*).

Visitor Info San Antonio de Areco Tourist Board (✉ *Bul. Zerboni at Arellano* ☎ *2326/453-165* 🌐 *www.pagosdeareco.com.ar* ⏲ *Weekdays 8–7, weekends 8–8*).

EXPLORING

1 **Museo Gauchesco y Parque Criollo Ricardo Güiraldes.** Gaucho life of the past is celebrated—and idealized—at this quiet museum on a small estate just outside town. Start at the 150-year-old *pulpería* (the gaucho version of the saloon), complete with dressed-up wax figures ready for a drink. Then head for the museum proper, an early-20th-century replica of a stately 18th-century *casco de estancia* (estancia house). Here, polished wooden cases contain a collection of traditional gaucho gear: *mates*, elaborately decorated knives, ponchos, and all manner of elaborate saddlery and bridlery. The museum is named for local writer Ricardo Güiraldes (1886–1927), whose romantic gaucho novels captured the imagination of the Argentinean people. Several rooms document his life in San Antonio de Areco and the real-life gauchos who inspired his work. ✉ *Camino Ricardo Güiraldes* ☎ *2326/455-839* 🎫 *4 pesos* ⏲ *Wed.–Mon. 11–5.*

3 **Museo Molina Campos de Areco.** Although iconic Argentinean painter Florencio Molina Campos was not from San Antonio de Areco, the foundation behind this museum felt that this was the most appropriate home for his humorous paintings of traditional pampas life. The works usually depict red-nosed, pigeon-toed gauchos astride comical steeds, staggering drunkenly outside pulperías (taverns), engaged

RANCH STAYS

You can visit most *estancias* (ranches) for the day—a *día de campo*—or stay for a day or two. Most are family-run setups and rates include all meals (and often drinks, too), which you usually eat with the hosts and other guests at a communal table. It's best to book by e-mail or phone several weeks in advance. Estancias are generally priced in dollars but usually accept payment in dollars or pesos; few accept credit cards.

Price, luxury, and overall vibe vary. For instance, La Porteña, 5 km (3 mi) east of San Antonio, is historically significant; Cabaña Los Dos Hermanos, 90 km (55 mi) northwest of Buenos Aires, is a place to, well, horse around; Juan Gerónimo, near the coast 120 km (75 mi) south of La Plata, appeals to nature lovers; and La Sofía Polo, between San Antonio and the small town of San Andrés de Giles, 25 km (15 mi) south, has the best accommodations.

$$$$ Cabaña Los Dos Hermanos. Horses—about 200 of them—are the focus at this low-key estancia, 90 km (55 mi) northwest of Buenos Aires and 35 km (22 mi) north of San Antonio de Areco. The owners, Ana and Pancho Peña, welcome you personally, and Don Juan, a gaucho with sideburns that rival those of Elvis, leads the lengthy horseback trips. If you're not up for the cowboy act, there are several sulkies in which to tour. You get unlimited riding if you stay over in one of the basic cabins, which are filled with a hodgepodge of furniture but are clean and functional. Meals are homey, revolving around lots of beef. A *día de campo* here costs $85 per person, including lunch but not transport from Buenos Aires. **Pros:** loads of horsey action; gorgeous peaceful fields. **Cons:** accommodation is rustic; no towns nearby. ✉ *Ruta 193, Km 10.5, Cuartel IV, Escalada, C.C. No. 50, Zárate* ☎ *11/4765–4320 in Buenos Aires, 3487/43–8903 estancia* 🌐 *www.estancialosdoshermanos.com* *5 cabins* *In-room: no a/c, no phone, kitchen, refrigerator. In-hotel: pool, laundry service* *No credit cards* *AI.*

$$$$ ★ Juan Gerónimo. This cattle ranch is said to have once belonged to a shipwrecked English bandit, but for several generations it's been in the hands of the same family. Some 4,000 Aberdeen Angus cattle reside on 10,000 acres in the middle of a UNESCO World Biosphere Reserve bordering the River Plate 120 km (75 mi) south of La Plata. It's said that you can ride here for three days without covering the same terrain. Basic rooms are a hallmark of a real estancia, although the more expensive ones have antiques and lake views. It's miles from anywhere, so a generator, battery-powered lights, and candles provide illumination. **Pros:** not at all pretentious; huge portions of delicious homemade food; great for nature-lovers, particularly bird-watchers. **Cons:** some rooms are small and rather basic, and not all have en suite bathrooms; transport costs to the estancia are high. ✉ *On RN 11, 5 km (3 mi) east of intersection with RP 36, 165 km (103 mi) south of Buenos Aires* *Arroyo 873, Buenos Aires 1007* ☎ *11/15–4937–4326* 🌐 *www.juangeronimo.com.ar* *8 rooms* *In-room: no a/c, no phone, no TV (some). In-hotel: pool, laundry service* *No credit cards* *AI.*

$$$$ **La Margarita de Morgan.** A winding avenue flanked by eucalypti opens onto the turreted, dusky-pink main house of this former sheep ranch, 8 km (5 mi) south of San Antonio de Areco. Staying here is a family affair: horseback trips are led by Matías, the original owner's great-great-grandson, and his mother and sister cook the meals, which are served in the original ranch kitchen. Open fireplaces or wood-burning stoves heat the rooms, which are fitted with mismatched antiques. Trendy wall colors—tomato red, ochre, or lavender—are the only hint of modernity; indeed, the century-old house is lit by candles and lamps when the generator is shut off each night. **Pros:** friendly owners; authentic, family-run estancia; few other guests. **Cons:** few structured activities; some might balk at lack of electricity; bathrooms are private but not en-suite. *R41, Km 57.5* *2325/1540–5343* *www.lamargaritademorgan.com.ar* *2 rooms* *In-room: no a/c, no phone, no TV. In-hotel: pool* *No credit cards* *AI.*

$$$$ **La Porteña.** San Antonio's most famous resident was writer Ricardo Güiraldes, and this 19th-century estancia 5 km (3 mi) east of San Antonio de Areco was where he lived and worked. Rooms have uneven wooden floors, plain white walls, and woven bedspreads; bathrooms are huge, if slightly worn. Some 500 acres of woods and farmland surround the buildings, so all riding expeditions stay entirely within the property. Paths through the trees and strategic benches make the grounds perfect for rambling, picnicking, and bird-watching, too. A día de campo here costs $85 and includes two riding trips and a midday asado. **Pros:** beautiful, grounds; rates include transport from San Antonio; historic building. **Cons:** rooms are basic for the price. *RP 41, 3 km (2 mi) northeast of intersection with RN 8 Km 110* *11/15–5626–7347* *www.laporteniadeareco.com* *6 rooms* *In-room: no a/c, no phone, no TV. In-hotel: pool* *No credit cards* *AI.*

$$$$ ★ **La Sofía Polo.** Horsing around in Argentina isn't just for gauchos—many of the world's best polo players also come from here. You can try your hand at the game at La Sofía, 15 km (9 mi) south of San Antonio de Areco, where a class with the owner, professional player and experienced instructor Marcos Antín Güiraldes, is included in your stay. Polo isn't the only thing that sets La Sofía apart: accommodations in both the renovated old estancia and new wing are well-appointed. Heavy wooden furniture and open fireplaces remind you you're at a ranch, but the firm beds (with crisp linens) and spacious bathrooms are worthy of a boutique hotel. A día de campo here costs $100 with riding and an asado; it's $130 if you include a polo class. **Pros:** beautiful accommodations; great quality food and wine; polo classes. **Cons:** few non-horse related activities. *4 km (2.5 mi) north of San Andrés de Giles, 103 km (64 mi) east of Buenos Aires on RN 7* *Calle Belgrano 321, 1ro San Andrés de Giles 6720* *2325/1541–5980* *www.lasofiapolo.com.ar* *6 rooms* *In-room: no a/c, no phone, no TV, Wi-Fi. In-hotel: pool* *No credit cards* *AI.*

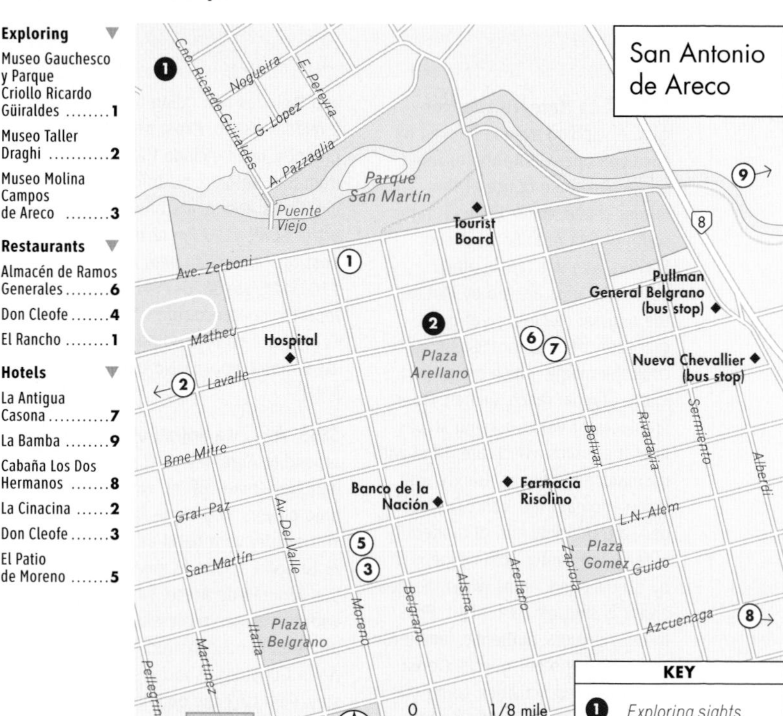

in cockfighting or folk dancing, and taming bucking broncos. The collection is fun and beautifully set out but too small to justify the unreasonably high entrance price, which seems more to reflect the no-expenses-spared renovation of the traditional house that contains the museum. Still, your ticket includes coffee and croissants in the jarringly modern café, which also does great empanadas and sandwiches. Behind its curtained walls lie huge theme park–style 3D recreations of three paintings, periodically revealed. Sadly, the lively and insightful voice-over explaining them is in Spanish only. ✉ *Moreno 279* ☎ *2326/456–425* 🌐 *www.museomcdeareco.org* 🎫 *20 pesos* ⏲ *June–Sept., Fri.–Sun. 10–6; Oct.–May, Fri.–Sun. 10–8.*

2 **Museo Taller Draghi.** San Antonio is famed for its silversmiths, and the late Juan José Draghi was the best in town. This small museum adjoining his workshop showcases the emergence and evolution of the Argentine silver-work style known as *platería criolla*. The pieces are mostly ornate takes on gaucho-related items: spurs, belt buckles, knives, stirrups, and the ubiquitous matés, some dating from the 18th century. Also on display is the incredibly ornate work of Juan José Draghi himself; you can buy original pieces in the shop. His son and a host of disciples keep the family business alive—they're often at work shaping new pieces at the back of the museum. ✉ *Lavalle 387* ☎ *2326/454–219* 🌐 *www.draghiplaterosorfebres.com* 🎫 *5 pesos* ⏲ *Daily 9–1 and 4–8.*

WHERE TO EAT

$$ ARGENTINE **Almacen de Ramos Generales.** This old general store is airy and charming, and its classic Argentine fare is consistently good. You can snack on *picadas* of salami, prosciutto, cheeses, olives, and eggplant *en escabeche* (pickled). The *bife de chorizo* (sirloin steak), meanwhile, is perfectly juicy, tender, and flavorful, all the more so when accompanied by wondrous french fries with basil. The atmosphere, too, is just right: it's country-store-meets-elegant-restaurant. No wonder locals and visiting porteños alike vie for tables—on weekends, reservations are essential. *Zapiola 143, between Lavalle and Sdo. Sombra 2326/456–376 www.ramosgeneralesareco.com.ar MC, V.*

$$ CONTEMPORARY **Café de las Artes.** The charismatic owner of this intimate restaurant clearly gets a kick out of breaking the rules. Instead of the country style most San Antonio eateries go for, the walls here are painted bordello red and are cluttered with art, crafts, photos, and souvenirs from all over the world. Pasta dishes are the specialty: expect unusual combinations like duck ravioli in a saffron and walnut sauce or tenderloin and carrot ravioli in spiced tomato. Only the wine list comes up short—literally so—though the few options on it are very reasonably priced, as is the food. *Bolívar 70 2326/456–398 No credit cards Closed Mon.–Thurs.*

$ CONTEMPORARY ★ **Don Cleofe.** Three things set Don Cleofe apart: a peaceful location just outside of town; a setting inside a century-old adobe house with buttercup-yellow walls hung with weavings and pottery from northwestern Argentina, where the chef is from; and the food. Forget about asado and *milanesas:* here the stars are *lomo* (tenderloin) in a Malbec reduction and rabbit stew with *papines* (small potatoes native to the Andes). Locals make the 10-block trek here on weekend nights, but consider coming at lunch for the fabulous views over surrounding fields. Note that this restaurant is officially open only Friday through Sunday, but as it's in a hotel (that's always open), the management has been known to open during off-hours (even for only two people); just call ahead. *Guido s/n, west of town over old train tracks 2326/455–858 www.doncleofe.com.ar No credit cards Closed Mon.–Thurs. except by reservation.*

$ ARGENTINE **Puesto La Lechuza.** Your first difficult decision is where to sit: the breezy outside tables overlook the river, and the rustic yellow-painted interior is hung with historic pictures of gauchos. Let gaucho-diet principles guide your order—go for the asado or *vacío* (beef on and off the bone, respectively), slow-cooked over hot coals. The little stage where folky guitar players perform in the evenings might look touristy, but locals love the sing-song here as much as visitors. Weekend reservations are essential. *Arrellano (at the river) 2326/452–351 AE, MC, V.*

WHERE TO STAY

$ **Don Cleofe.** Rolling farmland spreads out before this family-run establishment, which is only a few blocks out of town but feels a million miles from everywhere. Colorful cushions and bed throws from the north of Argentina warm up the small, ultrasimple rooms, which each has one wall painted a rich color like butter-yellow or crimson (but jarring with the Formica wardrobes). The owners are happy to customize your already generous breakfast, served in a sunny dining room that turns

Continued on page 157

THE COWBOYS at WORLD'S END

by Victoria Patience

Along a country road, you may come across riders herding cattle. Dressed in baggy pants and shirts, a knife stuck in the back of their belts, these are the descendants of the gauchos, Argentina's cowboys. These men of few words symbolize honor, honesty, and courage—so much so that a favor or good deed is known locally as a *gauchada*.

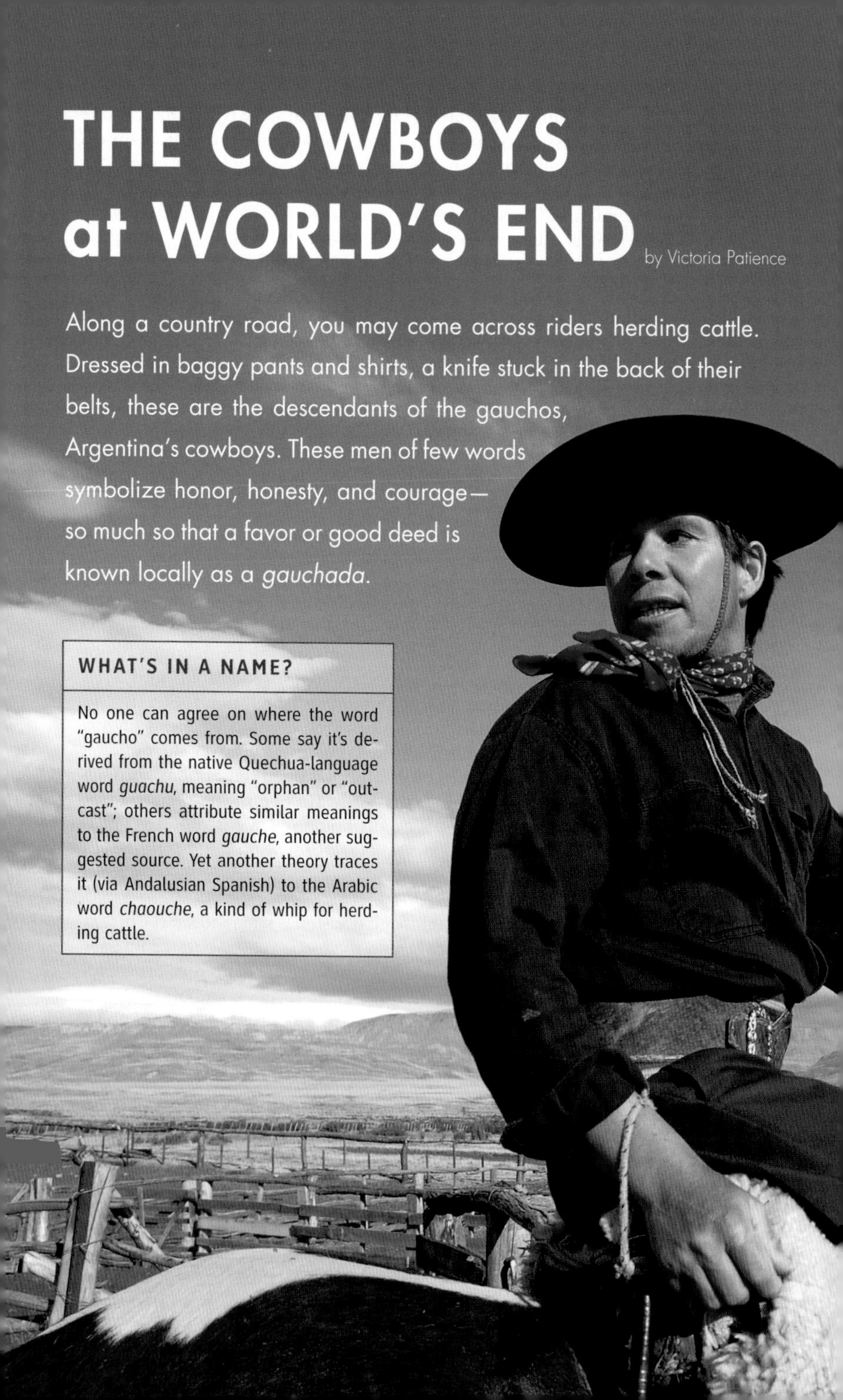

WHAT'S IN A NAME?

No one can agree on where the word "gaucho" comes from. Some say it's derived from the native Quechua-language word *guachu*, meaning "orphan" or "outcast"; others attribute similar meanings to the French word *gauche*, another suggested source. Yet another theory traces it (via Andalusian Spanish) to the Arabic word *chaouche*, a kind of whip for herding cattle.

Gauchos were the cattle-herding settlers of the pampas (grasslands), renowned for their prowess as horsemen. Most were criollos (Argentina-born descendants of Spanish immigrants) or mestizos (of mixed Spanish and native Argentine descent). They lived in villages but spent much of their time riding the plains, much like North American cowboys.

With the establishment of big estancias (ranches) in the early- and mid-19th century, landowners began taking on gauchos as hired hands. The sheer size of these ranches meant that the gaucho's nomadic lifestyle remained largely unchanged, however.

In the 1860s Argentina's president Domingo Faustino Sarmiento encouraged massive settlement of the pampas, and branded gauchos as barbaric, potentially criminal elements. (Despite being of humble origins, Sarmiento as a snob about anything he saw as uncivilized.) Laws requiring travelers to carry passes ended the gaucho's right to roam. Many more than ever signed on as permanent ranch hands; others were drafted into military service, at times becoming deserters and outlaws.

Vindication came in the late-19th and early-20th century, when a wave of literary works like José Hernández's Martín Fierro and Ricardo Guíraldes's Don Segundo Sombra captured the national imagination with their dramatic, romantic descriptions of gauchos and their nomadic lifestyle. The gaucho—proud, brave, and melancholy—has been a national icon ever since.

Gaucho on an estancia near El Calafate, Patagonia, Argentina

GAUCHO GEAR

SOMBRERO
Although a sombrero (flat-crowned, wide-brimmed hat) is the most typical style, conical felt hats (shown), berets, flat caps, and even top hats are also worn.

CAMISA
Traditionally smocked shirt with baggy sleeves. Modern gauchos wear regular long-sleeved cotton shirts.

BOMBACHA
Baggy pants cinched at the ankle; the story goes that after the Crimean War, surplus Turkish-style army pants were sold to Argentina by Britain and France. The fashion caught on: no gaucho is seen without these.

BOTAS
Early gauchos wore rough, rawhide boots with open toes or a flip-flop-style thong. Today, gauchos in colder parts of Argentina wear flat-soled, tapered boots, usually with a baggy pirate-style leg.

CHIRIPÁ
Before bombachas arrived, gauchos used to wind a large swathe of woven fabric (like an oversize loincloth) over thin, long underpants.

PAÑUELO
Large, brightly colored kerchief, worn knotted around the neck; some gauchos drape them under their hats to protect their necks from the sun or cold.

CHAQUETA
Jacket; often kept for special occasions, and usually worn short and unbuttoned, to better display the shirt and waistcoat underneath.

FAJA
A long strip of colorful woven fabric once worn to hold the pants up, now mainly decorative and often replaced by a leather belt. Either way, gauchos stick their knives in the back.

ESPUELAS
Spurs; most gauchos favor those with spiked wheel-like designs.

Gaucho traditionally dressed

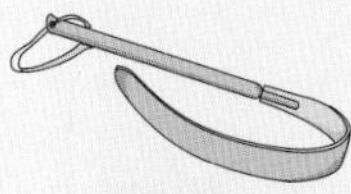

REBENQUE
A short rawhide crop, often with a decorative metal handle.

PONCHO
Woven from sheep's or llama's wool, usually long and often vertically striped. Some colors denote certain provinces.

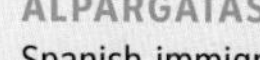

ALPARGATAS
Spanish immigrants in the 18th century popularized flat, rope-soled espadrilles in warmer parts of Argentina. Today, rubber-soled versions are more common.

BOLEADORAS
Gauchos adopted this native Argentinian device for catching animals. It's made of two or three stones wrapped in cowhide and mounted at the end of a cowhide cord. You whirl the boleadora then release it at the animal's legs.

LAZO
A braided rawhide lasso used for roping cattle.

CUCHILLO OR FACÓN
No gaucho leaves home without his knife. Indeed, most Argentine men have one to use at barbecues (early gauchos used theirs for fighting, too). Handles are made of wood or horn, blades are triangular.

SUPER GAUCHOS

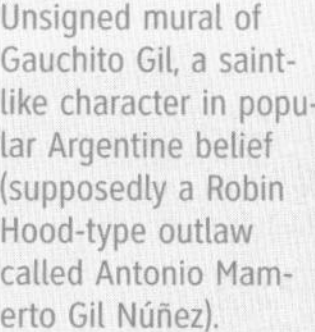

Unsigned mural of Gauchito Gil, a saint-like character in popular Argentine belief (supposedly a Robin Hood-type outlaw called Antonio Mamerto Gil Núñez).

EL GAUCHITO GIL: legend has it that this gaucho from Corrientes Province was hunted down by a sheriff over a woman. He was hung by his feet from a tree but, just before his throat was cut, he predicted that the sheriff would find his son at home mortally ill and only able to recover if the sheriff prayed to Gil. The prediction came true, and the repentant sheriff spread the word. Today, roadsides all over Argentina are dotted with red-painted shrines to this folk saint. Superstitious locals leave offerings, hoping for help with their problems.

MARTÍN FIERRO: the fictional hero of an eponymous 19th-century epic poem written by José Hernández. Fierro is a poor but noble gaucho who's drafted into the army. He deserts, and becomes an outlaw. His pride, independence, and love of the land embody the national ideal of what a man should be. Writer Jorge Luis Borges so loved the poem that he started a literary magazine with the same name.

JUAN MOREIRA: a real-life gaucho who married the daughter of a wealthy landowner, provoking the wrath of a jealous local judge. Wrongly accused of various crimes, Moreira became a fugitive and a famed knife-fighter, killing 16 men before eventually dying in a police ambush in 1874 in the town of Lobos in Buenos Aires Province. A 1973 biographical film by arty local director Leonardo Favio was a box-office smash.

UN DIA DE CAMPO

In the late 19th century, well-to-do European families bought huge blocks of pampas land on which to build estancias, often with luxurious houses reminiscent of the old country. The advent of industrial agriculture has led many estancias to turn to tourism for income; others combine tourism with small-scale farming.

The gauchos who once herded cows now have a new sideline shepherding visitors, putting on riding shows or preparing large-scale *asados* (barbecues). You can visit an estancia for a *día de campo* (day in the country) or to stay overnight or for a weekend. There are estancias for most budgets: some are ultraluxurious bed-and-breakfasts, others are homey, family-run farms.

A day at an estancia typically involves a late breakfast; horseback riding or a long walk; a full-blown asado accompanied by Argentine red wine; and afternoon tea. Longer stays at upscale establishments might also include golf or other sports; at working farms you can feed animals or help with the milking. Estancia accommodation generally includes all meals, and although some estancias are close to towns, it's rare to leave the grounds during a stay.

Gaucho on an estancia near El Calafate, Patagonia, Argentina

HORSEMANSHIP

During a visit to an estancia, you may see gauchos demonstrating traditional skills and games such as:

Zapateo Criollo: a complicated, rhythmic, foot-stomping dance.

Jineteada or Doma: rodeo, gaucho-style.

La Carrera de Sortija: riders gallop under a bar from which metal rings are hung, trying to spear a ring on a stick as they pass.

Carrera Cuadrera: a short horseback sprint that riders start from a standstill.

Boleadas and Pialadas: catching an animal using boleadoras or a lasso, respectively.

La Maroma: participants hang from a bar or rope and jump onto a horse that gallops beneath them.

GAUCHO GRUB

When gauchos were out on the pampas for weeks, even months, at a time, their diet revolved around one food–beef–and one drink–mate (a type of tea). Times may have changed, but most Argentines still consume a lot of both.

MAKING THE MOST OF AN ASADO

Whether you're just at someone's home or out on an estancia, a traditional Argentine asado is a drawn-out affair. All sorts of meats go on the grill initially, including chorizo sausage, black pudding, and sweetbreads. These are grilled and served before the larger cuts. You'll probably also be served a picada (cheese, salami, and other snacks). Follow the local example and go easy on these starters: there's lots more to come.

The main event is, of course, the beef. Huge, grass-fed chunks of it, roasted for at least two hours over hot coals and flavored with little more than salt. While the asador (barbecuer) does his stuff, it's traditional to admire his or her skills; interfering (criticism, touching the meat, or the like) is not part of this tradition. The first meat to be served is often thick-cut ribs, accompanied simply by a mixed salad and bread. Then there will be a pause for digestion, and the asador will serve the choicest cuts: flank or tenderloin, usually. All this is washed down with a robust red wine and, not surprisingly, followed by a siesta.

Gaucho *asado* (barbecue), Argentina

MATE FOR BEGINNERS

Mate (mah-tay) is a strong tea made from the dried leaves of *Ilex paraguariensis*, known as yerba. It's drunk from a gourd (also called a mate) through a metal straw with a filter on the end (the *bombilla*).

Mate has long been a traditional drink for the Guaraní people native to Argentina's northeast. They introduced it to Jesuit missionaries, who learned to cultivate it, and today, most yerba mate is still grown in Misiones and Corrientes provinces. The drink eventually became popular throughout Argentina, Uruguay, and southern Brazil.

Much like tea in England, mate serves as the basis of social interaction: people drink it at any hour of the day. Several drinkers share the same gourd, which is refilled and passed round the group. It's often extended to strangers as a welcoming gesture. If you're shown this hospitality be sure to wait your turn, drink all the mate in the gourd fairly quickly, and hand the gourd directly back to the *cebador* (server). Don't pour yourself a mate if someone else is the cebador, and avoid wiping or wiggling the straw around. Also, you don't say "gracias" until you've had your fill.

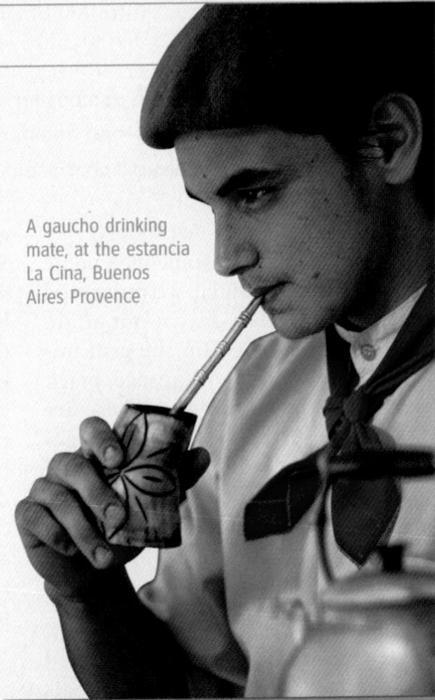

A gaucho drinking mate, at the estancia La Cina, Buenos Aires Provence

WHAT'S IN A MATE?

Caffeine: 30 mg per 8-oz serving (versus 47 mg in tea and 100 mg in coffee)

Vitamins:
A, C, E, B1, B2, B3, B5, B complex

Minerals:
Calcium, manganese, iron, selenium, potassium, magnesium, phosphorus, zinc

Antioxidant properties:
similar to green tea.

SERVING MATE

1) Heat a kettle of water to just before boiling (176°F/80°C)—boiling water ruins yerba.

2) Fill ⅔ of the gourd with yerba.

3) Without the bombilla in place, cover the gourd with your hand, and turn it quickly upside down (to get rid of any fine yerba dust that can block the bombilla).

4) For some reason, yerba never sits flat in the gourd; pour some hot water in the empty space left by the slightly slanting yerba leaves. Let the yerba swell a little, cover the top of the bombilla with your thumb, and drive it firmly into the leaves.

5) Finish filling the gourd with water, pouring it in slowly near the bombilla's base. (Some people also add sugar at this point.)

6) Drink all the mate in the gourd (the cebador traditionally drinks first, so the mate isn't so bitter when brewed for others) and repeat Step 5, passing the gourd to the next drinker—and so on—until the yerba mate loses its flavor.

into one of San Antonio's best restaurants on weekends. **Pros:** fabulous home cooking; fresh air and serious peace and quiet within walking distance of the main drag; friendly but nonintrusive owners. **Cons:** small rooms; only the best room has views of the fields; cold in winter. ✉ *Guido s/n, west of town over old train tracks* ☎ *2326/455–858* 🌐 *www.doncleofe.com.ar* *7 rooms* *In-room: no a/c, no phone, no TV. In-hotel: restaurant, bicycles* *No credit cards* *CP.*

$$$ ★ **El Patio de Moreno.** You might be in gauchoville but that doesn't mean you have to renounce creature comforts or slick design: hip hotel chain New Age has turned this 1910 town house into the coolest digs in town. You'll be loathe to get up from the comfy crimson sofas in the slate-gray atrium, whose checkered floors, exposed beams, and stained-glass windows hint at the building's past. At night, the lights dim and it becomes a wine bar. Cow-skin rugs bring just the right dose of country to the minimal beige-painted rooms, which have huge beds. Some rooms open directly onto the sunny patio, where tables, chairs, and outdoor sofas overlook a tiny pool. **Pros:** two blocks from main street; beautifully designed rooms and lobby; most bathrooms have double sinks and shower heads. **Cons:** rooms overlooking street can be noisy; kids might be uncomfortable with very adult vibe; service is professional but not personal. ✉ *Moreno 251, at San Martín* ☎ *2326/455–144* 🌐 *www.patiodemoreno.com* *11 rooms* *In-room: safe, no TV (some), Wi-Fi. In-hotel: room service, bar, pool, laundry service, Internet terminal* *AE, MC, V* *CP.*

B&BS $ **La Antigua Casona.** The dusky pink walls, brass bedsteads, antique wardrobes, and embroidered linens of this small B&B make you feel like you're staying in a Merchant-Ivory film. The owner-architect renovated the 1897 house himself, and the fittings are as period as the furnishings: think claw-foot bathtubs, vintage tiles, and doors and floors rescued from demolition sites. Thankfully, old-world charm comes with modern comforts like well-sprung beds and thick bathrobes. **Pros:** vintage furnishings; sunny, sheltered patio; two blocks from the main square. **Cons:** high ceilings make some rooms drafty in winter; getting to the bathroom of one room involves crossing the (admittedly pretty) kitchen. ✉ *Segundo Sombra 495, at Bolívar* ☎ *2326/456–600* 🌐 *www.antiguacasona.com* *5 rooms* *In-room: no phone, no TV. In-hotel: bicycles* *No credit cards* *CP.*

SPORTS

When you're ready to work off all that asado you've been eating, head to **Tragame Tierra** (✉ *Martínez, at the river* ☎ *11/15–6603–4066* 🌐 *www.sanantoniodeareco.com/tragametierra* ⏲ *Weekdays by reservation only*), which organizes bicycle tours around town and hiking and kayaking expeditions up the Areco River.

AFTER DARK

PULPERÍA (tavern), ALMACÉN (general store), and DESPACHO DE BEBIDAS (drinks counter) are some of the labels you might find on San Antonio's many traditional bars. Some genuinely haven't changed in 50 years (nor have their clientele), others are well-intentioned re-creations; all provide truly atmospheric surroundings for a coffee or a drink.

Silver and leather work aren't the only hand-crafted products in San Antonio. Seven varieties of artisanal beer, brewed on-site, have made a name for **La Cervecería** (✉ *Zapiola 76* ☎ *2326/456–408*). The amber-colored Scottish ale packs a punch in winter; the paler pilsner's ideal for cooling off in summer. There are pizzas, sandwiches, and other snacks to accompany them.

Candy jars, old bottles, and a gleaming antique cash register sit atop the decades-old zinc-topped bar of **La Esquina de Mertí** (✉ *Arellano at Segundo Sombra* ☎ *2326/456–705*), a gorgeous old café on Plaza Arellano. The owners seem more preoccupied with the charm of the building than that of the waitstaff, so stick with drinks—mugs of icy beer or Cinzano and soda are the local favorites.

SHOPPING

San Antonio de Areco is an excellent place to pick up high-quality handicrafts and gifts, especially traditional silverware and leather goods. Workshops that double as stores fill the old houses lining Calle Alsina and other streets leading off Plaza Arellano, the main square.

The handwoven belts and ponchos **Cristina Giordano** (✉ *Sarmiento 112* ☎ *2326/452–829* 🌐 *www.telarcriolloypampa.com.ar*) creates in soft, naturally dyed fibers are fit to hang on the wall as art, and have justifiably made her San Antonio's best-known exponent of the traditional craft of weaving.

Gustavo Stagnaro (✉ *Arellano at Matheu* ☎ *2326/454–801* 🌐 *www.stagnaro.com.ar*) is a big name in San Antonio silversmithing. His majestic corner store sells gaucho knives, no-nonsense silver jewelry, and mate paraphernalia.

All of the mouthwatering chocolates and alfajores (dulce de leche sandwiched between two cookies) at **La Olla de Cobre** (✉ *Matheu 433* ☎ *2326/453–105* 🌐 *www.laolladecobre.com.ar*) are handmade on the premises. Best of all, you can sample at leisure before you buy. All the gaucho accessories you can think of—including knives, belt buckles, and kerchief rings—are exquisitely made in silver at **Platería del Campo** (✉ *Alsina 86* ☎ *2326/456–825*).

It's not surprising that the smell of leather hits you even before you go into **Talabartería El Moro** (✉ *Alsina at San Martín* ☎ *2326/455–443*), as everything in this beautiful corner shop is made of the stuff.

THE ATLANTIC COAST

Southern Buenos Aires Province is synonymous with one thing—*la playa* (the beach). Every summer Argentines flock to resort towns along the coast, many of which were originally large estates. Now they all hinge around a long *peatonal* (a pedestrians-only street) or central avenue. It can be hard to see the sand in the summer months. However, by walking (or driving) a little farther, you can get some beach action in more-agreeable surroundings even in peak season. Locals prefer to be in the thick of things by renting a canvas tent at a *balneario* (beach club); weekly rents are extortionate but include access to toilets and showers, otherwise nonexistent on Argentine beaches. Happily, buying a drink at their snack bars earns you the same privilege.

Although the weather is usually hot and sunny December through February, the sea is usually bracing, and temperatures drop in the evenings. Off-peak, the beaches tend to be deserted, and luxury accommodations are half price or cheaper. Though the weather can get chilly, walks along the windswept sands—when followed by an evening in front of a warm log fire—can be very romantic. Bear in mind, though, that many hotels and restaurants open only on weekends April through November.

Busy resort town Pinamar has been *the* place for well-to-do porteños to buy vacation homes for decades. The nearby town of Mar de las Pampas is set among pine forests and has made its names as a more exclusive (and thus expensive) destination. Farther south is Mar del Plata, the grande dame of Argentine coastal resorts. Although unbelievably packed in summer, the city the only place on the coast to function more or less normally in low season.

GETTING HERE AND AROUND

Comfortable long-distance buses connect Buenos Aires with the Atlantic Coast. Although extra buses are added in January and February, tickets sell out fast. Plusmar and Expreso Alberino make numerous daily trips to Pinamar in high season; the five-hour trip costs 75–85 pesos. The best service to Mar del Plata is with Flechabus and Nueva Chevallier; there are 10–20 daily departures, and the five-hour trip costs 90–100 pesos. Local company Montemar runs buses every 15 minutes between Pinamar's bus station and Villa Gesell, the closest town to Mar de las Pampas. They also have buses that run along Avenida Bunge and within Pinamar.

Ferrobaires runs daily trains from Constitución to Mar del Plata (52–69 pesos; six hours). The most comfortable option is the Super-Pullman (90 pesos), which goes to Mar del Plata on Friday night and returns Sunday night.

The Aeropuerto Internacional Mar del Plata (Km 398 on AU 2, about five minutes outside the city) is the beach region's main airport. There are two daily flights (around 500 pesos) year-round to and from Buenos Aires on Aerolíneas Argentinas. Note that this is a coveted route in summer, so make reservations early.

Having your own wheels is a great boon on the coast. You can rent cars locally, or drive from Buenos Aires via Autopista La Plata and AU 2, a two-lane highway that continues straight to Mar del Plata (tolls of 18 pesos). The four- to five-hour drive is just one long straight highway, though that highway does get very busy in summer. To reach the northern coast, come off AU 2 at Dolores, continue 30 km (20 mi) on RP 63 to Esquina de Crotto, then turn onto RP 56. This takes you the 110 km (70 mi) to Pinamar. The Pinamar turn-off also intersects with RP 11, also known as the Interbalnearia, a two-lane coast road that connects Pinamar with Mar de las Pampas.

ESSENTIALS

Airline Contact **Aerolíneas Argentinas** (☎ *800/2228-6527* 🌐 *www.aerolineas.com.ar*).

Bus Contacts El Rápido Argentino (☎ *11/4314–7999* 🌐 *www.rapido-argentino.com*). **Expreso Alberino** (☎ *11/4576–7940* 🌐 *www.expresoalberino.com*). **Flechabus** (☎ *11/4000–5200* 🌐 *www.flechabus.com.ar*). **Nueva Chevallier** (☎ *11/4311–0033 in Buenos Aires* 🌐 *www.nuevachevallier.com*). **Plusmar** (☎ *810/999–1111* 🌐 *www.plusmar.com.ar*). **Montemar** (☎ *2254/404–501*). **Terminal de Ómnibus de Retiro** (☎ *11/4310–0700* 🌐 *www.tebasa.com.ar*).

Train Contact Ferrobaires (☎ *11/4304–0028* 🌐 *www.ferrobaires.gba.gov.ar*).

PINAMAR

342 km (212 mi) southeast of Buenos Aires via AU 2 and RN 11.

The resort town of Pinamar is a home away from home for wealthy porteños who haven't gone to the even snootier Punta del Este in Uruguay. A stay here puts you in the company of film and television stars, models, and politicians.

Top local-brand boutiques compete for space with family-run shops along the otherwise unattractive main street, Avenida Bunge, which is usually packed with browsing teens during peak season. Pretty redbrick summerhouses with well-kept lawns line the sandy, unpaved streets that make up the rest of the town; many follow curving lines inspired by the shapes of sea animals.

The beach has pale sands, though to get a view of the dunes Pinamar was once famous for you need to go much farther north or south of the main drag. Some of the best sands in the area are in Ostende, a small town that is officially 5 km (3 mi) south of Pinamar, but effectively one of its suburbs—the half-hour walk along the beach from Pinamar is a pleasant way to reach it.

ESSENTIALS

Bank Banco de la Nación Argentina (✉ *Av. Shaw 156* ☎ *2254/481–880* 🌐 *www.bna.com.ar*).

Bus Contact Terminal de Ómnibus Pinamar (☎ *2254/403–500*).

Medical Assistance Farmacia Bunge (✉ *Av. Bunge 794* ☎ *2254/497–078*). **Hospital de Pinamar** (✉ *Av. Shaw 255, at Las Medusas* ☎ *2254/491–670*).

Taxi Remises Pinamar (☎ *2254/404–600*).

Visitor Info Pinamar (✉ *Av. Bunge 654* ☎ *2254/491–680* 🌐 *www.pinamar.gov.ar* ⏲ *Jan. and Feb., daily 8 AM–10 PM; Mar.–Dec., Mon.–Sat. 8–8, Sun. 10–6*).

WHERE TO EAT

Note that most restaurants open only on weekends during low season (April through November).

$$ SEAFOOD ✕ **El Viejo Lobo.** Right on the beach, this has long been the most-popular seafood joint in town. The airy open-plan dining room doesn't offer intimacy, but the checkered tablecloths are as cheery as the waitstaff. *Gambas al ajillo* (deliciously garlicky chili prawns) are the must-have starter; follow them with a more unusual fish dish like *lenguado con alcaparras* (flatfish in a browned butter-and-caper sauce). Reservations are a must

Live snails litter the beach in coastal Pinamar.

if you want a table with a sea view. ✉ *Av. del Mar between Del Caracol and De las Almejas, 100 m from Av. Bunge* ☎ *2254/483–218* ▭ *V.*

$$$ ✕ **Tante.** Though this restaurant's huge menu offers food from all over
GERMAN the world, it's the signature German dishes that keep Pinamar residents coming back. The elegant white house the restaurant occupies is a lonely historical orphan among glitzy car showrooms and 1970s tower blocks—it was the home of soprano Bruna Castagna. At lunch or dinner, there's classic Alpine fare like fondues (meat, cheese, and chocolate), smoked pork ribs, or goulash, all artfully presented. Alternatively, come for an afternoon tea of Tante's calorie-filled homemade cakes, strudels, and pastries, as you watch the world pass on Avenida Bunge through the restaurant's big windows or from the large wooden tables on the sidewalk. ✉ *De las Artes 35* ☎ *2254/482–735* ▭ *AE, MC, V.*

$$ ✕ **Tritón.** This trendy beachfront restaurant attracts vacationing foodies
SEAFOOD looking to escape Pinamar's similar seafood menus. The restaurant's take on the seaside look is equally refreshing: the clapboard lining the walls and ceilings is painted a glossy white, as are the tables, chairs, and bar, punctuated by the occasional ultramarine tablecloth. During the day, light floods the airy, open-plan room through huge plate-glass windows. Candles, dimmed lights, and a great view of the moonlighted sea make for romance after dark. Although you could easily make a meal of tapas, it would be a shame to miss mains like the hake-and-salmon fillet in creamy leek sauce. Landlubberly standouts include garlicky lamb and sautéed vegetables brought to your table in a sizzling iron frying pan. ✉ *Av. del Mar at Los Tritones* ☎ *2254/495–074* ⚠ *Reservations essential* ▭ *MC, V.*

WHERE TO STAY

$$$ **Hotel las Calas.** Attention to design and a quiet adult atmosphere make this self-proclaimed boutique hotel the exception to Pinamar's family-oriented approach. Earth- and cinnamon-color stucco walls and sleek, polished wood furniture welcome you in the small lobby and bar. Plain white walls and drab linens mean that the rooms verge on the basic, though the bathrooms with their big bowl-style sinks are more of a step in the right direction. Avoid the four apartment-style suites, as their balconies look onto traffic-packed Avenida Bunge. Rooms are often discounted up to 70% in winter. **Pros:** slick design; perfect for couples; wooden loungers in gravel-and-bamboo patio are great for sunbathing. **Cons:** bang in the middle of Pinamar's busy main street; no pool; clueless (though amiable) staff. ✉ *Bunge 560* ☎ *2254/405–999* 🌐 *www.lascalashotel.com.ar* *13 rooms, 4 apartments* *In-room: refrigerator, dial-up. In-hotel: bar, gym, Wi-Fi, parking (no fee)* *AE, MC, V* *CP.*

$$$$ **Terrazas al Mar.** Right in front of the beach, and only a block or two from Pinamar's best restaurants and nightclubs, this huge hotel's location is its main draw. You can tell it's popular: guests file through the lobby continuously, flooding the willing but overworked staff with requests and lobbing their used towels at them. The rooms' plain ceramic floors, beige-and-slate walls, and rustic metal bedsteads are perfectly inoffensive, but they're not up to the hotel's high-season prices. Your own beach-club tent, the two pools, and small spa partly make up for it, as does the airy teal-wall restaurant where breakfast is served. Fully fitted apartments connecting to rooms on another floor are a boon for groups or families. **Pros:** right on the beach; close to shops and restaurants; prices halve when summer finishes. **Cons:** basic, uninspiring furnishings; unreasonably high prices and seven-night minimum stay in summer; pool-view rooms can be rowdy. ✉ *Av. del Mar and De las Gaviotas* ☎ *2254/480–900* 🌐 *www.terrazasalmar.com* *76 rooms* *In-room: safe, kitchen (some), refrigerator (some), Wi-Fi. In-hotel: 2 pools, gym, spa, beachfront, children's programs (ages 4–16; summer only), laundry service* *AE, DC, MC, V* *CP; MAP and FAP available in low-season.*

$$$$ ★ **Villa Ostende.** A block from the beach in a tranquil corner of Ostende, this good-value hotel is a five-minute taxi ride from Pinamar's brash center, but seems worlds apart. The breezy, uncluttered rooms and apartments have cream-color ceramic floors, simple wooden furniture, and crisp cotton bed linens. What rooms lack in serious luxury, the owners (themselves long-term Pinamar vacationers) have made up for in thoughtful touches. One of Villa Ostende's two mock-Tudor buildings contains apartments with beach-view balconies. Asado-addicted Argentine families are especially grateful for the dishwashing service and private barbecue decks. These look onto the large, sloping garden, and deck-edged pool, which the hotel shelters from strong sea winds. Couples usually opt for the quieter block of double rooms. Its indoor pool has windows onto the lawn and a rock-grotto Jacuzzi; a sauna and steam room round off the cold-weather comforts. **Pros:** one block from a quiet stretch of beach; in summer, the already reasonable rates include your own tent at the beach club; well appointed for winter visits. **Cons:** no decent restaurants within comfortable walking distance;

apartment bedrooms are slightly cramped; minimum seven-night stay in January and February. ✉ *El Cairo at Biarritz, Ostende* ☎ *2254/406–866* 🌐 *www.villaostende.com.ar* ⇨ *8 rooms, 18 apartments* 👍 *In-room: no a/c (some), kitchen (some), refrigerator, Wi-Fi. In-hotel: pools, gym, beachfront, no elevator, children's program (ages 6–12; summer only), Internet terminal* ▭ *AE, MC, V* 🍴 *CP.*

AFTER DARK

Seeing, being seen, and getting your photo in the social pages of a glossy mag is what Pinamar nightlife is all about. Most of it centers on the cafés, laid-back bars, and ice-cream parlors on Avenida Bunge and the streets branching off it.

The vibe is mostly laid-back and beachy, but it can feel like a frat party on weekends. Local guys often keep their board shorts on, although girls tend to doll up. The hottest bars belong to beach clubs north of Bunge—celebs are often present, but many events are invitation-only. Note that most people don't finish dinner until 1 or 2 AM, and clubs don't really fill up until 4 AM.

Dancers groove atop speakers at Pinamar's most-popular nightclub, **Ku–El Alma** (✉ *Av. Quintana at Corso* ☎ *2254/481–1314*). The seriously young and rowdy crowd don't seem to mind the wide variety of music—rock, techno, salsa, and cumbia—played on any given night.

The long line that forms outside **Munchi's** (✉ *Bunge at Av. Libertador* ☎ *2254/481–015*) is a sign that the ultracreamy ice cream is worth waiting for. The seating area functions as a kind of boozeless pre-bar, where locals flirt before they hit nearby dance floors.

Models and rock stars know that some of the best cocktails in town are at trendy beachfront bar **UFO Point** (✉ *Av. del Mar y Tobís* ☎ *2254/488–511*), which gets clubby later on.

MAR DE LAS PAMPAS

21 km (13 mi) south of Pinamar on RN 11.

The secret is out: this tiny town, once known only to campers and backpackers, has suddenly become the most sought-after vacation spot on the northern coast. Those willing to fork out the immense summer rents are generally rich, nature-loving porteños. They come for the quiet sandy streets, heavily wooded lots, and stylish stone-and-wood cabins that have become Mar de las Pampas's trademark. Most of these are really glorified hotels and include breakfast and maid service.

Huge dunes separate the town from the beach, and despite the fleets of new four-wheel drives that pack the few blocks around Avenida Cruz del Sur and El Lucero, the commercial center, the sands are wide and peaceful. Two smaller towns, Las Gaviotas and Mar Azul, lie south of Mar de las Pampas, and maintain an equally peaceful—if less-exclusive—back-to-nature vibe.

GETTING HERE AND AROUND

The nearest long-distance bus station to Mar de las Pampas is in Villa Gesell, a crowded, unattractive resort town 6 km (4 mi) north of Mar de las Pampas. Taxis depart from an official stand in the Villa Gesell terminal and cost around 20 pesos to Mar de las Pampas. Local bus company El Ultimo Querandí also connects the two: their groaning, sand-filled buses leave Avenida 3 in Villa Gesell every hour on the half hour, and return from Mar de las Pampas's main square on the hour.

As Mar de las Pampas has no supermarket or bank (only an ATM), a car is useful for stays of more than a day or two. If you don't fancy the drive from Buenos Aires, you can rent a car in Pinamar or Villa Gesell, then continue along RN 11 until you reach the clearly labeled left-hand turnoff to Mar de las Pampas.

ESSENTIALS

Bank (ATM only) Red Link (✉ *Av. Lucero at Santa María* 🌐 *www.redlink.com.ar*).

Medical Assistance Farmacia Pujol (✉ *In Paseo Sendas del Encuentro shopping center, Santa María between El Lucero and El Ceibo* ☎ *2254/451–827*). **Hospital General de Agudos** (✉ *Av. 8 at Paseo 124, Villa Gesell* ☎ *2255/462–618*).

Taxi Remises Sol (✉ *Villa Gesell* ☎ *2255/464–570*).

Visitor Info Mar de las Pampas Tourist Board (✉ *Av. 3 at Rotunda* ☎ *2255/470–324* 🌐 *www.mardelaspampas.info* ⏲ *Dec.–Mar. 10–8*).

EXPLORING

Faro Querandí. Picturesque Querandí Lighthouse about 24 km (15 mi) south of Mar de las Pampas, is surrounded by forest and sand dunes and can only be reached by quad-bike, which you can rent on the beach, or on organized four-wheel-drive excursion from Villa Gesell. The lighthouse itself is not open to the public.

Turismo Aventura (☎ *2255/466–797*), based in Villa Gesell, organizes trips to the Faro Querandí and along the dunes south of Mar de las Pampas. The costs are 80 pesos per person if you go by four-wheel-drive and 150 pesos per person by quad-bike; rates usually include some sandboarding.

WHERE TO EAT AND STAY

Mar de las Pampas has several campsites, which the tourist office can direct you to. Be warned that in summer they're often packed to bursting with noisy teenagers. Most other accommodations here are cabins and apart-hotels (a cross between a furnished apartment and a hotel—breakfast is usually offered as is maid service and each room has a private kitchen and living room). In January and February, the minimum stay is often one week.

$$$ ITALIAN ✕ **Amorinda.** Mom and dad are in the kitchen, and their grown-up daughters wait tables, but the real secret to this family-run restaurant are the killer pasta recipes grandma brought with her from Italy. The creamy whiskey-and-tomato sauce packs a punch, but it's not just flavors that knock you over here. Portions of pancetta-and-broccoli or ricotta ravioli easily serve two, while the mammoth lasagna, scattered with tiny meatballs, might fill even more. Their dense tiramisu might be too much to contemplate; the trembling panna cotta in marmalade sauce is easier to deal with. ✉ *Av. Lucero at Cerchunoff* ☎ *2255/479–750* ♨ *Reservations essential* ▬ *No credit cards* ⏲ *Closed Mon.–Thurs., no dinner Sun. Apr.–June and Aug.–Nov.*

$$ JAPANESE **Heiwa.** Some say the Japanese chef at the eponymous restaurant in the Heiwa hotel does the best sushi and sashimi on the coast, others say it's the best in Argentina. It seems only fair, given the restaurant's fabulous setting on the ground floor of a small hotel by the same name right on the quiet sands of Las Gaviotas. As if the sight and sound of the real sea weren't enough, a huge Hokusai wave decorates one of the walls; mismatched crockery, paper lamp shades, and sandy floors complete the backdrop. The dessert *de rigueur* is the orange-and-ginger spring rolls. If you just want a drink, Heiwa makes delicious juices and cocktails under the white canvas awnings of a beach bar, which opens to non-hotel guests at 9 PM and is lighted with torches after dark. ✉ *Calle 34 at beachfront, Las Gaviotas (3 km [2 mi] from Mar de las Pampas)* ☎ *2255/453–674* *Reservations essential* *No credit cards* *Dec.–Mar. dinner daily, Apr.–Nov. dinner Sat. only.*

$$ CAFE **Viejos Tiempos.** Teahouses abound in this area, but none have more tranquil surroundings than this one, which sits in a beautifully kept garden. In summer, hummingbirds hover over the flowers, while tea and cakes are served at heavy wooden tables set with floral-patterned china. Inside, the chintz-and-lace drapes and cloying red cloths look like something your great-grandma would love, but at least the open fireplace keeps things toasty in winter. After years of making some of the best cakes in town, Viejos Tiempos has added (bizarrely) Mexican dishes to the menu, but it's the sweets that remain the main draw here. ✉ *Leoncio Paina at Cruz del Sur* ☎ *2255/479–524* *No credit cards* *Closed weekdays Apr.–Oct.*

$$$ **Abedul.** Solid stone walls, oak fixtures, and handwoven drapes make the split-level cabins at Abedul very earthy. Outside each is a wooden deck with its own barbecue, and you can arrange for your breakfast to be brought here at the hour of your choice. The bedrooms look out over Mar de las Pampas's unspoiled woods, and the beach is only three blocks away. The sheltered indoor-outdoor pool is a boon when the wind whips up the sand and sea. **Pros:** close to the beach and even closer to restaurants in the town center; lovely wooded grounds; low-key and laid-back but staff still try hard to please. **Cons:** in summer, four-wheel drives roar up and down the road outside; limited nearby grocery stores make the kitchen redundant; beds are on the hard side. ✉ *Santa María between El Lucero and El Ceibo* ☎ *2255/455–819* *www.abedulmardelaspampas.com* *7 cabins* *In-room: no a/c, kitchen, refrigerator, DVD, Wi-Fi. In-hotel: pool, bicycles* *No credit cards* *Closed weekdays Apr.–June and Aug.–Nov.* *CP.*

$$$ ★ **Heiwa.** The sea breezes that ruffle the cotton drapes at this beachfront hotel are almost as calming as the owners' zenned-out approach. No wonder the low-key, simply furnished apartments are often booked up months in advance by returning devotees. With their colorful quilts, bright mosaic-tile bathrooms, and delicate table arrangements, you feel like you're staying with an attentive, arty relative than at a hotel. The incredible sea views more than compensate for the rather cramped bedrooms. The Japanese-Argentine couple who built the hotel have combined their heritages in the individual, bamboo-fenced patios, where solid-looking barbecues have pride of place. **Pros:** any closer to the sea and you're in

Mar del Plata isn't just surf and sand; explore some of the unique architecture.

it; breakfast is served on the beach; incredible sushi restaurant by the same name and beach bar on-site. **Cons:** far from other restaurants and the center of Mar de las Pampas; dead zone after midnight, aside from the in-house bar; tiny bedrooms. ✉ *Calle 34 at beachfront, Las Gaviotas (3 km [2 mi] from Mar de las Pampas)* ☎ *2255/453–674* 🌐 *www.heiwa.com.ar* *5 apartments* *In-room: no a/c, no phone, kitchen, refrigerator. In-hotel: restaurant, bar, beachfront* *No credit cards* *No lunch, closed weekdays Apr.–June and Aug.–Nov.* *CP, MAP.*

MAR DEL PLATA

400 km (248 mi) south of Buenos Aires via AU2.

Come summer, Argentina becomes obsessed with Mar del Plata. The city of 600,000 residents is the country's most popular beach resort—and at least five times as big as any runners-up. Dull gray sand and chilly water may not make for the best beach experience, but in Mar del Plata activities like people-watching, eating, shopping, and clubbing are just as important. The sands are comically crowded in January and February, when there's a carnival-like atmosphere day and night.

The tourist infrastructure hums, with more than 700 hotels and countless eateries. Off-season can get a bit lonely, though the windy sands and almost deserted boulevards feel cinematic. The city becomes literally cinematic each November, when it hosts the Festival de Cine de Mar del Plata, Argentina's biggest film festival.

Although most hotels are within walking distance of a beach, and the city center is navigable on foot, you'll need a taxi or bus to get to other parts of town, like the port. There are several downtown-area beaches; the summertime action revolves around Playa Bristol. The trendiest strip of sand is south of the lighthouse, but you need a car to get here comfortably.

ESSENTIALS

Bank Banco de la Nación Argentina (*Av. Independencia 2375 223/491-966 www.bna.com.ar*).

Medical Assistance Hospital Español de Mar del Plata (*San Luis 2562 223/410-8810*).

Taxi Tele Taxi Mar del Plata (*223/476-0012*).

Visitor Info Mar del Plata Tourist Board (*Blvd. Marítimo P. Peralta Ramos 2270, Local 51 223/495-1777 www.turismomardelplata.gov.ar Jan.–Mar., daily 8 AM–10 PM; Apr.–Nov., Mon.–Sat. 8–8, Sun. 10–5*).

EXPLORING

Aquarium Mar del Plata. More of a sea-theme amusement park than a true aquarium, this slick set-up has performing dolphins and sea lions, waterskiing shows, and a 3-D movie theater. Penguins, crocodiles, tortoises, and, yes, some fish, are also present. The place also has its own beach (open December through March) with beach chairs, umbrellas, and a bar. *Av. Martínez de Hoz 5600 223/467–0000 www.mdpaquarium.com.ar 55 pesos Jan. and Feb., daily 10–9, last ticket sold at 6; Mar. 1–15, daily 10–8, last ticket sold at 5; Mar. 16–30, daily 10–7, last ticket sold at 5; Apr.–Oct., Fri.–Sun. 10–6, last ticket sold at 4; Nov., daily 10–6, last ticket sold at 4; Dec., daily 10–7, last ticket sold at 5.*

El Puerto. Beaches aside, Mar del Plata's tourist action hinges around the port area, 7 km (4 mi) south of the city center. A cluster of tacky but fun seafood restaurants form the **Complejo Comercial Puerto** (*Av. Martínez de Hoz at 12 de Octubre*). A half-mile walk toward the sea along 12 de Octubre brings you to a stretch of souvenir shops and fishmongers, beyond which lies the **Barranca de Lobos**. This is the port proper, home to hundreds of brightly painted fishing vessels and a colony of lobos marinos (sea lions)—their powerful stench announces their presence well before you sight them. The huge creatures often haul themselves out of the water to sun themselves on the breakwater as happy crowds of holiday makers snap photos.

Museo del Mar. More than 30,000 seashells are the main exhibit at this attractive, modern museum. The four-story complex has numerous aquariums, including a petting pool as well as explanations of marine life and rock formations, a café, library, movie theater, and gift shop. The rooftop lookout provides panoramic city views. Puppet shows and kiddie-oriented theater are common during school vacations. *Av. Colón 1114 223/451-9779 www.museodelmar.com 18 pesos Jan.–Mar., daily 10–10; Apr.–June and Aug.–Nov., Tues.–Thurs. 10–6, Fri.–Sun. 10–8; July and Dec., daily 10–8.*

WHERE TO EAT AND STAY

$ SEAFOOD **Chichilo.** Fancy, it ain't: you line up cafeteria style to be served, then elbow your way to a Formica table, scattering the seagulls that peck at scraps from the floor. But the plates piled with calamari and fries and the huge portions of hake and sole cooked on griddles as you watch have made this friendly seafood joint a local favorite for over 40 years. ✉ *Complejo Comercial del Puerto Local 17 Av. Martínez de Hoz at 12 de Octubre* ☎ *223/489–6317* 💳 *No credit cards* ⏲ *Closed weekdays Apr.–June and Aug.–Nov.*

$$$ CONTEMPORARY ✕ **Sarasanegro.** The menu and portions might be small, but each dish is packed with enough flavor—and enough ingredients—to make variety moot. Mar del Plata staples like fried prawns and sole come in a lettuce sauce or bathed in clam juice. The *mollejas* (sweetbreads) are crisply caramelized in sherry. The two young chefs behind the restaurant are so intent on the food that they've left the restaurant rather bare. Still, by the time you're through your scallops with tomato couscous and are on to the apple millefeuille, you probably won't care. The eight-course tasting menu (80 pesos) is a great way to sample everything. ✉ *San Martín 3458* ☎ *223/473–0808* 💳 *No credit cards* ⏲ *No lunch. Closed Mon. and Sun. Apr.–Nov.*

$$$ SEAFOOD ✕ **Viento en Popa.** Word of mouth is the only advertising this restaurant seems to need: it doesn't even have a sign outside yet its tables are always full. Owner Ñeco Gioffi is a pioneer of so-called south Atlantic cuisine, aiming to show off the quality of ultra-fresh local fish and seafood, rather than bathe them in sauces. Dishes such as the *burriqueta en oliva* (burriqueta fish in olive oil and tarragon) or *lenguado con alcaparras* (sole with capers) are testament to the success of his formula. ✉ *Av. Martínez de Hoz 257* ☎ *223/489–0220* ✍ *Reservations essential* 💳 *No credit cards* ⏲ *Closed Mon.*

$$$$ 🏨 **Hotel Costa Galana.** This may be Argentina's most popular seaside resort, but the look at Costa Galana is anything but beachy: rooms are richly decorated with thick wool carpets, mahogany furniture, and heavy drapes. Although they're kept immaculately clean, the furnishings are beginning to look a little worn. The hotel's top-notch restaurant, La Bourgogne, is a favorite with the grandes dames of Argentine television, who often stay here, but the well-trained staff give everyone the star treatment. **Pros:** large pool protected from the wind, direct access to a (relatively) quiet beach through a small underpass, great service. **Cons:** far from the center of town; despite high prices, they charge for extras like Internet; standard rooms are a bit small. ✉ *Blvd. Marítimo P. Peralta Ramos 5725* ☎ *233/410–5000* 🌐 *www.hotelcostagalana.com* *186 rooms* *In-room: safe, Internet (some). In-hotel: 2 restaurants, room service, bar, pool, gym, spa, beachfront, laundry service* 💳 *AE, D, DC, MC, V* 🍽 *CP.*

$ 🏨 **La Casa del Balcón.** Grown-up backpackers more interested in a good night's sleep than all-night partying love this budget hotel. The ivy-covered house it's in dates from the 1920s—that's old by Mar del Plata standards—and the owners have carried the vibe into the double rooms, many of which have vintage wooden beds and wardrobes. The dorms are more basic, but half have their own bathrooms. Add the living room, with its comfy sofas, the huge dining room, and the kitchen (which you can use, hostel-style), and it feels a bit like you're staying at someone's house, but pleasantly so. **Pros:** downtown location one block from the beach, unbeatable prices, homey atmosphere.

Cons: bathrooms are small, and not all rooms have them; creaky floors can wake you up, staff often seem indifferent. ✉ *3 de Febrero 2538* ☎ *223/491–5609* 🌐 *www.lacasadelbalcon.com.ar* *5 rooms, 24 beds* *In-room: no a/c (some), no phone, no TV (some), Wi-Fi. In-hotel: Internet terminal* *No credit cards* *CP.*

AFTER DARK

In summer, a night out in Mar del Plata can feel like a marathon. Things kick off before sunset with what's known locally as "after beach"—drinks and dancing at the different *paradores* (beach clubs) along the sands. Eventually everyone heads home to get dolled up, have dinner sometime after midnight, and eventually head to one of the big clubs around 4 AM, before winding up on the beach to watch the sun rise.

Live music is also an option. In January and February open-air stages are set up on the beach at Punta Mogotes, 2 km (1 mi) southwest past the port. Top local radio stations such as La Rock and Pop host the gigs, which feature big Argentine bands.

The best beer in town comes from the on-sight tanks of established brew-pub **Antares** (✉ *Córdoba 3025* ☎ *223/492–4455*).The most popular night out for Argentines in their twenties and thirties is at **Sobremonte** (✉ *Constitución 6690* ☎ *223/479–2600* 🌐 *www.sobremonte.com.ar*), a complex made up of a Mexican restaurant, two dance clubs, and a quiet bar. Note that nothing really gets going here until 3 AM.

LOS ESTEROS DEL IBERÁ

119 km (74 mi) northeast of Mercedes, Corrientes, on RP 40; 857 km (530 mi) northeast of Buenos Aires; 264 km (164 mi) southwest of Posadas, Misiones; 576 km (358 mi) southwest of Puerto Iguazú, Misiones.

Few places in Argentina are more peaceful, or more magical, than this vast wetland reserve, which stretches over 13,000 square km (5,000 square mi)—an area almost the size of Connecticut—of Corrientes Province. "Iberá" is Guaraní (the local indigenous language) for "brilliant water," and the name couldn't be more apt. Set between Buenos Aires and Puerto Iguazú, they make a fascinating, albeit time-consuming, detour on trips to the falls.

The wetlands are made of more than 60 shallow shimmering *lagunas* (lagoons), separated by sandy banks and punctuated by dense floating "islands" of vegetation. Most aren't fed by rivers; instead, the water seeps into them from the underground tables of the Paraná River basin.

The esteros are home to an incredible variety of wildlife, including two species of *yacaré* (Argentine alligators), capybara (the world's largest rodents), long-legged marsh deer, and around 400 species of birds. Small, flat-bottomed launches take you alongside these animals and the colorful vegetation, into the heart of the Laguna Iberá, one of the biggest lagoons.

Although hunting is forbidden here, patrolling an area this size is almost impossible and some of the inhabitants, like the *aguará guazú* (maned wolf) and the *lobito de río* (neotropical otter), are close to extinction.

The tiny town of Colonia Carlos Pellegrini (population 800), on the eastern shore of Laguna Iberá, is the base for exploring the Esteros del Iberá. A handful of lodges and guesthouses are scattered about its dirt roads. Most of these places organize transfers, boat trips, hikes, and horseback riding. Many offer all-inclusive packages, an advantage as the town's few restaurants have limited offerings. Note that there's no bank in the town, and no credit card facilities, so bring ample cash supplies with you.

GETTING HERE AND AROUND

The unpaved, pothole-ridden Ruta Provincial 40 connects Colonia Carlos Pellegrini to Mercedes, a small city in Corrientes, and Posadas, the capital of Misiones Province. From Buenos Aires, you can reach Mercedes with Flechabus (9–10 hours; 120 pesos) and Posadas with Vía Bariloche (12 hours; 135–175 pesos). You can also take one of Aerolíneas Argentinas five weekly flights (1½ hours; 443 pesos) to Posadas.

Private **four-wheel-drive** transfers take two hours between Mercedes and Colonia Carlos Pellegrini; most accommodations in Colonia Carlos Pellegrini offer (or can arrange) transfers—expect to pay 300–450 pesos for up to four people. A cheaper—but slower, and much more uncomfortable—option is the local bus service Itatí II, which leaves the Mercedes bus terminal Monday to Saturday at noon. The trip takes three to four hours and costs 30 pesos.

ESSENTIALS

Bank Banco de la Nación Argentina (✉ *Rivadavia 602, Mercedes* 🌐 *www.bna.com.ar*).

Bus Contacts Flechabus (☎ *11/4000-5200* 🌐 *www.flechabus.com.ar*). **Itatí II** (☎ *3773/421-154*) .

Vía Bariloche (☎ *11/4315-7700* 🌐 *www.viabariloche.com.ar*).

Medical Assistance Hospital Colonia Carlos Pellegrini (✉ *Aguará at Timbá, Colonia Carlos Pellegrini* ☎ *3773/422-040*).

SAFETY AND PRECAUTIONS

Heavy rain can make the dirt road to Colonia Carlos Pellegrini treacherous. The alligators that live in the lagoon are all relatively young and aren't big enough to harm a human (still, swimming is forbidden). Corrientes becomes unbearably hot and humid between December and February, and few visitors come during these months. The town is busiest during Argentine winter holidays in July, when most accommodations are booked solid. Whenever you come, be sure to bring plenty of mosquito repellent.

EXPLORING

Centro de Interpretación. The detailed, up-to-date displays at Los Esteros de Iberá's Interpretation Center provide an excellent introduction to the local wildlife and the reserve's history. There's also a screening-

room showing different short documentaries about wetland flora and fauna. Families of capybara often sunbathe outside, sometimes joined by small alligators.

Across the road from the Interpretation Center is a short forest walk known as the **Sendero de los Monos** (Monkey Trail) for the families of howler monkeys that live high in its trees. It only takes 10 minutes to walk, but you'll need to linger longer (in patient silence) to see the monkeys. Early morning and evening are the best times to catch a glimpse of them. ✉ *Ruta Provincial 40, Km 118, Colonia Carlos Pellegrini* ☎ *No phone* 🌐 *www.camaraturismoibera.com* ⏱ *Daily 8–noon and 4–6.*

★ **Laguna Iberá.** The second-largest lagoon in the reserve has incredibly still waters that cover an area of 52 square km (20 square mi), but are on average only 10 feet deep. The lagoon is also home to more than 4,000 species of plants and animals. Every hotel and guesthouse in Colonia Carlos Pellegrini has its own small six- to eight-seater launch and arranges two- or three-hour guided trips (you can't visit the lagoon alone). Guides check in with the park rangers before speeding out into the center of the lagoon; when you're close to the floating islands of matted vegetation, they cut the motors and use long poles to maneuver the boat silently through the waters, gondolier-style.

Gaucho culture still permeates daily life in Esteros del Iberá.

Among the rushes, ferns, floating hyacinths, and water lilies, you'll certainly see glistening, half-submerged *yacarés,* paddling *carpinchos* (capybara), and lots and lots of birds. Bring binoculars to see them and more-timid animals like the *ciervo de los pantanos* (marsh deer), which rarely come close to the boats. Thankfully, Colonia Carlos Pellegrini is remote enough to keep visitor numbers to a minimum, so you're unlikely to encounter other launches. You see different animals at different times of day, so try to visit the lake more than once. Afternoon visits are the most dramatic, however: you return to the shore at dusk, when the still waters seem to burn a brilliant orange as they reflect the setting sun.

WHERE TO EAT AND STAY

¢ ARGENTINE ✕ **El Esquinazo.** The menu at this rough-and-ready *comedor* (canteen) runs to two dishes: empanadas and milanesas. Both are totally homemade—you can see the owners preparing them to order through a serving hatch—and go perfectly with the endless supplies of cheap beer from the shop they run in the other half of the house. ✉ *Curipí at Guaysú Virá, Colonia Carlos Pellegrini* ☎ *3773/1562–7548* ▭ *No credit cards.*

$$–$$$ **Irupé Lodge.** If this thatched yellow lodge was any closer to the Laguna Iberá you'd be sharing your bed with an alligator. Many rooms overlook the water (the pricier ones have their own lakeside balconies) and, although they're fairly simple, the well-made wooden furniture, shining wooden floors, and tangerine-painted walls lend them style. You should seriously consider the good-value-for-money all-inclusive option: one-, two-, and three-night packages include guided walks and boat trips (in

English), horse riding, and all meals. These are served in an airy dining area or on the breeze-swept veranda overlooking the lagoon, and feature hearty, mandioca-based dishes typical of Corrientes. **Pros:** location next to the lagoon; lakeside pool; reasonably luxurious (for the town). **Cons:** in-house transfers are expensive; alcoholic drinks aren't included in the AI rate; portions can be small. ✉ *Capivára between Irupé and Ysypá, Colonia Carlos Pellegrini* ☎ *3773/1540–2193* 🌐 *www.irupelodge.com.ar* *9 rooms* *In-room: no a/c, no phone, no TV. In-hotel: restaurant, pool, some pets allowed* *AE, MC, V* *AI, CP.*

¢ **Rancho Inambú.** Traditional materials—adobe, wooden beams, and thatching—were used to build this charming hostel, which is far and away the best budget accommodation in the Esteros. Hammocks swing from the veranda overlooking a lush garden. Local handicrafts decorate the white-walled rooms, which are plain but utterly spotless. The owner, Julieta Balparda, is a qualified guide and keen bird-watcher: fellow enthusiasts and nature-loving backpackers make up most of the guests. She organizes boat trips and horse-riding and leads many hiking expeditions herself (moonlight birding trips are a house specialty). A separate thatched building contains an airy lounge with a guest kitchen, bar, and a restaurant serving sandwiches and simple meals—handy, given Colonia Carlos Pellegrini's limited restaurants. **Pros:** traditional Corrientes architecture; knowledgeable, attentive owner; great breakfasts included in the rock-bottom price. **Cons:** shared bathrooms; not right on the lake; beds are a bit hard. ✉ *Yerutí between Aguapé and Peguajó, Colonia Carlos Pellegrini* ☎ *221/15542–4692* 🌐 *www.ranchoinambu.com.ar* *4 rooms* *In-room: no a/c, no phone, no TV. In-hotel: bar, restaurant, laundry service* *No credit cards* *CP.*

IGUAZÚ FALLS

1,358 km (843 mi) north of Buenos Aires; 637 km (396 mi) west of Curitiba; 544 (338 mi) west of Vila Velha.

Iguazú consists of some 275 separate waterfalls—in the rainy season there are as many as 350—that plunge more than 200 feet onto the rocks below. They cascade in a deafening roar at a bend in the Iguazú River (Río Iguazú/Río Iguaçu) where the borders of Argentina, Brazil, and Paraguay meet. Dense, lush jungle surrounds the falls: here the tropical sun and the omnipresent moisture produce a towering pine tree in two decades instead of the seven it takes in, say, Scandinavia. By the falls and along the roadside, rainbows and butterflies are set off against vast walls of red earth, which is so ubiquitous that eventually even paper currency in the area turns red from exposure to the stuff.

The falls and the lands around them are protected by Argentina's Parque Nacional Iguazú (where the falls are referred to by their Spanish name, the Cataratas de Iguazú) and by Brazil's Parque Nacional do Iguaçu (where the falls go by the Portuguese name of Foz do Iguaçu). The Argentine town of Puerto Iguazú and the Brazilian town of Foz do Iguaçu are the hubs for exploring the falls (the Paraguayan town of Ciudad del Este is also nearby).

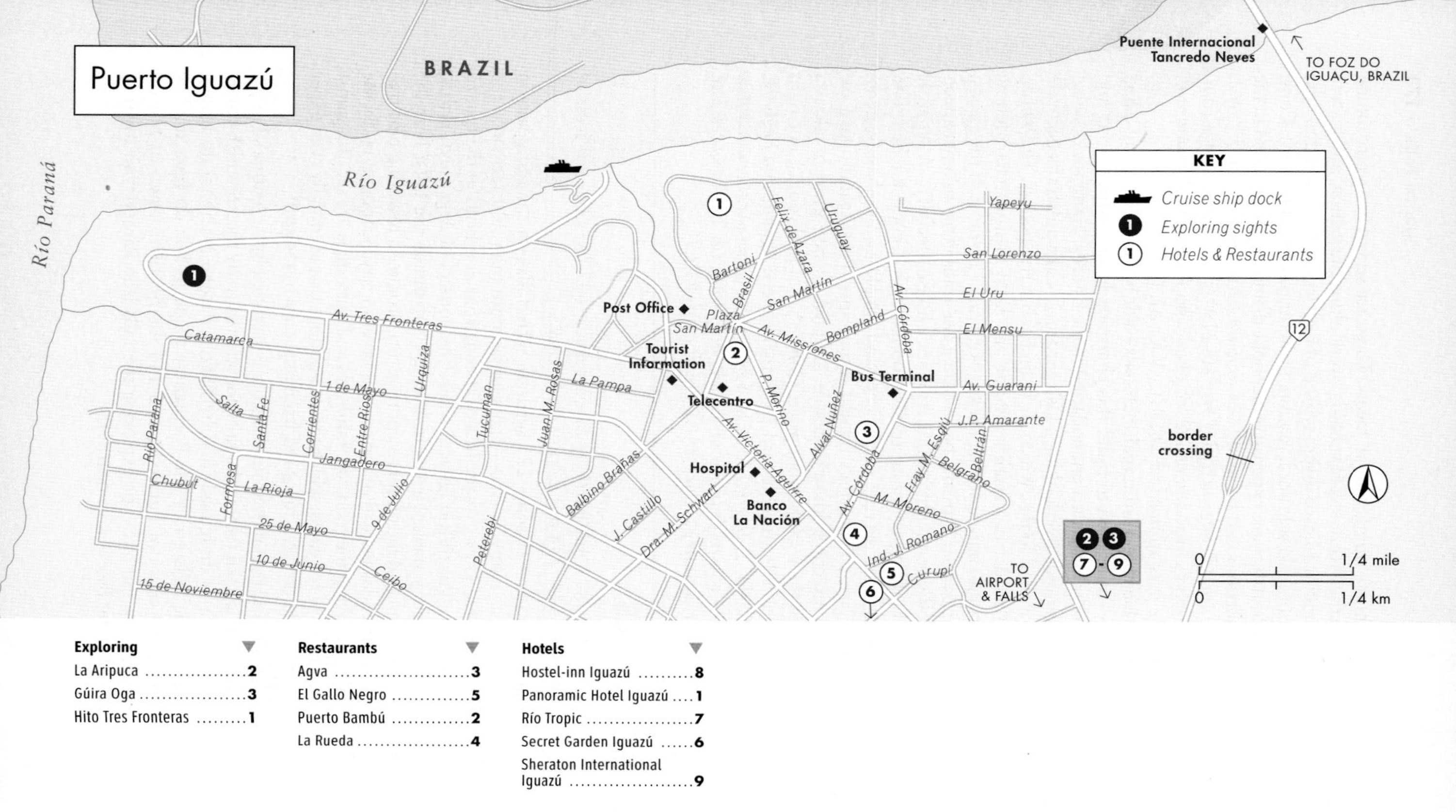

Puerto Iguazú
BRAZIL
Río Paraná
Río Iguazú
Puente Internacional Tancredo Neves
TO FOZ DO IGUAÇU, BRAZIL
KEY
Cruise ship dock
Exploring sights
Hotels & Restaurants
Yapeyu
San Lorenzo
El Uru
El Mensu
Av. Guarani
J.P. Amarante
Felix de Azara
Uruguay
Bartoni
Brasil
San Martín
Av. Córdoba
Post Office
Plaza San Martín
Av. Misiones
Bompland
Av. Tres Fronteras
Catamarca
Tourist Information
Telecentro
Bus Terminal
La Pampa
P. Morino
Alvar Nuñez
1 de Mayo
Urquiza
Tucuman
Juan M. Rosas
Salta
Santa Fe
Corrientes
Entre Rios
Río Paraná
Jangadero
Av. Victoria Aguirre
Fray M. Esqiú
Belgrano
Beltrán
Hospital
Banco La Nación
Chubut
Formosa
La Rioja
Balbino Brañas
J. Castillo
Dra. M. Schwart
M. Moreno
25 de Mayo
9 de Julio
Peterebi
Ind. J. Romano
10 de Junio
Ceibo
Curupí
15 de Noviembre
TO AIRPORT & FALLS
border crossing
12
0
1/4 mile
1/4 km
Exploring
La Aripuca 2
Gúira Oga 3
Hito Tres Fronteras 1
Restaurants
Agva 3
El Gallo Negro 5
Puerto Bambú 2
La Rueda 4
Hotels
Hostel-inn Iguazú 8
Panoramic Hotel Iguazú 1
Río Tropic 7
Secret Garden Iguazú 6
Sheraton International Iguazú 9

GETTING HERE AND AROUND

ARGENTINA INFO

Aerolíneas Argentinas flies four to five times daily between Aeroparque Jorge Newbery in Buenos Aires and the Aeropuerto Internacional de Puerto Iguazú (20 km/12 mi southeast of Puerto Iguazú); the trip takes 1¾ hours. LAN does the same trip two or three times daily. Normal rates are about 400–500 pesos each way. Four Tourist Travel runs shuttle buses from the airport to hotels in Puerto Iguazú. They leave after every flight lands and cost 15 pesos. Taxis to Puerto Iguazú cost 70 pesos.

DOOR-TO-DOOR

Argentinean travel agency **Sol Iguazú Turismo** (☎ *3757/421-008* 🌐 *www.soliguazu.com.ar*) organizes door-to-door transport to both sides of the falls, and can reserve places on the Iguazú Jungle Explorer trips. It also runs day trips to the Jesuit ruins in San Ignacio, the Itaipú Dam, and to other areas of Misiones Province.

Vía Bariloche operates several daily buses between Retiro bus station in Buenos Aires and the Puerto Iguazú Terminal de Omnibus in the center of town. The trip takes 16–18 hours, so it's worth paying the little extra for *coche cama* (sleeper) or *cama ejecutivo* (deluxe sleeper) services, which cost 220–260 pesos one-way (regular semi-cama services cost around 165 pesos). You can travel direct to Rio de Janeiro (22 hours) and São Paolo (15 hours) with Crucero del Norte; the trips cost 315 and 265 pesos, respectively.

From Puerto Iguazú to the falls or the hotels along RN 12, take El Práctico from the terminal or along Avenida Victoria Aguirre. Buses leave every 15 minutes 7–7 and cost 13 pesos round-trip.

There's little point in renting a car around Puerto Iguazú: daily rentals start at 200–250 pesos, more than twice what you pay for a taxi between the town and the falls. A hire car is useful for visiting the Jesuit ruins at San Ignacio, 256 km (165 mi) south of Puerto Iguazú on RN 12, a two-lane highway in excellent condition.

ARGENTINA ESSENTIALS

Airline Contacts Aerolíneas Argentinas (☎ *800/2228-6527* 🌐 *www.aerolineas.com.ar*). **LAN** (☎ *810/999-9526* 🌐 *www.lan.com*).

Banks and Currency Exchange Argencam (✉ *Av. Victoria Aguirre 1162*). **Banco de la Nación** (✉ *Av. Victoria Aguirre 179* 🌐 *www.bna.com.ar*).

Bus Contacts Crucero del Norte (☎ *11/5258-5000 in Buenos Aires, 3757/421-916 in Puerto Iguazú* 🌐 *www.crucerodelnorte.com.ar*). **Four Tourist Travel** (☎ *3757/422-962 at airport, 3757/420-681 in Puerto Iguazú*). **Vía Bariloche** (☎ *800/333-7575 in Buenos Aires, 3757/420-854 in Puerto Iguazú* 🌐 *www.viabariloche.com.ar*).

Internet Telecentro (✉ *Av. Victoria Aguirre 300* ☎ *3757/422-864*).

Medical Assistance Farmacia Bravo (✉ *Av. Victoria Aguirre 423* ☎ *3757/420-479*). **Hospital Samic** (✉ *Av. Victoria Aguirre 131, Puerto Iguazú* ☎ *3757/420-288*).

Taxis Remises Iguazú (✉ *Puerto Iguazú* ☎ *3757/422-008*).

Visitor Info Cataratas del Iguazú Visitors Center (✉ *Park entrance* ☎ *3757/420–180* 🌐 *www.iguazuargentina.com* ⏲ *Mar.–Aug. 8 AM–6 PM; Sept.–Feb. 8 AM–8 PM*). **Puerto Iguazú Tourist Office** (✉ *Av. Victoria Aguirre 311, Puerto Iguazú* ☎ *3757/420–800* ⏲ *Daily 7–1 and 2–9*).

CROSS-BORDER BUS

Crucero del Norte (☎ *3757/421–916 in Puerto Iguazú* 🌐 *www.crucerodelnorte.com.ar*) runs an hourly cross-border public bus service (3 pesos) between the bus stations of Puerto Iguazú and Foz do Iguaçu. Locals don't have to get on and off for immigration but be sure you do so. To reach the Argentine falls, change to local minibus service El Práctico at the intersection with RN 12 on the Argentine side. For the Brazilian park, change to a local bus at the Avenida Cataratas roundabout.

BRAZIL INFO

There are direct flights between Foz do Iguaçu and São Paulo (1½ hours; $180), Rio de Janeiro (2 hours; $360), and Curitiba (1 hour; $180) on TAM, which also has connecting flights to Salvador, Recife, Brasilia, other Brazilian cities, and Buenos Aires. Low-cost airline GOL operates slightly cheaper direct flights on the same three routes.

The Aeroporto Internacional Foz do Iguaçu is 13 km (8 mi) southeast of downtown Foz. The 20-minute taxi ride should cost R$40; the 45-minute regular bus ride about R$2.20. Note that several major hotels are on the highway to downtown, so a cab ride from the airport to these may be less than R$30. A cab ride from downtown hotels directly to the Parque Nacional in Brazil costs about R$50–R$70.

Via bus, the trip between Florianópolis and Foz do Iguaçu takes 15 hours with Pluma (R$120; R$230 for sleeper). The same company travels to Rio de Janeiro, which takes 11½ hours (R$175), and São Paolo, which takes 14 hours (R$144; R$215 for sleeper). The Terminal Rodoviário in Foz do Iguaçu is 5 km (3 mi) northeast of downtown. There are regular buses into town; they stop at the Terminal de Transportes Urbano (local bus station, often shortened to TTU) at Avenida Juscelino Kubitschek and Rua Mem de Sá. From here, buses labeled PARQUE NACIONAL also depart every 15 minutes (7–7) to the visitor center at the park entrance; the fare is R$4. The buses run along Avenida Juscelino Kubitschek and Avenida Jorge Schimmelpfeng, where you can also flag them down.

There's no real reason to rent a car in Foz do Iguaçu: it's cheaper and easier to use taxis or local tour companies to visit the falls, especially as you can't cross the border in a rental car. There are taxi stands (*pontos de taxi*) at intersections all over town, each with its own phone number. Hotels and restaurants can call you a cab, but you can also hail them on the street.

BRAZIL ESSENTIALS

Airline Contacts GOL (☎ *300/115–2121 toll-free, 45/3521–4230 in Foz do Iguaçu* 🌐 *www.voegol.com.br*). **TAM** (☎ *800/570–5700 toll-free, 45/3521–7500 in Foz do Iguaçu* 🌐 *www.tam.com.br*).

Bus Contacts Pluma (☎ *800/646–0300 toll-free, 045/3522–2515 in Foz do Iguaçu* 🌐 *www.pluma.com.br*).

Exploring

Ecomuseu de Itaipú **2**

Itaipú Dam and Hydroelectric Power Plant **1**

Parque das Aves **3**

Restaurants

Búfalo Branco ... **1**

Tempero da Bahia **3**

Zaragoza **2**

Hotels

Hotel das Cataratas **4**

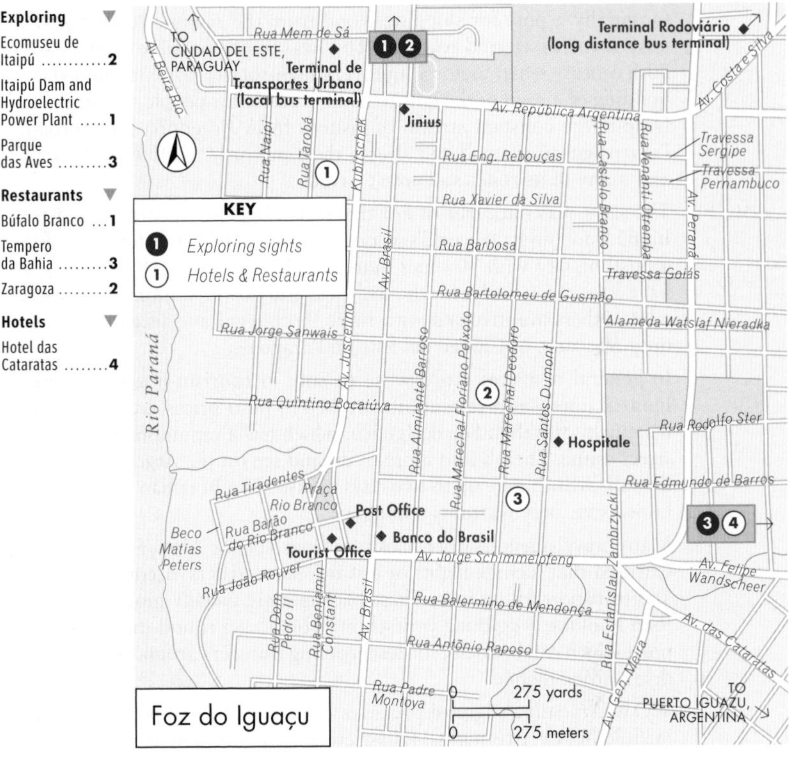

Banks and Currency Exchange Banco do Brasil (✉ *Av. Brasil 1377* 🌐 *www.bb.com.br*).

Internet Jinius (✉ *Av. Brasil 34* ☎ *45/3572-0078*).

Medical Assistance FarmaRede (pharmacy) (✉ *Av. Brasil 46* ☎ *45/3572-1363*). **Hospital Ministro Costa Cavalcanti** (✉ *Av. Gramado 580* ☎ *45/3576-8000*).

Taxis Ponto de Taxi 20 (☎ *45/3523-4625*).

Visitor Info Foz do Iguaçu Tourist Office (✉ *Praça Getúlio Vargas 69, Brazil* ☎ *45/3521-1455* 🌐 *www.iguassu.tur.br* ⏲ *8 AM–6 PM*).

EXPLORING

To visit the falls, you can base yourself in the small Argentine city of Puerto Iguazú, or its sprawling Brazilian counterpart, the city of Foz do Iguaçu. The two cities are 18 km (11 mi) and 25 km (15 mi) northwest of the falls, respectively, and are connected by an international bridge, the Puente Presidente Tancredo Neves. Another bridge links Foz do Iguaçu with Ciudad del Este in Paraguay. Together, the three cities form the Triple Frontera (Tri Border).

Originally a port for shipping wood from the region, Puerto Iguazú now revolves around tourism. This was made possible in the early 20th century when Victoria Aguirre, a high-society porteña, funded the building of a road to the falls to make it easier for people to visit them. Despite the constant stream of visitors from Argentina and abroad, Puerto Iguazú is small and sleepy: there are only 32,000 inhabitants, and many of its roads still aren't paved.

The same was once true of Foz de Iguaçu, but the construction of the Itaipú Dam (now the world's second largest) in 1975 transformed it into a bustling city with 10 times more people than Puerto Iguazú. Many have jobs connected with the hydroelectric power station at the dam, while others are involved with trade (both legal and illegal) with the duty-free zone of Ciudad del Este, in Paraguay.

In general it makes more sense to stay in tourism-oriented Puerto Iguazú: hotels and restaurants are better, peso prices are lower, and it's much safer than Foz do Iguaçu, which has a reputation for violent street crime. There's also more to do and see on the Argentine side of the falls, which take up to two days to visit. The Brazilian side, though impressive, only warrants half a day.

Many travel agencies offer packages from Buenos Aires, São Paulo, or Curitiba that include flights or bus tickets, transfers, accommodation, and transport to the falls. These packages are usually more expensive than booking everything yourself but you do get round-the-clock support, which can be useful for rescheduling transfers around Argentina's delay-prone flights.

WOW Argentina's Iguazú packages cost around $750 per person and include flights, two nights' falls-view accommodation at the Sheraton Iguazú, airport transfers, and a boat ride. Isabel at Buenos Aires Tours does a similarly priced package as well as one with accommodation in Puerto Iguazú that costs around $470 per person, including transport to the Argentine side of the park. Both can arrange add-on excursions to the Brazilian side.

If you're staying in town, rather than at the hotels in the parks, you can easily reach the falls on your side of the border by public bus, private shuttle (most hotels work with shuttle company), or taxi. Travel agencies and tour operators in Puerto Iguazú and Foz de Iguaçu also offer day trips to the opposite sides of the border. Most are glorified shuttle services that save you the hassle of changing buses and get you through immigration formalities quickly. Use them to facilitate getting to the park, but avoid those that include in-park tours: most drag you around with a huge group of people and a megaphone, which rather ruins the fabulous natural surroundings.

Both parks are incredibly well organized and clearly signposted, so most visitors have no trouble exploring independently. Once in the park, be sure to go on a boat trip, an unmissable—though drenching—experience that gets you almost under the falls. You can reserve these through tour operators or hotels, or at booths inside the parks.

Continued on page 186

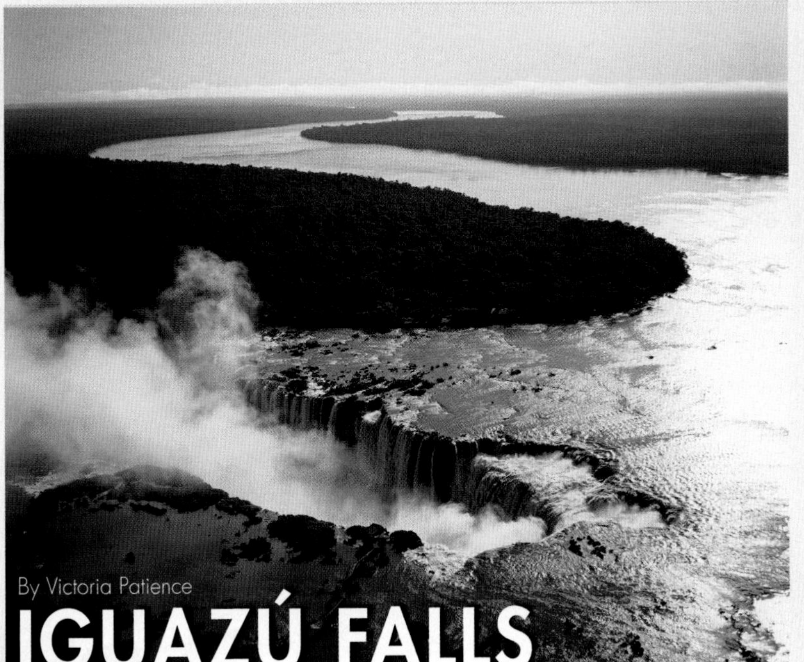

By Victoria Patience

IGUAZÚ FALLS

Big water. That's what *y-guasu*—the name given to the falls by the indigenous Guaraní people—means. As you approach, a thundering fills the air and steam rises above the trees. Then the jungle parts. Spray-soaked and speechless, you face the Devil's Throat, and it's clear that "big" doesn't come close to describing this wall of water.

Taller than Niagara, wider than Victoria, Iguazú's raging, monumental beauty is one of nature's most awe-inspiring sights. The Iguazú River, on the border between Argentina and Brazil, plummets 200 feet to form the Cataratas de Iguazú (as the falls are known in Spanish) or Foz do Iguaçu (their Portuguese name). Considered to be one waterfall, Iguazú is actually made up of around 275 individual drops, that stretch along 2.7 km (1.7 mi) of cliff-face. Ranging from picturesque cascades to immense cataracts, this incredible variety is what makes Iguazú so special. National parks in Brazil and Argentina protect the falls and the flora and fauna that surround them. Exploring their jungle-fringed trails can take two or three days: you get right alongside some falls, gaze down dizzily into others, and can take in the whole spectacle from afar. You're sure to come across lizards, emerald- and sapphire-colored hummingbirds, clouds of butterflies, and scavenging raccoonlike coatis. You'll also glimpse monkeys and toucans, if you're lucky.

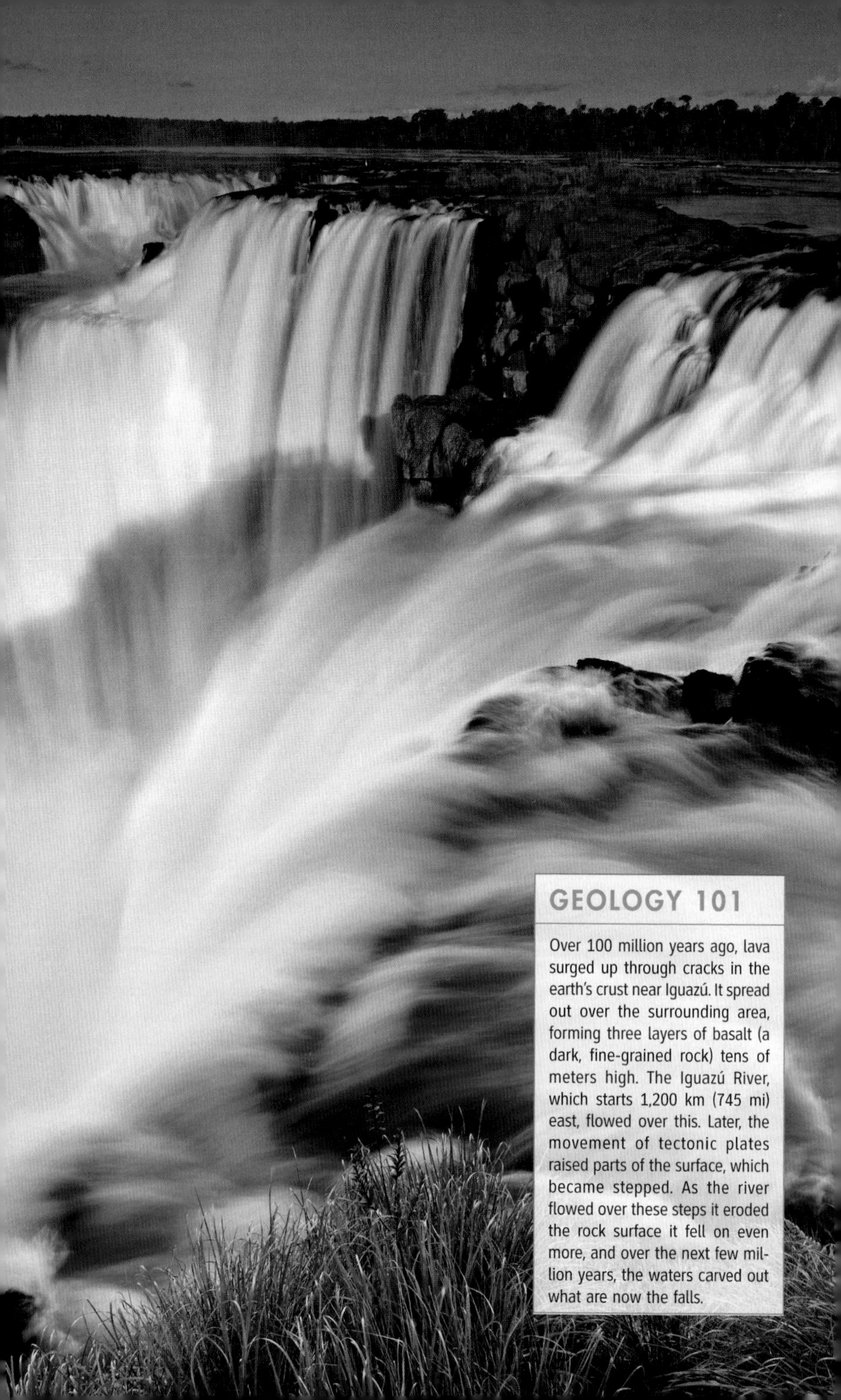

GEOLOGY 101

Over 100 million years ago, lava surged up through cracks in the earth's crust near Iguazú. It spread out over the surrounding area, forming three layers of basalt (a dark, fine-grained rock) tens of meters high. The Iguazú River, which starts 1,200 km (745 mi) east, flowed over this. Later, the movement of tectonic plates raised parts of the surface, which became stepped. As the river flowed over these steps it eroded the rock surface it fell on even more, and over the next few million years, the waters carved out what are now the falls.

WHEN TO GO

Time of year	Advantages	Disadvantages
Nov.—Feb.	High rainfall in December and January, so expect lots of water.	Hot and sticky. December and January are popular with local visitors. High water levels stop Zodiac rides.
Mar.—Jun.	Increasingly cooler weather. Fewer local tourists. Water levels are usually good.	Too cold for some people, especially when you get wet. Occasional freak water shortages.
Jul.—Oct.	Cool weather.	Low rainfall in July and August—water levels can be low. July is peak season for local visitors.

WHERE TO GO: ARGENTINA VS. BRAZIL

Argentines and Brazilians can fight all day about who has the best angle on the falls. But the two sides are so different that comparisons are academic. To really say you've done Iguazú (*or* Iguaçu), you need to visit both. If you twist our arm, we'll say the Argentine side is a better experience with lots more to do, but (and this is a big "but") the Brazilian side gives you a tick in the box and the best been-there-done-that photos. It's also got more non-falls-related activities (but you have to pay extra for them).

	ARGENTINA	BRAZIL
Park Name	Parque Nacional Iguazú	Parque Nacional do Iguaçu
The experience	Up close and personal (you're going to get wet).	What a view!
The falls	Two-thirds are in Argentina including Garganta del Diablo, the star attraction.	The fabulous panoramic perspective of the Garganta do Diablo is what people really come for.
Timing	One day to blitz the main attractions. Two days to explore fully.	Half a day to see the falls; all day if you do other activities.
Other activities	Extensive self-guided hiking and Zodiac rides.	Organized hikes, Zodiac rides, boat rides, helicopter rides, rafting, abseiling.
Park size	67,620 hectares (167,092 acres)	182,262 hectares (450,379 acres)
Animal species	80 mammals/450 birds	50 mammals/200 birds

VITAL STATISTICS

Number of falls: 160—275*	**Total length:** 2.7 km (1.7 mi)	**Average Flow:** 396,258 gallons per second **Peak Flow:** 1,717,118 gallons per second
Major falls: 19	**Height of Garganta del Diablo:** 82 m (270 feet)	**Age:** 120—150 million years

*Depending on water levels

IGUAZÚ ITINERARIES

LIGHTNING VISIT. If you only have one day, limit your visit to the Argentine park. Arrive when it opens, and get your first look at the falls aboard one of Iguazú Jungle Explorer's Zodiacs. The rides finish at the Circuito Inferior: take a couple of hours to explore this. (Longer summer opening hours give you time to squeeze in the **Isla San Martín.**) Grab a quick lunch at the Dos Hermanas snack bar, then blitz the shorter Circuito Superior. You've kept the best for last: catch the train from **Estación Cataratas** to **Estación Garganta del Diablo,** where the trail to the viewing platform starts (allow at least two hours for this).

Tren Ecologico de la Selva

BEST OF BOTH SIDES. Two days gives you enough time to see both sides of the falls. Visit the Brazilian park on your second day to get the panoramic take on what you've experienced up-close in Argentina. If you arrive at 9 AM, you've got time to walk the entire trail, take photos, have lunch in the Porto Canoas service area, and be back at the park entrance by 1 PM. You could spend the afternoon doing excursions and activities from Macuco Safari and Ma-

KEY

- Wheelchair-accessible
- Restaurant
- Scenic Viewpoint
- Walking/Hiking Trails
- Ferry Lines
- Rail Lines

Estación Garganta del Diablo

Garganta del Diablo

Garganta del Diablo

ARGENTINA

Parque Nacional do Iguaçu

BRAZIL

Isla San Martín

Río Iguazu

Walkway view at Garganta del Diablo

cuco EcoAventura, or visiting the Itaipú dam. Alternatively, you could keep the visit to Brazil for the afternoon of the second day, and start off with a lightning return visit to the Argentine park and see the **Garganta del Diablo** (left) with the sun rising behind it.

SEE IT ALL. With three days you can explore both parks at a leisurely pace. Follow the one-day itinerary, then return to the Argentine park on your second day. Make a beeline for the Garganta del Diablo, which looks different in the mornings, then spend the afternoon exploring the **Sendero Macuco** (and Isla San Martín, if you didn't have time on the first day). You'll also have time to visit Güira Oga bird sanctuary or La Aripuca (both on RN 12) afterwards. You could spend all of your third day in the Brazilian park, or just the morning, giving you time to catch an afternoon flight or bus.

Estación Central
Estación Cataratas
Circuito Superior
Parque Nacional Iguazú
Circuito Inferior
Dos Hermanas

VISITING THE PARKS

Visitors gaze at the falls in Parque Nacional Iguazú.

Argentina's side of the falls is in the **Parque Nacional Iguazú,** which was founded in 1934 and declared a World Heritage Site in 1984. The park is divided into two areas, each of which is organized around a train station: Estación Cataratas or the Estación Garganta del Diablo. (A third, Estación Central, is near the park entrance.)

Paved walkways lead from the main entrance past the **Visitor Center,** called *Yvyrá Retá*—"country of the trees" in Guaraní (☎ 3757/49-1469 🌐 www.iguazuargentina.com 🎫 60 pesos 🕐 Mar.–Aug. 8–6; Sept.–Feb. 8–8). Colorful visual displays provide a good explanation of the region's ecology and human history. To reach the park proper, you cross through a small plaza containing a food court, gift shops, and ATM. From the nearby Estación Central, the gas-propelled Tren de la Selva (Jungle Train) departs every 20 minutes.

In Brazil, the falls can be seen from the **Parque Nacional Foz do Iguaçu** (☎ 45/3521-4400 🌐 www.cataratasdoiguacu.com.br 🎫 R$21.15 🕐 Apr.–Sep 9–5; Oct.–Mar. 9–6). Much of the park is protected rain forest—off-limits to visitors and home to the last viable populations of panthers as well as rare flora. Buses and taxis drop you off at a vast, plaza alongside the park entrance building. As well as ticket booths, there's an ATM, a snack bar, gift shop, and information and currency exchange. Next to the entrance turnstiles is the small **Visitor Center,** where helpful geological models explain how the falls were formed. Double-decker buses run every 15 minutes between the entrance and the trailhead to the falls, 11 km (7 mi) away; the buses stop at the entrances to excursions run by private operators Macuco Safari and Macuco Ecoaventura (these aren't included in your ticket). The trail ends in the **Porto Canoas** service area. There's a posh linen-service restaurant with river views, and two fast-food counters the with tables overlooking the rapids leading to the falls.

VISAS

U.S. citizens don't need a visa to visit Argentina as tourists, but the situation is more complicated in Brazil. ⇨ See the planning section at the beginning of the chapter.

EXCURSIONS IN AND AROUND THE PARKS

A Zodiac trip to the falls.

Iguazú Jungle Explorer (☎ 3757/42-1696 ⊕ www.iguazujungleexplorer.com) runs trips within the Argentine park. Their standard trip, the Gran Aventura, costs 150 pesos and includes a truck ride through the forest and a Zodiac ride to San Martín, Bossetti, and the Salto Tres Mosqueteros (be ready to get soaked). The truck carries so many people that most animals are scared away: you're better off buying the 75-peso boat trip—Aventura Nautica—separately.

You can take to the water on the Brazilian side with **Macuco Safari** (☎ 045/3574-4244 ⊕ www.macucosafari.com.br). Their signature trip is a Zodiac ride around (and under) the Salto Tres Mosqueteros. You get a more sedate ride on the Iguaçu Explorer, a 3½ hour trip up the river.

It's all about adrenaline with **Iguazú Forest** (☎ 3757/42-1140 ⊕ www.iguazuforest.com). Their full day expedition involves kayaking, abseiling, waterfall-climbing, mountain-biking, and canopying all within the Argentine park.

In Brazil, **Cânion Iguaçu** (☎ 045/3529-6040 ⊕ www.campodedesafios.com.br) offers rafting and canopying, as well as abseiling over the river from the Salto San Martín. They also offer wheelchair-compatible equipment.

Argentine park ranger Daniel Somay organizes two-hour Jeep tours with an ecological focus through his Puerto Iguazú–based **Explorador Expediciones** (☎ 3757/42-1632 ⊕ www.rainforestevt.com.ar). The tours cost 120 pesos and include detailed explanations of the Iguazú ecosystem and lots of photo ops. A specialist leads the birdwatching trips, which cost US$100 and include the use of binoculars and hotel pick-up and drop-off.

Macuco Ecoaventura (☎ 045/3529-6927 ⊕ www.macucoecoaventura.com.br) is one of the official tour operators within the Brazilian park. Their Trilha do Pozo Negro combines a 9-km guided hike or bike ride with a scary boat trip along the upper river (the bit before the falls). The aptly-named Floating trip is more leisurely; shorter jungle hikes are also offered.

ON THE CATWALK

You spend most of your visit to the falls walking the many trails and catwalks, so be sure to wear comfortable shoes.

OTHER SITES TO SEE

Surprisingly, the falls are not the only site to see in these parts, though few people actually have time (or make time) to go see others.

IN ARGENTINA

Numbers in the margin correspond to numbers on the Puerto Iguazú map.

Güira Oga. Although Iguazú is home to around 450 bird species, the parks are so busy these days that you'd be lucky to see so much as a feather. It's another story at Güira Oga, which means "house of the birds" in Guaraní, although "bird rehab" might be more appropriate. Injured birds, birds displaced by deforestation, and birds confiscated from traffickers are brought here for treatment. The large cages also contain many species on the verge of extinction, including the harpy eagle and the red macaw, a gorgeous parrot. The sanctuary is in a forested plot just off RN12, halfway between Puerto Iguazú and the falls. The entrance price includes a 1½-hour guided visit (in English and Spanish). ✉ *RN12, Km 5, Puerto Iguazú* ☎ *3757/423–980* 🌐 *www.guiraoga.fundacionazara.org.ar* 🎫 *30 pesos* 🕒 *Daily 9–6 (last tour leaves 4:45).*

Hito Tres Fronteras. This viewpoint west of the town center stands high above the turbulent reddish-brown confluence of the Iguazú and Paraná rivers, which also form the *Triple Frontera,* or Tri Border. A mini pale-blue-and-white obelisk reminds you you're in Argentina; across the Iguazú River is Brazil's green-and-yellow equivalent; farther away, across the Paraná, is Paraguay's, painted red, white, and blue. A row of overpriced souvenir stalls stands alongside it. ✉ *Av. Tres Fronteras, Puerto Iguazú.*

La Aripuca. It looks like a cross between a log cabin and the Pentagon, but this massive wooden structure—which weighs 551 tons—is a large-scale replica of a Guaraní bird trap. La Aripuca officially showcases different local woods, supposedly for conservation purposes—ironic, given the huge trunks used to build it, and the overpriced wooden furniture that fills the gift shop. ✉ *RN12, Km 5, Puerto Iguazú* ☎ *3757/423–488* 🌐 *www.aripuca.com.ar* 🎫 *8 pesos* 🕒 *Daily 8:30–6.*

IN BRAZIL

Numbers in the margin correspond to numbers on the Foz do Iguaçu map.

1 **Itaipú Dam and Hydroelectric Power Plant.** It took more than 30,000 workers eight years to build this 8-km (5-mi) dam, voted one of the Seven Wonders of the Modern World by the American Society of Civil Engineers. The monumental structure produces 25% of Brazil's electricity and 78% of Paraguay's, and was the largest hydroelectric power plant on Earth until China's Three Gorges (Yangtze) Dam was completed. You get plenty of insight into how proud this makes the Brazilian government—and some idea of how the dam was built—during the 30-minute video that precedes hour-long guided panoramic bus tours of the complex. Although commentaries are humdrum, the sheer size of the dam is an impressive sight. To see more than a view over the spillways, consider the special tours, which take you inside the cavernous structure and includes a visit to the control room. Night tours—which

include a light-and-sound show—begin at 8 on Friday and Saturday (reserve ahead).

WORD OF MOUTH

"I've been to Niagra Falls and to Victoria Falls (Zambia *and* Zimbabwe sides). Niagra was lovely; Victoria was truly breathtaking... but Cataratas de Iguazu was the best. Both the Argentine and Brazilian sides were spectacular—even more powerful and exciting and gorgeous than the others. Each side has a different quality; each side is awesome." —MarnieWDC

3

❷ At the **Ecomuseu de Itaipú** (Itaipú Eco-Museum) (✉ *Av. Tancredo Neves 6001* 🎫 *R$8* ⏲ *Tues.–Sun 8–5:30*) you can learn about the geology, archaeology, and efforts to preserve the flora and fauna of the area since the dam was built. Note that it's funded by the dam's operator Itaipú Binacional, so information isn't necessarily objective. ✉ *Av. Tancredo Neves 6702* ☎ *800/645–4645* 🌐 *www.itaipu.gov.br* 🎫 *Panoramic tour R$13, special tour R$30* ⏲ *Regular tours daily 8:30–4:30 (hourly on the half hour). Special tours daily 8:30, 9, 10:30, 11* AM, *2, 2:30, 4, 4:30* PM.

❸ Flamingos, parrots, and toucans are some of the more-colorful inhabitants of the privately run **Parque das Aves** (Bird Park). Right outside the Parque Nacional Foz do Iguaçu, it's an interesting complement to a visit to the falls. A winding path leads you through untouched tropical forest and walk-through aviaries containing hundreds of species of birds. Iguanas, alligators, and other nonfeathered friends have their own pens. ✉ *Km 17.1, Rodovia das Cataratas* ☎ *045/3529–8282* 🌐 *www.parquedasaves.com.br* 🎫 *R$22* ⏲ *Daily 8:30–5:30.*

WHERE TO EAT

Booming tourism is kindling the restaurant scenes of Puerto Iguazú and Foz do Iguaçu, and each has enough reasonably priced, reliable choices to get most people through the two or three days they spend there. Neither border town has much of a culinary tradition to speak of, though most restaurants at least advertise some form of the local specialty *surubí* (a kind of catfish), although it's frequently out of stock. Instead, parrillas or churrascarias abound, as do pizza and pasta joints.

PUERTO IGUAZÚ

$$$ SEAFOOD ✕ **Aqva.** Locals are thrilled: finally, a date-night restaurant in Puerto Iguazú (reservations are essential on weekends). Although the high-ceilinged split-level cabin seats too many to be truly intimate, they make up for it with well-spaced tables, discreet service, and low lighting. Softly gleaming timber from different local trees lines the walls, roof, and floor. Local river fish like *surubí* and *dorado* are the specialty: have them panfried, or, more unusually, as pasta fillings. Forget being romantic at dessert time: the chef's signature dessert, fresh mango and pineapple with a *torrontés* sabayon, is definitely worth keeping to yourself. ✉ *Av. Córdoba at Carlos Thays* ☎ *3757/422–064* 💳 *AE, MC, V.*

$$$–$$$$ ARGENTINE ✕ **La Rueda.** This parrilla is so popular with visitors that they start serving dinner as early as 7:30 PM—teatime by Argentine standards. The local beef isn't quite up to Buenos Aires standards, but La Rueda's bife

de chorizo is one of the best in town. Surubí is another house specialty, but skip the traditional Roquefort sauce, which overwhelms the fish's flavor. The surroundings stay true to the restaurant's rustic roots: hefty tree trunks hold up the bamboo-lined roof, and the walls are adorned by a curious wooden frieze carved by a local artist. ✉ *Av. Córdoba 28* ☎ *3757/422–531* ✍ *Reservations essential* ▭ *AE* ⏲ *No lunch Mon.–Tues.*

FOZ DO IGUAÇU

$$$ BRAZILIAN ✕ **Búfalo Branco.** The city's finest and largest churrascaria does a killer *rodizio* (all-you-can-eat meat buffet). The *picanha* stands out from the 25 meat choices, but pork, lamb, chicken, and even—yum—bull testicles find their way onto the metal skewers they use to grill the meat. The salad bar is well stocked, a boon for vegetarians. ✉ *Av. Rebouças 530* ☎ *45/3523–9744* ▭ *AE, DC, MC, V.*

$$$$ SEAFOOD ✕ **Tempero da Bahia.** If you're not going as far as Bahia on your trip, you can at least check out its flavors at this busy tangerine-painted restaurant. It specializes in northeastern fare like *moquecas* (a rich seafood stew made with coconut milk and palm oil); their delicious versions are unusual for mixing prawns with local river fish. Spicy panfried sole and salmon are lighter options. The flavors aren't quite so subtle at the all-out seafood (and river food) buffets they hold several times a week, but at R$36 for all you can eat, they certainly pull in crowds. ✉ *Rua Marechal Deodoro 1228* ☎ *45/3025–1144* ▭ *DC, MC, V* ⏲ *No dinner Sun.*

$$$ SPANISH ✕ **Zaragoza.** On a tree-lined street in a quiet neighborhood, this traditional restaurant's Spanish owner is an expert at matching Iguaçu's fresh river fish to authentic Spanish seafood recipes. Brazilian ingredients sneak into some dishes—the *surubi à Goya* (catfish in a tomato-and-coconut-milk sauce) definitely merits a try. ✉ *Rua Quintino Bocaiúva 882* ☎ *45/3028–8084* ▭ *AE, DC, MC, V.*

WHERE TO STAY

Once you've decided which country to base yourself in, the next big decision is whether to stay in town or at the five-star hotel inside each park. If you're on a lightning one-night visit and you only want to see one side of the falls, the convenience of staying inside the park might offset the otherwise unreasonably high prices for mediocre levels of luxury. Otherwise, you get much better value for money at the establishments in town or on highways BR489 (Rodavia das Cataratas) in Brazil, or RN12 in Argentina. During the day you're a 20-minute bus ride from the falls and the border, and at night you're closer to restaurants and nightlife (buses stop running to the park after 7 or 8; after that, it's a 70-peso taxi ride into town from the park).

Hotels in Argentina are generally cheaper than in Brazil. During low season (late September–early November and February–May, excluding Easter) rooms are often heavily discounted. ⚠ **Staying on the Brazilian side (apart from at the Hotel das Cataratas in the park) is not recommended. It's dangerous, especially after dark, more expensive, and the hotels are worse.**

PUERTO IGUAZÚ

$ **Hostel-Inn Iguazú.** An enormous turquoise pool surrounded by classy wooden loungers and well-kept gardens lets you know this hostel is far from typical. Spacious double rooms with private bathrooms, huge windows, and lots of light attract couples and families. Partying backpackers love the great-value dorm accommodations (but be sure to book one with a/c) and organized weekend bar expeditions. The Hostel-Inn is on the road halfway between Puerto Iguazú and the falls so you can get to the park early, but you're only a short bus or taxi ride from the restaurants and bars in town. You can sort out excursions, including trips to the Brazil side, through the in-house travel agency. The kitchen churns out simple sandwiches, salads, and burgers, and there's an all-out asado several times a week. **Pros:** beautiful pool area; rooms are simple but clean and well designed; location between town and the falls gives you the best of both worlds. **Cons:** impersonal service from indifferent staff; lounge and kitchen are run-down; very basic breakfast. ✉ *Ruta 12, Km 5* ☎ *3757/421–823* 🌐 *www.hostel-inn.com* *52 rooms* *In-room: no phone, Wi-Fi. In-hotel: restaurant, pool, bar, laundry service, public Internet* *No credit cards* *CP.*

$$$$ ★ **Panoramic Hotel Iguazú.** The falls aren't the only good views in Iguazú: half the rooms of this chic hotel look onto the churning, jungle-framed waters of the Iguazú and Paraná rivers. The view inside the rooms is lovely, too. Taupe throws and ocher pillow shams offset the clean lines of the contemporary dark-wood furniture. You don't miss out on luxury by booking a standard, as all have king-size beds and flat-screen TVs. Even the pool, set on a large terrace, looks over the river. The view gets seriously panoramic from the top-floor bar, one of the best sundowner spots in town. **Pros:** river views; great attention to detail in the beautifully designed rooms; the gorgeous pool. **Cons:** the in-house casino can make the lobby noisy; indifferent staff aren't up to the price tag; it's a short taxi ride to the town center and in-house transport is overpriced. ✉ *Paraguay 372* ☎ *3757/498–100* 🌐 *www.panoramic-hoteliguazu.com* *91 rooms* *In-room: safe, Wi-Fi. In-hotel: 2 restaurants, bar, pool, public Internet, no-smoking rooms* *AE, MC, V* *CP.*

$ ★ **Río Tropic.** Friendly owners Rémy and Romina give you a warm welcome at this rootsy B&B, which is surrounded by a lush garden. Rooms open onto a shady veranda that runs all the way along the wooden building; from there it's a couple of more steps to the pool. Pine paneling gives the rooms a country vibe, and though simple, they're spotlessly clean and have firm beds. **Pros:** the wonderfully helpful and attentive owners; peaceful surroundings; abundant homemade breakfasts served on a terrace in the garden. **Cons:** too far from the town center to walk to; low on luxury. ✉ *Montecarlo s/n, at Km 5, RN12* ☎ *3757/15405–577* 🌐 *www.riotropic.com.ar* *10 rooms* *In-room: no phone, no TV, Wi-Fi. In-hotel: bar, pool, bicycles, public Internet* *No credit cards* *CP.*

$$ **Secret Garden Iguazú.** Dense tropical vegetation overhangs the wooden walkway that leads to this tiny guesthouse's three rooms, tucked away in a pale-blue clapboard house. There's nothing fancy about them, but the wood and wicker furniture and brightly painted paneling are

cheerful and welcoming. So is the owner, John Fernandes. He's full of information and advice about Iguazú, which he shares with you over high-octane caipirinhas at the nightly cocktail sessions. **Pros:** wooden deck overlooking the back-to-nature garden; knowledgeable owner John's charm and expert mixology; home-away-from-home vibe. **Cons:** the three rooms book up fast; no pool; comfortable but not luxurious. ✉ *Los Lapachos 623* ☎ *3757/423–099* 🌐 *www.secretgardeniguazu.com* *3 rooms* *In-room: no phone, no TV, Wi-Fi. In-hotel: public Wi-Fi* *No credit cards* *CP.*

$$$$ **Sheraton International Iguazú.** That thundering you can hear in the distance lets you know how close this hotel is to the falls. The lobby opens right onto the park trails and half the rooms have big balconies with fabulous falls views—be sure to reserve one of these well in advance (note that they're about 30% more expensive). The proximity is what you pay for: the rooms are perfectly serviceable, but the dated furniture, worn bathrooms, and drab linens aren't up to the price. And although the spa is a step in the right direction, with a gorgeous hot tub and treatment tents on an outdoor deck, you have to pay extra to use it. You can see the rising mist over the falls from the beautiful swimming pool, which is surrounded by palm trees and jungle. **Pros:** the falls are on your doorstep; great buffet breakfasts; well-designed spa. **Cons:** rooms are in need of a complete makeover; mediocre food and service at dinner; other restaurants are an expensive taxi-ride away. ✉ *Parque Nacional Iguazú, Argentina* ☎ *3757/491–800* 🌐 *www.sheraton.com* *176 rooms, 4 suites* *In-room: safe, Internet. In-hotel: restaurant, room service, bar, pool, gym, spa, tennis courts, laundry service, public Internet, airport shuttle, no-smoking rooms* *AE, MC, V* *CP.*

FOZ DO IGUAÇU

$$$$ ★ **Hotel das Cataratas.** Not only is this stately hotel *in* the national park, with views of the smaller falls from the front-side suites, but it also provides the traditional comforts of a colonial-style establishment: large rooms, terraces, vintage furniture, and hammocks. The main building, surrounded by verandas and gardens, is almost 100 years old and is a National Heritage Site. Although the rooms are comfortable, it's the setting and atmosphere that you pay for, rather than luxury fittings. Still, for many, the chance to wander the paths to the falls before and after the hordes of day visitors arrive is priceless. The hotel is undergoing extensive renovations through 2010: it will remain open, but with fewer rooms. At this writing, the traditional Brazilian Itaipú restaurant is due to re-open, and work is complete on the Ipê grill near the pool, which does an all-you-can-eat barbecue and salad buffet. **Pros:** right inside the park, a short walk from the falls; serious colonial-style charm; friendly, helpful staff. **Cons:** rooms aren't as luxurious as the price promises; far from Foz do Iguaçu so you're limited to the on-site restaurants; only the most-expensive suites have views of the falls. ✉ *Km 28, Rodovia das Cataratas* ☎ *045/2102–7000 or 0800/726–4545* 🌐 *www.hoteldascataratas.com.br* *198 rooms, 5 suites* *In-room: safe, Wi-Fi. In-hotel: restaurant, tennis courts, pool, gym, laundry service, Internet terminal, airport shuttle* *AE, MC, V* *CP.*

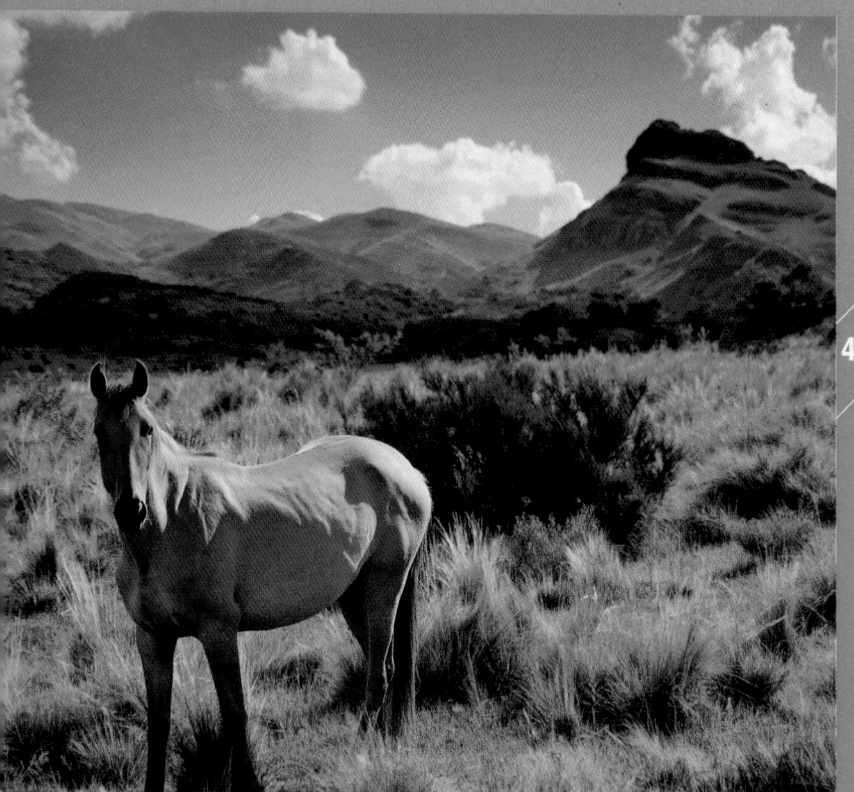

Córdoba and Environs

WORD OF MOUTH

"Cordoba is a vibrant city with a lot of history. The cathedral and Jesuit center around the central plaza highlight the rich colonial history. There's also a lot of music and nightlife. The nearby Sierras are lovely and there are a lot of small, interesting villages such as Alta Gracia (home of Che) to visit."

—alfisol

WELCOME TO CÓRDOBA

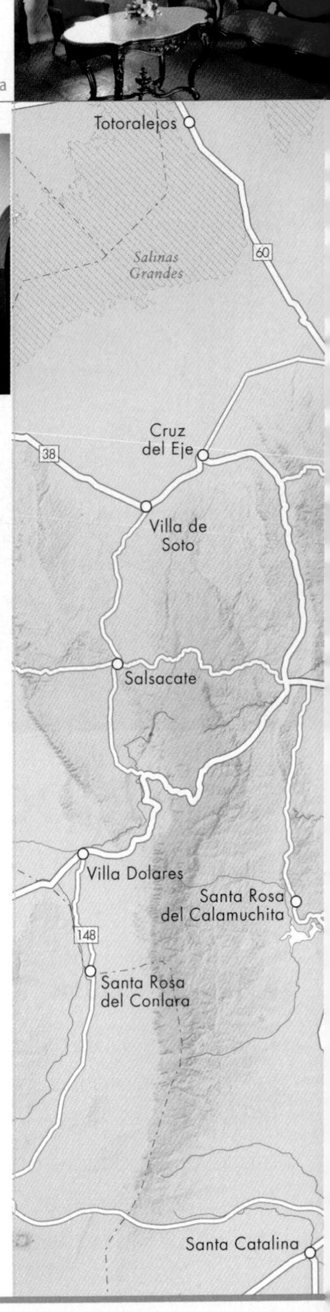

Jesuit Estancia, Alta Gracia

TOP REASONS TO GO

★ **The Second City:** Argentina's second-largest city has a beautifully preserved colonial downtown, great restaurants, a vibrant art scene, and hopping nightlife.

★ **Jesuit Estancias:** Grandiose stone buildings and stark colonial churches, set up by the Jesuits, stretch from the city to the mountains.

★ **Golfing and Gliding:** The region's hills and flats mean golfing and paragliding are huge—the former even more since Córdoban Angel Cabrera won the U.S. Open in 2007.

★ **Rivers and Mountains:** Small hill towns are within a short drive of Córdoba City. Soak in nature on foot, on horseback, or in a 4x4—but don't miss splashing in the region's crystalline rivers and lakes.

★ **The Musical Muse:** Córdoba produces music and musicians that define genres; evidence ranges from the annual folk-music festival in Cosquín down to the lilting *cordobés* accent itself.

National University of Cordoba

1 Córdoba City. Córdoba is known as La Docta (the Learned) for its nearly 400-year-old university, the Universidad Nacional de Córdoba. In true university-town fashion, the whole city's filled with students, parks, and some very innovative architecture.

2 Valle de la Punilla and Sierras Chicas. The big, green rolling landscapes on either side of the Sierras Chicas are lined with pleasant towns to the west and grand estancias to the east; the otherworldly landscape of Ongamira lies to the north.

3 La Valle de Calamuchita and Traslasierra. Follow the winding road toward Mendoza, past another Jesuit estancia and Che Guevara's old home to the quiet lands behind the hills where the rest of the world seems far, far away.

Valle de la Punilla

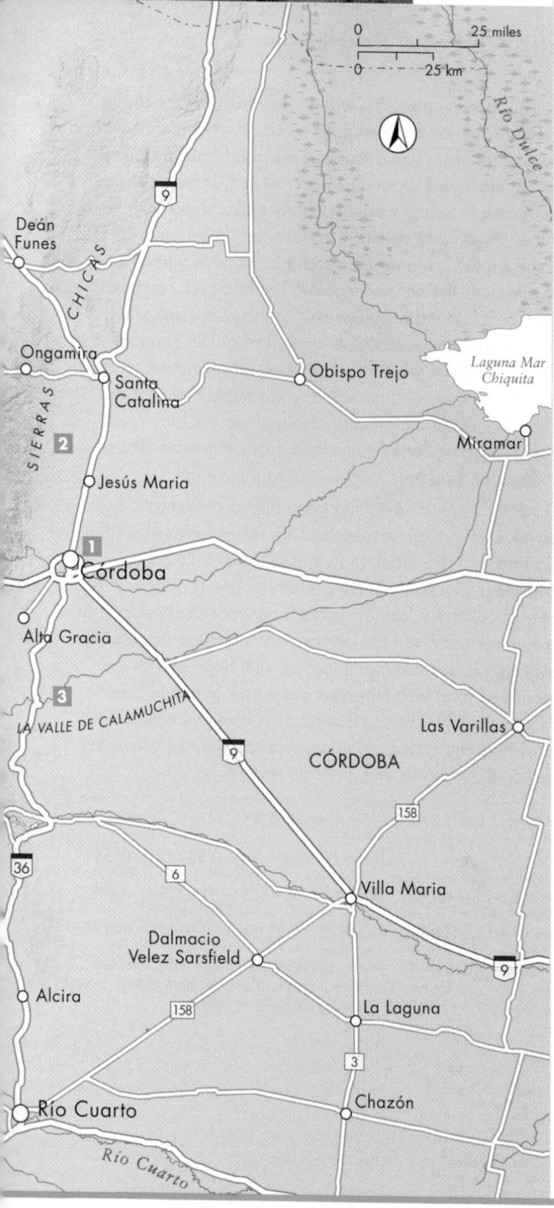

GETTING ORIENTED

Córdoba Province is the geographical center of Argentina, and its eponymous capital, 710 km (441 mi) northwest of Buenos Aires, is a chaotic, cosmopolitan hub filled with students and businesspeople. Unlike *porteños* (citizens of Buenos Aires), however, this city's inhabitants are only a short drive from cooling rivers, hills, and tranquillity; some say it's why people here are so pleasant. Indeed, a meandering drive from the city through the mountain towns is a lovely way to spend a day or two—or an entire summer. Córdoba City is served by daily flights from Buenos Aires as well as lots of long-distance bus companies, many of which have a comfortable *cama* (sleeper) service, or an even more comfortable—and not much more expensive—cama suite service. Within the city, hiring a car isn't necessary (or even advisable, given the chaotic traffic): the center is compact, and official black-and-yellow taxis abound.

CÓRDOBA PLANNER

When to Go

Córdoba is at its best in the spring and autumn, since in summer the sun parches the mountains. Even in summer, though, nights can be chilly in the mountain towns, so pack a warm jacket. Walking boots are also a good idea if you plan to do much hiking. During the summer holidays (January and February), porteños fill the mountain resorts, which means inflated prices and less peace and quiet. Temperatures rarely go below freezing in winter, and the snowcapped sierras are lovely.

Money Matters

There are ATMs all over Córdoba City (identifiable by a sign saying LINK or BANELCO) and in most, but not all, other towns. Although hotels in the towns outside Córdoba may accept U.S. dollars, it's safer to change any currency in the city: Citibank is a good bet. As in the rest of Argentina, banking hours are 10 AM to 3 PM weekdays. Note that neither La Cumbrecita nor Ascochinga has banks.

Emergency Services Ambulance (☎ *107*). **Fire** (☎ *100*). **Police** (☎ *101*).

Eat Well and Rest Easy

Surrounded by pampas, fertile farmland, and the strong Italian influence that pervades much of Argentina, Córdoba has a restaurant scene that stresses good fresh products and pride in one's culinary work; what Córdoba's restaurants lack in trendy innovation they make up for with flavor. When Argentines vacation in Córdoba their friends at home expect just one sample of this flavor in return: a box of *alfajores,* the national cookie. The alfajores *cordobés,* the Córdoban variety, have soft dough and come filled with homemade jam or *dulce de leche* (sort of like caramel) and dipped in a thin white frosting. There are hundreds of local varieties: many vendors will let you sample their goods. Other homemade foods are also high on the list of must-haves: organic honey, jams from every fruit under the sun, cheeses and salamis, and extra-virgin olive oil.

Córdoba's hotels have long been aimed at domestic holidaymakers in high season, and the resort towns like Villa Carlos Paz, Villa General Belgrano, and La Falda are swarming with them. There are other options and they're very good. In the last few years a network of estancias has grown up that might be 19th-century mansions or purpose-built top-class accommodation, all with huge estates to roam and most with their own horses for guests to ride. In the city are efficient and comfortable business hotels, and elsewhere are grand old idiosyncratic buildings converted into boutique hotels with first-rate service.

DINING AND LODGING PRICE CATEGORIES

	¢	$	$$	$$$	$$$$
Restaurants	under $8	$8–$12	$13–$18	$19–$25	over $25
Hotels	under $80	$80–$120	$121–$170	$171–$230	over $230

Restaurant prices are for a main course at dinner, excluding 7.4% tax. Hotel prices are for two people in a standard double room in high season, including 9.4%–11.7% tax but excluding service charges.

Getting Here and Around

Air Travel: The Aeropuerto Internacional Ingeniero Aeronáutico Ambrosio Taravella (phew!) is 13 km (8 mi) north of Córdoba City. Aerolíneas Argentinas (🌐 *www.aerolineas.com.ar*) runs more than 10 daily flights between Buenos Aires and Córdoba; Chilean carrier LAN Airlines (🌐 *www.lan.com*) does three to four daily. The flight takes just over an hour. Take a shuttle or the local bus into town.

Bus Travel: There are dozens of daily buses to Córdoba from Buenos Aires's Retiro bus station. Companies like Chevallier and General Urquiza run *semi-cama* services (standard with reclining seats, air-conditioning, and sometimes videos) as well as *cama* or *ejecutivo* services (sleeper services with fully reclinable seats, refreshments, videos, and shorter journey times). From Córdoba City local bus companies connect you with most mountain towns. Buses leave once or twice an hour from the central bus station, Nueva Estacion Terminal de Omnibus de Córdoba (NETOC). In Córdoba City itself most sights and hotels are within walking distance. This is a relief, as routes in the 24-hour electric trolley-bus system are messy, there are no maps, and drivers are unhelpful. If you do decide to brave the system, buy a *cospel* (token) or *tarjeta magnética* (multi-journey pass) from a *kiosco* (kiosk) before getting on.

Car Travel: Two roads act as the main north–south axis to the north of Córdoba City: running along the province's northeastern side is Ruta Nacional, or RN, 9, which takes you to Ascochinga, as does the winding E53 (also known as RN53), a longer, more scenic route. To the northwest, RN38 passes through the Valle de la Punilla. Ruta Provincial, or RP, 17 crosses the region's north and takes you past Ongamira. Farther south is RN156, which meanders through the mountains between Jesús María and La Cumbre. RP5 is the main access for Alta Gracia and the valley of Calamuchita, south of Córdoba City, and RN20 takes you to the Traslasierra and on towards Mendoza.

Taxi Travel: Taxis are a relatively cheap and convenient way of getting around Córdoba City. Official black-and-yellow cabs are everywhere, and all run on a meter, which includes luggage and all passengers. If you're looking to hire for the day, arrange a chauffeur-driven car; as well as avoiding expensive metered fares, you'll enjoy the driver's experience with popular visitor routes (which is sometimes a problem for local taxi drivers). In smaller towns, *remises* (private fixed-price taxis) do the job. You can call for one or go to an agency. Some remises may do longer trips or stick with you for a whole day; arrange fares in advance.

Tour de Force

With so many activity choices, it's a good idea to consider enlisting a tour company's expertise. Here's a list of some reputable ones to help you navigate everything from walking tours of the city to your first paragliding adventure.

Córdoba's Cabildo Tourist Office (✉ *Cabildo Deán Funes 15, Córdoba* ☎ *351/428–5856*) organizes free walking tours of downtown Córdoba; English-language tours leave at 9:30 AM and 4:30 PM daily (more often in high season).

Latitud Sur (✉ *Fructuoso Rivera 70, Córdoba* ☎ *351/425–6023* 🌐 *www.latitudsurtrek.com.ar*) specializes in adventure tourism, including rock climbing, paragliding, and skydiving. As well as all-inclusive day trips, they organize camping.

Nativo Viajes (✉ *27 de Abril 11, Córdoba* ☎ *351/424–5341* 🌐 *www.Córdobanativoviajes.com.ar* 🎫 *4-hour city tours, 55 pesos; all-day excursions 60 pesos–100 pesos, including transport and meals*) runs city tours and themed day trips with English-speaking guides; they'll arrange vehicle hire, transfers, and accommodations.

Sendas Travel (✉ *Chalet Ruca Malen Calle Dumas 110, La Cumbre* ☎ *3548/1553–2177* 🌐 *www.sendastravel.com*) is run by an English and Argentine couple; vacations include transport and accommodation. They specialize in horseback rides, treks, and tours, and paragliding.

4

JESUIT ESTANCIAS

The Jesuit estancias in and around Córdoba City aren't just atmospheric relics of a bygone era; they're UNESCO-listed monuments and museums that keep alive the region's history as a center of learning and production.

Estancia church, Alta Gracia. Bottom right: Estancia church, Santa Catalina. Top right: Main altar of Jesuit church, Alta Gracia.

In Córdoba, Jesuit estancias went beyond the self-contained centers of agriculture and crafts found elsewhere in Argentina, Paraguay, and Brasil. Beginning with Estancia Caroya's sale in 1661 to the founder of the Collegio Montserrat in the Manzana de Jesuitica, the estancias here became satellite farms, wineries, mule-breeding facilities, and summer boarding houses for the learned elite in town.

Whereas Jesuit missions in other places fell into disrepair when the Jesuits were ordered out of South America in 1767 (due to King Carlos III's nervousness about the Jesuits' increasing control over the culture and economy region), Córdoba's Jesuit estancias have gone on to have second, third, and fouth lives—as bayonet factories, repatriation stopovers, and even private homes.

GETTING AROUND

Rent a car or hire a guide (⇨ *see Essentials under Córdoba*) to explore what some call the Jesuit Trail: north from Cordoba on RA9, west into the hills on RN17, and then south on RA38. This 200 km (100 mi) loop passes the Caroya, Jesus Maria, and Santa Catalina estancias; head west from La Cumbre on a dirt road to get to La Candelaria, and drive a half hour south of the city to get to Alta Gracia.

TOP JESUIT ESTANCIAS

CAROYA

The first estancia built (1616) and one of the first to shift from Jesuit control, Caroya has worn many hats. In 1661, after the Jesuits sold it to Collegio Montserrat, the estancia became a **summer retreat** for students. During Argentina's war for independence, this was a **bayonet factory** (don't miss the display). In the mid-1800s, Italian immigrants lived here; their community blossomed into the town of Colonia Caroya.

JESÚS MARÍA

Just a few miles from Caroya on the edge of the Sierras Chicas is Estancia Jesús María. The Jesuits produced a light table **wine** here, quaffing thirsts as far-flung as the King of Spain's. Head to on-site Museo Jesuitico Nacional to learn about their methods and have a taste.

SANTA CATALINA

Gleaming white bell towers set against dramatic trees are impressive, but the real feat was what the Jesuits built underground. In 1622, Jesuits began a **subterranean irrigation system** that brought water from the hills in Ongamira to the cattle, sheep, and mills here; it's still a farming center.

ALTA GRACIA

The Jesuits turned a donation of land south of Córdoba into the nucleus of a small city. They bred mules for transporting goods to Alto Peru, and built **Tajamar, a lake** kept full by dams. After the Jesuits, former Viceroy of the River Plate Santiago de Liniers lived here. The **Casa del Virrey Liniers** museum runs frequent concerts in this atmospheric setting.

LA CANDELARIA

La Candelaria is a cross between a spiritual retreat and protected stronghold with only two small doorways and few windows. They reared cattle and mules—and provided safe haven from attacks from native Argentines. The original locals and the Jesuits are long gone, but the **haunting solitude** remains the same.

TIMING

Hours of operation. Opening dates and hours are liable to change, and estancias generally close for lunch and a siesta. Santa Catalina is still owned by the same family that took it over in 1767; full access to the estancia is dependent on whether they are at home or not.

Day Tripping. It's possible to see all of the estancias mentioned here in a single day. Jesús María and Caroya are in the same urban zone, and Santa Catalina is a further 20km drive away along scenic minor roads; head here if you have only half a day. La Candelaria is located on a dirt road roughly 70 k (45 mi) from the town of Jesús María (where three estancias are clustered), and can take longer to get to than expected if it's been raining.

Overnight. For an extended journey into estancia country and a more leisurely time covering the Jesuit Trail, consider staying overnight at (non-Jesuit) uber-luxurious Estancia La Paz in the town of Jesús María.

4

Updated by
Andy Footner

Although the rest of the country seems designed to take your breath away, Córdoba's the place to come to get it back. The region, roughly the size of the state of Florida, has long attracted visitors with the purported health effects of its cool, uplifting breezes, but now visitors from all over Argentina vacation here year after year to simply enjoy the peace of the natural surroundings with family and friends.

For the visitor from abroad, the unassuming natural charms of Córdoba face stiff competition from the waterfalls, glaciers, deserts, and jagged peaks found elsewhere in Argentina, but there are an increasing number of reasons to make Córdoba part of a wider itinerary through the country. And while avoiding frequently delay-ridden air travel in Argentina isn't the main reason to come here, it's admittedly a great excuse to fit Córdoba in—Córdoba City is an easy 10 or so comfortable hours via overnight bus journey from Buenos Aires, and well placed for connections to Mendoza and the Northwest.

Some would argue that the main reason to come might be not the natural landscape at all but instead Córdoba's historic and intellectual landscape. A slew of Jesuit estancias, added to the UNESCO World Heritage List in 2000, were first set up nearly 400 years ago to protect and support, among other things, the Jesuits' newly formed institution of higher learning, known today as the Universidad Nacional de Córdoba (UNC). It's recognized as the first degree-granting institution in Argentina, and was one of the first in South America. Córdoba is a real university town, filled with lots of art, music, lectures, and other cultural pursuits. Love of life and learning isn't the only thing that unifies the people, though; many buildings in the city center are linked via a network of underground tunnels.

The natural backdrop found just outside the city may lack the drama found elsewhere in Argentina, but for a more meditative type of sightseeing, it has much to offer. Most of what you'll want is held between the two low chains of mountains running north–south, known as the

Sierras Grandes and Sierras Chicas. North of the city you'll find historic Jesuit estancias galore, hiking paths, otherworldly burnt-red rock faces (near which many have experienced UFO sightings), and some of the best places in the world to paraglide. South of the city the atmosphere's even mellower, with crystal-clear mountain streams, swimming holes, lakes, gentle rambling opportunities, hilltop views, and fields that go on forever.

As for where to lay your head at night, there are few places in the world that can rival the setup, and the price, of Córdoba's estancias.

CÓRDOBA CITY

Stone buildings dating from the 17th and 18th centuries line the cobbled streets around shady Plaza San Martín in Córdoba's compact Centro Histórico, which has the highest concentration of colonial buildings in Argentina. The city's history stretches back to 1573, when Geronimo Luís de Cabrera first set foot here. His family was from Córdoba, Spain, and he named the town accordingly. Both north–south and east–west streets change names at the *cabildo* (town hall) on Plaza San Martín.

The tolling bells and cross-topped towers of downtown's 10 churches are evidence of the role the Jesuits played here. This was the center of their missionary work, from their arrival in 1599 until their expulsion from Argentina in 1767. Other architectural reminders of their presence abound, most notably at the Manzana Jesuítica (Jesuit Block), a block-long conglomeration of 17th-century buildings that has been declared a UNESCO World Heritage Site. For more than two centuries the city was Argentina's cultural and intellectual hub. Its national university, established in 1613, earned the city its nickname—La Docta, or the Learned. Today this provincial capital is the country's second-largest city (population 1.3 million).

The epicenter of Córdoba's emerging restaurant scene is the Nueva Córdoba neighborhood, a few blocks south of the center. Avenida Hipólito Yrigoyen is its main thoroughfare. Southeast of the center, on the other side of Avenida Poeta Lugones, is the Parque Sarmiento, home to the zoo and fine arts museum.

GETTING HERE AND AROUND

For suggestions on how to get here, see Getting Here and Around in the Córdoba Planner at the beginning of the chapter; most transit to the region stops in Córdoba City.

Once you get to the city, the best way to enjoy Córdoba's colonial architecture and slower pace of life is on foot: most places of interest are within easy walking distance of Plaza San Martín. The bus system is complicated and drivers are unhelpful, but there are plenty of taxis. These are also the best option at night, especially along La Cañada, which can get a bit lonely.

ESSENTIALS

Bank Citibank (✉ *Rivadavía 104*).

Bus Contacts **Bus Terminal** (✉ *Bul. Perón 380* ☎ *351/433–1982*). **Minibus Terminal** (✉ *Mercado Sud Bul. Illia 155* ☎ *351/425–2854*). **Ciudad de Córdoba** (☎ *351/424–0048 in Córdoba*). **General Urquiza** (☎ *11/4000–5222 in Buenos Aires; 351/421–0711 in Córdoba*). **Nueva Chevallier** (☎ *11/4000–5200 in Buenos Aires; 351/422–0936 in Córdoba*). **Pájaro Blanco** (☎ *351/425–2854 in Córdoba*). **Sarmiento** (☎ *351/433–2161 in Córdoba*). **Sierras de Calamuchita** (☎ *351/422–6080 in Córdoba*).

Medial Assistance **Hospital Privado de Córdoba** (✉ *Av. Chacabuco 4545* ☎ *223/499–0000*).

Post Office (✉ *Colón 210*).

Rental Cars **Budget Rentacar** (✉ *San Jeronimo 131/5* ☎ *351/421–1240* 🌐 *www.budgetargentina.com*).

Taxi **Transmitaxis** (✉ *Mariano Fragueiro 340* ☎ *351/470–0000*).

Visitor Info **Centro de Información Turistica** (✉ *Cabildo Deán Funes 15* ☎ *351/428–5856* ✉ *Cabildo, Independencia 30* ☎ *351/434–1200* ✉ *Airport* ☎ *351/434–8390* ✉ *Bus terminal, ground floor* ☎ *351/433–1982*).

EXPLORING

TOP ATTRACTIONS

3 ★ **Plaza San Martín.** The square has always been the heart of Córdoba; it's crossed by diagonal walkways, which from dawn to dusk are filled with busy-looking office workers and residents out for a more casual stroll. Of the many native trees shading it, the most spectacular are the bulging, thorn-covered *palo borracho* (literally, "drunken stick") and the jacarandas, which blaze with violet blossoms in spring. In the middle of the square an exuberant equestrian statue of General San Martín faces west, toward Pasaje Santa Catalina between the cathedral and the old city hall. ✉ *Rosario de Santa Fe at Independencia.*

2 **Catedral de Córdoba** (✉ *Calle Independencia 64, at Plaza San Martín* ⏲ *Daily 8–noon and 4:30–8*). Córdoban poet Luís Roberto Altamira called the Catedral de Córdoba, on the west side of Plaza San Martín, a "stone flower in the heart of the homeland." Construction began in 1577, though it wasn't until 1784 that the church was completed—which explains its disparate styles. Note the angelic musicians on the baroque front towers. They were sculpted by indigenous peoples in 1776, and they bear the faces of their sculptors.

7 Fodor's Choice ★ **La Manzana Jesuítica** *(The Jesuit Block)*. La Manzana Jesuítica is the city block whose four main buildings—the Catedral de Córdoba (see review), the Universidad Nacional de Córdoba, the Colegio Montserrat, and the Templo de la Compañía de Jesús—form the major sights of any visit here, even if you're not hugely into Córdoba's history. A decade after the foundation of Córdoba this city block was given to the Society of Jesus, testament to the order's political and social clout in the Americas at the time. From here the Jesuits held sway over the religious, educational, and cultural activities of the city and surrounding lands. Their church, the **Templo de la Compañía de Jesús** (*Temple of the*

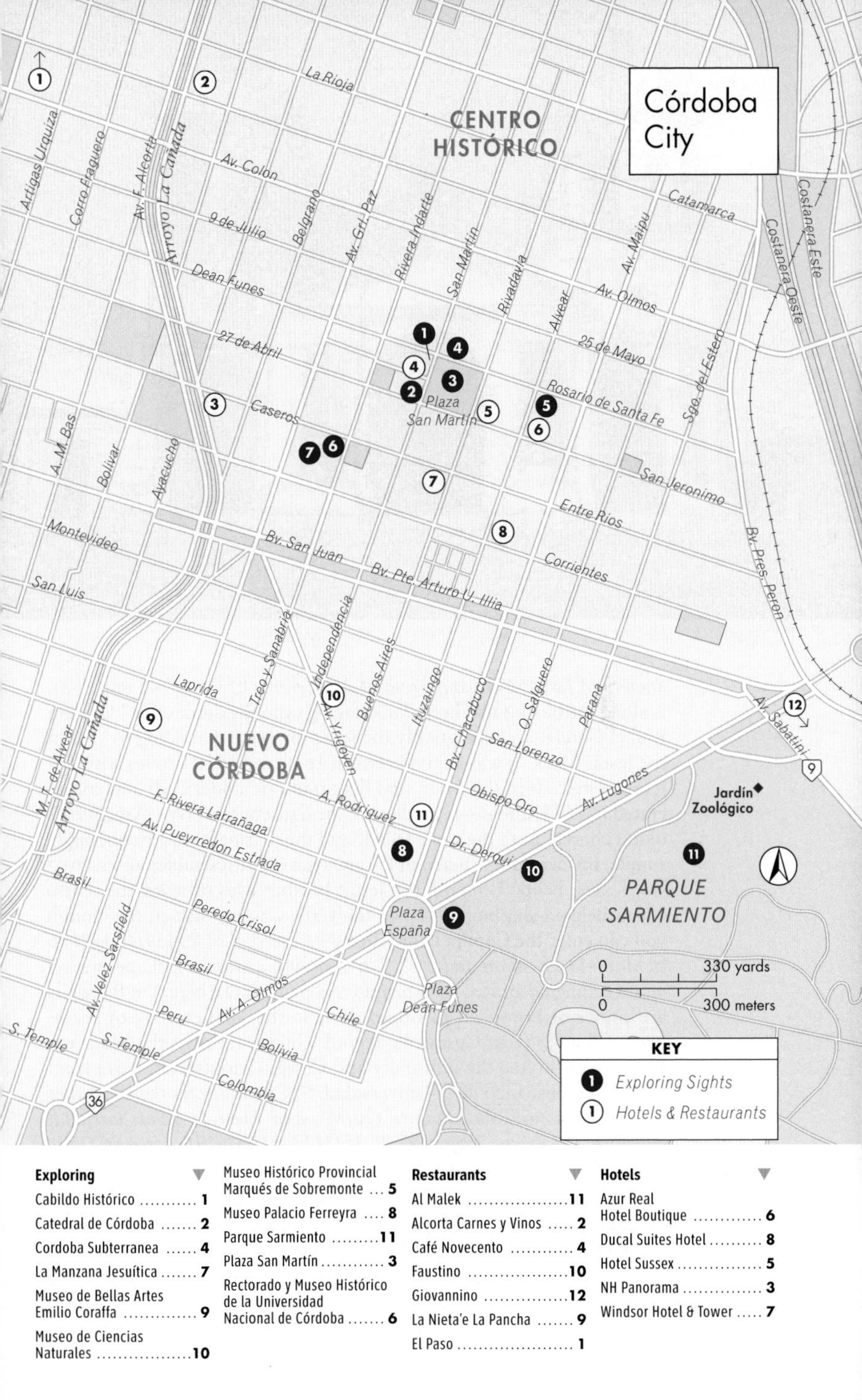

Exploring

Cabildo Histórico 1
Catedral de Córdoba 2
Cordoba Subterranea 4
La Manzana Jesuítica 7
Museo de Bellas Artes Emilio Coraffa 9
Museo de Ciencias Naturales 10
Museo Histórico Provincial Marqués de Sobremonte ... 5
Museo Palacio Ferreyra 8
Parque Sarmiento 11
Plaza San Martín 3
Rectorado y Museo Histórico de la Universidad Nacional de Córdoba 6

Restaurants

Al Malek 11
Alcorta Carnes y Vinos 2
Café Novecento 4
Faustino 10
Giovannino 12
La Nieta'e La Pancha 9
El Paso 1

Hotels

Azur Real Hotel Boutique 6
Ducal Suites Hotel 8
Hotel Sussex 5
NH Panorama 3
Windsor Hotel & Tower 7

The Catedral de Córdoba is the ornate focal point of the city's Plaza San Martín.

Society of Jesus ⊠ *Obispo Trejo at Av. Caseros* ⏲ *Daily 7–1 and 5–8*), is along the block's northern flank, facing onto the diminutive Plazoleta Rafael García, and is arguably the most impressive building to visit in the Jesuit Block. It was begun between 1640 and 1650 (stones with different dates adorn the front, and historians are undecided) and consecrated in 1671, and is—regardless of the date controversy—Argentina's oldest church. Both the stone facade and the soaring nave are soberingly simple. Inside, a dome made of Paraguayan cedar resembles an inverted ship's keel: Felipe Lemaire, the Jesuit brother who oversaw the work, was a Belgian shipbuilder. From the Calle Caseros side of the church you can enter the **Capilla Doméstica** (⊠ *Caseros 121* ☎ *351/423–9196* ⏲ *Mon.–Fri. 8–noon and 5–9, Sat. 8–noon*), a stunning chapel with a wood ceiling decorated with primitively painted rawhide. On the walls are copies of European paintings done in the 17th century by members of the Peruvian Cusqueña School. Guided tours of the Manzana Jesuítica, including the university and Colegio Montserrat, leave from the Museo Histórico de la Universidad. ⊠ *City block flanked by calles Casero, Obispo Trejo, Duarte Quirós, and Avenida Vélez Sarsfield, entrance at Obispo Trejo 242* ☎ *351/423–9196* 🎫 *10 pesos* ⏲ *Daily 9–1 and 4–8; guided tours at 10, 11, 5, and 6.*

4 ★ **Córdoba Subterranea** *(Underground Córdoba)*. This fascinating series of spooky subterranean constructions includes old jail cells and dates from 1588. You can visit only on guided tours, which leave at 9:30 Tuesday–Friday from the Obispo Mercadillo in the main plaza and take a couple of hours. ⊠ *Rosario de Santa Fe 39* ☎ *351/428–5600* 🌐 *guiasdeCórdoba.spaces.live.com* 🎫 *50 pesos* ⏲ *Mon.–Fri. 9–6.*

8 **Museo Palacio Ferreyra.** Hung with mostly Córdoban artists, this huge museum is a good place to see how the city is bringing its architectural history into the 21st century. The monumental old building has been largely redone inside, including the addition of a cowhide-covered staircase and some shiny new elevators. The vast hall with its original grand stairs, though, remains the museum's architectural centerpiece. The pictures run from classical to contemporary, with a large modernist section and even a couple of Pablo Picasso's graphic cartoons. Guided tours in English are available. ✉ *Hipólito Yrigoyen 511* ☎ *351/434–3629* 🎫 *3 pesos (Wed. free)* ⏲ *Tues.–Sun. 10–8.*

WORD OF MOUTH

"Driving in the city is a bit of a nightmare, but a car and driver or a rental will greatly add to your experience if you are moving around outside the city."

—Huentetu

11 **Parque Sarmiento.** In Nuevo Córdoba, the southern part of the city center, is the splendid Parque Sarmiento. It was designed by French landscape architect Charles Thays, and has a zoo, a lake skirted by palms and cypress where you can rent rowboats, an outdoor swimming complex, an amusement park, vast landscaped zones, wide lawns, and cafés. ✉ *Av. Poeta Lugones at Av. Amado Sabattini (R9 Sur).*

9 **Museo de Bellas Artes Emilio Caraffa.** On Parque Sarmiento's western corner, opposite Plaza España, is the city's leading visual-art space, the Museo de Bellas Artes Emilio Caraffa. The austere 1916 neoclassical facade has recently been boldly and blockily reworked to better suit the simple white-painted rooms, where you'll find a spry collection of 19th- and 20th-century paintings, engravings, and sculpture. Most of the artists represented are Argentine—including Córdobans Genaro Páez, Emilio Caraffa, and Fernando Fader. ✉ *Av. Hipólito Yrigoyen 651* ☎ *351/433–3412* 🎫 *Free* ⏲ *Tues.–Sun. 11–7.*

WORTH NOTING

1 **Cabildo Histórico.** Next to the cathedral on Plaza San Martín's western side, the Cabildo Histórico now houses municipal offices and holds occasional cultural events. Construction of the long, two-story, arcaded structure began in 1588 (excavated cells—including what was probably a prison—date from as early as the 17th century), but wasn't completed until the late 18th century; the facade dates from this time. For more than 300 years wealthy residents gathered here to discuss town affairs. The upstairs Salón Rojo (Red Salon) is still used for official receptions. The main floor houses an exhibition space, a café, a library, a tourist office, and a bookshop with literature about the city. In the summer, tango dances are held in the Patio de Tango late on Friday nights. A plaque in the Pasaje Santa Catalina alludes to a darker time in the building's history. It reads, THE CABILDO FUNCTIONED, BEGINNING IN 1976 DURING THE MILITARY DICTATORSHIP, AS A CLANDESTINE CENTER OF DETENTION, TORTURE, AND DEATH. ✉ *Calle Independencia at Plaza San Martín* ☎ *351/428–5600* 🎫 *Free* ⏲ *Daily 9–8.*

6 **Rectorado y Museo Histórico de la Universidad Nacional de Córdoba.** This two-story building's cream-colored facade features prominently on the

east side of the Jesuit Block; it's the formal administrative center of a sprawling campus whose educational standards rivaled those of any European university in its heyday. Early graduates of Latin America's second-oldest university became the doctors and lawyers who ran the fledging nation; some are even Catholic saints. Inside is a Jesuit library that includes such rarities as a 1645 Bible written in seven languages, as well as a spectacular collection of maps, religious works, and historical documents such as the first draft of the Argentine Civil Code. The interior patio contains a statue of Fray Fernando Trejo, who donated the money to build the university for Jesuit education in 1613. The museum and the Colegio Nacional de Nuestra Señora de Montserrat next door, a high school dating from 1687, are visitable by tour only: one-hour tours are 8 pesos and given daily in English at 11 AM and 6 PM (tours in Spanish are at 10 AM and 5 PM). ✉ *Obispo Trejo 242, between Av. Caseros and Av. Duarte Quirós* ☎ *351/433–2075* 🎫 *Free* ⏲ *Tues.–Sun. 9–1 and 4–8.*

10 **Museo de Ciencias Naturales.** This bright and airy natural-history museum is the newest of Córdoba's museums, where you'll find exhibits that feature objects from as far back as prehistoric times. It's mostly aimed at school children, but gives a good, quick overview of the flora, fauna, and minerals of the Sierras. ✉ *Av. Poeta Lugones 395* ☎ *351/434–4070* 🎫 *2 pesos* ⏲ *Mon.–Fri. 9–6, Sat., Sun. 11–7.*

5 ★ **Museo Histórico Provincial Marqués de Sobremonte.** The former home of the Marquis de Sobremonte, a Córdoban governor of the late 18th century, is a block east of Plaza San Martín. This is Córdoba's oldest private residence, and one of the country's best examples of colonial architecture. Five courtyards, a chapel, and 26 rooms are distributed over two floors; the rooms are furnished with period pieces, costumes, old photographs, and oil paintings of the Cusqueña School, a 17th- to 18th-century movement of artists based in Cuzco, Peru. Their baroque-style paintings are usually heavily gilded, and depict religious figures, often with indigenous features. A tour of the home's labyrinthine corridors can lead your imagination back in time. ✉ *Rosario de Santa Fé 218, at Ituzaingó* ☎ *351/433–1661* 🎫 *3 pesos* ⏲ *Tues.–Fri. 10–3, Sat. 9–2.*

WHERE TO EAT

$ MIDDLE EASTERN ✕ **Al Malek.** For a change from steak and pasta, Lebanese chef Tony Raphael serves up Middle Eastern dishes in a new location in Barrio General Paz. It's stylish and almost always busy, with most customers opting for the *picada árabe*—hummus, eggplant, tabouleh, empanadas, and stuffed grape leaves. Spice lovers should know that most dishes are prepared milder than usual to suit local taste, so don't be afraid to ask for condiments. ✉ *Lima 865* ☎ *351/425–6363* ▭ *No credit cards* ⏲ *No lunch Mon. No dinner Sun.*

$$$$ ARGENTINE ✕ **Alcorta Carnes y Vinos.** Alcorta is a great choice for a long, indulgent, and impeccable meal. The meat, including the *bife de chorizo* (sirloin), is simply excellent. The voluminous wine list has offerings from all over the country, including some hard-to-find reds. The service is attentive and deferential without ever seeming in the way. The wide-open,

Satisfy your hunger and your sweet tooth at once: Córdoban empanadas often contain ingredients like sugar and raisins.

airy interior is modern, elegant, and refined, spoiled only slightly by rather insipid piped music and unnecessary advertising. ✉ *Alcorta 330 at Cañada and Santa Rosa* ☎ *351/424–7916* 🌐 *www.alcortacarnes.com.ar* 💳 *AE, DC, MC, V.*

$$$ ARGENTINE ✕ **Café Novecento.** Owned by a Córdoban restaurateur who already had thriving restaurants in Buenos Aires and New York City's SoHo, but couldn't resist taking advantage of a calm courtyard in the Cabildo, this place couldn't be more hip or more central. The menu stays close to what Argentines do best—meat and pasta—but the chef takes obvious pleasure in throwing in a few Asian twists and adventurous salads. Lunch here makes a good stop on any sightseeing itinerary. ✉ *Cabildo, Deán Funes 33* ☎ *351/423–0660* 🌐 *www.bistronovecento.com* 💳 *No credit cards* 🕑 *Lunch only.*

$$$ ARGENTINE ✕ **El Paso.** It's an upscale place that does fantastic *parrilla* (Argentine barbecue) fare—and, yes, in endless quantities. The owner runs the show, ensuring friendly service despite the hordes of demanding Córdoba trendies. The 49-peso fixed-price menu includes as much sizzling beef as you can eat, as well as cabrito, salads, grilled vegetables, and even an empanada as a starter. The restaurant is northwest of downtown in the nightclub-laden Argüello district, but don't be put off: it's only a 10-minute taxi ride. ✉ *Av. Rafael Núñez 5652, Argüello* ☎ *354/342–0394* 💳 *No credit cards.*

$$$$ ARGENTINE ✕ **Faustino.** At first sight the Paseo del Buen Pastor, a remodeled former women's prison in the heart of Nueva Córdoba, seems like a shopping or cultural center, but the main focus turns out to be food. The new branch of Faustino, an upmarket *parillada* (barbecue) already established in Parque Sarmiento, is the best place to enjoy this new space,

with its clever architecture and extensive wine list from boutique bodegas. ✉ *Paseo del Buen Pastor, Av. Hipólito Yrigoyen 349* ☎ *351/598–2034* 🌐 *www.faustinoparrilla.com* 💳 *No credit cards.*

$$$ ITALIAN ✕ **Giovannino.** Unusual pasta dishes and divinely crisp wood-oven pizzas take this trattoria beyond most Argentine-Italian restaurants. Beef comes as mini-steaks in a creamy cress sauce. The *spaghettini con frutti de mare* (angel-hair pasta with shrimp, mussels, and salmon) or *cappelletti al forno* (pork-and-ricotta-filled pasta in a Parma ham sauce) are also good. Light from the huge plate-glass windows floods the spacious, open-plan dining room at lunchtime, when the three-course prix-fixe menu attracts visitors and businesspeople alike. ✉ *Av. Sabatini 2050* ☎ *351/455–5659* 🌐 *www.giovannino.com.ar* 💳 *AE, DC, MC, V.*

$$$ ARGENTINE ★ ✕ **La Nieta'e La Pancha.** You won't be disappointed by anything on the menu, written in the Córdoban dialect rather than straight Spanish, at this maverick restaurant that's fast becoming a Córdoban institution. Local specialties done with flair include *cabrito* (roast kid) in cream sauce, peppers, and sweet potatoes or *matambre* (roast pork) served with a "tower" of eggplant, onions, and cheese. Most memorable is the river trout, from the nearby Río Ceballos, with sautéed peppers and carrots in olive oil. The warm, rustic decor, soothing live guitar music, and the friendly owners all make for a perfect atmosphere. ✉ *Belgrano 783* ☎ *351/468–1920* 💳 *No credit cards* ⏲ *Dinner only.*

WHERE TO STAY

$ 🏨 **Azur Real Hotel Boutique.** The only question is how Córdoba managed to last so long without a boutique hotel, but the Azur, opened in late 2009, instantly made up for the omission. The furnishings come from Buenos Aires and Santiago del Estero—both ends of Argentina's sophistication spectrum—and a Córdoban architect has worked wonders with the building (which was once the university residence for Che Guevara). A fine restaurant ($$$) open to the public continues the fusion theme with chefs from Peru and Singapore, and the stylish terrace, with a tiny splash pool, attracts a cool crowd for after-office drinks. **Pros:** very central location, free slippers, attentive bilingual service. **Cons:** inward-facing windows. ✉ *San Jerónimo 243* ☎ *351/424–7133* 🌐 *www.azurrealhotel.com* *14 rooms* *In-room: safe, refrigerator, Wi-Fi. In-hotel: restaurant, room service, bar, pool, gym, laundry service, parking (free), no-smoking rooms* 💳 *AE, MC, V* 🍽 *BP.*

$$$$ 🏨 **Ducal Suites Hotel.** All basic but tasteful rooms at the Ducal include a kitchenette and small lounge area. Extras, like a lobby Internet connection, are appreciated. The location is also a pull: Plaza San Martín and the Manzana Jesuítica are just three blocks away. **Pros:** location; cook up a kitchenette-size storm in your pajamas. **Cons:** decor a little basic considering the price. ✉ *Corrientes 207* ☎ *351/570–8888* 🌐 *www.hotelducal.com.ar* *82 suites* *In-room: safe, kitchen. In-hotel: restaurant, room service, bar, pool, gym, laundry service, parking (free)* 💳 *AE, DC, MC, V* 🍽 *CP.*

$ 🏨 **Hotel Sussex.** The best rooms look over Plaza San Martín, the Cathedral, and the Cabildo, which has been the Sussex's big draw for nearly half a century. But the Hotel Sussex offers more than just its location and the views; rooms, though small, are functional and well equipped, and the staff are polite and helpful. They could probably do with a bar to join the grand piano in the retro lobby, but they're so central that guests can just as easily go out. **Pros:** location. **Cons:** small rooms, many rooms without views. ✉ *San Jeronimo 125* ☎ *351/421–8563* 🌐 *www.hotelsussexcba.com.ar* *110 rooms* *In-room: refrigerator, Wi-Fi. In-hotel: room service, laundry service, parking (free)* ▭ *AE, DC, MC, V* 🍽 *CP.*

$$$$ ★ **NH Panorama.** The beds are huge and so are the breakfasts at NH Panorama, which has world-class rooms at very local prices. Although all that bed acreage doesn't leave space for much else, the gleaming parquet, rich cotton sheets, and eminently covetable bathrobes more than make up for it. Another winning detail is the early-risers' breakfast, which comes in handy if you're doing day trips out of town. There are fabulous views of the Centro Histórico from the rooftop pool, hence the hotel's name. The hotel's restaurant, Tipuana ($$$), is in a glass-domed space between the two towers that house the rooms; go for the classic Córdoban dish *cabrito* (also *chivito*; roast goat) if you stay in for dinner. **Pros:** friendly, thoughtful service; good views. **Cons:** some rooms feel slightly cramped due to huge beds. ✉ *Marcelo T. de Alvear 251* ☎ *351/410–3900* 🌐 *www.nh-hotels.com* *138 rooms, 3 suites* *In-room: safe, refrigerator, Wi-Fi. In-hotel: restaurant, room service, pool, gym, spa, laundry service, parking (free)* ▭ *AE, DC, MC, V* 🍽 *BP.*

$$$$ **Windsor Hotel & Tower.** A central, comfortable, and solid option from the Windsor chain with a range of different rooms, suites, and prices. The pianist tinkling away in the lobby sets the tone, and it remains classic up to the gym, swimming pool, and *quincho* (barbecue area) on the rooftop terrace, where things relax a bit. Breakfast is served buffet-style. **Pros:** central location; well maintained; sauna; gym has a personal trainer. **Cons:** tiny swimming pool. ✉ *Buenos Aires 214* ☎ *351/422–4012* 🌐 *www.windsortower.com* *85 rooms* *In-room: refrigerator, DVD (some). In-hotel: pool, gym, laundry service, parking (free)* ▭ *AE, MC, V* 🍽 *CP.*

AFTER DARK

Córdoba is an around-the-clock city. For low-key nights on the town there are traditional *confiterías* (cafés) on practically every downtown street corner. Many stay open well into the wee hours, and serve alcoholic drinks, coffee, and sandwiches. The trendier hub for bars, cafés, and live-music venues is the Nueva Córdoba district, to the south of Boulevard San Juan/Illia, just a few blocks from the center.

The city is known for nightclubs where the action doesn't get going until 2 or 3 AM and continues well past dawn. Electronic music is big here, and international DJs play frequently, as do touring rock bands. The most popular drink in the province is *Fernet con coca,* also known as a "Fernando," a mixture of the sticky Italian apéritif Fernet Branca with Coca-Cola. The resulting witches' brew has brown froth and is sold by the bucket-sized glass. Most of the hot spots are north of the center, in the exclusive Chateau Carreras and Cerro de las Rosas neighborhoods or slightly lower-key Villa Belgrano and El Abasto. Córdoban nightclubs are in the habit of changing their names and locations regularly, but there'll always be a huge cluster of them in the park in Chateau Carreras around the intersection of Avenues Piamonte and Cárcano. Any barman in Cerro de las Rosas should be able to guide you to which one's best. Travel by taxi.

BARS

Galileo (✉ *Gauss 5700, Villa Belgrano* ☎ *354/344–4090*) is the artsy café of choice with theatrical events on weekends and other events during the week. Rub shoulders with young trendies and well-to-do intellectuals who come here as much for the drinks and sublime cakes as for the live music.

Mandarina (✉ *Obispo Trejo 171* ☎ *351/426–4909*) is actually a restaurant—you can watch the meals being made in the open-plan kitchen—but the live music, cultural goings-on, and tables in the pedestrian street outside make it seem more like a café-bar. It's laid-back, with simple rustic furniture. It's also open for breakfasts, including a long, late brunch on Sundays. **Villa Agur** (✉ *Tristán Malbrán 4355, at José Roque Funes, Cerro las Rosas* ☎ *351/481–7520*) is an ultracool bar in a happening part of town with low leather sofas and frequent live music shows. It also has a small restaurant and an open-air terrace.

DINNER SHOW

El Arrabal (✉ *Belgrano 899* ☎ *351/460–2990* 🌐 *www.elarrabal.com.ar*) is a restaurant and café with *milongas* (tango dancing) every evening from 10:30 PM and tango shows at midnight Thursday–Saturday. The cost is 79 pesos to watch the shows, including a fixed menu, or 18 pesos to join in the milongas on the other nights of the week (or if you're eating, not dancing, you pay just for food). Reservations are a must for the shows.

SHOPPING

Córdoba's main shopping area is the pedestrian-only street San Martín, which runs north from Plaza San Martín. Stores are shaded by awnings and bougainvillea, which provide a welcome relief from the sun in the summer. The street is particularly strong on surf and mountain wear, testament to the outdoors offerings just outside town. Three blocks southwest of here is the Patio Olmos mall, chock-full of fashions, food courts, and cinemas. For souvenirs, the staples are cookies and leather, though there are also two parallel streets that turn into antiques and crafts markets on weekends.

ALFAJORES

Perhaps the most famous alfajores in town are made by **Chammas** (✉ *Rivadavía 77* ☎ *351/426–5693*), a long-running establishment whose cookies go by the dozen.

LEATHER

One of the few shops among the restaurants, galleries, and open spaces of the Paseo del Buen Pastor is the high-quality leather shop **A'Gustino Cueros** (✉ *Paseo del Buen Pastor Av. Hipólito Yrigoyen 325, 1st fl.*

☎ *351/422–2003* 🌐 *www.agustinocueros.com.ar*), with all manner of accessories and a big choice of jackets.

ANTIQUES AND CRAFTS

A small collection of stalls selling genuine antiques and plain old stuff form the **Feria de Antigüedades** (✉ *Pasaje Revol at Belgrano* ☎ *No phone* ⏲ *Fri.–Sun. 6* PM*–11* PM). There doesn't seem to be any rule governing prices here, so shop around. Late on weekend afternoons, stalls fill a winding cobbled space near La Cañada to create the **Feria Paseo de las Artes** (✉ *Achával Rodríguez at La Cañada* ☎ *No phone* ⏲ *Fri.–Sun. 5* PM*–11* PM), the city's best crafts market. Bargaining isn't common practice, though you can expect a small discount if you buy in quantity.

MALLS

Posh **Patio Olmos** (✉ *Av. San Juan at Bul. Vélez Sarsfield* ☎ *351/570–4100* 🌐 *www.patioolmos.com*) is behind a sweeping stone facade that once belonged to an exclusive school. The mall is in the middle of downtown, and has a cinema multiplex and mostly Argentine-brand shops.

4

VALLE DE LA PUNILLA AND SIERRAS CHICAS

The highway from Córdoba City to the Jesuit country around the town of Ascochinga passes so many centuries-old estancias that it's been dubbed El Camino de la Historia (The History Trail). Farther afield, another 100 km (62 mi) north of Ascochinga is Cerro Colorado and its pre-Hispanic petroglyphs.

Northwest of the city is the Valle de Punilla with its many villages. In high season the southernmost places in this valley—Villa Carlos Paz, Cosquín, and La Falda—are flooded by vacationing porteños. A little farther north are less hectic La Cumbre and Capilla del Monte. Here rolling hills are interspersed with strange formations of rich red sandstone at the Cerro Uritorco and Parque Natural Ongamira. The weird and wonderful shapes make it easy to see why this is Argentina's favorite UFO spot. Trekking both on foot and on horseback, golf, and extreme sports like paragliding are other popular activities.

Between the Valle de la Punilla and Ascochinga are the Sierras Chicas (small mountains), traversed by a picturesque road. It's unpaved but any car can handle it; there are no bus routes.

JESÚS MARÍA AND ASCOCHINGA

48 km (30 mi) north of Córdoba on RN9.

Jesús María and Colonia Caroya are two towns divided by RN9. Colonia Caroya, whose restaurants betray the fact that the population is descended from immigrants from Friuli in northeast Italy, stretches out along a long tree-lined avenue to one side; Jesús María is a compact grid of streets on the other. Once an indigenous settlement, the area changed radically in 1616, when the Jesuits bought over 100 square km (38 square mi) of land here to build Estancia Caroya. Two years later came the Estancia Jesús María, and in 1622 the biggest of the lot, Estancia Santa Catalina, 20 km (12 mi) to the northwest. They also planted more

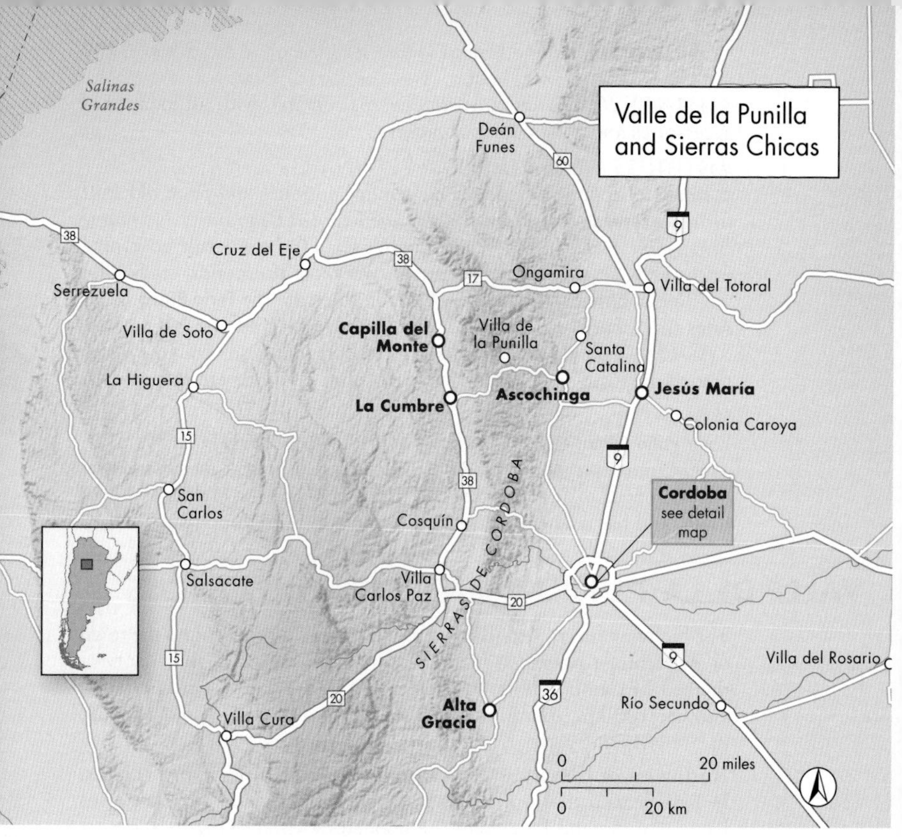

than 48,000 vines from which came Lagrimilla, the first New World wine to be presented at the Spanish court (it's still produced). In the first fortnight of January the town comes to life with the Festival Nacional de La Doma y el Folklore (National Rodeo and Folklore Festival), which is more about heavy drinking than cowboy activities.

These estancias were added to the UNESCO World Heritage list in 2000, but it's another type of estancia that's the biggest draw of these parts: the exclusive estates that offer lodgings to a privileged few. Also in the area is Ascochinga, whose bracing air and idyllic rolling hills and woods made the town a logical choice for a high-class tuberculosis sanatorium. These days it's a sleepy vacation spot, known for its 18-hole golf course that has incredible views of the Sierras Chicas.

GETTING HERE AND AROUND

Services leave every 15 minutes during the daytime from the minibus terminal in Córdoba—more frequent and quicker than regular bus services. From the Valle de Punilla there are no buses, but it's a pleasant and picturesque drive on an unpaved road from La Cumbre via Ascochinga or from Capilla del Monte via Ongamira.

ESSENTIALS

Banks Santander Rio (✉ *Colón 26*).

Bus Contacts Ciudad de Córdoba (☎ *352/542–3800 in Córdoba*). **Fono Bus** (☎ *352/542–3900*).

Medical Assistance Hospital Vincente Agüero (✉ *España 125* ☎ *352/542–6703*).

Taxi Remis Los Platenos (✉ *San Martín 188, Colonia Caroya* ☎ *352/546–3333*).

Visitor Info Municipalidad de Jesús María (✉ *RN9 at Av. San Martín* ☎ *352/546–5700* 🌐 *www.jesusmaria.gov.ar*).

EXPLORING

The stately three-wing **Estancia Jesuítica Jesús María** *(Estancia San Isidro Labrador)* was once the nerve center of the Jesuits' vast holdings in Jesús María. Two stories of arched galleries range around three sides of the main courtyard; behind them lie the priests' living quarters and communal rooms. The estancia's single-nave church is a beautiful example of the Jesuits' no-nonsense building style: the only adornment is the relief work of the cupola, which is thought to have been created by indigenous artisans. Inside the estancia is the **Museo Jesuítico Nacional** (National Jesuit Museum), which has a 10,000-piece collection that includes religious artifacts, colonial art and furnishings, and agricultural and wine-making paraphernalia. ✉ *Pedro de Oñate s/n* ☎ *3525/420–126* *2 pesos* ⏲ *Apr.–Sept., weekdays 8–7, weekends 10–noon and 2–6; Oct.–Mar., weekdays 8–7, weekends 10–noon and 3–7.*

The **Estancia Jesuítica de Caroya** was founded in 1616 and evolved over the centuries: the ascetic stone chapel dates from its founding, while the patio, cloisters, and outbuildings were added during the 18th and 19th centuries. During the wars of independence, the building had the brief but dubious honor of being Argentina's first knife and sword factory; later it became a sort of summer camp for the students of Córdoba's prestigious Colegio de Nuestra Señora de Montserrat. Heavy rustic furniture and religious paintings from the Cusqueña School fill the 10 rooms that were once the priests' cells, while more weapons—this time 18th-century rifles—fill the gallery. The patio is shaded by elms, orange trees, and palms—all rustled by cool breezes. ✉ *Av. 28 de Julio s/n* ☎ *3525/426–300* *2 pesos* ⏲ *Tues.–Fri. 9–6, weekends 8–2.*

★ Twenty kilometers (13 mi) northwest of Jesús María is the **Estancia Jesuítica de Santa Catalina**, once the Jesuits' largest estate. When the Jesuits acquired it in 1622, the first thing they did was construct an extensive underground irrigation system to water the dry lands. The area remains a massive agricultural center. The jewel in the estancia's crown is the **Iglesia de Santa Catalina** (Saint Catherine's Church), whose twin belfries tower over the estate. It took the Jesuits almost 100 years and more than three architects to complete the structure, which was finally consecrated in 1726. The stone they used—the local *piedra de sapo* (literally, toad stone)—is porous, and the church's baroque facade is regularly whitewashed to protect it from the elements: you may find it dazzling white or beautifully weather-stained, depending on when it was last painted. Inside, a spartan nave leads up to the building's only decoration, a gleaming gilded retable with a portrait of Saint Catherine. The estancia's arched galleries stretch off on either side of the church,

Built in the early 17th century, Estancia Caroya's chapel is a simple stone structure.

giving way to several shady courtyards with fountains. ✥ *6 km (4 mi) west of Jesús María on E66, then north on a dirt road for 13 km (8 mi)* ☎ *3525/421–600* 🌐 *www.santacatalina.info* 🎫 *3 pesos* ⏲ *Apr.–Sept., Tues.–Sun. 10–1 and 2–6; Oct.–Mar., Tues.–Sun. 10–1 and 2:30–7. One-hr guided tours available Tues.–Fri., except Jan., Feb., July, and Holy Week.*

OFF THE BEATEN PATH

Parque Arqueológico y Natural Cerro Colorado. This small reserve well north of Ascochinga is one of Argentina's most important pre-Hispanic sites, with over 30,000 petroglyphs painted on red rock formations. The oldest date to roughly AD 800, and include pictures of llamas, condors, *yaguaretés* (a jaguar species that used to roam the region), and human hunters, though most of the paintings remain uninterpreted. Later works represent mounted figures, a unique indigenous record of the arrival of the conquistadores. To visit the paintings, you must take one of the three daily guided walks that leave from the Archeological Museum at the entrance to tiny Cerro Colorado village. Two fords cross the dirt road into the village, so drive carefully. While you're there, make sure to stop in the house, now museum, of Cerro Colorado's most famous son, folk legend Atahualpa Yupanqui. ✉ *120 km (75 mi) north of Jesús María on RN9, then 10 km (6 mi) west on a dirt road north of Santa Elena* ☎ *3514/333–425* 🎫 *2 pesos* ⏲ *Daily 11–7; tours at 11:30, 2:30, and 4:30.*

WHERE TO EAT

$$ ARGENTINE ★

✕ **El Faro.** Local opinion is unanimous: this is the best parrilla in the north of Córdoba, and the perfect place to break up a day of estancia-seeing. All over the province, restaurants have begun to imitate El Faro's unusual serving style: *asadores* (barbecuers) carve slices from the sizzling beef sides on the grill and return time and again with dripping portions on wooden boards. They also do fantastic *chivito* (goat). ✉ *Juan Bautista Alberdi 245, Caroya* ☎ *352/466–258* ▭ *No credit cards.*

$$ ARGENTINE **La Ranchería.** Top-quality handicrafts surround you at this colorful restaurant-cum-shop, which has been owned by the same family since the late 18th century. Snack your way to a meal with a *picada* (platter of cold cuts) of locally cured ham and homemade cheeses washed down with some ice-cold beer—ask which *cervezas artesanales* (local microbrewed beers) are available. Hearty parrilla fare is also on offer if you need something more filling. ✉ *Next to Estancia Santa Catalina Santa Catalina* ☎ *352/542–4467* ▭ *No credit cards* ⊙ *No dinner Sun.*

$$$ ITALIAN **Macadam.** This fine old brick building 3 km (2 mi) down Caroya's tree-lined avenue is the place to come to try out northeast Italian sausages and cheeses, continuing traditions begun in Fruili. As you might expect, the wine list is rather good, too. ✉ *Av. San Martín 3210* ☎ *352/546–9777* 🌐 *www.macadam.com.ar* ▭ *No credit cards* ⊙ *Closed Mon. and Tues.; no lunch weekdays.*

WHERE TO STAY

$$$$ **El Puesto.** This is a traditional house on what was part of the estate of La Paz. It's run by adventurous hosts determined to help you make the most of your stay—whether that's riding horses around the large estate or swinging in the hammock. Contact them in advance to find out the options (there are a lot), and they'll tailor something special for your stay. They also offer accommodation in La Defensa, the main house on the estate, though the price is almost double. **Pros:** gorgeous countryside, own private bathing spots in the river. **Cons:** few facilities in the rooms. ✉ *Ruta E66, Km 14* ☎ *3525/1550–5623* 🌐 *www.elpuestoturismo.com.ar* *3 rooms* *In-room: no a/c, no phone, no TV (some), Wi-Fi. In-hotel: pool, bicycles, laundry service, parking (free), no-smoking rooms* ▭ *No credit cards* *AI.*

$$$$ **Estancia de Colibri.** The Fenestraz family is famous for luxury hotels in the Alps, so when son Raoul and his family undertook this venture they had a reputation to uphold. With not one but two polo fields, huge rooms and suites, a swimming pool and spa, and expansive living areas all done up with no expense spared, it earns its relatively hefty price tag. Kids will never be bored with horseback riding, survival courses, and treasure hunts on offer; if somehow they are, they can try working on the estate with the groundskeepers. **Pros:** luxury in all the details; many activities. **Cons:** costs much more than its neighbors; very popular with dove hunters (guests opposed to hunting might be uncomfortable). ✉ *Camino a Santa Catalina, Km 7* ☎ *352/546–5888* 🌐 *www.estanciaelcolibri.com* *2 rooms, 7 suites* *In-room: safe, DVD, Wi-Fi. In-hotel: restaurant, room service, bar, pool, spa, laundry service, parking (free), some pets allowed* ▭ *AE, MC, V* *AI.*

$$$$ Fodor's Choice ★ **Estancia La Paz.** Colonnaded galleries run around the outside of Estancia La Paz, which belonged to Argentine president Julio Roca at the end of the 19th century. The false wardrobe connecting his bedroom with that of his lover isn't the only reminder of the estancia's past: the owners' choice of antique furniture, period ornaments, and heavy silk

drapes all take you back in time. Ducks swim serenely on the huge lake behind the estancia, whose manicured grounds were designed by landscaper Carlos Thays and make for perfect picnic territory. When you sit down for dinner at the long, damask-clothed dining table, expect some surprises: as well as top-notch classic Argentine fare, chef Bruno Glaudo also prepares exotic national dishes that feature llama, deer, wild boar, capybara, and even *yacaré* (a local caiman species, similar to an alligator). **Pros:** historical feel; fantastic food; buffet breakfast; nighttime horseback riding. **Cons:** not appropriate for those opposed to hunting, as it's a popular offering. ✉ *Ruta E66, Km 14, Ascochinga* ☎ *352/549–2073* 🌐 *www.estancialapaz.com* *23 rooms* *In-room: no TV. In-hotel: room service, bar, tennis court, pool, spa, laundry service, parking (free)* *AE, MC, V* *AI.*

$$$$ ★ **Posada Camino Real**. A long and winding dirt track leads to the family-run Posada Camino Real, whose enormous grounds were once part of the Jesuits' holdings at Santa Catalina. Outside, the stucco buildings are a harmonious dusky rose; inside, rich chestnuts and ochers abound in rooms furnished with hefty iron bedsteads and chunky wooden furniture. Although the rooms and living area—complete with a huge hearth—are lovely, you'd be mad to stay indoors: the countryside is teeming with wildlife, and your hosts organize excursions on foot and horseback (included in the price). Top chefs come regularly to train the kitchen staff, an arrangement that produces modern takes on traditional Argentine fare and is also open to the public (with reservations). In true Argentine style, meals aren't confined to the kitchen: beef and whole goats are roasted over coals in the outdoor barbecue. **Pros:** price includes horseback riding; new area and playroom keep noisy kids at a distance from other guests; personal attention from the owners. **Cons:** as with many estancias in the region, there's an isolated feeling that may be off-putting if you're not seeking it. ✉ *10 km (6 mi) north of Santa Catalina on road from Ascochinga Santa Catalina* ☎ *351/552–5215* 🌐 *www.posadacaminoreal.com.ar* *12 rooms* *In-room: refrigerator. In-hotel: bar, golf course, pool, spa, restaurant, bicycles, laundry service, parking (free)* *MC, V* *BP.*

SPORTS AND THE OUTDOORS

There is a local debate over whether the pollution to the water supply from lead shot is worth tolerating for the tourist dollars it brings in, but dove hunting is still scarcely regulated and a huge draw to the region for North American hunters frustrated by regulations at home. The area around Ascochinga also has more than its fair share of polo grounds.

GOLF

Ascochinga Golf Club (✉ *Zona Urbana, Círculo Fuerza Aerea, Ascochinga* ☎ *352/549–2015* 🌐 *www.ascochingagolf.com.ar* *Green fees for non-members: 120 pesos for tournaments each Wed. and Sat., 85 pesos Sun., 60 pesos other days*) is a par-72, 18-hole golf course that looks over the rolling hills around Ascochinga.

LA CUMBRE

96 km (60 mi) north of Córdoba on RN 38.

Villa Carlos Paz, Cosquín, and La Falda are packed with hotels aimed at the Argentinian market and are close to Córdoba; for a similar valley landscape minus the crowds, head to quiet, refined La Cumbre. Formerly part of a massive Spanish hacienda, La Cumbre had become a mini British colony by the first half of the 20th century, filled with the summerhouses of investors involved with construction of the railway. Though their legacy remains in the mock-Tudor buildings at the town's snooty golf course, nowadays La Cumbre is synonymous with paragliding (it's near one of the country's best launching spots). The town itself has lots of good hotels and restaurants, making it a great base for exploring La Punilla or for taking hikes and horse treks into the surrounding hills.

EXPLORING TIPS

- Though day trips from the city are easy, spend at least a night or two in the sierras to really breathe in the mountain air.
- Consider renting a car or hiring a remis to avoid having the minibus routes and schedules rule your itinerary.
- Away from the highways, dirt roads are the norm—but you can visit all the places mentioned in this chapter without a four-wheel drive.

4

GETTING HERE AND AROUND

It's two hours by bus from Córdoba to La Cumbre. *Diferenciales* (minibuses) are usually cheaper and quicker, and run every hour or so. Buses run north–south along the valley, but to go east you'll need to hire a remis or a car of your own.

ESSENTIALS

Bank Banco de la Nación Argentina (✉ *25 de Mayo 255* ☎ *354/845–1351* 🌐 *www.bna.com.ar*).

Medical Assistance Hospital Municipal (✉ *López y Planes 83* ☎ *3548/451–100*).

Bus Contacts Transierras (☎ *351/424–3810 in Córdoba*). **Sarmiento** (☎ *351/433–2161 in Córdoba*).

Taxi Remises La Terminal (✉ *Av. Carraffa 217* ☎ *354/845–1500*).

Visitor Info La Cumbre Tourist Board (✉ *Ex-Estación de Ferrocarril Av. Caraffa 300* ☎ *354/845–2966* 🌐 *www.lacumbre.gov.ar*).

EXPLORING

El Paraíso, a museum that was once the home of writer Manuel Mujica Láinez, is nestled in the posh hilltop neighborhood of Cruz Chica, overlooking La Cumbre. Displays consist of his personal effects, including a 15,000-strong library and objects collected from his extensive travels, and exhibitions of work by local artists. But you should stop by just to soak up the atmosphere in its rooms and its gorgeous gardens, which were designed by Carlos Thays. ✉ *Cruz Chica, 2 km (1 mi) north of*

La Cumbre ☎ *3548/630–043* 🌐 *www.fundacionmujicalainez.org* *3 pesos* ⊙ *Daily 9:30–12:30 and 5–7:30.*

Cuchi Corral, in the hills west of La Cumbre, is a vast natural balcony with views over the Río Pinto valley. Once used by indigenous communities for spiritual rituals, it now sees another kind of natural high: paragliding. With a drop of 402 meters (1,319 feet), Cuchi Corral is Argentina's top spot for the sport, and international championships are held here every March. Even if you can't take the leap, stop by for the views, and if you've got transport, wind your way down to the riverside restaurant at the bottom—it's a very peaceful place and good for a dip in the water on a hot day. ✉ *8 km (5 mi) east of La Cumbre on RN38.*

WHERE TO EAT

$$ ECLECTIC ✕ **Kasbah.** Studiedly eclectic and executed with enthusiasm, Kasbah sits on a corner in the heart of town and serves pastas, fish, and pleasantly spicy *cocina étnica* ("ethnic" food). The decoration includes posters of local goings-on and artwork, and the service is helpful and bilingual. ✉ *Sarmiento 6* ☎ *3548/1540–1926* ▭ *No credit cards* ⊙ *Closed Tues. No lunch weekdays.*

$$ ARGENTINE ✕ **La Casona del Toboso.** The little cottage that houses La Cumbre's best-known restaurant looks a bit fairy-tale from the outside, though the sunny beer garden lessens the effect somewhat. The hard chairs and dubious artwork inside do nothing to put locals off: the food outweighs any complaints. The specialty is trout, fished locally and served baked or grilled. Other great grills and pastas are also on offer. ✉ *Belgrano 349* ☎ *3548/451–436* ▭ *AE, DC, MC, V.*

$$$ ECLECTIC ★ ✕ **Pajaro Goloso.** Inventive food prepared by a French-trained Madagascan-Chinese chef and a relaxed atmosphere have made Pajoro Goloso a key weekend spot (or all-week-long spot during the busy season). The menu is sophisticated yet simple. The restaurant has recently moved from the Aeroclub, where it forged strong links with La Cumbre's flying crowd. Sunday lunchtimes are the best time to visit if you can get a table. It's especially popular with families; after the meal, kids disappear into the garden while parents chat and relax. ✉ *Belgrano 564* ☎ *3548/1557–9952* *Reservations essential* ▭ *No credit cards* ⊙ *No lunch Mon.–Thurs. Jan., Feb., and July; closed Mon.–Thurs. Mar.–June and Aug.–Dec. No lunch Fri.*

WHERE TO STAY

$$$$ **Angelus.** Silver cutlery, feather duvets, original hundred-year-old inlaid wood floors, roaring log fires, wide-open views over the valley, and a hundred other details make this boutique hotel stand out. The kitchen is open to guests, or the staff will prepare meals to order in the main dining room. The long garden provides a secluded feel, despite being in the center of town, and also holds a fine swimming pool for lazy summer afternoons. **Pros:** accommodating service; beautiful views and shared spaces. **Cons:** sometimes closed for private parties (so check ahead). ✉ *Belgrano 560* ☎ *3548/451–324* 🌐 *www.angeluslacumbre.com* *6 rooms* *In-room: no a/c, no phone, Wi-Fi. In-hotel: pool, laundry service, parking* ▭ *AE, D, DC, MC, V* ⊙ *BP.*

The Córdoban music scene includes great *folklorica* (folk). You might see instruments decorated in *fileteado*, a flowery mode of painting, like the kind seen here on folk musician Leon Gieco's guitar.

$$$$ Castillo de Mandl. On the way up the hills at the back of town is this former private home, now sharing its curious architecture and "wow" views with guests in what feels like a low-key garden party at a castle. All the rooms are decorated differently and have huge wardrobes. The communal spaces are a highlight: there's a huge round dining table and a games room, while outside, paths meander through the gardens and up to the small but enticing swimming pool. Breakfast is served buffet-style. **Pros:** commanding views of the town. **Cons:** an uphill walk from the center. ✉ *San Josemaria Escrivá 73* ☎ *3548/452–001* 🌐 *www.elcastillodemandl.com* *10 rooms, 3 suites* *In-room: no a/c, safe (some), Wi-Fi. In-hotel: restaurant, bar, pool, laundry service, parking (free), no kids under 12, no-smoking rooms* 💳 *AE, MC, V* *CP.*

$ El Cóndor. Someday soon someone's going to coin a term for former backpacker hostels whose owners, exhausted by backpackers, are moving—just slightly—upmarket. El Condor is still in the transition phase, but with its rambling garden, homey kitchen, and a side business in restoring antique furniture, it's clearly more suited for its new direction. The six new apartments, with kitchenettes and en suites, are away from the main house (where you can still get a shared room for 50 pesos a night). **Pros:** quiet location, lots of character. **Cons:** few facilities. ✉ *Bartolome Jaime 204* ☎ *3548/452–870* *6 apartments, 3 dorms* *In-room: no a/c, no phone, kitchen (some), refrigerator (some), no TV. In-hotel: laundry facilities, no-smoking rooms* 💳 *No credit cards* *CP.*

$ Hostel La Cumbre. A family-run budget option in a big old house with a large garden and small swimming pool, Hostel La Cumbre has double and triple rooms, as well as dormitories, and all have good beds. The common areas are large and friendly; they also run a travel agency so there are lots of activities on offer. Breakfast is served buffet-style. **Pros:** roomy; well priced; close to the center. **Cons:** shared bathrooms. ✉ *Av. San Martín 186* ☎ *354/845–1368* 🌐 *www.hostellacumbre.com* *7 rooms* *In-room: no a/c, no phone, no TV, Wi-Fi. In-hotel: pool, laundry facilities, parking (free), no-smoking rooms* *No credit cards* *CP.*

$$$ **Posada Los Cedros.** Rooms in the century-old main house of this family-style hotel overlook sweeping lawns; in the apartments you open your curtains onto the Sierras. The flowery chintz and heavy wooden furnishings may feel a bit old-ladyish, but the place is very clean and well organized. Be sure to get up in time for breakfast, which includes mouthwatering homemade jams and is served on a veranda bathed in sunlight. **Pros:** efficiently run; very homey feel. **Cons:** very peaceful, but not as isolated as other lodgings. ✉ *Av. Argentina 837* ☎ *3548/451–028* 🌐 *www.posadaloscedros.com* *12 rooms* *In-hotel: room service, bar, pool, laundry service, parking (free)* *No credit cards* *CP.*

AFTER DARK

Gourmet pizzas and sandwiches and a warm and friendly atmosphere, as well as the four different lines of cerveza artesanal, draw La Cumbre's families to **The Owl Beer House** (✉ *Belgrano 437* ☎ *3548/452–314* 🌐 *www.theowlbeerhouse.com.ar*). They're open from 8 PM to 2 AM Thursday to Sunday year-round and every day during the high seasons.

Toby's (✉ *Dean Funes 323* ☎ *No phone*) claims to be the oldest *boliche* (bar) in the country, entertaining La Cumbre's nightbirds for over 60 years in a practically unchanged old colonial house, though now there's a disco ball reflecting on the fireplace. Things don't get started till well after 2 AM on weekends (it opens every day in high season), when the youth fill the place to bursting and spill out into the large garden outside.

SHOPPING

For local crafts and produce, drive along the winding Camino de los Artesanos (Craftsmen's Road), which is lined by more than a dozen workshop-cum-shops, each selling its own specialty. It runs parallel to RN38 between La Cumbre and Villa Giardino to the south.

See the world through purple-tinted spectacles at **Domaine de Puberclair** (✉ *RN38 Km 68.5* ☎ *3548/451–639*), a lavender plantation that distills the plant and sells its own soaps, perfumes, and creams. It's open afternoons only, from 4 PM to 8 PM.

Of the shops selling local produce, by far the best is **Jardines de Yaya** (✉ *Camino de los Artesanos* ☎ *3548/1563–7215*), a biodynamic farm with hundreds of different homemade jams, preserves, and liqueurs. It does a sideline in textiles and hand-carved housewares. The **Estancia del Rosario** (✉ *5 km [3 mi] from La Cumbre on Ruta E66 toward Ascochinga* ☎ *3548/451–257*) is an organic farm that has been making alfajores, jams, and homemade liqueurs for over 80 years.

SPORTS AND THE OUTDOORS

As pleasant as the town is, the green hills that surround it are the real attraction. Paragliding is an amazing way to experience them, but there are many ground-level options, too. Local guides **Sendas Travel** (✉ *Calle Dumas 110* ☎ *3548/1553–2177* 🌐 *www.sendastravel.com*) are a young Anglo-Argentine couple who organize biking, trekking, horseback riding, and picnics as well as booking hotels and making recommendations. They also have a stone cottage in the hills (fully furnished but without roads or electricity) that they use for lunch breaks or overnight stays.

GOLF

The pride of town, the 18-hole course of **La Cumbre Golf Club** (✉ *Belgrano 1095* ☎ *354/845–2283* 🌐 *www.lacumbregolf.com.ar* *Green fees for nonmembers: 100 pesos*) was built in 1924 by British railway families: the almost excessively English-looking Tudor-style clubhouse is vivid proof.

HORSEBACK RIDING

Of the many horseback-riding outfits the most recommended by locals is **Carmelo Cabalgatas** (✉ *Calle Belgrano s/n* ☎ *3548/1556–0076* 🌐 *www.carmelocabalgatas.com.ar*), who offer rides of two hours to two days in all directions from their ranch near the golf course. Their specialty is two-hour moonlit rides at full moon.

PARAGLIDING

Pablo Jaraba (✉ *RN38 at the turnoff to Cuchi Corral* ☎ *3548/1557–0951* 🌐 *www.cuchicorral.com*) is just one of many paragliders from around Argentina and the world who have settled in La Cumbre to be close to Cuchi Corral, a spot with excellent conditions and an awesome view. If he's busy, he'll fix you up with another pilot for a *vuelo de bautismo* (baptism flight), a 250-peso half-hour tandem flight where you have to do nothing but take two steps forward and be lifted into the air. A really stellar paragliding experience is dependent on the wind, and the morning is generally better here; the sport is suitable for all ages and really highly recommended.

CAPILLA DEL MONTE

20 km (12 mi) north of La Cumbre on RN38.

Shop windows filled with New Age books and T-shirts proclaiming close encounters of the third kind let you know that Capilla del Monte is synonymous with the out-of-this-world activity at nearby Cerro Uritorco, Argentina's number one UFO-spotting location. Locals are also proud of the *calle techada* (roofed street), which is just what it sounds like: in the 1970s the residents found themselves without a gallery for an upcoming photography exhibition, so they built a roof over part of the main drag. It was such a hit that it's never been dismantled. On one end of the street is a square where a small crafts market is held on weekends. Unusual area rock formations and several national parks make hiking one of the main activities here.

Visitors enjoy *cabalgatas* (horesback riding) outside of Jesus María, north of Córdoba City.

GETTING HERE AND AROUND

It's three hours by bus from Córdoba to Capilla del Monte, 20 km (12 mi) after La Cumbre.

ESSENTIALS

Bank Banco de la Nación Argentina (✉ *Av. Pueyrredón 438*).

Bus Contacts Ciudad de Córdoba (☎ *351/424-0048 in Córdoba*). **Sarmiento** (☎ *351/433-2161 in Córdoba*).

Medical Assistance Hospital Municipal Dr. Oscar Américo Luqui (✉ *Sarmiento 486* ☎ *3548/481-082*).

Taxi Remises Centro (✉ *Rivadavia 411, Capilla del Monte* ☎ *3548/481-844*).

Visitor Info Capilla del Monte Tourist Board (*Ex-Estación de Ferrocarril* ✉ *Av. Pueyrredón at Diagonal Buenos Aires* ☎ *3548/481-878* 🌐 *www.capilladelmonte.com.ar*).

EXPLORING

You may not see flying saucers, but you probably will catch stunning views over the valley to the west from the craggy top of **Cerro Uritorco** (*1 peso*). The 6-km (4-mi) climb up takes about three hours, following a well-signed path that starts near a small ticket booth at the *sendero* (trailhead), located on privare property on the other side of a small bridge near the Balneario La Toma on the Calabalumba River, north of Plaza San Martín. Although guides abound, it's a straightforward ascent. Take plenty of water and avoid walking in the midday sun.

Over the last 180 million years, air and water have eroded soft red sandstone to form the huge, bizarrely shaped formations in the park of **Los Terrones.** Although you can drive through the arid landscape, it's worth leaving your car at the entrance: the trail makes for a fascinating two-hour walk that culminates in great views of the Cerro Pajarillo and the valleys surrounding Capilla del Monte. Watch for condors, eagles, and falcons, which are often seen from the top. ✉ *18 km (11 mi) north of Capilla del Monte on RN38, then east on RP17* 🌐 *www.losterrones.com* 🎫 *5 pesos* 🕑 *Daily 9–dusk.*

The countryside surrounding **Ongamira**, a small town 1,408 meters (4,619 feet) above sea level, is one of the few places in the Punilla where you can see remains of the indigenous cultures that lived in the area before the Jesuits' arrival decimated their population. The valley of Ongamira was formed 130 million years ago, and over time the elements have carved its dusky sandstone into all manner of caves and grottos, known as **Grutas de Ongamira.** The people who eventually formed the Comechingón nation arrived here around AD 200, although other tribes lived here as long as 8,000 years ago. Their only legacy is rock paintings of animals and human figures. Follow the signs to the special viewpoint to see these pre-Hispanic works.

The Comechingones held out for a long time against the "civilizing" impulses of the Spanish invaders in what is now the privately owned **Parque Natural Ongamira** (✉ *Entrance on RP17* 🎫 *2 pesos* 🕑 *Daily 9–dusk*). Legend has it that the last point of resistance was the Cerro Colchequí, from which the defeated people flung themselves in 1574, preferring death to slavery. The park has views of both this hill and Cerros Pajarillo and Aspero, which inspired the likes of Chilean poet and Nobel Prize–winner Pablo Neruda, who once stayed here. A 3-km (2-mi) trail leads to the peak of Cerro Colchequí. ✉ *25 km (16 mi) from Capilla del Monte: 8 km (5 mi) north on RN38, then 17 km (11 mi) east on RP17.*

WHERE TO EAT AND STAY

$$$$ ARGENTINE ✕ **La Tramontana.** If you like your meals with a view, it's worth making the 5-km (3-mi) trip out of town for lunch at La Tramontana. The low pastel-colored buildings blend into the landscape, and house a small restaurant and a trout farm: no prizes for guessing what the specialty is. The whitewashed dining-room walls are hung with farming implements; the floors are a patchwork of colored concrete. ✉ *RN38 Km 89.5* ☎ *3548/1563–5049* 🌐 *www.granjalatramontana.com.ar* 💳 *No credit cards.*

$$$ 🏨 **La Guarida.** Individuality reigns at this small complex. The cabins and suites are all decorated differently, with a name to match: for example, the ocher-painted Mexicana cabin is surrounded by agave plants, and its exposed-stone walls are hung with Mexican artwork. The king-size beds in each suite face large hearths; private decks are the perfect places to devour the contents of the daily breakfast basket, complete with bread still warm from the oven. The freshest local produce is at the center of the nightly three-course meal, which may feature goat, venison, or even guinea pig. (There are also à la carte options, and vegetarians are well cared for.) If you stay in a cabin, you can arrange for the chef to come and cook there. **Pros:** incredible service for the price; a foodie's dream estancia; good vegetarian options. **Cons:** a slight hike

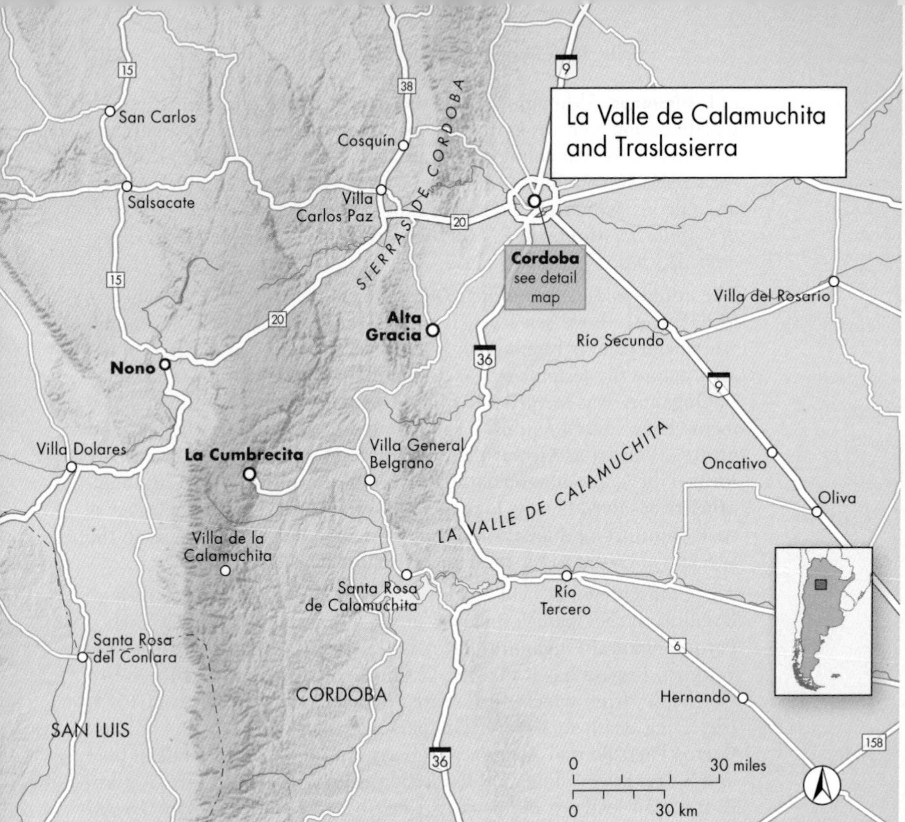

into town. ✉ *Los Terrones 1008* ☎ *3548/482–920* 🌐 *www.laguarida.com.ar* ↩ *4 rooms, 7 suites* 👍 *In-room: no phone, safe, refrigerator, Wi-Fi. In-hotel: restaurant, room service, bar, pool, laundry service, parking (free)* ▭ *MC, V* 🍽 *BP.*

SPORTS AND THE OUTDOORS

HIKING AND HORSEBACK RIDING

Nahuan Multiaventura (✉ *Diagonal Buenos Aires at Rivadavia* ☎ *3548/488–319* 🌐 *www.nahuanmultiaventura.com.ar*) know the best local spots and the best ways to see them. They offer horseback riding, trekking, caving, rappelling, and other ways to avoid crowds. Their half-day trip to the waterfalls at Cuchi Corral (near La Cumbre) involves a 4-km (2½-mi) hike uphill to a perfectly refreshing waterfall, following the stream back down to a simple lunch by the gentle Río Pintos.

LA VALLE DE CALAMUCHITA AND TRASLASIERRA

Small streams crisscross the pine-covered hills that line either side of La Valle de Calamuchita (Calamuchita Valley), where you'll find Jesuit town Alta Gracia and the tiny vacation town of La Cumbrecita. This area lies south of Córdoba City between the Sierras Chicas to the east and the Sierras Grandes and Sierras Comechingones to the west. In the first half of the 20th century German and Austrian immigrants made this their home, and among the chalet-style hotels and torte-filled tearooms you'd be forgiven for thinking yourself in the Alps. Myriad paths wind around the slopes of this part of Córdoba—trekking and viewpoint-climbing are the main attractions here (tearooms and Oktoberfest aside).

RP5 winds south from Córdoba City through Alta Gracia; once here, take RP45 north to RA20 west to get to Traslasierra. It may not seem that inspired, but the name for Traslasierra ("behind the hills") in a stroke sums up the simplicity of life here—especially when you're on holiday—and the compelling beauty of sitting at the feet of the Altas Cumbres hills, which keep the rest of the world at a safe distance. Certainly the pace of life is slower here but that just means there's more time for contemplation, especially outside of the local tourist season when the many cabanas and hosterias get booked out. The area boasts a few eclectic museums (which generally close "at sundown"), but the main attractions are as far away from other people as you can get, off in the mountains riding horses, bathing in little rivers, paragliding, or just finding a chair with a nice view.

ALTA GRACIA

38 km (24 mi) south of Córdoba on RP5.

The gateway to the Calamuchita Valley (and only a slight detour on the way to the Traslasierra), Alta Gracia grew up around a Jesuit estancia whose ruins are, in turn, clustered around Plaza Solares, in what is now the town center. The bracing air that sweeps over the low hills outside town made it a popular destination for rest cures in the early part of the 20th century; one of the town's most famous residents, Ernesto "Che" Guevara, was brought by his parents to live here in the hope that the mountain air would cure his asthma. Today many people come to hike, horseback ride, and fish in nearby rivers, which also make great swimming spots in summer. There are also two great golf courses here.

GETTING HERE AND AROUND

It's one hour by bus from Córdoba to Alta Gracia.

ESSENTIALS

Bank Banco de la Nación Argentina (✉ *Av. Belgrano 115*).

Bus Contacts Sarmiento (☎ *351/433–2161 in Córdoba*). **Sierras de Calamuchita** (☎ *351/422–6080 in Córdoba*).

Medical Assistance Hospital Alta Gracia (✉ *Av. Del Libertador 1450* ☎ *354/742–9282*).

Taxi Taxi-Run (✉ *Malvinas Argentinas 236* ☎ *354/742–0555*).

Visitor Info Alta Gracia Tourist Board (✉ *Av. del Tajamar at Calle del Molino* ☎ *354/742–8128* 🌐 *www.altagracia.gov.ar*).

EXPLORING

★ The massive stone walls of the main estancia buildings dominate one side of Plaza Solares. After the Jesuits' expulsion from Argentina, the buildings' most illustrious resident was Viceroy Santiago de Liniers, famous for defending Buenos Aires against invading British forces. Liniers lived here briefly in 1810, before his pro-Spanish sympathies cost him his life when Argentina became independent. Despite its name, the **Museo Casa del Virrey Liniers**, a well-organized museum, isn't just about Liniers, but also documents life on the estancia and includes some exhibits about the native Comechingón people who inhabited the area prior to the Europeans' arrival.

The entrance's crumbling baroque gate gives way to the main courtyard. Overlooking this are the priests' cells, which house period furniture, religious art, and Liniers's personal effects. Deeper within the building are the original kitchens, the forge, and the *areas comunes* (common areas)—a euphemism for the Jesuits' toilets. These were discovered by archaeologists in the 1970s, incongruously filled with porcelainware. Adjoining the museum to the south and worth checking out if you're at the museum is the **Iglesia Parroquial Nuestra Señora de la Merced,** finished only a few years before the Jesuits' expulsion. Unlike the museum, the church hasn't been well maintained or restored. Take a short walk north of the main building to see the **Tajamar** (breakwater), built by the Jesuits in 1643 to create a reservoir for their estate. ✉ *Padre Domingo Viero and Solares* ☎ *3547/421–303* 🌐 *www.museoliniers.org.ar* ⏲ *Apr.–Sept., Tues.–Fri. 9–1 and 3–7, weekends 9:30–12:30 and 3:30–6:30; Oct.–Mar., Tues.–Fri. 9–8, weekends 9:30–8. Guided tours in English at 10, noon, 5, and 7; call ahead to arrange.*

A few blocks north of the square in the Carlos Pellegrini neighborhood is the **Museo Casa de Ernesto "Che" Guevara**, in one of several houses rented by the future revolutionary's family during his youth. Thoughtful exhibits fill 10 rooms and include photographs and such personal possessions as school reports and the contents of his bookshelf—testaments to a precocious intellect. There are two films on rotation in a room in the back to fill in some of the historical context, but the exhibits make more sense if you already know a bit about his life, or have at least seen the film *The Motorcycle Diaries*—on display are a replica of the motorcycle in question and photos and articles from the voyage. ✉ *Avellaneda 501* ☎ *3547/428–579* 🎟 *3 pesos* ⏲ *Daily 9–7.*

WHERE TO EAT AND STAY

$$$ ARGENTINE ✕ **Morena**. Hearty Córdoban dishes like *cazuela de conejo* (rabbit stew) are great winter warmers, while the trout—best appreciated garnished with only a little herbed butter—is fished locally. If you're looking for something more elaborate, don't miss the *ravioles Morena,* squid-ink black pasta filled with pink prawn, leek, and ricotta mousse—as delicious as it is visually striking. The friendly young staff are happy to talk you through your options. ✉ *Av. Sarmiento 413* ☎ *3547/426–365* 🌐 *www.morena-ag.com.ar* ✍ *Reservations essential* 💳 *AE, MC, V* ⏲ *Closed Mon., no lunch Tues.–Thurs.*

$$$$ 🏨 **El Potrerillo de Larreta**. The heavyset main building of this hotel-cum-country-club was once part of the Jesuits' holdings. The grounds are

now Alta Gracia's prestigious golf club—you can wake up and step right out onto the green. The simple white-walled rooms certainly feel very colonial, with big brass bedsteads, floral curtains, and hardwood floors. Modern installations like air-conditioning assure that old doesn't mean uncomfortable. The downstairs dining room, which has huge windows looking over the greens, serves such traditional Argentine dishes as *medallón de lomo a la pimienta* (black pepper steak) and hearty gnocchi. **Pros:** exclusive and luxurious; staying here gives access to the golf course. **Cons:** a short drive outside of town. ✉ *Camino a los Paredones, Km 3* ☎ *3547/439–033* *3 rooms, 4 suites* *In-room: no phone, no TV. In-hotel: restaurant, golf course, pool, bicycles, parking (free)* *AE, V* *BP.*

4

$$$$ **Sierras Hotel.** This hotel put Alta Gracia on the map. The healthy climate and the Jesuit estancia played their part, but the visiting socialites from Buenos Aires in the 1930s came to stay here, with its magnificent gardens designed—as all good gardens in the region are—by Carlos Thays. The hotel has since seen worse times, having been abandoned, squatted in, and run down, but it's recently been overhauled and reopened in 2006. Its casino isn't as upmarket as it used to be, but it's still got the gardens, and the 26 rooms have all the comforts you can ask for. **Pros:** very roomy; very central; a distinguished history. **Cons:** lots of slot machines. ✉ *Velez Sarfield 198* ☎ *3547/431–200* 🌐 *www.cetsa.com.ar* *26 rooms, 4 suites* *In-room: safe, refrigerator, Wi-Fi. In-hotel: restaurant, bar, tennis courts, pool, gym, spa, parking (free)* *AE, DC, MC, V* *BP.*

SPORTS AND THE OUTDOORS

GOLF

Alta Gracia Golf Club (✉ *Av. Carlos Pellegrini 1000* ☎ *3547/422–922* 🌐 *www.aggc.com.ar* *Green fees for nonmembers: 50 pesos weekdays, 70 pesos Sat., 60 pesos Sun.*) is known as much for its 18-hole course (for which you need a recognized handicap to play on weekends) as for its fantastic restaurant. And, oh, yeah: Che Guevara played here.

LA CUMBRECITA

84 km (52 mi) southwest of Alta Gracia: 50 km (31 mi) south on RN5 to Villa General Belgrano, then 34 km (21 mi) west on an unnumbered provincial road.

Immigrants from Switzerland and Austria built this village in the 1930s, and its wooden chalets wouldn't look out of place in the Alps. La Cumbrecita is surrounded by tree-filled slopes, and well-marked trails lace the area. The peace extends right into La Cumbrecita, which is a car-free zone in the daytime (many residents use golf carts to get around). Two clean rivers, the Almbach and the Río del Medio, run close to the village; both have small cascades and *balnearios* (bathing spots). The village has a mild microclimate, with warm but not roasting summers; snow is a frequent sight in winter, which puts the finishing touches to La Cumbrecita's alpine look. The village has no main square and isn't laid out on a grid. Instead, two roads run through it, neither with street numbers; the lower Paseo Bajo has several restaurants and hotels along it.

GETTING HERE AND AROUND

Pájaro Blanco is a minibus company that makes several daily trips from Córdoba via Villa General Belgrano to La Cumbrecita and from Santa Rosa. The 38 km (24 mi) of unpaved windy road from Villa General Belgrano should be taken slowly and carefully as you enjoy the scenery.

ESSENTIALS

Banks Take note that there are no banks in La Cumbrecita—the nearest ones are in Villa General Belgrano.

Bus Contact **Pájaro Blanco** (☏ *351/425–2854 in Córdoba; 354/648–1096 in La Cumbrecita*).

Medical Assistance **Farmacia La Cumbrecita** (✉ *Calle Pública s/n* ☏ *035/4648–1004*).

Taxi **Federico Mayer Remis** (☏ *354/648–1012*).

Visitor Info **La Cumbrecita Tourist Board** (✉ *At village entrance, on first block after the parking lot* ☏ *354/648–1088* 🌐 *www.lacumbrecita.gov.ar*).

EXPLORING

North of town on Paseo Bajo, water from the peaks has created the small pools known as **La Olla.** They're over 8 meters (26 feet) deep, and even in summer the water temperature never exceeds 15°C (59°F), making this the perfect place to cool off on hot days. The rock face behind the pools is a favorite with local rock climbers. If that's too cold, follow the river for a couple of hundred yards to the slightly warmer Lago de las Truchas. In late afternoons, on the other side of the river, tea and rich German-style cakes await at Confitería Tante Liesbeth.

From La Olla a path continues up to the top of **Cerro Wank**, one of the most popular walks in La Cumbrecita. The peak is at 1,728 meters (5,669 feet) above sea level. The walk up takes about an hour, with fantastic views from the top over the Calamuchita Valley.

A brisk half-hour walk along the winding path that starts at the Hostería Kuhstall takes you through pine woods to **La Cascada**, a 14-meter-tall (46-foot-tall) waterfall on the Almbach. You can swim in the pool it forms.

WHERE TO EAT

$$$ GERMAN
✕ **Bar Suizo.** Consistently excellent Swiss-German fare makes this small wood-clad restaurant the best of the alpine eateries that line the Paseo Bajo. Pork dishes feature heavily on the menu, but the raclette (a relative of cheese fondue), trout in herb butter, and ravioli with wild mushroom sauce are other winning options. At teatime, berry cakes and apple strudel accompany Viennese *Eiskaffee* (iced coffee topped with whipped cream). ✉ *Las Truchas s/n* ☏ *3546/481–067* ▭ *No credit cards* ▭ *Closed from 8 PM out of season* ▭ *Reservations advised in season.*

$ CAFÉ ★
✕ **Confitería Tante Liesbeth.** The founder of La Cumbrecita's most famous teahouse was Liesbeth Mehnert, one of the region's original German immigrants. She passed her secrets on to her daughter-in-law, who continues to turn out the best confections in town. It's open daily from 3:30 to 7 PM. ✉ *North end of Paseo Bajo, crossing the Almbach River*

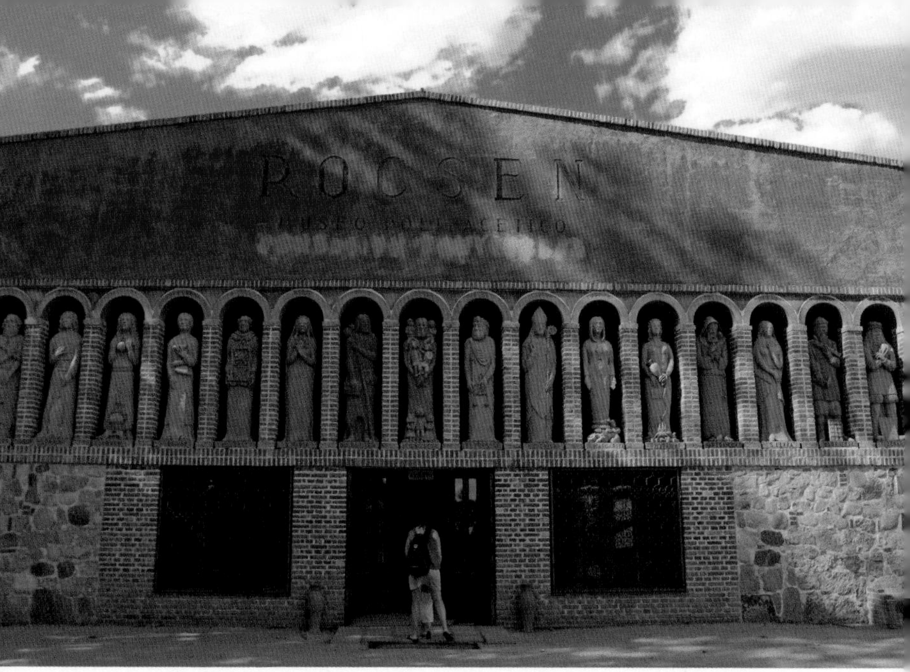

Museo Rocsen, in tiny Nono in the Traslasierra Valley, is a destination in itself.

3546/481–079 *No credit cards* *In season closed Mon.–Wed.; out of season closed weekdays.*

WHERE TO STAY

$$$ **Hotel La Cumbrecita.** The massive chalet is a local style icon, synonymous with the image of La Cumbrecita. Once the only house in the village, it was soon turned into a four-room hotel, and has grown, along with the village, ever since. Although its scale is still impressive, its heavy hardwood furniture, floral bedspreads, and rather dim lighting feel old-fashioned. All meals are served in the wooden-clad dining room: unsurprisingly, German and Austrian fare is the basis of the menu. **Pros:** hilltop setting provides stellar views. **Cons:** big spread-winged bird-of-prey taxidermy in the bar might be off-putting for some. *Calle Pública s/n, off Ruta 5* *3546/481–052* *www.hotelcumbrecita.com.ar* *33 rooms, 3 bungalows* *In-room: no a/c, safe. In-hotel: restaurant, room service, tennis court, pool, gym, laundry service, parking (free)* *AE, DC, MC, V* *CP.*

$$$ **La Colina.** Pine-filled hills are the first thing you see each morning at this small apart-hotel on a natural balcony over town. You can even bathe with a view: the stone-clad hot tubs are surrounded by massive plate-glass windows. The spacious suites all have bouncy king-size beds with rich cotton linens in soft colors like taupe and camel; the irregular woolen swaths that line the walls are a modern take on alpine style. You can also get an eyeful of the view from the hotel's restaurant ($$), where owner-chef Ricardo Nogueira does excellent nightly set menus of Central European dishes like pork ribs and sauerkraut. His son, Juan Pablo, organizes rappelling, rock-climbing, horseback-riding, and

4x4 excursions. **Pros:** decor and architecture are aesthetically sensitive to the landscape. **Cons:** a short drive from the city center; restaurant reservations essential. ✉ *Calle Pública s/n* ☎ *3546/481–063* 🌐 *www.suitesdelacolina.com* *4 suites* *In-room: no phone, refrigerator, Wi-Fi. In-hotel: restaurant, room service, bar, bicycles, laundry service, no kids under 18, no-smoking rooms* *No credit cards* *CP.*

EN ROUTE

About halfway between Villa Carlos Paz and Mina Clavero, the winding road through the mountains from Córdoba to Traslasierra passes through La Quebrada del Condorito—a grand-scale slice through the mountains where you can get a bird's-eye view of the condors. From the visitor center a well signed 9-km (5½-mi) path (accessible on foot or by bike) leads to the Balcón Norte, with a view over the gorge. Park rangers advise allowing four hours for the round-trip; longer routes are also marked. For more info, head to 🌐 *www.condoritoapn.com.ar* or call ☎ *3541/433–371*.

NONO

8 km (5 mi) south of Mina Clavero on RP14; 155 km (tk mi) southwest of Córdoba on RN20

There are other more lively towns in the Traslasierra and Valle de Calamuchita with more services, but Nono gets the nod precisely because of its low-key nature and lack of fuss. For a town that makes its living from tourism, everything is refreshingly unaffected, save that there's little sign of the donkey-breeding industry that tourism replaced. Nono's center is the main road that joins the larger towns of Mina Clavero to the north and Villa Dolores to the south, with a hint of a grid system on either side, but most of the town is stretched out along dirt tracks that follow the rivers and streams toward the hills.

GETTING HERE AND AROUND

The 150-km (93-mi) road from Córdoba comes via Alta Gracia or Villa Carlos Paz and takes 2½ hours, or 820 km (510 mi) from Buenos Aires, taking 12 hours.

ESSENTIALS

ATM YPF Service Station (✉ *Av Libertad 625, Nono*).

Bus Contacts Panaholma (☎ *351/428–0848 in Córdoba; 3544/498–912 in Nono*). **Chevallier** (☎ *3544/498–976 in Nono; 11/4000–5255 in Buenos Aires*).

Medical Assistance Centro de Salud Integral (✉ *San Martín 1550, Mina Clavero* ☎ *3544/472–351*).

Taxi Taxi Nono (*3544/555–856*). **Remis Herredia** (*3544/498–230*).

Visitor Info Nono Tourist Office (✉ *Sarmiento 365* ☎ *3546/429–654* 🌐 *www.vallecalamuchita.com*).

EXPLORING

Half the wonder of the **Museo Rocsen** is how it could possibly have come into existence in the first place. The other half is the sheer breadth and magnitude of the collection. In 40 years it has grown from a hundred-square-meter collection of odds and ends to almost 20,000 pieces in over 15 times the space (which is filled to bursting). The French owner and founder, now over 80 years old but still very much an active presence at the museum, imaginatively displays the overwhelmingly varied collection. ✉ *Av. de los Porteños s/n* ☎ *3544/498–218* *www.museorocsen.org* *14 pesos* *Open daily 9–sunset.*

WHERE TO EAT AND STAY

$$$$ **Casas del Arroyo.** Four fully furnished cabins are unobtrusively tucked into a slope that leads to the banks of the Arroyo Sanjuanino, beyond which there's an uninterrupted view of the hills. The owners recently moved from Buenos Aires, and set right to task building and refining the full set of facilities, inviting swimming pool, and in-room Jacuzzis with sweeping views. The cabins are quiet, well separated from each other, and have fully equipped kitchens (but the owners are on hand to arrange meals if you choose). **Pros:** peace and tranquillity, great views from the Jacuzzis. **Cons:** best suited to families of four. ✉ *Av. Los Porteños s/n* ☎ *3544/498–721* *www.casasdelarroyo.com.ar* *4 cabins* *In-room: no phone, safe, kitchen, refrigerator, DVD, Wi-Fi. In-hotel: pool, laundry service, parking (free)* *AE, MC, V* *BP.*

$$$$ **La Constancia.** Whatever peaches, plums, apricots, and nuts the birds don't take from the trees are used in cooking, one of the many strengths of La Constancia, an idyllic retreat cut off from the world by a bumpy dirt road that winds up the side of Mount Champaqui, the highest in the Sierras Grandes. A clear mountain stream provides water and electricity, fills the natural swimming pool, and provides 5 km (3 mi) of fly-fishing opportunities. The buildings are furnished with old restored furniture, hand-knitted woolen blankets warm the beds, and there's a huge private chapel with a belfry overlooking everything. Included in the price are horseback rides to the top of the mountain, full board (except cold drinks), and free roam of the 3,000-acre estate. Don Luis, your cordial host, will even throw in cooking lessons. **Pros:** lots of amenities; eco-friendly hydroelectric power. **Cons:** feels isolated (though for many, that's the point). ✉ *Ruta a Champaqui, Km 7, San Javier* ☎ *3544/482–826* *www.laconstancia.net* *9 rooms* *In-room: no a/c, no phone. In-hotel: restaurant, pool, laundry service, parking (free), no-smoking rooms* *AE, MC, V* *AI.*

$ **Manantial Hosteria.** Follow the garden down to the river and stop to admire the eucalyptus trees and poplars surrounding the big round pool—from here it's as if the rest of the world, and certainly its cares, just might not exist. The six rooms are smart but not too lavish, and the restaurant ($$$) is open to the public and run by the owner's daughter—who uses nuts and fruit from the garden to augment other locally sourced produce. At this writing, they're finishing up a yoga room, and they can also connect guests with trekking and horse-riding guides, but the Manantial's specialty is taking it easy. **Pros:** quiet and relaxed. **Cons:** rather isolated if you're without a car. ✉ *Camino a Poaso de las Tropas s/n* ☎ *3544/498–179* *www.hosteriamanantial.com.ar* *6 rooms* *In-room: no a/c, no phone, kitchen (some), refrigerator (some), Wi-Fi. In-hotel: restaurant, pool, laundry service, parking (free)* *No credit cards* *CP.*

SHOPPING

A short drive south to Villa de las Rosas is rewarded by a quick 15 minute tour of the plantation and factory and a tasting session of the much awarded **Olium** (☒ *RP14 El Valle, Villa de las Rosas* ☎ *3544/494–658* ☎ *www.olium.com.ar*) olive oils. You can buy small tasting bottles for gifts from the land.

Alfajores are a particular specialty of Córdoba, but there are few places that put their case as clearly as **El Nazareño** (☒ *Esmeralda s/n, Arroyo de los Patos* ☎ *3544/472–295*), which has shops in Nono and Mina Clavero. At this small factory on the side of the road between the two, the justifiably proud owners give delicious guided tours.

SPORTS AND THE OUTDOORS

HORSE RIDING

Luis Liste (☒ *Las Rabonas* ☎ *3544/15–552–926* ☎ *www.loslistecaballos.com.ar*) runs courses in horse whispering and is very experienced in introducing new riders to equitation. Two or three day treks in the mountains (overnighting in a refuge at the top of Mount Champaqui) are his thing, and there's really no better way to discover the area. **Fernando Neyer** (☎ *3544/471–046* ☎ *fernandoneyer@gmail.com*), a local guide, leads walking tours to the hills starting from Los Hornillos, just a few kilometers to the south.

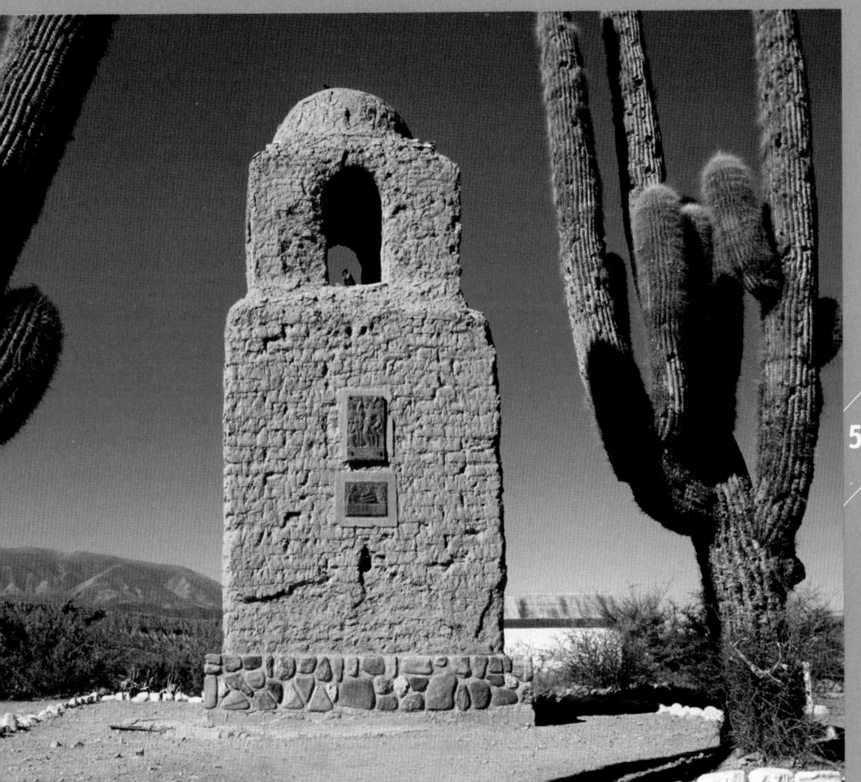

The Northwest

WORD OF MOUTH

Tilcara was more touristy than Purmamarca but both are pretty quiet when the buses have departed in the late afternoon. If you are into photography then stay in Purmamarca as the best time to photograph the Cerro de los Siete Colores is in the early morning 7–9 AM.

—crellston

WELCOME TO THE NORTHWEST

ceramics, Salta Province

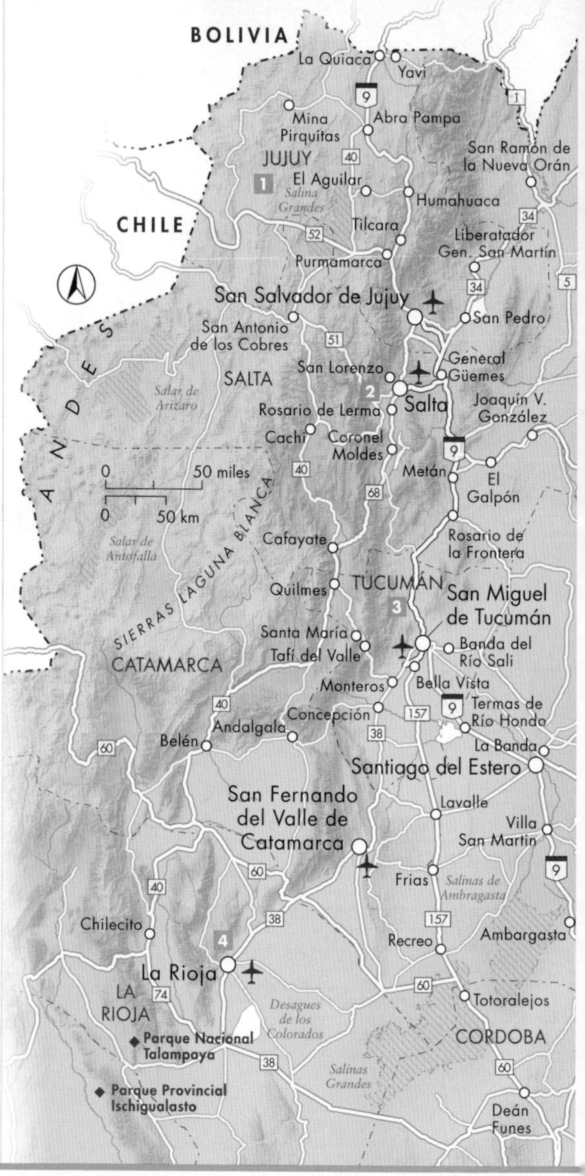

TOP REASONS TO GO

★ **The Quebrada:** In this craggy, vast, color-splashed landscape, gaze up from time to time at the eternity of stars or the otherworldly carved walls of the gorge.

★ **Sports and the Outdoors:** Mountains, valleys, lakes, streams, and plains make this region ideal for hiking, horseback riding, rafting, fishing, and rock climbing. Or you could take a spin in a kite buggy on the Salinas Grandes.

★ **Folk Music:** In this hub of Argentina's folkloric music scene, a trip to one of Salta's *peñas* (halls of food, music, and dancing) is essential. Wind instruments, diverse percussion, and soaring harmonies define the high-Andean sound track.

★ **Wine:** Though they usually take a backseat to wines from the central Mendoza Province, the wines of the north, especially in the Cafayate region of Salta, are gaining worldwide recognition.

Salta city center

1 Jujuy. Jujuy is a province of varied histories and geographies. Once the battleground of South America's struggle for independence, it's still home to the peoples who lived here before colonization by the Incas and the Spanish.

2 Salta. The city is the perfect base for exploring the wonders of the eponymous province. Chief of these is the Calchaqui Valley, which follows the Inca Trail and Ruta 40 through improbably charming towns in a dusty, cactus-studded wilderness. And in the midst of this are the world's highest vineyards.

3 Tucumán. Argentina's smallest province is also the most varied—deserts are just a short drive from jungle, and rich agricultural lands that have earned the region its title Garden of the Republic. Retreat from the capital city to the cooler Tafí del Valle or the ruins of Quilmes.

4 La Rioja. La Rioja has lots of off-the-beaten-track territory. It's not for tourists but rather for travelers who require very little logistical support. Its draws include vineyards, paleontological parks, a flamingo-flocked lake, and some very special places to stay.

GETTING ORIENTED

The landscape in Argentina's northwestern reaches is incredibly varied—from 22,000-foot-high Andean peaks to the high, barren plateau known as the Puna, from subtropical jungles to narrow sandstone canyons. Much of the area is desert, cut and eroded by raging brown rivers that wash away everything in sight during summer rains. It's inhabited by tough, resilient peoples who've got the land in their blood and their culture. The area also has some of the country's most vibrant cities, but even they close down each afternoon for a lengthy siesta.

iglesia (church) in Molinos

THE NORTHWEST PLANNER

When to Go

January and February are Argentina's summer vacation months, meaning hotels get booked up and prices rise. Ironically, these two months coincide with rainy season, when flooding and/or landslides can block mountain roads. (Both the Tucumán–Tafí del Valle and Salta–Cachi routes are notorious for this.) Other busy times are winter break (July), Easter week, and movable feasts such as Carnival in the Quebrada de Humahuaca. Most facilities remain open year-round.

Money Matters

Avoid people on the street who offer to change your currency to pesos; head to a bank instead. Banks are generally open weekdays 7–1 and 4–8. For ATMs, look for the maroon BANELCO sign of Argentina's largest ATM network. You can use your Plus or Cirrus card to withdraw pesos. Traveler's checks aren't recommended in the Northwest. Few places accept them, and with ATMs so easy to find there's little need for them. Outside the major towns many businesses don't accept credit cards and cash is sometimes the only option.

Eat Well and Rest Easy

The Northwest's indigenous heritage has influenced its cuisine: corn and potatoes are common ingredients. Some dishes worth trying include *locro,* a soup of corn, beans, and red peppers which becomes a stew when meat is added; tamales, ground corn baked with potatoes and meat and tied up in a corn husk; and *humitas,* grated corn with melted cheese cooked in a corn husk. Grilled *cabrito* (goat) is also a specialty of the region. For dessert you may come across *cayote,* an interesting concoction of green-squash marmalade served with nuts and local cheese.

Hotels in the Northwest's major cities tend to be modern and comfortable. Most accept credit cards, though several offer discounts if you pay in cash. Many estancias (ranches) in the foothills accept guests and are listed with local tourist offices. Although the whole region has really started to open up to the outside world, there are almost no chain hotels. Instead, a dazzling array of boutique hotels and estancias have been built—or reinvented—with a sense of history and location.

ACA (Automóvil Club Argentino) maintains good campgrounds with numerous amenities. Note that as you travel farther north into smaller towns English is rarely spoken at hotels.

DINING AND LODGING PRICE CATEGORIES (IN PESOS)

	¢	$	$$	$$$	$$$$
Restaurants	under 8 pesos	8 pesos–15 pesos	15 pesos–25 pesos	25 pesos–35 pesos	over 35 pesos
Hotels	under 80 pesos	80 pesos–140 pesos	140 pesos–220 pesos	220 pesos–300 pesos	over 300 pesos

Restaurant prices are based on the median main course price at dinner. Hotel prices are for two people in a standard double room in high season.

Getting Here and Around

Air Travel. Aerolíneas Argentinas/Austral (🌐 *www.aerolineas.com.ar*) has direct flights from Buenos Aires to San Salvador de Jujuy, Salta, La Rioja, and Tucumán, but is plagued by delays and cancellations. LAN Chile (🌐 *www.lan.com*) and Andes (www.andesonline.com) fly from Buenos Aires to Salta. There are no connecting flights within the region, except for a few weeks in high season when it's possible to fly with Aerolíneas between Salta and Jujuy—though including check-in times, the trip is faster by bus. All flights between Buenos Aires and the Northwest use the capital's Aeroparque Jorge Newbery, about 15 minutes north of downtown.

Bus Travel. Buses are reliable, affordable, and well used, though certain routes require a little advance planning. Some companies offer roadside pickup; others have luxury double-decker buses offering overnight services. Tourist offices can advise which companies go where. In peak season, buy tickets a day or two in advance.

Car Travel. Traveling outside of cities is often easiest by car. However, picking up a car in one city and dropping it off in another incurs significant extra costs, so rent cars for only parts of your journey or commit to a round-trip. Roads are generally good and not very crowded, but be prepared for paved roads turning *ripio* (unpaved) for long stretches. Very few routes require a 4x4. A Volkswagen Gol costs about 180 pesos per day; 4x4s start at 400 pesos per day.

Two main roads cross the area: the legendary Ruta 40, winding its unpaved way through small towns nearly 3,000 mi to the country's southern tip, and Ruta 9, the ancient road of the Incas, which takes you from Bolivia through San Salvador de Jujuy, Salta, Tucumán, Santiago del Estero, and on toward Córdoba. Before you set out, visit an ACA (🌐 *www.aca.org.ar*) office for maps and information, especially during the January–March rainy season.

Remis Travel. For short trips (e.g., Tucumán to Tafí del Valle or Salta to Cafayate), consider hiring a *remis* (fixed-price taxi). Some routes have shared services, where you split the cost with others making the same journey. You can find a remis at airports, bus stations, and on main plazas—or your hotel can call one for you.

Health and Safety

Be mindful of *soroche,* or altitude sickness, which results in shortness of breath and headaches. Walk slowly, eat carbohydrates, and drink plenty of fluids (but avoid alcohol). Locals swear by the *coqueando* remedy: sucking on coca leaves (sold at corner groceries and street vendors). Tear off the stems and stuff some leaves into the space between your teeth and cheek; leave them in for an hour or more, neither chewing nor spitting, but swallowing when you salivate.

Aside from being sold an overpriced tour (recommended rates are listed in Salta's tour office), you're unlikely to encounter crime. Many hotels pride themselves on not needing safety deposit boxes.

The many roadside shrines marking car accidents, especially on winding mountain routes, are a reminder to check your speed. Also take care on the many unpaved roads. And do wear your seat belt.

5

TREN A LAS NUBES

Approaching the tracks for the Tren a las Nubes, Salta Province
Top right: Car and engine, Tren a las Nubes
Bottom right: Famous La Polvorilla Viaduct, a highlight of the journey

With a bird's-eye view of its passage over the 210-foot-high Viaducto La Polvorilla, the Tren a las Nubes (Train to the Clouds) is probably the Northwest's most famous attraction. This train ride of a lifetime takes you on a 16-hour journey to the high, desolate Puna and back.

The trip begins at 4,336 feet as the train climbs out of the Lerma Valley from Salta into the mountains. It rattles over steel bridges that span wild rivers, winding ever upward through many turns and tunnels to reach the viaduct (13,770 feet), just beyond San Antonio de los Cobres, the only town of any size in the Puna. In San Antonio and at the viaduct you can disembark to test the thin air and visit a train-side market set up by locals for just this occasion.

The 217-km (135-mi) round-trip takes in 29 bridges, 21 tunnels, 13 viaducts, and a couple of hairpin bends and spirals, all of which are interpreted by the bilingual guides on board. Medical assistants take the ride with you to help with altitude sickness. Stop in at the dining car; breakfast and an afternoon snack are included in the fare.

WHEN TO GO

The heavy rains of summer mean the train stops running completely between the end of November and March, and in wintertime those that mind the cold might want to think twice about committing to 15 hours travel in the mountains. On August 1 the Festival of the Pachamama is celebrated in San Antonio de los Cobres.

WHAT'S OUT THE WINDOW

The infrastructure alone makes the trip incredible as the rack-and-pinionless train uses all the tricks in the book to gain altitude while avoiding steep grades. The trip isn't only for railway enthusiasts, though: an other-worldly landscape offers view after spectacular view as the train twists and turns along the route. For the parts where the train is accompanied by a road, or as it passes through infrequent villages, there are people to wave to. In San Antonio de los Cobres and on the lookout at the Viaducto la Polvorilla, locals gather round the train for a chat—and to sell handicrafts and trinkets. The guides in each carriage provide lots of information for each stage of the journey; when there's nothing more to be seen out the window, or once the sun's gone down on the return journey, they double as entertainers.

SAN ANTONIO DE LOS COBRES

San Antonio is like many small towns in rural Argentina, except that it's so heavily battered by sun and wind even the kids have wrinkles. It's also really difficult to get to and has very little oxygen in the air. Essential accessories for visitors are sunscreen, extra clothes for warmth at night, and coca leaves—they're chewed as an aide to digestion (which helps with altitude sickness). All that saliva production promotes swallowing, too, which will pop your ears (like sucking hard candies on a plane). Only since the last couple of years have there been lodging options; the basic **Hostal del Cielo** (✉ *Belgrano at Comandante Goulu* ☎ *387/490-9912* 🌐 *www.vivirenloscobres.com.ar*) and the smarter **Hosteria de las Nubes** (✉ *RN51 s/n* ☎ *387/490-9059* 🌐 *www.maresur.com*) are the best right now, and more hotels are being built. Renting a room of someone's house is an option, too. A small ethnographic and archaeological museum, ANTAPU, fills in some detail on the town's background and raison d'etre, but it's still very young and needs more work. The main business is making artesanías—handmade goods that can be sold to tourists.

RESERVATIONS

Reservations can be made at many agencies in Salta or with **Les Amis** (✉ *Cerrito 844* ☎ *11/5246-6666*) in Buenos Aires and cost 120 USD in low season, 140 USD in high season. ✉ *Salta Station, Ameghino and Balcarce, Salta* ☎ *0800/888-6823* 🌐 *www.ecotren.com.*

EXTENDING YOUR TRIP

Though you can only buy return tickets, there's nothing to stop you getting off in San Antonio and continuing north to the salinas (salt flats) and on to Purmamarca in Jujuy. Bear in mind, however, that there's no public transport, though for the right price drivers will take you in their own cars. Going south to Cachi isn't as easy; the road is narrow and dangerous. Make sure to tell the gendarmeria in San Antonio if you're going to attempt this route.

TUCUMAN'S CIRCUITO CHICO

You need only go a little way out of Tucumán City to get a feel for the province. The Circuito Chico (Short Circuit) is a 70-km (45-mi) drive that heads west, through the affluent suburb of Yerba Buena, through cane fields and citrus orchards, and up into the Selva Tucumana—a subtropical rain forest.

Top left: Be sure to scan the *selva*, or forest, for butterflies.
Top right: Paraglide at Loma Bola.
Bottom right: Find rugged civility golfing in the Andean foothills.

The commuter village Villa San Javier, complete with its own statue of Christ, is full of lookouts that double as paragliding launch points. From here, head south to the picturesque village of Villa Nouges, where you can stop for a round of golf, to gape at the mansions, or to hike or fish. The road winds perilously back down to the plains and Ingenio San Pablo, until recently a major cane-processing center, where the road splits: R301 goes straight back to Tucumán City; R339 returns to Yerba Buena past another golf club. If you don't have your own transport, most local tour agencies offer half-day trips for around 50 pesos.

GETTING AROUND

On Tuesday, Thursday, and Sunday the tourist office organizes a 5½-hour tour of the Circuito Chico, and public buses run frequently to San Javier. But if you have access to a car, it makes sense to go it alone and explore the villages and views along the way. Avoid days of heavy rain, don't rush the narrow mountain roads, and leave early so you can complete the trip in the daytime.

THINGS TO DO AND SEE ALONG THE WAY

As befits a business-oriented city in such verdant surroundings, golf is a big concern in Tucumán and there are four good courses open to the public in the hills along the Circuito Chico, two close to the city in Yerba Buena and two in the hills. The oldest course is the **Jockey Club** in Yerba Buena, a short but demanding 18-hole course. Also in Yerba Buena is **Las Yungas Country Club** with a more gentle 9-hole course in pleasant surroundings. Higher in the hills are two 9-hole courses with amazing views; they claim the ball travels farther in the air at **El Siambón** than at sea-level, while the most picturesque of the bunch, **Las Hortensias**, was left fallow for nearly 15 years until 1987, when it was rediscovered and brought it back to life.

The beauty of the hills is everywhere—lush vegetation and wildflowers seem to greet you at every turn. But to experience nature in more depth, turn to the right shortly after Yerba Buena and head toward the **Reserva Experimental Horco Molle**. Part of the Parque Sierra de San Javier (run by the University of Natural Sciences of Tucuman), Horco Molle is full of ocelotes, tapirs, suris, and other fantastical creatures. There's spectacular wildlife to be found in the **Reserva Natural Aguas Chiquitas,** too, but the main attraction are the waterfalls—the biggest of which plummets 40 meters into a wonderfully cool pool.

To really take advantage of the cool breezes in the hills, you have to try **paragliding** from the launch pad at Loma Bola, between San Javier and Villa Nougués. When you chose your guide, though, note how much time is spent on instruction; generally, the more the better. Don't be shy about asking for safety records. Find more information and weather conditions at 🌐 *www.lomabola.com.ar.*

BEST GUIDES FOR . . .

Golf. There are no golf guides per se, but don't hesitate to contact a club directly for information on additional info that will help you self-guide yourself from hole to hole. **Jockey Club** (✉ *Yerba Buena, Av. Solano Vera, Km 2* ☎ *381/425-1038* 🌐 *www.jockeyclubtucuman.com*), **Las Yungas Country Club** (✉ *Yerba Buena, Mendoza y Canal* ☎ *381/425-0244* 🌐 *www.lasyungas.com*), **El Siambón** (✉ *RP341, Km 26* ☎ *381/492-5064*), **Las Hortensias** (✉ *Villa Nougués* ☎ *381/431-0862*).

Selva Tucumana. **Reserva Experimental Horco Molle** (✉ *Av. Pte. Perón* ☎ *381/425-0936* ⏲ *Daily 9–7* 🎫 *Guided tours 5 pesos*) has guided tours for 5 pesos, while Reserva Natural Aguas Chiquitas (3 km [2 mi] from El Cadillal) features a self-led hike to the main waterfall.

Paragliding. **Eduardo Deheza** (☎ *381/425-1430* ✉ *eduardodeheza@hotmail.com*) is our favorite instructor in this area who can take you on a tandem flight.

Updated by Andy Footner

Argentina's history began in the Northwest, in the provinces of Jujuy, Salta, and Tucumán, along the ancient road of the Incas. In the late 1400s the Incan people traveled southward from Peru along this route to conquer the tribes of northern Argentina and Chile. Half a century later the Spaniards traveled the same route in search of gold and silver.

By 1535 the Royal Road of the Inca had become a well-established trade route between the mines in the north and the agricultural riches of Argentina to the south. Examples of the pre-Hispanic and colonial cultures remain in the architecture, music, language, dress, and craftsmanship found in small villages throughout the region. Churches built by the Jesuits in the 17th century dot the landscape; Incan ruins lie half buried in remote valleys and high plateaus; and pre-Inca mummies continue to be discovered in the highest peaks of the Andes near Salta.

Neighboring Bolivia calls the high-altitude Andean desert of this region by its Spanish name, the *altiplano,* but Argentina prefers the ancient Quechua Indian term: the Puna. The desert covers an area of 90,000 square km (34,750 square mi) from Catamarca north across the Andes into Bolivia, Peru, and Chile. Alpacas, guanacos, llamas, and vicuñas are the only animals you'll see; dry grasses and thorny shrubs with deep roots searching for moisture the only plants. The wind is relentless. Who could live here? Just as you've asked yourself this question, the colorful red poncho of a *coya* (native woman of this region) momentarily brightens the barren landscape as she appears out of nowhere, herding llamas into an unseen ravine. Many people can't breathe at this altitude, let alone walk or sleep: luckily, ordinary mortals can experience a taste of the Puna from El Tren a las Nubes (The Train to the Clouds) in Salta, or by car driving north from Humahuaca to La Quiaca on the Bolivian border.

The colonial villages of Cafayate and Cachi bask in the warm, sunny Calchaqui Valley on the border between Tucumán and Salta provinces. The soaring cliffs of the Talampaya Canyon in La Rioja, with its fossils from over 200 million years ago, the Quebrada de Las Conchas between Salta and Cafayate, and the Quebrada de Humahuaca in Jujuy Province

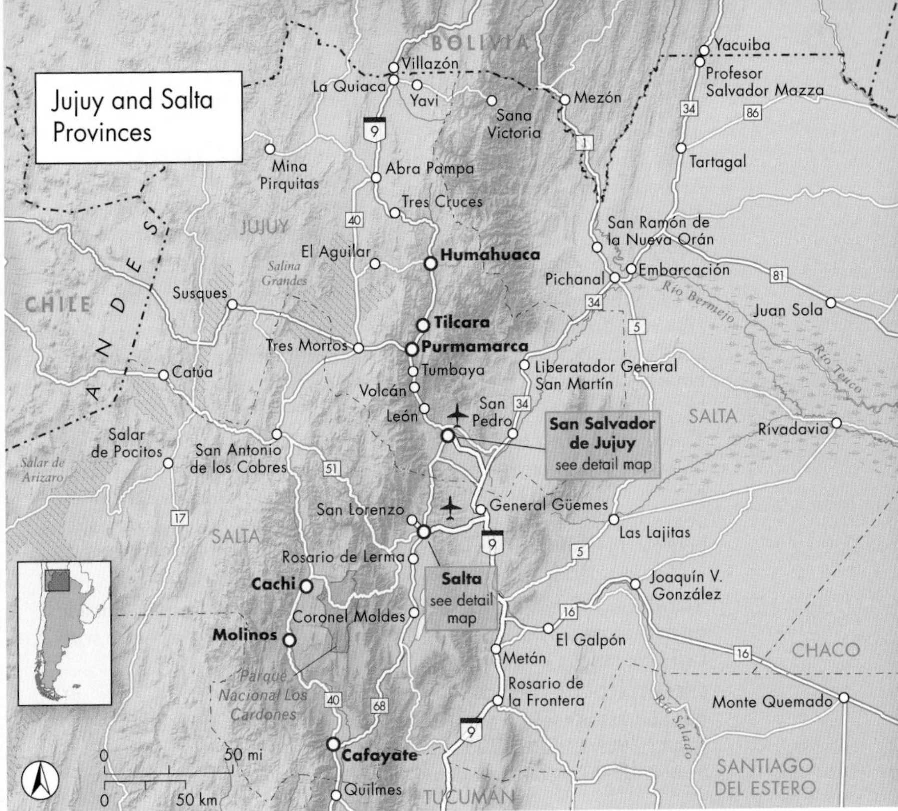

all impress with their peculiar rock formations. The peaks of the Andes run down the border with Chile, and subtropical jungle bursts out in Jujuy and Tucumán, which also has some of the most productive agricultural land in the country.

SAN SALVADOR DE JUJUY

1,643 km (1,020 mi) northwest of Buenos Aires; 97 km (60 mi) north of Salta on RN9; 459 km (285 mi) north of Tucumán on RN9.

Founded by Spaniards in 1593, San Salvador de Jujuy (simply Jujuy to most Argentines, and S. S. DE JUJUY on signs) was the northernmost town on the military and trade route between the Spanish garrisons in Peru and the northern cities of Argentina.

Today the quarter-million inhabitants—including a large indigenous population—of this city busy themselves with administration of the province's main sources of income (mining and tobacco). Just a few are beginning to deal with tourism, too. Although Jujuy lacks nearby Salta's colonial dreaminess (and hotel selection), it has a pleasant downtown, unadulterated local culture, and just a bit of frontier-town charm. And just outside town you can ride horses along mountain paths in the jungle or go boating in valley waterways.

GETTING HERE AND AROUND

Aerolíneas Argentinas flies once a day from Buenos Aires. The trip takes just over two hours. Jujuy's Aeropuerto Dr. Horacio Guzmán is 30 km (19 mi) southeast of town.

Andesmar and La Estrella run bus service from Tucumán and La Rioja to San Salvador de Jujuy. Andesmar also runs from Salta, as do Balut and Panamericano. These two also run north to Purmamarca, Tilcara, Humahuaca, and La Quiaca at the Bolivian border—a route also served by La Quiaqueño, which has nine departures a day.

Traffic builds up a bit around the beginning and end of the siesta, but otherwise Jujuy's one-way grid system is easy to navigate by rental car or by cabs, which are cheap. That said, most sights, restaurants, and hotels are within easy walking distance of the Plaza Belgrano, in the city center between the Río Grande and Río Xibi Xibi. The exception is the Alto de la Viña district, which is well worth the 7-peso taxi fare to reach.

You can arrange airport pickups, city tours, and excursions outside town through NASA, a family-owned and -operated travel office with two generations of experience.

WORD OF MOUTH

"I would suggest walking the loop first to get a close up look at the Cerro de los Siete Colores and then driving along the road towards the main highway for a panoramic view." —crellston

ESSENTIALS

Bus Contacts **Andesmar** (☎ *388/422–4888*). **Atahualpa** (☎ *387/431–9169*). **Balut** (☎ *388/422–2134*). **La Estrella** (☎ *388/422–4888*). **Panamericano** (☎ *388/423–7330*). **Terminal de Omnibus** (✉ *Dorrego and Iguazú*).

Banks and Currency Exchange **Banco Macro** (✉ *San Martín 789*). **HSBC** (✉ *Alvear 970*). **Cambio Dinar** (✉ *Belgrano 731*). **Horus** (✉ *Belgrano 722*).

Internet **Chat Bar** (✉ *Belgrano 678*).

Medical Assistance **Farmacia Siufi** (✉ *Alvear 1058* ☎ *388/422–3623 or 0800/222–5810*). **Hospital Pablo Soria** (✉ *Av. General Güemes 1345* ☎ *388/422–1228 or 388/422–1256*).

Rental Cars **Hertz** (✉ *Hotel Agustus Belgrano 715* ☎ *388/422–9582*).

Taxis **Parada Uno** (☎ *388/425–6500*).

Visitor and Tour Info **NASA** (✉ *Av. Senador Pérez 154* ☎ *388/422–3938* 🌐 *www.turismonorte.com.ar*). **Secretaría de Turismo y Cultura de la Provincia de Jujuy** (✉ *Gorriti 295* ☎ *388/422–1343* 🌐 *www.turismo.jujuy.gov.ar*).

EXPLORING

TOP ATTRACTIONS

❷ **Catedral de Jujuy.** The city cathedral dates from 1763, but has been augmented and remodeled so many times that it's now a hodgepodge of architectural styles. The interior contains an ornately carved, gold-plated pulpit, said to be the finest in South America. A close look reveals an intricate population of carved figures, biblical and otherwise. It was

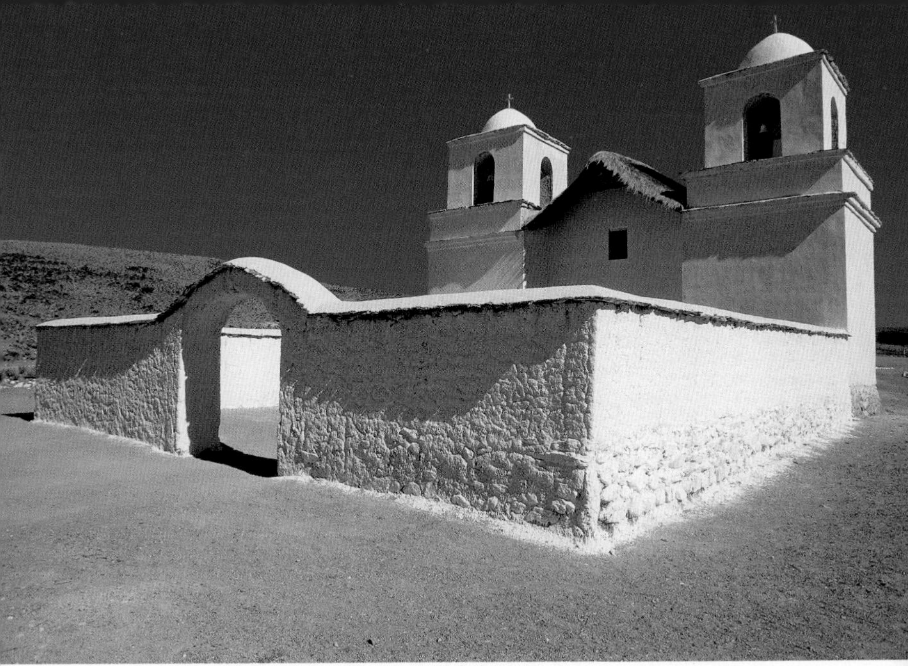

Head to Jujuy Province to see Puna architecture—like this church in Tafna—as stark as the landscape.

inspired by the Cusqueña school of art from Cuzco, Peru, as were the building's ornate doors and confessionals. ✉ *West side of Plaza General Belgrano* ☎ *388/423–5333* 🎫 *Free* 🕓 *Weekdays 10–noon and 5–10, weekends 7–noon and 5–10.*

6 **Centro Cultural y Museo Pasquini López.** Elevated on a natural balcony overlooking the city and with its own small patch of regenerated jungle, this mansion has a little museum of centuries-old ceramics and other artifacts found nearby. Better still, botanists have been developing a mile-long nature trail that buzzes with cicadas. Knowledgeable guides can enlighten you on the flora. Call ahead to organize tours in English. ✉ *Victor Hugo 45, Alto la Viña* ☎ *388/426–2569* 🎫 *1 peso* 🕓 *Weekdays 8 AM–9 PM, Sat. 9–1 and 3–7, Sun 9–1.*

3 **Iglesia de San Francisco.** An ornate 18th-century wooden pulpit with dozens of figures of monks is the centerpiece of the Church of St. Francis, two blocks west of Plaza General Belgrano. There's some debate about who carved the pulpit: it may have been local artisans, or the pulpit may have been transported from Bolivia. Although the church and bell tower look colonial, they date from 1930. ✉ *Belgrano and Lavalle* 🎫 *Free* 🕓 *Daily 10–1 and 5–9.*

4 **Museo Arqueológico Provincial.** The Provincial Archaeological Museum houses such treasures as a 2,600-year-old ceramic goddess and a mummy of a two-year-old child dating back 1,000 years. Ceramic pots painted with geometric designs from Yavi and Humahuaca are constantly being added to the collection, and a diorama shows what life was like here 9,000 years ago. ✉ *Lavalle 434* ☎ *388/422–1315* 🎫 *1 peso* 🕓 *Weekdays 8–8, weekends 9–1 and 4–8.*

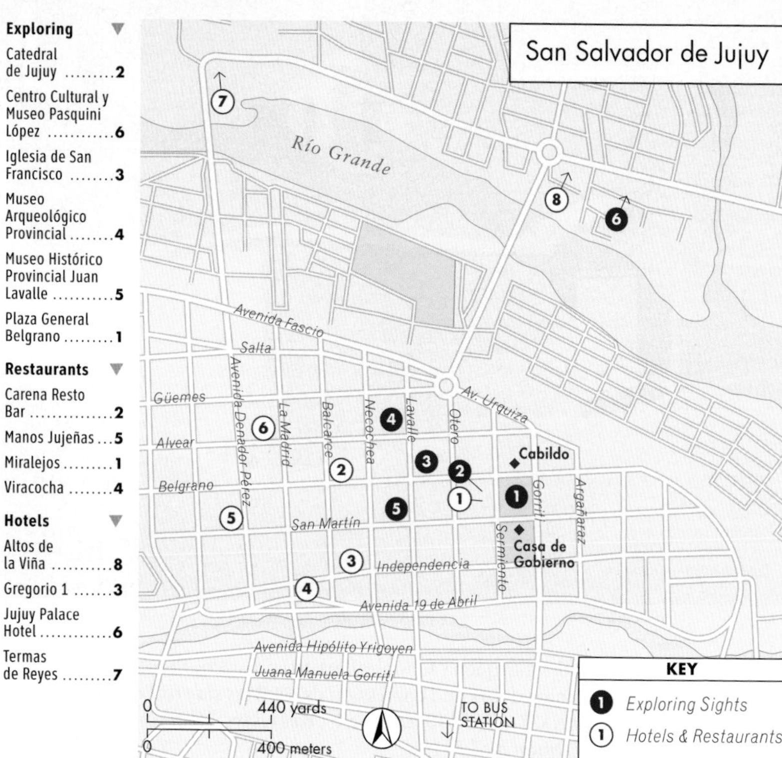

1 **Plaza General Belgrano.** Orange trees and vendors populate the central square, which is lined with colonial buildings—including the imposing government palace. It's empty by day, but in the early evening it fills with gossiping Jujeños. The 1907 **Casa de Gobierno** (Government House) fronts the plaza on San Martín and contains the provincial government offices. A second-floor hall, the Salón de la Bandera, displays the original Argentine flag donated by General Belgrano in 1813, a gift to the city after it cooperated with the Belgrano-headed Exodus of Jujuy during the War of Independence. The flag was replaced a couple of years later by the current white and sky-blue stripe version, and the one here is now used as the national coat of arms. ✉ *San Martín 450* ☎ *388/423–9400* 🎟 *Free* 🕒 *Weekdays 9–9, weekends 9–1 and 4–8.*

WORTH NOTING

5 **Museo Histórico Provincial Juan Lavalle.** Arms, trophies, and memorabilia from military campaigns collected from the 25 years of fighting for independence are on display at the Juan Lavalle Provincial History Museum. In this adobe building General Juan Lavalle, a hero of the wars of independence and an enemy of the dictator Juan Manuel de Rosas, was assassinated. A replica of the door through which Lavalle was shot in 1746 is part of the exhibit. ✉ *Lavalle 256* ☎ *388/422–1355* 🎟 *1 peso* 🕒 *Weekdays 8–8, weekends 9–1 and 4–8.*

WHERE TO EAT

$ ARGENTINE **Carena Resto Bar.** The muted lighting and slick furniture give this bar-restaurant a 1980s New York bond-trader look and feel. The clientele here is clearly the local bourgeoisie. Come for the Jujeña cuisine. *Belgrano and Balcarce 388/422–2529 DC, MC, V.*

$ ARGENTINE ★ **Manos Jujeñas.** Ponchos on the walls, old paintings, native artifacts, stucco archways, and Andean background music are clues that this might be a good place to sample authentic Northwestern cuisine. Try the locro: a soup of maize, white beans, pork, chorizo, pancetta, and a wonderful redpepper–oil glaze, all of which come together in a mélange of savory, starchy flavors. *Senador Pérez 379 388/424–3270 No credit cards No lunch Sun. No dinner Mon.*

$$ ARGENTINE **Miralejos.** Conveniently situated on the main square between the cathedral and the handicrafts market, Miralejos serves both Argentine standards and regional dishes. Enjoy them it with a home-brewed beer. *Sarmiento 268 388/422–4911 MC, V No lunch Mon.*

5

$ ARGENTINE Fodor's Choice ★ **Viracocha.** The menu at this unassuming *picanteria* (restaurant specializing in spicy foods) has everything from trout to rabbit, but llama or quinoa are the things to try. Less adventurous eaters can have one of the pasta dishes. Staffers are helpful, and the atmosphere amid the yellow walls and arches is happily relaxed. *Corner of Independencia and Lamadrid 0388/423–3554 AE, MC, V Closed Tues. No dinner Sun.*

WHERE TO STAY

$$ Fodor's Choice ★ **Altos de la Viña.** A former state-owned hotel a short ride out of town is now one of the best arguments for spending time in San Salvador de Jujuy. The view from the swimming pool takes in most of the city and the mountains beyond, and the facilities, including a spa and a very good and reasonably priced restaurant, mean there's plenty to keep you occupied. **Pros:** great pool; good for families; helipad. **Cons:** very little within walking distance. *Pasquini López 50, Alto la Viña 388/426–2626 www.altosdelavina.com.ar 60 rooms In-room: safe, refrigerator, DVD (some), Wi-Fi. In-hotel: restaurant, room service, bar, tennis court, pool, gym, spa, laundry service, parking (free), no-smoking rooms AE, DC, MC, V.*

$ **Gregorio 1.** This downtown boutique hotel has sober rooms with parquet floors and all the modern conveniences. Large ceramic pots and woven textiles decorate the public areas; the decor, with clean, simple lines, is well executed. **Pros:** close to everything; attentive service. **Cons:** few in-hotel services. *Independencia 829 388/424–4747 18 rooms, 1 suite In-room: refrigerator, Wi-Fi. In-hotel: laundry service, parking (paid) MC, V.*

$$ **Jujuy Palace Hotel.** Large rooms with impeccable facilities and balconies overlooking the street, a rooftop gym, a gated parking lot, and a formal second-floor dining room with first-class service are among the things that make this hotel exceptional. Views from the top floors take in the cloud-covered hills and Spanish colonial domes of the city center. **Pros:** comfortable; bilingual service. **Cons:** primarily a business hotel.

✉ *Belgrano 1060* ☎ *388/423–0433* 🌐 *www.jujuypalacehotel.com* 54 *rooms, 5 suites* *In-room: safe, refrigerator. In-hotel: restaurant, bar, gym, parking (free)* 💳 *AE, DC, MC, V.*

$$$ **Termas de Reyes.** This countryside complex (which was once run by Evita Perón's charity and twice paid host to the famed first lady) is on the edge of a spectacular river valley. Life here is all about relaxation and panoramic views. The centerpiece is the natural thermal baths, indoor and out, bubbling up from underground hot springs. **Pros:** the chance to take the cure and find inner peace. **Cons:** a location 19 km (12 mi) outside Jujuy on a partially paved road. ✉ *R4, Km 19* ☎ *388/492–2522* 🌐 *www.termasdereyes.com* *60 rooms* *In-hotel: restaurant, bar, pool, spa* 💳 *AE, DC, MC, V.*

AFTER DARK

For local music, head to **La Peluqueria** (✉ *Alvear 526* ☎ *388/424–0938* 🌐 *www.laspeluqueriapub.com*), a music hall where live bands perform every Wednesday to Saturday evening. Weeknights are for folk music; weekends are about covers of *rock nacional.*

In the **Babylonia Bar** (✉ *Independencia 946* ☎ *No phone*) they play electronic music and rock starting at around midnight. On weekends the bar's many rooms stay busy till 6 AM. For something more elaborate and traditional, try **Chung King** (✉ *Alvear 627* ☎ *388/422–2982*), a pizzeria that turns into an upscale dinner-entertainment venue with a good *peña* (folkloric music performance) on weekends.

SHOPPING

The modest **Paseo de los Artesanos** (✉ *Sarmiento 240* ☎ *No phone*) on Plaza General Belgrano has good prices on all kinds of woven and handcrafted souvenirs. And those *coca* tea bags, imported from Bolivia, are a curiosity that's hard to resist.

La Hilanderia (✉ *Belgrano 592* ☎ *388/424–2875* 🌐 *www.decotextil.com*) sells high-quality textiles. Look for bags, bedspreads, scarves, and whatever else you might want woven from sheep and llama wool brought down from the Puna to their factory just outside of town. They also work with cotton and design fabrics.

SPORTS AND THE OUTDOORS

With its jungles, lakes, waterfalls, and wild rivers, the area around San Salvador de Jujuy is great for hiking and horseback riding. There are a number of operators offering excursions, but very few are online, which makes things hard, as most trips must be booked a few days in advance. One notable exception is **Paisajes del Noroeste** (✉ *San Martin 132* ☎ *388/423–7565* 🌐 *www.noroestevirtual.com.ar*). The staff can arrange treks and horseback rides as well as paragliding and sandboarding (like snowboarding but on sand dunes) outings.

JUJUY PROVINCE

Although San Salvador de Jujuy is the provincial capital and the region's gateway, the star attraction of Jujuy (pronounced "hoo-*hoo*-wee"), Argentina's northernmost province, is the 161-km (100-mi) Quebrada de Humahuaca. In this breathtaking gorge, which has been used as a trade route for over 10,000 years, are the three towns of Purmamarca, Tilcara, and Humahuaca, each with a different feel. You can take in most of the region's attractions on day trips from these bases. Indeed, there are few visitor facilities elsewhere.

By far the largest part of Jujuy is the area known as the Puna: vast, high-altitude desert plains that merge into the Andes. Except for some villages built around exquisite adobe churches (most notably in the town of Yavi, near the Bolivian border), this area is pristine and tough, baked by day and chilled at night. The easiest way to experience it is on a trip to the Salinas Grandes (Great Salt Plains) from Purmamarca, a short drive with spectacular views.

For an otherworldly adventure, head to Laguna de los Pozuelos, with its exotic year-round colony of pink flamingos. Note, though, that it's a long way from the nearest hotel. The best approach is via Abra Pampa, the town where Ruta 9 and Ruta 40 meet, a 97-km (60-mi) drive from Humahuaca.

PURMAMARCA

65 km (40 mi) north of San Salvador de Jujuy.

Nestled in the shadow of craggy rocks and multicolored, cactus-studded hills—with the occasional low-flying cloud happening by—the colonial village of Purmamarca (altitude 7,200 feet/2,195 meters) is one of the best bases from which to explore the Quebrada. Its few lights and dry air also make it a great place for stargazing.

Here blazing red adobe replaces the white stucco used in architecture elsewhere, and the simple, square buildings play off the matching red rock. Come quick, before it's completely transformed from a one-horse town with basic stores and a few artisans selling their wares in the pleasant, tree-shaded plaza into an exclusive destination.

GETTING HERE AND AROUND

You get here via a clearly marked 3-km (2-mi) detour off Ruta 9 onto Ruta 52. Any of the many buses running from Jujuy to Humahuaca and beyond will drop you at the junction to wait for a local bus to take you the final 3 km (2 mi) into town. Evelina SA runs about 10 buses a day through here, to and from both Jujuy and Humahuaca.

Almost no place has its own street number (they're marked "s/n" or *sin numero* [no number] in addresses), but the town is so small that everything is either on or within one block of the main square, Plaza 9 de Julio. There's no bank or hospital, but there is a cash machine next to the tourist information office.

Continued on page 257

TOURING THE QUEBRADA DE HUMAHUACA

by Andy Footner

This rugged, windswept canyon connects Argentina's desert-like Puna near Bolivia with the city of San Salvador de Jujuy 150 km (93 mi) further south. It's a natural passage through the surrounding mountains, so it's no surprise that thousands of years of history have played out between its sandstone walls. For many, those very walls are the main attraction: colorful minerals, seismic activity, and a powerful river continue to shape one of Argentina's most fascinating geological formations.

Cardones, or cacti, and sandstone formations are a major part of the landscape in Argentina's northwest

HISTORY OF THE QUEBRADA

Jujuy Province, Quebrada de Humahuaca landscape near Purmamarca village

The Quebrada de Humahuaca continues to be carved into existence by the ever-changing Rio Grande. A roaring, splashing force in summer, the river in winter reduces to barely a trickle in its wide, dry riverbed. You'll have a good view wherever you are in the main canyon of the Quebrada; Route 9, the main north-south road through here, runs parallel to it. Like the river, people have come through this canyon in both trickles and torrents over the centuries—but unlike the river, the sense of history is strong whenever you visit.

PRE-INCAN TO THE CAMINO INCA

Ten thousand years ago, the first humans to inhabit the Southern Cone came from the north through this very canyon. Some stayed, becoming this area's original indigenous peoples. In the 15th and 16th centuries, the Incan Empire left its mark on the valley and the culture; the single road through this protected canyon became part of the hugely important Camino Inca—the Inca Trail, a system of roads used to travel through the empire which eventually spanned much of the Andes. Because of this unique Andean history, the culture here can seem to share more with those of Bolivia and Peru than with other parts of Argentina; keep your ears open in town squares: in this part of Argentina you can still hear people speaking Quechua and Aymara, two of the main languages of the Incas.

PEÑAS

Clubs, restaurants, and *peñas* attract both locals and tourists, who come to hear regional folk bands give it their all on small, cramped stages. Adding to the rowdy, dinner-theater atmosphere are the local dancers who entice (and often entrap) foreigners into strutting their stuff on stage; it's always a good laugh, no matter what language you speak.

Tilcara, Children's carnival, Quebrada de Humauaca

JESUITS AND VICEROYALTIES

The Incans weren't the only conquering force that found the protected valley appealing: in the 17th century, Jesuit priests used Aymara and Quechua to convert the locals to Catholocism, which helped the Spanish eventually use the Quebrada to connect the Viceroyalties (administration center) of Peru in Lima and La Plata in what would later become Buenos Aires. Today, the local mix of pre-Incan, Incan, and Christian traditions and symbols are reflected in everything from dress to architecture to the kinds of items you'll find for sale.

WORLD HERITAGE

Traditions and festivals celebrated along the Quebrada include a unique combination of ancient Andean rites and European religious celebrations. In 2003, UNESCO added the Quebrada to its World Heritage list for its continued legacy of pre-Hispanic and pre-Incan settlements in the area.

SHOPPING CULTURE

The best shopping is in Humahuaca. Numerous small shops sell tourist trinkets, and there's a daily handicrafts market on the steps leading up the hill to the monument. Most of the items for sale will be familiar to anyone who has traveled in the central Andean region, and there are a few artisans making jewelery and other items in more modern Argentine styles.

GEOLOGICAL COLORS: A TIMELINE

The hills in the Quebrada de Humahuaca are famous for their colors—caused by mineral deposits formed from 1 to 400 million years ago. The two best places to see the colors are the Paleta del Pintur (Painter's Palette, pictured) and the Cerro de los Siete Colores (Hill of Seven Colors).

ITINERARY

Salinas Grandes

DAY ONE

MORNING: Purmamarca

The smallest and most picturesque town in the Quebrada, Purmamarca is about two hours north of Salta or over an hour north of San Salvador de Jujuy on R9. The turnoff (left side) onto RA52 is well marked. Arrive as early as possible for the morning light. Get your bearings with a view of the Cerro de Los Siete Colores (Hill of Seven Colors) from a popular viewpoint on the north side of RA52; the trailhead is on your right as you approach town. You can also walk along Paseo de los Colorados, a dirt road (watch for vehicles) that winds around the base of hill itself; to get to it from Plaza 9 de Julio, head west on Florida for 3 blocks.

AFTERNOON: Siesta or Salinas Grandes

Purmamarca goes from quiet to dead during the afternoon siesta; take a siesta yourself, or head out on a half-day side trip. Drive further west on RA52 as it winds its way up the **Cuesta de Lipan** (the Lipan Slope, the Quebrada's mountainous western barrier) and on to the **Salinas Grandes** (Big Salt Flats). If you're without your own transport, there are plenty of taxis, remises, or guides to take you. Technically, the Salinas Grandes themselves are outside of the Quebrada, but the drive there takes you through a dramatic mountain pass—and the highest driveable point in the Quebrada; look for a sign marking your altitude of 4170 m (13,681 ft). After an hour or two (depending on your vehicle's horsepower and photo stops), you'll take unpaved EX-RN40 south to the turnoff (right side) for the Salinas Grandes. Drive until you're on the salt flats themselves—this is the parking lot. This is a working salt flat; don't miss gazing into the clear blue harvesting pools.

NIGHT: Purmamarca

Once back in Purmamarca, explore some nouveau Andean cuisine at **Los Morteros**. After dinner, head to **El Rincon de Claudia Vilte**, a friendly peña where the musicians like to find out where the audience is from in between renditions of folk songs about the Quebrada.

DAY TWO

MORNING: Tilcara

Set out early and take R9 north to Tilcara; head straight to the **Pucará de Tilcara**. This partially reconstructed pre-Columbian fort shows one of the most complex ruins in Argentina. Make time to visit the botanical garden next door. Wander through the central square's market, one of the best in the region. Leave to arrive in Humahuaca before noon.

AFTERNOON: Humahuaca to Maimara

Every day at noon at San Francisco Solano church, a statue of the church's namesake pops out of the clock tower and, as the story goes, delivers a blessing. Catch this if you can, then have lunch and explore the market near the monument steps. Stop in at the small yet atmospheric folklore museum. On your way back to Salta or Jujuy, make brief photo stops at the **Tropic of Capricorn** at Huacalera, the church at Uquia (known for its Cuzco School angel paintings), and the photogenic cemetery of the town of Maimara. If sunset is approaching, however, simply head straight for Maimara—visible behind the cemetary is the Painter's Palette. This flat segment of the east canyon wall contains colored layers of mineral deposits that attain stunningly rich hues as the light shines in from the west.

Pucará de Tilcara

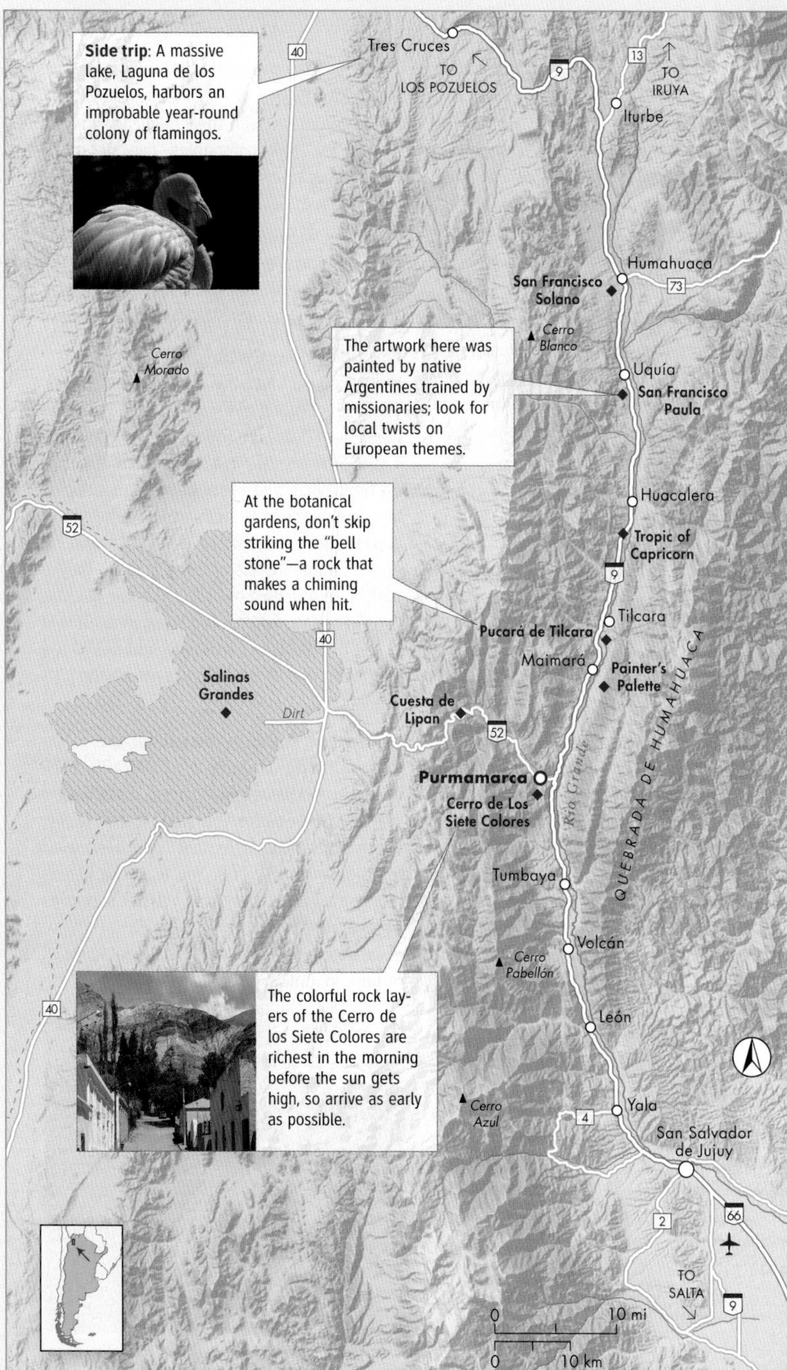

Side trip: A massive lake, Laguna de los Pozuelos, harbors an improbable year-round colony of flamingos.
Tres Cruces
TO LOS POZUELOS
TO IRUYA
Iturbe
Humahuaca
San Francisco Solano
Cerro Blanco
Cerro Morado
The artwork here was painted by native Argentines trained by missionaries; look for local twists on European themes.
Uquía
San Francisco Paula
Huacalera
Tropic of Capricorn
At the botanical gardens, don't skip striking the "bell stone"—a rock that makes a chiming sound when hit.
Pucará de Tilcara
Tilcara
Maimará
Painter's Palette
Salinas Grandes
Dirt
Cuesta de Lipan
Purmamarca
Cerro de Los Siete Colores
Río Grande
QUEBRADA DE HUMAHUACA
Tumbaya
Volcán
Cerro Pabellón
The colorful rock layers of the Cerro de los Siete Colores are richest in the morning before the sun gets high, so arrive as early as possible.
León
Cerro Azul
Yala
San Salvador de Jujuy
TO SALTA
0
10 mi
0
10 km

PLANNING YOUR VISIT

PUBLIC TRANSIT

A good and frequent bus system and shared taxis between the main towns mean hitchhiking isn't common or necessary. However, although buses reach all destinations described, renting a car or going with a guide mean you can stop at any point to explore, take pictures, and admire the views.

SELF-DRIVE LOGISTICS

Cars can be rented in Salta and Jujuy. Check the conditions for off-road driving and the options for crossing a pass into Chile—these are not automatically included in the rental.

Good to Know:

- Car hire agencies like to calculate the price on the spot and there's little transparency in their calculations. Many destinations from Salta and San Salvador de Jujuy involve unpaved roads that are punishing on cars, so it might help to let them know your itinerary if you're only visiting the Quebrada (where all the roads are paved). Pricing systems favor round trips (i.e. there's a big surcharge for dropping off a car in another city).
- Gas stations can be found in most of the towns, but they don't all take credit cards. Except for in Humahuaca (ACA—the Automovil Club Argentino) and San Salvador de Jujuy, plan for cash only. As well as providing gas and good maps, ACA is the Argentine equivalent of the AAA and can help you out if your car breaks down somewhere.
- The roads in the Quebrada are better than most in the area—they're well marked and have clear passing lanes—but during the rainy season (between October and February), falling rocks or mudslides can block the roads.

Car Rental Agencies: In Salta, **Hertz** (✉ Caseros 374 4400 ☎ 387/421-6785) and **Localiza** (☎ 387/431-4045; 0800/999-2999 central reservations) are reputable companies. In Jujuy, contact **Hertz** (✉ Hotel Agustus Belgrano 715 ☎ 388/422-9582).

GUIDED TOURS

Personal guides, with their own cars or ones owned by their companies, can be found through the tourism offices of Salta and Jujuy. From Salta in particular, a sure bet is:

Angélica Vasquez de Zaleski (☎ 387/4964-0658 ✉ langie_guide@hotmail.com). There are also many, many bus trips from Salta or Jujuy, taking in the Quebrada sights in a day or longer.

For Indigenous Culture:
When you pull into the town of Humahuaca, you'll see a group of locals waiting under the main sign. These are tour guides; if you know a little Spanish, they're a wealth of information on how Wichí and other indigenous peoples live and work in Humahuaca today. Even if you're here with a tour guide of your own, he or she might hire one of these guides—they're part of an initiative to provide career alternatives in a place where drug smuggling (Bolivia is just a few clicks north, after all) has in the past been one of the only decent-paying jobs available.

For Getting Out Into the Landscape:
Caravana de Llamas (☎ 0388/495-5326 🌐 www.caravanadellamas.com.ar), out of Tilcara, offers an experience you won't get at home: llama treks along trails that have been used for thousands of years. You lead the llamas along; they carry everything you need for trips that can last from 1 to 10 days. On overnight excursions, you're hosted by the inhabitants of remote mountain huts.

Llamas, Jujuy Province

ESSENTIALS

Transportation Contacts Evelina SA buses (☎ *388/423–6975*). Taxi (☎ *388/490–8030*).

Visitor and Tour Info Tourist Office (✉ *Belgrano s/n, on Plaza 9 de Julio* ☎ *388/155–808–352*).

EXPLORING

The most notable feature downtown on the central plaza is the landmark 1648 **Iglesia de Santa Rosa de Lima**, which was constructed from adobe and thistle wood.

★ Looming above Purmamarca is the **Cerro de Siete Colores**, Hill of Seven Colors, with its lavenders, oranges, and yellows. Look closely and see if you can find all seven—most people can pick out only four. ■ **TIP→ The colors are most clearly visible in the morning.** The best way to see the hill is by walking a 3-km (2-mi) loop called the **Paseo de Siete Colores,** which starts to the left of the church on the main square. This one-lane gravel road winds through bizarre, humanlike formations of bright, craggy, red rock, before passing a series of stark, sweeping, Mars-like vistas with stands of trees in the river valley. The road then passes a few family farms and ends with a striking view of the Cerro itself before bringing you back to the center of Purmamarca. You can also drive the route, though the ride is a bit bumpy. The tourist office has a map showing the best points for photos.

5

Sixty-four km (40 mi) west of Purmamarca lie the **Salinas Grandes**, over 200 square km (80 square mi) of dazzling salt crystals. To get here you travel Ruta 52 over the majestic Cuesta de Lipan (Lipan Rise)—which tops out at 4,170 meters (13,700) above sea level—and cross Ruta 40. The salty landscape is surreal, and it's made even more so by a building (once a restaurant but now closed, as there's currently no water source) constructed entirely out of slabs of salt turned a brownish color. A series of small pools have been cut out of the salt flats' surface, revealing a layer of water and freshly forming crystals underneath. Take a camera, a hat, and sunblock.

WHERE TO EAT

$$ ARGENTINE

✕ **La Posta de Purmamarca.** Empanadas, llama dishes, and other regional specialties dominate the menu at this eatery on the main square. Take a seat by the window and watch the scene at the market stalls outside while enjoying such Jujeño staples as *picante de pollo* (spicy chicken). La Posta also has a boutique and some rooms to stay in, but it's the restaurant that's the draw. ✉ *Rivadavia s/n, on Plaza 9 de Julio* ☎ *388/490–8040* 🌐 *www.postadepurmamarca.com.ar* ▭ *No credit cards* 🕒 *Closed Mon.*

$$ ARGENTINE Fodor's Choice ★

✕ **Los Morteros.** Even if it didn't have a multicolored hill, Purmamarca would be an essential stop in the Quebrada de Humahuaca just for this restaurant. Its insistence on regional products helped to start a trend in the area, but the food is still highly inventive and delicious. There's plenty of quinoa and llama on the menu, and ceramic pots, adobe, and earthy tones provide the decoration. Reservations are a good idea. ✉ *Salta s/n* ☎ *388/490–8063* ▭ *MC, V* 🕒 *Closed Mon.*

"Rectangles have been dug out [of Salinas Grandes] to allow the water to seep through and salt to crystallize for the miners to harvest. The clearest water and the whitest salt I have ever seen." —Clive Ellston, Fodors.com member

WHERE TO STAY

$ **El Cardon.** It's small and no-frills, but if you're just looking for a place to sleep in between excursions, this friendly lodging a short walk from the main square is a good bet. Its seven rooms are arranged around a small courtyard, and are decorated sparingly. **Pros:** a reliable, in-town option. **Cons:** few facilities; often booked in high season. ✉ *Belgrano s/n* ☎ *388/490–8672* *7 rooms* *In-room: no a/c, no phone, no TV* *No credit cards.*

$$$$ ★ **El Manantial del Silencio.** At this tranquil retreat weeping willows, red rocks, and gardens filled with birdsong are hemmed in by the craggy Quebrada and its utter calm. Inside the colonial-style stucco mansion local artifacts and earth tones make things warm and harmonious throughout. The restaurant offers sophisticated takes on local fare. **Pros:** the grandest lodging in the Quebrada; great gardens and pool. **Cons:** the most expensive lodging in the Quebrada. ✉ *RN52, Km 3.5* ☎ *388/490–8080* ⊕ *www.hotelmanantialdesilencio.com.ar* *18 rooms, 1 suite* *In-room: no a/c, safe, no TV, Wi-Fi. In-hotel: restaurant, room service, bar, pool, bicycles, laundry service, parking (free)* *AE, DC, MC, V.*

$$$$ **La Comarca.** The various rooms, cabins, and houses (which can sleep up to six people) here surround a garden of flowers and cacti. All accommodations are built with traditional local materials—adobe, cane, wood—and decorated with a contemporary eye. A similar aesthetic is reflected in the restaurant, which is one of the best in town. The small pool is so warm you can even take a dip on a cool evening. **Pros:** quiet; well decorated; good restaurant. **Cons:** showers not designed for tall people. ✉ *RN52, Km 3.8* ☎ *388/490–8001* ⊕ *www.*

lacomarcahotel.com.ar ⊲ *12 rooms, 2 houses, 2 cabins, 1 suite* ♁ *In-room: no a/c, kitchen (some), refrigerator (some), no TV, Wi-Fi. In-hotel: restaurant, room service, bars, pool, gym, spa, laundry service, parking (free)* ▭ *AE, MC, V.*

$$$ **Los Colorados.** All the reddish adobe walls of the cabins here, on the Cerro de Siete Colores, have rounded corners, giving the whole place a look of having been sculpted straight from the earth. They say imitation is the greatest form of flattery, and in that spirit several similar structures have been built in the valley since this hotel opened in 2006. It's perfect for kicking back, whether you're in your room curled up by the fireplace or on the common terrace stargazing. **Pros:** quiet retreat; a six-person Jacuzzi. **Cons:** small bathrooms. ✉ *El Chapacal s/n* ☎ *388/490–8182* ⊕ *www.loscoloradosjujuy.com.ar* ⊲ *7 rooms* ♁ *In-room: no a/c, no phone, safe, kitchen, no TV (some). In-hotel: parking (free)* ▭ *MC, V.*

AFTER DARK

At **El Rincon de Claudia Vilte** (✉ *Libertad s/n, close to corner of Belgrano* ☎ *388/490–8088* ✉ *7-peso cover*) the crowd is fairly cosmopolitan, but on the small stage of this intimate peña it's pure Jujeño, with pan pipes, drums, and guitars as well as the occasional storytelling session with tales about local traditions and happenings.

At the town's only late-night bar, **El Heriberto** (✉ *Sarmiento s/n, close to corner of Libertad* ☎ *No phone*), you get a good mix of locals and visitors. In high season it's open from 10 PM until the last customer leaves or until 5 AM, whichever comes first.

5

TILCARA

85 km (53 mi) north of San Salvador; 18 km (11 mi) northeast of Purmamarca via RN9.

The town of Tilcara (altitude 8,100 feet), founded in 1600 and witness to many battles during the War of Independence, is on the eastern side of the Río Grande at its confluence with the Río Huasamayo. Purveyors of local crafts crowd the main plaza, and artists and musicians escaping the big cities fill the cafés and bars. Several things make it a main stop in the Quebrada: an interesting museum; nearby Inca ruins, caves, and waterfalls; and a good selection of accommodations.

GETTING HERE AND AROUND

You get here along the Ruta 9, which is well served by buses running between San Salvador de Jujuy and Humahuaca or La Quiaca. Arriving from the south, look out for the surprisingly large cemetery of Maimará, which sprawls on either side of the road outside town. If you're heading to San Salvador de Jujuy from Tilcara, consider taking one of the shared taxis that are available at the bus terminal; they cost about the same as buses.

ESSENTIALS

Bank Banco Macro (✉ *Lavalle s/n, at Marcelino Vargas*).

Bus Contacts Atahualpa (☎ *387/431–9169*). **Evelia SA** (☎ *388/495–5216*).

Medical Assistance Hospital (✉ *Lavalle 552* ☎ *388/495-5001*).

Visitor Info Tourist Office (✉ *Belgrano s/n, at Padilla* ☎ *No phone*).

EXPLORING

At the **Museo Arqueológico**, run by the University of Buenos Aires, you're often left wondering what you're looking at due to a lack of labels. The two mummies on display are considerably less well explained and cared for than those in Salta's Museum of High Altitude Archaeology, but no less fascinating. The clothes, hair, and skin of the first, found in San Pedro de Atacama in Chile, are well preserved. Other rooms show Nazca, Inca, Aguada, and other remains from the last 2,000 years. Keep your ticket stubs, as they'll get you in to the nearby Pucará de Tilcara ruins, where some of the artifacts here were found. ✉ *Belgrano 445* ☎ *388/495-5006* *5 pesos* *Daily 9-12:30 and 2-6.*

★ On a hill above the left bank of the Río Grande about a mile south of town are the **Pucará de Tilcara** ruins. This fortified, pre-Inca settlement is the best preserved of several in the Quebrada de Humahuaca. You can clearly see the different parts of the village (some have been rebuilt) among the cacti on the hill. Allow at least 90 minutes to walk around where the Omaguaca lived, worshipped, kept their animals, and threw away their waste. Turn left at the entrance to the fort for the Jardin Botanico (Botanical Garden), with a large array of cacti among its plantings. Don't turn down the invitation on a sign to strike the Piedra Campana with another stone—true to its name (Bell Stone) it rings like a bell. Note that ticket stubs from a visit to the Museo Arqueológico in town get you free entrance to both the ruins and the botanical garden. *5 pesos* *Daily 9-12:30 and 2-6.*

Seven kilometers (4 mi) west of town is **La Garganta del Diablo** (The Devil's Throat), a red-rock gorge with waterfalls (the number depends on the season). The tourist office in Tilcara can point you in the right direction; ask about the path that knocks about half the distance off the journey. Ask, too, for directions to the wind-eroded caves that are a similar distance east of town.

WHERE TO EAT

$$ ARGENTINE Fodor's Choice ★ ✕ **El Nuevo Progreso.** The food is superb; the wine list is good and fairly priced; and the wooden floors, fairy lights, and artwork make the space appealing. What's more, every evening around 9:30 there's live music, generally performed by friends of the owners. It's right in the center of town, with windows looking out on the small plaza. ✉ *Lavalle 351* ☎ *388/495-5237* *MC, V.*

$$ ARGENTINE ✕ **El Patio Comidas.** With three dining rooms, a patio out back, a location just yards from the central plaza, and well-priced regional cuisine, El Patio is one of Tilcara's most recommended restaurants. The menu is an unpretentious mix of regional specialties and standard Argentinian fare, and service is friendly. ✉ *Lavalle 352* ☎ *388/495-5044* *MC, V* *Closed Tues.*

$$ ARGENTINE ✕ **Los Puestos.** A poetic narrative in the menu describes this place as "a haven for parched travelers," along the lines of the watering holes used for centuries by area shepherds. As well as water and wine, they offer bread and empanadas baked in the oven right by the entrance

PARTY TIME, QUEBRADA-STYLE

If you time your trip to Salta and Jujuy provinces right, you'll get to see some of the most unique partying this side of the Paraná Delta.

CARNIVAL

Where? All over the province, but especially in Humahuaca.
When? The week before lent.
Go if you like . . . dancing with a lot of strangers and some dressed-up devils.
The north of Argentina has a few good options for Carnaval, not to mention neighboring Brazil, but the Quebrada de Humahuaca's take on the festival is a treat to witness. Local papers carry lists of performance times and places for carnival bands and people get dressed up and dance all day and all night, encouraged by plentiful chicha (a potent spirit made from fermented corn or peanuts).

PACHAMAMA

Where? All over the Quebrada.
When? August 1.
Go if you like . . . ecological awareness and age-old tradition.
The Pachamama is the time for giving thanks to *Madre Tierra* (Mother Earth) for all she has given during the year. The best corn, potatoes, meat and other vegetables are dried and stored in preparation for the first of August, when they are prepared in a *tijtincha* (stew) and "fed" to the earth—they're buried under stones in a hole in the ground—along with other food, cigarettes, coca leaves, alcohol, and trinkets. The festival stresses the dependence on the earth for subsistence and is as much to ask the land to provide for the year to come as to thank her for what she has given. During the rest of the year, the Pachamama is honored through the gradual construction of *apachetas* (piles of stones) by the side of the road or on tops of hills, which passers-by add one stone to each time.

INTI RAYMI

Where? Huacalera.
When? June 20–21.
Go if you like . . . sunshine in the wintertime.
On the eve of the winter solstice at the monument marking the Tropic of Capricorn they light fires for the Festival of the Sun, standing round big fires sharing hot alcoholic drinks and trying to keep warm on the midwinter night. It's a huge festival in Peru, reintroduced to the Quebrada in the '90s and getting bigger each year.

EXODO JUJEÑO

Where? All over the province.
When? August 22 and 23.
Go if you like . . . history and celebrating strategic retreats.
In commemoration of General Belgrano's decision to evacuate Jujuy in 1812 in the face of a large Spanish advance, a drastic step which served to disorientate the enemy and ultimately gain vital ground. It's now become the focal point of the province's pride and is celebrated with parades in the streets and re-enactments.

FIESTA DE LA VIRGEN DE LA CANDELARIA

Where? Humahuaca.
When? February 2.
Go if you like . . . low-key processions, traditional music.
The patron saint of Humahuaca is honored on February 2, with preparations building up in the days before. Bands of young men playing *sikuris* and *cajas* (Andean flutes and drums) while a statue of the Virgin is carried through the streets.

and delicate cuts of meat. Try the fillet of llama with orange sauce and Andean potatoes. ✉ *Belgrano, corner of Padilla* ☎ *388/495–5100* ▭ *MC, V* ⊙ *Closed Mon.*

$$ ARGENTINE ✕ **Yacón**. The friendly service, wooden tables and chairs, cane roof, and stone walls all suggest tradition. Yet the kitchen shows some innovation by serving llama meat on skewers and a shepherd's pie made with quinoa. It's just a block from the main square. ✉ *Rivadavia 222* ☎ *388/495–5611* ▭ *No credit cards* ⊙ *No dinner Sun.*

WHERE TO STAY

$$$ **Las Terrazas**. A few blocks from the square and in a less touristed area, Las Terrazas has nine spacious rooms, each with its own balcony. The bar serves snacks and regional wines; at this writing, a restaurant and a small swimming pool are in the works. Check out the ingenious water feature that flows inside and out and a perfectly circular well that dates back at least a thousand years and was discovered during construction. **Pros:** good-size rooms and bathrooms; great views; a good breakfast. **Cons:** not very central. ✉ *La Sorpresa s/n, at San Martín* ☎ *388/495–5589* 🌐 *www.lasterrazastilcara.com.ar* *9 rooms* *In-room: no a/c, safe, DVD (some), Wi-Fi. In-hotel: room service, bar, parking (free)* ▭ *AE, MC, V.*

$$$ **Refugio del Pintor**. The building that houses this hotel (look carefully for the sign, or you'll miss it) was formerly used by a painter from Jujuy, hence the name and the local artworks on the walls. The garden and the sweeping views have been here a while; everything else has been redone with style and imagination. Rooms are small but efficient, with wooden beams, striped fabrics, and big windows. Common spaces are light and welcoming. There's a *fogón* (open fireplace) for cooking in the courtyard. **Pros:** switched-on staff; great views; good common spaces; good breakfast. **Cons:** small rooms. ✉ *Alverro s/n, between Jujuy and Ambroseti* ☎ *388/495–5695* 🌐 *www.elrefugiodelpintor.com* *13 rooms* *In-room: no a/c, TV, Wi-Fi. In-hotel: restaurant, room service, bar* ▭ *AE, DC, MC, V.*

$ **Uwa Wasi**. The name means "a house with grapes," and it does, indeed, have a few vines in its rambling back garden, where there's also space to relax and get to know your hosts, whose grandparents built the house. Rooms are small and basic, some share bathrooms, but all have personal touches. **Pros:** good location; friendly service, nice garden. **Cons:** small rooms; few facilities. ✉ *Lavalle 564* ☎ *388/495–5368* 🌐 *www.uwawasi.com.ar* *6 rooms* *In-room: no a/c, no phone, no TV* ▭ *No credit cards* *CP.*

$$$ **Viento Norte.** This long, thin, adobe boutique hotel overlooks a decent-size swimming pool. Rooms have simple decorations and low lighting. A special emphasis was placed on getting the bathrooms right; those in superior rooms have hot tubs. There's a snack bar but no restaurant. It's not a bother, though, thanks to all the eateries in the town center, just a couple of blocks away. **Pros:** central yet quiet; a good breakfast. **Cons:** pool is visible from the street. ✉ *Jujuy 536* ☎ *388/495–5605* 🌐 *www.hotelvientonorte.com.ar* *11 rooms* *In-room: no a/c, safe, refrigerator, no TV (some), Wi-Fi. In-hotel: room service, bar, pool, no-smoking rooms* ▭ *MC, V.*

Cardones (cacti) grow amid the ruins of the Pucará de Tilcara in Jujuy Province.

AFTER DARK

It's hard to miss rustic, characterful **La Peña de Carlitos** (✉ *Lavalle 397* ☎ *388/495–5331* 🌐 *www.lapeniadecarlitos.com.ar*): it's the place with the large murals on the main square. The music is great; the food isn't. **Rincon del Colla** (✉ *Lavalle s/n, at Alverro* ☎ *388/495–5618*) has live folk music every night starting at about 9:30.

SHOPPING

The central plaza fills with stalls selling Andean-type souvenirs and gifts, some handcrafted by the stall holder, some imported from Bolivia. The best of the local stuff includes knitted hats and scarves. On a Saturday afternoon there's also an old woman with a cart selling *chicha*—an alcoholic drink made from fermented corn—you won't want a lot, but it's a rare opportunity to try it.

SPORTS AND THE OUTDOORS

Caravana de Llamas (☎ *0388/495–5326* 🌐 *www.caravanadellamas.com.ar*) offers an experience you won't get at home: llama treks along trails that have been used for thousands of years. You lead the llamas along; they carry everything you need for trips that can last from 1 to 10 days. On overnight excursions you're hosted by the inhabitants of remote mountain huts.

HUMAHUACA

126 km (78 mi) north of San Salvador de Jujuy; 42 km (26 mi) north of Tilcara on RN9.

Humahuaca (9,700 feet) is the gateway to the Puna. Its narrow stone streets hark back to pre-Hispanic civilizations, when aboriginals fought the Incas who came marauding from the north. The struggle for survival continued into the 16th century, when the Spanish arrived.

Given its location, Humahuaca is a bit touristy, flooded with vendors hawking artisan wares. Things are busiest at midday, when an automated carving of Saint Francisco Solano emerges like a cuckoo from a clock to bless visitors in the main plaza with his mechanized arm. Despite all this, the town is very short on visitor amenities: the tourist board is less than organized, and there are only a few lodgings. These include a couple of small, basic hotels (some downright run-down and depressing) and one large hotel that, at this writing, is falling into disrepair while the municipality decides what's to be done with it.

You're much better off staying in Tilcara. And, indeed, most people visit Humahuaca on a day trip from there, Purmamarca, or San Salvador de Jujuy, or as a stop en route to Iruya. That said, if you're nearby around the time of Carnaval (40 days before Easter), it's worth putting up with whatever lodgings you can get to participate in the wonderful festivities that are a complicated mix of Catholicism and paganism.

GETTING HERE AND AROUND

You can easily visit the town and nearby gorge as a day trip from San Salvador de Jujuy or Salta, either with a car or with a tour group. RN9 leads straight here on its way from San Salvador to La Quiaca, and Balut, Panamericano, and other lines have buses going each way almost every hour during the day.

ESSENTIALS

Bank Banco Macro (✉ *Jujuy 327*).

Medical Assistance Farmacia (✉ *Cabildo, central plaza*).

Visitor Info Tourist Office (✉ *Cabildo, central plaza* ☎ *388/421–375*).

EXPLORING

Humahuaca's picturesque **cabildo** (town hall), on the main square, is the most striking building in the village, with a beautifully colored and detailed clock tower. Each day at about noon, everyone crowds into the plaza to watch as a life-size mechanized statue of San Francisco Solano pops out of the tower—it's kitschy fun. You can't go inside, but you can peer into the courtyard. ✉ *Central plaza.*

The 1641 **Iglesia de la Candelaria** contains fine examples of Cusqueño art, most notably paintings depicting elongated figures of Old Testament prophets by 18th-century artist Marcos Sapaca. ✉ *Calle Buenos Aires, west side of central plaza.*

★ At first sight the **Museo Folklórico Regional** is a dusty collection of stones and strange objects, but allow a guide (arrange in advance for one who speaks English) to show you around, and you'll learn a lot about the indigenous population. The museum has been put together by one man over the last forty years with a huge amount of passion and imagination, and each exhibit—from dolls made of dried apricots to musical instruments made from armadillos—provides a new insight. ✉ *Buenos Aires 435* ☎ *388/421–064.*

WHERE TO EAT

$$ ARGENTINE ✕ **Hostel El Portillo.** This restaurant-café (which also has seven modest double rooms to rent for about 100 pesos a night) caters to the Quebrada- or Puna-bound travelers. That said, it retains a rustic, local feel. Friendly service puts you at ease, and a cute adobe courtyard allows for a lazy lunch in the midday sun. You can get a llama steak or a hearty version of the classic regional dish *locro* (here it's made with yellow squash, pureed beans and corn, and various types of pork). There's even a short wine list. ✉ *Tucumán 69* ☎ *3887/421–288* 🌐 *www.elportillohumahuaca.com.ar* 💳 *V.*

$ ARGENTINE ★ ✕ **K'allapurca.** At lunch the best tables are taken by groups of tourists being serenaded by a band of minstrels, but don't let that put you off. The food is well-presented, simple Andean fare, and the prices are very reasonable. The kitchen can cater to vegetarians, too. The courtyard is very picturesque, especially in spring. ✉ *Buenos Aires 175* ☎ *3887/421–318* 💳 *MC, V.*

SHOPPING

The shops just east of the plaza are full of the same ponchos, bags, hats, and shirts sold elsewhere in the Quebrada. Though things are reasonably priced, they're more expensive than they would be in Bolivia, which is where most of the stock originates. There are also some interesting original articles on sale in the main plaza.

5

SALTA

92 km (57 mi) south of San Salvador de Jujuy on RN9 or 311 km (193 mi) south of San Salvador de Jujuy on R34 (La Cornisa Rd.); 311 km (193 mi) north of Tucumán on RN9 or 420 km (260 mi) north of Tucumán on RN68 via Tafí del Valle.

It's not just "Salta" to most Argentines, but "Salta la Linda" (Salta the Beautiful). That nickname is actually redundant: "Salta" already comes from an indigenous Aymara word meaning "beautiful." But for the country's finest colonial city, it's worth stating twice. Walking among its well-preserved 18th- and 19th-century buildings, single-story houses, and narrow streets, you could easily forget that this is a city of 500,000 people. But the ever-increasing traffic, the youthful population, and the growing contingent of international itinerants also give the city a cosmopolitan edge. All in all, it's a hard place to leave. For its friendliness, its facilities, its connections, and its central location, Salta is also the best base for a thorough exploration of the Northwest. Do make good use of the tourist office, which has very helpful staff armed with a wealth of maps and useful information.

Salta is hardly an urban jungle, but some visitors opt to stay in the quieter hillside suburb of San Lorenzo, 10 km (6 mi) to the northwest

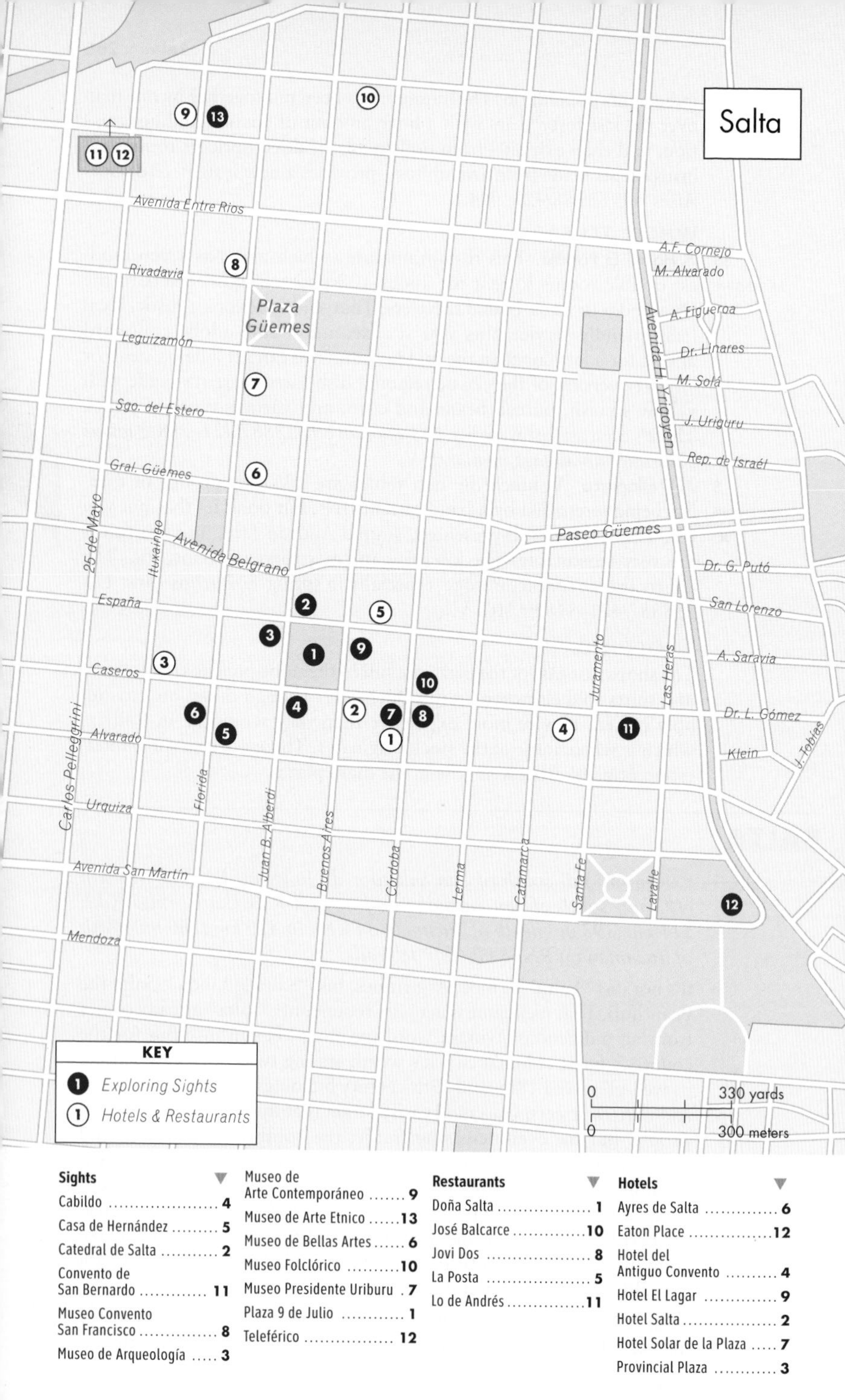

Salta
Avenida Entre Rios
Rivadavia
Plaza Güemes
Leguizamón
Sgo. del Estero
Gral. Güemes
Avenida Belgrano
25 de Mayo
Ituxaingo
España
Caseros
Alvarado
Carlos Pelleggrini
Florida
Urquiza
Juan B. Alberdi
Buenos Aires
Córdoba
Lerma
Catamarca
Santa Fe
Lavalle
Avenida San Martín
Mendoza
A.F. Cornejo
M. Alvarado
A. Figueroa
Dr. Linares
M. Solá
J. Uriguru
Rep. de Israél
Avenida H. Yrigoyen
Paseo Güemes
Dr. G. Putó
San Lorenzo
A. Saravia
Dr. L. Gómez
Klein
J. Tobías
Juramento
Las Heras
KEY
Exploring Sights
Hotels & Restaurants
0
330 yards
0
300 meters
Sights
Cabildo 4
Casa de Hernández 5
Catedral de Salta 2
Convento de San Bernardo 11
Museo Convento San Francisco 8
Museo de Arqueología 3
Museo de Arte Contemporáneo 9
Museo de Arte Etnico 13
Museo de Bellas Artes 6
Museo Folclórico 10
Museo Presidente Uriburu 7
Plaza 9 de Julio 1
Teleférico 12
Restaurants
Doña Salta 1
José Balcarce 10
Jovi Dos 8
La Posta 5
Lo de Andrés 11
Hotels
Ayres de Salta 6
Eaton Place 12
Hotel del Antiguo Convento 4
Hotel El Lagar 9
Hotel Salta 2
Hotel Solar de la Plaza 7
Provincial Plaza 3

and a cooler 980 feet higher. It's a great place if you have a car or can adhere to the every-30-minute bus service to and from Salta.

WORD OF MOUTH

"The Salta region is a must, even though it's not promoted as such—maybe that's what makes it so special. There's diversity, color, sunshine, good food and wine, beautiful architecture. April is the perfect month: the rainy period has finished, and the scenery is still green." —Flintstones

GETTING HERE AND AROUND

It's a two-hour flight to Salta from Buenos Aires. Aerolíneas Argentinas flies four times a day; Andes and LAN both once a day. From Aeropuerto El Aybal it's a 10-km (6-mi) drive southeast into Salta, 15 pesos by taxi or 5 pesos by bus.

Balut buses (12 trips daily) connect Salta to San Salvador de Jujuy, Humahuaca (six trips daily), and Tucumán (once a day). El Indio has two buses a day to Cafayate (four hours). Marco Rueda has one or two buses daily to Cachi (4½ hours); check the day before, as most leave early in the morning.

In the city most sights are within walking distance of one another, and taxis are cheap and easy to find. Renting a car does make exploring the province much easier. That said, many roads are unpaved and can be dangerous in bad weather, so the price of cars is rather high, approaching 200 pesos per day.

MoviTrack offers excursions around Salta, but is best known for its Bus to the Clouds, an oxygen-equipped vehicle that follows the same route as the Tren a las Nubes. Trips last 15-plus hours, and depart daily in winter and nearly every day in summer. Check the MoviTrack Web site for schedules and prices. A very active member of the Fodors.com forums (known as "Flintstones"), Angélica Vasquez de Zaleski is an independent tour guide with years of experience, a passion for the region, and loads of good recommendations.

ESSENTIALS

Bus Contacts **Balut** (☎ *387/432–0608*). **El Indio** (☎ *387/432–0846*). **Panamericano** (☎ *387/431–1957*). **Marco Rueda** (☎ *387/421–4447*). **Terminal de Omnibus** (✉ *Av. Hipólito* ☎ *387/401–1143*). **El Tucumano** (☎ *387/431–7004*).

Banks and Currency Exchange **Banco de la Nación** (✉ *Mitre 151 at Belgrano*). **Cambio Dinar** (✉ *Mitre 101, on Plaza 9 de Julio*).

Medical Assistance **Farmacia Belgrano** (✉ *Belgrano 700, Salta* ☎ *387/431–1331*). **Hospital San Bernardo** (✉ *Tobís 69, Salta* ☎ *387/431–0241*).

Post Office (✉ *Dean Funes 160*).

Rental Cars **Hertz** (✉ *Caseros 374* ☎ *387/421–6785*). **Localiza** (☎ *387/431–4045; 0800/999–2999 central reservations*).

Taxis **Remisol** (☎ *387/431–7317*).

Visitor and Tour Info **Angélica Vasquez de Zaleski** (☎ *387/4964–0658 angie_guide@hotmail.com*). **MoviTrack** (✉ *Buenos Aires 68* ☎ *387/431–6749* 🌐 *www.movitrack.com.ar*). **Salta Tourist Office** (✉ *Buenos Aires 93* ☎ *387/431–0950* 🌐 *www.turismosalta.gov.ar*).

5

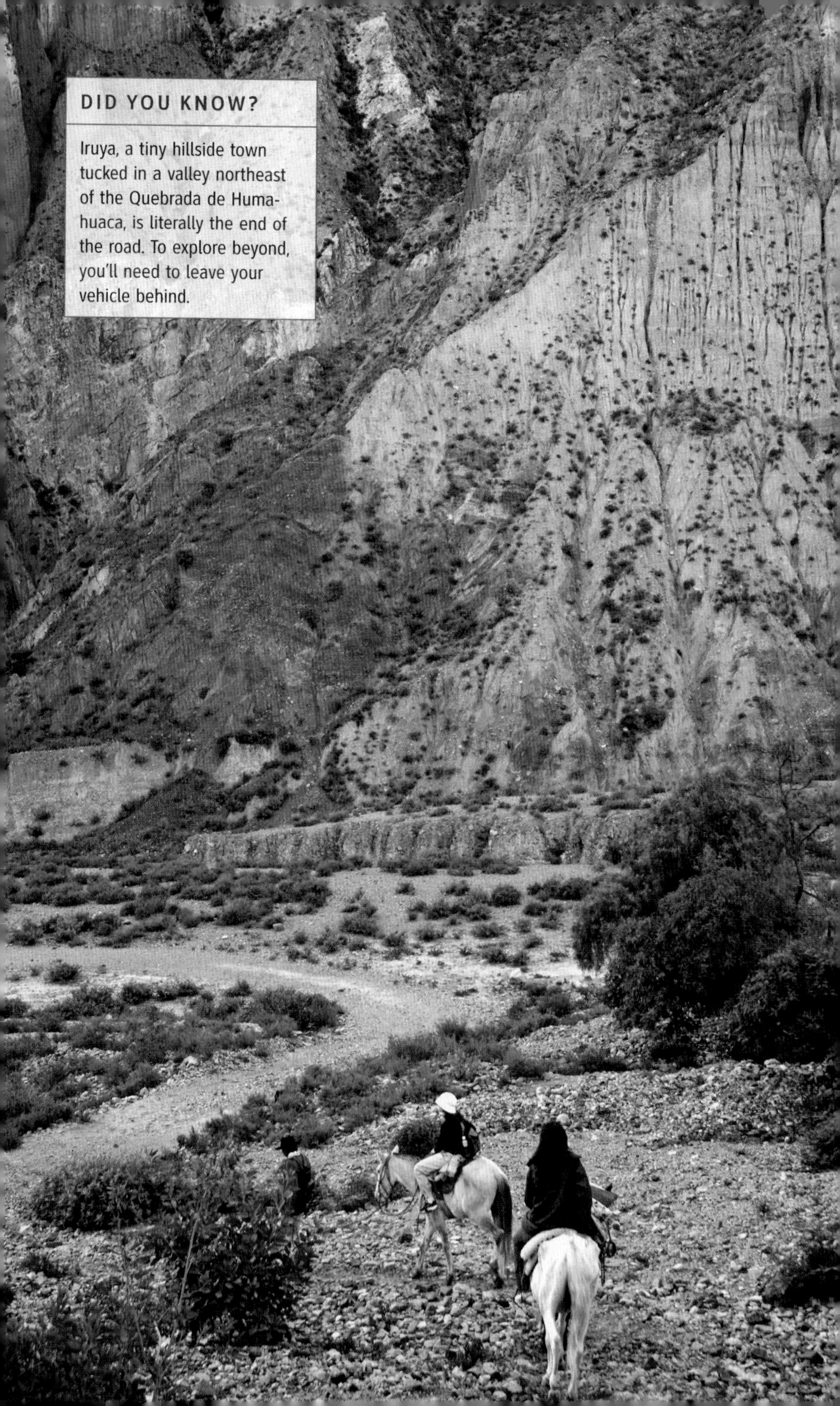

DID YOU KNOW?

Iruya, a tiny hillside town tucked in a valley northeast of the Quebrada de Humahuaca, is literally the end of the road. To explore beyond, you'll need to leave your vehicle behind.

EXPLORING

TOP ATTRACTIONS

4 **Cabildo.** The whitewashed town hall, first constructed in 1582 and rebuilt many times since, still houses Salta's municipal government. *Caseros 549 ☎ 387/421–5340 🌐 www.museonor.gov.ar 🎫 2 pesos ⏲ Tues.–Fri. 9:30–1:30 and 3:30–8:30, Sat. 9:30–1:30 and 3:30–8, Sun. 9:30–1.*

2 **Catedral de Salta.** The city's 1882 neoclassical cathedral fronts the central plaza, and is notable for the enormous frescoes portraying the four gospel writers on the portico around the altar. Inside the entrance is the Panteón de las Glorias del Norte, enclosing the tombs of General Martín Miguel de Güemes and other heroes from the War of Independence. ✉ *España 558 🎫 Free ⏲ Weekdays 6:30–12:30 and 4:30–8:30, Sat. 7:30–12:30 and 4–8:30, Sun. 7:30–1:15 and 5–9:30.*

5

11 **Convento de San Bernardo.** The Convent of St. Bernard, Salta's oldest religious building, served as a chapel first, then a hospital. Today a cloistered order of Carmelite nuns lives here, so the convent is closed to the public except for morning Mass. The wooden rococo-style door, carved by indigenous craftsmen in 1762, contrasts markedly with the otherwise stark exterior of this 1625 structure. ✉ *Caseros 73 🎫 Free ⏲ Mass Mon.–Sat. at 7:45 AM, Sun. at 8 AM and 10 AM.*

8 ★ **Museo Convento San Francisco.** Every Salteño's heart and soul belongs to the town's landmark St. Francis Church, with its white pillars and bright terra-cotta-and-gold facade. The first temple and convent were built in 1625; the second, erected in 1674, was destroyed by fire; the present church was completed in 1882. The 173-foot-high belfry houses the Campaña de la Patria, a bell made from the bronze cannons used in the War of Independence. It rings with an atonal, strangely hypnotic rhythm for more than 20 minutes each afternoon at 5:30. In the sacristy, the **Museo Convento San Francisco** displays religious art. ✉ *Córdoba 33 ☎ 387/432–1445 🎫 Church free, museum 1 peso ⏲ Church daily 7:30–noon and 5–9, museum daily 9–noon and 5–8.*

3 Fodor's Choice ★ **Museo de Arqueología de Alta Montaña.** The fascinating Museum of High Mountain Archaeology has the mummified remains of three children—ages 6, 7, and 15—and the objects buried with them in Incan sacrificial services almost 600 years ago. They were discovered at the summit of the 22,058-foot Volcán Llullaillaco, on the Argentine–Chilean border, in 1999. The high altitude and freezing temperatures kept their skin, hair, and clothes in pristine condition, though the face of one was damaged by lightning. The museum also contains an exhibition about the Qhapaq Ñan Inca trading route and another mummy, the Reina del Cerro (Queen of the Mountain), which was for decades illegally in the hands of private collectors and has deteriorated significantly. ✉ *Mitre 77 ☎ 387/437–0499 🌐 www.maam.org.ar 🎫 10 pesos, free Tues.–Fri. 9 AM–10 AM ⏲ Tues.–Sun. 11–8.*

13 **Museo de Arte Etnico Americano Pajcha.** The small, private Museum of Ethnic American Art Pajcha has artifacts and illustrations from the pre-Columbian world and later. Enthusiastic one-hour guided tours explain exhibits in six small rooms, each exploring a separate topic, from religion

to the Mapuche culture. There's enough reason to linger for hours, and there's also a good café. ⊠ *20 de Febrero 838* ☎ *387/422–9417* 🌐 *www.museodearteetnico.com.ar* 🎫 *10 pesos* ⏲ *Mon.–Sat. 9–8.*

10 ★ **Museo Folclórico Pajarito Velarde.** The two rooms of this museum are full of curiosities and background information on the cultural and artistic elite that were the constant companions of Guillermo "Pajarito" Velarde Mors, the consummate bohemian who lived here from 1930 to 1965. Pay just two pesos for a gentle recital of this eccentric's tale and a look at the hat that Carlos Gardel gave him and the bed that folk singer Atahualpa Yupanki slept on. If you're not au fait with Argentine culture from half a century ago, you'd imagine there's not much interest, but this museum is a delightful tribute to a real character. ⊠ *Pueyrredón 106* ☎ *387/421–2921* 🎫 *2 pesos* ⏲ *Mon.–Sat. 9–8.*

1 **Plaza 9 de Julio.** The heart of Salta is quintessential Latin America: a leafy central plaza named for the date of independence. Arcaded buildings, many housing cafés, line the streets surrounding the square, providing perfect spots to while away a warm afternoon.

NEED A BREAK?

The Parisian-style Van Gogh café, with reproductions of works by its namesake master, is one of the best places on Plaza 9 de Julio to enjoy great coffee and cakes while writing postcards to folks back home. ⊠ ***España 502*** ☎ ***387/431–4659*** 💳 ***AE, MC, V.***

12 **Teleférico a Cerro San Bernardo.** The Cerro San Bernardo rises east of downtown Salta, a cool 880 feet higher than the city center. This cable car takes you up the hill from a station across from Parque San Martín in less than 10 minutes. Views of the entire Lerma Valley reward you at the top. If you're in the mood for a little light exercise, take the staircase back down. ⊠ *San Martín and H. Yrigoyen* ☎ *387/431–0641* 🎫 *20 pesos each way* ⏲ *Daily 10–7.*

WORTH NOTING

5 **Casa de Hernández/Museo de la Ciudad.** Inside an 1870 neocolonial house is the City Museum. The first floor displays an exceptional collection of musical instruments. Rooms upstairs document the history of Salta through paintings and photographs. ⊠ *La Florida 97* ☎ *387/437–3352* 🎫 *1 peso* ⏲ *Weekdays 9–1 and 4–8:30, Sat. 5 PM–9:30 PM.*

9 **Museo de Arte Contemporáneo.** In a priviledged position on a corner of the plaza, the Contemporary Art Museum opened in 2004, and has already won an award as Museum of the Year from the Association of Argentine Art Critics. It changes the shows on both its floors each month. ⊠ *Zuviria 90* ☎ *387/437–0498* 🎫 *2 pesos* ⏲ *Tues.–Sat. 9–8, Sat. 4–8.*

6 **Museo de Bellas Artes.** The 18th-century home of General Félix Árias Rengel now holds the Fine Arts Museum. Its collection of colonial-era religious art includes figures from Argentina's Jesuit missions as well as Cuzco-style paintings from Peru and Bolivia. Another hall of the museum highlights 20th-century works by Salteño artists. ⊠ *La Florida 20* ☎ *387/422–1745* 🎫 *5 pesos* ⏲ *Mon.–Fri. 10–8, Sat. 11–7.*

7 **Museo Presidente José Evaristo Uriburu.** Fine examples of late-colonial architecture—an interior courtyard, thick adobe walls, a reed-and-tile

roof—abound in this simple building, the 19th- and 20th-century home of the Uriburu family, which gave Argentina two presidents. Furniture, costumes, paintings, and family documents are on display in six rooms. ✉ *Caseros 417* ☎ *387/421–5310* 🎫 *1 peso* ⏲ *Tues.–Sat. 9:30–1:30 and 3:30–8:30.*

WHERE TO EAT

SALTA

$$ ✕ **Doña Salta.** This warm, festive, family-friendly locale serves dishes quite typical of Salta and the Northwest. You'll dine in a room steeped in local tradition, amid wine jugs and old wooden implements. Try classics like *humitas* (steamed corn husks filled with cheese) or one of the local stews, like *locro*. Empanadas and meats are also reliable; the pastas are unremarkable, though. The location, across from Iglesia San Francisco, couldn't be more central. ✉ *Córdoba 46* ☎ *387/432–1921* 🌐 *www.donasalta.com.ar* 💳 *AE, DC, MC, V.*

5

$$ ✕ **José Balcarce.** In 2001 a group of chefs launched a restaurant and catering service for high Andean cuisine—"high" referring to both the altitude and the gourmet techniques. The result is José Balcarce, in a brick-and-wood building with large windows just two blocks from bustling Balcarce Street. The menu is short, and the service can be slow, but the food is fresh and delicious. ✉ *Necochea 590* ☎ *387/421–1628* ⏲ *No lunch. Closed Sun.* 💳 *AE, DC, MC, V.*

$$ ✕ **Jovi Dos.** It's an eclectic, great-value restaurant on a quiet downtown corner. The big, high-ceilinged room, with wood beams and plate-glass windows, is crammed with local businesspeople at lunch. Noteworthy starters include marinated eggplant and baked meat empanadas. Grilled meats, seafood, pizza, and pasta have equal billing on the ridiculously long menu. Dishes such as the *ravioles mixtas* (ravioli filled with spinach and cheese and topped with a creamy pink sauce) are big enough for two people. The waitstaff is attentive, and the wine list is solid. ✉ *Balcarce 601* ☎ *387/432–9438* 💳 *AE, DC, MC, V.*

$$$ ✕ **La Posta.** A crimson-and-cream color scheme and a checkerboard floor lend personality to this bright, cavernous downtown eatery. Start with a salad from the salad bar and perhaps one of the outstanding cheese empanadas, and then move on to *cabrito al asador* (goat grilled over an open fire), a luscious, salty indulgence. Pair it with a local Cabernet. For dessert there's the unique *dulce de cayote*, a molasseslike marmalade served with walnuts atop local goat cheese. ✉ *España 456* ☎ *387/421–7091* 🌐 *www.guiagastronomica.com* 💳 *AE, DC, MC, V.*

SAN LORENZO

$$ ARGENTINE ✕ **Lo de Andrés.** Folks from Salta and San Lorenzo favor this bright, airy semi-enclosed brick-and-glass building with a vaulted ceiling for weekend dining. Andrés prepares a lightly spiced Argentine-style parrillada, but if you're not up for such a feast, there are empanadas and *milanesas* (breaded steak) as well. ✉ *Juan Carlos Dávalos and Gorriti* ☎ *387/492–1600* 💳 *AE, DC, MC, V* ⏲ *No lunch Mon.*

WHERE TO STAY

SALTA

$$$ **Ayres de Salta.** Conveniently located between the main plaza and Balcarce Street, Ayres de Salta has a small pool and fitness center on the roof and a good little restaurant on the ground floor. Rooms are large and well equipped. The staff can arrange excursions to the rest of the province and parts of Jujuy. **Pros:** efficient, professional staff; good location; buffet breakfast. **Cons:** some rooms look into the windows of other rooms. ✉ *General Güemes 650* ☎ *387/422–1616* 🌐 *www.ayresdesalta.com.ar* *40 rooms* *In-room: safe, refrigerator, Wi-Fi. In-hotel: restaurant, room service, bar, pool, laundry service, parking (free), no-smoking rooms* 💳 *AE, MC, V.*

$$ **Hotel del Antiguo Convento.** This charming property is in a former convent and run by a cheerful and attentive young staff. Rooms are clean, bright, and well priced. You can opt for a more private, apartment-style suite in the back with its own *parrilla* (barbecue). The hotel is on a lively street just a few blocks from many downtown attractions. **Pros:** staffers go out of their way to be helpful; convenient location. **Cons:** small courtyard and pool. ✉ *Caseros 113* ☎ *387/422–7267* 🌐 *www.hoteldelconvento.com.ar* *15 rooms* *In-room: safe, kitchen (some), refrigerator. In-hotel: room service, bar, pool, laundry service, parking (paid)* 💳 *No credit cards.*

$$$$ ★ **Hotel El Lagar.** The wrought-iron door is always locked, and there's barely any sign to indicate there's a hotel here on this quiet street a few blocks north of the city center. But inside you'll find Salta's most exclusive—though not at all stuffy—bed-and-breakfast, owned by the Etchart family. Cusqueño religious art decorates the walls, and plush upholstered furniture and a cozy fireplace decorate the living room. Rooms all have canopy beds; the suite is simply magnificent. **Pros:** charming garden; wine cellar; large breakfast. **Cons:** a few blocks from the main plaza. ✉ *20 de Febrero 877* ☎ *387/431–9439* *10 rooms* *In-room: safe, refrigerator, Wi-Fi. In-hotel: pool, parking (free)* 💳 *AE, DC, MC, V.*

$$$ ★ **Hotel Salta.** The Salta is in a handsome neocolonial building, a National Historic Monument, in the heart of the city. Antique furniture and views of either the plaza or the surrounding mountains make every room attractive. You'll also find wooden balconies, blue-and-white tiling, sitting rooms on every floor, and a poolside bar-restaurant with an area for barbecues. Local master Ernesto Scotti painted the frescoes in the dining room. **Pros:** ideal location; access to Salta Polo Club; spa; breakfast buffet. **Cons:** rooms facing the plaza can be noisy. ✉ *Buenos Aires 1* ☎ *387/426–0740* 🌐 *www.hotelsalta.com* *99 rooms* *In-room: safe, refrigerator, Wi-Fi. In-hotel: restaurant, bar, pool, gym, spa, laundry service, parking (free), no-smoking rooms* 💳 *AE, DC, MC, V.*

$$$$ ★ **Hotel Solar de la Plaza.** The exterior of this beautiful old house belies the modern comforts within. An elegant lobby leads to a beautifully appointed sitting room, airy courtyard spaces, and a good (though expensive) restaurant. The rooftop pool area has great city views. The slightly pricier superior rooms have balconies overlooking a quiet plaza; suites have Jacuzzis. **Pros:** high comfort; buffet breakfast. **Cons:** rather

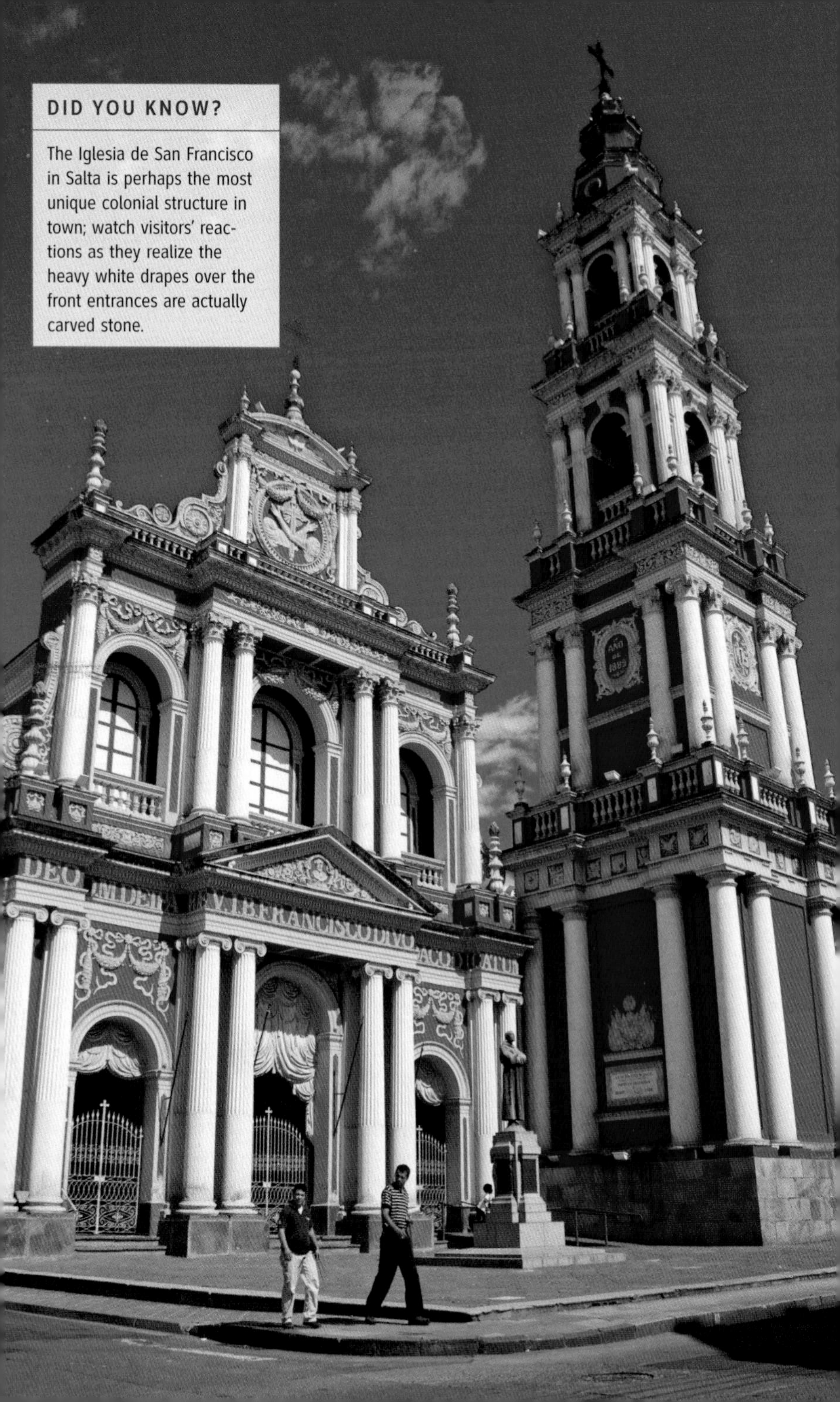

DID YOU KNOW?

The Iglesia de San Francisco in Salta is perhaps the most unique colonial structure in town; watch visitors' reactions as they realize the heavy white drapes over the front entrances are actually carved stone.

pricey. ✉ *Leguizamón 669* ☎ *387/431–5111* 🌐 *www.solardelaplaza.com.ar* ↺ *28 rooms, 2 suites* ♨ *In-room: safe, Wi-Fi. In-hotel: restaurant, room service, bar, pool, gym, laundry service* ▭ *AE, MC, V.*

$$ **Provincial Plaza.** This hotel is on a corner just blocks from Plaza 9 de Julio. Only a few standard rooms have not been renovated; superior and executive floors are spruced up and have good facilities. Views from the top floor are nice. There are also views from a pool that's sized more for a cooling plunge than for actual swimming. **Pros:** central location; full buffet breakfast. **Cons:** lower floors get street noise. ✉ *Caseros 786* ☎ *387/432–2000* 🌐 *www.provincialplaza.com.ar* ↺ *88 rooms* ♨ *In-room: refrigerator (some), Wi-Fi. In-hotel: restaurant, room service, bar, pool, children's programs (ages 2–14), laundry service, parking (free)* ▭ *MC, V.*

SAN LORENZO

$$ **Eaton Place.** Despite appearances, this elegant Georgian-style mansion and its beautiful gardens date only from the 1980s, when it was built as a home. The owner, who runs the property almost as a one-man show, converted it into a hotel in 1994, but it still feels like a private house. The bright and airy rooms in the main house and guesthouse have huge windows, hardwood floors, and period furniture. The huge, dark-wood-paneled penthouse suite has a vaulted ceiling. Two of the double rooms in the guesthouse share a sitting room, making them ideal for a family or group. **Pros:** well appointed; large breakfast. **Cons:** a long way from the center of town. ✉ *San Martín 2457* ☎ *387/492–1347* 🌐 *www.eatonplacesalta.com.ar* ↺ *8 rooms, 1 suite* ♨ *In-room: no a/c (some), kitchen (some), refrigerator (some), no TV (some). In-hotel: pool* ▭ *No credit cards.*

AFTER DARK

Salta is a young and lively city, with a bar district along a few blocks of Balcarce Street that can get quite busy. Clubs, restaurants, and peñas attract both locals and tourists, who come to hear regional folk bands give it their all on small, cramped stages. Adding to the rowdy, dinner-theater atmosphere are the local gaucho dancers who entice (and often entrap) foreigners into strutting their stuff on stage; it's always a good laugh, no matter what language you speak.

A top spot for music, gaucho dancers, and the like is **La Vieja Estacion** (✉ *Balcarce 877* ☎ *387/421–7727* 🌐 *www.la-viejaestacion.com.ar*). At **Macondo** (✉ *Balcarce 980* ☎ *387/431–7191*), a raucous and smoky pub where blues and beer are always on tap, you're as likely to meet back-packing Aussies as you are local law students.

El Rastro Peña (✉ *Av. San Martín 2555* ☎ *387/434–5427*) is an auditorium-like dining hall in the Mercado Artesanal—that is, until the lights dim and the beat of a drum, the warble of *quenas* (bamboo flutes), and the strumming of a guitar begin. National folk groups appear regularly. Shows start at 10:30 PM, and reservations are advised. **La Casona del Molino** (✉ *Luis Burela 1* ☎ *387/434–2835*), 20-odd blocks down Caseros Street from the main plaza, is renowned for its nightly folk performances and its good food.

SHOPPING

The one thing Salta fails to excel at (apart from soccer) is shopping. It has all the usual main street shops where you can stock up on sundries, but for souvenirs and regional products you'll probably do better in provincial villages. The proud exceptions to that rule are the huge 1882 Jesuit monastery that holds the **Mercado Artesanal** (✉ *Av. San Martín 2555* ☎ *387/434–2808*) and the open stalls across the street. Look for red-and-black Salteño ponchos, alpaca knitwear and weavings, leather goods, wooden animal masks, and fine silver. Everything is open daily 9–9.

SPORTS AND THE OUTDOORS

Salta has just a few outfitters, but the options they offer feel fresh and exciting. Horseback riding is a growing activity, as are rafting, paragliding, and mountain biking. Fifteen km (10 mi) west of Salta, **Finca Lesser** (✉ *4 km [2½ mi] past Castellanos, San Lorenzo* ☎ *387/155–827–321* 🌐 *www.redsalta.com/fincalesser*) provides horseback-riding tours on their huge private estate. Trips can last anywhere from a few hours to two days. They can also organize a folk-music performance and a tour showing gauchos at work.

Salta Rafting (✉ *Buenos Aires 88, Local 13* ☎ *387/401–0301* 🌐 *www.saltarafting.com*) operates from a base 35 km (21 mi) south of Salta by the Cabra Corral dam. They offer much more than just getting wet in exciting circumstances. They also offer tandem paragliding jumps and have a "death slide"—a network of zip-line cables that crosses high above the Río Juramento. **Sayta** (✉ *Chicoana* ☎ *387/156–836–565* 🌐 *www.sayta.com.ar*) offers horseback treks lasting from 1 to 10 days for riders of all levels. The estancia of its owner, Enrique Carbia in Chicoana, 40 km (24 mi) south of Salta, has meals and accommodation.

EN ROUTE

When the road to Cachi starts ascending toward Piedra de Molina—a lookout point at 11,000 feet above sea level—it winds up the spectacular Cuesta del Obispo (Bishop's Rise) and, shortly before the top, reaches the **Parque Nacional Los Cardones.** Almost nothing other than *los cardones* (the cardon cacti) for which the park is named can thrive here, and even they've been threatened. (People were chopping them down for use as "wood" at a faster rate than they could grow back; they're now protected). Try to make the journey in the morning, as clouds descend in the afternoon and the road becomes difficult to navigate; never drive the route at night, and seek advice before setting out in the rainy season. Halfway through the park the road splits: the quicker route is via Payogasta to the north, but R42 takes you on a fantastic but unpaved road through red mountains nicknamed Los Colorados.

SALTA PROVINCE

The city of Salta, the unofficial capital of the Argentine north, is known throughout the country for its colonial architecture and its unassuming provincial appeal. It's also a hot spot for international visitors, and compared to its neighbors it's really got its tourism act together. That said, most of the province of Salta has yet to be discovered by outsiders. Even the main circuit, the Valles Calchaquíes (Calchaqui Valley), involves long drives on unpaved roads with no one else in sight.

Only the central third of the province has much in the way of population (the east and the west being vast, uninhabitable wilderness) but within that there's great variety. Although new circuits are being opened up that take in the Cabra Corral dam and thermal waters of Rosario de la Frontera, the main destinations outside the city of Salta are Cafayate for its wine, Cachi for its landscape and archaeological sites, and San Antonio de las Cobres—the destination of the Tren a las Nubes (Train to the Clouds).

CACHI

157 km (97 mi) southwest of Salta.

Cachi is a tiny village on Ruta 40 that's developing into a base for exploring the north of the Calchaqui Valley. The town also has a charming church, a small archaeological museum, and couple of very nice hotels and restaurants, though nothing at all in the way of nightlife. Watching over it all is the 6,340-meter (20,800-foot) Nevado de Cachi, a few miles away.

The area around town is loaded with archaeological sites that have scarcely been explored. El Tero is a site of pre-colonial dwellings, and within 15 km (10 mi) are two more important sites: Puerta La Paya to the southwest and Las Pailas to the north (at the foot of the Nevado de Cachi). A little farther north, en route to La Poma, are the Graneros Incaicos (Incan Graneries), a cave in a stunning setting used by the Incas for storing grain.

GETTING HERE AND AROUND

Just one bus company, Maria Rueda, serves Cachi from Salta. You're advised to buy tickets the day before for the journey that takes just over four hours on a good day. For more flexibility, Remis San José runs a fixed-price taxi service four times a day. The cost is about 150 pesos. They also offer transfers to Cafayate and the villages in between and sightseeing tours of the area. Local guide Santiago Casimiro is a former mountain rescuer who offers treks and tours by car. What he has to show is fascinating, but he doesn't speak much English. Check with the tourist office about other tour options.

ESSENTIALS

Bus Contacts Maria Rueda (☎ *387/421–4447*).

Banks Banco Macro (✉ *General Güemes s/n, on the plaza*).

Medical Assistance Hospital Regional (✉ *Benjamín Zorrilla s/n* ☎ *3868/491–085*).

Taxis Remis San José (☎ *3868/491–907*).

Visitor and Tour Info Santiago Casimiro (☎ *3868/1563–8545*). **Tourist office** (✉ *General Güemes s/n* ☎ *3868/437–0039*).

THE NORTHWEST SHOPPING EXPERIENCE

Throughout the Northwest, you'll find nearly every town has a main area where vendors sell *artisenías*—crafts that are emblematic of the local materials and culture. Spending time at these markets isn't just a great way to find the perfect souvenir; it's also a great opportunity to interact with locals and learn about some of the traditions that permeate the region.

Do note, however, that Andean *artisenías* come in two forms: mass-produced products (generally imported from Bolivia) and locally produced handmade items. Often, stall owners will sell a mix of the two; ask which are locally made, and opt for them when you can as they do more to support the local community. Bolivian goods get cheaper the farther north you go.

Also, you'll see lots of dimpled *cardon* (cactus) wood carved into all manner of souvenirs, but there's no system right now for verifying the origins of the wood (only souvenirs carved from already-dead cardones are legal). At this writing, we encourage asking your guide or another local for vendor recommendations, or steering clear of cardon and choosing a different kind of craft.

Alpaca knits. Alpacas look like a cross between a llama and a sheep with a glossy, silky fleece. Textiles from alpaca feel lovely and are unmistakably Andean, especially with the traditional designs.

Silver. It was its position on the road to the silver mines of Potosi that made the Quebrada so important in colonial days, but don't count on the silver on sale now being locally sourced. What you do have, though, are traditional motifs and symbols cast into silver as jewelry and, borrowing traditions from elsewhere, tableware.

Leather. Unless there's an item that particularly catches your eye, save your leather purchases for the pampas. They do use cows and leather in the Quebrada, but not in the decorative ways of elsewhere in the country.

Masks. If you don't witness Humahuaca at carnival time, you might be surprised by the number of masks—of humans and animals, made of wood or pottery—among the souvenir stalls. If you do go in carnival time, it'll make more sense.

Coca. Especially useful for those going on to the higher altitudes of Bolivia, coca here is medicine rather than narcotic and freely available. Easier than chewing the leaves, a coca tea is neatly packaged and doesn't taste too bad. But don't try taking it home without checking customs regulations first.

Ponchos. They go well with anything, are useful against the cool cloudless nights in the Quebrada and make a great souvenir or gift from the region. Made of wool from sheep or llama, and available with hats and gloves in matching patterns. Just don't try wearing one in Buenos Aires if you're hoping to blend in.

Musical instruments. Pan pipes are easy to play for anyone (though harder to play well) and instantly evocative of the windswept Quebrada. There are more intricate instruments available for musicians or the curious. For some tips on how to play, take it to a peña in the evening and corner one of the performers.

Iglesia San Pedro de Nolasco, Molinos

WHERE TO EAT AND STAY

$ ARGENTINE **Luna Cautiva.** The white-walled building may date from 1796, but the restaurant has been around only since 2005, and is owned by two women, one from Buenos Aires, the other from Rosario. The menu is strong on regional dishes and has a good selection of tapas. ✉ *Pasaje Borje s/n (next to church)* ☎ *3868/491–029* ▭ *No credit cards.*

$$$ **ACA Hosteria.** For most of the last 40 years this Argentine Automobile Club hosteria was the only decent place to stay in Cachi, but it's now facing some stiff competition. Still, it has a pool, a good restaurant, and a nice garden. **Pros:** good facilities; buffet breakfast; children's play area. **Cons:** small rooms. ✉ *Av. Automóvil Club Argentino s/n* ☎ *3868/491–105* 🌐 *www.soldelvalle.com.ar* *33 rooms* *In-room: safe refrigerator (some). In-hotel: restaurant, room service, bar, pool, laundry service, parking (free)* ▭ *MC, V.*

$$$ **El Cortijo.** This rustic boutique hotel was converted from an old house, and is, at this writing, a work in progress. It stands out for its friendly service, but it also has a great view from the balcony of its courtyard, a wine cellar, a restaurant, and well-decorated rooms. **Pros:** good service; artistic decoration; buffet breakfast. **Cons:** construction work is slated to continue indefinitely. ✉ *Av. Automóvil Club Argentino s/n* ☎ *3868/491–034* 🌐 *www.elcortijohotel.com* *12 rooms* *In-room: Wi-Fi. In-hotel: bar, laundry service, parking (free), no-smoking rooms* ▭ *AE, DC, MC, V.*

$$$$ Fodor's Choice ★ **La Merced del Alto**. The stately white-adobe building looks like it's been here forever. In fact, it was built in 2006. It sits on a good-size patch of land between two streams, with the Nevada de Cachi on one side, the Parque Los Cardones on the other, and the town spread out

below. Rooms are huge and comfortable; common areas include an enormous reading room, a well-stocked bar, a wine cellar, and a really good restaurant. There's also a fully equipped spa in a separate building, and hotel staff can arrange trekking, horseback riding, and visits to archaeological sites. **Pros:** expansive grounds with great views; attention to detail; accessible for people with disabilities; buffet breakfast. **Cons:** 3 km (2 mi) from Cachi; echoing corridors. ✉ *Fuerte Alto s/n* ☎ *3868/490–020* 🌐 *www.lamerceddelalto.com* *13 rooms, 1 suite* *In-room: no a/c, safe, no TV, Wi-Fi. In-hotel: restaurant, room service, bar, pool, spa, bicycles, laundry service, no-smoking rooms* ▭ *AE, DC, MC, V.*

MOLINOS

206 km (128 mi) southwest of Salta (via Cachi); 50 km (31 mi) south of Cachi.

5

Molinos has a photogenic church and a small farm breeding vicuñas, an animal similar to a llama but one whose fur makes a much finer (and more expensive) wool. Its main draw, however, is a location on the way to Cafayate, with its many *bodegas* (wineries), and to Colomé, Argentina's oldest bodega, with one of the world's highest vineyards and a luxury hotel.

Molinos is also just a few miles from the Camino de Artesanos (Road of the Artisans) of Seclantás, who weave ponchos and scarves by the roadside on contraptions improvised from wood and old bicycle parts. The Laguna de Brealito, 10 km (6 mi) due west of Seclantás, is a picturesque lake in the middle of nowhere. Eight kilometers (5 mi) east of Molinos are the pre-Columbian ruins of Chicoana.

WHERE TO EAT AND STAY

$ ARGENTINE ✕ **Inti Ray**. It's an honest little restaurant in Seclantás, with some fine old photos on the walls and good, oven-baked empanadas. Other attractions are a delicious goat stew, regional breads and jams, and a warm welcome from your host, Alejandro Diaz. ✉ *Cornejo s/n Seclantás* ☎ *No phone* ▭ *No credit cards.*

$$$$ ★ **Estancia Colomé**. Remote hotels are one thing; Colomé, set up by Swiss winemaker Donald Hess and his wife, is another. Arriving puts the miles upon miles of driving along bumpy, unpaved roads firmly into perspective: each room has uninterrupted views of the lavender and cactus gardens, the vineyards, and the great expanse beyond. A world-class winery helps to continue a wine-making tradition that dates from 1831. Rooms are enormous, with bathrooms so huge and enticing that you'd never imagine water to be in short supply. The restaurant is, of course, excellent. Since 2009 the Estancia is also home to the James Turrell Museum, showcasing the artist's works with light and space. It's open between 2 and 6 daily, though you're advised to make a reservation in advance. **Pros:** luxurious; an irresistible pool; a full range of activities; buffet breakfast. **Cons:** a long way from anywhere; very bumpy road for the last 50 km (30 mi). ✉ *RP53 Km 20* ☎ *3868/494–200* 🌐 *www.estanciacolome.com* *9 rooms* *In-room: safe, refrigerator, Wi-Fi.*

In-hotel: restaurant, room service, bar, pool, bicycles, laundry service, parking (free) ▭ *AE, DC, MC, V.*

CAFAYATE

185 km (115 mi) southwest of Salta via RN68; 340 km (211 mi) southwest of Salta via R40; 230 km (143 mi) northwest of San Miguel de Tucumán.

Thanks to a microclimate and fertile soil, the area around Cafayate is one of Argentina's wine-growing regions. Cafayate itself is very civilized and orderly, with free tours of boutique bodegas, lots of good restaurants, and some exquisite hotels. But wander a couple of blocks from the central plaza and you're back on unpaved roads. Take a bit of a hike and you're in the mountains—probably enjoying a wine-tasting session at a tiny *finca* and trying hard to get your camera to do justice to the view. There are also some authentic handicrafts to buy, a five-aisle cathedral, and a world-famous ice-cream man.

GETTING HERE AND AROUND

El Indio runs three bus services a day from Salta (four hours). It's best to buy your ticket the day before if you can, especially in summer. From Tucumán (five hours), Aconquija has three buses a day. In town, many agencies and hotels offer bicycle rental, and there are some good bodegas and sights to visit within a few miles of town. There are also lots of opportunities to explore the countryside on horseback or go on a hike, either organized or by yourself.

ESSENTIALS

Bank Banco de la Nacion (✉ *Nuestra Señora del Rosario 103* ☎ *3868/421–215*).

Medical Assistance Farmacia Cafayate (✉ *Mitre 24* ☎ *3868/421–299*).

Visitor Info Tourist Office (✉ *Plaza 20 de Febrero* ☎ *3868/422–224* 🌐 *www.turismosalta.gov.ar*).

EXPLORING

For 66 years, Rodolfo Bravo collected and catalogued funerary and religious objects from local excavations. These objects, made of clay, ceramic, metal, and textiles, are on display at the **Museo Regional y Arqueológico Rodolfo Bravo** (Rudolfo Bravo Regional and Archaeological Museum). Artifacts from the Incas (15th century) and Diaguitas of the Calchaqui Valley are also part of the collection. ✉ *Colón 191* ☎ *3868/421–054* 🎫 *1 peso* ⏲ *By appointment only.*

Learn about wine making at the **Museo de la Vid y del Vino** (Museum of Grapevines and Wine), which is in a building dating from 1881. Machinery, agricultural implements, and old photographs tell the history of wine making in this area. ✉ *R40, Av. General Güemes* ☎ *3868/421–125* 🎫 *1 peso* ⏲ *Mon.–Sat. 8:30–12:30 and 1–7.*

NEED A BREAK?

Helados Miranda is an essential stop in Cafayate. In 1994, at the age of 60, Ricardo Miranda decided that he wasn't going to make it as a painter and that he could only make a living out of something he wasn't passionate

about. It took him two years to perfect his creation: wine sorbets. Sweet Torrontés arguably makes sense as a sorbet; the Cabernet makes a good match for it and his fruit-flavored ice creams. All are made organically on the premises. ✉ *Av. Güemes Norte 170* ☎ *3868/421-106.*

Quebrada de las Conchas. The first 50 km (30 mi) of the direct road to Salta (or the last stretch if you don't come via Cachi and Molinos), known as the Gorge of the Shells, takes in such dramatic scenery that it's become an attraction in itself. The various rock formations have been eroded into wildly different shapes that have been nicknamed the Windows, the Castles, the Frog, the Friar—each name seems truly fanciful, that is until the road winds around the corner and you're actually confronted by the formation itself. The climax is the Amphitheater, which is sometimes used as a venue for proper orchestras; wandering minstrels offer impromptu performances. ✉ *RN68, Km 6–Km 46.*

5

BODEGAS

Though Salta makes only 1% of Argentina's wines, the province accounts for 15% of the country's exports. Most of the production is in or around Cafayate, which has a dozen bodegas, ranging from small family businesses to small branches of multinational concerns.

Bodega Nanni. Nanni has been in the same family and in the same building—just a block from the main square—for more than a century. It has the only organic certification in Cafayate, and nearly half of its small production of Torrontés, Malbec, Cabernet Sauvignon, and Tannat is exported to the United States. Tours and tastings are only $5. ✉ *Silverio Chavarria 151* ☎ *3868/421–527* 🌐 *www.bodegananni.com* 🎫 *$5* 💳 *MC, V* ⏲ *Mon.–Sat. 9–1 and 2–6, Sun. 11–6.*

Domingo Hermanos. With vineyards to the north, west, and south of Cafayate and more right next to the bodega, just a few blocks from the center of town, Domingo Hermanos is one of Cafayate's biggest operations. They started in the 1960s, and increased production in the mid-'90s to 3 million liters per year. ✉ *Nuestra Señora del Rosario s/n, at 25 de Mayo* ☎ *3868/421–225* 🌐 *www.domingohermanos.com* 🎫 *Free* ⏲ *Weekdays 9–12:30 and 2:30–6:30, Sat. 9–12:30, Sun. 10:30–12:30.*

El Esteco. Producers of several lines of well-received wines, El Esteco is just as famous for being the home of the Patios de Cafayate Hotel & Spa (⇨ *Where to Stay, below*). The bodega is 3 km (2 mi) from the center of Cafayate, so it's easy to drop in for a tour and/or tasting or to try out the restaurant. ✉ *RN40 at RN68* ☎ *3868/1556–6019* 🌐 *www.elesteco.com.ar* 🎫 *15 pesos* ⏲ *Tours weekdays at 10, 11, noon, 2:30, 3:30, 4:30, 5:30 and 6:30, weekends at 10, 11, and noon.*

Etchart. Founded in 1850 and taken over in 1996 by Pernod Ricard, the Etchart Bodega is a large estate 10 km (6 mi) south of town. As well as the chance to take a tour, a visit is an opportunity to taste some of the area's most successful wines. ✉ *RN40, Km 1,047* ☎ *3868/421–310* 🌐 *www.vinosetchart.com* 🎫 *Free* ⏲ *Weekdays 9–noon and 1–4.*

Finca de las Nubes. In 1996 there was nothing on the land of the Bodega José Luis Mounier in El Divisadero, 4 km (2 mi) out of town. Now this is one of Salta's best boutique wineries. Almost half of its small line of reds, whites, rosés, and sparklings is sold in the bodega itself. The small fee for tours is discounted against any purchases, and they also offer lunch if you book ahead (65 pesos per person). *El Divisadero, Km 4* *3868/422–129* *www.bodegamounier.com.ar* *15 pesos per group* *Mon.–Sat. 9:30–5.*

Peña Veyrat Durbex. This getaway for the bon vivant has eight well-appointed guest rooms (450 pesos double room with garden view, 650 pesos with vineyard view), a wine cellar, a restaurant, and a small organic winery. They also offer wine tours and tastings to day visitors. It's 18 km (11 mi) from the center of Cafayate and on the way to the Quebrada de las Conchas. *RN68, Km 18* *3868/421–555* *www.lacasadelabodega.com.ar* *25 pesos* *Daily 10–2 and 2–6.*

HOME STAYS

Ruta 40 continues unpaved most of the way to Cafayate, with a public transport gap between Molinos and Angastaco. If you're going this way, look into the **Red de Turismo Communitario** (*Network of Community Tourism* *www.turismocampesino.org*), which puts visitors within communities, not only staying with families but joining in their daily tasks. There are places to stay in Angastaco, Santa Rosa, San Carlos, Animaná, and Divisadero. The cost is about 60 pesos per person per night. It helps to know some Spanish—to understand the Web site and your host family.

San Pedro de Yacochuya. Head out of town toward the hills to find Arnaldo Etchart's small-scale winery that's still in its early years. Supplement a free tour and tasting with a meal at the restaurant (220 pesos for a fixed menu with wine) and enjoy the views back over the valley, or head on toward waterfalls in the hills. *Yacochuya* *3868/421–233* *www.yacochuya.com* *Free* *Weekdays 10–5, Sat. 10–1.*

El Transito. Inside a blocky concrete building in the center of town is the bodega and visitor center of El Transito, a business run by a family that shares common ancestors with the folks at Bodega Nanni just around the corner. Come for a tour and the chance to sample Malbec, Cabernet Sauvignon, and Torrontés. *Belgrano 102* *3868/422–385* *www.bodegaeltransito.com* *Free* *Mon.–Sat. 9–1 and 3–8, Sun. 10–1 and 2–7.*

Vasija Secreta. On the northern edge of town, Bodega La Banda is in a grand 150-year-old building with a small museum displaying imported oak barrels and machinery for pumping and bottling wine. Short tours fill in some history and show how production methods have changed. There are also 10 very beautiful but facility-free guest rooms (600 pesos double). *RN40 s/n* *3868/421–850* *www.vasijasecreta.com* *Free* *Daily 9–1 and 2:30–6:30.*

WHERE TO EAT

$ ARGENTINE

El Patio Peña. This place makes the list for its music rather than its food—though the barbecued meats and empanadas are good deals. Singers, musicians, and sometimes dancers bring the place to life each night. *Mitre 86* *3868/421–043* *No credit cards* *Closed Tues.*

Drying chili near Cachi, Calchaquí Valley

$$ ARGENTINE — **El Rancho.** This big barn of a restaurant faces the main plaza, and offers big portions of regional specialties and classic Argentinian steaks and pastas. Expect a bustling atmosphere, occasional live music, and wines from Bodega Rio Colorado, just a block away. ✉ *Vicario Toscano 4* ☎ *3868/421–256* 🌐 *www.elranchocafayate.com.ar* ▭ *No credit cards* ⏲ *Closed Mon.*

$$$ ARGENTINE ★ — **Macacha Gourmet.** In a 100-year-old former school building is Cafayate's most ambitious restaurant, hosted by a very friendly husband-and-wife team. The three dining rooms are themed after the Nanni, Domingo Hermanos, and Etchart bodegas, with wine displays and special cutlery. The decoration is from all around the world, but the food is strictly local, with llama, quinoa, rabbit, and Andean potatoes playing starring roles. The convivial wine bar stays open late to serve its wines from every bodega in town. ✉ *Av. Güemes Norte 28* ☎ *3868/422–319* 🌐 *www.macachagourmet.com.ar* ▭ *AE, MC, V* ⏲ *Closed Sun.*

WHERE TO STAY

$$$ — **Cafayate Wine Resort.** Three kilometers (2 mi) from the plaza on a straight dusty road lined with vineyards and in the shadow of San Isidro is this big white adobe building with 12 rooms around a wide courtyard. Highlights include huge rooms with walk-in closets, a well-stocked cellar with tastings and talks, and an elevated swimming pool with views of vineyards and mountains. **Pros:** spacious shared areas and access to veranda from all rooms; vineyards right up to the hotel, buffet breakfast. **Cons:** a little isolated from the town. ✉ *25 de Mayo s/n, Camino Al Divisadero* ☎ *3868/422–272* 🌐 *www.cafayatewineresort.com* *12 rooms* *In-room: no a/c (some), safe, DVD, Wi-Fi. In-hotel:*

restaurant, room service, bar, pool, bicycles, laundry service, parking (free) ▭ *AE, MC, V.*

$ **El Hospedaje.** This 100-year-old building used to be a youth hostel until the owner got tired of the noise and chaos. If you can relate to that, you might enjoy this modest little place. Rooms are pretty basic, but they're set around a pleasant courtyard or around an inviting swimming pool. **Pros:** quiet and close to center; Continental breakfast. **Cons:** few facilities; other places offer bigger breakfasts. ✉ *Camila Quintana de Niño s/n, at Salta* ☎ *3868/421–680* *12 rooms* *In-room: no a/c, no phone, no TV (some). In-hotel: bar, pool, laundry facilities* ▭ *No credit cards.*

$$ **Hotel Asturias.** The swimming pool is terrific, the garden is ample, and the hotel—the biggest and oldest in town—is comfortable. Half the rooms are standard, the other half superior, with better views and decoration. All have delicate touches, big bathrooms, and lots of storage space. **Pros:** great garden and pool; two art galleries; close to the center; buffet breakfast. **Cons:** superior rooms more expensive; restaurant open only in high season. ✉ *Av. General Güemes 154* ☎ *3868/421–328* *www.hotel-asturias.com.ar* *66 rooms* *In-room: no a/c (some), safe (some), refrigerator (some), Wi-Fi. In-hotel: room service, bar, pool, laundry service, parking (free)* ▭ *MC, V.*

$$$$ **Patios de Cafayate Hotel & Spa.** Creature comforts and a fine restaurant make this luxury Starwood property a top choice. The rustic rooms are decorated in rich red and green tones and overlook vineyards. In the Wine Spa, the first of its kind in Argentina and open only to hotel guests, local blends are used for treatments that are sure to replenish your body and soul. **Pros:** very exclusive; good facilities. **Cons:** very expensive. ✉ *R40 at RN68* ☎ *3868/421–747* 🌐 *www.starwoodhotels.com* *30 rooms* *In-room: safe, refrigerator, Wi-Fi. In-hotel: restaurant, bar, pool, gym, parking (free)* ▭ *AE, DC, MC, V.*

$$ ★ **Portal del Santo.** Just two blocks from the plaza but already on the edge of town, this place feels like a hideaway. Behind the large building, with its big guest rooms and its fireplace-warmed common area, is a garden with a blue-and-white swimming pool and great views. There's also a well-stocked *quincho*—a sheltered barbecue area with tables, chairs, and an oven. **Pros:** both central and quiet; good bathrooms; big breakfast. **Cons:** many guests are families, which tends to disturb the peace. ✉ *Silvero Chavarria 250* ☎ *3868/422–500* 🌐 *www.portaldelsanto.com.ar* *12 rooms* *In-room: safe, refrigerator, Wi-Fi. In-hotel: bar, pool, laundry service, parking (free)* ▭ *V.*

SHOPPING

Besides wine, *cesteria* (weaving with cane), *tejidos* (weaving with fabric), and *cerámica* (pottery) are the local specialties. You can find all these goods in the Paseo de Artesanos on the main plaza, or in individual workshops. Ask staff in the tourist office opposite the Paseo de Artesanos for details. **Calchaquitos** (✉ *Güemes Sur 118* ☎ *3868/421–799*), just next to the plaza, sells cookies and chocolates, local jams, wine, and clothes.

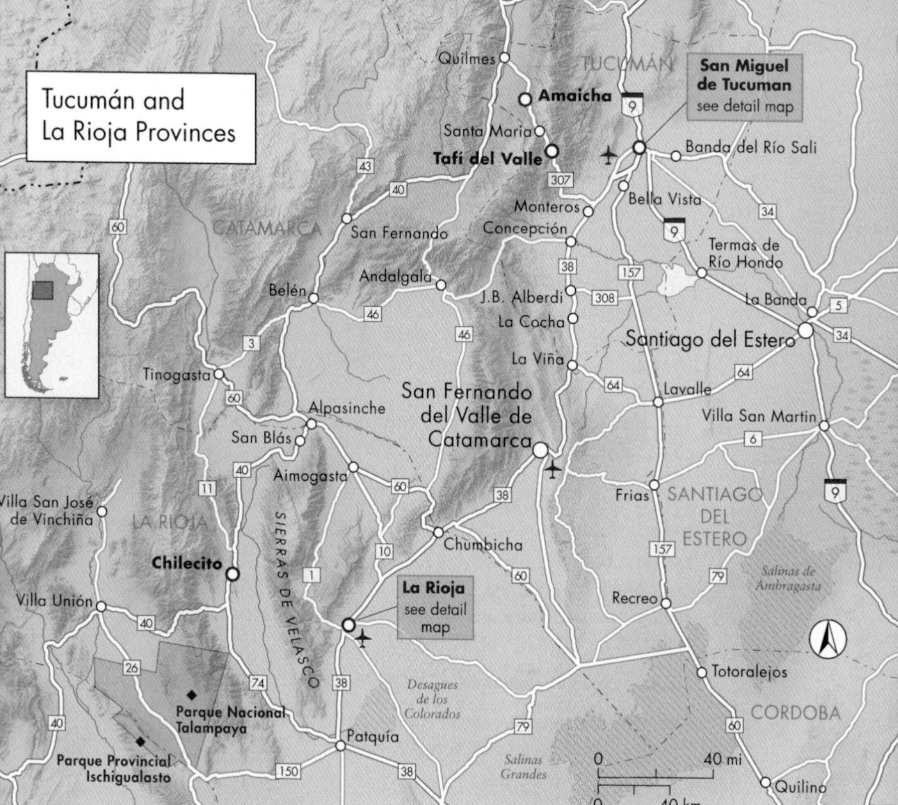

SPORTS AND THE OUTDOORS

Getting active in Cafayate involves the gentler end of adventure tourism: there are lots of opportunities for hikes, horseback rides, and bike excursions but nothing too extreme. The waterfalls in the Río Colorado make a good excursion on a bike or on foot. **Turismo Cordillerano** (✉ *Av. General Güemes 28* ☎ *3868/422–137* 🌐 *www.turismocordillerano.com.ar*) rents bikes and offers half-day to five-day treks and horseback rides.

SAN MIGUEL DE TUCUMÁN

1,310 km (814 mi) northwest of Buenos Aires; 597 km (371 mi) north of Córdoba; 311 km (193 mi) south of Salta via RN9; 392 km (244 mi) northwest of La Rioja on R38.

Tucumán Province's bustling capital and Argentina's fourth-largest city is San Miguel de Tucumán, or just Tucumán in local parlance. The streets are often crowded with both students from the local university and businesspeople, and the traffic is often heavy, though everything grinds to a halt each afternoon when the heat gets too intense.

The city is full of grand colonial architecture, broad avenues, and leafy plazas, all of which are lined with buildings done in a bewildering mix of architectural styles. Although the center of Tucumán isn't beautiful by conventional standards, it bursts with good restaurants, bars, outdoor cafés, and nightlife.

GETTING HERE AND AROUND

Aeropuerto Benjamín Matienzo is 13 km (8 mi) east of Tucumán. Flights from Buenos Aires take an hour and 40 minutes. Aerolíneas Argentinas has three to five flights a day. There are frequent buses departing from Buenos Aires (15 hours), especially between 4 and 10 PM. The bus company Aconquija links Tucumán to Tafí del Valle (six to eight departures daily, 2½ hours) and Cafayate (two to three times daily, 5½ hours); to continue on to Salta you must change to El Indio in Cafayate. Balut is the best for San Salvador de Jujuy (five departures daily, five hours).

The city is laid out in a grid and easy to navigate. Note that streets change their names either side of the main street, 24 de Setiembre. Taxis are cheap and plentiful except during rush hour, when people line up at taxi stands. Duport Turismo runs four-hour city tours and three- to four-day excursions to Tafí del Valle and other areas of interest.

ESSENTIALS

Bus Contacts Aconquija (✉ *Lavalle 3395* ☎ *381/433-0205 in town; 381/422-7620 at terminal*). **Balut** (☎ *381/430-7153*). **Terminal de Omnibus** (✉ *Brígido Terán 250* ☎ *381/430-4696*).

Currency Exchange Maguitur (✉ *San Martín 765* ☎ *381/431-0032*).

Medical Assistance Farmacia Molina 24 (✉ *24 de Setiembre 621* ☎ *381/421-8090*). **Hospital Angel C. Padilla** (✉ *Alberdi 550* ☎ *381/424-0848*).

Post Office (✉ *25 de Mayo and Córdoba*).

Rental Cars Localiza (☎ *381/421-5334; 0800/999-2999 central reservations*). **Móvil Renta** (✉ *San Lorenzo 370* ☎ *381/421-8635*).

Taxis Remitur (☎ *381/422-0008*).

Visitor and Tour Info Tucumán Tourist Office (✉ *24 de Septiembre 484* ☎ *381/422-2199 or 381/422-0000* 🌐 *www.tucuman.gov.ar* ✉ *Duport Turismo Congreso 160* ☎ *381/422-2199 or 381/422-0000*).

EXPLORING

3 On July 9, 1816, congressmen from all over the country gathered in what is now called the **Casa Histórica de la Independencia** (Historic House of Independence) to draft Argentina's declaration of independence from Spain. Most of what you see here is a faithful reconstruction, not the original house, but the exterior is authentic, built from 1761 to 1780. A nightly sound-and-light show at 8 PM (each evening except Thursdays, 15 pesos) reenacts the arrival of these representatives and the historic signing. It's quite moving—even more so if you understand Spanish. ✉ *Congreso 151* ☎ *381/431-0826* 🎫 *8 pesos* ⏲ *Wed.–Mon. 9–1 and 3:30–7.*

2 **Museo Histórico de la Provincia.** At the Historical Museum of the Province a collection of hats, maps, coins, and letters is on display in the

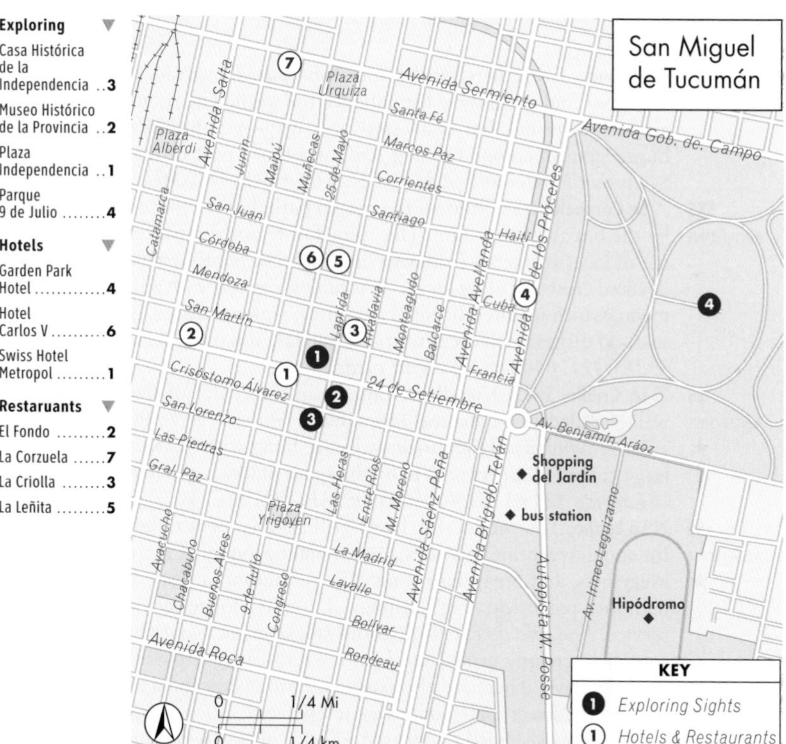

birthplace of former President Nicolás Avellaneda. ✉ *Congreso 66* ☎ *381/431–1039* 🎫 *Free* 🕓 *Daily 9–noon and 3–8.*

1 **Plaza Independencia.** The monumental 1912 art nouveau Casa de Gobierno, which houses Tucumán's provincial government and whose monumental white stateroom is open for visits, sits on one side of the central Plaza Independencia, the city's heart. Other buildings here are the Iglesia Catedral, with its bulbous domes, the Iglesia de San Francisco, and the Centro Cultural Dr. Alberto Rougés. In addition to hosting conferences and book launches (it curates an unusual collection of English novels, 10,000 titles strong), the center offers guided tours in the morning.

4 **Parque 9 de Julio.** It has an artificial lake for boating, tennis courts, a polo field, and lovely gardens and was designed in 1916 by celebrated landscaper Carlos Thays, whose parks also grace Mendoza, Córdoba, and Buenos Aires. The park incorporates the house of Bishop Colombres, which now holds the **Museo de la Industria Azucarera** (Museum of the Sugar Industry), whose exhibits demonstrate the processes behind one of the region's most important crops. ✉ *Av. Soldati and Av. Benjamín Aráoz* ☎ *381/452–2332* 🎫 *Free* 🕓 *Daily 8–1 and 3–8.*

WHERE TO EAT

$$ ARGENTINE **El Fondo**. Come here for the impressive *parrilla* spread. A self-service salad bar and good wine list enhance the meal. The room and service are rather formal, but in an enjoyable way—you feel like you're in a huge, Spanish-colonial dining hall, and that's part of the experience. ✉ *Av. San Martín 848* ☎ *381/422–2161* ▭ *AE, DC, MC, V.*

$$$ ARGENTINE **La Corzuela**. It's a little off the beaten path, but the journey is justified by the fine Argentine fare. This, piped in regional music, and all manner of local artifacts—from weavings to horse paraphernalia—attract a devoted crowd of older locals. You can't go wrong with anything on the menu, which features, in equal measures, regional dishes, grilled meats, seafood dishes (including trout and paella), and pasta. ✉ *L'Aprida 866* ☎ *381/421–6402* ▭ *No credit cards.*

$$ ARGENTINE ★ **La Criolla**. It's a friendly restaurant in the center of the city with a well-rounded menu that includes some inventive vegetarian options and a decent wine list. High brick walls are hung with huge canvases, and large groups of diners tend to fill the space at lunch and in the evenings. ✉ *Laprida 181* ☎ *381/400–0854* ▭ *AE, DC, MC, V.*

$$ ARGENTINE ★ **La Leñita**. This wonderful, lively grill also happens to be a great spot for some Argentine folk music: each night around 11 the waiters drop everything and break into song. The restaurant is rustic but welcoming, with red bricks, high ceilings, a country-lodge feel, and friendly service. The *bife de chorizo* (sirloin steak) is juicy and tender, but the sublimely creamy grilled *mollejas* (sweetbreads), a parrilla appetizer, steal the show. There are also pasta and fish dishes and a salad bar. For dessert, the sweet, rich *panqueque* (crepe) with *dulce de leche* (a spread made from sweetened condensed milk) is glazed with burnt sugar for an unusual taste combination. ✉ *Av. 25 de Mayo 377* ☎ *381/422–9241* ▭ *AE, DC, MC, V.*

WHERE TO STAY

$$$ **Garden Park Hotel**. Garden Park is a smart, busy hotel looking out onto Parque 9 de Julio. Rooms are comfortable, well equipped, and have park or city vistas. The staff is helpful. **Pros:** good views; easy access from airport, bus station, and center. **Cons:** tiny swimming pool. ✉ *Av. Soldatti 330* ☎ *381/431–0700* ⊕ *www.gardenparkhotel.com.ar* *80 rooms, 5 suites* *In-room: safe, refrigerator, Wi-Fi. In-hotel: restaurant, room service, bar, pool, gym, laundry service, parking (free), no-smoking rooms* ▭ *AE, DC, MC, V.*

$$ ★ **Hotel Carlos V**. Central and popular, Carlos V has a bustling lobby and street-side café under an arched brick facade. Cream-color walls, dark wood, and well-appointed bathrooms make rooms feel more like an escape than just a place to drop your bags. The full-service restaurant is good in its own right. **Pros:** good location; good bar. **Cons:** some rooms have no natural light. ✉ *25 de Mayo 330* ☎ *381/431–1666* ⊕ *www.hotelcarlosv.com.ar* *70 rooms* *In-room: refrigerator, Wi-Fi. In-hotel: restaurant, bar, laundry service, no-smoking rooms* ▭ *AE, MC, V.*

$$$ **Swiss Hotel Metropol.** Modernity and taste pervade this Swiss-owned hotel. Rooms are airy and have pastel color schemes. The English-speaking staff is friendly, and it's hard to beat the location only one block from the plaza. **Pros:** location; efficient service; buffet breakfast. **Cons:** noisy in the morning. ✉ *24 de Septiembre 524* ☎ *381/431–1180* 🌐 *www.swisshotelmetropol.com.ar* *75 rooms, 5 suites* *In-room: safe, refrigerator, Internet. In-hotel: room service, bar, pool, laundry service, no-smoking rooms* *AE, DC, MC, V.*

AFTER DARK

There's plenty of nightlife in or near the city center, mostly in the form of late-night cafés, bars, and dance clubs. With a large student population, nights out here generally don't start until around 10 or 11; everything shuts down at 4 AM. If you head out of the center on Avenida Mate de Luna, a continuation of 24 de Septiembre, you'll eventually find yourself on Aconquija Street. After a 15-minute drive you'll end up in the Yerba Buena neighborhood, where Aconquija is lined by restaurants, musical peñas, bars, and nightclubs.

5

At **Plaza de Almas** (✉ *Maipú 791, at Santa Fe* ☎ *381/430–6067* 🌐 *www.plazadealmas.com*), a warmly lighted, art nouveau bar (that also serves food), the multiple levels, nooks, crannies, and courtyards keep you guessing—happily. **The Belfast** (✉ *Santa Fe 506* ☎ *381/431–0391*) is a rugby-loving pub with food.

SHOPPING

Tucumán doesn't have many souvenir shops, but the few there are are worth visiting. Be sure to try the local version of the *alfajores* chocolate-covered cookies; here they're filled with a nougat-like paste made from the province's abundant sugarcane, rather than with the jam or dulce de leche used elsewhere. On the pedestrian Paseo de la Independencia is a modest artisan fair with stalls of knitwear and homemade foods. **Ajwenchey Artesanias** (✉ *Laprida 137* ⏲ *Daily 9–7*) has three shops in the city center that sell leather goods, ponchos, and other clothes, and well-crafted jewelry.

SPORTS AND THE OUTDOORS

Pablo Zelaya and his team at **Montanas Tucumanas** (✉ *Laprida 196, Oficina 5* ☎ *381/15–467–1860* 🌐 *www.montanastucumanas.com*) have a passion for the great outdoors and a thorough knowledge of the mountains of Tucumán. Whether you want to explore on foot, bike, horseback, or suspended from a paraglider, they can accommodate you, but for big trips try to reserve 30 days in advance. They also arrange climbing excursions as well as organized hikes with overnight stays in remote homes of indigenous locals. Trips last four to nine days and have been completed by hikers ages 5 to 79.

El Campito (✉ *Avenida Aconquija 3138* ☎ *381/425–7768* 🌐 *www.elcampitocabalgata.com.ar*) is a riding school in Yerba Buena that offers four-hour guided rides into the mountains and forests. Tours

Tucumán City's ornate Casa de Gobierno (government house) dominates Plaza Independencia.

take place daily, though they request that you set things up at least 24 hours in advance.

TUCUMÁN PROVINCE

Small Tucumán Province is rich in industry, commerce, and variety of landscapes. The capital city may be a sweltering sun trap, but it's a lively and industrious one. And just a short drive through jungles and over mountains is Tafí del Valle, a getaway with some beautiful small hotels and temperatures that never rise above 26°C (78°F).

The next valley over could be another country. In Amaicha every day is sunny, there's no water, and the pace of life couldn't be any slower. It's on the map primarily for its proximity to the ruins at Quilmes. Farther south, on the province's western edge, are some mountains rising to 16,000 feet or so, while in the east you'll find the fertile plains that have earned the province the title Garden of the Nation. Sugarcane, tobacco, livestock, and citrus fruits are all abundant here—in fact, Tucumán is the world's largest producer of lemons. Who knew?

TAFÍ DEL VALLE

143 km (89 mi) west of Tucumán via R38 and R307.

Tafí del Valle is a cool retreat that seems to specialize in tea and cakes for Tucumán's overheated gentry. Its history goes back to the Diaguita people, who arrived around 400 BC. They were follwed by the Incas, and, in 1700, the Jesuits. That said, the area remained isolated from the rest of the country until 1943, when a road was built from Tucumán.

Thanks to the altitude, it's often as much as 20 degrees cooler here than San Miguel de Tucumán. In January and February, during Easter week (when the whole town stages a passion play), and in July it's an overcrowded resort; during the rest of the year it's peaceful. The town is a great base for hiking, horseback riding, and windsurfing—the last thanks to the artificial lake, Angostura, created to generate electricity but never used for that purpose.

GETTING HERE AND AROUND

It's a short distance from San Miguel de Tucumán, but the road winds upward slowly, and the journey takes over two hours. It's a simple drive south from Cafayate on Ruta 40, crossing to Amaicha on Ruta 357 and on to Tafí on Ruta 307. Aconquija is the only bus company with service: six trips a day from Tucumán and two a day from Cafayate. La Cumbre agency and the tourist office can help you arrange outings to Lago Angostura and elsewhere in the region.

ESSENTIALS

Bus Contacts Aconquija (☎ *381/422-7620*).

Bank Caja Popular de Ahorro (✉ *Los Faroles s/n*).

Medical Assistance Hospital (✉ *Av. San Martín s/n* ☎ *3867/421-031*).

Visitor and Tour Info Tourist Office (✉ *Los Faroles s/n* ☎ *3867/421-084*). **La Cumbre** (✉ *Av. Perón 120* ☎ *3867/421-768*).

EXPLORING

The Sierra de Aconquija to the west and the Cumbres de Calchaquíes to the north enclose the high (6,600-foot) oval-shaped valley and its artificial lake, Lago Angostura. You can best appreciate the size of this often fog-shrouded valley from El Pinar de los Ciervos (The Pine Grove of the Deer), just above the actual town of Tafí del Valle.

A 45-km (28 -mi) circuit starts crossing the river toward La Banda and continues around the back of Cerro Pelado (Bald Mountain), which rises from the side of the lake to 2,696 meters (8,844 feet). The road goes past Estancia Las Carreras, a working farm, cheese factory, and museum with a fine hotel and restaurant, and leads to the town of El Mollar, with its Menhir Park, which is at the south at the other end of the valley and the lake. The return journey is 12 km (7 mi) along the straight main road alongside the lake.

Parque de los Menhires (Menhirs Park) is an area the size of a football field studded with hundreds of menhirs, or stone monoliths, said to be more than 2,000 years old. Before being collected in this park, most had been moved many times, obscuring their intended purpose and meaning. Some are over 6 feet tall and carved with primitive animal or human motifs, while others are just plain phallic. ✉ *Park entrance 5 km (3 mi) from Ruta 307, toward village of El Mollar* 🎫 *3 pesos* ⏲ *Mon.–Sat. 9–6, Sun 9–noon.*

WHERE TO EAT

> **WORD OF MOUTH**
>
> "We drove to the Museo Pachamama in Amaicra in Tucuman province, a little less than an hour south of Cafayate. Museo Pachamama is not to be missed—it was one of the highlights of the trip and one of the most spectacular human constructions I have ever seen in my life."
>
> —yestravel

¢ ARGENTINE **Doña Maria.** Probably the least formal restaurant in this whole guide, Doña Maria doesn't even have a sign outside, and the eating space is still used as a garage. Through the little hatch window in the back, though, is a kitchen where Doña Maria and her family work wonders with local specialties—empanadas, tamales, and the like. *Los Palenques s/n (opposite Camping Los Palenques) No phone No credit cards No dinner.*

$$ ARGENTINE **Popey.** There are lots of decent restaurants on Avenida Perón, but to choose just one we've followed the lead of Tafí's well-heeled residents, who congregate here. The Argentine fare is good, and the red-and-white-check tablecloths and helpful waitstaff make the place cheery. *Av. Perón 258 381/155–605–191 No credit cards Closed Mon.*

WHERE TO STAY

$$$$ Fodor's Choice ★ **Estancia Las Carreras.** This estancia has been in the same family since 1779. It's still a working farm, with more than 2,000 cows whose milk is used to make cheese both here and elsewhere. There's also a little museum with displays on the history of the valley and the estancia. The guest rooms in the main house are decorated with local textiles and such unique touches as bedside tables that were once used for making bread. Rooms open onto a peaceful courtyard, as do the cozy living room and the restaurant, which is open to nonguests with a reservation. Activities include horseback riding, hiking, and mountain biking. Ask a staffer to arrange a massage for after your exertions. **Pros:** tranquillity; a privileged position in history and in the valley; buffet breakfast. **Cons:** doesn't take credit cards; separated from town by a 12-km (7-mi) dirt track. *R325, Km 13.5 3867/421–473 www.estancialascarreras.com 10 rooms In-room: no a/c, refrigerator (some), no TV, Wi-Fi. In-hotel: restaurant, room service, bar, laundry service, parking (free), some pets allowed No credit cards.*

$$ **Estancia Los Cuartos.** Mercedes Chenaut, the current owner, explains that everything in this estancia is original, brought here by her ancestors over the last 200 years. Even the enormous wardrobes were transported up in pieces on the backs of mules. There are three bedrooms in the original building and four more in an extension. Breakfast includes artisanal cheese made in the small dairy and eggs from chickens in the garden (the five llamas are more decorative). With reservations, day visitors can have lunch and/or afternoon tea. **Pros:** great library; authentic antique details; close to center. **Cons:** doesn't accept credit cards; extension can't compete with the original building. *Miguel Critto s/n 381/155–874–230 www.estancialoscuartos.com 9 rooms In-room: no a/c, no phone, no TV. In-hotel: restaurant, laundry service, parking (free) No credit cards.*

$$ **La Guadalupe Posada.** It's a hotel and teahouse at the base of the Mala Mala mountains. Rooms, which are named for local plants, are cozy and have valley views. On warm days you can cool off in the small pool. Horseback riding can be arranged at neighboring stables. **Pros:** beautiful location; good garden; friendly service; Continental breakfast. **Cons:** outside of town; few facilities. ✉ *Av. Lola Mora 650* ☎ *3867/421–329* 🌐 *www.posadalaguadalupe.com.ar* *10 rooms* *In-room: no a/c, no phone, no TV. In-hotel: restaurant, pool, laundry service, parking (free)* *No credit cards.*

$$ **Las Tacanas.** It's surprising to come across a 17th-century Jesuit estancia at the end of Avenida Perón, Tafí's commercial street. There are nine rooms here; ask for the one with the four-poster bed so large it has wooden steps to get into it. The hotel is set back from the road in a delightful garden. **Pros:** charming old property and gardens; buffet breakfast. **Cons:** few in-room amenities. ✉ *Av. Perón 372* ☎ *3867/421–821* 🌐 *www.estancialastacanas.com* *9 rooms* *In-room: no a/c, no phone, no TV. In-hotel: bar, laundry service, parking (free)* *No credit cards.*

5

AFTER DARK

If you're here out of season, after dark is a time for looking at the stars. In season there aren't too many more options, but if anything is happening, it's happening in bars along Avenida Perón or Avenida Belgrano. **Los Nuevos Arcos** (✉ *Av. Perón s/n* ☎ *381/156–455–691*) is a restaurant that serves drinks and has live music starting at 10 on weekends in high season.

SHOPPING

This region is famous for its cheeses, ponchos, blankets, and leather goods—all sold in shops along Avenida Perón. Over the last decade the **Arte Alter Nativo** (✉ *Galeria Popey Local 8, Av. Perón* ☎ *3867/421–876* 🌐 *www.artealternativo.com*) cooperative has grown from supporting 5 to 45 families with its textiles. Expect traditional techniques and all natural materials (llama and sheep wools dyed with roots and leaves and rust) in the beautiful scarves, ponchos, and blankets sold here. The staff can ship things home for you, too.

El Blanquito (✉ *R307, Km 62* ☎ *3867/421–559*) is primarily a teahouse where Tafí's residents gather in the afternoon for a cuppa and a valley view. That said, they also sell some rather sweet souvenirs, including chocolate "menhirs," with dulce de leche and peanuts, and conical "Ñuñorquitos," named after the mountain you can see through the window.

SPORTS AND THE OUTDOORS

You can fish for trout or *pejerrey* (a narrow, silver fish similar to a trout), sail, windsurf, water-ski, or row on Lago Angostura. **Jeronimo Critto** (✉ *Av. Lola Mora s/n* ☎ *3867/421–257* 🌐 *www.tafidelvallerural.com.ar*) organizes horseback rides lasting from two hours to five days.

EN ROUTE

The drive out of Tafí on Ruta 307 takes you toward the Calchaqui Valley over a 10,000-foot pass. Here you get a glimpse of stone ruins and isolated menhirs. When cacti replace the valley's green sweep, you know that you've reached the desert landscape of the Puna. About 6 km

(4 mi) before Amaicha is the village of Ampimpa, with an observatory and a hotel, the Uno Cabañas.

AMAICHA

165 km (100 mi) northwest of San Miguel de Tucumán on R307.

Amaicha del Valle is so hot and dry that it feels like a world away from the towns on either side of it. The Ruins of Quilmes are the big draw, and although its indigenous inhabitants were long ago forcibly evicted, much of their way of life is continued in Amaicha. The area has 360 days of sunshine, but the best time to visit is in February, during Pachamama, a celebration of Mother Earth, with festivities led by the oldest woman in the town and lots of music.

GETTING HERE AND AROUND

From San Miguel de Tucumán, Ruta 307 continues past Tafí del Valle for another 40 km (25 mi). The route is covered by the Aconquija bus company *(⇨ San Miguel de Tucumán Essentials, above)* five or six times daily, stopping in the center of Amaicha. From Cafayate, take Ruta 40 south to Ruta 357, just after the Ruinas de Quilmes (20 km [12 mi] from Amaicha).

ESSENTIALS

Bank Caja Popular de Ahorro (✉ *M. Aráoz s/n*).

Medical Assistance Farmacia El Cóndor (✉ *Ernesto Padilla s/n* ☎ *3892/421–210*).

EXPLORING

The **Museo Pachamama** was established on the main road from Amaicha to the Ruinas de Quilmes by Hector Cruz, the man behind the Parador de Quilmes hotel next to the ruins. In the courtyards are some huge stone and wood sculptures; inside, look for exhibits on geology, art, and the daily life and traditions of the local indigenous community. ✉ *R307, Km 118* ☎ *3892/421–004* 🎫 *8 pesos* ⏲ *Mon.–Sat. 8–1 and 2–6, Sun. 9–1 and 2–5.*

The main attraction is the **Ruinas de Quilmes**, about 20 km (13 mi) down the road from the Museo Pachamama. Argentina's best-preserved ruins were home to a community of indigenous Quilmes between the 11th and 17th centuries. Some 5,000 people lived within this walled city at its peak (late 1600s). Only one part of the 75 acres of ruins has been partially reconstructed.

The best way to experience the ruins is to contact a guide from Amaicha; tours start at the back of the mountain and involve some climbing to reach the unrestored refuge at the peak. From here, with a view in all directions, it's easy to see how the Quilmes community could hold out against the Spanish for so long. In the end, the Spaniards cut off their water supply to force a surrender, then deported the whole community on foot toward the area in Buenos Aires that now bears their name. According to most reports, not one of them survived the trip. ✉ *5 km off R40* ☎ *3892/421–075* 🎫 *5 pesos* ⏲ *Daily 9–dusk.*

WHERE TO STAY

There are some very basic eateries within a couple of blocks of Amaicha's plaza and above the service station on the main road. For anything special in the way of food or decoration, though, make reservations at restaurants in the hotels listed below.

$$$$ **Altos de Amaicha.** Here, on a plateau above Amaicha, the views go on to the hills of Quilmes 20 km (12 mi) away. The hotel is in a smart, modern building and has a spirited and knowledgeable staff; they also have horses on which guests can explore the wide-open landscape. The restaurant is open to all, but it's best to let them know you're coming. **Pros:** by far the most comfortable place to stay in Amaicha; frequent barbecues for guests; Continental breakfast. **Cons:** doesn't take credit cards; far from town for those without rental cars. ✉ *R307, Km 117* ☎ *3892/421–430* 🌐 *www.altosdeamaicha.com.ar* *8 rooms* *In-room: no phone, refrigerator, Wi-Fi. In-hotel: restaurant, pool, parking (free)* *No credit cards.*

$ **Casa Uno.** On the road from Tafí, 6 km (4 mi) before Amaicha is Ampimpa, a tiny village with an observatory and this amazing place to stay. Its three cabins can sleep two to six people and have fully equipped kitchens, Wi-Fi, and satellite TV. There's also a swimming pool. It's run by a multilingual German wanderer who's chosen his place in the world for "the silence of the view." It's set up for self-catering, but meals can be prepared with advance notice. **Pros:** amazing views by day and night; tranquillity; Continental breakfast. **Cons:** credit cards aren't accepted; you need your own transport. ✉ *R307, Km 111, Ampimpa* ☎ *381/155–883–946* 🌐 *www.uno.travel* *3 rooms* *In-room: no a/c, no phone, kitchen, refrigerator, Wi-Fi. In-hotel: restaurant, pool, parking (free)* *No credit cards.*

¢ **Hostal del Sol.** Owners Mónica and Julio either made or found many of the decorative items here, from the 600-year-old mortar stones to the 120-year-old wooden trays for bread making to the cardon-wood bedside tables. It's a peaceful place. There's a large garden and a pleasant common area that serves as a restaurant (order meals in advance). **Pros:** peaceful; very good value; Continental breakfast. **Cons:** small rooms; few facilities. ✉ *Hipólito Yrigoyen s/n (3 blocks from the plaza)* ☎ *3892/421–435* *8 rooms* *In-room: no a/c, no phone, no TV. In-hotel: restaurant, laundry service* *No credit cards.*

AFTER DARK

After dark, most of the townsfolk gather in the plaza. They tend to sit at the corner near the police station. Photogenic **Bar La Esquina** (✉ *M. Aráoz s/n, at H. Yrigoyen* ☎ *No phone*) is on the corner of the plaza opposite the police station. They don't stand on ceremony here. The clientele consists mainly of locals, many of whom are happy to chat with strangers.

SHOPPING

There are souvenir shops at the entrance to the village on the main road. **El Artesano** (✉ *R307, Km 117* ☎ *3892/421–273*), next to the service station, is piled high with every type of local products you could wish

5

for: herbs, nuts, ceramics, leather, stones, carvings. There are also wall hangings made by the owner, Heriberto Ocampos.

SPORTS AND THE OUTDOORS

As well as tours of the ruins at Quilmes, Sebastian Pastrana of **Sumajpacha Ecoturismo** (✉ *Ernesto Padilla s/n, 1st fl.* ☎ *3892/421–433* 🌐 *www.sumajpacha.com*) arranges horseback rides, hikes, and excursions to the Tiu Punco petrified forest in the desert, the remains of the Los Cardones fort, and a nearby waterfall.

LA RIOJA

1,167 km (725 mi) northwest of Buenos Aires; 460 km (286 mi) northwest of Córdoba; 388 km (241 mi) southwest of Tucumán via R38.

The city of Todos los Santos de la Nueva Rioja—always shortened to just La Rioja—was founded in 1591 by Juan Ramírez de Velasco, a Spanish conqueror of noble lineage who named the city after his birthplace in Spain. Three hundred years later there were only 8,000 inhabitants, and the city was relatively untouched by the big immigrations of the early 20th century. It started to grow in the 1970s with increased industrialization, and now has 150,000 citizens. The super-relaxed nature of those inhabitants suggests that one day it's going to be a great place for a holiday, but it still lacks a clincher. Unless you can adjust to taking a siesta, the afternoons are hot and boring, and in the evening the streets are flooded with the sound of broken exhaust pipes as the locals circle the plazas on mopeds. So make good use of the mornings and late afternoons when the museums are open. If you want to get out and about, hire a rental car here: the rest of the province is hard to reach by public transport, and there's nowhere else in the province to rent cars.

GETTING HERE AND AROUND

Aeropuerto Vicente Almandos Almonacid is 7 km (4 mi) east of La Rioja. Aerolíneas Argentinas runs three flights a week (three hours). Andesmar offers bus service between La Rioja and Tucumán (three times a day, six hours) and Salta (four times a day, 11 hours).

In the city the bus system is good, taxis are cheap, and most attractions are within easy walking distance of the center. For the rest of the region, though, careful planning is needed if you don't rent a car, as public transport is sporadic and private tour operators are few and far between.

In addition to providing area information, the staff at La Rioja's tourism office can help you arrange hikes, camping trips, and tours by four-wheel-drive vehicle to Parque Nacional Talampaya.

ESSENTIALS

Bus Contacts Andesmar (☎ *3822/422–430*).**Terminal de Omnibus** (✉ *Artigas at Av. Ortiz de Ocampo* ☎ *3822/425–453*).

Bank Banco de Galicia (✉ *S. Nicolás de Bari at Buenos Aires*).

Working at a loom, La Rioja Province

Medical Assistance **Farmacia Americana** (✉ *San Martín 334* ☎ *3822/427–009*). **Hospital Presidente Plaza** (✉ *Av. San Nicolás de Bari Este 97* ☎ *3822/427–814*).

Post Office (✉ *Av. Perón 764*).

Rental Cars **King's Rent a Car** (✉ *Av. F. Quiroga 1070* ☎ *3822/422–122*). **Winner** (✉ *H. Yrigoyen 412* ☎ *3822/431–318* 🌐 *www.winner-rentcar.com.ar*).

Taxis **Remises La Rioja** (☎ *3822/426–666*).

Visitor and Tour Info **Tourist Office** (✉ *Pelagio B. Luna 345* ☎ *3822/426–384 or 3822/426–384* 🌐 *www.larioja.gov.ar/turismo*).

EXPLORING

❷ **Convento de Santo Domingo.** An earthquake in 1894 destroyed most of the town's colonial buildings, save the 1623 convent church, which is the oldest building in Argentina (it's one block from the plaza).

❸ **Museo Folklorico.** Displays on daily life and traditions at this museum are well presented but short on explanations. The museum has been adding to the collection of spades, clothes, and musical instruments since opening in 1969, and there's a good exhibit on the making of *vino patero* (homemade wine). ✉ *Pelagio B. Luna 811* ☎ *3822/457–035 or 3822/428–500* 🎟 *2 pesos* ⏲ *Tues.–Fri. 9–noon and 5–9, weekends 9–noon. Closed Mon.*

❹ **Museo Inca Huasi.** It was originally housed in the School of San Francisco when it was founded by Father Gomez, a Franciscan missionary,

CLOSE UP

The Leaders of La Rioja

Though underpopulated and unadorned, La Rioja has played a large role in Argentina's history and development through its *caudillos* (the term used for charismatic and self-appointed leaders throughout Latin America in the 19th century). Juan Facundo Quiroga and his protégé "El Chacho" Peñaloza were major players in the battles for Federalism and are honored with streets and statues throughout the province. In the 1990s La Rioja produced another influential political son, President Carlos Menem, who oversaw the decade of privatization and unbounded prosperity that led to the economic crisis of 2001. Always a theatrical figure, Menem cultivated his whiskers in homage to the enormous sideburns of La Rioja's caudillos, and then immersed himself in the high life—hanging out with celebrities and driving a red Ferrari.

in 1926. It moved to the present building in 1949, and is currently run by Father Pugliese, a protégé of Father Gomez who is well over 90 years old, and one part-time assistant. The indigenous artifacts of stone, metal, bone, and clay, all with typewritten explanatory cards, number more than 9,000 pieces—there's even a cabinet of human skulls in a back room. ✉ *Juan B. Alberdi 650* ☎ *3822/427–310* *2 pesos* ⏲ *Tues.–Sat. 9–1.*

❶ **Plaza 25 de Mayo.** The central plaza is named for the date the town was established.

WHERE TO EAT AND STAY

$$ ARGENTINE ✕ **La Construcción.** On a quiet corner in a building that looks unfinished—there's a wheelbarrow above the door—is a restaurant serving some of the city's best food. The aging waiters can steer you through the menu of pasta, fish, and vegetarian dishes to the sizzling parrillada. ✉ *Buenos Aires y Urquiza* ☎ *3822/434–838* ▭ *No credit cards.*

$$ ARGENTINE ✕ **L'Stanzza.** Clearly the goal at this small restaurant is raising the standard of eating out in La Rioja. There's a refreshing range of seafood and Asian dishes, in addition to the more familiar pasta and meat options. ✉ *Dorrego 164* ☎ *3822/430–809* ▭ *MC, V* ⏲ *Closed Mon. No dinner Sun.*

$$ **Hotel Plaza.** Although the exterior looks unexciting, inside everything is polished, and rooms are carpeted, quiet, and simply furnished. Drinks and snacks (excellent olives!) are served in the reception area, the small bar, and the restaurant-café, which are on the central plaza. The rooftop pool takes in a grand sweep of the city and the mountains beyond. **Pros:** good location. **Cons:** rooms overlooking the plaza can be noisy. ✉ *San Nicolás de Bari 502* ☎ *3822/425–215* 🌐 *www.plazahotel-larioja.com* *65 rooms, 3 suites* *In-room: refrigerator, Internet, Wi-Fi (some). In-hotel: restaurant, room service, bar, pool, gym, laundry service, parking (free)* ▭ *AE, DC, MC, V.*

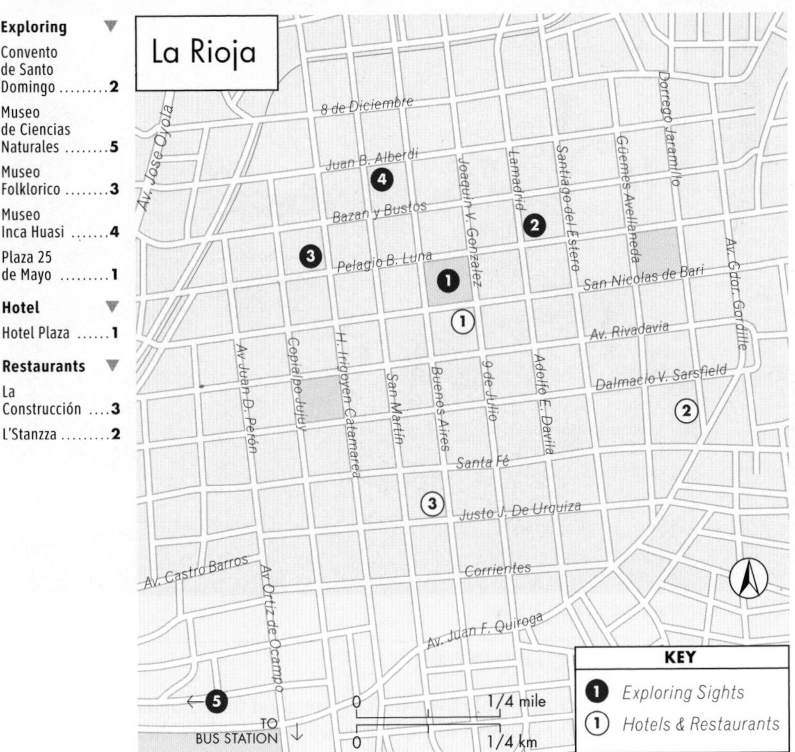

5

AFTER DARK

Unless you hire a moped and circle the plazas, there's not a whole lot to do at night. There are a few bars around the old railway station at the end of Avenida Rivadavia, but not much else. On Friday and Saturday nights from around 10 PM to around 3 AM, there's usually something in the way of live rock music or theater at **Centro Cultural El Pasillo** (✉ *Pelagio B. Luna 875* ☎ *3822/429–868*), a friendly cultural center.

SHOPPING

The locally produced olives (*aceitunas en Aimugasta*) are outstanding, as are the dates and the date liqueur; you can buy all three in shops around the main plaza. A **crafts market** (✉ *Pelagio B. Luna 782* ☎ *3822/468–433*) occupies a room in a building shared with the Museum of Sacred Art, and takes place Tuesday–Friday 9–noon and 5–9 and weekends 8–noon. The ceramics come from the capital, the textiles are sourced from the province, and the prices are excellent. **Casa Grande de Pinchas** (✉ *Buenos Aires 254* ☎ *3822/463–913*) has a rich selection of local produce, especially olives and homemade wines.

Parque Nacional Talampaya, La Rioja Province

SPORTS AND THE OUTDOORS

The mountains visible from the city are good for paragliding. Around 100 km (60 mi) north of the city toward Aimogasta there are opportunities for guided horseback rides or to rent bikes, motorcycles, and 4x4s. Hugo "Rubio" Avila of **Aguila Blanca** (✉ *Av. Ramirez de Velazco, Km 7* ☎ *3822/451–635* 🌐 *www.vuelosaguilablanca.com.ar*) offers tandem flights and courses in both hang-gliding and paragliding.

Condorcuna (✉ *Rivadavia 747* ☎ *3822/1536–6743* 🌐 *www.condorcuna.com.ar*) can arrange guides for trips to the olive- and grape-growing villages north of La Rioja as well as to Talampaya and Ischigualasto.

Once a month **Corona del Inca** (✉ *Pelagio B. Luna 914* ☎ *3822/422–142* 🌐 *www.coronadelinca.com.ar*) runs day trips to the Corona del Inca crater, a lake with a diameter of 5 km (3 mi) situated 5,500 meters (18,000 feet) above sea level. They need a minimum of five passengers, so they can take two 4x4s, and you need some warm clothes. They also run shorter trips to a number of far-flung destinations, including Laguna Brava, with its flamingo colony.

OFF THE BEATEN PATH

Tough to get to but unforgettable when you're there is a hilltop in the **Quebrada del Condor,** where you can stand and watch condors circling just meters away. Arriving involves a long off-road drive, a night in a posada with no electricity, a 90-minute horseback ride the next morning, and then a short hike. Don't forget batteries for your camera. Other activities on offer include trout fishing and a 6-hour nature walk where the only signs left by humans are pre-Hispanic cave paintings. For more information, see 🌐 *www.postaloscondores.com.ar*.

LA RIOJA PROVINCE

With a population of fewer than 300,000 in the province, no community shakes off the small-town feeling, and huge areas are completely deserted. The capital city itself is not much to get excited about—it stops completely for a siesta each afternoon, and in the evening there's nowhere to go. But the province has some wild surprises in store—if you are adventurous and don't need a lot of visitor facilities.

The Top Attractions have hardly changed in 250 million years: the national park of Talampaya and the provincial Ischigualasto Park (across the border in San Juan Province) have otherworldly landscapes of wind-eroded rocks where dinosaurs used to roam. A more recent development, and still almost completely off the radar, are the wineries of Chilecito and the Famatina Valley. Here you'll find mostly small productions of *vino patero*—handmade, or rather foot-made, wines. The province is also a place with high-altitude lakes, low-altitude condors, glaciers, mines, flamingos, centuries-old olive trees, and a tradition of extravagantly whiskered politicians.

PARQUE NACIONAL TALAMPAYA AND PARQUE PROVINCIAL ISCHIGUALASTO

230 km (143 mi) southwest of La Rioja.

Between them, the parks of Talampaya and Ischigualasto cover just under 700,000 acres, and contain the world's most complete fossil record of the Triassic period (245–208 million years ago), giving palaeontologists a clear picture of the evolution of dinosaurs, plants, and mammals. The importance of the parks and the finds in them went unnoticed until the 1950s; both parks were made UNESCO World Heritage Sites in 2000.

To help preserve the parks, entry is limited to 1,350 visitors a day, so arrive early in peak periods of January, February, July, and Easter Week. Ischigualasto (also known as Valley of the Moon, though the Quechua name prevents confusion with its namesake in Chile) is 80 km (50 mi) from Talampaya in the province of San Juan, and generally considered to be the more impressive of the two. That said Talampaya's vast walls of rock, whittled by wind and rain into strange formations, may be unlike anything you've ever seen. Besides strange rocks and fossils, both parks bear witness to human presence, with petroglyphs from thousands of years ago.

GETTING HERE AND AROUND

From La Rioja take Ruta 38 south to Patquía, head west on Ruta 150, and then northwest on Ruta 76. The roads are well signed and in good condition, and you leave your vehicle at the entrance, so there's no need for a 4x4 or a guide, as all tours are conducted by private operators. For Ischigualasto, head back along Ruta 76 to Ruta 150 and turn south. A member of the park staff must accompany you in your vehicle for tours of the valley.

There's a bus to Villa Union that leaves La Rioja early in the morning. It passes Talampaya then and later in the day on the return journey.

Just make sure you check the timings carefully. Most travel agencies in La Rioja, Chilecito, or Villa Union will take you to the parks; fees depend on group size. Use the ATM before you leave those towns, as you won't find one on the road or at the parks; transactions outside of towns are often cash only.

EXPLORING

Just five years ago, visitors could turn up in and explore the parks alone, but for the sake of conservation, all visits are now guided. In Talampaya two companies offer excursions to different areas.

Rolling Travel (✉ *R76, Km 145* ☎ *351/570–9909* 🌐 *www.talampaya.com*) has two tours in air-conditioned buses with guides: the main 2½-hour tour of the Talampaya Canyon (65 pesos), which takes in the petroglyphs known as the Cathedral and the Monk, and the longer tour (4 hours, 95 pesos), which continues for another 25 km (15 mi) to Los Cajones, where the canyon narrows to just 23 feet. Note that credit cards are not accepted.

Cooperativa Talampaya (✉ *R76, Km 133* ☎ *3825/470–384* 🌐 *www.turismoentalampaya.com.ar*) operates a 4-hour journey in a labyrinth of rock known as the Ciudad Perdida (Lost City) and a 3½-hour trip to Cañon Arco Iris (Rainbow Canyon), a multicolored ripple of rocks among myriad strange forms and stranger wildlife. Tours cost 120 pesos for two people, and an additional 50 pesos for each extra person. Credit cards are not accepted.

Ischigualasto's formations are imaginatively named after animals, stories, games—even a submarine. You should really brush up on some basic geology before your visit, though there's an explanatory 90-minute talk in the museum at the entrance to give you some context. Then there's the park itself, a 40-km (25-mi) circuit undertaken in a convoy of private vehicles with a park ranger riding in each.

You can visit both parks in a day, but it's worth considering a night in Villa Union (45 km [28 mi] from Talampaya) in between.

If you are doing both in one day, the light and the colors make it advisable to see Talampaya in the morning and Valley of the Moon in the afternoon. There's a campsite (3 pesos per person per night) and a basic snack bar at Talampaya. Take extra drinking water, hats, and sunblock, as there's very little shade.

WHERE TO STAY

$$ ★ **Pircas Negras.** Pircas Negras, named after Chile's *Pircas Negras* (black peaks) visible from here, is a surprise: who would expect to find such a high-quality hotel in the middle of nowhere? Well, that's only half true; this hotel is well-placed between Talampaya (50 km [30 mi]) and Ischigualasto (85 km [52 mi]), and also serves as a staging post for visiting Laguna Brava. Rooms have marble bathrooms. The food in the restaurant (evenings only, 30 pesos for a main dish) is very good. **Pros:** good service; marvelous pool; buffet breakfast. **Cons:** isolated. ✉ *RN76, Acceso Sur Villa Union* ☎ *3825/470–611* 🌐 *www.hotelpircasnegras.com* *47 rooms* *In-room: safe, Wi-Fi. In-hotel: restaurant, room service, bar, pool, laundry service, parking (free)* *MC, V.*

Throughout the northwest, there are places where it's possible watch wild pink flamingos.

CHILECITO

198 km (123 mi) west of La Rioja.

Chilecito, the province's second city (actually more of a small town), is not much closer to Talampaya than the capital, but it is the main nexus of the wine-making Famatina Valley and on the scenic route—the Cuesta de Miranda, a disorienting and uphill sequence of more than 200 turns—to Villa Union. The town has the rusting remains of the world's longest cable car, built to transport minerals from far-off mines.

GETTING HERE AND AROUND

Frequent buses run from La Rioja's terminal, but it's quicker to take a *diferencial* minibus; they run every couple of hours from both La Rioja and Chilecito and can drop you exactly where you want to go. There are no car-rental agencies in Chilecito.

ESSENTIALS

Bank Banco Macro (✉ *Adoblfo Dávila s/n, opposite central plaza*).

Medical Assistance Farmaworld (✉ *Libertad 48* ☎ *3825/426–049*).

Minibuses Chilecito diferenciales (✉ *El Maestro 61* ☎ *3825/424–710*). **La Rioja diferenciales** (✉ *Buenos Aires 154* ☎ *3822/435–279*).

Visitor Info Tourist Office (✉ *Castro y Bazan 52* ☎ *3825/422–688* 🌐 *www.larioja.gov.ar/turismo*).

EXPLORING

You need less than a day to wander around Chilecito. If you have a rental car you can make it a full day by heading out to nearby villages with their picturesque little chapels. The tourist office can provide useful information on such towns.

La Riojana is a cooperative of over 500 small and medium-size wine producers in the Valle de Famatina, Catamarca, and Mendoza. Its wines reach not only the Argentine market but also those in the United States, United Kingdom, China, and Africa. Its main production is of the sweet, white Torrontés Riojano—an appellation that's had some opposition from the original La Rioja in Spain—but they also have Malbec, Merlot, Tempranillo, Pinot Gris, and many other varieties and blends. Tours are held weekdays every 90 minutes from 9:30 to 4:30 and on Saturday at 9:30 and 11:30. ✉ *La Plata 646* ☎ *3825/423–150* 🌐 *www.lariojana.com.ar* 🎫 *Free* 🕒 *Weekdays 8–6, Sat. 9–1.*

The **Museo Chirau Mita** is a botanical garden that over 20 years has gathered more than 1,700 different species of cacti from all over the Americas. It's an immense undertaking by its two owners, and is very well presented. You can enter only via a guided tour, which spends about 90 minutes in the terraces of cacti and 20 minutes in the museum. ✉ *Av. Primera Junta s/n* ☎ *3825/424–531* 🎫 *10 pesos* 🕒 *Tues.–Fri. 9–noon and 3–7, Sat. 9–noon.*

WHERE TO EAT AND STAY

$ ARGENTINE ✕ **La Plaza.** This old-fashioned restaurant on the main plaza serves fresh food and local wine. The large windows provide a good view of Chilecito's social scene, which consists of what seems to be all the town's cars and motorbikes circling the square for hours each evening. ✉ *25 de Mayo 58* ☎ *3825/422–696* 💳 *No credit cards.*

$ 🏨 **ACA.** It's a quiet, spacious hotel run by the Argentinian Automobile Club. Prices are reasonable for the medium-size rooms with simple bathrooms and decoration. There's a large swimming pool and a garden, and it's just a few blocks from the plaza. **Pros:** large, airy building with lots of space; Continental breakfast. **Cons:** no English spoken. ✉ *Timoteo Gordillo 101, at Alberto Campo* ☎ *3825/422–201* *44 rooms* *In-room: safe. In-hotel: restaurant, room service, bar, pool, children's programs, laundry service, parking (free)* 💳 *MC, V.*

SPORTS AND THE OUTDOORS

The old cable-car line, which has a museum at the first station next to the bus terminal, makes a good walking route, though not all of it is accessible. There are also some demanding walks with great views on the Cuesta de Miranda, not far out of town.

Inka Ñan (✉ *25 de Mayo 37, Local 2* ☎ *3825/422–418* 🌐 *www.inkananturismo.tur.ar*) offers treks and excursions around Chilecito and the province, including day trips to Talampaya and Ischigualasto via the Cuesta de Miranda, and to Laguna Brava. Inka Ñan also rents bikes and sells plane tickets.

6

Wine Regions

MENDOZA AND SAN JUAN: THE HEART OF WINE COUNTRY

WORD OF MOUTH

We stayed in the suburbs of Mendoza (think Napa Valley), at a finca which we loved. All the big wineries are in this area with the Andes as a backdrop. We loved having a car/driver and doing the tour; ending with a 3 hour wine lunch and didn't have to worry about where we were or how we were getting back.

—owlwoman

WELCOME TO WINE REGIONS

TOP REASONS TO GO

★ **Scenic Wonders:** Wherever you go—over the pass to Chile, north to San Juan, south to San Rafael—the sight of those towering white Andean peaks never ceases to amaze.

★ **Fun in the Sun:** This sun-soaked land will delight, whether you pedal a bike along flat vineyard roads, ride a horse along Andean trails, or go skiing.

★ **Bed and Bodega:** Country inns with gourmet restaurants, vineyard visits and tastings, cooking classes, and discussions with oenologists make wine touring a pure pleasure.

★ **Food and Wine:** Some of Argentina's premier chefs have left resorts on the coast and the bistros of Buenos Aires for wine country inns and wineries.

★ **Unique Terroir:** All the big-name wineries have planted in the high-altitude region of the Uco Valley, where grapes ripen slowly and varieties show tremendous fruitiness.

Top left: Familia Zuccardi Winery
Top right: Las Lenas, Mendoza

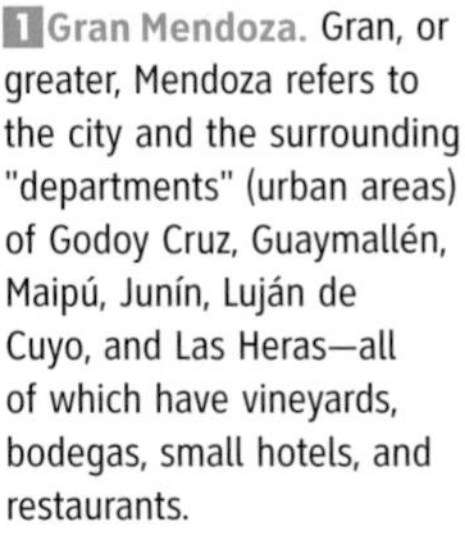

1 Gran Mendoza. Gran, or greater, Mendoza refers to the city and the surrounding "departments" (urban areas) of Godoy Cruz, Guaymallén, Maipú, Junín, Luján de Cuyo, and Las Heras—all of which have vineyards, bodegas, small hotels, and restaurants.

2 Valle de Uco. At the foot of the Cordón del Plata, between the towns of Ugarteche and Pareditas, the Uco Valley spreads its green mantle of vineyards and fruit orchards for 125 km (78 mi). The Río Tunuyán and its many arroyos (streams) create an oasis in this otherwise dry, desert region.

3 San Rafael. The vineyards and olive groves that surround this growing agricultural town in the southern portion of Mendoza Province are irrigated by the Ríos Atuel and Diamante, which flow from the nearby Andes.

4 San Juan. From this historic town surrounded by three important wine-producing valleys—Tulum, Ullum, and Zonda—you can travel west up the Río San Juan into a landscape of mountains, valleys, and desert.

GETTING ORIENTED

The provinces of Mendoza and San Juan, in the central west portion of Argentina, lie at the foot of the highest Andean ranges along the border with Chile. The city of Mendoza and its surrounding departments are in Mendoza Province's northern portion, 1,040 km (646 mi) from Buenos Aires but only 360 km (224 mi) from Santiago, Chile. The east–west Ruta Nacional 7 (RN7 Pan Americano or Panamerican Highway) crosses the Andes from Mendoza to Chile and links Argentina and neighboring countries (Brazil, Uruguay, Paraguay) with Pacific ports. Ruta Nacional 40 runs north–south the length of the country, passing through San Juan and down to Mendoza, the Valle de Uco, and San Rafael.

lunch at Cava de Cano, Mendoza

WINE REGIONS PLANNER

Wine Tours

Andesmar (☎ *261/405-0800 in Mendoza* 🌐 *www.andesmar.com*) owns the bus company of the same name. Among their offerings are seven wine tours.

Aventura and Wine (Bacchus Tours) (☎ *261/429-3014 in Mendoza* 🌐 *www.aventurawine.com*) customizes winery tours to include a visit with the owner or winemaker. They can also arrange anything from cooking classes to golf.

Aymará Turismo (☎ *261/420-2064 in Mendoza* 🌐 *www.aymara.com.ar*) offers 4- to 11-day tours with an oenologist and even longer tours to Chilean wineries.

Trout&Wine Tours (☎ *261/425-5631 cell, 261/155-413-892 in Mendoza* 🌐 *www.troutandwine.com*) has both private and group tours to top bodegas in Mendoza and the Uco Valley.

Joker Viajes (☎ *2627/436-982-282 in San Rafael* 🌐 *www.jokerviajes.com.ar*) does wine and recreational tours.

Mendoza Viajes (☎ *261/461-0210 in Mendoza* 🌐 *www.mdzviajes.com.ar*) offers wine tours, rafting, and horseback riding.

Money Tur (☎ *264/420-1010 in San Juan* 🌐 *www.moneytur.com.ar*) has a combination olive oil, jam, and wine tour.

Visiting Wineries

Most wineries prefer reservations. It's even better to arrange tours to vineyards through your hotel, a tourist office, or a local tour operator. Tours are particularly good if there's a specific bodega you wish to visit or if you're traveling with a group and/or during the harvest. If you do head out yourself, don't be put off by security precautions such as a locked gate or a uniformed guard. The guards are there to help, and will call up to the winery to announce your arrival.

SELF-GUIDED WINE TOURS

Each area has its own unique *caminos del vino* (wine routes). San Juan wineries have pooled their resources to print a booklet, *Ruta del Vino,* with maps, photos, and information in Spanish. In San Rafael, pick up information in your hotel or at the tourist office. Mendoza's caminos del vino are featured on several maps. The WINEMAP, available at bookstores and wineries, consists of four maps and a guidebook (in Spanish).

Getting Here and Around

Mendoza, San Juan, and San Rafael all have bus stations, car-rental agencies, cheap taxis, and *remises* (hired cars with drivers). If you're combining a ski vacation in Las Leñas with wine tours, fly from Buenos Aires to San Rafael, then travel north through the Valle de Uco to Mendoza. If you're skiing in Chile, fly from Santiago (or take a bus) to Mendoza.

Hiring a remis for an hour or a day is a good use of money, as frequent detours, road construction or washed-out roads, and misleading (or nonexistent) signs can make driving yourself frustrating and time consuming. Further, finding wineries on your own requires not only a good map but also a working knowledge of Spanish. That said, if you have the time and the temperament for it, exploring on your own—stopping for photos and to chat with locals—has its rewards. Driving to small Andean villages and the border with Chile is a particularly remarkable experience.

Eat Well and Rest Easy

Most of the region follows national culinary trends—beef, lamb, chicken, and pork *a la parrilla* (grilled). Second- and third-generation Italian restaurants serve family recipes enhanced with fresh ingredients like wild asparagus and mushrooms. Olive oil, garlic, melons (ripe February–March), and many other fruits and vegetables are grown locally. Hearty Spanish soups, stews, and casseroles are a connection to the region's past, as is *clérico,* a white-wine version of sangria. You may also have the opportunity to attend an *asado* (a traditional outdoor barbecue) while you're here. Malargüe, southwest of San Rafael, is famous for its *chivito* (goat)—cooked a la parrilla or *al asador* (skewered on a metal cross stuck in the ground aslant a bed of hot coals).

Tourist offices can recommend all kinds of *hospedajes* (lodgings), apart-hotels (rooms with cooking facilities and sometimes a sitting area), *cabañas* (cabins), hostels, and *residenciales* (bed-and-breakfasts), all of which are generally well maintained and offer good bargains. In the countryside you'll find everything from campgrounds to *hosterías* (inns), estancias (ranches), and even a spa hotel. *Posadas* (country inns) can be cozy and old-fashioned, sprawling and ranchlike, or sleek and modern. Some have first-rate restaurants and an extensive wine list. Afternoon tea, wine tastings, and custom tours, horseback rides, and evening entertainment are all possible activities.

Mendoza City has lively hostels, many medium-size hotels and apart-hotels, and the Hyatt and the Diplomat for luxury. San Rafael has two modern hotels, a few smaller ones, a golf and tennis resort, bodega and hotel, and the inimitable Finca Los Alamos—a charming and historic country home family-owned and -operated since 1890.

DINING AND LODGING PRICE CATEGORIES (IN PESOS)

	¢	$	$$	$$$	$$$$
Restaurants	under 8 pesos	8 pesos–15 pesos	15 pesos–25 pesos	25 pesos–35 pesos	over 35 pesos
Hotels	under 80 pesos	80 pesos–140 pesos	140 pesos–220 pesos	220 pesos–300 pesos	over 300 pesos

Restaurant prices are based on the median main course price at dinner. Hotel prices are for two people in a standard double room in high season.

When to Go

The wine harvest ends in autumn and is celebrated with a week of festivities that culminate in the *vendimia* (wine festival). In Mendoza this takes place during the last days of February and first week of March. A parade circles the Plaza Independencia and ends in the soccer stadium in San Martín Park with a grand finale of music, dancing, and religious ceremonies to ensure a good harvest. People shop and graze at food stands in the parks and plazas.

Winter is time for pruning and tying vines. Ski season begins in July, the month with the best weather and the one most favored by Argentines and Brazilians. August usually has plenty of snow, and September offers spring conditions. Weather in the Andes is unpredictable; pack clothes for all conditions, and get reports from ski areas. Springtime in the Valle de Uco brings trees covered in pink and white blossoms and new life in the vineyards. The snowcapped Andes form a spectacular backdrop, so bring your wide-angle lens.

Emergency Contacts

Ambulance–Medical Emergencies (☎ *107*). **Fire** (☎ *100*). **Police** (☎ *101*).

6

CERRO ACONCAGUA VIA THE USPALLATA PASS

At 6,957 meters (22,825 feet), it's the highest mountain in the Americas and in the southern hemisphere. It towers over the Andes with its five glaciers gleaming in the sun. Every year, from late November through March, hundreds try to conquer the so-called Giant of America.

Top left: Sunset on Aconcagua from Plaza de Mulas base camp Bottom right: Look up: condor sightings are common in this area Top right: Poplar trees en route to the Uspallata Pass

However, you don't have to be a mountaineer to enjoy the wild beauty here. Although guided climbing expeditions require two weeks of hiking and acclimating, a worthy alternative is to park at the rangers' cabin right off Ruta Nacional 7 just beyond the Puente del Inca, pay the park fee, and hike three hours the Río Horcones to a lagoon. If this seems like a short hike for such a drive out, you can take, or simply relax knowing that the journey to this place is as breathtaking as Aconcagua itself.

While fauna isn't thick, sight lines are unobstructed and you might see foxes or shy guanacos; look up for condors, too. Alpine meadows bloom in the spring, and lichen are up to 500 years old.

DRIVE SAFELY

Ruta Nacional 7 is the only road that connects the Pacific ports of Chile with Argentina, Brazil, and Uruguay. Be prepared for heavy truck traffic.

Note that roads become icy in winter and can close for days due to snow.
The altitude jumps from 762 meters (2,500 feet) in Mendoza to 3,184 meters (10,446 feet) at the top of the pass; winds can sometimes pickup.

ALONG THE USPALLATA PASS (RN7, THE PANAMERICAN HIGHWAY)

Leaving Mendoza, green vineyards give way to barren hills and scrub brush as you follow the river for 30 km (19 mi). If you find yourself engulfed in fog and drizzle, don't despair: you'll likely find brilliant sunshine when you reach the Potrerillos Valley 39 km (24 mi) along. The road passes a long dam and then follows the Río Mendoza for 105 km (65 mi) to Uspallata, the last town before the Chilean frontier.

Along the way, the Ríos Blanco and Tambillos rush down from the mountains into the Río Mendoza, and remnants of Inca *tambos* (resting places) remind you that this was once an Inca route. They're marked by signs along the way; if you're traveling with a guide, she or he will stop for you to check them out. At Punta de Vacas corrals that held cattle on their way to Chile lie abandoned alongside defunct railway tracks. Two kilometers (1 mi) beyond the army barracks and customs office three valleys converge. Looking south, the region's third-highest mountain, Cerro Tupungato, an inactive volcano (6,800 meters/22,310 feet), reigns above the Valle de Uco.

After passing the ski area at Los Penitentes (⇨ *Skiing under Sports and the Outdoors, below*), you arrive at Puente del Inca (2,950 meters/9,680 feet). Legend has it that, long before the Spaniards arrived an Inca chief traveled here to cure his paralysis in the thermal waters. Today, in addition to the thermal springs, you'll see a natural bridge of red rocks encrusted with yellow sulphur that spans the Río Cuevas; what's left of a spa hotel, built in the 1920s and destroyed in a 1965 flood and landslide, is covered in copper and gold sediment below the bridge. A few miles farther west, past the Argentine customs check, is the entrance to the park and the park rangers cabin. Fifteen kilometers (9 mi) farther along, the highway passes Las Cuevas, a settlement where the road forks right to Chile or left to the statue of Cristo Redentor (Christ the Redeemer) on the Chilean border (at 4,206 meters /13,800 feet), commemorating the 1902 peace pact between the two countries.

GUIDES AND LOGISTICS

While it's possible to hike any time of year, aim for November–March. Two- or three-day treks with guides take you to the Plaza de Mulas base camp at 4,325 meters (14,190 feet), where there's a *refugio* (mountain cabin with bunk beds; ☎ *261/423–1571* in Mendoza for reservations). **Inka Expeditions** (☎ *261/425–0871* 🌐 *www.inka.com.ar*) has 10 years of experience leading tours to base camp. Purchase a permit at **Cuba House** on San Martin Park in Mendoza City (✉ *Las Tipas at Los Robles Avenue* 🎫 *Trekking permits US$50–$110, depending on season and permit level; Ascent permits $160–$500* ⏲ *Mon.–Fri. 8–6, Sat.–Sun. 9–1*).

CONTINUING TO CHILE

Some tours and independent travelers continue on through to Chile to explore the vintages there. A visa is required of US citizens, but they can be purchased at the border. (⇨ *See the Crossing the Andes section of the* Wines of Chile and Argentina *feature in this chapter.*)

6

Updated by Eddy Ancinas

In the center of Argentina, in the provinces of Mendoza and San Juan, melting snow from the Andes flows into rivers, streams, and underground aquifers, and transforms this semi-arid region into the largest area under irrigation in Argentina. Eighty percent of the country's wine is produced here, as are olive oil, garlic, and a cornucopia of fruits and vegetables.

Argentina is the world's fifth-largest wine producer; in Mendoza alone, more than 200,000 hectares (494,200 acres) of vineyards bask in the sun from the suburbs of Mendoza City south through the Valle de Uco (Uco Valley) to San Rafael. The grapes are protected from the humid winds of the Pacific by the Andes, and grow at altitudes between 609 and 1,524 meters (2,000 to 5,000 feet), where they ripen slowly during long, hot summer days and cool nights and maintain acidity for long-lasting taste. Since there's little rain, irrigation of the mineral-rich snowmelt is controlled, and pests are minimal. Indeed, many vineyards could be classified as organic, as chemicals are seldom used or needed.

This wine-growing region is often referred to as the Cuyo—a name passed down from the early indigenous Huarpe people, who called it Cuyum Mapu (Land of Sand). *Acéquias* (canals) built by the Huarpes and improved upon by the conquering Incas and Spaniards, as well as by modern engineers, continue to capture the flow of the region's great rivers and channel it along the shady streets of the regions major cities: Mendoza, San Juan, and San Rafael.

Jesuit missionaries crossed the Andes from Chile to plant the first grape vines in 1556, followed by Spanish settlers who founded the city of Mendoza in 1561 and San Juan a year later. At that time the Cuyo was part of the Spanish Viceroyalty of Peru. Most of the area was cattle country, and ranchers drove their herds over the Andes to markets in Santiago. Although the Cuyo became part of the eastern Viceroyalty of the Río de la Plata in 1776, the long, hard journey across the country by horse cart to Buenos Aires kept the region economically and more culturally tied to Chile until 1884, when the railroad from Buenos Aires reached Mendoza.

The area is known not only for its wine but also for its outdoor activities. River rafting, horseback riding, and hiking in the highest range of the Andes, including Aconcagua, soaking in thermal baths, and skiing at Las Leñas and Penitentes, attract people year-round. In addition, one of the world's richest paleontological areas—the Parque Provincial Ischigualasto in San Juan Province—is a UNESCO World Heritage Site ⇨ *Parque Nacional Talampaya and Parque Provincial Ischigualasto under La Rioja Province in Chapter 4, The Northwest.*

GRAN MENDOZA

Mendoza Province, its eponymous capital, and the capital's environs (departments) are home to about 1,600,000 people, roughly 110,000 of whom live in Mendoza City. Most of the major vineyards and bodegas are in departments south of the city (Maipú, Godoy Cruz, Luján de Cuyo) and farther south across the Río Mendoza, in the regions of Agrelo and Perdriel. Still more vineyards are farther south in the Uco Valley. Each department has its own commercial areas, with shopping centers, hotels, and restaurants.

MENDOZA CITY

1,060 km (659 mi) southwest of Buenos Aires; 250 km (155 mi) east of Santiago, Chile.

Mendoza is shaded from the summer sun by a canopy of poplars, elms, and sycamores. Water runs along its sidewalks in acéquias, disappears at intersections, then bursts from fountains in the city's 74 parks and squares. Many acéquias were built by the Huarpe Indians and improved upon by the Incas long before the city was founded in 1561 by Pedro del Castillo.

Thanks to the booming wine and tourism industry, Mendoza bustles with innovative restaurants and lodgings that range from slick high-rises with conference rooms for serious wine tasting to low-key inns and B&Bs for serious relaxing. Low-rise colonial buildings with their high ceilings, narrow doorways, and tile floors house restaurants and shops. In the afternoon, shops close, streets empty, and siesta-time rules—until around 5, when the city comes back to life and goes back to work.

GETTING HERE AND AROUND

Mendoza's Aeropuerto Internacional Francisco Gabrielli is 6 km (4 mi) north of town on Ruta Nacional 40. Aerolíneas Argentinas has flights (about two hours) from Buenos Aires. LAN Chile has 55-minute flights from Santiago, Chile.

Busy Terminal del Sol is in Guaymallén, an eastern suburb about a 10-minute cab ride to or from town. From here buses travel to every major Argentine city and to Santiago, Chile. Transport companies include Andesmar and La Cumbre, with service to San Juan (3 hours);

Chevallier with daily service to Buenos Aires (14 hours); El Rápido, with daily buses to Buenos Aires and Santiago, Chile (8 hours).

Driving from Buenos Aires (along lonely but paved Ruta Nacional 7, aka Ruta Pan Americano or the Panamerican Highway) or Santiago (again, on Ruta Nacional 7, which is sometimes closed along this stretch in winter) is an option, provided you have plenty of time and speak some Spanish. There's little need of a car in town, and it's hard to find wineries in outlying areas on your own—even when you *do* speak Spanish. Further, Mendocinos are known for their cavalier attitude toward traffic rules. Pay attention to weather and road information. If you fear getting lost or breaking down in remote areas, hire a remis (a car with a driver) or arrange a tour. ⚠ **Downtown streets have ankle-breaking holes, steps, and unexpected obstacles, so watch where you're going. Jaywalkers may find they have to leap across a gutter to reach the sidewalk.**

ESSENTIALS

Air Contacts Aerolíneas Argentinas (✉ *Paseo Sarmiento 82* ☎ *261/420-4101*). **LAN Chile** (✉ *Rivadavia 135* ☎ *261/448-4411 in Mendoza; 0800/222-2424 elsewhere*).

Banks Banelco (✉ *Av. San Martín at San Lorenzo* ✉ *San Martín at Sarmiento*). **Banco de la Nación** (✉ *Av. San Martín at Gutiérrez*). **Citibank** (✉ *Av. San Martín 1098*).

Bus Contacts Andesmar (☎ *261/438-0654* 🌐 *www.andesmar.com*). **Chevallier** (☎ *261/431-0235*). **El Rápido** (☎ *261/431-4094*). **Terminal de Ómnibus** (✉ *Av. Gobernador Videla at Av. Acceso Oeste* ☎ *261/448-0057*).

Car Rentals Avis (✉ *Primitivo de la Reta 914* ☎ *261/447-0150* 🌐 *www.avis.com*). **Hertz** (✉ *Espejo 415* ☎ *2627/423-0225*). **Localiza** (✉ *Primitivo de la Reta 0800* ☎ *261/429-6800* 🌐 *www.localiza.com*).

Internet Cyber Café (✉ *Garibaldi 7 at Av. San Martín*). **Locutorio Internet** (✉ *Av. Villanueva 570*).

Medical Assistance Farmacia del Puente (✉ *Av. Las Heras 201* ☎ *261/423-8800*). **Hospital Central** (✉ *José F. Moreno and Alem, near the bus station* ☎ *261/449-0500*).

Taxis La Veloz del Este (☎ *261/423-9090*).

Visitor Info Mendoza Tourist Board (✉ *Av. San Martín 1143, at Garibaldi* ☎ *261/420-1333* ⏲ *Weekdays 9-1 and 4-8, Sat. 9-1* 🌐 *www.turismo.mendoza.gov.ar*).

EXPLORING

In 1861 an earthquake destroyed the city, killing 11,000 people. Mendoza was reconstructed on a grid, making it easy to explore on foot. Four small squares (Chile, San Martín, Italia, and España) radiate from the four corners of Plaza Independencia, the main square. Their Spanish tiles, exuberant fountains, shaded walkways, and myriad trees and flowers lend peace and beauty. Avenida San Martín, the town's major thoroughfare, runs north–south out into the southern departments and wine districts. Calle Sarmiento intersects San Martín at the tourist office and becomes a *peatonal* (pedestrian mall) with cafés, shops, offices, and bars. It crosses the Plaza Independencia, stops in front of the Hyatt Plaza, then continues on the other side of the hotel.

NEED A BREAK?

For a fresh cup of coffee, stop at Bonafide Espresso (✉ *Peatonal Sarmiento 102* ☎ *261/423–7915*) on the corner of Sarmiento and 9 de Julio. *Medialunas* (croissants) and *alfajores* (cookies with dulce de leche, sweet carmelized milk) add to the enjoyment of this lively café.

TOURING TIPS

In winter, a *bus turístico* (tourist bus) departs at 9:30 AM and 2:30 PM from the tourist office (where you can buy tickets for 15 pesos) and travels along a tour route, letting you on and off at designated stops. Also, you can pick up a free walking-tour map (the Circuitos Peatonales) at hotels or the tourist office.

TOP ATTRACTIONS

Plaza Independencia. In Mendoza's main square you can sit on a bench in the shade of a sycamore tree and watch children playing in the fountains, browse the stands at a weekend fair, or take a stroll after lunch to the historic Plaza Hotel (now a Hyatt) on your way to the shops and outdoor cafés on the pedestrian-only Calle Sarmiento, which bisects the square. **The Museo Arte Moderno** (☎ *261/425–7279* *45 pesos* *Mon.–Sat. 9–1 and 4–9, Sun. 4–9*), right in the plaza, exhibits paintings, ceramics, sculptures, and drawings by Mendocino artists from 1930 to the present.

Parque General San Martín. This grand public space has more than 50,000 trees from all over the world. Fifteen kilometers (9 mi) of paths and walkways meander through the park, and the rose garden has about 500 varieties. You can observe nautical competitions from the rowing club's balcony restaurant, visit the zoo, or play tennis or golf. Scenes of the 1817 Andes crossing by José de San Martín and his army during the campaign to liberate Argentina are depicted on a monument atop Cerro de la Gloria (Glory Hill) in the park's center. The soccer stadium and Greek theater (capacity 22,500) attract thousands during Vendimia, the annual wine-harvest festival.

WORTH NOTING

Museo del Area Fundacional. On the site of the original *cabildo* (town hall), the Foundation Museum explains the region's social and historical development. Of note is the display of a mummified child found on Aconcagua, with photos of his burial treasures. Excavations, made visible by a glass-covered viewing area, reveal layers of pre-Hispanic and Spanish remains. ✉ *Beltrán and Videla Castillo* ☎ *261/425–6927* *5 pesos* *Tues.–Sat. 8 AM–10 PM, Sun. 3–8.*

Museo del Pasado Cuyano. This 26-bedroom, 1873 mansion, the home of former governor and senator Emilio Civit, was the gathering place of the Belle Epoque elite. Today it's the Museum of the Cuyo's Past, a gallery and archive with paintings, antiques, manuscripts, and newspapers. ✉ *Montevideo 544* ☎ *261/423–6031* *Donation suggested* *Weekdays 9–12:30.*

6

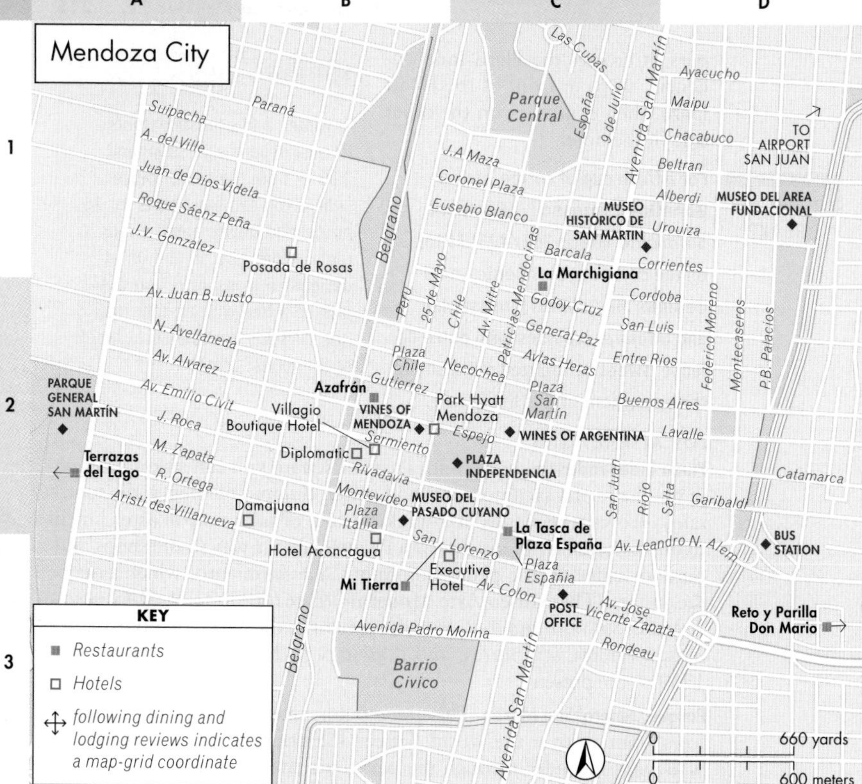

Museo Histórico de San Martín. The San Martín Historical Museum has a decent library and a token collection of artifacts from campaigns of the Great Liberator. ✉ *Av. San Martín 1843* ☎ *261/425–7947* *3 pesos* ⏲ *Weekdays 8:30–1:30.*

NEED A BREAK?

More than 40 ice-cream flavors, including *dulce de leche* (sweet caramelized milk) with *granizado* (chocolate chip) and many fresh berry and chocolate concoctions, merit a visit to Soppelsa (✉ *Emilio Civit and Belgrano Mendoza*).

WINERIES

The department of Maipú, south and slightly east of Mendoza City, has some 12 wineries in the districts of General Gutierrez, Coquimbito, and Cruz de Piedra. To the south, the department of Luján de Cuyo borders both banks of the Mendoza River and has 27 wineries in the districts of Agrelo, Carodilla, Chacras de Coria, Drummond, Perdriel, Ugarteche, and Vistalba. **TIP→ Aceso Sur (Ruta Nacional 40), the main highway south, is the fastest way to get to the area. RP15 runs parallel to 40, and most of the wineries are on this route.**

INSIDER INFO

Before heading out to the wineries, stop by the **Vines of Mendoza** (✉ *567 Espejo, between Chile and 25 de Mayo, Mendoza* ☎ *0261/438–1031* 🌐 *www.vinesofmendoza.com* ⏲ *Daily 11–11)* tasting room and information center. (Their Web site is a great place to get info before you even leave home.) It's owned by two American entrepreneurs who visited the area and fell enough in love with it to quit their jobs, move down, and establish a central place where English-speaking visitors can get insider wine and winery information. Their monthly newsletter, also available at the Park Hyatt, describes wine tours, tastings, and tips on favorite restaurants and bodegas.

In addition to offering 50 boutique wines by the glass and by the flight, they have weekly wine events and classes. Their knowledgeable staff can offer guidance on area tour guides, wineries, and wine stores.

Through Vines of Mendoza you can continue your wine experience at home. By joining the Acéquia Wine Club you receive shipments of four to six bottles of locally produced wine four times a year (each shipment costs US$145–US$245).

Feel like investing in a really big way? Through the Vines' private vineyard program you can buy 4- to 12-acre parcels of a Valle de Uco vineyard. As an owner, you—in consultation with a team of vineyard managers and winemakers—would participate in everything from choosing what to plant to designing your own label. It's the ultimate way to be an insider.

6

GODOY CRUZ

1 **Bodega Escorihuela.** Founded in 1884 by Spaniard Miguel Escorihuela Gascón, the oldest bodega in Mendoza features a 63,000-liter French barrel—the largest in the province. In 1993 a group of investors led by pioneer vintner Nicolás Catena bought the interests in the Bodega Escorihuela. Experimentation and innovation continue here with art exhibits and Francis Mallmanns' renowned restaurant, 1884. ✉ *Belgrano 1188, Godoy Cruz* ☎ *261/424–2282* 🌐 *www.escorihuela.com.ar* ⏲ *Weekdays 9:30–5:30; guided tours on the hour.*

MAIPÚ

3 **Bodega la Rural.** In 1855, Felipe Rutini left the hills of Italy to found a winery in the raw land of Coquimbito, Argentina. His descendants planted the first grapes (Chardonnay and Merlot) in the now-popular Tupungato District of the Valle de Uco. Today, Bodega la Rural is still family-owned and -operated. The winery's well-known San Felipe label was created by Alejandro Sirio, a famous Spanish artist. Inside the original adobe barns the Museo del Vino (Wine Museum) displays leather hoppers, antique pressing machines, vintage carriages; 100-year-old leather, wood, and copper tools; and even an amazing mousetrap. ✉ *Montecaseros 2625, Coquimbito, Maipú* ☎ *261/497–2013* 🌐 *www.bodegalarural.com.ar* ⏲ *Tours every 30 mins Mon.–Sat. 9–1 and 2–5; Sun. 10–1 with reservations.*

4 **Bodegas y Viñedos López.** Wines up to 60 years old are stored in the main cellar of this traditional family winery, established in 1898 and

Bodega Catena Zapata, Lujan de Cuyo

still owned by the same family. After a tour of the winery, tastings take place in the cave, where lunches can be arranged with a two-day notice. ✉ *Ozamis 375, Maipú* ☎ *261/497–2406* 🌐 *www.bodegaslopez.com.ar* ⏲ *Weekdays tours hourly 9–5; Sat. tours at 9:30, 10:30, 12:30; Sun. open only by appt.*

2 Fodor's Choice ★ **Familia Zuccardi.** In 1950 Don Alberto Zuccardi, a civil engineer, developed a more modern system of irrigation for his vineyards in Maipú and later in Santa Rosa. He and his team of 450 workers continue to discover new approaches to viniculture and wine tourism; their newest innovation, the Cava de Turísmo, is an air-conditioned cave where you can join tours of the bodega led by family members or an oenologist. A soft, soothing light glows on cobblestone floors, concrete walls, and warm woodwork in the tasting room and gift shop. Outside, you can walk shoulder to shoulder with the neatly labeled vines to the garden restaurant for a wine-tasting lunch or tea. During harvest time (February and March), Vení a Cosechar (Come and Harvest) is a program for wannabe grape-pickers that includes an early-morning pickup at your hotel, breakfast, and a morning of hard work in the vineyards (guided by agronomists and oenologists). This is followed by a wine tasting and lunch. From June to August a similar program teaches the art of pruning. Cooking classes, music, balloon rides, and art exhibits are also offered. ✉ *RP33, Km 7.5, Maipú* ☎ *261/441–0000* 🌐 *www.familiazuccardi.com* ⏲ *Mon.–Sat. 9–5:30.*

10 **Finca Flichman.** In 1873 Don Sami Flichman, a Jewish immigrant, planted the first vines in the stony soil of a former riverbed in the *barrancas* (ravines) next to the Mendoza River. His son Isaac acquired the

property during the 1930s Depression and had the foresight to produce only high-quality grapes. In 1983 the Wertheim family bought the winery, introduced new technology, and added another winery, installing stainless-steel tanks and computerized temperature controls in the underground cellars. ⊠ *Munives 800, Maipú* ☎ *261/497–2039* 🌐 *www.flichman.com.ar* ⏲ *Wed.–Sun. 10–5.*

LUJÁN DE CUYO

12 **Achával Ferrer.** With a score of 97 from *Wine Spectator* for their 2007 Malbec, Santiago Achaval's winery on the banks of the Mendoza River continues to score high points for their red wines. Guided visits include pre-paid barrel and bottle tastings. Quimera is a blend of red grapes (Malbec, Merlot, Cabernet Sauvignon, and Cabernet Franc) grown on three different *fincas,* including one in the Uco Valley. Quantities of each grape are adjusted to the quality of the grapes. The tasting fee is discounted from any wine purchase. ⊠ *Calle Cobos 2601, Perdriel, Lujan de Cuyo* ☎ *261/448–1131* 🌐 *www.achavalferrer.com* ⏲ *Weekdays tours 9, 11:30, 2:30, and 3* with reservaiton

20 ★ **Bodega Catena Zapata.** A faux Mayan pyramid rising from the vineyards fronts the towering Andes at this landmark winery where the architecture rivals the wine. You descend from a crystal cupola through concentric spaces to the tasting room, which is surrounded by 400 oak barrels. Founding father, Nicola Catena, arrived in 1898 and planted his first vineyard of Malbec grapes in 1902. Sons Domingo and Nicolás (the latter an economics professor at Columbia University) manage the vineyards planted at varying altitudes, blending varietals from these different microclimates to create complex, distinctive wines. Special tastings with meals can be arranged for groups by prior notice. ⊠ *Calle J. Cobos s/n, Agrelo Luján de Cuyo* ☎ *261/490–0214* 🌐 *www.catenawines.com.*

7 **Bodega Lagarde.** Built in 1897, Lagarde is one of the oldest and most traditional wineries in Mendoza. The third generation of the Pescarmona family now cultivates the grapes, producing limited quantities of quality wine and searching for ways to improve while avoiding fleeting trends. A five-course tasting lunch is served in the 19th-century *casona* (farm house). ⊠ *San Martín 1745, Mayor Drummond, Luján de Cuyo* ☎ *261/498–0011* 🌐 *www.lagarde.com.ar* ⏲ *Weekdays 9–5:30 with reservations, Sat. 9:30–2.*

14 **Bodega Norton.** In 1895, English engineer Sir Edmund Norton built the first winery in the valley south of the Mendoza River. Part of the old adobe house and a wing of the winery demonstrate the traditional construction of beamed ceilings with bamboo reeds under a zinc roof. In 1989 an Austrian businessman purchased the company, and his son continues to modernize and expand the 100-year-old vineyards. La Vid, their restaurant, has a 6-plate tasting menu, picnics, and even a children's menu. ⊠ *RP15, Km 23.5, Perdriel Luján de Cuyo* ☎ *261/490–9700* 🌐 *www.norton.com.ar* ⏲ *Hourly tours daily 9–noon and 3–4:30.*

5 **Bodegas Nieto y Senetiner S.A.** White adobe walls, tile roofs, flower-bed-lined walkways, and huge shade trees welcome you to this bodega. From March 10 to mid-April volunteer pickers arrive for breakfast,

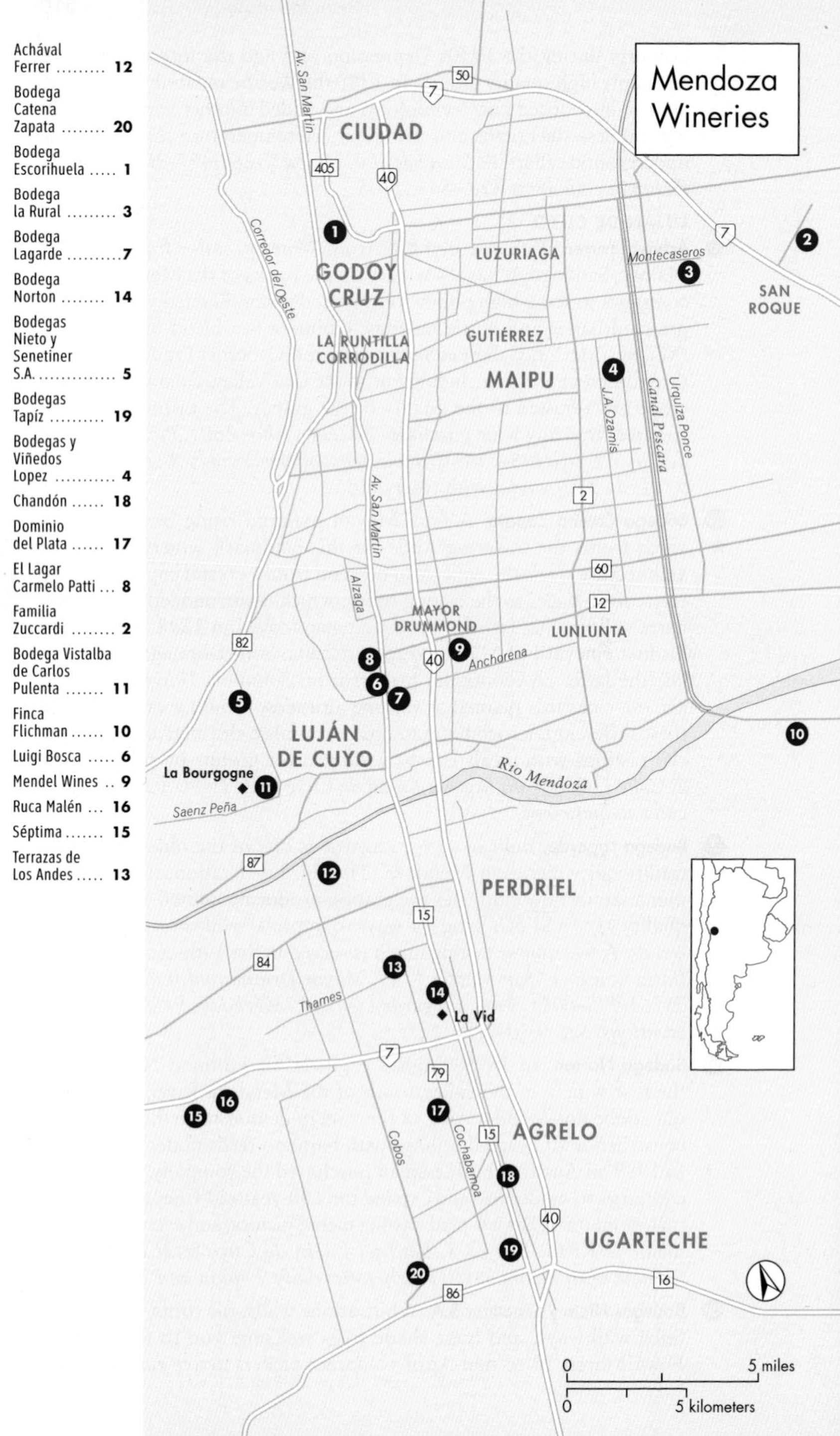

Mendoza Wineries
Achával Ferrer 12
Bodega Catena Zapata 20
Bodega Escorihuela 1
Bodega la Rural 3
Bodega Lagarde 7
Bodega Norton 14
Bodegas Nieto y Senetiner S.A. 5
Bodegas Tapíz 19
Bodegas y Viñedos Lopez 4
Chandón 18
Dominio del Plata 17
El Lagar Carmelo Patti ... 8
Familia Zuccardi 2
Bodega Vistalba de Carlos Pulenta 11
Finca Flichman 10
Luigi Bosca 6
Mendel Wines .. 9
Ruca Malén ... 16
Séptima 15
Terrazas de Los Andes 13
CIUDAD
GODOY CRUZ
LA RUNTILLA CORRODILLA
LUZURIAGA
GUTIÉRREZ
MAIPU
SAN ROQUE
MAYOR DRUMMOND
LUNLUNTA
LUJÁN DE CUYO
PERDRIEL
AGRELO
UGARTECHE
Av. San Martín
Corredor del Oeste
Montecaseros
J.A.Ozamis
Canal Pescara
Urquiza Ponce
Alzaga
Anchorena
Río Mendoza
Saenz Peña
Thames
Cobos
Cochabamoa
La Bourgogne
La Vid
50
7
405
40
2
60
12
82
87
15
84
79
16
86
0
5 miles
0
5 kilometers

a brief explanation of harvest technique, and an introduction to their foreman. Then, with tools in hand, it's off to the vineyards with the agronomist until baskets are inspected to see who wins the prize for the best pick. From mid-August until the end of September pruning (*podar*) takes place, and you can join the experts in cutting, tying, and modifying vines. Perhaps the most unusual tour is a three-hour, 2-km (1-mi) horseback ride to a hilltop for a view of the mountains and vineyards. During a maté (a tealike beverage) and muffin break, an oenologist explains the varietals growing around you. All of these activities include lunch at the bodega, tasting, and a tour, and all require reservations. ✉ *Guaradia Viaje, between RN7 and Rosque Sáenz Peña s/n, Vistalba Luján de Cuyo* ☎ *261/498–0315* 🌐 *www.nietosenetiner.com.ar* ⏲ *Summer: tours weekdays at 10, 11, 12:30, and 4; Other seasons: tours weekdays at 10, 11, 12:30, and 3.*

WORD OF MOUTH

"When you go to wineries in Luján de Cuyo—they are all very close together. Probably, the longest drive is 15–20 minutes apart. If you wanted to go to four wineries in a day—you can easily do that in this area."

—julieod

6

19 **Bodegas Tapíz.** When the Ortiz family bought this modern bodega from Kendall Jackson in 2003, CEO Patricia Ortiz and oenologist Fabián Valenzuela decided to make "happier wines" that are easier to drink and more food-friendly. Inside the bodega, walls of loose river rocks held in place by wire mesh contrast with the slick granite walls and long corridors. Tours begin in the vineyard, followed by tank, barrel and bottle tastings. In summer a two-horse carriage driven by a local gaucho takes you on a learning tour of the vineyard. Club Tapiz, a seven-room inn with a spa and the restaurant Terruño, is only 20 minutes away. ✉ *RP15, Km 32, Agrelo Luján de Cuyo* ☎ *261/490–0202* 🌐 *www.tapiz.com* ⏲ *Weekdays 9–4, Sat. 10–12.*

18 **Chandón.** The president of Moët & Chandon was so impressed by the *terroir* (soil, climate, and topography that contribute to making each wine unique) in Agrelo that he decided to build the first foreign branch of his family's company here. Today the winery is producing wine and *vino spumante* (sparkling wine) in great quantities. In a one-hour class for groups of 2 to 15, an oenologist will guide you through the process of blending wine, and you can take your new private label home with you. During harvest (February, March, and April) an agronomist takes groups to work in the vineyard with modern equipment; lunch is included. Special workshops can be arranged for business groups, wine clubs, and wannabe winemakers. ✉ *RN40, Km 29, Agrelo Luján de Cuyo* ☎ *261/490–9968* 🌐 *www.chandon.com.ar* ⏲ *Hourly tours weekdays; winter weekday tours at 11:30, 2, 3:30, and 5. Sat. tours require reservation.*

17 **Dominio del Plata.** Since 2001 Susana Balbo and her husband, viticulturalist Pedro Marchevsky, have combined their formidable skills with the newest technology and a passion for the care and cultivation of their land. Balbo, Argentina's first licensed female oenologist and an

internationally known winemaking consultant, can look out her living room window across a sea of vineyards to the sparkling Cordón de Plata mountain range. From her dining-room window she can see the stainless-steel tanks and pipes of the bodega she designed. ✉ *Cochebamba 7801, Agrelo, Luján de Cuyo* ☎ *261/498–6572* ⏲ *Weekdays 10, 12, and 3:30* ✍ *Reservations essential.*

11 Fodor's Choice ★ **Bodega Vistalba.** During his seven years as president of Salentein, a Dutch company with three bodegas, Carlos Pulenta increased the number of European varietals, installed the latest technology, and put Salentein wine on the tables of the world. He left in 2004 and returned to his family's land in Vistalba. Surrounded by vineyards, the courtyard entrance frames a perfect view of the 4,900-meter (16,000-foot) Cordón de Plata mountain range. Underground in the bodega, glass walls expose the tumbled rocks and dirt that Malbec thrives in. Pulenta and his team of family advisers and oenologists have created three blends using Malbec, Cabernet, Merlot, and Bonarda, plus a delicate Sauvignon Blanc and a Torrontés from their vineyard in Salta. Day tours include lunch at La Bourgogne, the award-winning restaurant. The light stone and polished concrete complex houses two ultra-modern rooms for overnight guests. ✉ *Roque Saenz Peña 3531, Vistalba, Luján de Cuyo* ☎ *261/498–9400* 🌐 *www.carlospulentawines.com.*

8 **El Lagar Carmelo Patti.** He answers the phone, greets you at the door and personally conducts tours (in Spanish only), drawing wine from the barrel and entertaining guests with anecdotes and entertaining facts about everything from growing grapes to winemaking and how to drink it, to the preservation of corks. Carmelo Patti, a legendary winemaker of the old school, is famous for his Cabernet Sauvignon. Producing only 5,000 bottles at a time, he notes the harvest and bottling dates on the label. ✉ *San Martín 2614, Mayor Drummond* ☎ *261/498–1379* ⏲ *By appointment.*

6 **Luigi Bosca.** Alberto, Raul, and Roberto Arizú—descendants of Leoncio Arizú, who brought the original vines from Spain in 1890—believe that a winemaker's job is to preserve what nature has delivered. Here nature is on their side. The terroir has much to do with the unique character of Luigi Bosca's wine. This bodega is an architectural gem, with 14 carved reliefs depicting the history of winemaking in Argentina, tile floors, inlaid wood ceilings, and painted arches. ✉ *San Martín 2044, Mayor Drummond, Luján de Cuyo* ☎ *261/498–1974* 🌐 *www.luigibosca.com.ar* ⏲ *Daily tours at 10, 11, 12:30.*

9 **Mendel Wines.** Every year since 2004, both *Wine Spectator* and Robert Parker's *Wine Advocate* have awarded over 90 points to Mendel's Malbec, as well as to their Malbec–Cabernet Sauvignon blend (Unus). This is testimony to the expert winemaking of one of Argentina's best know winemakers, Roberto de la Mota, and to the dedicated owners of this limited-production winery, where quality, not quantity, is their mantra. In this unassuming 80-year-old adobe building, informal tours point out the loving care grapes receive—from hand-picking to hand-crushing to storage. ✉ *Terrada 1863, Mayor Drummond* ☎ *261/524–1621* 🌐 *www.mendel.com.ar* ⏲ *Weekdays 9–12:30.*

16 **Ruca Malén.** Jon Pierre Thibaud brings 10 years of experience as president of neighboring Chandón vineyards to this modern, compact boutique winery situated just back from Ruta Nacional 7. Thibaud and his French partner, Jacques Louis de Montalembert, have dedicated their collective skills and passion to selecting the finest grapes for quality wines. Wine tours, tastings, and blending seminars can be followed by a gourmet lunch and wine tasting, after which a quick siesta on the balcony looking up at the Andes revives visitors before continuing on to the next bodega. ✉ *RN7, Km 1059, Agrelo Luján de Cuyo* ☎ *261/410–6214* 🌐 *www.bodegarucamalen.com* ⏲ *Weekdays 10–5, Sat. 10–1.*

15 ★ **Séptima.** When the Spanish wine group Codorniú decided that Argentina would be their seventh great wine investment, they constructed their winery in the *pirca* style, in which natural stones are piled one atop the other. The Huarpe natives used this technique to build walls, dwellings, and sacred places. Inside the massive walls is a state-of-the-art winery with sleek wood and glass corridors. Visitors climb over hoses and machinery while they follow the grapes from vineyard to bottle in a natural working atmosphere. A rooftop terrace is available for private lunches, weddings, or sunset wine tastings, and a restaurant (María) uses local ingredients infused with Arabic, Jewish, Greek, and African culinary traditions. ✉ *RN7, Km 6.5, Agrelo Luján de Cuyo* ☎ *261/498–5164* 🌐 *www.bodegaseptima.com.ar* ⏲ *Weekdays 10–5* ✍ *Reservations essential.*

13 **Terrazas de Los Andes.** Four vineyards situated at different heights (terraces)—Syrah at 800 meters (2,600 feet), Cabernet Sauvignon at 980 meters (3,200 feet), Malbec slightly higher, and Chardonnay at 1,200 meters (3,900 feet)—take advantage of different microclimates, allowing each varietal to develop to its maximum potential. Bare brick walls, high ceilings, and a labyrinth of soaring arches shelter premium wines in stainless-steel tanks and oak barrels. Built in 1898 and restored in the mid-1990s, everything in the tasting room—from the bar to the tables to the leather chairs—is made with recycled barrels. A six-room guesthouse and a dining room are available for family or business gatherings with reservations one day in advance by phone or e-mail. ✉ *Thames and Cochebamba, Perdriel, Luján de Cuyo* ☎ *261/448–0058* 🌐 *www.terrazasdelosandes.com* ⏲ *Weekdays 10, 12, and 3 PM.*

WHERE TO EAT

MENDOZA CITY

$ WINE BAR/ RESTAURANT ★ ✕ **Azafrán.** It's as much a gourmet grocery and wineshop as it is a restaurant—one that offers a break from parrilla fare, at that. Eighty wineries are represented by more than 400 labels in the wine bar, where an old wine press has been converted into a tasting table. Outside on the sidewalk or inside this 19th-century brick building you can enjoy cheeses, pâtés, and hot and cold tapas served on wooden platters. Shelves are stocked with olive oils, smoked meats, dried herbs, mushrooms, olives, jams, and breads. ✉ *Sarmiento 765, Mendoza* ☎ *261/429–4200* ✉ *Villanueva 287* 💳 *AE, MC, V* ⏲ *Closed Sun.* ✥ *B2.*

$$$ ITALIAN ✕ **La Marchigiana.** They've served homemade pasta since 1950, and Nonna Fernanda, whose cookbooks are available to purchase, often dines here with her family. The old restaurant burned down in 2006,

DID YOU KNOW?

There are two main pruning methods for grape vines. Spur (or head) pruning involves allowing only two shoots per branch to bear grapes; this is most common in older vineyards or in the warmest growing climates. Cane pruning trains up to four shoots per branch along a trellis so that up to sixteen new shoots will bear fruit along the trellis the next season.

but a modern version with underground parking is just as popular with Mendocinos looking for a reasonably priced meal (and a great lasagna). ✉ *Patricias Mendocinas 1550, Mendoza* ☎ *261/423–071* ✉ *Palmares Shopping Mall, Godoy Cruz* ☎ *261/439–1961* ▭ *AE, DC, MC, V* ✣ *C1.*

$$ MEDITERRANEAN ✕ **La Tasca de Plaza España.** If the bright red walls, the strange faces painted above the entrance, and the eclectic art inside don't grab you, the tapas and Mediterranean dishes probably will. Seafood tapas, veal-and-artichoke stew, and a casserole of zucchini, onions, and peppers in a cheese sauce are a few of the tempting dishes served in this venerable—though irreverent—old house. ✉ *Montevideo 117, Mendoza* ☎ *261/423–3466* ▭ *AE, MC, V* ✣ *C2.*

$$$ ARGENTINE ✕ **Mi Tierra.** It's in an old house with tall narrow doors, high ceilings, and five dining rooms, each dedicated to a particular winery. Chicken or rabbit *al disco* (in a wok) comes with grilled vegetables. Leave room for the *volcan de frutas* (fruit in a merengue). ✉ *Mitre 794, at San Lorenzo, Mendoza* ☎ *261/425–0035* ▭ *AE, MC, V* ⏲ *Weekdays 12–3:30 and 8–12* ✣ *B3.*

$$ ARGENTINE ✕ **Restaurant y Parilla Don Mario.** Mendocinos have been coming here for years for their basic beef fix. *Bife de lomo* and *bife de chorizo* are grilled to perfection at this comfortable country-style restaurant with pastas, grilled vegetables, and a good wine list. ✉ *25 de Mayo 1324, Mendoza, Guyaymallén* ☎ *261/431–0801* ▭ *AE, DC, MC, V* ✣ *D3.*

$$ ARGENTINE ✕ **Terrazas del Lago.** It's only a 15-minute taxi ride from downtown to this restaurant in Parque General San Martín. The long wood-and-glass building overlooks a lake and two pools that are part of an aquatic club (open for day use by nonmembers). A buffet fills one room. The master of the pasta bar waits to help you—first with choosing from four kinds of ravioli and eight types of noodles, then with selecting a sauce from a simmering pot, and finally with piling your plate with all kinds of other treats. Seating is outdoors on a deck or indoors with air-conditioning (essential for summer lunches). Reservations are a good idea. ✉ *Av. Las Palmeras s/n, on Parque Gral San Martín, Mendoza* ☎ *261/428–3438* ▭ *AE, MC, V* ⏲ *No dinner Sun.; no lunch Mon.* ✣ *A2.*

GODOY CRUZ

$$$$ ARGENTINE ★ ✕ **1884 Restaurante Francis Mallman.** The soft glow of candles on the patio at the 100-year-old Bodega Escorihuela sets the tone for superchef, Francis Mallman, whose version of Patagonian cuisine has won him many awards and international acclaim. You can dine on the patio, where empanadas and traditional meats, including goat, are baked in mud ovens, a custom derived from the Incas. The 36-page wine list has detailed information on grapes and bodegas. ✉ *Belgrano 1188, Godoy Cruz* ☎ *261/424–2698* ▭ *AE, DC, MC, V.*

MAIPÚ

$$$$ ARGENTINE ★ ✕ **Terruños.** Light from a whimsical chandelier high in the timbered ceiling highlights the Malbec-color walls and worn floors of this 1890 vintner's elegant residence. Seasonal dishes marrying beef, pork, or veal with Mediterranean and Asian influences creates unforgettable meals that have won many awards for chef Max Casá. An experienced staff knows how to pair local wine with each course, including dessert. ✉ *Club Tapiz, Pedro Molina (RP60) s/n Maipú* ☎ *261/496–0131* ✍ *Reservations essential* 🌐 *www.tapiz.com.*

LUJÁN DE CUYO

$$$$ FRENCH Fodor's Choice ★ ✕ **La Bourgogne.** "Cooking comes from regional traditions. My cuisine is tied to the land," says Jean-Paul Bondoux, Argentina's Relais Gourmand chef, who oversees this restaurant along with two others by the same name. He applies his French culinary skills to the best local produce in this casually elegant restaurant at Carlos Pulenta's winery. After a winery tour you can select your own herbs from the garden to complement the menu. ✉ *Roque Sáenz Peña 3531, Vistalba, Luján de Cuyo* ☎ *261/498–9400* ⏲ *Lunch only (1–3). Closed Sun.* 🌐 *www.carlospulentawines.com* ✍ *Reservations essential* ▭ *AE, MC, V.*

$$$ ARGENTINE ✕ **La Vid.** At the Norton winery, this restaurant, with its pleasing contemporary design, welcomes guests from all over Mendoza—with or without the wine tour. You can spend the afternoon tasting wines with a six-course tasting menu, or opt for the daily special with a glass of wine, or sample a cheese and cold-cut plate. Of course, there is also à-la-carte fare, with unusual dishes like rabbit lasagna and salmon ravioli. They even have a kids' menu and pack-up picnics. ✉ *RP15, Km 23, Perdirel, Luján de Cuyo* ☎ *260/490–9790* 🌐 *www.norton.com.ar* ✍ *Reservations essential* ▭ *AE, MC, V* ⏲ *Open Mon.–Sat. 10–6.*

WHERE TO STAY

6

MENDOZA CITY

¢ **Damajuana.** It's easy to feel at home inside or out: a bar, restaurant, fireplace, and TV are in the living room, and the spacious backyard has a grill and hammocks. It's a popular hostel with rooms for two, four, or six people that are half the price per person of the one double. All rooms have lockers and shared baths. The neighborhood—steps from bars, boutiques, and cafés—is popular with young Mendocinos. **Pros:** great neighborhood, especially for young people; clean; safe; fun. **Cons:** can be noisy at night. ✉ *Aristedes Villanueva 282, Mendoza* ☎ *261/425–5858* 🌐 *www.damajuanahostel.com.ar* *8 rooms* *In-hotel: restaurant, bar, pool, public Wi-Fi* ▭ *MC, V* ✥ *A2.*

$$$$$ **Diplomatic.** At last, Mendoza has a big luxury hotel with plenty of rooms for meetings, parties, wine tastings, and events, plus a famous restaurant (La Bourgogne), and an inviting wine bar. Polished wood floors in all the rooms, gleaming marble in the lobby, twinkling chandeliers—all elements of luxury and refined taste—raise the bar for luxury lodgings in Argentina's wine capital. **Pros:** everything you could possibly want in luxury, design, comfort, amenities; big picture windows in rooms. **Cons:** price; pictures or rugs in rooms would make them a little friendlier. ✉ *Belgrano 1014* ☎ *261/405–1900, 0810/122–5000 reservations* 🌐 *www.parksuites.com.ar* *116 rooms* *In-room: safe, a/c, Wi-Fi. In-hotel: meeting and event rooms, restaurant, room service, bar, lobby wine bar, pool, gym, spa, Wi-Fi, parking (fee)* ▭ *AE, D, DC, MC, V* *CP* ✥ *B2.*

$$$$ ★ **Executive Hotel.** The tall, elegant tower of this downtown hotel looks out on the Plaza Italia in a quiet residential area just blocks from shops and restaurants. The lobby and dining area are all slick marble, glass, and mirrors. The staff is welcoming—from the front-desk staff to the waiters to the concierge. If you're here for a longer stay, opt for a suite; each has a sitting room with a couch, a desk, and a counter

Difficult choices at Mendoza City's Mercado Central

for snacks or drinks. **Pros:** sauna, tasting rooms with free wine from local vinters. **Cons:** windowless bar-restaurant. ✉ *San Lorenzo 660, Mendoza* ☎ *261/524–5000* 🌐 *www.parksuites.com.ar* ⇨ *49 rooms, 32 suites* ☝ *In-room: safe, Wi-Fi. In-hotel: restaurant, pool, gym, parking (paid)* ▭ *AE, DC, MC, V* 🍴 *CP* ✣ *B3.*

$$$$ **Hotel Aconcagua.** The service is friendly and efficient at this modern hotel on a quiet street near shops and restaurants. Classic gray granite creates a businesslike atmosphere in the lobby and in meeting rooms. Check their Web site for promotions, including a free night. Los Parrales restaurant uses a mud oven and wood-fired grill to create typical Mendocino meals. **Pros:** central location; business suites with attendant on top floor. **Cons:** public areas often crowded with wine-business and tour groups. ✉ *San Lorenzo 545, Mendoza* ☎ *261/520–0500* 🌐 *www.hotelaconcagua.com* ⇨ *159 rooms, 9 suites* ☝ *In-room: Wi-Fi. In-hotel: restaurant, pool, public Wi-Fi, parking (free)* ▭ *AE, DC, MC, V* 🍴 *CP* ✣ *B3.*

$$$$ **Park Hyatt Mendoza.** Hyatt has preserved the landmark Plaza Hotel's
Fodor's Choice ★ 19th-century Spanish colonial facade: a grand pillared entrance and a wide veranda that extends to either side of the street. Lunch, afternoon tea, and dinner are served on this gracious terrace overlooking Mendoza's main square. A two-story wine wall separates Bistro M, the restaurant, from the lobby. Minimalist bedrooms are softened by plump white pillows and duvets covering the simple ebony beds. **Pros:** weekly events such as ladies night with wine and tapas (Wednesday), Sunday buffet lunch at Grill Q, wine and tapas nights at The Vines (Thursday), and special wine-tasting dinners. **Cons:** glass walls in bathroom don't allow for privacy. ✉ *Calle Chile 1124, Mendoza* ☎ *261/441–1234*

mendoza.park.hyatt.com *171 rooms, 15 suites* *In-room: safe, Internet. In-hotel: restaurant, bar, pool, gym, spa, parking (free)* *AE, DC, MC, V* *CP* *B3.*

$$$ **Posada de Rosas.** Don't be fooled by this ordinary house on an ordinary street—inside, bright rooms are decorated with modern art and ancient Andean weavings, and have just the places to enjoy breakfast (inside or out on the patio) or tea or to curl up with a *New Yorker* or one of the English-language wine magazines that are set out. American expat owners Ellen and Riccardo share their knowledge and passion for Mendoza through their tour company, Amazing Mendoza (*www.amazingmendoza.com*). Three rooms with kitchenettes in an outside building face the garden. **Pros:** nice neighborhood with good shops and restaurants; helpful English-speaking owners who know the territory. **Cons:** long walk to town. *Martínez de Rozas 1641, Mendoza* *261/423–3629* *www.posadaderosas.com* *8 rooms* *In-room: refrigerator, Wi-Fi. In-hotel: pool, Wi-Fi* *AE, MC, V* *CP* *B1.*

$$$$ **Villagio Boutique Hotel.** There's a high-tech Italian feel to this modern boutique hotel a block from the main plaza and shopping street. Expect such details as polished wood or stainless-steel trim; beige, black, and tan furnishings; and modern artwork throughout. **Pros:** spacious rooms; artful architecture and design; sauna; Jacuzzi with a mountain view. **Cons:** small rooms; some guests complain of thin walls and noise from neighbors; some rooms have views of air shaft. *25 de Mayo 1010, Mendoza* *261/524–5200* *hotelvillaggio.com.ar* *26 rooms* *In-room: Wi-Fi. In-hotel: restaurant, bar, pool, gym, public Wi-Fi* *AE, DC, MC, V* *CP* *B2.*

6

MAIPÚ

$$$ ★ **Club Tapiz.** This 1890 governor's mansion surrounded by vineyards feels like a private villa. Stroll through the old winery, lounge on the enclosed patio, or gaze at the Andes from the outdoor pool or indoor Jacuzzi. Evening wine tastings will whet your appetite for dinner in Terruña (Terroir). **Pros:** great restaurant; close to vineyards. **Cons:** far from shops or town. *Pedro Molina (RP60) s/n, Maipú* *261/496–4815* *www.tapiz.com* *7 rooms* *In-hotel: restaurant, bar, spa, bicycles* *AE, MC, V.*

LUJÁN DE CUYO

$$$$ ★ **Cavas Wine Lodge.** Inside a gracious colonial villa surrounded by mountains and vineyards, a reception hall is washed in sunlight from high windows, and common areas are appointed in white, gold, wood, and leather. Imagine yourself in one of the white adobe guesthouses, with your own patio and plunge pool, and your own roof deck with a fireplace. Bedrooms are painted a soothing cream that contrasts with the bold red throws and pillows. Bathrooms have natural stone walls and what seem like all the amenities ever invented. Enjoy the Jacuzzi or an aromatherapy or vinotherapy treatment in the on-site spa. Ask the concierge to arrange visits to nearby bodegas; make reservations at restaurants; or organize horseback-riding, rafting, or biking excursions. **Pros:** luxurious; private; spacious; good service. **Cons:** expensive; far from shops, restaurants, and other urban activities. *RN40 south, west on RN7, turn off onto Cosa Flores just before Ruca Malen Winery.*

Follow signs for 2.2 km (1.4 mi) ✉ *Luján de Cuyo* ☎ *261/410–6927* 🌐 *www.cavaswinelodge.com* ⇨ *14 cottages* 👍 *In-room: safe, DVD, Internet. In-hotel: restaurant, bar, pool, gym, spa, bicycles* ▭ *AE, DC, MC, V* ⊗ *Closed June* 🍴 *CP.*

$$$ **Chacras de Coria Lodge.** A stay at this lodge puts you in an upscale residential area 15 minutes from Mendoza and close to wineries in Maipú and Luján de Cuyo. The staff can arrange custom tours with oenologists as well as catered meals, golf, tennis, horseback riding, mountain biking—even tango lessons. The atmosphere is intimate and friendly, from outdoor *asados* (barbecues) to candlelit dinners on the veranda. **Pros:** personalized tours; close to vineyards; good restaurant. **Cons:** in a residential suburb. ✉ *Viamonte 4762, Chacras de Coria, Luján de Cuyo* ☎ *261/496–1888* 🌐 *www.postalesarg.com* ⇨ *6 rooms, 1 apartment* 👍 *In-hotel: restaurant, bar, pool, Wi-Fi* ▭ *AE, MC, V* 🍴 *CP.*

$$$$$ Fodor's Choice ★ **La Posada Carlos Pulenta.** One large room on the second floor of this Tuscan terra-cotta building faces east, where the sun rises over the vineyards; the other faces west where it sets behind the Andes. Inside, cream-colored tile floors, dark wicker furniture, and taupe-and-café-au-lait-covered furnishings complement the refined architecture. The restaurant, La Bourgogne, offers long, leisurely lunches—each course paired with the proper wine. At night, when the restaurant is closed, a helpful staff will recommend nearby restaurants and arrange transportation; they can also deliver a light snack and wine to your room. **Pros:** good views; lunch, wine tour, and airport pickup included in rate. **Cons:** few rooms; no pool; lonely at night. ✉ *Roque Sáenz Peña 3531, Vistalba, Luján de Cuyo* ☎ *261/498–9400* 🌐 *www.carlospulentawines.com* ⇨ *2 rooms* 👍 *In-room: Wi-Fi. In-hotel: restaurant, bar, conference room for private parties* ▭ *AE, MC, V* 🍴 *MAP.*

NIGHTLIFE

Avenida Arístedes Villanueva wakes up at around 11 PM, when the bars, boutiques, wineshops, and cafés open their doors. As the evening progresses crowds get bigger, and the music—rock, tango, salsa—gets louder. The action peaks after midnight. Inexpensive, casual **El Bar del José** (✉ *Arístedes Villanueva 740, Mendoza* ☎ *No phone*) was the first gathering place in the trendy Villanueva neighborhood.

Por Acá (✉ *Arístedes Villanueva 557, Mendoza*) attracts a cosmopolitan crowd of locals and Europeans. Live rock music begins after 10 PM. The **Regency Casino** (✉ *25 de Mayo and Sarmiento, Mendoza* ☎ *261/441–2844*) at the Park Hyatt Mendoza has blackjack, stud poker, roulette tables, slot machines, and an exclusive bar.

SHOPPING

Pick up leather goods, shoes, and clothing along the pedestrian part of Sarmiento and its cross streets, or on Avenida La Heras, where you'll find regional products to eat, drink, wear, or decorate your house with. On weekends Plaza Independencia becomes a market, with stands selling jewelry, handmade sweaters, ponchos, maté gourds, olive oil, and other regional wares.

CLOTHES AND ACCESSORIES

Talabarterías sell fine leather goods and everything equestrian, from saddles and handmade tack to hats, vests, and other gaucho-inspired items. Mendocinos shop at **La Matera** (✉ *Villanueva 314, Mendoza* ☎ *261/425–3332*) for boots, vests, belts, scarves, and riding gear. On the peatonal, **Cardón** (✉ *Sarmiento 224, Mendoza*) carries gaucho clothing and accessories: *bombachas* (baggy, pleated pants), leather jackets and vests, boots, belts, scarves, ponchos, and knives.

FOOD AND WINE

There's a huge selection of wine and olive oil at **La Casa del Vino** (✉ *Aristedes Villanueva 160, Mendoza* ☎ *261/425–0659*). **Pura Cepa** (✉ *Peatonal Sarmiento 664, Mendoza*) conducts in-store wine tastings. Before your picnic, grab a bottle of Malbec at **Juan Cedrón** (✉ *Peatonal Sarmiento 278, Mendoza*). **Azafrán** (✉ *Sarmiento 765, Mendoza* ☎ *261/429–4200*) is a wine bar, café, wineshop, and delicatessen with regional olive oil, jams, meats, and cheeses.

In a beautiful old country house, **Historias & Sabores** (*Histories and Flavors* ✉ *Carril Gómez 3064, Coquimbito-Maipú* ☎ *261/155–744–614 reservations* ⏲ *Mon.–Sat. 11–6*) conducts guided tours and tastings of fruits, olives, chocolates, and liquors. Learn how chocolate-covered cordials are made.

MALLS

For all the things you forgot to pack, the **Mendoza Plaza Shopping Center** (✉ *Lateral Accesso Este 3280, Guaymallén*) has Falbella, an American-style department store (actually Chilean owned), plus shoe stores, cafés, and a bookstore (Yenny) with English titles. The indoor amusement park has a roller coaster, carousel, rides, and games. South of Mendoza, **Palmares Shopping Mall** (✉ *Panamericano 2650, Mendoza*) has 10 movie theaters and many shops and restaurants.

MARKET

The 1884 **Mercado Central** (✉ *Av. Heras and Patricias Mendocinas, Mendoza*) is the oldest market in Mendoza. Ponchos, Indian weavings, olive oil, fruit, and handicrafts are sold in open stalls daily from 9 to 1:30 and 4:30 to 9.

SPORTS AND THE OUTDOORS

The high peaks of the Andes provide a natural playground of ski slopes in winter, mountains to climb in summer, and miles of trails to hike, bike, or ride on horseback. Rivers roar out of the mountains in spring, inviting rafters and kayakers to test the water. Country roads in and around the vineyards make great bike paths.

Some of the wildest and most remote mountain areas are made accessible by the Ruta Nacional 7, which crosses the Andes right by Parque Provincial Aconcagua (⇨ *below*). Uspallata offers lodging and a base close to the action.

Tour operators in Mendoza City offer a variety of adventures. **Aymara-Turismo** (✉ *9 de Julio 1023, Mendoza* ☎ *261/420–2064* 🌐 *www.aymara.com.ar*) handles guided horseback rides, trekking, mountain climbing, and river rafting on the Mendoza River.

6

Tras Andino Turismo (✉ *Chile 1443, Loc. 04, Mendoza* ☎ *261/425-425-6726* ✉ *R82, Km 38, Cacheuta* ☎ *262/449-0159* 🌐 *www.trasandinoturismo.com.ar*) has operations in Mendoza City and in the mountains. They offer trekking to a base camp at Aconcagua as well as 15-day ascents. They also offer mountain-biking, rock-climbing, rafting, and horseback trips.

HORSEBACK RIDING

Cabalgata (horseback riding) is an enjoyable and natural way to explore the mountains west of Mendoza. You can ride to the foot of Aconcagua or Tupungato, or follow the hoofprints of San Martín on a seven-day trip over the Andes. **Cordon del Plata** (✉ *Av. Las Heras 341, Mendoza* ☎ *261/423-7423* 🌐 *www.cordondelplata.com*) offers horseback rides from a day to a week, combination horseback-riding/trekking/rafting trips, and mountain-biking trips.

MOUNTAIN BIKING

Many of Mendoza's back roads lead through the suburbs and vineyards into the Andean foothills and upward to mountain villages—or all the way to Chile.

Bikes and Wines (✉ *Urquiza 1606, Maipú* ☎ *261/410-6686* 🌐 *www.bikesandwines.com*) rents motorbikes and three kinds of mountain bikes for full- or half-day self-guided tours in the wine district of Maipú. Trips include a map, water bottle, lunch, and medical and mechanical assistance. You begin at La Rural winery and museum and along the way visit three wineries, a chocolate and liquor factory, and an olive oil company. The lunch stop is at a deli, where you can eat on a patio.

WHITE-WATER RAFTING

Mendoza-based adventure-tour companies offer half- to two-day Class II to Class IV rafting and kayaking trips on the Río Mendoza near Potrerillos *(⇨ Parque Provincial Anconcagua, below).*

With **Argentine Rafting** (*Office:* ✉ *Primitivo de la Reta 992, Loc. 4, Mendoza* ☎ *262/429-6325* 🌐 *www.argentinarafting.com*) you can raft the Río Mendoza, take a kayak class, or combine rafting, horseback riding, and mountain biking in a two-day multisport outing, spending the night in a mountain refugio. **Betancourt Rafting** (✉ *Lavalle 36, Galería Independencia, Loc. 8, Mendoza* ☎ *261/429-9665* ✉ *RN7, Km 26, Luján de Cuyo* ☎ *261/15-559-1329* 🌐 *www.betancourt.com.ar*) has three small cabins and a lodge at the Cacheuta Hot Springs.

USPALLATA

125 km (78 mi) west of Mendoza City.

At the crossroads of three important routes—Ruta Nacional 7 from Mendoza across the Andes to Ruta 57 from Mendoza via Villavicencio, and Ruta 39 from San Juan via Barreal—this small mountain town lies in the Calingasta Valley between the foothills and the front range of the Andes. It's a good base for excursions into the mountains by 4x4 or on horseback to abandoned mines, a desert ghost town, and spectacular mountain scenery where the 1997 movie *Seven Years in Tibet* was filmed. Metals have been forged at **Las Bóvedas,** the pointed adobe

Hikers traverse a low portion of the south face of Cerro Aconcagua.

cupolas a few miles north of town, since pre-Columbian times. Arms and cannons for San Martín's army were made here.

GETTING HERE AND AROUND

Head south from Mendoza on Avenida San Martín to the Ruta Nacional 7 and turn west. You can make this 195-km (121-mi) trip from Mendoza by bus (long, with many stops), on a guided tour (advised), or by rental car. You can make it an all-day drive, or break it up with an overnight in Uspallata.

SAFETY

An adventurous way to explore the dramatic landscape around Uspallata is by driving yourself. There are things to keep in mind, though, if you want to have a safe, stress-free time. Always leave town with a full tank of gas, as there are no services available, and traffic is minimal. Carry a flashlight if you leave late in the day, and be aware of weather conditions (not recommended in winter snow storms). Good maps are available at ACA (the automobile club in Mendoza) and at the tourist office.

EXPLORING

Fodor's Choice ★ **Parque Provincial Aconcagua.** This provincial park extends for 66,733 hectares (164,900 acres) over wild, high country with few trails other than those used by expeditions climbing the impressive Cerro Aconcagua (Aconcagua Mountain), the main attraction. For permits to enter the park, stop at Cuba House, near Parque San Martín, before you leave Mendoza City. ✉ *Las Tipas at Av. Robles, Mendoza* 🎫 *Trekking permits US$50–$110, depending on season and permit level; Ascent permits $160–$500* ⏲ *Mon.–Fri. 8–6, Sat., Sun., and holidays 9–1.*

SCENIC DRIVES AND LOOKOUTS

Uspallata Pass on Ruta Nacional 7 (Panamerican Highway). This route heads west on R13 and then RN7 and takes you straight into the mountains. You'll go from vineyards to barren hills until you reach the Potrerillos Valley, then head farther west on R7 into the heart of the Andes. This was a major Inca route, so keep your eyes peeled for Inca *tambos* (resting places). You'll pass ancient thermal springs and the ruins of a spa from the 1920s. This is the only route between Chile and Argentina for miles and miles, so if you're self-driving be ready to share the road with cargo trucks.

WORD OF MOUTH

"[The drive from Mendoza to Aconcagua] is an amazing drive, and if you drive yourself you can stop where and when you what. I reserved the car before we left and per day with all the insurance it was approximately $50 a day. It is approximately 380km r/t, about 4-5 hours each way. Go for the drive, it is awesome. It was the first time I saw purple mountains, yellow mountains, green mountains, and snow-covered mountains together." —sandiej

★ **Camino del Año.** From Mendoza traveling 47 km (29 mi) north on Ruta Provincial 52, passing through Canota, you arrive at Villavicencio, the source of mineral water sold throughout Argentina. The nearby Hostaria Villavicencio serves lunch and dinner.

Farther up the road, the Camino del Año begins its ascent around 365 turns to El Balcón atop the pass at Cruz de Paramillo (3,000 meters/9,840 feet). Look for the ruins of a Jesuit mine, the Arucarias de Darwin (petrified trees found by Darwin in 1835), and the 1,000-year-old petroglyphs on Tunderqueral Hill. From the top of the pass you can see three of the highest mountains outside of Asia, all over 6,000 meters (20,000 feet): Aconcagua to the west, Tupungato to the south, and Mercedario (6,770 meters/22,211 feet) to the north.

At Km 67, the road straightens and descends into Uspallata, where you can continue west on Ruta Nacional 7 to Chile or take the lonely road north on Ruta 39 to Barreal in San Juan Province (108 km/67 mi). The road to Barreal crosses a high desert valley, where the only sign of life is an occasional ranch obscured by a grove of alamo trees.

At Los Tambillos, about 40 km (25 mi) north of Uspallata, the route is intersected by the Inca road that ran from Cusco, Peru, through Bolivia and into northern Argentina. The site is surrounded by a fence that protects traces of the original road and remains of an Inca *tambo* (resting place). A map shows the route of the Incas.

The mountains to the west get higher and more spectacular as you approach Barreal. At the San Juan Province border, the road becomes Ruta 412, and is paved the remaining 50 km (31 mi) to Barreal.

WHERE TO EAT

¢ ARGENTINE ✕ **Lo de Pato.** This casual roadside spot serves cafeteria-style lunches and grilled meat and pasta dinners; get yourself a cold drink from the refrigerator. The souvenir shop sells candy bars, postcards, T-shirts, and other mementos. ✉ *RN7, Uspallata* ☎ *264/420–249* ▭ *AE, MC, V.*

WHERE TO STAY

¢ **Hostería Puente del Inca.** Vintage photos in the dining room reveal this hostel's history as a mountaineering outpost. Climbers still gear up here before attempting Aconcagua, and gather afterward to relate their adventures. Guides and mules can be arranged. **Pros:** the only place to sleep atop the pass; close to hot springs. **Cons:** more a shelter for climbers than an actual hotel; preoccupied staff; no amenities. ✉ *RN7, Km 175, Puente del Inca* ☎ *261/420–2064* *82 beds in doubles and 4- to 6-person dorms* *In-hotel: restaurant* ▭ *MC.*

$$$$ **Hotel Termas Cacheuta.** Hot mineral springs have been bubbling forth at this historic spa next to the Mendoza River since 1885, when visitors arrived by train from Buenos Aires. Today hotel guests and day-trippers begin their day with a steamy sauna in the grotto, followed by a high-powered hot shower, and then a Jacuzzi. Next they get slathered with hot mud, then wait until it dries in the sun (or via heater if nature's taking a day off). After rinsing off in another shower, a variety of indoor and outdoor pools kept at varying temperatures invite long soaks. Lunch is a huge buffet, featuring vegetables grown on-site. Rooms overlook the lawn and warm mineral pool. Rates include three meals, two thermal baths, and a massage. Hiking, river rafting, and mountain biking can be arranged. **Pros:** scenic surroundings; delicious and nutritious food. **Cons:** watch your head in the grotto. ✉ *RP82, Km 38, Luján de Cuyo* ☎ *2624/490–152* 🌐 *www.termascacheuta.com* *16 rooms* *In-hotel: restaurant, pool, spa, Internet access on lobby computers* ▭ *MC, V* *FAP.*

6

$$$$ **Hotel Uspallata.** In spite of the cavernous hallways, minimal decor, barren walls, and dim lighting (legacies of the Perón era, when the government built grand hotels for its employees), this grand old hotel offers comfortable refuge en route to Aconcagua, Chile, or Barreal in the opposite direction. The surrounding scenery, grounds, and gardens invite long walks; the dining room is huge; and the bedrooms have closets large enough to accommodate a month's worth of clothes. **Pros:** large rooms; proximity to outdoor activities including skiing. **Cons:** impersonal decor. ✉ *RN7, Km 1149, Uspallata* ☎ *2624/420–066* 🌐 *www.granhoteluspallata.com.ar* *74 rooms* *In-hotel: restaurant, bar, bowling, pool table, Ping-Pong, Wi-Fi, swimming pool, paddle tennis* ▭ *AE, MC, V* *CP.*

$$ **Hotel Valle Andino.** As you approach Uspallata on Ruta Nacional 7, this brick building with a pitched tile roof and wood trim sits beside the road surrounded by scenic vistas in all directions. Inside, an open, airy living room has places to sit around a woodstove. Outside, a large glass-enclosed swimming pool is surrounded by a lawn big enough for a soccer game. Rooms are modern; some have bunk beds, and all have brick walls and minimalist furniture. **Pros:** family-friendly (kids under 4 stay free; 20% discount for those ages 4–10). **Cons:** facilities are spread out; need a car to visit nearby sights and town. ✉ *RN7, Uspallata* ☎ *2624/420–095; 261/425–8434 in Mendoza* 🌐 *www.hotelvalleandino.com* *26 rooms* *In-hotel: restaurant, bar, pool* ▭ *MC, V* *CP.*

SPORTS AND THE OUTDOORS

HORSEBACK RIDING

El Rincón de los Oscuros (✉ *Av. Los Cóndores s/n, Potrerillos* ☎ *2624/483–030* 🌐 *www.rincondelososcuros.com*) has gentle horses and experienced guides at their ranch outside of Potrerillos. Two-hour or all-day rides take you to panoramic vistas, waterfalls, and high-altitude sites where condors and guanacos are often seen.

HIKING AND MOUNTAINEERING

November through March are the best months for hiking and climbing. You can arrange day hikes with area tour operators. Of the longer treks, the most popular lasts four to seven days and begins at Puente del Inca, at 2,950 meters (9,680 feet), where you spend a night to get acclimated, and then set out for Aconcagua's base camp. On the first day, a steady climb takes you to Confluencia, where most people spend two nights and enjoy a day hike to the south wall and its incredible glacier. The hike continues to the Plaza de Mulas (4,260 meters/13,976 feet) and ends at the base camp for climbers making a final ascent on Cerro Aconcagua.

You can get permits for climbing Aconcagua through your tour operator or on your own in Mendoza at **Centro de Visitantes** (✉ *Av. de Los Robles and Rotondo de Rosedal, Mendoza*), in Parque San Martín near the entrance. The center is open weekdays 8–6 and weekends 9–1.

Fernando Grajales (☎ *261/429–3830; 800/516–6962* 🌐 *www.grajales.net*) is an experienced guide and veteran of many Aconcagua summits. His company leads 18-day excursions to the summit of Aconcagua, weather permitting, December 1–February 12. **Inka Expeditions** (✉ *Av. Juan B. Justo 345, Mendoza* ☎ *261/425–0871* 🌐 *www.inka.com.ar*) has 10 years of experience leading tours to base camp at Aconcagua.

Termas Cacheuta. Spend a day with your kids at this hot (65–102 degrees F) thermal water park, within walking distance of its namesake hotel. Slide into the wave pool, swim along the 270-meter canal through a tunnel and under a waterfall, or just loll about in the myriad indoor and outdoor pools. Even toddlers will enjoy the shallow pools with small slides. Picnic tables and covered eating areas are located along the river. You can grill your own *bife* in the many parillas provided or visit the restaurant. This park accommodates over 1,000 visitors on holidays. ✉ *RP82, Km 38, Cacheuta* ☎ *2624/490–139, 261/429–9133* 🌐 *www.termascacheuta.com* 🎫 *25 pesos* ⏲ *Daily 10–6:30.*

SKIING

Skiers bound for Mendoza's resorts arrive from early July through September at the airports of Mendoza or San Rafael (the latter for Las Leñas only ⇨ *below*). Los Penitentes is a medium-size ski area that attracts mostly Argentines, particularly Mendocinos who can drive up for a day. Vallecitos, the province's oldest ski center, is where most Mendocinos made their first turns.

Los Penitentes. Popular as a day destination for Argentine skiers, this uncrowded ski area, 153 km (95 mi) northwest of Mendoza on Ruta Nacional 7, is named for the rock formations that resemble penitent monks. Despite the elevation of 2,580 meters (8,465 feet) at the base and 3,194 meters (10,479 feet) at the top, the snow here is often thin. When it does snow, the danger of avalanches is severe. The base village has hotels, restaurants, bars, discos, medical services, a ski school, and guides.

Facilities: 700-meter (2,300-foot) vertical drop; 300 hectares (741 acres); 20% beginner, 30% intermediate, 50% advanced; two double chairs, one T-bar, five surface lifts. Cross-country ski trails, extreme and off-piste snocat skiing, sledding, and *pato* (snow polo).

Lessons and Programs: Ski school, mountain gui\des, and a children's school and day care.

Lift Tickets: Adults 95 pesos a day.

Rentals: Rental shops at the base area.

Contact information: ☎ *261/429–9953* ⏲ *DailyMid-June to late August*

Vallecitos. Situated at 2,900 meters (9,514 feet) in a glacial valley of the Cordón de Plata range, 80 km (50 mi) from Mendoza and 26 km (16 mi) from Potrerillos, this small ski area owned and operated by Ski Club Mendoza has great off-piste skiing.

Facilities: 400-meter (1,312-foot) vertical drop; 100 hectares (247 acres) of skiable terrain plus unlimited out-of-bounds skiing; 20% beginner, 60% intermediate, 30% advanced; three double chairs, one single chair, three surface lifts.

Lift Tickets: 41 pesos per day.

Rentals: Equipment rental and sales at base lodge.

Contact Information: ✉ *Av. Acceso Este 650, Luján del Cuyo* ☎ *261/312–799* ⏲ *Daily July 1–Sept. 30.*

VALLE DE UCO

The Valle de Uco extends southwest of Mendoza along the foothills of the Cordón de Plata and the Andes, whose two highest peaks, Tupungato Volcano and El Plata, rise over 580 meters (19,000 feet) on the western horizon. The Ríos Tunuyán in the north and Las Tunas in the south bring mineral-rich melted snow from the glaciers to the potato fields, apple and cherry orchards, olive groves, and vineyards planted across this immense valley. Old family ranches that once extended all the way to Chile are being sold off or converted to vineyards in what is now the country's fastest-growing wine area.

It's also one of the world's highest wine-growing regions, with approximately 81,000 hectares (200,000 acres) planted at altitudes between 900 and 1,200 meters (3,000–3,900 feet). Cool nights and warm days cause an average temperature range of 14 degrees, allowing grapes to ripen slowly while developing excellent fruit flavor, good acidity in white wines, and the formation of strong tannins in reds.

Wineries vary from traditional family-run operations to ultramodern facilities, and many names long associated with Argentina's wine industry are building innovative ventures here. Wineries tend to be scattered about in infrequently traveled areas, making reservations highly

Continued on page 350

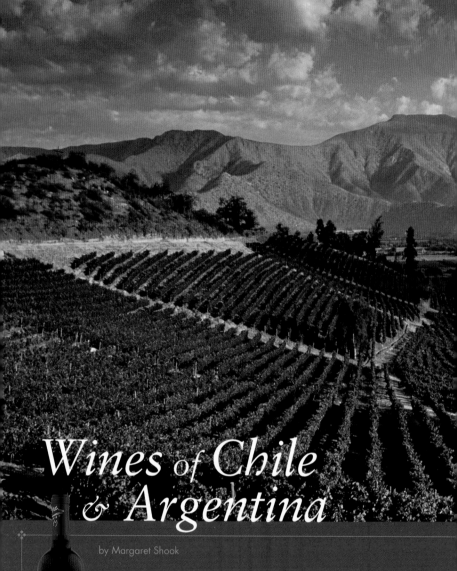

Wines of Chile & Argentina

by Margaret Shook

The wine regions of both Chile and Argentina are set against the backdrop of the Andes. And while these mountains do play an important role in the making of wine in both countries, Chile and Argentina have very different traditions and strengths.

Although wine-loving Spaniards settled both countries in the 16th century, only Chile's wine industry developed quickly, largely because the land around Santiago was particularly good for growing grapes. Buenos Aires, on the warm and humid Atlantic coast, however, was hardly an ideal place for viticulture. Mendoza, Argentina's present-day wine wonderland, was impossibly far away to be a reliable supplier of wine to the capital until the railroad united it with the coast in the mid-19th century.

Chile also experienced a boom in the 19th century as new, French-inspired wineries sprang up. Both countries continued without significant change for more than 100 years, until the 1990s international wine boom sparked new interest in South American wines. Big investments from France, Spain, Italy, the United States, and elsewhere—plus some extraordinary winemakers—have made this an exciting place for oenophiles to visit.

(left) Bottle of Maradona red wine; (above) Errazuriz Winery, Chile

NEIGHBORS ACROSS THE ANDES

CHILE

In the early days, the emphasis was on growing cheap wine to consume domestically. Then, in the middle of the 20th century, Chile's political turmoil caused the business to stagnate. It wasn't until the 1980s that wine exports became a major business, and today Chile exports more than it imports.

Chile's appellation system names its valleys from north to south, but today's winegrowers stress that the climatic and geological differences between east and west are more significant. The easternmost valleys closest to the Andes tend to have less fog, more hours of sunlight, and greater daily temperature variations, which help red grapes develop deep color and rich tannins while maintaining bright acidity and fresh fruit characteristics. On the other hand, if you're after crisp whites and bright Pinots, head to the coast, where cool fog creeps inland from the sea each morning and Pacific breezes keep the vines cool all day.

Interior areas in the Central Valley are less prone to extremes and favor varieties that require more balanced conditions, such as Merlot, and Chile's own rich and spicy Carmenère. Syrah, a relatively new grape in Chile, does well in both cold and warm climates.

BE SURE TO TASTE:

Sauvignon Blanc: Cool-climate vineyards from Elqui to Bío Bío are producing very exciting Sauvignon with fresh green fruit, crisp acidity, and often an enticing mineral edge.

Carmenère: Chile's signature grape arrived in Chile during the mid-19th century from France, where it was usually a blending grape in Bordeaux. Over time Chileans forgot about it, mistaking it for Merlot, but during the Chilean boom times of the 1990s they realized that they had a very unique grape hidden amongst the other vines in their vineyards.

Cabernet Sauvignon: The king of reds grows well almost anywhere it's planted, but Cabernets from the Alto Maipo are particularly well balanced, displaying elegance and structure.

Syrah: Chile produces two distinct styles of this grape. Be sure to try both: luscious and juicy from Colchagua or enticingly spicy from coastal areas, such as Elqui or San Antonio.

Malbec: True, this is Argentina's grape, but Chile produces award-winning bottlings that have appealing elegance and balance.

Vina Cousino Macul, Santiago, Chile

Miguel Torres, Chile

Winery tour, Chile

Bodega Tres Erres, Chile

ARGENTINA

Unlike Chile, Argentina exports far less wine than it consumes, and much of its wine is produced in accordance with local tastes and wallets. The 1990s wine boom sparked a greater emphasis on export, and following new investments, the country is now widely recognized for the quality of its red wines, particularly its signature Malbec.

Broad-shouldered Argentina looks west to the Andes for a life-giving force. Its wine regions receive no cooling maritime influence, as Chile's do, and its vineyards rely on the mountain altitudes not only to irrigate its lands, but also to attenuate the effects of the blazing sun. The climate here is capricious, so producers must be ever-prepared for untimely downpours, devastating hailstorms, and scorching, dehydrating Zonda winds.

BE SURE TO TASTE:

Malbec: Just one sip of Argentina's most widely known wine evokes gauchos and tangos. Deep, dark, and handsomely concentrated, this is a must-try on its home turf.

Cabernet Sauvignon: Argentine Cabs are big, bold, and brawny, as is typical of warmer climates. They're perfect with one of those legendary Argentine grilled steaks.

Red Blends: The red blends here may be mixtures of classic Bordeaux varietals with decidedly Argentine results, or audacious combinations that are only possible in the New World.

Torrontés: Argentina's favorite white has floral overtones, grown most often in Cafayate, in the northwestern province of Salta.

Monteviejo Winery, Clos de los Siete, Mendoza

Estancia San Pablo Tupungato

Colome Winery, Molinos, Salta

TASTING TIPS ON BOTH SIDES OF THE BORDER

1. The number one wine travel rule in Chile and Argentina? Make reservations! Unlike wineries in the U.S., most wineries are not equipped to receive drop-in visitors.

2. Don't expect wineries to be open on Sunday. Winery workers need a day off too.

3. The distances between wineries can be much longer than they look on the map. Be sure to allot plenty of travel time, and plan on no more than three or four wineries per day.

4. Do contact the wine route offices in the region you're visiting. They can be extremely helpful in coordinating visits to wineries and other local attractions.

5. Hire a driver, or choose a designated driver. That's sage advice in any wine region.

6 IN FOCUS WINES OF CHILE & ARGENTINA

GREAT WINE ITINERARIES

SEE CHAPTER FOR WINERY CONTACT INFORMATION

Chile's wine industry was affected by the 8.8-magnitude earthquake that hit the country on February 27, 2010. Early estimates put the total loss at 125 million liters (14 million cases); equal to roughly 12% of the nation's wine output for 2009. Although older adobe structures didn't fair well, most cellars and bottling lines in modern, more quake-resistant buildings were able to be repaired.

Vineyards reported little damage to the vines themselves; the grape harvest began on schedule, though damaged roads initially slowed transport. Wine regions most affected were Cachapoal, Colchagua, Curicó and Maule; Maipo (closest to Santiago) faired comparatively well, and areas farther north sustained little to no damage. Call ahead; at this writing, details had not yet been released for which facilities would be temporarily unavailable to the public.

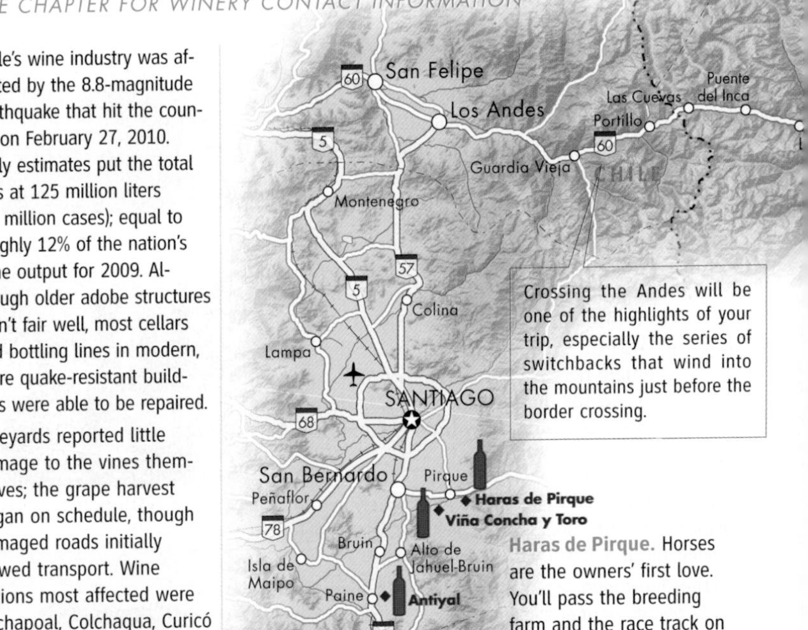

Crossing the Andes will be one of the highlights of your trip, especially the series of switchbacks that wind into the mountains just before the border crossing.

ALTO MAIPO ITINERARY

Plenty of wineries are a day trip from Santiago. You can go solo and hire a taxi ($70 for a half day), but for around US$160 (full day) a guide provides better access.

Concha y Toro. Start the day at one of Chile's oldest and best known wineries, located just outside of the capital in Pirque.

Antiyal. One of Chile's first boutique-garage wineries, Antiyal only makes two red blends, both of which are organic and biodynamic.

Haras de Pirque. Horses are the owners' first love. You'll pass the breeding farm and the race track on the way to this horseshoe-shaped winery tucked up into the Andean hills.

COLCHAGUA ITINERARY

If it's Saturday, book a ride on the Wine Train, which travels from San Fernando to the heart of the Colchagua Valley in Santa Cruz.

Viña Bisquertt. This family-run winery houses several 15-foot-tall wooden casks from the 1940s.

Clos Apalta. Viña Casa Lapostolle built this gravity-flow wonder exclusively for their red blend, Clos Apalta.

Viña Santa Cruz. More than just a winery, this is an entire wine complex. Take the a cable car to the "indigenous village."

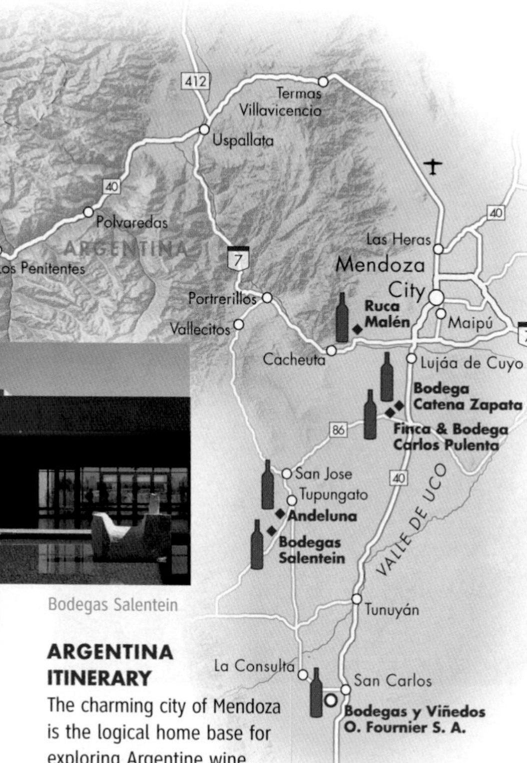

Bodegas Salentein

ARGENTINA ITINERARY

The charming city of Mendoza is the logical home base for exploring Argentine wine country, and the country's finest wineries surround the city.

Ruca Malén. This smallish winery is less than 10 years old and offers a friendly, personalized tour with tastings of its Malbec, Cabernet, and Chardonnay wines. The restaurant is a good place to stop for lunch.

Bodegas Vistalba de Carlos Pulenta. Owned by one of Argentina's most renowned winemakers, Carlos Pulenta, this elegantly modern winery has glass walls that expose the vineyard's soil profiles.

Bodega Catena Zapata. Rising like a Mayan temple from the fertile soil, this winery produces some of Argentina's most memorable blended wines.

Familia Zuccardi, Mendoza

Harvest time at Andeluna

WINERY-ARCHITECTURE ITINERARY

Fans of spectacular architecture will enjoy visiting Argentina's wineries. Big, modern, sometimes whimsical, and often surprising, many of these enormous high-tech facilities have restaurants and even lodgings to make the long distances between them bearable. Plan for a long day in the beautiful Valle de Uco visiting some striking examples.

Bodegas Salentein. A perfect example of the "winery-plus" experience in South American wine tourism, this property is a work of art set against a natural backdrop of the Andes, complete with cultural center, restaurant, chapel, and award-winning wines.

Andeluna. The Rutini family has long made wine in Argentina, and its newest endeavor is at the relatively high altitude of 1,300 meters (4,265 feet). Check out the house wines at the wine bar or one of the other tasting centers, or chat in the kitchen as the chef prepares your meal.

Bodegas y Viñedo O. Fournier S.A. End your day at this highly unusual building that looks, from a distance, like a city of Oz for the new millennium. An enormous, flat roof seems to hover over the building, and the large U-shaped ramp accommodates gravity-flow winemaking.

CROSSING THE ANDES

Mendoza, Argentina; Andean foothills, wine harvest.

■ If you're coming all the way to South America to taste wine, be sure to visit both sides of the Andes. There are frequent hour-long jet flights between Santiago and Mendoza for US$200–$300 that provide a spectacular condor's-eye view of the craggily snow-covered peaks below.

■ If you are visiting in the summer months and have time for the day-long 250 km (155 mi) overland route, by all means take it. Know that you will most likely have to get a roundtrip car rental. Most companies will not allow one-way international crossings. Better to rent a car in Santiago or Buenos Aires to see the wineries in each country, then fly or catch a bus to cross the border. On the Argentina side, a flight from Buenos Aires to Mendoza can save time.

■ Roads are well-maintained and reasonably marked. Take Ruta 57 north from Santiago to the small city of Los Andes, then head east on Ruta 60 toward the mountains and the Argentine border, where the highway's name changes to Ruta 7, to Mendoza.

■ Crossing the Andes will be one of the highlights of your trip, especially the series of switchbacks that wind into the mountains just before the border crossing some 8,200 feet above sea level. Be aware that the Libertadores Pass is often closed for days at a time during the winter months, so don't risk it unless you're willing to spend several days sleeping in your car while you wait for things to clear up. Be sure to bring a jacket any time of year, as it can be very chilly at that altitude.

■ Plan a couple of stops along the way; make the Portillo Ski Resort your last stop on the Chilean side, where you can visit the Laguna del Inca at nearly 10,000 feet. The ski resort is a great place to stop for lunch. On the Argentine side, stop for gas and a bite to eat in Upsallata, about 100 km (65 miles) before reaching Mendoza.

WINE TASTING PRIMER

Ordering and tasting wine—whether at a winery, bar, or restaurant—is easy once you master a few simple steps.

LOOK AND NOTE

Hold your glass by the stem and look at the wine in the glass. Note its color, depth, and clarity.

For whites, is it greenish, yellow, or gold? For reds, is it purplish, ruby, or garnet? Is the wine's color pale or deep? Is the liquid clear or cloudy?

SWIRL AND SNIFF

Swirl the wine gently in the glass to intensify the scents, then sniff over the rim of the glass. What do you smell? Try to identify aromas like:

- **Fruits**—citrus, peaches, berries, figs, melon
- **Flowers**—orange blossoms, honey, perfume
- **Spices**—baking spices, pungent, herbal notes
- **Vegetables**—fresh or cooked, herbal notes
- **Minerals**—earth, steely notes, wet stones
- **Dairy**—butter, cream, cheese, yogurt
- **Oak**—toast, vanilla, coconut, tobacco
- **Animal**—leathery, meaty notes

Are there any unpleasant notes, like mildew or wet dog that might indicate that the wine is "off?"

SIP AND SAVOR

Prime your palate with a sip, swishing the wine in your mouth. Then spit in a bucket or swallow.

Take another sip and think about the wine's attributes. Sweetness is detected on the tip of the tongue, acidity on the sides of the tongue, and tannins (a mouth-drying sensation) on the gums. Consider the body—does the wine feel light in the mouth, or is there a rich sensation? Are the flavors consistent with the aromas? If you like the wine, try to pinpoint what you like about it, and vice versa if you don't like it.

Take time to savor the wine as you're sipping it—the tasting experience may seem a bit scientific, but the end goal is your enjoyment.

WINERY CHART

Winery	Reservations	Restaurant	Hotel	Cabernet Franc	Cabernet Sauvignon	Gamay	Italian Varietals	Malbec	Merlot	Petit Verdot	Pinot Noir	Syrah	Tannat	Tempranillo
				REDS										
Mendoza														
12 Achával Ferrer	✔			✔	✔			✔	✔					
★ 20 Bodega Catena Zapata	✔	✔			✔			✔						
1 Bodega Escorihuela	✔				✔		✔	✔	✔			✔		
3 Bodega La Rural	✔				✔		✔	✔	✔		✔	✔	✔	
7 Bodega Lagarde				✔	✔			✔	✔	✔	✔	✔		✔
14 Bodega Norton	✔				✔		✔	✔	✔			✔		✔
★ 11 Bodega Vistalba	✔	✔	✔		✔		✔	✔	✔					
5 Bodegas Nieto y Senetiner S.A.	✔				✔			✔						
19 Bodegas Tapíz	✔	✔	✔		✔			✔	✔			✔		
4 Bodegas y Viñedos López	✔				✔		✔	✔			✔	✔		
18 Chandón	✔				✔			✔	✔		✔	✔		
17 Dominio del Plata	✔				✔		✔	✔				✔		
8 El Lagar Carmelo Patti	✔				✔									
★ 2 Familia Zuccardi	✔	✔			✔		✔	✔	✔		✔	✔		✔
10 Finca Flichman					✔			✔				✔		
6 Luigi Bosca	✔				✔			✔	✔		✔	✔		✔
9 Mendel Wines	✔				✔			✔						
16 Ruca Malén	✔				✔			✔						
★ 15 Séptima	✔				✔		✔	✔						✔
13 Terrazas de Los Andes	✔		✔		✔			✔						

★ = Fodor'sChoice

Rose	Chardonnay	Chenin Blanc	Gewurztraminer	Muscat	Pinot Grigio	Riesling	Sauvignon Blanc	Semillion	Tocai Friulano	Torrontes	Viognier	Labels
	WHITES											
												Altamira, Quimera (blends)
	✓											Nicolás Catena Zapata, Catena, Catena Alta, Álamos
	✓						✓	✓			✓	Cavas San Julián, Pinar del Rio, Pont L'Eveque, Carcassonne, Gascón
	✓	✓	✓			✓						San Felipe, Trumpeter, Felipe Rutini
	✓			✓			✓	✓			✓	Henry, Lagarde, Altas Cumbres, Sémillon 1942
	✓						✓	✓		✓		Privada, Reserva, Barrel Select, Espumante Extra Brut
							✓					Corte A, Corte B, Corte C
	✓											Cadus, Don Nicanor, Santa Isabel, Reserva Nieto
	✓						✓					Tapíz, Zolo
	✓	✓					✓	✓				Montchenot, Chateaux Vieux, Rincón Famoso, López, Vasco Viejo, Traful
	✓						✓	✓				Valmont, Latitud 33°, Beltour, Clos du Moulin, Castel, Insignia, O2, Dos Voces
		✓					✓					BenMarco, Susana Balbo, Crios de Susana Balbo
												Carmelo Patti
	✓						✓			✓	✓	Santa Julia, Vida Orgánica, Malamado, Zeta, "Q"
	✓	✓				✓	✓					Dedicado, Caballero de la Cepa, Viña Plata, Paisaje de Tupungato, Paisaje de Barrancas
	✓		✓			✓	✓				✓	Reserva, Alta Gama, La Linda, Finca Los Nobles, Boheme
												Finca Remota, UNUS
	✓											Kinien, Ruca Malén, Yauquén, Terruño
												Séptima
	✓											Terrazas, Afincado, Reserva

WINERY CHART

Winery	Reservations	Restaurant	Hotel	Cabernet Franc	Cabernet Sauvignon	Gamay	Italian Varietals	Malbec	Merlot	Petit Verdot	Pinot Noir	Syrah	Tannat	Tempranillo
				REDS										
Valle de Uco														
❸ Andeluna					✔				✔					
❷ Atamisque	✔	✔						✔	✔		✔			
❹ La Azúl S.A.		✕						✔	✔					
❽ Bodega Aconquija	✔											✔		✔
❶ Bodega Bombal	✔		⌂				✔	✔						
❻ Bodega J&F Lurton	✔				✔		✔	✔				✔		
❿ Bodega y Viñedos O. Fournier S.A.	✔							✔	✔			✔		✔
❺ Bodegas Salentein	✔		⌂		✔			✔	✔		✔	✔		
★ ❼ Clos de Los Siete	✔							✔						
❾ Finca La Celia				✔	✔			✔	✔			✔		
San Rafael														
❻ Algodón Wine Estates	✔		⌂		✔		✔	✔		✔				
❸ Balbi					✔			✔				✔		
❺ Bodega Suter, S.A.					✔			✔	✔		✔			
★ ❶ Bodegas y Viñedos Valentín Bianchi	✔				✔			✔	✔		✔	✔		
★ ❼ Goyenechea	✔				✔			✔	✔			✔		
❹ Jean Rivier	✔				✔			✔						
❷ Jorge Simonassi Lyon	✔				✔		✔	✔	✔			✔		
❽ Lavaque	✔				✔			✔			✔			
San Juan														
❶ Bodegas Santiago Graffigna S.A					✔		✔	✔	✔					
❺ Bodegas y Viñas de Segisa					✔			✔			✔			
❽ Callia	✔				✔		✔	✔						
❾ Casa Montes Bodegas y Viñedos	✔			✔	✔			✔	✔			✔		✔
★ ❸ Cavas de Zonda S.A					✔			✔	✔		✔			
❼ Champañera Miguel Ángel Mas					✔						✔			
❻ Fabril Alto Verde					✔			✔			✔			
❹ Las Marianas					✔				✔		✔		✔	✔
❷ Museo Antigua Bodega de San Juan					✔						✔			

★ = Fodor's Choice

WHITES												
Rosé	Chardonnay	Chenin Blanc	Gewürztraminer	Muscat	Pinot Grigio	Riesling	Sauvignon Blanc	Sémillion	Tocai Friulano	Torrontés	Viognier	Labels
	✔											Andeluna
✔	✔								✔			Catalpa, Atamisque, Picaflor
												Azul, Reserva, Gran Vino
✔	✔											Aconquija, Alberto Furque, Furque
	✔						✔					Estancia Ancón, Bombal
✔	✔				✔					✔	✔	Lurton, Finca Las Higueras
												Acrux, Bcrux, Urban Uco
												Salentein, Primus, Finca El Portillo
	✔											Clos de Los Siete, Lindaflor, Petite Fleur, Festivo, Val de Flor
	✔				✔		✔	✔				Reserva, La Consulta, Furia, Magallanes, Angaro
												Viñas Del Golf
	✔											Calvet, Balbi
	✔	✔										Rojo, Etiqueta Marrón, Fritzwein
	✔	✔				✔	✔		✔	✔	✔	Famiglia Bianchi, Enzo Bianchi, Elsa, Elsa's Vineyard, 1887, Don Valentín Lacrado
✔	✔						✔		✔			Marquez de Nevado, Vasconia, Centenario, Quinta Generación
✔		✔										Jean Rivier, Inti Valley
												Andrea's Cavas, Tempo, Finca Simonassi
		✔										Rincón Privado, Lavaque Roble
		✔			✔		✔				✔	Graffigna, Colón, Santa Silvia, Casa de Cubas, Centenario, Tío Paco
	✔									✔		Premium, Fronda
												Magna, Alta, Signos
✔	✔										✔	Alzamora, Don Baltazár, Ampakama
	✔											Gran Cava
	✔									✔		Miguel Mas, Maria Martín
	✔											Buenas Ondas, Nuestra Escencia, Montgallard
												Fray Justo
	✔						✔	✔				Viñas de Chirino, Ensamblache, Antigua Bodega 1929

recommended. The easiest way to see the area is to take a tour or stay in a local lodge that offers tours. ■ **TIP→ If you're on your own, be sure to get the WINEMAP at local wineries or before you leave Mendoza.**

TUPUNGATO

78 km (48 mi) south of Mendoza.

Tupungato is a sleepy agricultural town most of the year. During the wine harvest (February and March), though, the roads in and around it overflow with carts and tractors loaded with grapes from the 24 area wineries. The population doubles from its official number of 28,420 as pickers arrive. Tupungato Volcano rises above the valley in snowbound splendor.

GETTING HERE AND AROUND

The most direct route from Mendoza to the Valle de Uco is south on Ruta Nacional 40 for 37 km (23 mi) to Ugarteche, where you turn west onto Ruta 86 for another 37 km (23 mi), passing through the village of San José just before arriving in Tupungato. Although buses arrive several times a day from Mendoza, the best way to get around the area is to join a tour or rent a car. If you're driving north, turn off RN40 on to RP88 at Zapata. RP86 runs north; RP89 runs south along the foot of the mountains, and most of the important bodegas are on or near these routes. O. Fournier in San Carlos is the southernmost bodega in the Uco Valley.

WORTH NOTING

If you have some time and aren't put off by driving on a dirt road, a scenic way here is south on Ruta Nacional 40 from Mendoza and west on to Ruta Nacional 7 to the dam at Potrerillos, where you exit and take Ruta Provincial 89 (a dirt road) south through the villages of Las Vegas and El Salto, where clusters of vacation cottages brim with flowers in summer and are covered with snow in winter. The road climbs steeply out of the canyon and over a pass, then crosses a high valley with magnificent view of the Andes. Soon the great expanse of the Valle de Uco lies before you, with its miles of vineyards and orchards of peaches, almonds, and chestnuts, adding wide swaths of pink and white blossoms in spring (late September–October). This drive is equally impressive in reverse.

ESSENTIALS

Bank Banco de La Nación (✉ *Belgano 1397, Tupungato*).

Medical Assistance Hospital General Las Heras (✉ *General Las Heras and M. Fernandez, Tupungato* ☎ *2622/422–325*).

Visitor Info Oficina de Turismo de Tupungato (✉ *Av. Belgrano 348, Tupungato* ☎ *2622/488–007* 🌐 *www.tupungato.mendoza.gov.ar*).

WINERIES

❸ Fodor's Choice ★ **Andeluna.** Surrounded by miles of vineyards, with the majestic Andes as a backdrop, the redbrick bodega blends comfortably into the scenery and the vineyards that climb the foothills of the Andes from 1,097 to 1,300 meters (3,600 to 4,265 feet). Inside, the large reception and

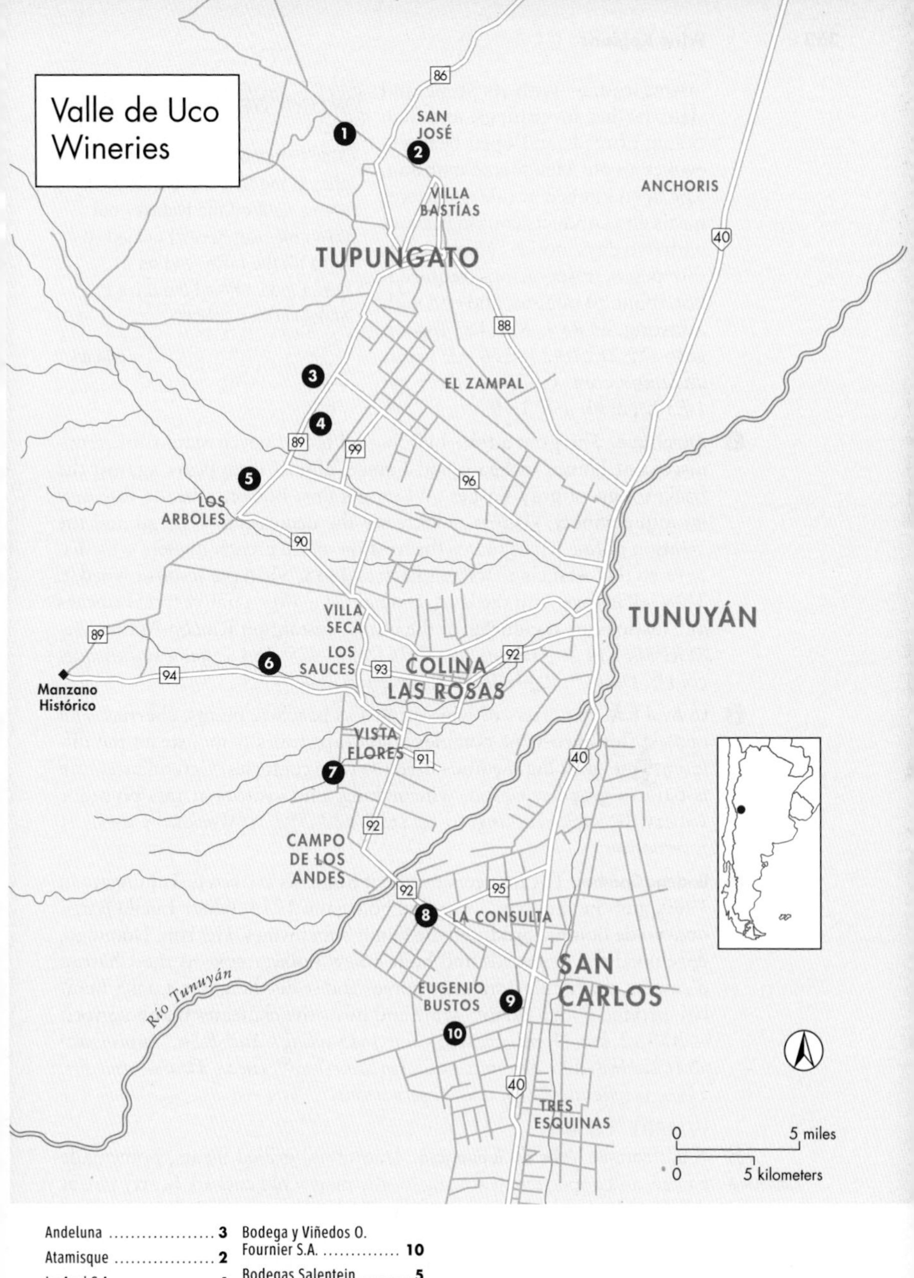

Andeluna **3**
Atamisque **2**
La Azul S.A. **4**
Bodega Aconquija **8**
Bodega Bombal **1**
Bodega J&F Lurton **6**
Bodega y Viñedos O. Fournier S.A. **10**
Bodegas Salentein **5**
Clos de los Siete (Monteviejo) **7**
Finca La Celia **9**

tasting room—with its stone and slate, leather furnishings, and high ceiling of reeds and open beams—evokes an old Mendocino mansion. The open kitchen at one end serves meals and conducts cooking classes with two days' notice. Winery tours (30 pesos, reservations required) last about 90 minutes and end with a tasting. ✉ *R89, Km 11, Tupungato* ☎ *2622/423–226* 🌐 *www.andeluna.com* ⏲ *Tours daily at 10:30, 12:30, and 3:30.*

WORD OF MOUTH

"Don't attempt driving to the wineries in the Uco Valley. Salentien seems right off the highway but O'Fournier was several unmarked turns off the main road on a gravel road. I heard the drive to Andeluna was similar."

—julieod

❷ **Atamisque.** The grey adobe building with its uneven slate roof, reminiscent of houses in Spain and France, almost disappears against the background of gray bushes and mountains. But once inside this new boutique winery, visitors quickly see the dedication to detail and the creation of fine wines that is the mission of the French owners who discovered this estancia that dates back to 1658, when the Jesuits owned it. They fell in love with the land, and named it after a native tree. Lunches and tastings are conducted at the nearby restaurant Rincón Atamisque. ✉ *RP86, Km 30, Tupungato* ☎ *261/156–855–184* 🌐 *www.atamisque.com* ⏲ *Daily 9:30–4:30, by reservation.*

❹ **La Azul S.A.** Exporters of wine as well as peaches, plums, cherries, and apples, this agro-wine complex's vineyard tours demonstrate the different vine-growing methods used over the centuries. Careful attention is paid to grape selection, winemaking, and visitors at this boutique winery. ✉ *R89, Tupungato* ☎ *2622/423–593* ⏲ *Weekdays 9–5, by reservation.*

❶ **Bodega Bombal.** The first generation of Bombals arrived in Tupungato in 1760, and the family built its first bodega in 1914, where Lucila Barrionuevo de Bombal produced the family's first wines. Her son, Domingo, developed the vineyards and built a new bodega next to the Château d'Ancón, the family's summer home. Today his daughter, Lucila Bombal, produces high-quality wine and hosts the château's many visitors. ✉ *R89, 2 km (1 mi) west of San José village and R86, Tupungato* ☎ *2622/488–245* 🌐 *www.estanciancon.com* ⏲ *Tues., Thurs., and Fri. 11–5, weekends 11–6, with reservations.*

WHERE TO EAT

$$ ARGENTINE ✕ **Restaurante Valle de Tupungato.** Traditional grilled meats, homemade pastas, and appetizers featuring locally made cold cuts are hearty fare at this friendly family-style restaurant. On Friday you can help yourself to steak, lamb, chicken, and goat at the open grill. Crowds of locals show up on weekends, overflowing onto the Astroturf lawn. ✉ *Belgrano 542, Tupungato* ☎ *2622/488–421* 💳 *MC, V.*

$$$ ARGENTINE ★ ✕ **Tupungato Divino.** High on a hillside, surrounded by vineyards, with the mighty Cordón del Plata extending across the horizon, this romantic restaurant/lodge awaits the determined traveler looking for peace, natural beauty, and great food. Some of the ingredients for lunch or dinner are

picked from gardens when you arrive. The menu, which changes according to what's ripe and appealing, is hand-written on a blackboard. Fresh-baked bread, a variety of cheeses, and innovative appetizers precede the excellent entreés, and desserts are not to be denied. ✉ *RP89 and Calle Los Europeos s/n* ☎ *2622/15448948* 🌐 *www.tupungatodivino.com.ar* *Reservations essential* ▭ *MC* ⊙ *Closed Tues.*

WHERE TO STAY

$$$$ **Château d'Ancón.** Inside, curved oak doors open onto marble halls filled with antiques, statues, paintings, tapestries, and family photographs. You can taste estate-bottled wine in the English pub and dine in an exquisite room furnished with Bombal family antiques shipped from Europe in 1933. Lucila Bombal, the granddaughter of the original owners, entertains guests with stories of her family's history. This place isn't cheap, but the price includes all meals, tea, cocktails, a wine tasting, a 4x4 vineyard tour, and a horseback ride. **Pros:** stately decor; romantic (no children under 10); lots of personal attention from owner. **Cons:** high price tag, yet doesn't accept credit cards; not good for families (no children under 10). ✉ *R89, 2 km (1 mi) west of the village of San José and R86* ☎ *261/4235–8455 in Mendoza; 2622/488–245 in Tupungato* 🌐 *www.estanciancon.com* *6 rooms* *In-hotel: bar, pool* ▭ *No credit cards* ⊙ *Closed mid-May–mid-Oct.* *FAP.*

6

$ **Don Romulo.** Don Romulo is the president of the local gaucho association. His sons run this hotel and restaurant with warmth and enthusiasm, and organize horseback rides, hikes, 4x4 excursions, and visits to wineries. Rooms are clean and basic, and the food is pure *criollo* (country cooking): empanadas, grilled meat, sausages, and salads. On weekends lamb, goat, and beef are cooked out back on the *asador* (barbecue). **Pros:** great bargain, especially considering the excursions. **Cons:** low-tech; staff speaks little English. ✉ *Almirante Brown 1200, Tupungato* ☎ *2622/489–020* 🌐 *www.donromulo.com.ar* *10 rooms* *In-room: no a/c, no phone. In-hotel: restaurant* ▭ *No credit cards.*

$$$$ **Posada Salentein.** Fifteen kilometers (9 mi) south of Tupungato on Ruta Nacional 89, and close to the ultramodern Bodega Salentein, this inn consists of cottage complexes with large rooms and a kitchen. The original farmhouse has been updated into a modern conference room. The high per-person room rates (950 pesos) include not only meals in the fine on-site restaurant but also a horseback ride, a visit to the Salentein winery, and a visit to the Killka art gallery (which features works by Argentine and Dutch painters). **Pros:** lovely hillside setting; great Andes views. **Cons:** cottages far apart; desultory staff. ✉ *RN89, at Elias Videla, Los Arboles, Tupungato* ☎ *2622/424–722; 261/423–8514 reservations* 🌐 *www.bodegasalentein.com* *8 rooms in 3 cottages* *In-hotel: restaurant, pool* ▭ *AE, MC, V* *FAP.*

$$$$ ★ **Tupungato Divino.** This mountainside retreat in the vineyards at the foot of the Cordón del Plata range is close to some of the best bodegas in the Uco Valley, yet seems to be in a world of its own—largely due to the architecture of owner/architect Sergio Viegas. He and an economist friend from college, Pablo, left their successful practices in Buenos Aires and moved with their families to start new lives as a restaurateur and inn-keeper. The property's two rooms, each with a woodstove, open out

to their own porches, where you can swing in a hammock and watch the grapes grow. **Pros:** serenity, mountain views, super restaurant, attentive owners **Cons:** remote location, only 2 rooms. ✉ *RP89 and Calle Los Europeos s/n* ☎ *2622/1544–8948* 🌐 *www.tupungatodivino.com.ar* ➪ *2 rooms* ♁ *In-room: safe, kitchen, wine. In-hotel: wine bar, restaurant, vegetable garden, swimming pool* ▭ *No credit cards* 🍽 *CP.*

SHOPPING

At **KDS Hecho a Mano** (✉ *South of town on RP92, Km 5, Tupungato* ☎ *2622/488–852* 🌐 *kdscuchillos.com.ar*) five members of the da Silva family have been designing and selling handmade knives and leather cases since the 1970s. You can watch the process and choose the right knife for your next asado from many designs in their showroom or on their Web site.

SPORTS AND THE OUTDOORS

Snowcapped Tupungato Volcano (6,800 meters/9,200 feet) looms above the high peaks that march along the border between Chile and Mendoza Province. Tupungato Provincial Park covers 110,000 hectares (272,000 acres) in the wesern portion of the departments of Luján de Cuyo, Tupungato, and Tunuyán. There are no roads into the park, but local tour companies lead horseback rides and hikes into the area. Some offer six-day horseback rides to the Chilean border. Mules can be hired to climb to South Glacier at 2,000 meters (6,562 feet).

Make arrangements for horseback riding, hiking, and fishing through area ranches and hotels. **Estancia Rancho e' Cuero** (☎ *261/496–4042 or 261/155–692–364* 🌐 *ranchoecuero.com.ar*), near Tupungato, offers ranch stays with riding, hiking, fishing, and excursions into the mountains to view condors and guanacos.

TUNUYÁN

81 km (50 mi) south of Mendoza.

Tunuyán is twice the size of Tupungato, and makes a good base for touring the Valle de Uco wineries. Downtown consists of two traffic circles on either side of two blocks, where most of the shops cater to the needs of local agricultural pursuits. Along with grape growing, said pursuits include growing cherries, pears, and apples, and making apple cider.

GETTING HERE AND AROUND

There's bus service here from Mendoza, but you'll have a hard time getting around without a car unless you're on a tour. From Mendoza City you can take RN40 directly to Tunuyán, then use Ruta 88, 89, 90, or 96 to reach Tupungato (your choice will depend on which wineries you want to visit). Consult the WINEMAP before heading out on your own.

Bodega Lurton is on the road to Manzano Histórico, and Clos de los Siete, Monteviejo, and Doña Elvira are south and east of Tunuyán, in the districts of Los Sauces and Vista Flores. Although San Carlos, a dusty agricultural town 25 km (15 mi) south of Tunuyán, isn't yet on the tourist map, it does have several noteworthy wineries near it.

Medical Assistance **Farmacia Galencia** (✉ *San Martín 650* ☎ *2622/422–826*).

Bodegas in Argentina's wine region often have restaurants with dedicated chefs and stellar cuisine. Some prepare food using traditional methods, like this charcoal grill.

Tourist Information Oficina de Turísmo (✉ *San Martín at Dalmau* ☎ *2622/425–810* 🌐 *www.tunuyan.mendoza.gov.ar*).

WINERIES

TUNUYÁN VICINITY

6 **Bodega J&F Lurton.** Jacques and François Lurton began searching for an Argentine vineyard in 1992. Three years later they planted their grapes in Vista Flores, where low yields and a wide temperature range would ensure premium wines with a defined varietal identity. The arched doorways of the wood-and-stucco colonial-style winery lead into three functional areas—one for winemaking, one for storage, and one for sales and tastings. Grapes are harvested by hand and carefully selected by experts—including Marco Toriano, who also leads wine tours and directs tastings. Horseback rides in the vineyards are an added attraction. ✉ *Camino al Manzano, RP94, Km 21, Tunuyán* ☎ *261/441–1100 for tastings and lunch* 🌐 *www.JFLurton.com* 🕒 *Weekdays 10–5 with reservations.*

5 **Bodegas Salentein.** On a knoll with an Andean backdrop, this ultramodern winery is built in the shape of a cross. Each of its four arms operates as a separate winery with two divisions: one at ground level housing stainless-steel tanks and one belowground where wine matures in oak barrels. These four wineries meet at a circular atrium where visitors are greeted and tastings, sales, and large events are held. Bottling and labeling take place underground. ✉ *R89 at Videla, Tunuyán* ☎ *2622/429–000* 🌐 *www.bodegasalentein.com* 🕒 *Daily 10–4.*

7 ★ **Clos de los Siete: Monteviejo, Flecha de Los Andes, Cuvelier de Los Andes.** Three wineries owned by seven partners, under the expert supervision of

Michel Rolland, share these vineyards equally, each choosing his particular grape variety. The grapes mature at different times because they're planted at different altitudes (this prolongs the harvest over five weeks). These three wineries, notable for their architecture as much as for their wine, all receive visitors, and lunch is included at Flecha de Los Andes. High-end wine tastings are charged by the bottle. ⊠ *Clodomiro Silva s/n, Vistaflores, Tunuyán* ☎ *2622/422–054 Monteviejo; 261/405–5640 Flecha de Los Andes; 261/405–5610 Cuvelier de los Andes* ⊕ *www.monteviejo.com* ✉ *turismo@clos7.com.ar* ⊙ *Weekdays 8–4 with 2 days' reservation.*

SAN CARLOS VICINITY

8 **Bodega Aconquija.** Handmade labels and dedication to quality characterize this boutique winery, where only 80,000 bottles are produced annually. Aconquija means "snow near the moon"—an apt description, given the location of the vineyards. Blessed with sandy soil and wide temperature variation, grapes ripen slowly on the meticulously pruned 30-year-old vines. Their fruity Syrah and Rosé blend is interesting. ⊠ *España 1094, La Consulta* ☎ *2622/470–379* ⊕ *www.aconquija.com* ✉ *bodega-aconquija@ar.net* ⊙ *Weekdays 9–noon, 4–6 with e-mail reservations.*

10 **Bodega y Viñedos O. Fournier S.A.** As you approach this winery on a lonely dirt road it looks like a flying saucer has landed in the middle of a vineyard, and when you take the tour through the bodega you understand that the shape has a purpose: making best use of gravity. Grapes are delivered by truck to rolling vats on the roof, then are hand sorted, then slide down to the first floor, where they are gently crushed, then down to the next floor into fermenting tanks and finally to the basement to age in oak barrels. Using both local and international expertise, the Spanish Ortega Gil-Fournier family aims to produce the highest-quality wines. Grapes are planted in rocky, sandy soil on three estates at an altitude of 1,200 meters (3,940 feet), producing red wines that consistently score in the 90s in *Wine Spectator* magazine. Tours end in the visitor center where there's a small charge for tasting. Blending classes with critique and tasting are available. ⊠ *Los Indios s/n, La Consulta* ☎ *2622/451–579* ⊕ *www.ofournier.com* ⊙ *Daily 9:30–4:30 (by reservation only).*

9 **Finca La Celia.** Eugenio Bustos built this winery in 1890, and it flourished under his daughter Celia's leadership, producing an excellent Malbec. CCU, a Chilean company, now owns the winery and has invested in the latest technology and machinery from France and Italy. ⊠ *Circunvalación Celia Bustos de Quiroga 374, San Carlos* ☎ *2622/451–010* ⊕ *www.fincalacelia.com.ar* ⊙ *Weekdays 9–4 (by reservation only).*

WHERE TO EAT AND STAY

$$$$ SPANISH-ARGENTINE ★

✕ **URBAN at O. Fournier.** Though she won an award for best restaurant in a winery in 2007, chef Nadia de Ortega doesn't rest on her laurels; she's consistently creating innovative entrées that pair gracefully with the six wines served at the wine-tasting lunch. "Wine by the bite" describes this epicurean odyssey—from delicate appetizers to simple yet perfect mains (think pastas, risottos, or grilled steak with imaginative garnish),

Torrontés sherbet with chocolate chips to serious desserts like coffee ice cream or the chocolate mousse volcano erupting with almonds. Big glass windows frame the mountains, and frogs serenade from the pond in the evening. ✉ *Los Indios s/n, La Consulta* ☎ *2622/451–579* 🌐 *www.ofournier.com* ✍ *Reservations essential* ▭ *AE, MC, V.*

> **TRIUMPHAL MARCH**
>
> The **Manzano Histórico**, 40 km (25 mi) west of Tunuyán, is the site of an apple tree under which General San Martín camped during his return from liberating Chile in 1823. Several local outfitters offer horseback rides that follow the hoofprints of San Martín's triumphal march across the Andes.

$$$$ **Valle de Uco Lodge.** If wine touring is all about good wine, good food, beautiful surroundings, and like-minded people, then this cozy lodge has it all. The low mission-style buildings are on a quiet country road and look across vineyards to Andean peaks. Modern rooms have down comforters and soft beige walls. **Pros:** engaged staff can help you arrange activities; lovely country setting. **Cons:** far from any kind of action. ✉ *Calle Tabanera, near Corredor Productivo, Colonia de Las Rosas, Tunuyán* ☎ *261/496–1888* 🌐 *www.postalesdelplata.com* *9 rooms* *In-room: safe. In-hotel: room service, bar, restaurant, pool, laundry service, Wi-Fi* ▭ *AE, MC, V* *CP.*

SPORTS AND THE OUTDOORS

HORSEBACK RIDING

You can ride in the foothills of the Andes for a day or cross the Andes to Chile in a six-day adventure that takes you into a treeless landscape of rocky trails, roaring rivers, tiny green meadows, and lofty peaks. Argentine horses aren't allowed in Chile, so you'll have to either change horses at the border or return.

Estancia El Puesto (✉ *Los Árboles* ☎ *261/439–3533* 🌐 *www.estanciaelpuesto.com.ar*) is a large ranch near Manzano Histórico, where you're pampered with food, wine, river swimming, and day rides. Raul Labat, the owner and veteran of more than 30 crossings to Chile, still finds each trip rewarding. He offers three six-day journeys a year in January and February for 3,200 pesos.

SAN RAFAEL REGION

Numerous dams and acres of irrigated land have created a vigorous agro-industrial oasis in the departments of San Rafael and General Alvear (90 km/56 mi southeast of San Rafael). San Rafael is one of the country's smallest regions to claim a Denominación de Origen (DOC). This is a point of pride for local vintners, and the quality of wine produced in this area speaks for itself.

San Rafael has a nearly perfect climate for growing grapes: low humidity, cold and dry winters, ample temperature variation, just enough rainfall, and plenty of water from the Ríos Diamante and Ateul. But into every vineyard a little rain must fall—and when it comes in the form of hail (*granizo*), it can be devastating, destroying one year's crop and the next year's tiny buds in one short shower. Most vineyards now

San Rafael Wineries

- Algadón **6**
- Balbi **3**
- Bodega Suter, S.A. **5**
- Bodegas y Viñedos Valentín Bianchi **1**
- Goyenechea **7**
- Jean Rivier **4**
- Jorge Simonassi Lyon **2**
- Lavaque **8**

protect their crops with expensive heavy netting that lets the water drip through and shades the grapes, aiding ripening.

SAN RAFAEL

240 km (150 mi) south of Mendoza.

Southern Mendoza would be vast arid plains were it not for the ríos Atuel and Diamante, which flow from the Andes and irrigate the fine alluvial soil that attracted the first inhabitants, who came from Chile in 1594. As they attempted to farm in the Diamante River Valley, Indian raids made it necessary to build a fort in 1805.

After the area was made safe from Indian raids in 1879, immigrants from Italy, Switzerland, and France brought their advanced viticulture skills and new grape varieties to this frontier region. When the railroad arrived in 1903 the fledgling wine industry was connected to Buenos Aires and the rest of the world. Today, with more than 80 wineries and a population of 173,000, San Rafael is the second-largest city in Mendoza Province. Wide avenues lined with leafy sycamores and tall poplars fed by streetside canals give this city a bucolic charm.

GETTING HERE AND AROUND

Take Ruta Nacional 40 south from Mendoza to Pareditas, where you pick up Ruta Nacional 143 to San Rafael. There are three flights a week to San Rafael from Buenos Aires, but since Mendoza has daily flights, many visitors fly there first, then drive or take a bus through the Valle de Uco to San Rafael. Locals drive or take overnight buses to and from Buenos Aires (1,000 km/621 mi), as the bus fare is less than half that of flying. The airport is about 15 minutes west of downtown San Rafael on Ruta 150, and the bus station is a block south of Avenida Yrigoyen at Avellaneda.

San Rafael is flat and laid out on a grid, which makes it easy to tour on foot. At Km 0, Avenida Yrigoyen crosses the downtown area (north–south) and becomes Bartolome Mitre. At this same intersection (east–west), Avenida El Libertador becomes San Martín—the main shopping street. Hotels are scattered about on the edge of residential areas but still close enough to walk or take a short cab ride to downtown or the tourist office. Note that siesta time lasts from lunch until 4:30. Also, beware of the acéquias—canals between sidewalk and streets. At night people riding bicycles with no lights or reflectors on narrow dirt roads can be a hazard.

6

Joker Viajes offers city tours, wine tours, and excursions into the surrounding mountains and lakes. Rafting, horseback riding, and hiking are some of the active sports they arrange nearby or in the vicinity of Las Leñas ski resort.

ESSENTIALS

Air Contact **Aerolíneas Argentinas** (☎ *2627/438–808 in San Rafael; 2627/435–156 at the airport*).

Banks **Banco Galicia** (*Banelco* ✉ *H. Yrigoyen 28*). **Banco de la Nación** (*Link* ✉ *El Libertador 30* ☎ *2627/423–854* ✉ *H. Yrigoyen 113* ☎ *2627/43009*).

Bus Contacts **Andesmar** (☎ *2627/427–720* 🌐 *www.andesmar.com*). **TAC** (☎ *2627/422–209*). **Terminal de Ómnibus** (✉ *Colonel Suarez and Avellaneda*).

Car Rentals **Alamo** (✉ *H. Yrigoyen 1240* ☎ *2627/445–656*). **Hertz** (✉ *25 de Mayo 450* ☎ *261/436–959*).

Internet **Locutorio Moreno I** (✉ *Av. M. Moreno 60* ☎ *2627/43321*). **Locutorio TELEFAX** (✉ *Avellaneda 76* ☎ *2627/433–321*).

Medical Assistance **Farmacia 16 Horas** (✉ *Libertador 206* ☎ *2627/430–214*). **Hospital Schestakow** (✉ *Emilio Civit 150* ☎ *2627/424–290*).

Taxi **Fono-taxi/Remises del Sur** (☎ *2627/420–200 or 2627/430–646*).

Visitor and Tour Info **Joker Viajes** (✉ *San Martín 234* ☎ *2627/436982* 🌐 *www.jokerviajes.com.ar*). **San Rafael Tourist Board** (✉ *Av. H. Yrigoyen 745, at Balloffet* ☎ *2627/424–217* 🌐 *www.sanrafaelturismo.gov.ar*).

WINERIES

Most of the wineries in this region are family-owned; consequently, the owners are busy in the vineyard, working in the bodega, testing wine with the oenologist, or tending to customers. As a courtesy, it's best to make an appointment. Road signs are scarce in the region, although the municipality is working to correct that.

3 **Balbi**. Founded in 1930 by Juan Balbi and now owned by Allied Domecq, this winery has a reputation for making a French Bordeaux-style wine. Changes in winemaking techniques seem to be moving their wine toward a more readily drinkable style, as they blend grapes from the Valle de Uco and San Rafael. ✉ *BA, Jensen & Sarmiento, Las Paredes, San Rafael* ☎ *2627/430–027* ⏲ *By reservation only.*

5 **Bodega Suter, S.A.** In 1900 the Suter family journeyed to Argentina from Switzerland and planted the first Riesling variety in the country. Today the fourth generation of the family continues to produce fine white wines, Malbec, Cabernet Sauvignon, and Spumante. A tour through this spotless winery leads you through a labyrinth of underground caves filled with huge oak casks—used more to evoke atmosphere than to store wine. ✉ *Hipólito Yrigoyen 2850, near the airport, El Toledano, San Rafael* ☎ *2627/421–076* 🌐 *www.bodegasuter.com* ⏲ *Mon.–Sat. 9–6 with reservation.*

1 ★ **Bodegas y Viñedos Valentín Bianchi**. Valentín Bianchi came to Argentina from Italy in 1910, and threw himself into a variety of endeavors until 1928, when he realized his dream of owning a winery and a vineyard. He struggled until 1934, when one of his fine wines won a gold medal in Mendoza and high praise in Buenos Aires. His legacy of hard work continues at this bodega, known as *La Champañera* (the sparkling wine house). Built on a hilltop in the style of a Roman villa, its colonnaded entrance looks out over formal gardens, fountains, and the vineyards. ✉ *R143 at Calle El Salto, Las Paredes, San Rafael* ☎ *2627/435–600* 🌐 *www.vbianchi.com* ⏲ *Daily 9–12:30 and 3–6.*

6 **Algadón**. When Ricardo Jurado, son of famous Argentine golf pro José Jurado, was invited to San Rafael to consult on a golf course, he bought a small Bonarda and Malbec vineyard at the foot of the Sierra Pintada range. Over the years he added Merlot, more Bonarda, and Cabernet Sauvignon, and also created a blend. Formerly known as Viñas de Golf, this 2,050 acre vineyard is owned today by Algodón Wine Estates, a U.S. real estate development company, with plans to sell home sites with vineyards and golf. Visits to the bodega include a special wine tour for two to 14 guests with a three-hour class in creating, tasting, bottling, and labeling your own blend. A tasting seminar (5 hours) takes you from grape to glass. Both tours include lunch. ✉ *RN144, Km 674, Cuadro Benegas, San Rafael* ☎ *627/429–020* ⏲ *Winter: Tues.–Sat. 11, 12, and 4. Summer: Mon.–Sat. 10, 11, 4, 5, and 6* 🌐 *www.algodonwineestates.com.*

7 ★ **Goyenechea**. One of the country's oldest wineries, Goyenechea was founded in 1868 by a Basque immigrant family who had the foresight to build not only a solid brick winery, but also 60 houses for the working families, a school for their children, a repair shop, and a chapel. Today fifth-generation families live in the houses, and the school still rings with the laughter of their children. As you pass through the arched caves where wine ages in bottles, you can see the *piletas,* huge concrete vats that held 8,976 gallons of wine when the industry was focused on

quantity, not quality. English-speaking family members often lead tours, and visitors are sometimes invited for wine tastings and snacks next door on the family's patio. ✉ *Sotero Arizú s/n, Villa Atuel, San Rafael* ☎ *2625/470–005* 🌐 *www.goyenechea.com* 🕒 *Weekdays 8–noon and 3–6, weekends by reservation.*

4 **Jean Rivier.** The Swiss-French brothers who own this winery produce a limited quantity of quality wines from their own grapes. Tours of their spotless winery include crushing, fermentation, and tasting. ✉ *Hipólito Yrigoyen 2385, Rama Caída, San Rafael* ☎ *2672/432–676* 🌐 *www.jeanrivier.com* 🕒 *Weekdays 8–11 and 3–6, Sat. 8–11.*

2 **Jorge Simonassi Lyon.** This old-fashioned bodega warmly guides you through winemaking, from grape to glass. A lovely house on the premises can occasionally be rented. Jorge's knowledge of growing grapes and blending wines was passed down from his Asti ancestors in northern Italy. ✉ *RN143, Km 657, Rama Caída, San Rafael* ☎ *2627/436–076* 🌐 *www.bodegasimonassi.com.ar* 🕒 *Weekdays 9–11 and 3–6.*

8 **Lavaque.** The Italo-French Lavaque family planted their first vineyards in Cafayate, Salta, in 1870. Their sons and grandsons carry on the tradition in San Rafael; their long white stucco and terra-cotta Spanish winery houses an aesthetically designed interior with Spanish tiles and adobe walls. ✉ *R165, Cañada Seca, San Rafael* ☎ *2627/497–044* 🌐 *www.vinasdealtura.com* 🕒 *Weekdays 7:30–4:30 by appointment only. Reservations by e-mail or fax only.*

6

WHERE TO EAT

$$$ ARGENTINE ✕ **Algodon.** This clubhouse/restaurant, nestled between a golf green and tennis courts, is the center of culinary activity in this new and expanding golf resort about 20 minutes' drive from the center of town. Surrounded by olive groves and vineyards, tables are set inside and out on the brick patio, where pine-log tables are surrounded by couches with puffy white cushions. Here you listen to birdsong while sipping wine and dining on such regional dishes as goat from Malargüe (spring and summer) with quinoa. Reservations are a good idea. ✉ *Cuadro Benegas, San Rafael* ☎ *2627/429–020* 💳 *AE, MC, V.*

$$ ARGENTINE ✕ **Bonafide.** Freshly ground coffees served at round wooden bistro tables or on the leather window seats make this Internet café a pleasant spot for lunch or a break. Homemade jams and breads are nice touches. ✉ *San Martín 102, San Rafael* ☎ *2627/437–331* 🕒 *Closed Sun.*

$ ARGENTINE ✕ **El Restauro.** Two tall doors open into this colonial building owned by the Spanish Club since 1910. There's nothing old-fashioned, however, about the menu. New owners are committed to regional cuisine, using fresh ingredients in recipes handed down from local families. *Tomaticán,* for instance, is a blend of fresh tomatoes and spices pureéd over toast with melted cheeses. Roasted goat from nearby Malargüe, trout from the Río Atuel, and quinoa (originally planted by the Incas) are used creatively. ✉ *Comandante Salas at Colonel Day, San Rafael* ☎ *2627/445–482* 💳 *AE, DC, MC, V.*

$ ARGENTINE ✕ **Sr. Café.** The sidewalk tables fill with a young local crowd at this popular spot for coffee, a light lunch, or a late-night snack. Try the *barroluco* sandwich: steak, ham, cheese, and tomato compressed between thin slices of white bread. ✉ *H. Yrigoyen and San Martín, San Rafael* ☎ *No phone* ▭ *No credit cards.*

$$$$ ARGENTINE **L'Obrador-Casa de Campo.** About 20 minutes from town, at a typical ranch house, Daniel Ancina, his wife Graciela, and a team of cooks are waiting to greet you, fill your wineglass, introduce you to the other guests, and seat you family-style at a long table. Little pots of spreads and sauces for dipping or spreading on *pan casero* (homemade bread) line the center of the table. Out of the mud-brick oven comes a platter of crisp baked empanadas and then some type of meat—goat, lamb, beef, chicken, or chorizo. Everything is cooked on the spot. Don't even try to find this place on your own. Call to be picked up or inquire at the tourist office for directions and reservations. ✉ *Camino Bentos 50, San Rafael* ☎ *267/4322–723 or 267/1560–1347* *Reservations essential* ⏲ *Tues., Thurs., Fri., or by appointment* ▭ *No credit cards.*

$$$ ARGENTINE **Malbec.** There's a lot more than just beef on the menu of this small restaurant next to the Hotel San Martín. Crepes with sautéd vegetables and giant *raviolines* (ravioli) are two tasty entrées. There's also a good selection of salads and brochettes. Taupe tablecloths and upholstery pick up the hues in the rock wall that defines the space between restaurant and hotel. Don't confuse this restaurant with the Parilla Malbec. ✉ *Av. San Martín 433* ☎ *2627/445–495* ▭ *No credit cards.*

$$ ARGENTINE **Nina.** At this casual café in an appealing colonial building, the menu is mostly sandwiches, snacks, and *milanesas* (breaded steak). Beware the giant barrolucos—one order is sufficient for two hungry people. Live music picks up the beat each Wednesday at 11 PM. ✉ *Av. San Martín 98* ☎ *No phone* ▭ *No credit cards.*

WHERE TO STAY

$$ **Algodón.** The thick adobe walls of this modern version of a 1920s *casona* (farm house) are decorated with colorful weavings. Red tones rule in carpets, drapes, and bed-coverings—the earth tones of the surrounding mountains. A row of ponchos hangs in the entrance to the living room—to be borrowed on cool evening walks (or drives) to the restaurant for dinner. Guests can gather for a drink, a good book, breakfast, or wine tastings in the living room or on any of the shady porches accessible from each room. **Pros:** golf, tennis, vineyards; olive and fruit trees. **Cons:** walk or drive to breakfast (and other meals), unless you order room service the night before. ✉ *RN144, Km 674–Cuadro Benegas, San Rafael* ☎ *2627/429–020* 🌐 *vinasdegolf.com.ar* ▭ *AE, MC, V* *8 rooms, 2 suites in 2 houses* *In-room: safe, Wi-Fi. In-hotel: restaurant (nearby), golf cart, room service, golf course, tennis courts, pool, Wi-Fi, parking (free)* ▭ *AE, D, MC, V* *CP.*

$$$$ **Finca los Alamos.** When this 150-year-old estancia was established by the great-grandparents of César and Camilo Aldao Bombal in 1830, San Rafael was still a fort. The ranch house is filled with objects from around the world, and many of Argentina's foremost writers (including Jorge Luis Borges) and artists have stayed here; they left their paintings on walls and their poetry in books scattered around the premises. You dine with the owners, and a fireplace glows in every room on cool nights. Prices include all meals, plus tea on the veranda, an open bar, and wine from the family's 100-year-old vineyard. Horses are available

for an extra charge. **Pros:** eclectic furnishings; Old World surroundings; intimate family experience. **Cons:** outside town; hard to find. ✉ *Bombal (R146), 10 km (6 mi) from town* ⌧ *Box 125, San Rafael 5600* ☎ *2627/442–350* ⊕ *www.fincalosalamos.com* *7 rooms* *In-hotel: bar, pool* ▭ *No credit cards* *FAP.*

$ **Hotel San Rafael.** Just off busy Avenida San Martín, this basic hotel has views of the mountains and vineyards from the top floor, where it's quietest. The reception area has plants, native stone floors, and wood trim. A pool and café are new additions on the second floor. Rather pedestrian decor and picture-less walls make rooms a bit dreary, but adequate. **Pros:** close to everything in town. **Cons:** pedestrian decor and pictureless walls make rooms dreary. ✉ *Colonel Day 30, San Rafael* ☎ *2627/430–125* ⊕ *www.hotelsarafael.com.ar* *60 rooms* *In-hotel: restaurant, parking (free)* ▭ *AE, DC, MC, V* *CP.*

$$$$ **Hotel Tower Inn and Suites.** Across the street from the tourist office, this tower hotel has spacious rooms, with big picture windows that let in light and a view of the main street and mountains in the distance. Breakfast, lunch, tea, and wine tastings take place in the restaurant off the lobby, and meals are served outside by the pool, where there's live music in summer. The spa offers olive-oil massages, the hotel arranges wine tours, and the travel agency, Mendoza Viajes, has an office next door. **Pros:** spacious rooms with plenty of places to stow your stuff; helpful staff. **Cons:** on a busy street at the edge of town. ✉ *H. Irigoyen 744, San Rafael* ☎ *2627/427–190* ⊕ *www.towersanrafael.com* *89 rooms, 6 suites* *In-hotel: restaurant, bar, pool, gym, spa, casino, public Wi-Fi* ▭ *AE, DC, MC, V.*

$$ **Microtel Inn & Suites, Malargüe.** A large lobby with casual furniture, a fireplace, and a sitting room lend a homey feel. The restaurant's wine list is longer than the menu, and summer sees barbecues. Modern rooms have yellow walls and large windows. **Pros:** good restaurant; a stay gets you a 50% discount on lift tickets at Las Leñas. **Cons:** long walk to town; pool isn't heated. ✉ *RN40 Norte, Malargüe* ☎ *2627/472–300* ⊕ *www.microyel-malargue.com.ar* *29 rooms, 4 suites* *In-hotel: restaurant, bar, pool* ▭ *AE, MC, V* *CP.*

$$$ **Tierra Mora.** San Rafael's newest apart-hotel is a compact five-story building overlooking a large park. It's about 14 blocks from downtown but within walking distance of an up-and-coming area with restaurants and shops. All rooms have floor-to-ceiling windows and kitchenettes with counters for eating or writing. Breakfast (with excellent *medialunas,* that is, croissants), drinks, and snacks are served in the adjoining café. **Pros:** large rooms; in a nice part of town with park. **Cons:** not a ton of amenities. ✉ *Ameghino 350, San Rafael* ☎ *2627/447–222* ⊕ *www.tierramora.com* *17 apartments, 2 rooms* *In-room: Wi-Fi. In-hotel: restaurant, parking (free)* ▭ *AE, DC, MC, V* *CP.*

SHOPPING

Toca Madera (✉ *San Martín 170, San Rafael* ☎ *2627/1567–4604*) is one of many shops on San Martín selling *artesanías*—pottery, weavings, carved wooden items, shoes, and cotton clothing. Local wines and olive oils are available on the same street.

CLOSE UP

A Recreational Drive

Cañón del Atuel (Atuel Canyon). The best way to dive into this very photogenic, 160-km (99-mi) canyon with its four hydroelectric stations along the Atuel River is to start at the top of the canyon in the village of El Nihuel, 75 km (47 mi) west of San Rafael. Take RP144 from San Rafael in the direction of Malargüe, turning south at el Desvío onto 180. At the dam, Ruta 173 descends into a labyrinth of red, brown, and gray sandstone rock formations. Unfortunately, the river disappears into underground pipes—supplying much-needed energy for the growing population and the vineyards of Mendoza Province. At Valle Grande the water is collected in a large dam, after which the river runs freely between sandstone cliffs, beneath shady willows and poplar trees. Swimming holes, sheltered picnic spots, and rafting adventures offer escape from the city on hot summer days. Small hotels, cottages, campsites, and shops renting rafting and kayaking equipment line the road before it returns across the desert to San Rafael.

LAS LEÑAS

200 km (124 mi) south of San Rafael.

Las Leñas is the largest ski area served by lifts in the Western Hemisphere—bigger than Whistler/Blackcomb in British Columbia, and larger than Vail and Snowbird combined. Although it should be thriving, the area has suffered bankruptcies, absentee owners, and several management teams. You must go through tour operators and travel agents to book into area hotels, all of which require a minimum stay of one week. Accommodations range from dorm-style houses and apart-hotels—some in disrepair—to deluxe hotels with indoor/outdoor pools, nice restaurants, bars, casinos, and a ski concierge. Travel offices in Buenos Aires, Mendoza, and San Rafael sell ski packages with lift tickets, equipment, and, in some cases, transportation—which may involve a combination of bus rides and charter flights.

The ski season runs from June through October. Most South Americans take their vacation in July, the month to avoid if you don't like crowds and high prices, although the weather is more benign. August has the most reliable snow conditions, September the most varied. Prices for lifts and lodging are lowest from mid-June to early July and from mid-September to early October; rates are highest from mid- to late July.

GETTING HERE AND AROUND

It takes 1½ hours to fly from Buenos Aires to San Rafael, then a 3-hour drive to Las Leñas. During high season (July–August) there are 2 charter flights a day from Buenos Aires to Malargüe, a town 80 km (50 mi) from the resort. There are no commercial flights to Malargüe. Some ski packages include the 1½-hour flight from Buenos Aires.

From San Rafael, take RP144 for 141 km (88 mi) to El Sosneado, then pick up RN40 to the turnoff onto RP222 that passes through Los Molles, 20 km (12 mi) from Las Leñas.

DID YOU KNOW?

The first incarnation of Las Leñas ski resort was built in a mere 4 months; construction began January 20, 1983, and by June 16 they were welcoming 400 beds-worth of guests. It's since expanded to over 3000 beds and has become one of the most successful resort complexes in Latin America.

The town of Malargüe is 45 km (28 mi) south of the turnoff at Ruta 144 on RN40, roughly 80 km (50 mi) from Las Leñas. Carry chains and be aware of weather conditions. This is a dramatically beautiful drive with hot springs at Los Molles.

You can sleep the whole 11 hours from Buenos Aires in a "Coche-cama" bus—not a bad option if you want to save your pesos for lift tickets and good accommodations.

ESSENTIALS

Visitor Info Malargüe Tourist Board (✉ *Dirección de Turísmo, R40 Norte–Parque del Ayer* ☎ *2627/471–659* 🌐 *www.malargue.gov.ar*).

SKIING

Las Leñas Ski Resort. From the top (3,429 meters/11,250 feet), a treeless lunar landscape of white peaks extends in every direction. There are steep, scary, 610-meter (2,000-foot) vertical chutes for experts; machine-packed routes for beginners; and plenty of intermediate terrain. A new terrain park for snowboarders has jumps and a half pipe. There's also a free-style slope. Off-piste skiing can be arranged through the ski school.

Facilities: 3,300 hectares (8,154 acres) skiable terrain; 1,230-meter (4,035-foot) vertical drop; 64 km (40 mi) of groomed runs, the longest is 8 km (5 mi); 15% beginner, 40% intermediate, 45% expert; 1 quad, 6 double chairs, 5 surface lifts. There are no detachable quad chairs or high-speed lifts.

Seasonal Rate Information: Low: June 13–26. Medium: July 4–10, August 8–September 4. High: July 11–August 7. Special: June 27–July 3, September 5–closing. Prices below in pesos.

Lessons and Programs: Multilingual ski and snowboard instructors give 2½-hour classes or two-hour private lessons for all levels. Good intermediate skiers to experts can experience untracked slopes with heli-ski and off-piste skiing accompanied by trained guides and avalanche experts.

Three-day 5-hour/Private Adult Lessons: Low, Medium, High: 645/338, Special: 398/238.

One-Day Adult Lift Tickets: Low: 137, Medium: 182, High: 210, Special: 158

Rentals: The following one-day rental packages are for three types of skis or snowboards, boots, and poles. Low: 73–130, Medium: 83–153, High: 94–173, Special: 112–205. To rent just one of these items, you must inquire at the shop. "Fat skis" for deep-powder and off-piste skiing are scarce, so bring your own.

Contact Information: ☎ *11/4819–6000 in Buenos Aires; 2627/471100 in Mendoza* 🌐 *www.laslenas.com* ⏲ *Weekdays 9–6, June–late September, depending on snow.*

WHERE TO STAY

The village at the ski area has six full-service hotels, eight apart-hotels (condominium complexes), and four dorm-style houses with small rooms and kitchenettes. Shuttle buses run between lifts, hotels, restaurants, and shops. Hotels in Malargüe, 70 km (43 mi) from Las Leñas, offer 50% discounts on lift tickets, and the hot-springs resort town of Los Molles, 19 km (12 mi) away, offers less expensive lodging options. Both towns offer bus service to and from the ski area. Day-trippers can lunch slopeside at the central El Brasero (cafeteria by day, grill at night), hotel restaurants, or the Pirámide shopping center. Hotel reservations can be made on their Web site or by phone. ✉ *Mitre 401, 4to piso, Buenos Aires* ☎ *11/ 4819–6000 or 11/4819–6099, Mendoza: 2627/471–1000* 🌐 *www.laslenas.com.*

$$$$ **Aries.** This slope-side luxury hotel has plenty of diversions for stormy days: a space for children's games and activities, a piano bar in the lobby, a wine bar serving cheese and regional smoked meats, and a movie theater. Rooms are spacious, and have large windows overlooking the slopes. **Pros:** proximity to slopes and non-ski alternatives. **Cons:** no direct reservation service and one-week minimum stay. ✉ *Las Leñas Ski Resort* ☎ *11/4819–6099 in Buenos Aires (off-season); 2627/471–1000 in Mendoza (ski season)* 🌐 *www.laslenas.com* *97 rooms, 5 suites* *In-hotel: 2 restaurants, bar, pool, spa, Wi-Fi, children's programs (ages 1–12)* *AE, MC, V* *CP, EP, FAP, MAP.*

$$$$ **Escorpio.** This small, intimate ski lodge is right on the slopes. Watch the action from the terrace while having lunch, or hit the cozy piano bar for après-ski board games with tea or cocktails. A movie lounge for families is nearby. Many rooms have balconies and mountain views. **Pros:** proximity to slopes. **Cons:** can't make reservations directly. ✉ *Las Leñas Ski Resort* ☎ *11/4819–6099 in Buenos Aires (off-season); 2627/471–1000 in Mendoza (ski season)* 🌐 *www.laslenas.com* *47 rooms, 1 suite, 2 apartments* *In-hotel: restaurant, bar* *AE, DC, MC, V* *MAP.*

$$$$ **Piscis.** This deluxe hotel pampers its guests with spa services, ski-equipment delivery, and an indoor-outdoor pool. There are supervised indoor activities for kids as well as ski instruction for all levels. Complimentary wine and hot chocolate are served in the afternoon. **Pros:** lots of services. **Cons:** can't make direct reservations for less than one week. ✉ *Las Leñas Ski Resort* ☎ *11/4819–6099 in Buenos Aires (off-season); 2627/471–1000 in Mendoza (ski season)* 🌐 *www.laslenas.com* *90 rooms* *In-hotel: 2 restaurants, bar, pool, gym, Internet terminal* *AE, DC, MC, V* *MAP.*

6

SAN JUAN REGION

In the Tulum Valley in the foothills of the Andes, the city of San Juan lies in an oasis of orchards and vineyards, surrounded by the Andes to the west and monotonous desert in every other direction. People here work hard in the fields during the day, take long siestas in the afternoon, and head back to the fields until sundown.

Although San Juan wineries have been slow to make the shift from quantity to quality, some 160 wineries have converted (or are converting) from producing bulk wine, and a new generation of oenologists and vintners is taking the lead. The province produces more wine than Napa and Sonoma combined, and you'll likely find the fine Cabernets,

Bonardas, and Syrahs—as well as the whites and sparkling wines—of San Juan on the world's wine lists in short order.

SAN JUAN

167 km (104 mi) northwest of Mendoza.

San Juan was founded in 1562 as part of the Chilean viceroyalty. On January 18, 1817, General José de San Martín gathered his army of 16,000 men in the town's plaza and set out on his historic 21-day march over the Andes to Chile, where he defeated the royalist army at the battles of Chacabuco and Maipú.

San Juan has been producing wine since 1569, though it wasn't until the 1890s, when Graffigna and other major wineries put down roots here, that production increased. At that point wineries began offering varieties other than the sweet white table wines, sherries, and ports that the area had been known for.

A 1944 earthquake destroyed San Juan (but helped to establish Juan Perón as a national figure through his relief efforts, which won him much popularity). A second earthquake in 1977 was as devastating. The low-rise buildings, tree-lined plazas, and pedestrian walkways you see today are the results of reconstruction. The streets and plazas of this easygoing agricultural town are shady, and the city is further cooled by Spanish-built canals that still run beneath the streets.

San Juaninos enjoy sharing their knowledge with visitors. In fact, you're often greeted at bodegas by the owner or a member of the family. In 2004 the tourist office and guide association formed a commission to evaluate wineries for membership in the Ruta del Vino de San Juan. Members guarantee knowledgeable personnel, tasting rooms, public restrooms, and reasonable hours. Eight wineries joined, and their booklet with maps is available at the tourist office.

GETTING HERE AND AROUND

There are daily flights to San Juan from Buenos Aires (1¾ hours), which is 10 hours away by car, slightly longer by bus. The Chacritas Airport is 11 km (7 mi) southeast of town. The 15-minute ride in a taxi or remis costs about 100 pesos. The drive from Mendoza is 1½ hours on Ruta Nacional 40.

It's easy to get around San Juan. There's one main shopping area in a three-block radius around the Plaza 25 de Mayo, from which most hotels are within walking distance or a quick cab ride.

Anna Maria de Montes and her partners at Dante Montes Turismo are experienced local agents with a full-service agency for lodging and transportation. They offer guided tours to bodegas, Valle Fertí (where they own their own cabins), Ischigualasto Park, and beyond. Moneytur conducts local tours of bodegas, including lunch; tours to Ischigualasto, Talampaya, Las Quijades, Jachal, as well as rafting trips on the Río San Juan, and horseback trips in the Calingasta Valley.

ESSENTIALS

Air Contacts Aerolíneas Argentinas (✉ *Av. Libertador San Martín Oeste* ☎ *264/427–4444*).

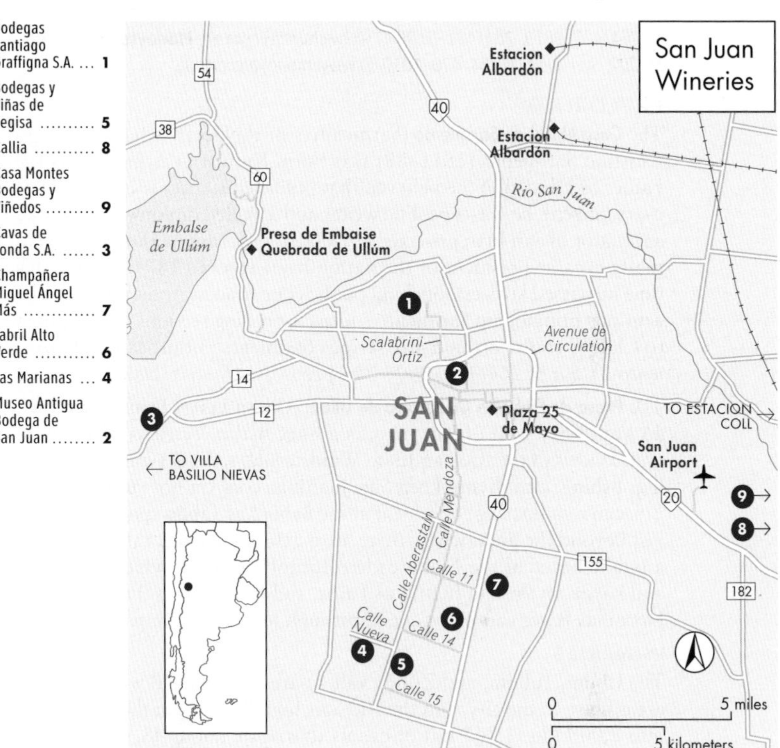

Banks **Banco de Galícia** (✉ *General Acha at Rivadavía* ☎ *264/421–2490*). **Citibank** (✉ *Av. J.I. de la Roza 211 Oeste* ☎ *264/427–6999*). **Lloyd's Bank** (✉ *General Acha 127 Sur* ☎ *264/420–6480*).

Bus Contacts **Autotransportes** (☎ *264/431–1000 San Juan office; 264/422–1105 in terminal* 🌐 *www.atsj.com.ar*). **Chevalier** (☎ *264/422–2871*). **CATA** (☎ *264/421–4125*). **Terminal de Ómnibus** (✉ *Estados Unidos 492, between Santa Fe and España 985*).

Car Rentals **Avis** (✉ *Av. Lib. Gral. San Martín 685 Oeste, San Juan* ☎ *264/422–4622* 🌐 *www.avis.com*). **Hertz** (✉ *Sarmiento 164 (sur), San Juan* ☎ *261/423–0225* 🌐 *www.milletrentacar.com.ar*).

Internet **Casino Cyber Café** (✉ *Rivadavía 12 Este* ☎ *264/420–1397*). **Interredes** (✉ *Laprida 362 Este* ☎ *264/427–5790*). **Telefónica** (✉ *Laprida 180 Oeste*).

Medical Assistance **Farmacia Echague** (✉ *Sarmiento 290* ☎ *264/427–6110*). **Hospital Dr. G. Rawson** (✉ *General Paz at E.E.U.U.* ☎ *264/422–2272*).

Taxis **Argentina Remise** (☎ *264/422–5522 or 264/421–3837*). **Radio Taxi** (✉ *Tucumán 1220* ☎ *264/422–3561 or 264/421–6677*).

Visitor Info **San Juan Secretaria de Turismo** (✉ *Sarmiento 24 Sur* ☎ *264/421–0004* 🌐 *www.sanjuan.gov.ar*). **Dante Montes Turismo** (✉ *Mendoza 360, Loc 11*

☎ *264/422-9019, 264/421-5198* 🌐 *www.chuncay.com.ar*). **Moneytur** (✉ *Santa Fe 202, San Juan* ☎ *264/420-1010* 🌐 *www.moneytur.com.ar*).

EXPLORING

The **Casa Natal de Sarmiento** (Sarmiento's Birthplace) is where Domingo Faustino Sarmiento (1811–88) was born. Known in Argentina as the Father of Education (he believed that public education was the right of every citizen), he was a prolific writer and a skilled diplomat. He served as senator of San Juan province in 1857, as governor in 1862, and eventually became president of the nation from 1869 to 1874. During this time he passed laws establishing public education in Argentina. (Just be cautious bringing up Sarmiento's ideas for ceding sections of Patagonia to Chile if you're around any serious Sarmiento enthusiasts). ✉ *Sarmiento 21 Sur* ☎ *264/421–0004* 💵 *3 pesos, free Sun.* ⏲ *Daily 9–7*

The **Presa de Embalse Quebrada de Ullum** (Ullum Valley Dam Reservoir), 15 km (9 mi) west of San Juan, is a huge hydroelectric complex with grand views of the Río San Juan. Windsurfing, sailing, swimming, rowing, fishing, and diving keep San Juaninos cool on hot summer days. You can rent boating equipment at the Bahía Las Tablas sports complex, just beyond the dam, where there are a café and change cabins. There's a public beach at the Embarcadero turnoff. You can white-water raft and kayak on the San Juan, Los Patos, and Jachal rivers. Fishing in Las Hornillas River can be arranged through local tour companies.

WINERIES

The Ullum, Tullum, and Zonda valleys are the principal wine-growing areas close to the city, and the Río San Juan flows from the mountains into 2,000 km (1,243 mi) of canals to irrigate about 48,500 hectares (120,000 acres) of vineyards. Other growing areas include El Perdenal, southeast near the Mendoza border, and Jachal, to the north.

❶ **Bodegas Santiago Graffigna S.A.** Italian wine expert Don Santiago Graffigna founded this winery in 1870 and planted Tulum Valley's first vines. You can learn the history of his family and their vineyard in the excellent museum on the premises. Today the company is owned by Allied Domecq, and grapes arrive at the winery from vineyards in many valleys. An enormous barrel serves as a sitting area in the tasting room. ✉ *Colón 1342 Norte, Desamparados, San Juan* ☎ *264/421–4227* ⏲ *Mon.–Sat. 9–6, Sun. 10–8.*

❺ **Bodegas y Viñas de Segisa.** The original stucco building constructed in 1906 was destroyed by earthquakes and abandoned. In 1995 the present owners resurrected what they could and built a new, anti-seismic facility, using the traditional high ceiling of bamboo canes held in place by crossed timbers and thick brick walls and floors. ✉ *Aberastain at Calle 15, La Rinconada, Pocito, San Juan* ☎ *264/492–2000* 🌐 *www.saxsegisa.com.ar* ⏲ *Mon.–Sat. 10–8, Sun. 10–2.*

❽ **Callia.** In a hot, dry, wide open valley 35 km (22 mi) from town and with new vineyards planted in every direction, this winery produces some of Argentina's best Syrah. It looks modern, but inside its superstructure is the old bodega (albeit with all new equipment). It's owned by Salentein, a Dutch company that also makes wine in the Valle de Uco.

Callia is open by appointment only on weekedays. ✉ *Calle de los Ríos s/n, Caucete, San Juan* ☎ *264/496–0000* 🌐 *www.bodegascallia.com.*

9 **Casa Montes Bodegas Y Viñedos**. Across the road from Callia, in a white cube surrounded by vineyards, Don Francisco Montes cultivates high quality grapes, and his Ampakama label is widely distributed in Argentina and abroad, including the U.S. Tours are by appointment two days in advance. ✉ *Pozo de los Algarrobos, Calle Colón y Caseros Caucete, San Juan* ☎ *264/423–6632* 🌐 *www.casamontes.com,ar.*

3 ★ **Cavas de Zonda S.A.** This winery isn't on the Caminos del Vino, but it should be; it is a temple. As you enter, Gregorian chant echoes through the whitewashed chambers, creating a sense of drama. Storage, winemaking, bottling, and tasting all take place in a labyrinth of caves, allegedly carved out of the mountain by Yugoslav prisoners in 1932. Outside, a large park is an ideal place to enjoy a picnic lunch with a newly purchased bottle—a good idea, since it's the farthest winery from town. ✉ *RP12, Km 15, Rivadavía, San Juan* ☎ *264/494–5144* 🌐 *www.cavasdezonda.com.ar* ⏲ *Daily 9–1 and 3–7.*

7 **Champañera Miguel Ángel Más**. There's a lot going on at this small, unassuming little winery. There isn't a fancy tour, but workers will stop to show you how they make sparkling wine, turning the bottles slowly on the many racks. Everything is certified organic—from the wine to the champagne to the garlic and tomatoes that grow out back. ✉ *Calle 11 s/n, 300 meters (328 yards) east of RN40, San Juan* ☎ *264/422–5807* ⏲ *Daily 10–5.*

6 **Fabril Alto Verde**. Grapes from this spotless winery are grown organically, and the wine and Spumante are stabilized without preservatives or additives. Internationally certified as organic, the wines are made in small quantities, and a great deal of care and control go into producing the best product. ✉ *RN40, between Calles 13 and 14, San Juan* 🌐 *www.fabril-alatoverde.com.ar* ☎ *264/492–1905* ⏲ *Mon.–Sat. 9–6, Sun. 10–6.*

4 **Las Marianas**. Founded in 1922, this winery is a fusion of tradition and technology. Gold adobe walls, arched doorways, and wine casks filled with flowers give it an Old Spanish air, but inside everything is state-of-the-art. Lots of care goes into irrigation, growing the grapes on *espalderas altos* (espaliers) or *parrales* (trellises), selecting grapes on the vine, hand harvesting, and hand crushing. The owner leads tours. ✉ *Calle Nueva s/n, La Rinconada, Pocito, San Juan* ☎ *264/423–1191* 🌐 *bodegalasmarianas.com.ar* ⏲ *Daily 10–1 and 2–8.*

2 **Antigua Bodega 1929.** At this landmark bodega and museum great concrete wine-storage tubs are exposed in a cavernous old building that survived three earthquakes and now functions as part of the museum. Wine and Spumante are served in the lovely garden or at a wine bar in the front room. ✉ *Salta 782 Norte, Capital, San Juan* ☎ *264/421–6160* 🌐 *www.antiguabodega.com* ⏲ *Mon.–Sat. 11–1 and 6–9.*

WHERE TO EAT

$$$ ECLECTIC ✕ **de Sanchez Libros y Discos.** What fun to find a gourmet restaurant with good books (*libros*) and old CDs (*discos*) lining one wall, larger-than-life photos of Rita Moreno on the other, and beaded chandeliers lighting

Taking a rest at Cerro Aconcagua's Camp Two.

the open booths (each papered in a subtle floral print). The menu's unlikely yet delicious fusions include lots of seafood and fresh vegetables like asparagus, artichoke hearts, and green beans—a welcome relief in this country of carnivores. The vibe is hip and healthy; wine glasses (and pours) are large. You can browse and/or buy the books and CDs. ✉ *Rivadavia 61 Oeste* ☎ *264/420–3670* 🌐 *www.desanchezrestoran.com.ar* 💳 *AE, DC, MC, V* ⏲ *closed Sundays.*

$$ ARGENTINE ✕ **Las Leñas.** This large, popular grill can serve up to 200 people under its high wooden roof and spinning fans. *Civito* (goat) is the specialty (it's best in March and April). Otherwise, enjoy a *bife de chorizo* (New York steak), sausages, and chicken, which arrive at your table sizzling on their own grill. If you don't like the music, ask them to play Argentine folklore. On Sunday afternoon families fill the long tables; live musicians often play Friday night. ✉ *Av. Libertador 1670 Oeste, San Juan* ☎ *264/423–5040* 💳 *AE, DC, MC, V.*

$$$ ARGENTINE ✕ **Remolacha.** Good smells from the outdoor grill lure locals off the streets and into this popular smoke-free restaurant in the center of town. Saffron-yellow tablecloths throughout brighten the low-ceilinged dining room and add a splash of color to the outdoor patio. A variety of typical dishes—grilled goat, beef, chicken, and vegetables, pasta, and crepes—are served for lunch and dinner. ✉ *Av. J.I. de la Roza 199 Oeste, at Sarmiento, San Juan* ☎ *264/422–7070* 💳 *AE, DC, MC, V.*

$$ ARGENTINE ✕ **Restaurante Palito—Club Sirio Libanés.** Tiled walls that look straight out of the Middle East mark the entrance to this popular eatery; in fact, you pass through a small mosque to enter the restaurant. Don't be dismayed by the bright lights and TV showing soccer games; just order a bottle of Malbec, head for the table of appetizers, and fill your plate with crab

brochettes, pickled eggplant, fresh tomatoes, and sliced tongue. Entrées include pastas, chicken, and beef prepared with a Mediterranean touch. ✉ *Entre Ríos 33, San Juan* ☎ *264/422–9884* 🌐 *hostaldepalito.com.ar* 💳 *AE, V* ⏲ *No dinner Sun.*

WHERE TO STAY

$$ **Albertina.** Bright white walls with colorful art, glass partitions, and slick modern furniture have rejuvenated this venerable four-story hotel on the main square in the center of town. Rooms are being updated floor by floor—about 60% are finished at this writing. **Pros:** convenient location. **Cons:** tiny windows; stairway down to entrance is inconvenient, although elevator access from street to second floor is available. ✉ *Mitre 31/41 Este, San Juan* ☎ *264/421–4222* 🌐 *hotelalbertina.com* *35 rooms* *In-hotel: restaurant, bar, Wi-Fi* 💳 *AE, DC, MC, V* *CP.*

$$$$ **Alkazar.** Polished granite floors, chrome, and glass lend this hotel's lobby a businesslike air. There are plenty of gathering places on the main floor, including a lively lobby bar, a street-side café, and a restaurant. Some rooms have views across the city to the mountains. **Pros:** professional staff; good location and business amenities. **Cons:** rooftop pool is small; floral bedroom decor a bit dated. ✉ *Laprida 82 Este, San Juan* ☎ *264/421–4965* 🌐 *www.alkazarhotel.com.ar* *104 rooms, 8 suites* *In-room: safe Wi-Fi. In-hotel: restaurant, bar, pool, conference rooms, parking (free)* 💳 *AE, DC, MC, V* *CP.*

6

$$$$ **Del Bono Park.** Light shines from a skylight four stories above the registration area, lobby, bar, and gathering spaces. A third-floor glass bridge connects rooms by spanning the atrium, and a circular staircase winds around a glass cylinder down into the basement bar, restaurant, and casino. Breakfast is served in a sunny room by the pool. Polished hardwood floors, contemporary art, glass, steel, leather upholstery, and lots of light bring an element of creative luxury to San Juan. **Pros:** San Juan's newest, sleekest ultra-modern hotel. **Cons:** just off the Circunvalación (Ring Road). ✉ *Av. J. I. de La Roza 1946* ☎ *0800/333–5266; 264/426–2300* *101 rooms* *In-room: safe, Wi-Fi. In-hotel: restaurant, bar, café, room service, business center, casino, pool, gym, spa, Wi-Fi, parking (free)* 💳 *AE, D, DC, MC, V* *CP.*

$$ **Deolinda.** The helpful owners of this new apart-hotel, outside of the ring road (Av. De Circunvalación), have created a friendly complex of cabins with outdoor patios, backyard grills, and a swimming pool. The casual outdoor ambience compensates for the lack of nearby shops, offices, or restaurants. **Pros:** friendly helpful owners, spacious grounds with open-air pool, nice for families. **Cons:** 15 minutes by car or taxi to town; no public transportation. ✉ *25 de Mayo and Lateral Oeste* ☎ *264/422–2923* 🌐 *www.ladeolinda.com.ar* *8 apartments (for 2–6), 4 rooms* *In-room: safe, kitchen), refrigerator, Wi-Fi. In-hotel: café, pool, Wi-Fi, parking (free)* 💳 *AE, D, DC, MC, V.*

$$$ **Provincial.** Soft sand colors, dark wood floors and trim, new carpets, and contemporary lighting have transformed this conventional building into a modern, businesss-oriented hotel just steps from shops, restaurants, and the green plaza. Brown and beige carpets and upholstery contrast pleasantly with clean white walls in the simple but adequate

bedrooms. **Pros:** location off main plaza in city center; some city views. **Cons:** institutional dining room/bar. ✉ *Av. Ignacio de la Roza 132 Este, San Juan* ☎ *264/422–7501* 🌐 *www.granhotelprovincial.com* *99 rooms, 2 suites* *In-room: a/c, safe, Wi-Fi. In-hotel: conference rooms, private dining room, restaurant, bar, pool, parking (free)* *AE, D, DC, MC, V.*

$$ **Villa Don Tomás.** If you're tired of downtown streets with traffic, crowds, and noise, and if you have active children who need to get out and play, consider this resort-like hotel on the outskirts of town. The spacious lawn, pool with swim-up bar, and casual restaurant are a safe haven to come home to after a day of touring bodegas or the surrounding countryside. **Pros:** huge lawn; pool; dedicated staff. **Cons:** 15-minute ride in taxi or rental car to town; no nearby shops or restaurants. ✉ *Comandante Cabot 568 Oeste, 5400* ☎ *264/428–3842* 🌐 *www.hotelensanjuan.com.ar* *32 rooms, 11 cottages, 8 apts* *In-room: safe, refrigerator, Internet, Wi-Fi. In-hotel: restaurant, room service, gym, bar, pool, Internet terminal, Wi-Fi, parking (free), no-smoking rooms* *AE, D, DC, MC, V.*

BARREAL

136 km (85 mi) northwest of San Juan.

Beyond the streets of Barreal that hide in the shade of *sauce llorones* (weeping willows) and alamos, lie apple orchards, vineyards, and fields of mint, lavender, and anise. Using this tranquil village as your headquarters, you can mountain bike, horseback ride, hike, climb, or drive a 4x4 east into the Sierra Tontal, where at 3,999 meters (13,120 feet) you can see the highest ranges of the Andes, including Aconcagua (6,957 meters [22,825 feet]) and Mercedario (6,768 meters [22,205 feet]).

GETTING HERE AND AROUND

You can reach Barreal by bus in three hours. By car it's three hours or more. Leave San Juan on Ruta Nacional 40 driving north, then veer west on 436 to Talacasto, which becomes 149 to the Calingasta Valley then continues south to Barreal.

Another option is the long, lonely, but scenic drive from Uspallata (⇨ *Scenic Drives in Parque Provincial Anconcagua under Mendoza Province, above*) on north–south Ruta 414 all the way to Barreal. The best way to explore Barreal, the Calingasta Valley, and the surrounding area is by car, using a 4x4 for forays into the mountains, or by joining a tour and letting them drive.

ESSENTIALS

Medical Assistance **Hospital-Calingasta** (☎ *264/842–1022*).

Visitor Info **Tourist Office** (✉ *Municipalidad, Presidente Roca, Barreal* ☎ *264/844–1066*).

EXPLORING

Twenty-two kilometers (14 mi) south of Barreal on Ruta 412 toward Uspallata, a dirt road turns off into **Reserva Natural El Leoncito** (Little Lion Natural Reserve), a vast, rocky area with little vegetation. You can continue on this road for 17 km (11 mi) to the CASLEO observatory, known for its exceptional stargazing. Overnight visits are available through Territorios Andinos. ✉ *Marioano Moreno s/n* ☎ *264/503–2008* 🌐 *www.territoriosandinos.com.ar*. Near the turnoff, on the western side of Ruta 412 at Pampa Leoncito, the sport of *carrovelismo* (landsailing) is practiced during summer months in wheeled sand cars called wind yachts that can sail up to 150 KPH (93 MPH) across a cracked clay lake bed.

An all-day drive (160 km/100 mi round trip) in a 4x4 to Las Hornillas at 3,300 meters (9,500 feet) takes you along the Río Los Patos into a red rock-walled canyon. The road narrows, clinging to the canyon walls, as it winds around closed curves, eventually opening into a small valley where, in 1817, General San Martín's troops gathered before crossing the Andes over the Los Patos Pass on one of his historic liberation campaigns.

A brief glimpse of Aconcagua looming in solitary splendor about 100 miles south is a preview of coming attractions: six peaks over 6,000 meters (20,000 feet) are visible in the Ramada Range to the northwest: Polaco 6000 meters, Alma Negra 6,180 meters, La Ramada 6,460 meters, and Mercaderio 6,770 meters (fourth highest peak in the Americas). As the road winds ever higher, herds of guanacos graze on the steep slopes, pumas prowl in the bush, and condors soar above.

6

WHERE TO STAY

$$ **El Mercedario.** The young owner (Luís) of this old adobe farmhouse (1928) on the main street is determined to create a gathering place for like-minded lovers of all that Barreal has to offer, as his passion is taking guests in his 4x4 to mountains, rivers, and local sights. Good books and music are noticeable in the living room, and good food (with an assist from his partner studying at the culinary academy in San Juan) is served in the dining room or outside on warm summer days. The cold simplicity of brick or cement floors contrasts with collections of folk art and themed rooms: Argentine and American heroines—from Evita to Mercedes Sosa, gaucho artifacts, historical men, art, and indigenous animals. **Pros:** enthusiastic owner/guide Luís speaks English. **Cons:** messy yard is a work in progress. ✉ *Av. Presidente Roca and Calle Los Enamorados* ☎ *264/155–090–907* 🌐 *www.elmercedario.com.ar* *3 rooms* *In-room: no phone, no TV. In-hotel: parking (free)* *No credit cards* *CP.*

$$$ **La Querencia.** Situated just beyond the south end of town, this Southwest style inn looks west to the Andes and east to the pre-Cordillera, washed in red tones at sunset. Adela and Carlos, the attentive owners, help plan day trips, suggest restaurants, and serve a farm-fresh breakfast (homemade yogurt, bread, jams) in the casual dining room. A fireplace in every room, puffy down comforters, books, records, afternoon tea on the veranda—what could feel more like home? **Pros:** big back yard, Andes view with sunset. **Cons:** need car, bike, or horse. ✉ *Florida s/n* ☎ *264/15–436–4699* 🌐 *www.laquerenciaposada.com* *6 rooms* *In-room: no phone, no TV, parking (free), 2 bicycles* *No credit cards* *CP.*

$$$ Fodor's Choice ★ **Posada San Eduardo.** A yellow adobe house with closed green shutters sits on the shady corner of Calle Los Enamorados (Lover's Lane). Inside, spacious rooms decorated with local weavings and rustic pine furniture open on to a colonial patio. Lunch is served on the lawn by the pool. Ricardo Zunino, former Formula One racer—now endurance horse competitor—inherited this 150-year-old estate from his family and converted it to an intimate country retreat. Winery owners from Mendoza mingle with guests. Lights are low at night to enhance star-gazing. **Pros:** peaceful setting; attentive staff and owners; good base for mountain forays. **Cons:** rooms are dark. ✉ *Av. San Martín at Los Enamorados, Barreal* ☎ *2648/441–046 in Barreal; 264/423–0192 in San Juan* *14 rooms* *In-hotel: restaurant, bar, pool* *no credit cards* *CP.*

SPORTS AND THE OUTDOORS

HIKING AND MOUNTAINEERING Tour offices in San Juan, Barreal, and as far away as Mendoza offer day hikes and rides or weeklong treks and horseback rides in the Parque Nacional El Leoncito or the high mountain ranges of the Cordillera Ansilta, where seven peaks from 5,160 to 6,035 meters (16,929–19,800 feet) challenge hikers and horseback riders. You can ride for four days to the Paso de Los Patos (Ducks Pass), as San Martín did with 3,200 men in 1817 on his way to liberate Chile.

Fortuna Viajes (✉ *Mariano Moreno s/n, Barreal* ☎ *264/844–1004* ⊕ *fortunaviajes.com.ar*) has 20 years of experience in outdoor adventure tourism. They offer horseback trips from one day to nine, including hiking and/or riding to Valle Colorado, where you can climb (or admire from your saddle) six peaks over 6,000 meters (20,000 feet). Hiking, mountaineering, rafting, fishing, sand-surfing, and 4x4 excursions are other offerings.

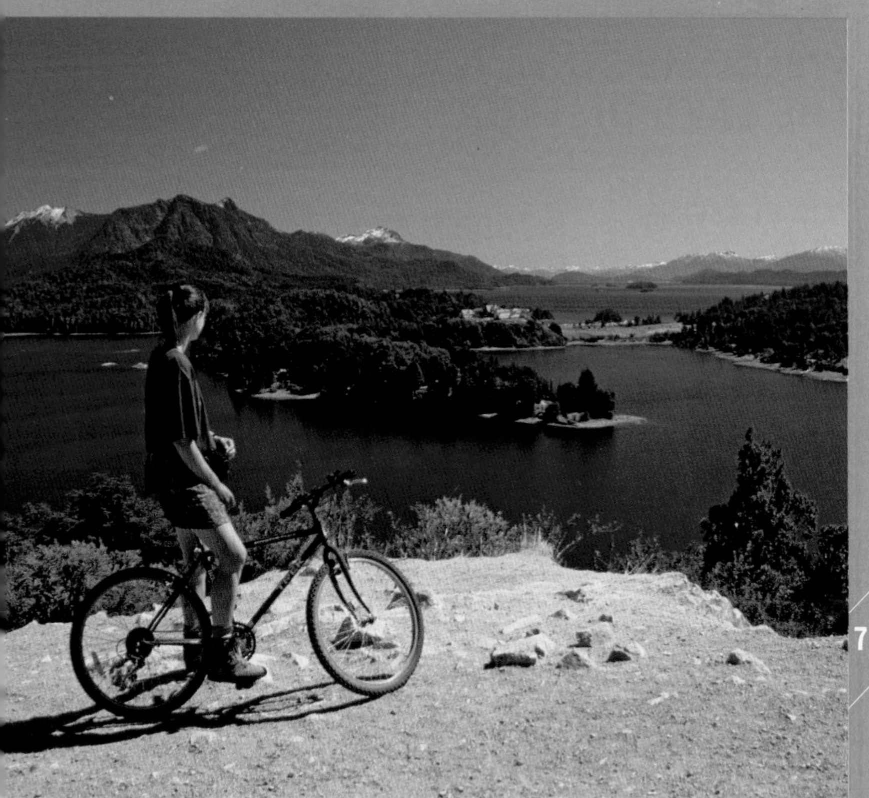

7

The Lake District

WORD OF MOUTH

"Villa la Angostura is an hour north of Bariloche; it's a small town with a cute Alpine-themed shopping district (one street). There's a recommended hike on the Arrayanes Peninsula from the forest back to town (about 7 miles/3 hours..take the boat to the tip and hike back)."

—WayneY

WELCOME TO THE LAKE DISTRICT

Lanín Volcano

TOP REASONS TO GO

★ **Savage Beauty:** One day a lake is silent, a mirror of its surrounding mountains. Another day waves are crashing on its shores, wind tears limbs from trees.

★ **The Great Outdoors:** Well-marked trails in the national parks lead into a world of strange forests, leaping waterfalls, and magnificent vistas. Commercial river rafting or kayaking might carry you to Chile.

★ **Water, Water Everywhere:** 40 different lakes, seven major rivers flowing into two oceans, and you can spend days just staring at Nahuel Huapi Lake with its shoreline disappearing under distant peaks and volcanoes.

★ **Ski in Summer:** In the northern Lake District of Patagonia, June through September is ski season on the slopes of Cerro Catedral near Bariloche, and Cerro Chapelco, near San Martín de los Andes.

Ashy-headed Goose

1 In and Around San Martín. This Andean town is a good base for exploring Parque Nacional Lanín and its nearby rivers and streams. A good variety of accommodations makes this a logical stopover on the Seven Lakes Route.

2 Route of the Seven Lakes. The best part of this 105-km (65-mi) drive is between Villa La Angostura and San Martín de los Andes, where the road winds up and around lake after lake—all of them different in shape, size, and setting.

3 Bariloche. Full of shops, shoppers, and skiers in winter, this unashamedly touristy city on the southeastern shore of Nahuel Huapi Lake welcomes the world with all levels of hostelry, restaurants, and tour offices. The best part of Bariloche is beyond the city limits.

4 Parque Nacional Nahuel Huapi. It's the oldest (founded in 1934), the biggest (272 square mi), and the most popular national park in Patagonia. Buses, boats, and private vehicles transport visitors to its far-flung corners to explore high mountain glaciers, hundreds of lakes, and trails.

5 In and Around El Bolsón. Known to some as a refuge for hippies and ex-urbanites, this amiable little town in a wide valley between two high mountain ranges straddles RN40 just north of Parque Nacional Lago Puelo on the Chilean border. Acres of hops and berry farms thrive in the microclimate along the Río Azul.

house on the shore of Lago Nahuel Huapi

cozy cabin lodging

46
L. Tromen
Volcán Lanín
L. Paimún
Río Aluminé
60
Lago Huechulafquen
Lago de Epuiafquen
Junín de los Andes
Lago Lolog
62
L. Escondido
San Martín de los Andes
Río Collon Cura
48
Lago Lacar
1
108
Cerro Chapelco
L. Falkner
Cerro Negro
L. Hermoso
234
L. Miluquina
CHILE
Parque Nac. Lanín
L. Traful
65
63
40
2
231
Villa la Angostura
L. Nahuel Huapi
Parque Nac. Nahuel Huapi
Route of the Seven Lakes
Ruta de los Siete Lagos
4
23
Pilcaniyeu
Mte. Tronadór
Circuito Chico
3
Cerro Catedral
Bariloche
L. Moreno
L. Gutiérrez
Manso
L. Mascardi
Lago J.H. Roca
RÍO NEGRO
40
40
ANDES
Norquinco
6
Parque Nacional Lago Puelo
5
El Bolsón
El Maitén
Arroyo Fitatamen
4
L. Puelo
Lago Epuyén
Epuyén
15
Lago Menéndez
Cholila
CHUBUT
Lago Rivadavia
40
Parque Nacional Los Alerces
71
L. Futalaufquen
12
Esquel
Trevelín
Embalse Amutui Quimei
259
0
30 mi
0
30 km
40

GETTING ORIENTED

The Lake District lies in the folds of the Andes along the Chilean border in the provinces of Neuquén, Río Negro, and Chubut, where myriad glacial lakes lap at the forest's edge beneath snowcapped peaks.
The area includes four national parks, with towns in each. Bariloche is the base for exploring Parque Nacional Nahuel Huapi, and the departure point for the lake crossing to Chile. North of Bariloche is Parque Nacional Lanín, with the towns of San Martín de los Andes and Junín de los Andes. South of Bariloche and El Bolsón on RN40 is Parque Nacional Lago Puelo in the Pacific watershed.

Lake Traful, submerged forest

LAKE DISTRICT PLANNER

When to Go

From June through September the weather is typical of any ski region—blowing snowstorms, rain, and fog punctuated by days of brilliant sunshine. August and September are the best months for skiing, as the slopes are crowded with vacationers in July.

In December the weather can be cool, breezy, overcast, or rainy, but the rewards for bringing an extra sweater and rain gear are great: an abundance of wildflowers and few tourists. January and February are the peak summer months, with long (sunsets at 10 PM) warm days. March and April are good months to visit, although rainy, cloudy days and cold nights can curtail some activities.

Health and Safety

There are good doctors and clinics in Bariloche, and San Martín de los Andes. Emergency Services: **Coast Guard** (☎ *106*). **Fire** (☎ *100*). **Forest Fire** (☎ *103*). **Hospital** (☎ *107*). **Police** (☎ *101*).

Eat Well and Rest Easy

Restaurant reservations are seldom needed except during school, Easter, and summer holidays (July, January, and February). Attire is informal, and tipping is the same as in the rest of the country (about 10%).

Idyllic lake-view lodges, cozy *cabañas* (cabins), vast *estancias* (ranches), and inexpensive *hospedajes* or *residenciales* (bed-and-breakfasts) are found in towns and in the countryside throughout northern Patagonia. Super-luxurious hotels in Bariloche and Villa La Angostura attract outdoor enthusiasts from all over the world, as do small family-run hostels where backpackers squeeze five to a room. Fishing lodges near San Martín de los Andes, Junín de los Andes, and in the Cholila Valley are not only for anglers; they make great headquarters for hiking, boating, or just getting away. Most of them include all meals and cocktails. Guides are extra. *Apart-hotels* have small, furnished apartments with kitchenettes. Local tourist offices are helpful in finding anything from a room in a residence to a country inn or a downtown hotel. Advance reservations are highly recommended if you're traveling during peak times (December–March; July–August for the ski resorts). Note: lodging prices include tax (IVA—which is 21%) unless otherwise noted.

DINING AND LODGING PRICE CATEGORIES (IN PESOS)

	¢	$	$$	$$$	$$$$
Restaurants	under 8 pesos	8 pesos–15 pesos	15 pesos–25 pesos	25 pesos–35 pesos	over 35 pesos
Hotels	under 80 pesos	80 pesos–150 pesos	150 pesos–250 pesos	250 pesos–400 pesos	over 400 pesos

Restaurant prices are for one main course at dinner. Hotel prices are for two people in a standard double room in high season.

Getting Here and Around

The most efficient way to get here is by air from Buenos Aires or Calafate. The most scenic way to arrive is from Puerto Montt, Chile, by boat through the lakes. Buses are the new trains—fast, inexpensive, with varying degrees of luxury, including beds, meals, and attendants. A car or bus is the best way to travel between cities in the Lake District, and once you've settled in a destination, you can use local tours, taxis, or a *remis* (car with driver).

Air Travel. Aerolíneas Argentinas (🌐 *www.aerolineas.com.ar*) flies from Buenos Aires to Bariloche, Esquel, San Martín de los Andes, and Neuqúen; it also connects Bariloche and Calafate. LAN (🌐 *www.lan.com*) also flies to Bariloche from Buenos Aires, as well as from Santiago, Chile.

Boat Travel. Traveling between Bariloche and Puerto Montt, Chile, by boat is one of the most popular excursions in Argentina. It requires three lake crossings and various buses, and can be done in a day or overnight. Travel agents and tour operators in Bariloche and Buenos Aires can arrange this trip.

Bus Travel. Buses arrive in Bariloche from every corner of Argentina—from Jujuy in the north, Ushuaia in the south, and everywhere in between.

Car Travel. Driving to the Lake District from Buenos Aires is a long haul (more than 1,500 km [930 mi] and at least three days) of interminable stretches with few hotels, gas stations, or restaurants. In Bariloche, unless you're on a tour or a ski-only vacation, renting a car gives you the freedom to stop when and where you want. The Seven Lakes Route closes when weather is bad; for winter travel, rent a 4x4. Hiring a remis is another option.

Visitor Information

The comprehensive Inter Patagonia Web site (🌐 *www.interpatagonia.com*) is an excellent resource for tourist information for every city and region in Patagonia. Local tourist offices (Direcciónes de Turismo) are helpful, easy to find, and usually open late every day.

Money Matters

There are ATMs in all towns and cities—even little villages. Many hotels and shops give a discount for cash (*efectivo*), and give good exchange rates for U.S. dollars.

Lake District Tours

Alunco Turismo specializes in trips around Bariloche for individuals and groups, and can help with reservations. Causana Viajes does custom tours for groups or individuals all over Argentina.

In San Martín the companies Turismo Messidor, El Claro Turismo, and Siete Lagos run horseback-riding, river-rafting, mountain-biking, lake, and land excursions around San Martín and to Lanín Volcano. In El Bolsón, Huara Viajes y Turismo offers guided fishing, rafting, and horseback-riding trips and excursions to Lago Puelo.

Tour Operators: Alunco (✉ *Moreno 187, 1st fl.,* ☎ *2944/422-283* 🌐 *www.aluncoturismo.com.ar*).

Causana Viajes (✉ *Moreno 390, Puerto Madryn* ☎ *2965/455-044* 🌐 *www.causana.com.ar*).

El Claro Turismo (✉ *Colonel Diaz 751* ☎📠 *2972/428–876 or 2972/425-876* 🌐 *www.elclaroturismo.com.ar* ✉ *elclaro@smandes.com.ar*).

Huara Viajes y Turismo (✉ *Dorrego 410, El Bolsón* ☎ *2944/455-000* 🌐 *www.huaraviajesyturismo.com.ar*).

Siete Lagos Turismo (✉ *General Roca 826* ☎📠 *2972/427-877* ✉ *sietelagostmo@smandes.com.ar*).

Turismo Messidor (✉ *Av. Arrayanes 21, piso 2, Villa La Angostura* ☎ *2944/495-265* 🌐 *www.turismomessidor.com.ar*).

RUTA DE LOS SIETE LAGOS

To fully experience the Lake District, head north of Bariloche past Nahuel Huapi Lake to the Ruta de Los Siete Lagos (Seven Lakes Route). This excursion has it all: lake after lake, mountains, wildflowers, waterfalls, hiking trails, and small towns along the way.

Top left: You'll pass lots of big-leaf lupine, or Lupus polyphyllus—an invasive species here.
Top right: rainbow trout
Bottom right: One of many stunning views along the way

The Route itself links Bariloche and San Martín de los Andes. Start in Bariloche and follow the Circuito Grande along R237 and R231 to Villa La Angostura, then pass Lagos Espejo and Correntoso on R231 to get to mostly unpaved R234; take this north to San Martín.

For a day trip, return from San Martin de Los Andes through Junin de Los Andes and Alicura (routes 234, 40, and 237) on 260 km (161mi) of paved road. If you have the time, though, overnight in San Martín de los Andes then take RP63 to Confluéncia, and then join R237 south along the Río Limay to Bariloche.

Renting a car is best, but even on a group tour it's spectacular. Buses are available from Bariloche or Villa La Angostura; you can also rent bicycles in these towns and take to the road on two wheels instead of four.

TIPS

Ask about road conditions before you leave Villa La Angostura; The route's unpaved portion north of there is often closed during heavy rains, winter storms, or construction.

Best bets for picnic spots or campsites are the beaches of lakes Villarino, Falkner, and Hermoso.

For maps, pick up *Guía Busch and Viajar Hoy (tour pamphlets in English and Spanish),* both available at car-rental agencies, kiosks, and hotels in Bariloche.

HIGHLIGHTS OF THE DRIVE

Rivers. Just past Villa La Angostura, the **Río Correntoso**—one of the world's shortest rivers at 300 m (984 ft.)—flows from the lake of the same name into Nahuel Huapi. This is a classic mouth-of-the-river fishing spot; you can watch the action from the glassed-in deck at the Hotel Correntoso or from the old fishing lodge on the shore of Nahuel Huapi Lake. To join in, contact **Patagonia Fly** (✉ *Av. Arrayanes 282* ☎ *2944/494–634* 🌐 *www.patagonfly.com*) at the Banana Fly Shop in Villa La Angostura.

Lakes. Traveling north from Villa Angostura to San Martín de Los Andes is the most scenic part of the drive, and it's no coincidence that this is where you'll find the region's most scenic namesake natural features—lakes. **Lago Correntoso** (Rapid Water) is the first one you'll pass, and you'll do so immediately after you cross over the Río Correntoso. Drive along its northern shore to arrive at a spooky abandoned hotel site; from here you'll see a side road that leads to **Lago Espejo Chico** (*Little Mirror*), with a beach, a campground and trails to nearby lookouts. Return to the main road and after a bit you'll come to **Lago Espejo** (Mirror)—head to the panoramic viewpoint for a good lunch spot, or use the camping area's benches and tables. **Lago Falkner** (east side of the road) has sandy beaches and a popular campground. It is linked by a stream and an isthmus, which you will cross to **Lago Villarino** (west side of the road). Here, at the Hostería Lago Villarino (☎ *2972/425–274*), you can rent fishing boats, buy supplies, dine, or spend a night. **Lago Hermoso** (*beautiful*) is a small sheltered lake. A sunny beach faces west, with nearby camping and a few vacation cabins. Finally, before you reach San Martin de los Andes, enjoy **Lago Machónico**'s dry landscape via the scenic overlook, or take the 2 km (1 mi) walk down to the shoreline.

Waterfalls. Between Lakes Villarino and Faulkner, **Cascada Vulignanco,** a 20-meter (66-foot) waterfall, is visible on the left-hand side of the road, where you can pull off at the *mirador* (overlook).

DETOURS

Four km (2.5 mi) south of Lago Villarino, jade green **Lago Escondido** (Hidden Lake) lies veiled in a thick forest of coíhue, ñire, and radale trees. You'll need to park and walk in.

At Pichi Trafúl, turn east on to a bumpy road for 2 km (1 mi) and walk to the sandy beach at **Pichi Trafúl Lake** (aka Brazo Norte of Lago Traful). Fishermen, mountain bikers, and hikers enjoy camping or picnicking here.

About 30 km (18 mi) north of the junction of RP234 and RP65, look on your left for a sign indicating the trail to **Casacada Ñivinenco** (*Whispering Falls*). The 2 km trail crosses a river (though in November and December the river is high; check conditions ahead of time), then follows the river into a silent forest of caña colihue, ñire, and coíhue.

If you pass through **Confluencia,** take RP 65 along the Trafúl River west a few km to **Cuyín Manzano,** a dirt road that continues along the river into a world of strange limestone rock formations, caves, and maybe even a condor sighting.

CIRCUITO CHICO Y CIRCUITO GRANDE

If you're in Bariloche, get out of town to take in some of the spectacular scenery and old-school resort feel of the area on either the Circuito Chico (small circuit) or Circuito Grande (large circuit) by rental car, hired driver, or tour group.

Top left: "We drove the Circuito Chico and stopped at this overlook." –HappyTrvlr, Fodors.com
Top right: "With flowers in full bloom it couldn't get much better." –Josh Roe, Fodors.com member
Bottom right: Hotel Llao Llao

The Circuito Chico is a 70-km (43 ½ mi) half-day round-trip from Bariloche along the southern shore of Lago Nahuel Huapi. Vistors head out to the Llao Llao Peninsula to ski or take in the lake views and waterfalls without ever being too far from a cup of tea.

The Circuito Grande covers 250 km (155 mi) and is an all-day excursion across the lake from Bariloche. This drive is more about wooded hikes and hidden lakes, and includes two towns where you could spend a night.

You can do the Circuito Chico on one tank of gas. Circuit Grande, however, has longer unpopulated spans. Leave Bariloche with a full tank and re-fuel at Confluencia or Villa La Angostura.

WEATHER TIPS

The Circuito Chico has lots of traffic but is otherwise an easy drive whatever the weather. The Circuito Grande is another story. The roads to Villa La Angostura and Confluencia are good, but RP 65 past Lago Traful is unpaved and can be treacherous in bad weather. Always check road conditions with ACA (Automobil Club Argentina), the park office, or your hotel.

CIRCUITO CHICO

From Bariloche's Centro Cívico (km 0), follow the shore of Lago Nahuel Huapi west on R237. At km 7, stop at **Playa Bonita**'s sandy beach. At km 10, take the chairlift to the top of **Cerro Campanario**. When you reach the Península Llao Llao (km 25.5), bear right to **Puerto Pañuelo** where boats embark on lake excursions to Isla Victoria, Puerto Blest and the boat crossing to Chile. Across from the Puerto Pañuelo, **Hotel Llao Llao** sits on a lakeside knoll with a backdrop of sheer cliffs and snow-covered mountains. Admire it from afar or make a lunch reservation. Continue following R77 to **Bahía Lopez**; you'll approach through a forest of ghostly, leafless lenga trees. After Bahía Lopez, the road crosses **Arroyo Lopez** (Lopez Creek); stop to hike to the waterfall or continue on R77 to **Punto Panoramico**, one of the most scenic overlooks on the peninsula. Just before you cross the Moreno Bridge (which separates Lago Moreno east and west), an unmarked dirt road off to the right leads to the rustic village of Colonia Suiza, a perfect stop for tea or lunch. Backtrack to cross Moreno Bridge, then leave R77 for R237 back to Bariloche.

CIRCUITO GRANDE

Leaving Bariloche on R237 heading east, follow the Río Limay into the **Valle Encantado** (*Enchanted Valley*) with its magical red rocks. Before crossing the bridge at Confluéncia (where the Río Traful joins the Limay), turn left onto R65 to Lago Traful. Five kilometers (3 mi) beyond the turnoff, a dirt road to Cuyín Manzano leads to **astounding sandstone formations**. Return to R65 and follow Lago Traful's shore. When you see the sign indicating a *mirador* (lookout), stop and climb the wooden stairs toone of the loveliest views in the region. Descend to Villa Traful, follow the lake shore, then dive into a dense forest of *caña colihue* and lenga trees. At the intersection with R237, turn left and follow the shore of Lago Correntoso to the paved road down to Villa La Angostura. The road skirts Lago Nahuel Huapi back into Bariloche.

NEED A BREAK?

Circuito Chico: Cheddar Casa de Te (✉ *Av. Bustillo (R237), Km 25* ☎ *2944/448–152* ⌚ *Closed Tues.*) is a little log house with a corrugated metal roof, a stone terrace and red umbrellas hanging out over the lake. Views are through the gnarly branches of a giant coihué tree to blue water and distant mountains. The trout sorrentinos in pesto sauce are as good as the view.

Circuito Grande: If you chose to visit Lago Trafúl in the morning, chances are you'll arrive in the Villa Trafúl in time for lunch at Nancu Lahuen, a casual spot in the middle of town with home cooking—a place you can depend upon to be open and ready for tourists. If you've had the foresight to bring a picnic, continue on past the town to the beach, where the road leaves the lake for R234 and Villa La Angostura. In Villa La Angostura, head to La Casita de la Oma (✉ *Cerro Inacayal 303* ☎ *2544/494–602*), which serves homemade cakes, pies and scones. Any dulce de leche item is a sure bet.

Revised by
Eddy Ancinas

Hundreds of sapphire lakes lie hidden amid the snow-covered peaks of the Andes on the western frontier with Chile, in what has become the most popular tourist area in Patagonia—the northern Lake District. Despite its growing popularity and accessibility from developed towns like Bariloche and San Martín de los Andes, visitors are constantly amazed at how easy it is to lose yourself in a silent forest, or by a still lake with no houses, no boats, no piers—just you and the natural surroundings.

Parque Nacional Lanín, in Neuquén Province, and the neighboring Parque Nacional Nahuel Huapi, in Río Negro Province, add up to 2.5 million acres of natural preserve—about the size of New England. South of Bariloche and the Cholila Valley and northwest of Esquel, the Parque Nacional los Alerces, named for its 2,000-year-old *alerce* trees, covers 1,610 square km (1,000 square mi) of mountains, forests, and lakes, with only one dirt road leading into it. Lago Puelo National Park near El Bolsón also has only one access road in Argentina, with a trail out the other side into Chile.

Outdoor activities and a wide variety of lodgings in extraordinary settings attract visitors year-round. In winter, skiers come to Cerro Catedral for its size and terrain, its superb setting overlooking Nahuel Huapi Lake, and its proximity to Bariloche. Smaller areas such as Chapelco in San Martín de los Andes and Cerro Bayo in Villa La Angostura attract mostly Argentines, lots of Brazilians, and a few other foreigners.

BARILOCHE

1,615 km (1,001 mi) southwest of Buenos Aires (2 hrs by plane); 432 km (268 mi) south of Neuquén on R237; 1,639 km (1,016 mi) north of Río Gallegos; 876 km (543 mi) northwest of Trelew; 357 km (221 mi) east of Puerto Montt, Chile, via lake crossing.

Bariloche is the gateway to all the recreational and scenic splendors of the Northern Lake District and headquarters for 2-million-acre Nahuel Huapi National Park. Although planes, boats, and buses arrive daily, you can escape on land or water—or just by looking out a window—into a dazzling wilderness of lakes, waterfalls, mountain glaciers, forests, and meadows.

The town of Bariloche hugs the southeastern shore of Nahuel Huapi Lake, expanding rapidly east toward the airport and west along the lake toward Llao Llao, as Argentines and foreigners buy and build without any apparent zoning plan. Being the most popular vacation destination in Patagonia has not been kind to the town once called the "Switzerland of the Andes." Traffic barely moves on streets and sidewalks during holidays and the busy months of January–March, July, and August.

Nevertheless, the Centro Cívico (Civic Center), with its gray-green stone-and-log buildings, has not lost its architectural integrity. Designed by Alejandro Bustillo, this landmark square, with its view of the lake and mountains, is a good place to begin exploring Bariloche.

7

GETTING HERE AND AROUND

For long excursions, such as the Seven Lakes Route, Circuito Grande, or Tronadór (⇨ *below*), sign up for a tour through your hotel or with a local tour agency. If you prefer the independence of figuring out maps and driving yourself, rent a car. Tour operators for fishing, rafting, and bike trips will pick you up and transport you to your destination. For good maps and a list of tour operators, look for *Guía Busch* at local bookstores, car-rental agencies, and kiosks. A local bus picks up skiers in Bariloche, and many hotels have their own shuttle.

SAFETY AND PRECAUTIONS

Driving in Bariloche requires total attention to blind corners, one-way streets, and stop signs where no one stops. Never leave anything in your car. Bariloche's challenging sidewalks are riddled with uneven steps, broken pavement, and unexpected holes—all potential ankle-breakers. When students hit Bariloche during holidays, they party until 5 or 6 in the morning, resulting in serious drunk-driving auto accidents.

ESSENTIALS

Bus Contacts **Bariloche Bus Terminal** (✉ *Av. 12 de Octubre* ☎ *2944/432–860*). **Algarrobal** (✉ *9 de Julio 1800* ☎ *2944/427–698*). **Andesmar** (✉ *Mitre 385* ☎ *2944/430–211*). **Don Otto** (✉ *At the bus terminal in Bariloche, Mitre 321* ☎ *2944/429–012*). **VIATAC** (✉ *Moreno 138* ☎ *2944/434–727*). **El Valle** (✉ *Av. 12 de Octubre 1884* ☎ *2944/431–444*). **Via Bariloche** (✉ *Mitre 321* ☎ *2944/432–444*).

Currency Exchange **Banco Frances** (✉ *Av. San Martín 332* ☎ *2944/430–325*). **Bansud** (✉ *Mitre 427* ☎ *2944/424–210*).

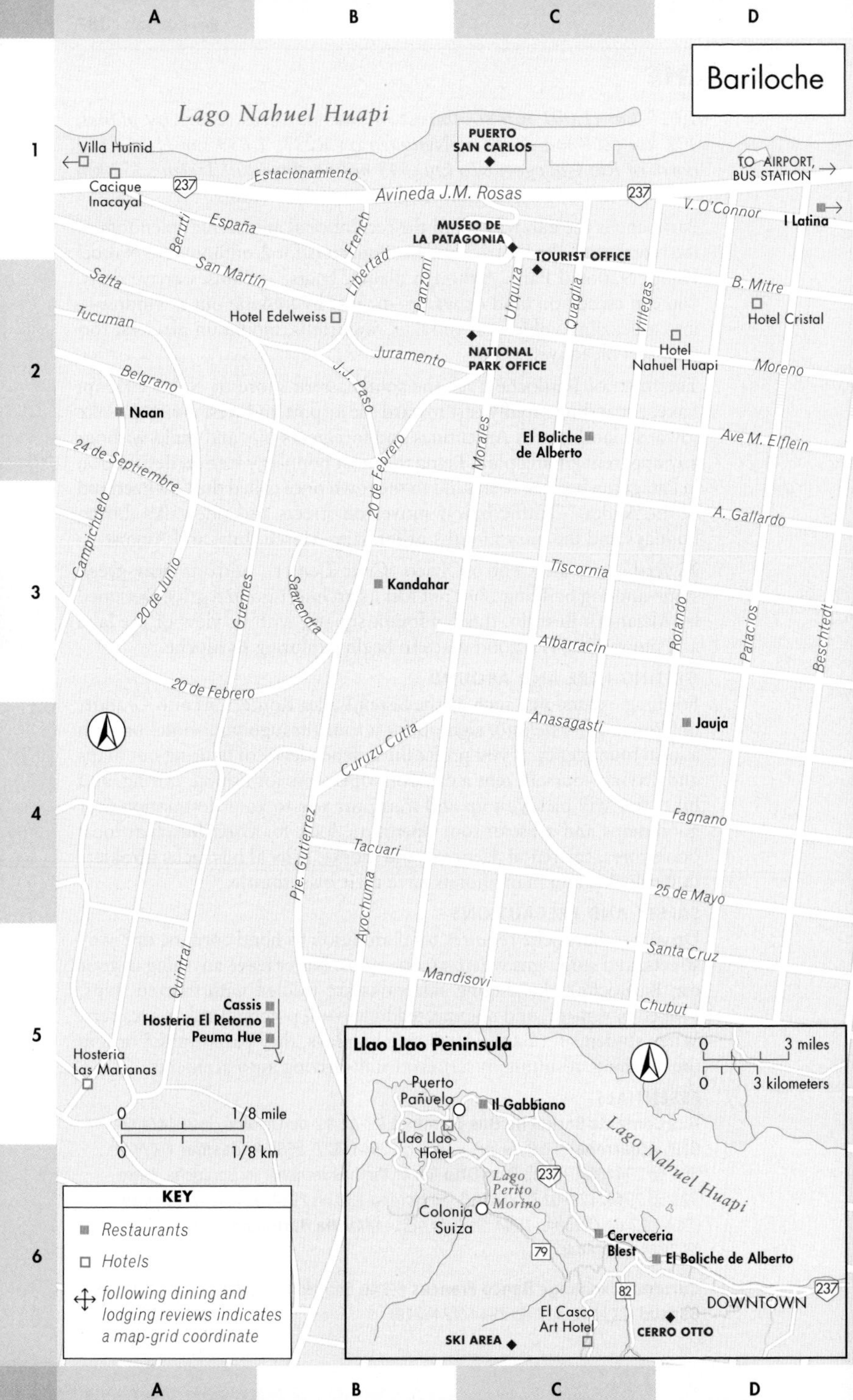
A
B
C
D
Bariloche
Lago Nahuel Huapi
PUERTO SAN CARLOS
Villa Huinid
TO AIRPORT, BUS STATION
Cacique Inacayal
Estacionamiento
237
Avineda J.M. Rosas
V. O'Connor
I Latina
España
Beruti
French
MUSEO DE LA PATAGONIA
TOURIST OFFICE
San Martín
Libertad
Panzoni
Urquiza
Quaglia
Villegas
B. Mitre
Salta
Hotel Cristal
Tucuman
Hotel Edelweiss
Hotel Nahuel Huapi
NATIONAL PARK OFFICE
Juramento
Moreno
J.J. Paso
Belgrano
Naan
Morales
El Boliche de Alberto
Ave M. Elflein
24 de Septiembre
20 de Febrero
A. Gallardo
Campichuelo
Tiscornia
Kandahar
20 de Junio
Guemes
Saavendra
Rolando
Palacios
Beschtedt
Albarracin
20 de Febrero
Anasagasti
Jauja
Curuzu Cutia
Fagnano
Tacuari
Pje. Gutierrez
Ayochuma
25 de Mayo
Santa Cruz
Mandisovi
Quintral
Chubut
Cassis
Hosteria El Retorno
Peuma Hue
Hosteria Las Marianas
0
1/8 mile
0
1/8 km
KEY
Restaurants
Hotels
following dining and lodging reviews indicates a map-grid coordinate
Llao Llao Peninsula
0
3 miles
0
3 kilometers
Puerto Pañuelo
Il Gabbiano
Llao Llao Hotel
Lago Perito Morino
Lago Nahuel Huapi
Colonia Suiza
Cerveceria Blest
El Boliche de Alberto
79
82
DOWNTOWN
El Casco Art Hotel
SKI AREA
CERRO OTTO
1
2
3
4
5
6

Medical Assistance **Angel Gallardo** (✉ *Gallardo 701* ☎ *2944/427-023*). **Farmacia Detina** (✉ *Bustillo 12,500* ☎ *2944/525-900*). **Hospital Zonal Ramón Carillo** (✉ *Moreno 601* ☎ *2944/426-119*). **Hospital Sanatorio del Sol** (✉ *20 de Febrero 598* ☎ *2944/525-000*).

Post Office **Bariloche** (✉ *Moreno 175*).

Remis (Car & Driver) **Patagonia Remises** (✉ *Av. Pioneros 4400* ☎ *2944/443-700*).

Rental Cars **Baricoche** (✉ *Moreno 115* ☎ *2944/427-638* 🌐 *www.baricoche.com.ar*). **Localiza** (✉ *Emilio Frey & V.A. O'Conner* ☎ *2944/435-374; 2944/1562-7708 cell* 🌐 *www.autosurpatagonia.com.ar*).

Visitor and Tour Info **Oficina Municipal de Turismo** (✉ *Centro Cívico, across from clock tower* ☎ *2944/429-850* 🌐 *www.barilochepatagonia.info* *secturismo@bariloche.com.ar*) is open daily 8:30 AM–9 PM.

EXPLORING

The **Museo de la Patagonia** tells the social and geological history of northern Patagonia with displays of Indian and gaucho artifacts and exhibits on regional flora and fauna. The histories of the Mapuche and the Conquista del Desierto (Conquest of the Desert) are explained in detail. ✉ *Centro Cívico, next to arch over Bartolomé Mitre* ☎ *2944/422-330* *2.50 pesos* *Mon. and Sat. 10–1, Tues.–Fri. 10–12:30 and 2–7.*

For an aerial view of the area around Bariloche, don't miss **Cerro Otto** (✉ *Av. de los Pioneros* *30 pesos* *Daily 10–5*)(Mt. Otto; 4,608 feet). The ride to the top in a little red gondola takes about 12 minutes. The cable car is owned by **Teleférico Cerro Otto**, and all proceeds go to local hospitals. The mountain is 5 km (3 mi) west of town; a free shuttle bus leaves from the corner of Mitre and Villegas, and Perito Moreno and Independencia. You can also hike or mountain bike to the top, or drive 8 km (5 mi) up a gravel road from Bariloche. In winter, cross-country skis and sleds are for rent at the cafeteria. In summer, hiking and mountain biking are the main activities. For a real thrill, try soaring in a paraplane out over the lake with the condors. Call for information (☎ *2944/441-035*) on schedules and sled or ski rentals.

WHERE TO EAT

$$$$ ARGENTINE Fodor's Choice ★ — ✕ **Cassis.** Chef Mariana began her culinary career in Argentina's best resorts, until she and her husband found the perfect spot to showcase her considerable talent: on lovely Lago Gutiérrez, across the road from the Arelauquen resort (a 30-minute drive from Bariloche). Together they have created dishes like venison baked in rhubarb and black-currant sauce; carrot, lime, and lemongrass soup; and fantastic desserts such as crispy quince tart with cardamom ice cream or crepes and cakes smothered with fresh berries. ✉ *R82 Arelauquen Point, Lago Gutiérrez* ☎ *2944/476-167* 🌐 *www.cassis.com.ar* *Reservations essential* *No credit cards* *B5.*

$–$$ ARGENTINE — ✕ **Cerveceria Blest.** This lively spot claims that it was the first brewpub in Argentina, and its relaxed bustle hits the spot after a day on the slopes. Don't miss the excellent bock beer, with a toasty coffee flavor, or if you

CLOSE UP

Chilean Lakes Crossing

The **Cruce a Chile por Los Lagos** (Chile Lake Crossing) is a unique excursion by land and lakes. You can do the tour in one or two days in either direction.

Board the boat at Puerto Pañuelo west of Bariloche, you'll stop for lunch in Puerto Blest, then travel by bus up to Laguna Frías, a cold glacial lake frozen in winter. After crossing that lake to Puerto Fríos, you pass Argentine customs, then board another bus that climbs through lush rain forest over a pass before descending to **Peulla.** Clear Chilean customs just before a lodge by Lago Todos los Santos. You may spend the night at the lodge (recommended) or head straight to Chile by catamaran from Peulla, with volcano views. The boat trip ends at the port of Petrohué. Your final bus ride skirts Lago Llanquihue, stopping at the Petrohué waterfalls, passing the town of Puerto Varas, and arriving, at last, at Puerto Montt. Guides on the Argentina side speak little English, and passenger literature in English isn't available; if your Spanish is shaky, do this trip with a tour group. ✉ *In Argentina: Puerto Blest S.A. Mitre 415, 1st fl., Bariloche* ☎ *2944/427–143* ✉ *In Chile: Puerto Varas/Turismo Peulla San Juan 430, 2nd fl., Puerto Varas* ☎ *65/236–150* ⏲ *Daily 8:30–3* 🌐 *www.crucedelagos.com.*

If you're pressed for time, return to Bariloche by paved road via Osorno, crossing at Cardenal Samoré (aka Paso Puyehue) to Villa La Angostura (125 km [78 mi] from the border to Bariloche on RN231).

OTHER CROSSINGS

Paso Hua Hum is the only crossing open year-round. It may be the shortest route—only 47 km (29 mi) from San Martín de los Andes on RP48—as the condor flies, but it's the longest journey by road, after factoring in the 1½-hour ferry ride across Lake Pirehueico on the Chilean side. There are three ferries daily, and buses leave regularly from San Martín de los Andes. You can also make this crossing by raft on the river Hua Hum.

Farther north, and accessible via Junín de los Andes, are two passes that require a longer excursion. Mamuil Malal (aka Paso Tromen) is 67 km (41½ mi) northwest of Junín de los Andes on RP60. This dirt road crosses Lanín National Park and passes through a forest of ancient araucaria trees as it heads for the foot of Lanín Volcano. Just before the park office, a road leads to good picnic spots and campsites on Lago Tromen. If you continue on to Chile, you'll see the Villarrica and Quetupillán volcanoes to the south and Pucón to the north.

Paso Icalma is 132 km (82 mi) west of Zapala on RN13. Villa Pehuenia, 10 km (6 mi) before the pass, is a small village on the shore of Lake Alluminé with modern accommodations and restaurants. Rafting or fishing the Alluminé River, a visit to an araucaria nursery, plus horse, bike, and raft rentals might tempt you to stay awhile.

No fresh fruits, meats, or vegetables are allowed across the border, so bring a power bar for long stretches without food. Lake crossings are not fun in driving rain and high waves. Snow may close some passes in winter. If you're driving, double-check with your rental agent that you have all the necessary paperwork. It's also a good idea to have some Chilean pesos with you, as it can be expensive to change them at the border.

—Eddy Ancinas

prefer hard cider, the Fruto Prohibido. You can come in just for an après-ski beer sampler or stay for dinner, which might include *costillitas de cerdo ahumadas con chucrut* (smoked pork chops with sauerkraut—is there a more classic beer food than that?). Pizzas, steak potpies, and other Anglophile options round out the menu. ✉ *Av. Bustillo, Km 11.6* ☎ *2944/461–026* ▭ *AE, MC, V* ✣ *C6.*

$ ARGENTINE ✕ **El Boliche de Alberto.** Leather place mats, calfskin menus, and the smell of beef all hint heavily at steak house. Alberto has the best beef in Bariloche. Grilled chicken, lamb, and chorizos all arrive sizzling on a wooden platter, accompanied by empanadas, *provoleta* (fried provolone cheese), salad, fried potatoes, and chimichurri sauce (slather it on the bread). Three locations: ✉ *Elflein 158* ☎ *2944/43–4864* ✉ *Villegas 347* ☎ *2944/43–1433* ✉ *Bustillo 8800* ☎ *2944/462–285* 🌐 *www.elbolichedealberto.com* ▭ *AE, DC, MC, V* ✣ *C2.*

$$$ LATIN AMERICAN ✕ **I latina.** The walls and even the radiators are painted hot tamale colors—red, orange, yellow—bringing a bright, cheerful Latin look to this restaurant across from the Cathedral. Food and drinks (pisco sours, margaritas, mojitos) are inspired by the cuisines of Peru, Cuba, Columbia, and Brazil. Columbian chef Carlos Pardo uses Caribbean flavors to enhance Argentine beef, chicken, and fish, and his stir-fry vegetables are *al punto.* ✉ *Vice Alte. O'Connor 541* ☎ *2944/428–520* ▭ *AE, MC, V* ⊙ *Closed Sun.* ✣ *D1.*

$$$–$$$$ ITALIAN ✕ **Il Gabbiano.** "We don't serve lunch," the folks at this cozy, candlelit house on the Circuito Chico near Llao Llao boast, "because preparing dinner takes all day." It's hard to argue with that after you sample the exquisite pastas, which change daily. Look for *tortelli* stuffed with wild boar, or pumpkin ravioli; they also have a way with fresh trout. A beautiful wine cellar is open to guests. ✉ *Av. Bustillo, Km 24.3* ☎ *2944/448–346* ⚠ *Reservations essential* ▭ *No credit cards* ⊙ *Closed Tues. No lunch* ✣ *C5.*

$$–$$$ ARGENTINE ✕ **Jauja.** Locals and families come to this friendly restaurant for its outstanding pastas and variety of entrées listed on an 8-page menu: meats from Patagonia to the pampas, fish from both oceans, local game, fresh vegetables including local mushrooms. Smokers have a separate room, and an upstairs dining room is available for special events. Empanadas and take-out items can be ordered at the entrance. (☎ *2944/429–986)* ✉ *Elflein 148* ☎ *2944/42–2952* ▭ *AE, DC, MC, V* ✣ *D4.*

$$$$ ARGENTINE ✕ **Kandahar.** A rustic wood building with a woodstove and cozy window seats in alcoves is the perfect setting for sipping a pisco sour and savoring a plate of smoked trout or salmon and guacamole. Start with the *tarteleta de hongos* (mushroom tart) and *rosa mosqueta* (rose hip) soup, followed by wild game and profiteroles with hot chocolate sauce. ✉ *20 de Febrero 698* ☎ *2944/424–702* ▭ *AE, MC, V* ✣ *B3.*

$$$$ ECLECTIC ✕ **Naan.** You can go around the world in six courses at this small private home–cum-restaurant in Bariloche's upscale hillside neighborhood, Barrio Belgrano. Vegetarian Vietnamese rolls, Italian panini, French mushroom gratin, Thai soup, Lebanese baba ghanoush—even Tex-Mex quesadillas make great shared appetizers. Then come the main courses: Moroccon pilaf, Chinese beef with shiitake mushrooms and asparagus, a Brazilian seafood plate, Greek lamb kebab, French grilled trout.

7

Desserts are equally creative concoctions of local berries and chocolate whipped, moussed, meringued, or creped. ✉ *Campichuelo 568, Barrio Belgrano* ☎ *2944/421–785* ✍ *Reservations essential* ▭ *AE, MC, V* ⊙ *Closed Mon. and 3 weeks in Nov.* ✣ *A2.*

WHERE TO STAY

If you don't have a car, it's better to stay in town. If you're looking for serenity, consider a lake-view hotel or cabins along the route to the Llao Llao Peninsula. Locations of out-of-town dining and lodging properties are measured in kilometers from the Bariloche Civic Center.

$$$$ ★ **Cacique Inacayal.** Looking out from your bedroom window when the wind whips up the waves on Nahuel Huapi Lake, you'll be glad you're on land. Perched on a cliff overlooking the lake, Cacique Inacayal has the reception, bar, and an outdoor patio on the top; a fine dining room for hotel guests down one floor; and lakeview rooms on the three floors below. In the middle of it all a glass-covered atrium six stories high allows light into all floors and interior spaces. Dinner consists of a cold buffet, soup, and two entrées to choose from. **Pros:** the maître d' makes every dinner seem like a party; dinner's included in the room rate. **Cons:** five rooms on the east side of the building, next to the disco, throb to the beat until late at night during holidays. ✉ *Juan Manuel de Rosas 625* ☎ *2944/433–888* 🌐 *www.hotelinacayal.com.ar* *57 rooms* *In-room: Wi-Fi. In-hotel: bar, indoor pool, spa, public Wi-Fi, parking (no fee)* ▭ *AE, DC, MC, V* *MAP* ✣ *A1.*

$$$$ Fodor's Choice ★ **El Casco Art Hotel.** Intriguing sculptures perched on marble stands, wooden ledges, or freestanding in the garden are part of a collection of over 200 artworks displayed throughout the hotel. All public spaces—halls, wine bar, gourmet restaurant—even the downstairs gym, indoor-out swimming pool, and large Jacuzzi—face the lake, where the hotel's private launch is docked at the pier. The rooms are huge, done in the same natural colors, and good art and a great view are major attractions. The hotel is only 15 minutes from the ski area, Bariloche, and two 18-hole golf courses. **Pros:** art everywhere; activities galore; self-contained luxury. **Cons:** perhaps too much extravagance for some. ✉ *Av. Bustillo, Km 11.5* ☎ *2944/463–131* 🌐 *www.hotelelcasco.com* *57 suites* *In-hotel: restaurant, bar, pool, gym, public Wi-Fi* ▭ *AE, DC, MC, V* *FAP* ✣ *C6.*

$ **Hosteria El Retorno.** Just 20 minutes from Bariloche, on the west shore of lovely Lago Gutiérrez, this venerable old lodge has been spruced up with new paint, new carpeting, and a profusion of flowers around its vast lawns and woods. Kayaks and bikes invite you to take off across the lake or into the woods. A summer bike ride from the Catedral ski area is all downhill, with a dip in the lake and a beer or tea and cakes at the end of the ride. Skiers have a back road (unless it's closed) up to the ski area, thus avoiding the traffic from Bariloche. Guests tend to stay on the premises, enjoying the many activities as well as the quiet and solitude at this country lodge. **Pros:** lots of room for kids to play; stargazing is tough to beat. **Cons:** no nightlife. ✉ *Western end of RP82 on Lago Gutiérrez, near Villa Arelauken* ☎ *2944/467–333* 🌐 *www.*

Whether it's sunbathing weather or ski season, the Lake District delivers.

hosteriaelretorno 24 rooms, 5 apartments In-hotel: restaurant, bar, golf course, tennis court, water sports, bicycles, Wi-Fi hotspot, parking (free), some pets allowed AE, MC, V Closed May CP B5.

$$ **Hosteria Las Marianas.** A perfectly proportioned Tyrolean villa, this B&B on a sunny hillside in Barrio Belgrano, the nicest neighborhood in town, is only four blocks from the city center, but it's in a world of its own on a quiet street surrounded by well-tended gardens. The owners are mountaineers and skiers, and their photos decorate the walls of the breakfast room, where homemade breads and jams are served to guests who gather at breakfast or teatime. **Pros:** away from the crowds. **Cons:** uphill haul from city center. *24 de Septiembre 218* *2944/439–876* *www.hosterialasmarianas.com.ar* *16 rooms* *In-hotel: Internet terminal* *No credit cards* *CP* *A5.*

$–$$ **Hotel Cristal.** A basic businesslike downtown hotel, this recycled old standby in the center of Bariloche has been greatly improved with modern furnishings and better facilities, as tour groups and independent travelers discover the flavor of being on the street with all the chocolate shops. The lobby has a nice fireplace and bar. The standard no-frills rooms are tidy and adequate. **Pros:** central downtown location; good value. **Cons:** small bathrooms; desultory reception; popular with tour groups. *Mitre 355* *2944/422–442* *www.hotelcristal.com.ar* *50 rooms* *In-hotel: restaurant, bar, public Wi-Fi* *AE, DC, MC, V* *CP* *D2.*

$$$$ **Hotel Edelweiss.** Fresh flowers from the owner's nursery are a tradition throughout this medium-size hotel, which is within walking distance of everything in town. Rooms on the upper floors have lake views from bay windows. Ski and tour buses, whether arranged through the hotel or other

travel agencies, pick up passengers at the front door. **Pros:** great location; helpful staff. **Cons:** bar has no windows; so-so street-side restaurant. *✉ Av. San Martín 202 ☎ 2944/445–500 🌐 www.edelweiss.com.ar ⇨ 94 rooms, 6 suites ♿ In-room: safe. In-hotel: restaurant, bar, pool, gym, parking (no fee), spa, public Wi-Fi ▭ AE, DC, MC, V 🍴 CP ✥ B2.*

$$$–$$$$ **Hotel Nahuel Huapi.** This slick city hotel on a busy downtown street in Bariloche has a spacious lobby with a wine bar in one corner and a sit-around fireplace in another. Locally made ceramics decorate the interior. Textured beige wallpaper in the large bedrooms show off the deep reds and browns of the woven bedspreads and upholstered chairs. Some rooms have a nice view into the neighbor's garden. **Pros:** central location; good accessibility for people with disabilities. **Cons:** rooms overlooking street might be noisy. *✉ Moreno 252 ☎ 2944/433–635 🌐 www.hotelnahuelhuapi.com.ar ⇨ 80 rooms ♿ In-hotel: restaurant, bar, parking (no fee) Wi-Fi ▭ AE, DC, MC, V 🍴 CP ✥ D2.*

$$$$ **Hotel Tronadór.** Named for the mountain that towers above the wild landscape of lakes and forests only 25 km (15½ mi) up the road, this stone and log lodge overlooking Lago Mascardi and surrounded by a profusion of flowers has been owned and cared for by the Vereertbrugghen family since 1929. The main attraction is a visit to Monte Tronodór and a walk up to its glaciers or through the forest to waterfalls that tumble from the frozen snow above. Ambitious hikers can climb to a refugio and return in a day. **Pros:** practically in the lap of the region's highest mountain glacier; airport transfers available for a fee; organic garden; game and video room. **Cons:** the road here is one-way heading towards the hotel 10:30 AM–2 PM, one-way heading away from 4 PM–7:30 PM, and two-way from 7:30 PM–10:30 AM only. *✥ RN40 west from Bariloche 66 km, past Villa Masacardi, turn right on dirt road to west end of Lago Mascardi ☎ 2944/490–550 🌐 www.hoteltronodor.com ⇨ 30 rooms, 7 apartments ♿ In-hotel: 2 restaurants, bar, beachfront, laundry service, Wi-Fi hotspot, parking (free) ▭ No credit cards ⊗ Closed mid-Apr.–mid-May 🍴 FAP.*

$$$$ **Llao Llao Hotel & Resort.** This masterpiece by architect Alejandro Bustillo sits on a grassy knoll surrounded by three lakes with a backdrop of rock cliffs and snow-covered mountains. Local wood—alerce, cypress, and hemlock—has been used for the walls along the 100-yard hallway, where paintings by local artists are displayed. Every room has a view worth keeping the curtains open for. A lunch or dinner reservation will also get you inside to see one of the most beautiful hotels in the world. **Pros:** beautiful setting; helpful staff; lots of activities. **Cons:** the public is allowed to visit this landmark hotel only on a guided tour on Wednesday at 3 PM. *✉ Av. Ezequiel Bustillo, 25 km (15½ mi) west of Bariloche ☎ 2944/448–530 🌐 www.llaollao.com ⇨ 153 rooms, 12 suites, 1 cabin ♿ In-room: safe. In-hotel: 2 restaurants, bar, golf course, pool, gym, spa, water sports, bicycles, children's programs (ages 2–12), no-smoking rooms ▭ AE, DC, MC, V 🍴 CP ✥ B5.*

$$$$ **Peuma Hue.** Inside, it's pine beams overhead, kilim rugs on wood floors, a lace table cloth on the dining table, guests gathered around the stone fireplace—a sense of rustic luxury prevails. Outside, Lago Gutiérrez shimmers through the trees across the lawn. No need to read

brochures or call tour operators—just sign up in the lobby for the days' or weeks' activities. Of course, you can loll in a hammock, read a book, or watch the birds any time of day. **Pros:** massage, yoga, and wine tastings just the tip of the activities iceberg. **Cons:** remote location. ⊠ *R258, Km 25* ✣ *Enter dirt road, 1½ mi to Lago Gutiérrez,Bariloche* ☎ *2944/50–1030* 🌐 *www.peuma-hue.com* *27 rooms* *In-room: phone, safe, DVD, Wi-Fi. In-hotel: restaurant, room service, bar, beachfront, bicycles, laundry service, Wi-Fi hotspot, parking (free)* ▭ *AE, MC, V* ⊙ *Closed June* 🍽 *FAP* ✣ *B5.*

$$$$ **Villa Huinid.** This peaceful complex consists of a grand hotel with a lake-view pool and spa and older two-story log-and-stucco cottages (one-, two-, or three-bedroom) on the lawns below. Cottages have stone chimneys and wooden decks that give them the appearance of private homes with well-tended gardens. You'll enjoy cypress-plank floors with radiant heat, carved wooden counters, and a view of Nahuel Huapi Lake. **Pros:** like renting a cabin with all the amenities of a hotel. **Cons:** outdoor hike to breakfast in hotel. ⊠ *Av. Bustillo, Km 2.6* ☎ *2944/523–523* 🌐 *www.villahuinid.com.ar* *46 rooms, 17 cabins* *In-room: kitchen. In-hotel: restaurant, bar, pool, gym, public Wi-Fi* ▭ *AE, MC, V* ✣ *A1.*

SHOPPING

Along Bariloche's main streets, Calles Mitre and Moreno, and the cross streets from Quaglia to Rolando, you can find shops selling sports equipment, leather goods, hand-knit sweaters, and gourmet food like homemade jams, dried meats, and chocolate. **Ahumadero Familia Weiss** (⊠ *Palacios 401* ☎ *2944/435–789* ⊠ *Av. Bustillo, Km 20* ☎ *2944/435–789*) sells pâtés, cheeses, smoked fish, and wild game.

Talabarterís sell items for the discerning equestrian or modern gaucho. **Cardon** (⊠ *Av. San Martín 324*) is a fine leather store whose leather jackets, coats, vests, bags, belts, and boots are sold all over Argentina. At **El Establo** (⊠ *Mitre 22*), look for shoes, handbags, belts, wallets, and wall coverings with distinctive black-and-white Mapuche designs.

SPORTS AND THE OUTDOORS

HORSEBACK RIDING

Argentine horses are sturdy and well trained, much like American quarter horses. *Tábanas* (horseflies) attack humans and animals in summer months, so wear long sleeves on *cabalgatas* (horseback outings). **Carol Jones** (🌐 *www.caroljones.com* ☎ *2944/426–508*) is the granddaughter of an early pioneering family, and her ranch north of town does day rides and overnights from the Patagonian steppes into the mountains. **El Manso** (☎ *2944/523–641 or 2944/441–378*) combines riding and rafting over the border to Chile. **Tom Wesley** (⊠ *Av. Bustillo, Km 15.5* ☎ *2944/448–193* 🌐 *www.cabalgatastomwesley.com*) at the **Club Hípico Bariloche** does rides lasting from one hour to a week.

Evening shoppers on Avenida Bartolomé Mitre, Bariloche

SKIING

Cerro Catedral (Mount Cathedral), named for its Gothic-looking spires, is the largest and oldest ski area in South America, with 39 lifts, 4,500 acres of mostly intermediate terrain, and a comfortable altitude of 6,725 feet. The runs are long, varied, and scenic. One side of the mountain has a vertical drop of 3,000 feet, mostly in the fall line. At the top of the highest chairlift a Poma Lift transports skiers to a weather station at 7,385 feet, where a small restaurant, **Refugio Lynch,** is tucked into a wind-sculpted snow pocket on the edge of an abyss with a stupendous 360-degree view of Nahuel Huapi Lake. To the southwest, Monte Tronadór, a 12,000-foot extinct volcano, straddles the border with Chile, towering above lesser peaks that surround the lake. August and September are the best months to ski. A terrain park, Nordic skiing in a forest of lenga trees, and online ticket purchasing are all new additions. Avoid the first three weeks of July (school vacation). (☎ *2944/409–000* 🌐 *www.catedralaltapatagonia.com*).

Villa Catedral (🌐 *www.catedralaltapatagonia.com*), at the base of the mountain, has ski retail and rental shops, information and ticket sales, ski-school offices, restaurants, and even a disco. Frequent buses transport skiers from Bariloche to the ski area. For information and trail maps, contact **La Secretaría de Turismo de Río Negro** (✉ *12 de Octubre 605* ☎ *2944/423–188*).**Club Andino Bariloche** (✉ *20 de Febrero 30* ☎ *2944/422–266*) also has information and trail maps. ✢ *46 km (28½ mi) west of town on Av. Bustillo (R237); turn left at Km 8.5 just past Playa Bonita.*

IN AND AROUND SAN MARTÍN DE LOS ANDES

260 km (161 mi) north of Bariloche on R237, R40, and R234 via Junín de los Andes (a 4-hr drive); 158 km (98 mi) north of Bariloche on R237 and R63 over the Córdoba Pass (69 km [42 mi] is paved); 90 km (56 mi) northeast of Villa La Angostura on R234 (Seven Lakes Rd., partly unpaved and closed for much of winter).

In the southeastern corner of Parque Nacional Lanín, San Martín de los Andes is the largest town within the park, with roads leading south to Bariloche on the Seven Lakes Route, north on a good paved road to Junín de los Andes (41 km [29 mi]), and west on a dirt road to the Hua Hum crossing into Chile (47 km).

Although Junín doesn't have the tourist infrastructure that San Martín has, and it's on the flat Patagonian steppe with no lake in sight, dirt roads leading west take you up the Chimehuin River to Lakes Curruhue, Huechulaufquen, and Paimún—all well known to sports fishermen. As you drive west, the perfect white cone of Lanín Volcano towers in the distance at 12,474 feet. Northwest of Junín, RP60 takes you north of Lanín Volcano to Paso Tromen (67 km [41½ mi]).

SAN MARTÍN DE LOS ANDES

Surrounded by lakes, dense forests, and mountains, San Martín de los Andes lies in a natural basin at the foot of Lago Lácar. It's a small, easygoing town, much like Bariloche was 30 years ago, with many small hotels and houses reflecting the distinctive Andean alpine architecture of Bustillo. Wide, flat streets lined with rosebushes run from the town pier on the eastern shore of Lago Lácar to the main square, Plaza San Martín, where two parallel streets—San Martín and General Villegas—teem with block after block of ski and fishing shops, chocolatiers, trinket shops, clothing boutiques, and cafés.

The Mapuche lived in the area long before the town was founded in 1898 by immigrants of Chilean, French, Dutch, and Italian descent. Because all of the water from this area runs into the Pacific, the territory was disputed by Chile, which claimed it as its own until 1902, when it was legally declared Argentinean.

After Lanín National Park was established in 1937 and the ski area at Chapelco developed in the 1970s, tourism replaced forestry as the main source of income. Today San Martín is the major tourist center in Neuquén Province—the midpoint in the Seven Lakes Route, and the gateway for exploring the Parque Nacional Lanín.

GETTING HERE AND AROUND

Aerolíneas Argentinas and LADE have flights from Buenos Aires, but most people arrive from Bariloche via Junín de los Andes or along the Seven Lakes Route. Buses from Bariloche are frequent and dependable. San Martín is a pleasant walking town, as it's flat. To access nearby beaches, hiking trails, or the ski area in winter, you need to rent a car, join a tour, or be an energetic cyclist. Taxis are inexpensive, and remises can be arranged through your hotel. There are no gas stations on the Seven Lakes Route.

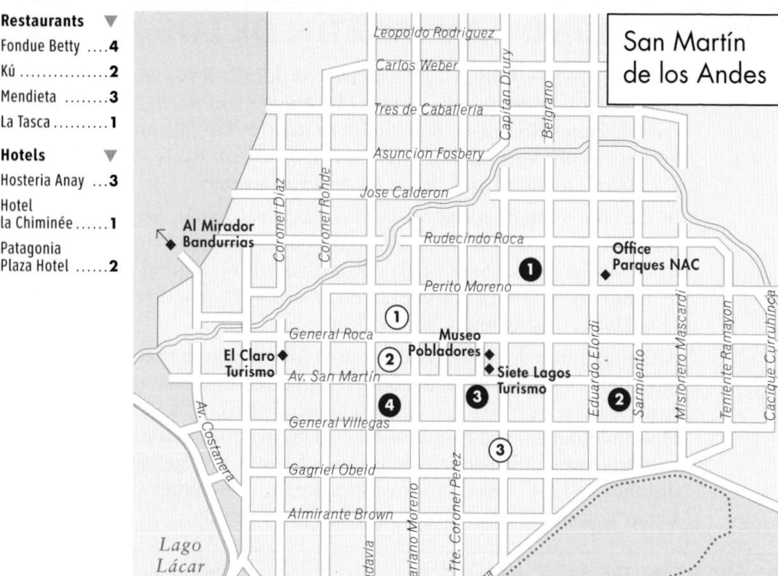

ESSENTIALS

Bus Contacts **San Martín de los Andes Bus Terminal** (✉ *Villegas at Juez de Valle* ☎ *2972/427-044*).

Currency Exchange **Banco de la Nación Argentina** (✉ *Av. San Martín 687* ☎ *2972/427-292*). **Banco Macro Bansud** (✉ *Av. San Martín 850* ☎ *2972/423-962*).

Medical Assistance **Farmacia del Centro** (✉ *San Martín 896, at Belgrano* ☎ *2972/428-999*). **Hospital Ramón Carillo** (✉ *San Martín at Rodhe* ☎ *107 emergencies; 2972/427-211*).

Post Office **San Martín de los Andes** (✉ *At the Civic Center, General Roca at Pérez*).

Remis (Car and Driver) **Del Oscar** (✉ *Av. San Martín 1254* ☎ *2972/428-774*).

Visitor and Tour Info **Dirección Municipal de Turismo** (✉ *J.M. de Rosas 790, at Av. San Martín* ☎ *2972/427-347* 🌐 *www.sanmartindelosandes.gov.ar*). Open daily 8 AM–9 PM.

EXPLORING

The **Museo Pobladores** (Pioneer Museum) is a tiny building next to the tourist office that was the original city council lodge. It is mainly dedicated to Mapuche ceramics and weavings, and a collection of

13,000-year-old tools and fossils gives an idea of ancient life in the region. ✉ *J.M. de Rosas 700* ☎ *2972/428–676* 🎫 *1 peso* ⏲ *Varies—check at the tourist office.*

From town you can walk, mountain bike, or drive to the **Mirador de las Bandurrias** (Bandurrias Overlook). It's a half-day hike round-trip (5 km [3 mi]) up a steep hill through a dense forest of cypress and oak. The reward is a view of town and the lake and a visit to a Mapuche village (**Paraje Trompul**) of about 40 families, most of whom work in town. You can visit the village for a peso, buy refreshments in the *quincho* (café), and see weavings and wood carvings (also for sale). If you're walking, take Avenida San Martín to the lake, turn right, cross the bridge behind the waterworks plant over Puahullo Creek, and then head uphill on a path around the mountain. By car, leave town on RP48 and drive about 4 km (2½ mi) to a turnoff (no sign) on your left. Take the turn and continue 3 km (2 mi) to the Curruhuinca Community, where you pay a fee to arrive at the lookout (about two hours round-trip).

WHERE TO EAT

$$ ARGENTINE ✕ **Fondue Betty.** It wouldn't be a ski town without a fondue restaurant. Fondues are uniformly excellent; the cheese fondue is smooth and rich, while the meat fondue comes with cubes of Argentine beef in assorted cuts and up to 12 condiments. The wine list is also great. The two rooms are cozy and intimate, equally well suited to children and honeymooners; and there's warm, familiar service from a genial older couple. ✉ *Villegas 586* ☎ *2972/422–522* 💳 *DC, MC, V.*

$$$$ ARGENTINE ★ ✕ **Kú**. Dark-wood tables and booths, a friendly staff, and a chalkboard—good building blocks for a restaurant. The smoked-meat plate with venison, boar, trout, salmon, and cheese is a good starter. Patagonian lamb *al asador* (on the open fire) and a good assortment of parrilla classics are paired with a fine wine list. ✉ *Av. San Martín 1053* ☎ *2972/427–039* 💳 *AE, DC, MC, V.*

$$$$ ARGENTINE ✕ **La Tasca**. This is one of the traditional top-end choices in town for locals and tourists. With tables scattered about the black-stone floor, and wine barrels, shelves, and every other imaginable surface stacked with pickled vegetables, smoked meats, cheese rounds, dried mushrooms and herbs, olive oils in cans and bottles, and wine bottles, you might think you're in a Patagonian deli. Diners should try local wild game dishes; especially good is the "La Tasca" appetizer platter of smoked salmon, venison, boar, and trout pâté. ✉ *Moreno 866* ☎ *2972/428–663* 💳 *AE, MC, V.*

$$$ ARGENTINE ✕ **Mendieta**. This may be the friendliest parrilla in Patagonia: cooks, waiters, and even the owners scurry about with sizzling meats from the grill and fresh steaming pasta with various sauces. By 2 PM the tables are filled with chatty locals. Pine racks around the dining room display a good selection of Argentina wines, and you can watch three or more Patagonian lambs being slowly roasted *a la cruz* (on the cross) in the streetside window. ✉ *Av. San Martín 713* ☎ *2972/429–301* 💳 *DC, MC, V.*

7

WHERE TO STAY

$$$ **Hosteria Anay.** *Anay* means "friendship," and that's what you feel inside this small, white stucco–and-log house. Guests gather around the fireplace for tea in the cozy sitting area or in the bright, cheerful breakfast room. Rooms have simple whitewashed walls, beamed ceilings, and carpeted floors. **Pros:** good value. **Cons:** small rooms. ✉ *Cap. Drury 841* ☎ *2972/427–514* 🌐 *www.interpatagonia.com/anay* *15 rooms* *In-hotel: laundry service, public Wi-Fi, parking (free)* *No credit cards* *CP.*

$$$$ ★ **Hotel la Cheminée.** Two blocks from the main street is this comfortable inn with pink-floral chintz and lace curtains. Plump pillows, fresh flowers, and fireplaces in some rooms add to the coziness. A sumptuous breakfast and an afternoon tea of homemade breads, scones, cakes, cookies, and jams are served. **Pros:** great breakfast; helpful tour options on bulletin board. **Cons:** no bar. ✉ *M. Moreno at General Roca* ☎ *2972/427–617* *lacheminee@smandes.com.ar* *15 rooms, 3 suites, 1 cottage* *In-hotel: pool, public Wi-Fi, parking (free)* *AE, MC, V* *CP.*

$$$–$$$$ **Patagonia Plaza Hotel.** Good-bye genteel rusticity. Hello modern downtown hotel with all the amenities. Shops, tourist offices, and restaurants are around the corner from this centrally located oasis with a lobby fireplace and soaring atrium full of light and plants. Note the paintings on display—each floor presents a different local artist. The staff caters well to the frequent fishermen, families, business travelers, and pleasure-types who stop here. **Pros:** location; big rooms with modern bathrooms. **Cons:** atmosphere deficient in restaurant. ✉ *Av. San Martín at Rivadavia* ☎ *2972/422–280* 🌐 *www.hotelpatagoniaplaza.com.ar* *15 rooms* *In-hotel: restaurant, bar, pool, laundry service, public Wi-Fi, parking (free)* *AE, DC, MC, V* *CP.*

SPORTS AND THE OUTDOORS

The following tour agencies arrange rafting trips on the Hua Hum or Aluminé rivers, guided mountain-biking, horseback-riding, and fishing tours, visits to Mapuche communities, and excursions to lakes near and far in both Lanín and Nahuel Huapi national parks. An all-day excursion to **Lago Huechulafquen** (✉ *General Roca 826* ☎ *2972/427–877*) with an extension to the hot-springs spa at **Epulaufquen** is a new addition. Fernando Aguirre, a lifelong resident of the area, offers two- to four-day camping trips with combinations of hiking, riding, rafting, biking, and kayaking. **Siete Lagos Turismo. El Claro Turismo** (✉ *Col. Diaz 751* ☎ *2972/428–876 or 2972/425–876* 🌐 *www.elclaroturismo.com.ar*) and **El Refugio** (✉ *Tte. Col. Perez 830* ☎ *2972/425–140* 🌐 *www.elrefugioturismo.com.ar*) offer similar excursions throughout the area.

BEACHES

Playa Catrite, 4 km (2½ mi) from San Martín on R234, on the south side of Lago Lácar, is a sandy beach with a campground, a store with picnic supplies, and a café. **Playa Quila Quina**, 18 km (11 mi) from San Martín, is reached by turning off R234 2 km (1 mi) before the road to Catrite and then getting on R108.

BOATING

You can rent small boats, canoes, and kayaks at the pier from **Lacar Nonthue** (✉ *Av. Costanera* ☎ *2972/427–380*). You can also rent a bicycle and take an all-day excursion to the other side of Lake Lácar, where there is a nice beach and woods to explore. Another option is the boat tour to **Hua Hum** at the western end of the lake, where the river of the same name runs to the Chilean border. ⇨ *White-Water Rafting, below.*

FISHING

During the fishing season (November 15–April 15, extended to the end of May in certain areas) local guides take you to their favorite spots on Lakes Lácar, Lolog, Villarino, and Falkner and on the Caleufu, Quiquihue, Malleo, and Hermoso rivers, or farther afield to the Chimehuín River and Lakes Huechulafquen and Paimún. Permits are available at the **Parque Nacional Intendencia** (✉ *Emilio Frey 749* ☎ *2972/427–233*) or any licensed fishing stores along Avenida San Martín. Most stores and tour operators can suggest guides.

Jorge Cardillo (✉ *Villegas 1061, behind the casino* ☎ *2972/428–372* ✉ *cardillo@smandes.com.ar*) is a well-known local guide. **Sidy Casa y Pesca** (✉ *Villegas 570* ☎ *2972/420–646l* ✉ *sidycazapesca@hotmail.com.ar*) rents and sells equipment and offers guidance on wading and trolling for all experience levels as well as fly-fishing trips for experts.

HORSEBACK RIDING (CABALGATAS)

Hour-, day-, and week-long organized and guided rides, often with an *asado* (barbecue) included, can be arranged through local tour offices. **Cabalgatas Abuelo Enrique** (✉ *Callejón Ginsgins* ☎ *2972/426–465* ✉ *abueloenrique@smandes.com.ar*) offers rides with a guide for two hours or all day, asado included. To get there, take Avenida Dr. Koessler (R234) toward Zapala, turn left at the polo field, and head toward Lago Lolog, then take a right past the military barracks to Callejón Ginsgins.

MOUNTAIN BIKING

San Martín is flat, but from there everything goes up. Dirt and paved roads and trails lead through forests to lakes, waterfalls, and high mountain valleys. In town you can rent bikes at **HG Rodados** (✉ *Av. San Martín 1061* ☎ *2972/427–345*). Bikes are also at **Enduro Kawa & Bikes** (✉ *Elordi at Perito Moreno* ☎ *2972/427–093*). **Chapelco Ski Area** has good trails and mountain-biking lessons.

SKIING

The ski area and summer resort of **Cerro Chapelco** (✉ *Information Office: San Martín at Elordi* ☎ *2972/427–845* 🌐 *www.cerrochapelco.com*) is 23 km (14 mi) from town—18 km paved and 5 km of dirt road. Ideal for families and beginner to intermediate skiers, the area has modern facilities and lifts, including a high-speed *telecabina* (gondola) from the base. On a clear day almost all the runs are visible from the top (6,534 feet), and Lanín Volcano dominates the horizon. Lift tickets run 55 pesos–96 pesos per day, and equipment-rental facilities are available at the base camp (32 pesos–51 pesos per day for skis, boots, and poles). On some days cars need chains to get up to the mountain, so call and check the latest conditions before driving up. Taxis can also take you up or down

7

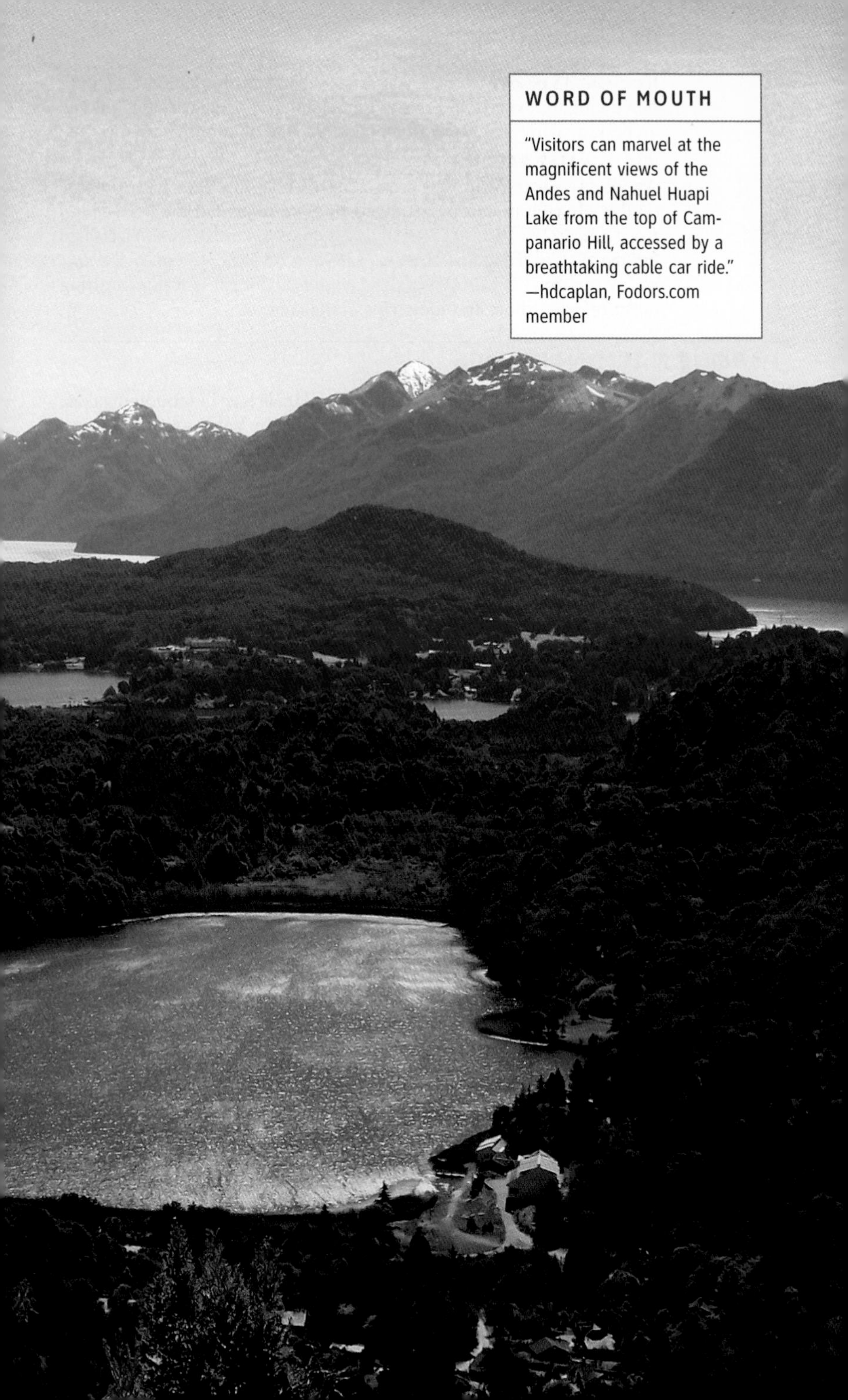

WORD OF MOUTH

"Visitors can marvel at the magnificent views of the Andes and Nahuel Huapi Lake from the top of Campanario Hill, accessed by a breathtaking cable car ride." —hdcaplan, Fodors.com member

for about 35 pesos each way. The summer Adventure Center has mountain biking for experts and classes for beginners, horseback rides, hiking, archery, a swimming pool, an alpine slide, and children's activities.

WHITE-WATER RAFTING

An all-day rafting trip that crosses into Chile on either Río Aluminé or Río Hua Hum can be arranged by **Siete Lagos Turismo** (✉ *General Roca 826* ☎ *2972/427–877* ✉ *sietelagostmo@smandes.com.ar*). **El Claro Turismo** (✉ *Col. Diaz 751* ☎ *2972/428–876 or 2972/425–876* 🌐 *www.elclaroturismo.com.ar* ✉ *elclaro@smandes.com.ar*) is a good rafting outfit offering short and long trips in the area.

PARQUE NACIONAL LANÍN

The dramatically beautiful **Parque Nacional Lanín** has 35 mountain lakes, countless rivers, ancient forests, and the Lanín Volcano. Tucked into the folds of the Andes along the Chilean border, it stretches 150 km (93 mi) north–south, covering 3,920 square km (1,508 square mi), and is the third-largest national park in Argentina. The area is home to the Mapuche, and you can learn about their history and buy their handicrafts in one of the 50 communities throughout the park.

GETTING HERE AND AROUND

Three towns have access to the park. The northernmost section is reached from the town of Aluminé (145 km [90 mi] west of Zapala on RP46), a typical Andean town with no paved streets but an abundance of nearby lakes (Aluminé, Quillén, and Mohquehue being the most accessible). The resort town of Pehuenia is a good base for exploring. Junín de los Andes, in the middle section, is at the end of the paved roads from either San Martín or Bariloche. San Martín, the major town in the park, is in the southern portion. All three of these towns have roads leading to the border with Chile (⇨ *Chilean Lakes Crossing box, below*). For information on the park, go to the **Intendencia de Parques Nacionales** (National Park Office) in San Martín. They have maps and information on all the parks and trails in the region, as well as fishing permits and information on big-game hunting. ✉ *E. Frey 749* ☎ *2972/427–233* ✉ *lanin@smandes.com.ar* ⏲ *Weekdays 8–1:30.*

EXPLORING

Found only in this part of the Andes, the ancient **Araucaria Araucana** tree grows to 100 feet, and has long spiny branches. Cones the size of bowling balls full of pinon nuts provided nourishment to the Mapuche, who call these trees *pehuenes*. The northern portion of the park near Lago Huechulaufquen and Aluminé is the best place to view these peculiar giants.

Volcán Lanín rises 12,378 feet in solitary snow-clad splendor on the western horizon, towering over the entire park and visible from every direction. The closest access is from Junín, but the northern route to Paso Tromen also offers endless photo ops through the tangled branches of the araucaria trees. You can climb Lanín in four days round-trip with a guide—or fly over it with **Aero Club de Los Andes** (✉ *Chapelco in San Martín de los Andes* ☎ *2972/491–379*).

SPORTS AND THE OUTDOORS

BOATING

You won't find piers or marinas on any of these lakes except at designated resorts. At Puerto Canoa on Lake Huechulafquen a catamaran takes about 50 passengers on a three-hour excursion to Lake Epulafquen, where you can view huge deposits of lava covered with vegetation at the end of the lake. The culprit, a large volcano minus its cone, looms in the distance. The fishing lodge at Paimún Lake has a dock, and in Villa Pehuenia you can rent boats and kayaks. The best way to organize a boating excursion is at the dock (arrive early) or through a tour operator.

FISHING

Professional fishing guides in San Martín de los Andes, Junín, and Aluminé have their favorite fishing spots, and they offer excursions for a day or a week. To contact a guide, go to 🌐 *www.neuquentur.gov.ar*. Fishing lodges lie concealed along the Chimihín River near Junín de los Andes and deeper into the lakes at Paimún. Smaller rivers such as the Malleo, Quillén, Meliquina, and Hua Hum are ideal for wading. In larger rivers like the Aluminé, Chimihuín, and Caleufu, guides provide rubber float boats.

HIKING

Besides climbing Lanín Volcano, trails throughout the park wind around lakes and streams, mostly at lower elevations. Signs are intermittent, so hiking with a guide is recommended. The best hikes are out of Lago Paimún to a waterfall, Lago Quillén near Aluminé, and Lácar near San Martín. For information, check out 🌐 *www.sendasybosques.com.ar*.

RAFTING

From San Martín you can run the Caleufu River from October through November, then move on to the Hua Hum in December through March. Both are Class II rivers. *Aluminé* in the Mapuche language means "clear," and this wide river in the northern section of the park provides a thrilling descent through dense vegetation and a deep canyon.

VILLA TRAFUL

60 km (37 mi) north of Villa La Angostura on R231 and R65; 39 km (23 mi) from Confluéncia on R65; 100 km (60 mi) northwest of Bariloche on R237 and R65.

If there were a prize for the most beautiful lake in the region, Lago Traful would win for its clarity, serenity, and wild surroundings. Small log houses peek through the cypress forest along the way to Villa Traful, a village of about 500 inhabitants. The town consists of log cabins, horse corrals, two fishing lodges, shops for picnic and fishing supplies, a school, a post office, and a park ranger's office. Well-maintained campgrounds border the lake, and ranches and private fishing lodges are hidden in the surrounding mountains. By day swimmers play on rocky beaches on the lake, a kayak cuts the still blue water, and divers go under to explore the mysteries of a submerged forest. Night brings silence, stars, and the glow of a lakeside campfire.

Continued on page 412

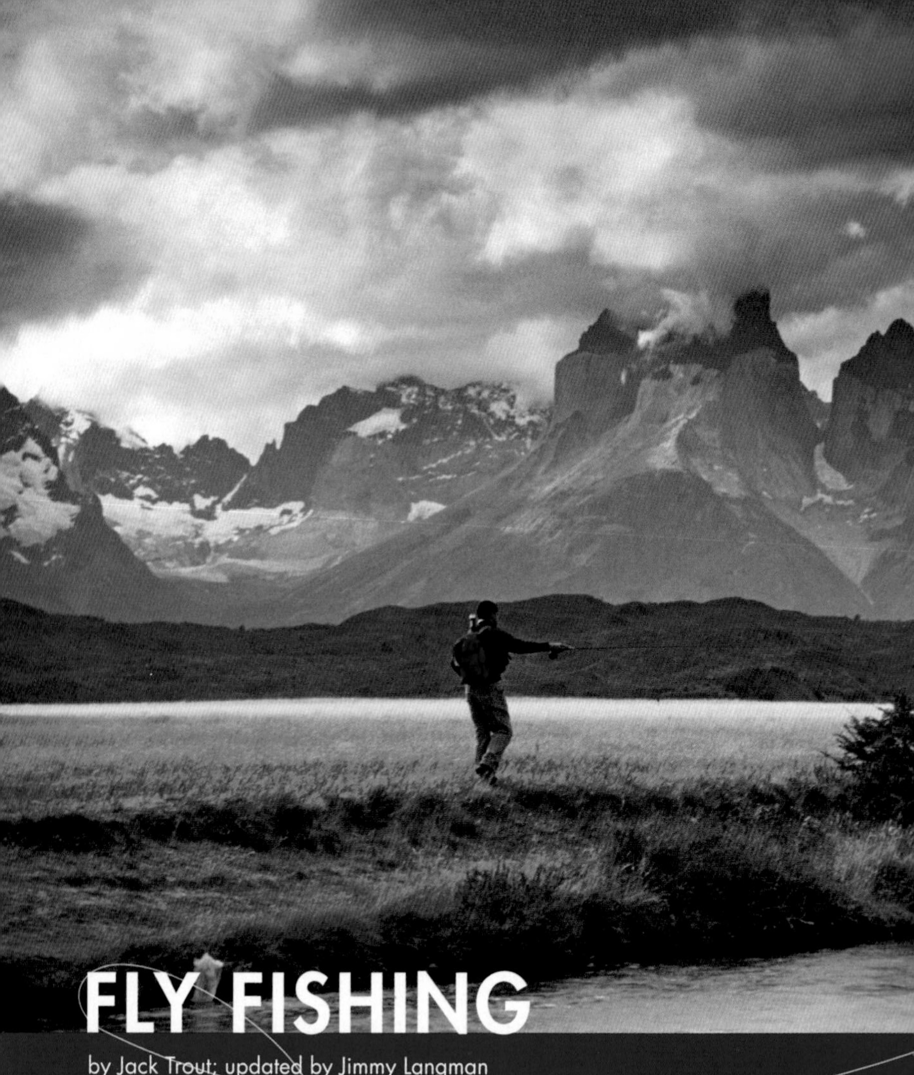

FLY FISHING

by Jack Trout; updated by Jimmy Langman

Chile and Argentina are the final frontier of fly fishing. With so many unexplored rivers, lakes, and spring creeks—most of which are undammed and free flowing to the ocean—every type of fishing is available for all levels of experience. You'll find many species of fish, including rainbow trout, browns, sea-run browns, brooks, sea trout, and steelhead.

Above: Flyfishing in Torres del Paine National Park, Patagonia, Chile

The Southern Cone has endless—and endlessly evolving—rivers, streams, and lakes, which is why they're so good for fly fishing. These waterways formed millions of years ago, as volcanic eruptions and receding glaciers carved out the paths for riverbeds and lakes that feed into the Pacific or Atlantic Oceans. With more than 2,006 volcanoes in Chile alone (including South America's most active mountain, Volcano Llaima, outside of Temuco), the Lake Districts of both countries are still evolving, creating raw and pristine fishing grounds.

Why choose Chile or Argentina for your next fly fishing adventure? If you're only after huge fish, stick to California. What these two South American countries offer is a chance to combine fishing, culture, and food in a unique package during the northern hemisphere's off season. With the right guide, you just might find yourself two hours down a dirt road, fishing turquoise water in the shadow of a glacial peak, with not a soul in sight but the occasional gaucho or huaso. It's an experience you will find nowhere else.

WHAT TO EXPECT ON THE GROUND

Fishing, Chile

LOGISTICS

You'll probably fly into Bariloche, Argentina, or Puerto Montt, Chile. You won't need more than two weeks for a good trip, and hiring a guide can make a big difference in the quality of your experience. Since most rivers are un-dammed, you'll need the extra help managing your drift boat or locating foot access for wading that stream you've spotted around the bend.

If you're fishing in Chile, be aware that the February 2010 earthquake affected some of the region's guides and lodges; call ahead to prevent planning a trip around a river or lodge that might be temporarily unavailable.

GUIDES VS. LODGES

You can purchase your trip package (usually between US $2,900 and US $5,500) through either an independent guide or a specific lodge property. In both cases, packages usually last one week to 10 days, and include breakfast, lunch, and dinner. If you opt to purchase through a lodge, you have the benefit of property-specific guides who know every nook and cranny of stream surrounding the lodge. On the other hand, hiring an independent guide will give you more power to customize your trip and go farther afield.

TIMING

Contact your guide or lodge in October or November, during the southern hemisphere's spring; the upcoming season's peak fishing times depend on snow melt. Plan on traveling in February or March.

CHOOSING YOUR GUIDE

What type of fishing suits you best? Do you like to fish from a boat, or do you prefer wading the river as it rushes by? Ask guides these questions to find the best one for you.

WHAT TO ASK A GUIDE

- How early do you start in the morning?
- Do you mainly spin cast or fly fish?
- How long have you been in business?
- Do you always catch and release?
- Will I fish with you or another guide?
- Can I see pictures of your raft or drift boat?
- Do you supply the flies?
- Where do you get your flies?
- Can we fish a river twice if we like it?
- Which rivers and lakes do you float?
- Can we set an itinerary before I arrive?

WHAT TO BRING

5 to 7 Weight Rod: at least 9 foot (consider bringing 9½ foot for larger rivers, windy days, lakes, and sink-tip streamer fishing).

Floating Lines: for dry fly fishing and nymphing.

Streamers: for use while wading to or from the drift boat.

Lines: 15 to 20 foot sink-tip lines with a sink rate of 5.5 to 8 inches per second. It's good to carry two to four different sink rate lines.

Intermediate sink lines: for lakes and shallow depth fishing.

Line Cleaner: because low-ozone areas (the hole in the ozone is close to Antarctica) will eat up lines if you don't treat and clean the lines daily.

Hook sharpener: most guides don't have this very important item.

Small gifts: for the people you meet. Gift-giving can help you gain access to private rivers and lakes. Chocolates, such as Hershey Kisses, or some unique fly pattern, such as a dragon fly, always go over well.

Good map: Turistel, in Chile, puts out the best maps and internal information for that country (w www.turistel.cl). Check Argentina Tourism (w www.turismo.gov.ar) for help with that country.

Coffee: Chile has Nescafé instant coffee just about everywhere you go. So if you like a good cup of joe, bring a filter and your favorite coffee. That way all you need is a cup and hot water, and you're all set for your morning fishing.

FLIES

■ Ask your guide where he or she gets flies. Those bought at a discount in countries outside of the United States are often sub-par, so get good guidance on this.

■ If you can, get a list of flies for the time of year you're scheduled to arrive and buy them in the United States before you go. Pay particular attention to the size as well type of insect.

■ The big fish and the quality catches are fooled by the flies that are tied by the guides themselves, because the guides know the hatches and the times they occur.

■ Flies are divided up into similar categories in Chile and Argentina since South America has many of the same insects as we do in North America. Check and see what time each insect is hatching. Note their sizes and colors. **You'll need both dry and nymph versions of the following, in a variety of sizes, colors, and patterns:**

Royal Wulff

Bead Head Pheasant Tail

Mudder Minnow

Living Damsel

Bitch Creek

Adams

ARGENTINA FLY-FISHING GUIDES AND RIVERS

Region, Trip Length, Season & Lake or Stream	Guides, Lodges, and Hostel Names	Phone	Web
SAN MARTIN DE LOS ANDES 5 to 7 days December–February Río Filo Huaum/ Parque y Reserva Nacional Lanin Río Careufu Río Collon Cura Río Quiquihue	Alejandro Bucannan	2972/424-767	www.flyfishing-sma.com
	Jorge Trucco	2972/427-561 or 429-561	www.jorgetrucco.com
	Pablo Zaleski / San Huberto Lodge	2972/422-921	www.chimehuinsp.com
	Estancia Tipiliuke	2972/429-466	www.tipiliuke.com
	La Chiminee	2972/427-617	n/a
	Lucas Rodriquez	2972/428-270	n/a
JUNIN DE LOS ANDES 5 to 7 days December–February Río Malleo Río Chimehuin Río Alumine	Alejandro Bucannan	2972/424-767 or 2944/1530-9469	www.flyfishing-sma.com
	Estancia Quemquemtreu	2972/424-410	www.quemquemtreu.com
	Redding Fly Shop Travel	800/669-3474 (in US)	www.flyfishingtravel.com
BARILOCHE 4 to 6 days December–February Río Limay Río Manso Río Traful Lago Fonk Parque y Reserva Nacional Nahuel Huapi	Martin Rebora / Montan Cabins	2944/525-314	www.patagoniasinfronteras.com
	Río Manso Lodge	2944/430-154	www.Ríomansolodge.com
	Estancia Peuma Hue	2944/501-030	www.peuma-hue.com
	Estancia Arroyo Verde	5411/4801-7448	www.estanciaarroyoverde.com.ar
	Hotel Piedras	2944/435-073	www.laspiedrashotel.com.ar
ESQUEL 5 to 7 days December–February Río Rivadavia Arroyo Pescado Río Carrileufu Río Pico – Lago Senquer Parque Argentino Los Alerces	Esquel Outfitters	2944/462-776 or 406/581-1760 (in US)	www.esqueloutfitters.com
	Guided Connections	307/734-2448 (in US)	www.guidedconnections.com
	Patagonia River Guides	2945/457-020 (in Argentina) or 406/835-3122 (in US)	www.patagoniariverguides.com
	Angelina Hostel	2945/452-763	n/a
	Hotel Tehuelche	2945/452-420	n/a

NOT NATIVE

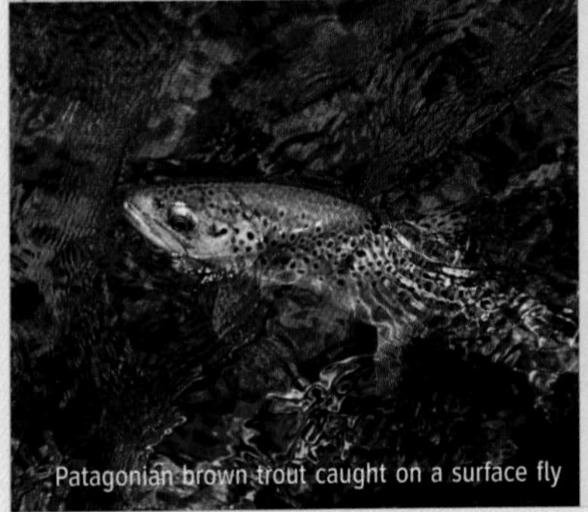
Patagonian brown trout caught on a surface fly

Trout, salmon, and other common species aren't indigenous to South America. These fish were introduced during the late 19th century, mostly as a result of demand from European settlers. Germans, Scots, and others needed trout-filled rivers to survive, so they stocked the New World streams in the image of those in the Old World. For more information, consult *Fly Fishing in Chilean Patagonia* by Gonzalo Cortes and Nicolas Piwonka or *Fly Fishing the Best Rivers of Patagonia Argentina* by Francisco Bedeschi.

CHILE FLY-FISHING GUIDES AND RIVERS

Region, Trip length, Season & Lake or Stream	Guides, Lodges, and Hostel Names	Phone	Web
PALENA AREA 5 to 7 days December–April Río Palena Río Rosselott Río Yelcho Río Futaleufu Lago Yelcho Parque y Reserva Nacional Palena Parque y Reserva Nacional Corcovado	Jack Trout	530/926-4540 (in US) 65/511-673 (in Chile)	www.jacktrout.com
	Chucao Lodge	2/201-8571	www.chucaolodge.com
	Yelcho Lodge	65/576-005	www.yelcho.cl
	Tres Piedras / Francisco Castano	65/330-157 or 9/7618-7526	www.trespiedras.cl
	Martin Pescador Lodge	207/350-8178 (in US)	martinpescadorfishing.com
PUERTO VARAS AREA 4 to 6 days December–March Río Petrohue Río Puelo Río Maullin Parque y Reserva Saltos de Petrohue	Jack Trout	530/926-4540 (in US) 65/511-673 (in Chile)	www.jacktrout.com
	Tres Piedras / Francisco Castano	65/330-157 or 9/7618-7526	www.trespiedras.cl
	Fundo Santa Ines	9/9430-1030 or 9/9235-5648	www.fundosantaines.cl
	Hotel Licarayen Puerto Varas	65/232-305	www.hotellicarayen.cl
	Hotel Puerto Pilar	65/335-378	www.hotelpuertopilar.cl
	Fish-Haus	65/438-973	www.fish-haus.com
COYHAIQUE AREA 4 to 7 days December–April Río Simpson Río Nirehuoa Río Paloma Río Azul Río Manihuales Lago Pollux Parque y Reserva Nacional Simpson Parque y Reserva Nacional Cerro Castillo	La Pasarela Lodge & Cabins	9/981-87390	www.lapasarela.cl
	Heart of Patagonia Lodge		www.patagoniachileflyfish-ing.com
	Esteban Osorio	9/9342-5562	n/a
	Eduardo Otarola	99/946-1943	n/a
	Rex Bryngelson	67/236-402	www.chilepatagonia.com
	Alex Príor	98/920-9132	www.flyfishingcoyhaique.com
	El Saltamontes Lodge	67/232-779 or 67/211-111	www.elsaltamonteslodge.com
	Troy Cowles	99/992-3199	n/a
RÍO BAKER & COCHRANE AREAS 4 to 6 days Janurary–April Río Baker Río Cochrane Parque Reserva Nacional Cerro Castillo	David Frederick	406/842-7158 (in US) 98/138-3530 (in Chile)	www.southernlatitudes.com
	Alex Príor	98/920-9132	www.flyfishingcoyhaique.com
	Green Baker Lodge – Río Baker	72/491-418 or 2/196-0409	www.greenbakerlodge.com
LAKES DISTRICT: PUCON & VILLARRICA 2 to 4 days Nov–Dec., then Mar.–May Río Trancura, Parque Villarrica Lago Quillen, Parque Nacional Lanin Río Quillen, Parque Nacional Lanin	Marío's Fishing Zone	99/760-7280	www.flyfishingpucon.com
	Off Limits	45/444-327	www.offlimits..cl
	Alma Verde	45/444-324	www.almaverde.cl

ESSENTIALS

Visitor Info Oficina Municipal de Turismo (✉ *Across from municipal pier* ☎ *2944/479–099* ✉ *trafultruismo@ciudad.com.ar*).

WHERE TO EAT AND STAY

During the slow season (October–November) some resaurants close, so call first.

$–$$ ARGENTINE ✕ **Alto Traful.** You'll be ready for a hearty dinner of steak, local game, or trout after you climb the stairs to this hillside aerie built by affable owner/craftsman Daniel. A potbellied woodstove sits in the middle of the room, and the view from floor-to-ceiling windows inspires guests to linger over homemade cakes and coffee. You can drive up a steep road and park in back. ✉ *R65, Km 32.5* ✣ *West of town* ☎ *2944/479–073* ✉ *altotraful@yahoo.com.ar* ▭ *MC, V.*

$$–$$$ ARGENTINE ✕ **La Terraza.** This is the local parrilla, with Patagonian lamb and goat plus all the usual beef cuts served in a brightly lighted dining room that looks through the forest to the lake. ✉ *RP65, Km 35.5* ✣ *Across the bridge west of town* ☎ *2944/479–077* ▭ *MC, V.*

$$$$ **Estancia Arroyo Verde.** Situated in the Andean foothills an hours' drive from the Bariloche airport, this 12,500 acre working cattle ranch in the Traful Valley borders a rocky cove at the end of Lago Traful, where the river of the same name runs across the property, providing some of the best fishing in Patagonia. Testimonials from expert anglers and pleased equestrians praise the scenery, accommodations, guides, and the quality of fishing and riding. The camaraderie between guests and owners, as they gather for drinks and meals in the historic ranch house or for an asado by the lake is part of an experience that brings visitors back year after year. You'll need to reserve, tough; guests are picked up at the airport, driven an hour north of Confluencia on a tough-to-navigate dirt road, and escorted through the two locked addressless gates. **Pros:** old world charm; unique setting; warm hospitality. **Cons:** 2-night minimum stay; accessible only with reservation. ✉ *Billinghurst 2586, piso 3, Buenos Aires* ☎ *5411/4801–7448* 🌐 *www.estanciaarroyoverde.com.ar* *4 rooms; 1 suite; 1 cabin* *In-room: no a/c, no phone, no TV. In-hotel: bar, water sports, no kids under 12* ▭ *No credit cards* ⊙ *Closed May–Oct.* *FAP.*

$$–$$$ **Marinas Puerto Traful.** Across the road from the lake is this bright-blue lodge with flower boxes lining the wooden porches of the seven upstairs rooms. Inside, the newly refurbished rooms have quiet beige carpeting, white walls and linens, and a bright-orange Mapuche blanket folded across the bed for a splash of color. All the decoration you need is outside the window. Breakfast is served in an all-purpose room that opens onto the deck facing the lake. **Pros:** lake views. **Cons:** no telephone; no Internet. ✉ *R65, Villa Traful* ☎ *2944/475–284* 🌐 *www.marinaspuertotraful.com.ar* *16 rooms, 1 suite* ▭ *No credit cards.*

SPORTS AND THE OUTDOORS

HIKING

Arroyo Blanco and Arroyo Coa Có. Drive, walk, or pedal about 3 km (2 mi) up from the village to the trailhead at Pampa de los Alamos, a clearing where the trail to Arroyo Blanco descends into a forest of 1,000-year-

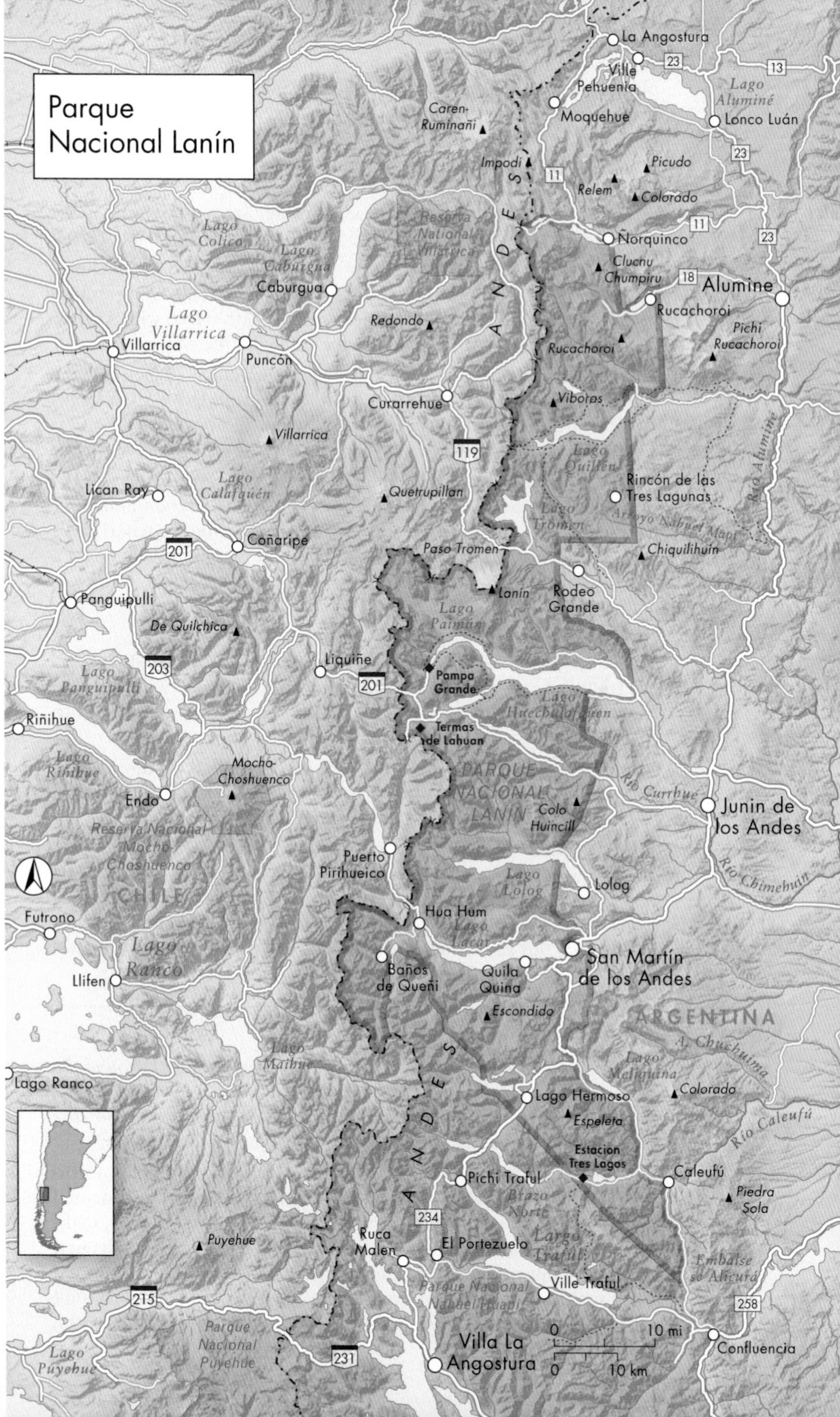
Parque Nacional Lanín
La Angostura
Ville Pehuenia
Moquehue
Lago Aluminé
Lonco Luán
Caren-Ruminañi
Impodi
Picudo
Relem
Colorado
Reserva National Villarrica
Lago Colico
Lago Caburgua
Ñorquinco
Clucnu Chumpiru
Alumine
Caburgua
Rucachoroi
Lago Villarrica
Redondo
Pichi Rucachoroi
Villarrica
Puncón
Rucachoroi
Curarrehue
Viboras
Villarrica
Lago Quillen
Río Alumine
Lago Calafquén
Rincón de las Tres Lagunas
Lican Ray
Quetrupillan
Lago Tromen
Arroyo Nahuel Mapi
Coñaripe
Paso Tromen
Chiquilihuin
Rodeo Grande
Panguipulli
Lanín
Lago Paimún
De Quilchica
Liquiñe
Pampa Grande
Lago Panguipulli
Lago Huechulafquen
Riñihue
Termas de Lahuan
Lago Riñihue
Mocho-Choshuenco
Parque Nacional Lanín
Río Currhue
Endo
Colo Huincill
Junin de los Andes
Reserva Nacional Mocho-Choshuenco
Puerto Pirihueico
Lago Lolog
Río Chimehuin
Chile
Lolog
Futrono
Hua Hum
Lago Lacar
Lago Ranco
Baños de Queñi
Quila Quina
San Martín de los Andes
Llifen
Escondido
Argentina
Lago Maihue
A. Chuchuima
Lago Meliquina
Lago Ranco
Lago Hermoso
Colorado
Espeleta
Río Caleufú
Estacion Tres Lagos
Pichi Traful
Caleufú
Brazo Norte
Piedra Sola
Ruca Malen
El Portezuelo
Largo Traful
Puyehue
Embalse so Alicurá
Ville Traful
Parque Nacional Nahuel Huapi
Parque Nacional Puyehue
Lago Puyehue
Villa La Angostura
Confluencia
Andes
0
10 mi
0
10 km
23
13
23
11
11
23
18
119
201
201
203
234
215
231
258

old *coihué* trees with their ghostly naked trunks, gigantic *lenga* (deciduous beech), and *ñires* that grow only at high altitudes. The trail leads to a wooden walkway along a steep cliff—the only way one could possibly view the waterfall tumbling 66 feet into a dark chasm. Follow the wooden trail along the cliff for increasingly frightening glimpses of this wild gorge, then return up the same route. Arroyo Coa Có is in the opposite direction, with a view of both the waterfall and Lago Traful.

A strenuous hike (seven hours) from the village to **Cerro Negro** climbs up through forests of cypress, coihués, lenga, and ñires, passing strange rock formations, then it reaches the summit at 6,000 feet, with a splendid view of Lago Traful and across the Andes all the way to Lanín.

Casacada Co Lemú thunders with a deafening roar down 20 meters at the end of an arduous trail (19 km [12 mi] round-trip). Drive 8 km (5 mi) west toward the Seven Lakes Route to the bridge over Arroyo Cataratas. Before you cross the stream, on your left, the trail climbs slowly at first, then straight up 1,500 meters to the falls.

Laguna Las Mellizas y Pinturas Rupestres (The Twins Lagoon and Cave paintings). A 15-minute boat trip across the lake from the wharf takes you to a sandy beach on the northern shore. A two-hour walk down a trail into a steep gully leads to the pools. Nearby caves with 600-year-old Tehuelche cave paintings are worth exploring.

FISHING

This area is famous for its landlocked salmon and record-breaking-size trout in Lago Traful and the Laguna Las Mellizas (Twins Lagoon) 5 km (3 mi) north of town. Fishing season runs from November 15 to April 15.

Osvaldo Brandeman (✉ *Villa Traful* ☎ *2944/479–048* ✉ *pescaosvaldo@hotmail.com*) is a local fishing guide. **Andrés Quelín** (✉ *Villa Traful* ☎ *2944/479–005*) is a fishing guide and rents boats at the marina.

SCUBA DIVING

In 1975 a violent earthquake caused half a mountain and its forest of cypress trees to slide to the bottom of the lake, creating the **Bosque Submergido**. You can dive to 30 meters (98 feet) in crystalline water and explore this sunken forest. Boat trips can be arranged at Cabañas Aiken (☎ *2944/479–048*).

VILLA LA ANGOSTURA

81 km (50 mi) northwest of Bariloche (a 1-hr drive on R231 around the east end of Lago Nahuel Huapi; also accessible by boat from Bariloche); 90 km (56 mi) southwest of San Martín de los Andes on R234 (the Seven Lakes Rte., partly unpaved and closed for much of winter).

Once a lakeside hamlet on a narrow *angostura* (isthmus) on the northern shore of Lake Nahuel Huapi, this small resort town has benefited from thoughtful planning and strict adherence to business codes, making it the second-most popular tourist area in the Lake District. Its first hotel was built in 1923, 10 years before the town was founded, and today some of the most luxurious hotels and resorts in Patagonia look out on the lake from discreet hiding places along its wooded shores.

Lanín Volcano, an ice-clad, cone-shaped stratovolcano, in Parque Nacional Lanín.

Shops and restaurants line the Avenida Arrayanes, where you can stop for homemade ice cream or cakes while window-shopping in the three-block-long commercial area. The tourist office and municipal buildings are at El Cruce (the Crossroads), where R231 from Bariloche to the Chilean border intersects with the road to the port and the Seven Lakes Route, R234, to San Martín de los Andes.

GETTING HERE AND AROUND

Buses from Bariloche are fast and frequent, but a car is the best way to get around the area and visit the town, which is creeping slowly from Lago Correntoso to Puerto Manzano. Bicycles are often available in hotels or can be rented in town.

ESSENTIALS

Visitor and Tour Info Secretaría de Turismo y Cultura (✉ *Av. Siete Lagos 93, at southern end of Av. Arrayanes* ☎ *2944/494–124*). **Villa La Angostura** (✉ *Siete Lagos at Av. Arrayanes* ☎ *2944/494–124* 🌐 *www.villalaangostura.gov.ar*).

WHERE TO EAT

$$$ ARGENTINE ✕ **Australis.** This is one of the best microbreweries in Patagonia. The excellent cuisine integrates beer, all the way through to dessert—a memorable flan is made with chocolate and a delicious stout. The restaurant will cook up your own freshly caught fish if you bring it in. ✉ *Av. Arrayanes (R231) 2490* ☎ *2944/495–645* 💳 *AE, DC, MC, V.*

$ ARGENTINE ✕ **La Casita de la Oma.** Between the bay and the main street, this teahouse, with its award-winning garden, serves homemade cakes, pies, and scones. Moist chocolate brownie cake with dulce de leche (sweet carmelized milk) is a winner, as is a pile of filo leaves with dulce de leche and meringue on top. Jars of jam line the shelves. ✉ *Cerro Inacayal*

303 ☎ 2544/494–602 ▭ MC, V ⊙ Closed May.

$$$ ARGENTINE ✕ **Waldhaus.** This Hansel and Gretel dark-timbered log house outside of town is open for lunch, tea, and dinner. It serves Argentine food with a Germanic flavor: goulash, spaetzle, fondue, and Patagonian lamb. The interior is a riot of hearts and flowers, with Swiss canton shields on the walls and ceilings. ✉ *Av. Arrayanes (R231) 6431 ☎ 2944/495–123 ▭ No credit cards ⊙ Closed Mar.–June and Mon.–Tues. July–Oct. No lunch Mon.–Thurs. and July–Oct.*

LOCAL SHOPS

One of the best of the many chocolate shops is **En El Bosque** (✉ *Av. Arrayanes 218 ☎ 2944/495–738*), a delicious artisanal producer where the smells of homemade sweets waft out onto the sidewalk; this one also doubles as a little teahouse. Delicious homemade jams (*dulces caseros*) are sold in nearly every shop. **Tanino** (✉ *Av. Arrayanes 172 ☎ 2944/494–411*) has the best selection of furs and leather goods—boots, belts, jackets, bags, and purses—in town.

WHERE TO STAY

$$$$ **Costa Serena.** Every room at this complex in Puerto Manzano has a lake view. A-frame *cabañas* (cabins) with decks, kitchens, and outdoor barbecues sleep up to seven. Suites have huge wooden Jacuzzis with views to the water. During high season a one-week minimum stay is required in cabins. A large swimming pool and deck with grill, kayaks, and boats are on the lake. **Pros:** good family reunion spot. **Cons:** far from town and tourist attractions. ✉ *Los Pinos 435, Puerto Manzano ☎ 2944/494–053 ⊕ www.costaserenavla.com.ar ⇨ 7 rooms, 3 suites, 4 cabins ☝ In-hotel: restaurant, bar, pool, gym, beachfront ▭ AE, MC, V ⍘ CP.*

$$$$ Fodor's Choice ★ **Hotel Correntoso.** You can see the fish jump from your bedroom window, your dining table, the glass-paneled deck, or from the refurbished 100-year-old fishing bar down by the lake. Perched on a hill where the Correntoso River runs into Nahuel Huapi Lake, this landmark hotel celebrates its place in history with old photos, light fixtures made from colihué branches, handwoven Mapuche fabrics, and custom-made furniture. The bar often has live music, and the restaurant ($$$$) overlooking the lake serves Patagonian specialties such as hare, wild boar, lamb, beef, and, of course, fish from local lakes and streams. A downstairs playroom, conference room, indoor-outdoor pool, and spa with a riveting view from the massage table all look out onto blue Nahuel Huapi Lake. Children under 10 who are not hotel guests are not allowed in the dining room, but they are welcome in the original fisherman's shack on the lake, which has been converted to a casual café-bar serving snacks and sandwiches. **Pros:** great location, food, spa; well-organized excursions. **Cons:** expensive. ✉ *RN231, Km 86, Puente Correntoso ☎ 2944/1561–9727; 11/4803–0030 in Buenos Aires ⊕ www.correntoso.com ⇨ 16 rooms, 16 suites ☝ In-hotel: restaurant, bar, pool, spa, children's programs, public Wi-Fi ▭ AE, MC, V.*

$$ **Naranjo en Flor.** This tranquil mountainside retreat in Puerto Manzano looks like a Norman hunting lodge, yet feels like home with a fireplace in the living room and a piano bar and playroom for bad-weather days. The restaurant offers interesting modern French cuisine. The modern

carpeted bedrooms have big windows and tasteful antiques. **Pros:** personal attention. **Cons:** off the main route; requires a car. ✉ *Chucao 62, Puerto Manzano* ☎ *2955/494–863* *naranjoenflor@infovia.com.ar* *8 rooms* *In-hotel: restaurant, bar, pool* *AE, V* *CP.*

$$$$ Fodor's Choice ★ **Puerto Sur.** Stone and wood merge throughout the angular space of this hotel in Puerto Manzano. Built into the side of a hill, with views of the lake and mountains from enormous windows, every room has a lake view, Jacuzzi, and restrained modern art. The spa, indoor-outdoor pool, and private beach, plus impeccable service make the reasonable prices a pleasant surprise—near the bottom of the $$$$ range. A few extra pesos get you a private deck. **Pros:** quiet, secluded spot. **Cons:** far from town and tourist activities. ✉ *Los Pinos 221, Puerto Manzano, Villa La Angostura* ☎ *2944/475–399* *www.hosteriapuertosur.com.ar* *7 rooms, 3 suites, 4 cabins* *In-hotel: restaurant, bar, pool, gym, beachfront, public Wi-Fi* *AE, MC, V* *CP.*

SPORTS AND THE OUTDOORS

FISHING

The **Río Correntoso,** reputed to be the shortest river in the world (260 meters), flows from Lago Correntoso beneath a bridge into Nahuel Huapi Lake, where fly-fishermen from the world over have been coming since the 1920s to catch and release record-breaking-size trout. Trolling, spinning, or fly-fishing from land or by boat in the lagoons and inlets of Nahuel Huapi will take you to spots of incredible scenic beauty and solitude. To arrange a one- to five-day fishing excursion, rent or purchase equipment, or hire a guide, contact **Patagonia Fly** (✉ *Av. Arrayanes 282* ☎ *2944/494–634* *www.patagonfly.com*) at the **Banana Fly Shop.**

HORSEBACK RIDING

Most trails used for hiking and mountain biking are also used for horseback riding. Horses are available from **Los Saucos** (✉ *R231, Km 61.8 [Av. Arrayanes 2500]* ☎ *2944/494–853*). Another good riding outfit is **Cahuel Hueñi** (✉ *Av. Siete Lagos* ☎ *2944/1561–4034*). **Cabalgatas Correntoso** (✉ *Cacique Antriao 1850, on the road toward Mirador Belvedere* ☎ *2944/1560–4903 or 2944/1551–0559* *www.cabalgatacorrentoso.com.ar*) offers three day trips—a 2-hour lakeside jaunt, a 3½-hour waterfall riding-hiking trip, or a 9-hour circuit to the valley of Cajón Negro, which includes lunch and a swim; there are also two- to four-day trips into the mountains.

HIKING

Access to the Río Bonito trail is 1 km (½ mi) from the base of the ski area at Cerro Bayo. It climbs 500 meters to a waterfall. The trailhead for a longer hike, to Inacayal Fall, is on the right-hand side of R231 just before you arrive at El Cruce. After climbing 1,200 meters (¾ mi), you arrive at a 50-meter-high (164-foot-high) waterfall. Continue another 300 feet to a lookout over Lake Correntoso.

MOUNTAIN BIKING

The area has more bike-rental shops than gas stations. You can easily ride from the village to Laguna Verde, near the port, or off the Seven Lakes Route to Mirador Belvedere and on to the waterfalls at Inacayal. The tourist office has a brochure, *Paseos y Excursiones,* with maps, distances, and descriptions (in Spanish) of mountain-biking, hiking, and horseback-riding trails.

Maps, information, and rentals are at **Free Bikes** (✉ *Las Fucsias 268* ☎ *2944/495–047* 🌐 *www.freebikes.com.ar*) in Las Cruces. **IAN Bikes** (✉ *Topa Topa 102, at Las Fucsias* ☎ *2944/495–005*) rents bikes, too, as does **Mountain Bike Cerro Bayo** (☎ *2944/495–047* ✉ *angosturafreebikes@yahoo.com.ar*) at the base of Cerro Bayo.

SKIING

Cerro Bayo (☎ *2944/494–189* 🌐 *www.cerrobayoweb.com*) is 9 km (5½ mi) from El Cruce via R66. During ski season (July–September) skiers and boarders glide over 12 km (7½ mi) of skiable terrain—most of it on 21 easy to intermediate groomed runs. With a 6,000-foot uninterrupted vertical drop and scenic off-piste skiing, this small ski area is much less crowded than neighboring Bariloche. Six double chairlifts, four tele-ski, and two surface lifts access the mid-station and the summit (5,000 feet), where a panoramic trail (open in summer for mountain biking) wends its way down 5 km (3 mi) around the mountain, offering a wide view of Nahuel Huapi Lake. Rental equipment and lessons are at the base facility next to El Refugio Chaltén, where goulash, lamb stew, snacks, and beverages are served. At mid-mountain, Tronadór café has snacks and lunch.

PARQUE NACIONAL NAHUEL HUAPI

Created in 1934, the Parque Nacional Nahuel Huapi is Argentina's oldest national park. The park extends over 2 million acres along the eastern side of the Andes in the provinces of Neuquén and Río Negro, on the frontier with Chile. It contains the highest concentration of lakes in Argentina. The biggest is Lago Nahuel Huapi, an 897-square-km (346-square-mi) body of water whose seven long arms (the longest is 96 km [60 mi] long, 12 km [7 mi] wide) reach deep into forests of *coihué* (a native beech tree), *cyprés* (cypress), and *lenga* (deciduous beech) trees. Intensely blue across its vast expanse and aqua green in its shallow bays, the lake meanders into distant lagoons and misty inlets where the mountains, covered with vegetation at their base, rise straight up out of the water. Every water sport invented and tours to islands and other lakes can be arranged through local travel agencies, tour offices, and hotels. Information offices throughout the park offer help in exploring the miles of mountain and woodland trails and the lakes.

Having landed in Bariloche, you can explore the park on an organized tour or on your own. Nearby excursions such as the Circuito Chico, Circuito Grande, a trip to Tronadór, or the ski area at Catedral can be done in a day. Since much of the park is covered by Nahuel Huapi Lake (it's 96 km [57 mi] long, covering 346 square mi), some of your exploration will be by boat to islands, down narrow fjords, or to distant shores on organized excursions. Small towns like Villa La Angostura and Villa Traful are excellent destinations for further explorations on foot or horseback to smaller lakes with their connecting streams, waterfalls, and surrounding forests and high peaks. Since most of the park is at a low elevation (under 6,000 feet), getting around in winter is not difficult—just cold. Fall foliage, long, warm summer days, and spring flowers are the rewards of other seasons. Park entry is 12 pesos.

GETTING AROUND

The easy way to get around is to plan your days with a local tour operator or remis, or hire a rental car, mixing up excursions between land and lake. When planning all-day or overnight trips, remember that distances are long and unpaved roads slow you down.

ESSENTIALS

Visitor Info **Intendencia del Parque Nacional Nahuel Huapi** (✉ *Av. San Martín 24 [at the Civic Center], Bariloche* ☎ *2944/423–111* 🌐 *www.parquesnacionales.gov.ar*).

EXPLORING

The most popular excursion on Lago Nahuel Huapi is the 30-minute boat ride from Puerto Pañuelo at Llao Llao to **Isla Victoria**, the largest island in the lake. A grove of redwoods transplanted from California thrives in the middle of the island. Walk on trails that lead to enchanting views of emerald bays and still lagoons. Then board the boat to sail on to the Paraque Nacional los Arrayanes.

The **Parque Nacional los Arrayanes** (✉ *12 km [7½ mi] along a trail from the Península Quetrihué* ☎ *2944/423–111*) is the only forest of arrayanes in the world. These trees absorb so much water through their thin skins that all other vegetation around them dies, leaving a barren forest of peeling cinnamon-color trunks. A one-hour stroll up and down wide wooden steps and walkways is a unique experience, as light filters through the twisted naked trunks, reflecting a weird red glow. You can make this excursion from the pier at Bahía Brava in Villa La Angostura (or by boat from Bariloche via Isla Victoria). In summer months you can walk (three hours) or ride a bike, after registering at the *Guardaparque* office (ranger station) near the pier. Leave in the morning, as entrance to the park closes at 2 PM. A nice combination is to go by boat and return by bicycle (it's all downhill that way). If returning by boat, buy your return ticket at the pier before you leave.

Boats to Isla Victoria and Parque Nacional los Arrayanes leave from Puerto Pañuelo, on the Península Llao Llao. They run twice daily (more in high season), at 10 AM and 2 PM. The earlier departure includes time for lunch on the island in a cafeteria-style restaurant. The later departure is a shorter trip. Boats are run by **Cau Cau** (✉ *Mitre 139, Bariloche* ☎ *2944/431–372* 🌐 *www.islavictoriayarrayanes.com*) and **Turisur** (✉ *Mitre 219, Bariloche* ☎ *2944/426–109* 🌐 *www.bariloche.com/turisur*).

A visit to **Monte Tronadór** (Thunder Mountain) requires an all-day outing covering 170 km (105 mi) round-trip from Bariloche. The 12,000-foot extinct volcano, the highest mountain in the northern Lake District, straddles the frontier with Chile, with one peak on either side. Take R258 south along the shores of Lago Gutiérrez and Lago Mascardi. Between the two lakes the road crosses from the Atlantic to the Pacific watershed. At Km 35, turn off onto a road marked TRONADÓR and

DID YOU KNOW?

Church bells sounding in clear air, wide streets leading to lakefront vistas—Bariloche is hard to dislike.

PAMPA LINDA and continue along the shore of Lago Mascardi, passing a village of the same name. Just beyond the village the road forks, and you continue on a gravel road, R254. Near the bridge the road branches left to Lago Hess and Cascada Los Alerces—a detour you might want to take on your way out.

As you bear right after crossing Los Rápidos Bridge, the road narrows to one direction only: it's important to remember this when you set out in the morning, as you can only go up the road before 2 PM and down it after 4 PM. The lake ends in a narrow arm (Brazo Tronadór) at the Hotel Tronadór, which has a dock for tours arriving by boat. The road then follows the Río Manso to **Pampa Linda,** which has a lodge, restaurant, park ranger's office, campsites, and the trailhead for the climb up to the Refugio Otto Meiling at the snow line. Guided horseback rides are organized at the lodge. The road ends 7 km (4½ mi) beyond Pampa Linda in a parking lot that was once at the tip of the now receding **Glaciar Negro** (Black Glacier). As the glacier flows down from the mountain, the dirt and black sediment of its lateral moraines are ground up and cover the ice. At first glance it's hard to imagine the tons of ice that lie beneath its black cap.

WHERE TO STAY

$$$$ **Isla Victoria Lodge.** The stone and wood structure on a cliff overlooking the lake and forests of coihues and cypresses, with its clean architecture and quiet interior of white walls, pine trim, leather upholstery, and fine Mapuche woven rugs, conveys a sense of peace and unity with the natural surroundings. Using some of the foundations of the original lodge, built in 1937 and destroyed by fire in 1982, the whole project is a labor of love by its owners, who bought the site and transformed it into a unique spa hotel in one of the most beautiful settings on earth. **Pros:** price includes alcoholic drinks and on-site activities (including horseback riding); hiking trails. **Cons:** nightlife is relegated to stargazing. ✉ *IslaVictoria CC 26, Nahuel Huapi National Park* ☎ *11/4394–9605* 🌐 *www.maresur.com* *20 rooms, 2 suites* *In-room: safe, Internet, Wi-Fi. In-hotel: restaurant, room service, bar, pool, spa, beachfront, water sports, bicycles, laundry service, Wi-Fi hotspot, no kids under 12* ▭ *AE, MC, V* *FAP.*

SPORTS AND THE OUTDOORS

For information on mountain climbing, trails, *refugios* (mountain huts), and campgrounds, visit the **Intendencia del Parque Nacional Nahuel Huapi** (✉ *Av. San Martín 24* ✥ *at the Civic Center, Bariloche* ☎ *2944/423–111* 🌐 *www.parquesnacionales.gov.ar*).

HIKING

Nahuel Huapi National Park has many forest trails near Bariloche, El Bosón, and Villa La Angostura. For day hikes in the forest along the shore of Nahuel Huapi Lake or to a nearby waterfall, search for trails along the Circuito Chico in the Parque Llao Llao. For altitude and grand

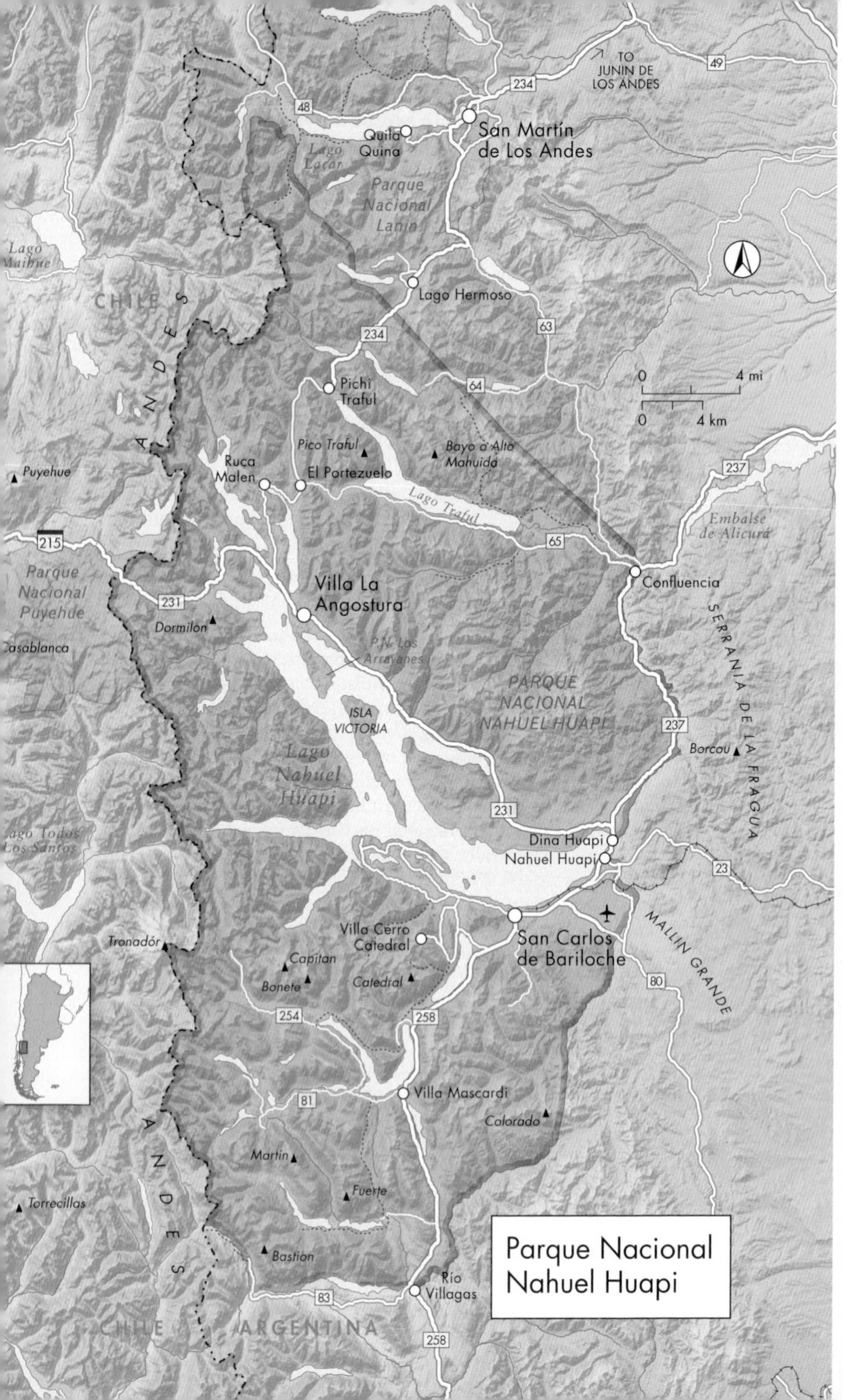

Parque Nacional Nahuel Huapi

panoramas, take the ski lift to the top of Cerro Catedral and follow the ridge trail to Refugio Frey, returning down to the base of the ski area.

West of Bariloche, turn right at Villa Mascardi onto the dirt road to Pampa Linda (⇨ *Exploring; Monte Tronadór, above*). From there you can hike a long day or overnight to Otto Meiling hut, or make shorter forays to the glacier or nearby waterfalls. A three-day trek will take you right past Tronadór and its glacier, along the Alerce River, and over the Paso de los Nubes (Clouds Pass) to Puerto Bless, returning to Bariloche by boat. Hiking guides can be recommended by local tour offices. For trail maps and information on all of the Lake District, look for the booklet (in Spanish) *Guía Sendas y Bosques* (Guide to Trails and Forests) sold at kiosks and bookstores. For ambitious treks, mountaineering, or use of mountain huts and climbing permits, contact **Club Andino Bariloche** (✉ *20 de Febrero 30* ☎ *2944/422–266* 🌐 *www.clubandino.org*). Click on the *mapas* link on the Web site.

MOUNTAIN BIKING

The entire Nahuel Huapi National Park is ripe for all levels of mountain biking. Popular rides go from the parking lot at the Cerro Catedral ski area to Lago Gutiérrez and down from Cerro Otto. Local tour agencies can arrange guided tours by the hour or day and even international excursions to Chile. Rental agencies provide maps and suggestions and sometimes recommend guides.

Dirty Bikes (✉ *Vice Almirante O'Connor 681* ☎ *2944/425–616* 🌐 *www.dirtybikes.com.ar*) offers local day trips all over the Lake District, including long-distance trips to Chile and back, for all ages and abilities. **La Bolsa del Deporte** (✉ *Diagonal Capraro 1081* ☎ *944/433–111*) rents and sells bikes.

WHITE-WATER RAFTING

With all the interconnected lakes and rivers in the national park, there's everything from your basic family float down the swift-flowing, scenic Río Limay to a wild and exciting ride down Río Manso (Class II), which takes you 16 km (10 mi) in three hours. If you're really adventurous, you can take the Manso all the way to Chile (Class IV). **Alunco** (✉ *Moreno 187* ☎ *2944/422–283* 🌐 *www.aluncoturismo.com.ar*) arranges rafting trips throughout the area. **Aguas Blancas** (✉ *Morales 564* ☎ *2944/432–799* 🌐 *aguasblancas.com*) specializes in the Manso River and offers an overnight trip to Chile with asado and return by horseback. They also rent inflatable kayacks (*duckies*). **Extremo Sur** (✉ *Morales 765* ☎ *2944/427–301* 🌐 *www.extremosur.com*) arranges trips on the Ríos Limay and Manso.

IN AND AROUND EL BOLSÓN

EL BOLSÓN

131 km (80 mi) south of Bariloche via R40.

El Bolsón ("the purse") lies in a valley enclosed on either side by the jagged peaks of two mountain ranges. You catch your first glimpse

7

Take in the view of Lago Nahuel Huapi on your way to Villa La Angostura.

of the valley about 66 km (41 mi) from Bariloche, with the glaciers of Perito Moreno and Hielo Azul (both more than 6,500 feet) on the horizon south and west. The spot was once a Mapuche settlement, then Chilean farmers came in the late 1800s in search of arable land. The town remained isolated until the 1930s, when a long, winding dirt road (often closed in winter) connected it to Bariloche. Attracted by the microclimate (about 7 degrees warmer than other Patagonian towns), young Argentines, as well as immigrants from Europe, the Americas, and the Middle East contribute to the cultural identity of this community of about 11,000. The first in Argentina to declare their town a non-nuclear zone, they have preserved the purity of its air, water, and land. Red berry fruits thrive on hillsides and in backyard *chacras* (farms), and are canned and exported in large quantities as jams and syrups. The exploding Patagonian microbrew beer industry is based on the largest crops of hops planted in Argentina.

GETTING AROUND

The main street, San Martín, has shops, restaurants, and some lodgings within a two- to three-block area. A grassy plaza next to the tourist office is the center of activities, with a crafts market on weekends and some weekdays. The sheer rock face of **Cerro Piltrequitrón** (from a Mapuche word meaning "hanging from the clouds") dominates the horizon on the southeast side of town. Trails along the Río Azul or to nearby waterfalls and mountaintops are a short taxi or bike ride from the plaza. In spring (late November–December) the roads are lined with ribbons of lupine in every shade of pink and purple imaginable.

CLOSE UP

Beer Sampling

This region has long been the biggest producer of hops in Argentina, and with a local population dedicated to agricultural pursuits, it's logical that entrepreurial *cervezarís artesanales* (artisanal breweries) would become a growing industry. **Otto Tipp** was a German immigrant who opened the first local brewery in 1890. Beers here include the classic triumvirate of blonde, red, and black—plus non-alcoholic malt beer and a fruity wheat beer. You can watch beer being brewed and bottled from a bar stool. This brewery is four blocks from the tourist office. ✉ *Islas Malvinas at Roca* ☎ *No phone* 💳 *AE, DC, MC, V.*

About 2 km (1 mi) north of town, **Cervezería El Bolsón** is the brewery that started the Patagonian "cerveza artesanal craze," and even if it's now the least artisanal of the bunch, it has become a local landmark. Every night from December through March, and Fridays and Saturdays for the rest of the year, the brewery's tasting room turns into a hopping bar and restaurant, where *picadas* (kind of like tapas), pizzas, sausages with sauerkraut, and a hearty goulash are listed on one side of the menu with suggested beers on the other. For instance, black beer is suggested with smoked meats; chocolate beer with dessert. There are 14 types of beer for you to taste, and descriptions of their ingredients are provided. A large campground is conveniently located by the river in back. ✉ *RN40, Km 123.9* ☎ *2944/492–595* 🌐 *www.cervezaselbolson.com* 💳 *AE, DC, MC, V* ⏱ *Restaurant closed Wed. Apr.–Nov.*

7

Berries are picked December–March. Summers are warm and lazy, and campgrounds at nearby lakes attract backpackers and families.

Huara Viajes y Turismo (✉ *Dorrego 410* ☎ *2944/455–000* 🌐 *www.huaraviajesyturismo.com.ar*) is a full-service travel and tour office that offers guided hiking, fishing, rafting, horseback, and mountain-bike trips. They also arrange day tours to Lago Puelo that include a boat trip. Rock climbing with rappels is offered on a multi-adventure trip near Lago Puelo.

ESSENTIALS

Visitor and Tour Info Secretaría de Turismo (✉ *Plaza Pagano at Av. San Martín* ☎ *2944/492–604 or 2944/455–336* 🌐 *www.elbolson.gov.ar*).

EXPLORING

The **Cascada de la Virgen** (Waterfall of the Virgin), 18 km (11 mi) north of El Bolsón, is most impressive in spring, when the runoff from the mountain falls in a series of three cascades visible from the road coming from Bariloche. Nearby is a **campground** (☎ *2944/492–610 information*) with cabins, grills, and a restaurant.

The **Cascada Mallín Ahogado** (Drowned Meadow Waterfall), 10 km (6 mi) north of El Bolsón on R258, makes a great picnic spot.

The **Bosque Tallado** (carved forest), about 1 km (½ mi) from the base of Piltriquitrón, is a forest of dry beech trees (resulting from a fire in 1978) that have been carved over the years by 13 of Argentina's notable

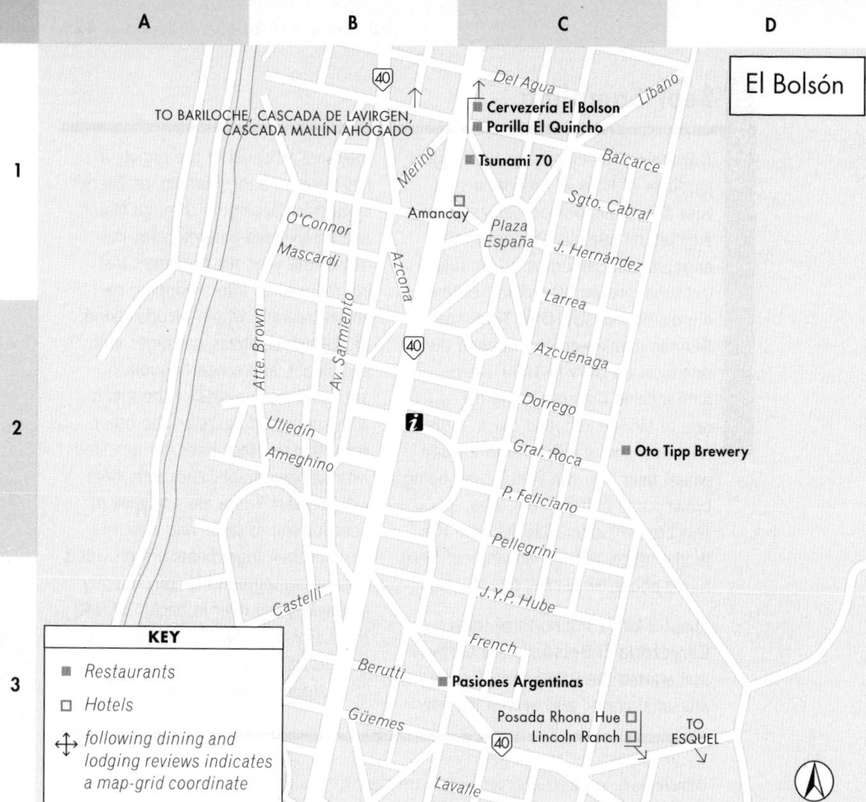

artists. Thirty-one monumental sculptures transform the dead forest into a living gallery.

The Bolsón International Jazz Festival takes place in December on the streets and in restaurants around town. The Fiesta Nacional de Lúpolo (National Hop Festival) is celebrated in February.

Don't leave the area of Bolsón or El Hoyo (15 km south) without a jar of jam! You can try all the flavors at **Cabaña Mico** (✉ *Islas Malvinas at Roca* ☎ *2944/492–691* 🌐 *www.mico.com.ar*). Not to be outdone by the beer tasting next door at Otto Tipp, little pots of jam are lined up for sale on a long table with disposable sticks for tasting the 40 different flavors.

WHERE TO EAT

$–$$ ARGENTINE ✕ **Parrilla El Quincho**. About 10 minutes north of town, on the bank of the river Arroyo del Medio, this is the place to try *cordero patagónico al asador* (lamb roasted slowly on a metal cross over a fire), along with sizzling platters of beef. From El Bolsón, follow RN40 north, and get off at the left exit for Catarata Mallín Ahogado. Follow that winding road north, then follow signs for El Quincho; you'll exit to the right after the Catarata exit (if you come to the Iaten K'aik museum, you've gone too far). ✉ *Mallín Ahogado* ☎ *2944/492–870* ▭ *No credit cards* ✥ *C1*.

$$$ ARGENTINE ✕ **Pasiones Argentinas Resto Bar.** Paintings of passionate tango dancers enliven the brick walls of this popular restaurant near the Villa Turismo. Vegetarian dishes, pastas, pizzas, even hamburgers fill the menu. Patagonian wine, local beer, Wi-Fi, and take-out food are added attractions. ✉ *Av. Belgrano at Berutti* ☎ *2944/483–616* ▭ *No credit cards* ✣ *B3.*

$$$$ SPANISH ★ ✕ **Tsunami70.** The front room is red, the back room is chartreuse, the bathrooms are blue, and the hallway is turquoise—yes, it's colorful! Spanish chef Juan Gonzalez creates seafood selections unheard of in this land of parrillas and asados. His seafood platter (*Degustación de Mariscos*) is a seven-course extravaganza of deliciously prepared seafoods flown in from Patagonia's Atlantic ports. ✉ *Av. San Martín 3275* ☎ *2944/483–562* ▭ *MC, V* ✣ *C1.*

CRAFTS FAIR

At the local **mercado artesanal** (artisanal crafts fair), which takes place on the main plaza on Tuesday, Thursday, Saturday, and Sunday from 10 to 5, local artisans sell ceramics, leather goods, wood handicrafts, objects made from bone and clay, and agricultural products—plus the famous local beers. El Bolsón is also known for its delicious small strawberries.

WHERE TO STAY

The hotel selection in downtown El Bolsón is woefully inadequate. Numerous small guesthouses take small groups, and the Hotel Amancay is the only full-service hotel worth recommending. About 2 km (1½ mi) south of town, off Avenida Belgrano, is **Villa Turismo,** a hillside community of cabins, bed-and-breakfasts, and small inns. Lodges in the surrounding mountains open for fishing season in summer (November–April) and close in winter (May–October).

7

$$ **Hotel Amancay.** A rose garden and masses of flowers greet you at the door of this yellow-stucco hotel three blocks from the center of town. The lobby has tile floors and dark-wood furniture with bright cushions. Rooms are clean but fairly basic, and showers are iffy, but this is about the best you can do in humble downtown El Bolsón. We hope new owners will remodel. **Pros:** walk to downtown restaurants. **Cons:** rooms are small and slightly run-down. ✉ *Av. San Martín 3207* ☎ *2944/492–222* *15 rooms* *In-hotel: parking (free)* ▭ *AE, DC, MC, V* *CP* ✣ *C1.*

$$ **Lincoln Ranch.** Perched higher than all the other cabin complexes, these modern cottages have plenty of room and all the accoutrements of a vacation home. Mountain views and an opulent garden will soothe your soul while you plan activities. **Pros:** lots of space; easy walk up to Piltriquitrón. **Cons:** far from restaurants and downtown shops. ✉ *Villa Turismo, Subida Los Maitenes* ☎ *2944/492–073* *10 1- and 2-bedroom cabins, 1 3-bedroom cabin* *In-hotel: pool, parking (free)* ▭ *MC, V* ✣ *C3.*

$$ **Posada Rhona Hue.** Formerly the headquarters for a fruit and berry farm, this farmhouse has been converted by Anabella Gouchs into a B&B where every room is filled with an eclectic mixture of antiques and recycled objects used as furniture. Bedrooms are toned-down versions of the three front rooms, and the only sound you'll hear is birdsong. **Pros:** country living; homemade jams and scones for breakfast; walking distance to Piltriquitrón. **Cons:** out of town. ✉ *Villa Turismo,*

DESTINATION HOTELS

Far from all the usual tourist sights, shops, and restaurants, usually on a dirt road and often with no real address, the Lake District's destination hotels are almost as soothing and inspiring as the very wilderness they're hidden in. Similar to the all-inclusive resort concept but without the resort-y feel, these hotels are focused on getting you as close to nature as possible. They often require a minimum stay of two or more nights—but this makes sense for guests because getting to these places can be a production. Once you've arrived, the staff at these hotels will facilitate a relazing nature-oriented stay where stargazing is the main evening event and hiking trails into the mountains are at your doorstep. Come with a group, as a couple, or with anyone you're eager to share some down time with.

If you're based in Bariloche, consider **Hosteria El Retorno, Hotel Tronadór, or Peuma Hue.** In Villa Traful, **Estancia Arroyo Verde** is our favorite destination hotel. The one with arguably the best location, though, is **Isla Victoria Lodge** in Nahuel Huapi National Park, right on Isla Victoria.

Subida de Juan Marqués ☎ *2944/493–717* 🌐 *www.interpatagonia.com/rhonahue* *4 rooms, 1 apartment, 1 cabin* *In-hotel: pool, parking (free)* ▭ *MC, V* *CP* ✣ *C3.*

SPORTS AND THE OUTDOORS

HIKING

There are 10 *refugios* (mountain huts) with beds and meals in the mountains around Bolsón. A few easy hikes begin but a short taxi ride from the center of town. The Río Azul (Blue River) drops down from the high mountains north of town and runs through the valley to Lago Puelo. Most of the hiking trails are in this area. To reach the Mirador Azul (5 km [3 mi] from the town center), ride or drive west on Azuénaga Street, cross the bridge over the River Quemquemtreu, and follow the signs. From here you can look down the valley to Lago Puelo and up at the snow-covered mountains to the west. A 6-km (4-mi) walk will take you to the **Cabeza del Indio** (Indian Head) and **Cascadas Escondidas** (Hidden Falls). A strenuous two-day trek to the **Hielo Azul** (Blue Glacier) climbs through forests to a refugio next to the glacier. Another overnight hike through the forest and past hidden lagoons is to the refugio by the glacier at **Cerro Lindo.** Easier to climb it than to say it, the summit of **Cerro Piltriquitrón** (pronounced pill-tree-quee-tron) offers stupendous views of lakes and mountains all around you, including Tronadór on the Chilean border near Bariloche. There's a refugio at the top with beds and meals.

HORSEBACK RIDING (CABALGATAS)

Riding a horse is a fun way to access most of the areas described in the hiking section, especially the area around **Cascada Mallín Ahogado,** or the Río Azul to the Azul Canyon or all the way to the glacier. You can arrange these trips with **Huara Viajes y Turismo** (✉ *Dorrego 410*

Cerro Lindo, near El Bolsón, is a hiker's dream.

☎ *2944/455–000* 🌐 *www.huaraviajesyturismo.com.ar*) or **Cabalgatas El Azul** (☎ *2944/483–590*).

MOUNTAIN BIKING

Hardy bikers ride all the way from Bariloche, enjoying the long descent into Bolsón. Once there, getting around is pretty easy, as there's not much traffic on the mostly flat dirt roads on the outskirts of town. Most of the waterfall walks and a long trail along the Azul River make pleasant day trips. Epuyén and Puelo lakes require more effort. For guided trips, contact **Huara Viajes y Turismo**(✉ *Dorrego 410* ☎ *2944/455–000* 🌐 *www.huaraviajesyturismo.com.ar*). To rent a bike and leave it at another destination in the region, contact **Patagonia Rent a Bike** (☎ *2944/1550–6198 or 2944/1567–3347* ✉ *lacomarcabike@hotmail.com*).

SKIING

The ski area at **Cerro Perito Moreno,** 25 km (15 mi) northwest of El Bolsón, is owned and operated by **Club Andino Piltriquitrón** (✉ *Sarmiento at Roca* ☎ *2944/492–600*), which also runs a restaurant at the base, where you can rent skis, snowboards, and sleds. The ski area is open from mid-June to mid-October and is used mainly by local families. Four short tows for beginners and one T-bar access the 750 meters (2,460 feet) of skiable terrain on east-facing slopes. Since storms approach from the west, snowfall can be minimal, so it's best to call the tourist office or Club Andino before you go.

PARQUE NACIONAL LAGO PUELO

19 km (12 mi) south of El Bolsón on RN40 and RP16.

One of the smallest national parks in the southern Andes, Lago Puelo has the warmest water for swimming, the largest salmon (coming all the way from the Pacific Ocean), and many hiking possibilities—the most interesting of which are at the other end of the lake on the Chilean border.

GETTING AROUND

Information is at the **Parque Nacional Lago Puelo** (☎ *2944/499–183* 🌐 *www.lagopuelo.gov.ar*), and picnic and fishing supplies can be purchased at the roadside store, 4 km (2½ mi) before you reach the sandy beach at Lago Puelo.

SPORTS AND THE OUTDOORS

BOAT EXCURSIONS

On Lago Puelo three launches, maintained by the Argentine navy, wait at the dock to take you on one- to three-hour excursions. The trip to El Turbio, an ancient settlement at the southern end of the lake on the Chilean border, is the longest. One side of the lake is inaccessible, as the Valdivian rain forest grows on steep rocky slopes right down into the water. Campgrounds are at the park entrance by the ranger's station, in a bay on the Brazo Occidental, and at the Turbio and Epuyén river outlets. **Juana de Arco** (✉ *San Martín at Juez Fernández* ☎ *2944/493–415 or 2944/1563–3838* 🌐 *www.interpatagonia.com/juanadearco*) is one of the boat-tour operators.

HIKING

Arriving at the water's edge, you will have three trails to explore: one is an easy stroll in the woods on a wooden walkway; another involves a steep climb to an overlook; and the third is an all-day trek (eight hours round-trip) to **Los Hitos** on the Chilean border, where you can admire the rapids on the Puelo River. It's possible to camp there at **Arroyo Las Lagrimas** and continue on for five or six days across Chile to the Pacific Ocean. You can also take a boat to **El Turbio** at the other end of the lake, where a tough two- to three-day day trek climbs to Lago Esperanza. Another option would be to hike to El Turbio from **El Desemboque** on **Lago Epuyén.** For a guide, contact Fabio Barreiro at **Puelo Extremo** (☎ *2944/499–588 or 2944/1541–999*) or one of the tour offices in El Bolsón.

Patagonia

WORD OF MOUTH

"We drove to Puerto Pyramides where we spent 2 hours on our whale watching trip. It was wonderful. We had many mother whales with their calves come right up to our boat. The water is very clean and clear so you can see them under water as well as when they surface and look at us."

—crzn1

WELCOME TO PATAGONIA

Torres del Paine, Chile

TOP REASONS TO GO

★ **Marine Life:** Península Valdés is home to breeding populations of sea lions, elephant seals, orcas, and the star of the local sea show, the southern right whale. Punta Tombo is the world's largest Magellanic penguin colony.

★ **Estancia Stay:** Visit an estancia, a working ranch where you can ride horses alongside tough-as-nails gaucho cowboys and dine under the stars on spit-roasted lamb.

★ **Glaciers and Mountains:** Set yourself opposite an impossibly massive wall of ice and contemplate the blue-green-turquoise spectrum trapped within. Meanwhile, stark granite peaks planted like spears in the Cordillera beckon extreme mountain climbers and casual trekkers alike.

★ **Brushing Up on Your Welsh:** In the largest Welsh colony outside Wales, the people of Gaiman have preserved their traditions and language. Gaiman's historic teahouses serve scones, cakes, and tarts from century-old recipes.

1 Puerto Madryn and Península Valdés. Puerto Madryn provides easy access to Península Valdés, one of the world's best places for marine wildlife viewing.

2 Trelew, Gaiman, and Punta Tombo. Gaiman and Trelew's teahouses and rose gardens date back to the original 19th-century Welsh settlers. Head south to Punta Tombo, the largest penguin rookery in South America.

3 Camarones and Bahía Bustamante. Traveling south along RP1 to colorful Camarones and Bahía Bustamante is like having a national park to yourself.

4 Sarmiento. This small, friendly town is a green oasis. There are stunning petrified forests nearby and a paleontology "park" with life-size dinosaur replicas.

5 El Calafate and the Parque Nacional los Glaciares. The wild Parque Nacional Glaciares dramatically contrasts nearby boomtown El Calafate. North is El Chaltén, base camp for hikes to Cerros Torre and Fitzroy.

6 Puerto Natales and Torres del Paine, Chile. Border town Puerto Natales is the last stop before one of the finest national parks in South America, Parque Nacional Torres del Paine.

7 Ushuaia and Tierra del Fuego. This rugged, windswept land straddles Chile and Argentina. Ushuaia, in Argentina, is the world's southernmost city.

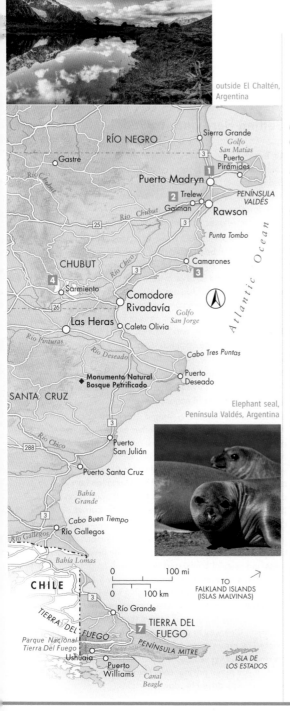

outside El Chaltén, Argentina

GETTING ORIENTED

Most of Patagonia is windswept desert steppe inhabited by rabbits, sheep, guanacos, and a few hardy human beings. The population centers—and attractions—are either along the coast or in a narrow strip of barely fertile land that runs north to south along the base of the Andes mountain range, where massive glaciers spill into large turquoise lakes. In nearby Chile, Puerto Natales is the gateway town to Parque Nacional Torres del Paine. At the bottom end of the continent, separated by the Magellan Strait and split between Chile and Argentina, lies Tierra del Fuego. The resort town of Ushuaia ("westward-looking bay" in local Yamana dialect), Argentina, base camp for explorations of the Beagle Channel and the forested peaks of the Cordillera Darwin mountain range, is far and away the leading tourist attraction of the region.

Elephant seal, Península Valdés, Argentina

PATAGONIA PLANNER

When to Go

Late September to February—spring and summer in the Southern Hemisphere—is high season in Patagonia. Reservations are advised, especially September and October in Atlantic and December–February in Southern Patagonia. Although the summer sun can be strong, the winds whistle year-round, so always bring extra layers and a windbreaker. In Atlantic Patagonia, many properties close in April and May to prepare for the first whale-watchers in June and July. Southern Patagonia all but shuts down June–August.

Health and Safety

Most mountains are not high enough to induce altitude sickness, but the weather can turn nasty very quickly. Sunglasses and sunscreen are essential. Although tap water is safe to drink throughout the region, most travelers still choose to drink bottled water. Do not approach or let your children approach sea lions, penguins, or any other animals, no matter how docile or curious they might seem.

Emergency Services: Coast Guard (☎ *106*). **Fire** (☎ *100*). **Forest Fire** (☎ *103*). **Hospital** (☎ *107*). **Police** (☎ *101*).

Getting Here and Around

Air Travel. Flying is the best way to reach Patagonia from Buenos Aires—flights from other parts of the country also go through here. The most popular route is between Aeroparque Jorge Newberry in Palermo, a short cab ride from downtown, and Trelew's tiny airport, which is the gateway to Atlantic Patagonia.

Aerolíneas Argentinas (🌐 *www.aerolineas.com.ar*) flies (along with its subsidiary Austral) several times daily between Buenos Aires and Trelew, Comodoro Rivadavia, or El Calafate and once or twice a day between Trelew and El Calafate and Ushuaia. LADE (Líneas Aéreas del Estado 🌐 *www.lade.com.ar*) connects Trelew and Comodoro Rivadavia to other parts of Patagonia, including Bariloche, El Calafate, and Ushuaia. Andes Líneas Aéreas (🌐 *www.andesonline.com*) has direct flights between Buenos Aires and Puerto Madryn three times per week.

Although Aerolíneas Argentinas offers cheaper tickets to Argentineans than to visitors, tickets with LADE are at one flat price regardless of nationality.

Bus Travel. Comfortable overnight sleeper buses connect Patagonia to Buenos Aires (and other major cities). However, as getting to even the closest city in Atlantic Patagonia, Puerto Madryn, takes 20 hours, most travelers feel it's worth the price to fly both to and within Patagonia. All the same, buses are a major form of transportation between destinations up to about 600 km (370 mi) apart. Don Otto (🌐 *www.donotto.com.ar*) is the most reliable carrier.

Car Travel. If you truly enjoy the call of the open road, there are few places that can rival the vast emptiness and jaw-dropping beauty of Patagonia. Be prepared for miles and miles of semi-desert steppes with no gas stations, towns, or even restrooms. Always carry plenty of water, snacks, a jack and tire-changing tools, with at least one spare. Take extra care when driving on *ripio* (gravel roads): it's easy to flip small cars at speeds over 80 kmh (55 mph). One way to prevent your windshield from being cracked by errant stones is to press your hand to it when passing oncoming vehicles. Fill your tank at every opportunity. If you're not driving, consider simply paying for a *remis* (car with driver) for day excursions.

Eat Well and Rest Easy

With so many miles of coastline, it's not surprising that Atlantic Patagonia is famous for its seafood, notably sole and salmon, *mejillones* (mussels), and *pulpo* (octopus). *Centolla* (king crab) is another specialty, especially south of Comodoro Rivadavia. Most restaurants are sit-down-and-take-your-time affairs that don't open for dinner until at least 8, and despite all the seafood on offer, steak still reigns supreme at most. The other carnivorous staple in the area is *cordero patagónico,* local lamb, usually served barbecued or stewed. Dining prices in most Patagonian cities rival those of upper-end Buenos Aires restaurants. Thankfully, so do the skills of local chefs, although expect more basic offerings of pizza, milanesas, and greasy empanadas in smaller towns. Whenever possible, accompany your meal with a bottle of wine from one of the increasing number of Patagonian wineries.

Huge numbers of foreign visitors mean that vegetarian options are getting better, even if most are carb-heavy. Still, *woks de verdura* (vegetable stir-fries) are a healthy and newly ubiquitous option. Most cafés and bars serve quick bites known as *minutas.* The region is also famous for its stone fruits, which are used in various jams, preserves, sweets, and *alfajores* (a chocolate-covered sandwich of two cookies with jam in the middle).

Although there are large, expensive hotels in Puerto Madryn, Trelew, and Comodoro Rivadavia, bed-and-breakfasts and other smaller *hosterías* offer the best deals and often the best lodging throughout the region. Punta Arenas has many historic hotels offering luxurious amenities and fine service. A night or two in one of them should be part of your trip. Several good resorts and lodges skirt Puerto Natales or are within Parque Nacional Torres del Paine. The terms *hospedaje* and *hostal* are used interchangeably in the region, so don't make assumptions based on the name. Many *hostals* are fine hotels—not youth hostels with multiple beds—just very small. By contrast, some *hospedajes* are little more than a spare room in someone's home.

DINING & LODGING PRICE CATEGORIES (IN PESOS)

	¢	$	$$	$$$	$$$$
Restaurants	under 8 pesos	8 pesos–15 pesos	15 pesos–25 pesos	25 pesos–35 pesos	over 35 pesos
Hotels	under 80 pesos	80 pesos–150 pesos	150 pesos–250 pesos	250 pesos–400 pesos	over 400 pesos

Restaurant prices are based on the median main course price at dinner. Hotel prices are for two people in a standard double room in high season.

Border Crossing

The border between Chile and Argentina is still strictly maintained, but crossing it doesn't present much difficulty beyond getting out your passport and waiting in a line to get the stamp. Most travelers end up crossing the border by bus, which means getting out of the vehicle for 30–45 minutes to go through the bureaucratic proceedings, then loading back in. Crossing by car is also quite manageable (check with your car-rental company for restrictions on international travel). Chilean customs officers are extremely strict about bringing food into the country, especially compared to their Argentine counterparts.

Literary Patagonia

The British writer Bruce Chatwin achieved widespread acclaim with his work *In Patagonia* (1977), a lyrical journey many consider among the greatest travel books of all time, despite criticism related to Chatwin's embellishments. Much of Charles Darwin's classic *Voyage of the Beagle* (1839) takes place in Patagonia, where the young naturalist marveled at the region's stark geology during a boat trip up the Río Santa Cruz.

CALENDAR OF FAUNA ON PENINSULA VALDES

Although few wildlife-viewing experiences are as grandiose as seeing whales breach or witnessing orcas charge the beaches in a hunt for sea lions, there are numerous special moments throughout the yearly cycles of all Atlantic Patagonian fauna. Regardless of what time you visit, you'll be witnessing something memorable.

Top left: Elephant seal bull with Snowy Sheathbill
Top right: Dolphin Gull
Bottom right: Southern Right Whale off Puerto Piramides

Since practically everyone who visits Península Valdés is here for the wildlife, any guide we recommend (⇨ *see Península Valdés Essentials section, below*) will know where to go for the best views of the wildlife that's most active. Renting a car is a possibility, but going with a guide service makes things easier—your guide will be able to navigate the unpaved roads while you scan the land and water for creatures.

Here is a Península Valdés wildlife primer to get you acquainted with what you'll see when.

WHEN TO GO

Birds: June–Dec.

Whales: June–Dec.

Dolphins: Dec.–Mar.

Elephant Seals: year round

Sea Lions: year round

Orcas: Sept.–Apr.

Penguins: Sept.–Mar.

SCOPE IT OUT

Consider purchasing or renting binoculars or a scope; your guide might provide them as part of the package.

LOOK TO THE WATER FOR . . .

Southern Right Whales. The first southern right whales arrive in Golfo Nuevo between the end of April and the beginning of May, and can be observed from beaches in and along Puerto Madryn as well as the Península Valdés. Your best chance of seeing them will be from a whale-watching point at Puerto Pirámides. These whales are between 36 and 59 feet long, and have several endearing behaviors such as "sailing," where they hold their fins up in the air, and when a mother uses her flippers to teach calves how to swim.

Elephant Seals. Elephant seals are larger mammals than sea lions, and have a different way of moving—using their flippers to waddle along on land, whereas sea lions use both front and back flippers to thrust themselves forward. Adult males can reach up to 6 meters (20 feet) in length and weigh up to 4 tons, and after four years develop a proboscis, or elephant-like appendage on their noses, which inflates to help produce sounds. The biggest elephant-seal colonies are in Península Valdés, at Punta Cantor, and Punta Delgada.

Sea Lions. In January and February sea lions begin to form "harems," with each dominant male taking up to a dozen females. The fights to maintain these harems can be bloody and violent, and sometimes it's possible to witness an invading male drag off one of the females from the harem with his teeth. Most of the year, however, sea-lion colonies appear peaceful: the animals sun themselves or swim, and the pups are especially curious and playful. They can be observed year-round all along the Atlantic Coast.

Orcas. Summertime (which in the Southern Hemisphere begins on December 21) up until April is when sea lions and elephant seals are reproducing and raising pups. It's possible to see the black fins of orcas cutting through the water along the coastline, occasionally storming the beach in violent and spectacular chases. The best place to see orcas is at the extreme northern tip of Península Valdés, Punta Norte, in April.

LOOK TO THE AIR AND LAND FOR . . .

Seabirds. Among the many seabirds found in Patagonia—including dolphin gull, kelp goose, southern giant petrel, rock and blue-eyed cormorant, snowy sheathbill, blackish oystercatcher, and steamer duck—one species, the arctic tern, has the longest migration of any bird. Each year it flies over 21,750 mi (round-trip) from the Arctic to Antarctica.

Penguins. At several places in Atlantic Patagonia—most notably Punta Tombo—there are large rookeries of Magellanic penguins, with up to 500,000 of these flightless birds. The males arrive from the sea at the rookery each August. A month later the females arrive and the males begin fighting territorial battles. In October and into November the nesting pairs incubate the eggs. Once the chicks hatch in November, the parents make continual trips to the ocean for food. In January the chicks leave the nest, learning to swim in February. Their plumage matures throughout the fall, when the penguins begin migrating north to Brazil.

Patagonia is a hybrid of the cultures of primarily European immigrants, who came here in the 19th century, and the cultures of the indigenous peoples, mainly the Tehuelche and Mapuche. The native Tehuelches fished and hunted the coast and pampas, and their spears and arrowheads are still found along riverbeds and beaches.

The first Spanish explorer, Hernando Magallanes, arrived in Golfo Nuevo in 1516, and was followed by several other Spanish expeditions throughout the 17th and 18th centuries. From 1826 to 1836 two English captains, Parker King, of the *Adventure,* and Robert Fitzroy, sailing the *Beagle,* made the first accurate nautical maps of the region. The indigenous populations are nearly all gone since the genocidal four-year military campaign (1879–83) led by General Roca and known euphemistically as the Conquest of the Desert.

Inland, a Welsh pioneer named Henry Jones explored the Chubut River valley in 1814. Fifty years later a small group of Welsh families—fleeing religious persecution in Great Britain—became the first Europeans to move to this area permanently, clearing the way for waves of Welsh immigrants that forged colonies in Gaiman, Trelew, Rawson, and Puerto Madryn. Beginning in the mid-19th century the Argentinian government courted settlers from all over Europe, including Italy, Spain, and Germany, as well as Boers from South Africa, offering land as a strategy for displacing indigenous populations and fortifying the young nation against neighboring Chile. These settlers adapted their agrarian traditions to the Patagonian terrain, planting windbreaks of Lombardy poplar along with fruit trees and flower gardens. They set up dairy farms and sheep ranches, and continued their cultural traditions and cuisine, such as Welsh tea, still found throughout Patagonia today.

Atlantic Patagonia is where the low windswept pampas meet the ocean. It's a land of immense panoramic horizons and a coastline of bays, inlets, and peninsulas teeming with seabirds and marine wildlife. The region is most famous for Península Valdés, a UNESCO Natural World Heritage Site where travelers can see southern right whales, orcas, southern elephant seals, and sea lions. There are seemingly endless dirt roads where you won't see another person or vehicle for hours, only guanacos, rheas, and other animals running across the steppe.

Farther south and inland to the Andes, the towns of El Calafate and El Chaltén come alive in summer (December–March) with the influx of visitors to the Parque Nacional los Glaciares, and climbers headed for Cerro Torre and Cerro Fitzroy. Imagine sailing across a blue lake full of icebergs, or traversing an advancing glacier in the shadow of the end of the Andes mountain range, watching a valley being formed before your eyes. A trip here is like a trip back to the Ice Age. It is that glacier, Perito Moreno, that is bringing tourists to this region in unprecedented numbers.

Experiencing Patagonia, however, still means crossing vast deserts to reach isolated population centers. It means taking deep breaths of mountain air and draughts of pure stream water in the shadow of dramatic snowcapped peaks. Most of all, it means being embraced by independent, pioneering souls just beginning to understand the importance of tourism as traditional industries—wool, livestock, fishing, and oil—are drying up.

PUERTO MADRYN AND PENÍNSULA VALDÉS

Updated by Victoria Patience

Visiting populations of whales, orcas, sea lions, elephant seals, and penguins all gather to breed or feed on or near the shores of this unique peninsula—at 132 feet below sea level, it's the lowest point on the South American continent. The wildlife isn't only water-based. Wandering the Patagonian scrub are guanacos, grey foxes, *maras* (Patagonian hares), skunks, armadillos, and rheas, while myriad bird species fill the air. There are also three inland salt lakes, and the curving gulf at Puerto Pirámides is one of the few places in Argentina where the sun sets over the water, not the land. With nature putting on such a generous display, it's not surprising that the 3,625-square-km (1,400-square-mi) peninsula has been designated a UNESCO World Heritage Site and is the main reason visitors come to Atlantic Patagonia.

Puerto Madryn is where you'll head first for organized excursions onto the peninsula. While a major part of the town's identity is as a staging ground for these trips, it's also well worth exploring and has an interesting history. The first economic boom came in 1886, when the Patagonian railroad was introduced, spurring port activities along with the salt and fishing industries. Although it isn't likely that the original Welsh settlers who arrived here in 1865 could have imagined just how much Puerto Madryn would evolve, a large part of the town's success is owed to their hardworking traditions, which continue with their descendants today. The anniversary of their arrival is celebrated every 28th of July here and in other Chubut towns. Only a statue—the Tehuelche Indian Monument—serves as a reminder of the indigenous people who once lived here and who helped the Welsh survive.

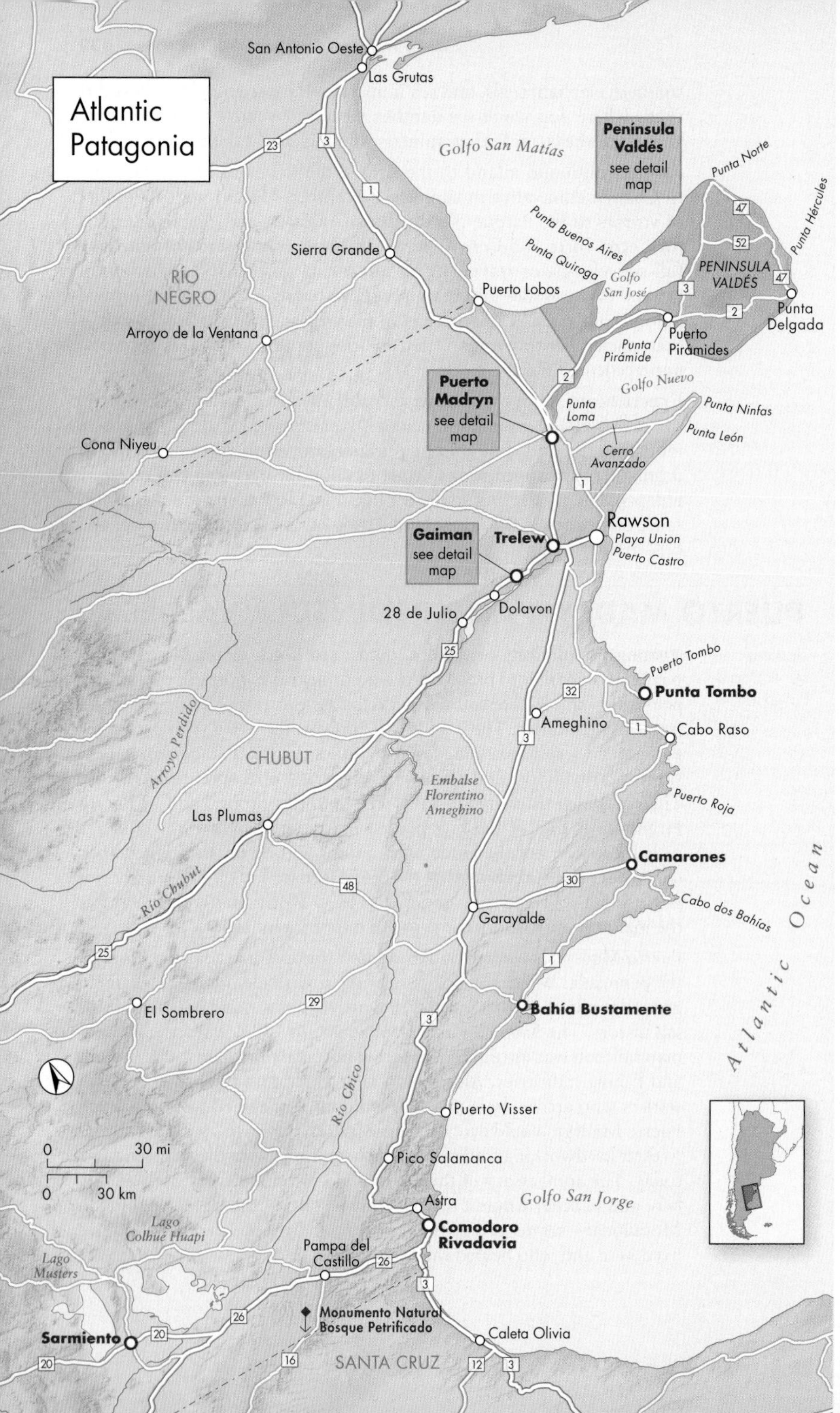
Atlantic Patagonia
San Antonio Oeste
Las Grutas
Golfo San Matías
Península Valdés see detail map
Punta Norte
Punta Hércules
Punta Buenos Aires
Punta Quiroga
Golfo San José
PENINSULA VALDÉS
Sierra Grande
RÍO NEGRO
Puerto Lobos
Arroyo de la Ventana
Punta Delgada
Puerto Pirámides
Punta Pirámide
Golfo Nuevo
Puerto Madryn see detail map
Punta Loma
Punta Ninfas
Punta León
Cerro Avanzado
Cona Niyeu
Rawson
Playa Union
Puerto Castro
Gaiman see detail map
Trelew
Dolavon
28 de Julio
Puerto Tombo
Punta Tombo
Ameghino
Cabo Raso
CHUBUT
Arroyo Perdido
Embalse Florentino Ameghino
Puerto Roja
Las Plumas
Camarones
Río Chubut
Garayalde
Cabo dos Bahías
Atlantic Ocean
El Sombrero
Bahía Bustamente
Río Chico
Puerto Visser
Pico Salamanca
0 30 mi
0 30 km
Golfo San Jorge
Astra
Comodoro Rivadavia
Lago Colhué Huapi
Lago Musters
Pampa del Castillo
Monumento Natural Bosque Petrificado
Sarmiento
Caleta Olivia
SANTA CRUZ

PUERTO MADRYN

67 km (41½ mi) north of Trelew; 450 km (279 mi) north of Comodoro Rivadavía; 104 km (64 mi) west of Puerto Pirámides.

Approaching from Ruta 3, it's hard to believe that the horizon-line of buildings perched just beyond the windswept dunes and badlands is the most successful of all coastal Patagonia settlements. But once you get past the outskirts of town and onto the wide coastal road known as the Rambla, the picture begins to change. Ranged along the clear and tranquil Golfo Nuevo are restaurants, cafés, dive shops, and hotels, all busy—but not yet overcrowded—with tourists from around the world.

Puerto Madryn is more a base for visiting nearby wildlife-watching sites like Península Valdés and Punta Tombo than a destination in its own right. The town's architecture is unremarkable, and beyond a walk along the coast, there isn't much to do. Indeed, even the few museums serve mainly to introduce you to the fauna you'll see elsewhere. The exception is the very beginning of whale season (May–July), when the huge animals cavort right in the bay before heading north—you can even walk out alongside them on the pier. During these months it's worth the extra expense for a room with a sea view.

The many tour agencies and rental car companies here make excursion-planning easy. Aim to spend most of your time here on one- or two-day trips exploring the surroundings. ⚠ **Note that competition is fierce between tourism operators in Puerto Madryn and other Patagonian destinations (including Puerto Pirámides on Península Valdés). Take information that tour operators and even the tourism office give you about these with a pinch of salt: they often exaggerate Madryn's virtues and other areas' flaws.**

8

GETTING HERE AND AROUND

Madryn is just small enough to walk around in, and many hotels are on or near the 3½-km-long (2-mi-long) Avenida Alte. Brown—often referred to as La Rambla—which runs alongside the bay and has a wide pedestrian walkway. Renting a bicycle is great way to reach the EcoCentro and (if you're feeling fit) the Punta Loma nature reserve. Otherwise, to get to either of these, to El Doradillo beach north of town, and to Península Valdés and Punta Tombo you'll need to either rent a vehicle, travel with a tour, or take a *remis*. Mar y Valle also run two to three daily bus services between Puerto Madryn's bus terminal and Puerto Pirámides on the Península Valdés.

For those flying in and out of Trelew, Transportes Eben-Ezer operates a shuttle service direct to any hotel in Puerto Madryn (35 pesos). The buses are timed to leave after the arrival of each Aerolíneas Argentinas flight. They fill up fast, so call ahead to book your seat. There are roughly hourly services between Puerto Madryn and Trelew and Gaiman with 28 de Julio. Andesmar and Don Otto connect Puerto Madryn to Buenos Aires, Bariloche, Río Gallegos, and Puerto Montt in Chile.

TOURS Puerto Madryn is a useful base for exploring nearby wildlife sites such as Península Valdés and Punta Tombo. If time is tight, or you don't feel like driving the several hundred kilometers to get to either, consider taking an organized day tour. The regular services offered by the many agencies around town vary little in price and content. Try to book a couple of days ahead if you can, although mid-week many companies accept bookings the night before the tour leaves.

Note that the English spoken by most guides ranges from amusing to downright unintelligible, so read up on the area first. Drinks, snacks, and meals are never included: bring plenty of your own along, and be prepared to spend a long, long time on your minibus.

Standard tours to Península Valdés typically include a stop at the visitor center, a whale-watching boat trip (June through December), and a visit to two other wildlife spots on the peninsula. Time is often tight, and tours can feel more like working through a fauna checklist than getting close to nature. All companies can drop you off in Puerto Pirámides on the way back if you've decided to stay there overnight.

Day trips to Punta Tombo stop off at Rawson for dolphin-watching (not always included in the tour price), then continue south to the penguin reserve where you get a scant hour or so. They usually return via Gaiman (with a visit to a Welsh teahouse) or Trelew (to see the dinosaur museum). Most companies are happy to drop you at the Trelew airport on the way back if you have an evening flight.

For more information, see the Getting Here and Around sections for Península Valdés and Punta Tombo.

Botazzi is the only Madryn-based tour operator with its own whale-watching boats—their tours to Península Valdés are slightly more expensive than those of other companies, but they guarantee you 1½ hours on the water. Nievemar and Miras del Mar are two other reliable operators—the latter's Punta Tombo tours are particularly good value. If you're after a more personal experience, talk to Causana Viajes, who create custom special-interest trips.

ESSENTIALS

Bus Contacts 28 de Julio (✉ *Terminal de Ómnibus* ☎ *2965/472–056*). **Andesmar** (✉ *Terminal de Ómnibus* ☎ *2965/473–764* 🌐 *www.andesmar.com*). **Don Otto** (✉ *Terminal de Ómnibus* ☎ *2965/451–675* 🌐 *www.donotto.com.ar*). **Mar y Valle** (✉ *Terminal de Ómnibus* ☎ *2965/450–600*). **Transportes Eben-Ezer** (☎ *2965/472-474*).

Currency Exchange Banco de la Nación (✉ *9 de Julio 127* ☎ *2965/474–466* 🌐 *www.bna.com.ar*). **Banco del Chubut** (✉ *25 de Mayo 154* ☎ *2965/471–250* 🌐 *www.bancochubut.com.ar*). **Thaler Cambio** (✉ *Av. Roca 497* ☎ *2965/455–858*).

Post Office Puerto Madryn (✉ *Belgrano at Maíz*).

Rental Cars Sigma Rent A Car (✉ *Av. Roca 27, Local 33* ☎ *2965/471–379* 🌐 *www.sigmarentacar.com*).

Visitor Info Puerto Madryn (✉ *Av. Roca 223* ☎ *2965/453–504 or 2965/456–067* 🌐 *www.madryn.gov.ar/turismo*).

Continued on page 452

INTO THE WILD

by Tim Patterson

Patagonia will shatter your sense of scale. You will feel very small, surrounded by an epic expanse of mountains and plains, sea, and sky. Whether facing down an advancing wall of glacial ice, watching an ostrich-like rhea racing across the open steppe, or getting splashed by a breaching right whale off the Valdez Peninsula, prepare to gasp at the majesty of the Patagonian wild.

GLACIERS OF PATAGONIA

Cruise on Lago Argentino, Santa Cruz province, Glaciers National Park, Argentina

The Patagonia ice field covers much of the southern end of the Andean mountain range, straddling the Argentina–Chile border. The glaciers that spill off the high altitude ice field are basically rivers of slowly moving ice and snow that grind and push their way across the mountains, crushing soft rock and sculpting granite peaks.

Most of Patagonia's glaciers spill into lakes, rivers, or fjords. Chunks of ice calve off the face of the glacier into the water, a dramatic display of nature's power that you can view at several locations. The larger pieces of ice become icebergs that scud across the water surface like white sailboats blown by the wind.

TRAVEL SHRINKS

The link between high-impact activities—such as air travel—and climate change is clear, leading to a disturbing irony: the more people come to see the glaciers of Patagonia, the more carbon is released into the atmosphere, and the more the glaciers shrink.

WEATHER

Weather is unpredictable around glaciers: it's not uncommon to experience sunshine, rain, and snow squalls in a single afternoon.

ICE COLORS

Although clear days are best for panoramas, cloudy days bring out the translucent blue of the glacial ice, creating great opportunities for magical photographs. You'll also see black or gray streaks in the ice caused by sediment picked up by the glacier as it grinds down the mountain valley. When that sediment is deposited into lakes, it hangs suspended in the water, turning the lake a pale milky blue.

ENVIRONMENTAL CONCERN

There's no question that human-induced climate change is taking its toll on Patagonia's glaciers. Although the famous Perito Moreno glacier is still advancing, nearly all the others have shrunk in recent years, some dramatically. The retreat of the Upsala glacier near El Calafate is featured in Al Gore's award-winning documentary, *An Inconvenient Truth*.

Right: Glacier Grey, Paine Circuit, Torres del Paine National Park, Chile

GLACIERS TO SEE

- Perito Moreno Glacier, Santa Cruz, Argentina
- Upsala Glacier, Santa Cruz, Argentina
- Martial Glacier, Tierra del Fuego, Argentina
- Serrano Glacier, Tierra del Fuego, Chile
- O'Higgins Glacier, Southern Coast, Chile

FIRE AND ICE: MOUNTAINS OF PATAGONIA

A trekker takes in the view of Cerro Torre (left) and Fitz Roy in Los Glaciares National Park, Patagonia.

In Patagonia, mountains mean the Andes, a relatively young range but a precocious one that stretches for more than 4,000 miles. The Patagonian Andes are of special interest to geologists, who study how fire, water, and ice have shaped the mountains into their present form.

CREATION

Plate tectonics are the most fundamental factor in the formation of the southern Andes, with the oceanic Nazca plate slipping beneath the continental South American plate and forcing the peaks skyward. Volcanic activity is a symptom of this dynamic process, and there are several active volcanoes on the Chilean side of the range.

GLACIAL IMPRINT

Glacial activity has also played an important role in chiseling the most iconic Patagonian peaks. The spires that form the distinctive skylines of Torres del Paine and the Fitzroy range are solid columns that were created when rising glaciers ripped away weaker rock, leaving only hard granite skeletons that stand rigid at the edge of the ice fields.

MOUNTAIN HIGH BORDERS

Because the border between Chile and Argentina cuts through the most impenetrable reaches of the ice field, the actual border line is unclear in areas of the far south. Even in the more temperate north, border crossings are often located at mountain passes, and the officials who stamp visas seem more like mountain guides than bureaucrats.

MOUNTAINS OF THE SEA

Tierra del Fuego and the countless islands off the coast of southern Chile were once connected to the mainland. Over the years the sea swept into the valleys, isolated the peaks, and created an archipelago that, viewed on a map, looks as abstract as a Jackson Pollack painting. From the water these island mountains appear especially dramatic, misty pinnacles of rock and ice rising from the crashing sea.

Right: Mt. Fitzroy

PROMINENT PEAKS AND RANGES

- Mt. Fitzroy and Cerro Torre, Santa Cruz, Argentina
- Cuernos of Torres del Paine, Chile
- Beagle Channel Mountains, Tierra del Fuego, Chile/ Argentina
- Cerro Piltriqitron, El Bolson, Argentina
- Osorno Volcano, Lake District, Chile

YAY, PINGÜINOS!

Magellanic Penguin walking to his nest in Peninsula Valdes

Everyone loves penguins. How could you not feel affection for such cute, curious, and loyal little creatures? On land, their awkward waddle is endearing, and you can get close enough to see the inquisitive gaze in their eyes as they turn their heads from side to side for a good look at you. In the water, penguins transform from goofballs into Olympic athletes, streaking through the waves and returning to the nest with mouthfuls of fish and squid for their chicks.

TYPES

Most of the penguins you'll see here are Magellanic penguins, black and white colored birds that gather in large breeding colonies on the beaches of Patagonia in the summer and retreat north to warmer climes during winter. Also keep an eye out for the red-beaked Gentoo penguins that nest among the Magellanics.

If your image of penguins is the large and colorful Emperor penguins of Antarctica that featured in the documentary *March of the Penguins*, you might be slightly underwhelmed by the little Magellanics. Adults stand about 30 inches tall and weigh between 15 and 20 pounds. What they lack in glamour, Patagonia's penguins make up in vanity—and numbers. Many breeding sites are home to tens of thousands of individuals, all preening and strutting as if they were about to walk the red carpet at the Academy Awards.

PENGUIN RELATIONS

Male and female penguins form monogamous pairs and share the task of raising the chicks, which hatch in small burrows that the parents return to year after year. If you sit and observe a pair of penguins for a little while you'll notice how affectionate they appear, grooming each other with their beaks and huddling together on the nest.

HUMAN CONTACT

Although penguins are not shy of humans who keep a respectful distance (about 8 feet is a good rule of thumb), the history of penguin-human relations is not entirely one of peaceful curiosity. Early pioneers and stranded sailors would raid penguin nests for food, and in modern times, oil spills have devastated penguin colonies in Patagonia.

Magellanic Penguins

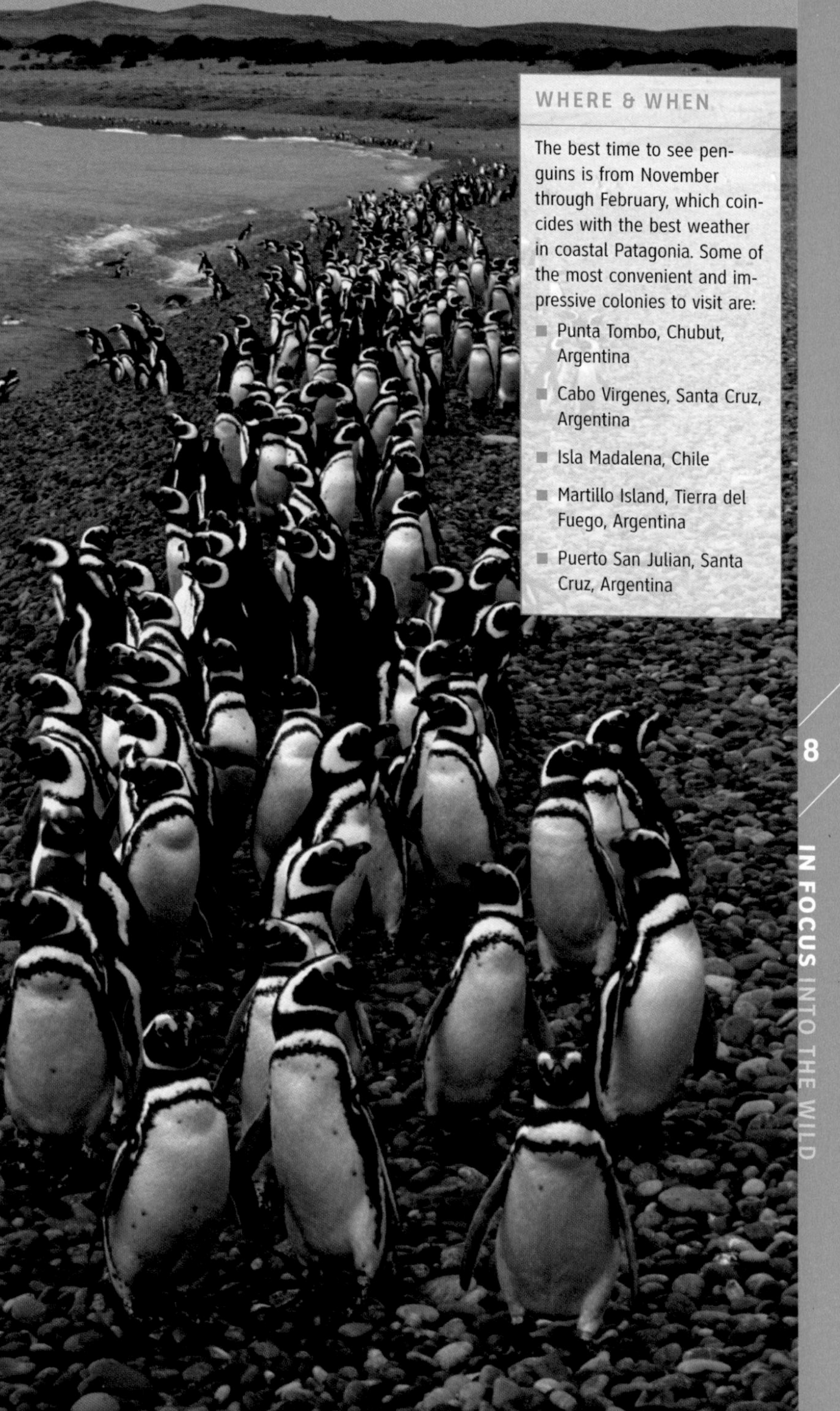

WHERE & WHEN

The best time to see penguins is from November through February, which coincides with the best weather in coastal Patagonia. Some of the most convenient and impressive colonies to visit are:

- Punta Tombo, Chubut, Argentina
- Cabo Virgenes, Santa Cruz, Argentina
- Isla Madalena, Chile
- Martillo Island, Tierra del Fuego, Argentina
- Puerto San Julian, Santa Cruz, Argentina

IN THE SEA

The Patagonian coast teems with marine life, including numerous "charismatic megafauna" such as whales, dolphins, sea lions, and seals.

❶ Seals & Sea Lions

In the springtime massive elephant seals and southern sea lions drag themselves onto Patagonian beaches for mating season—hopefully out of range of hungry orcas. These giant pinnipeds form two groups in the breeding colonies. Big, tough alpha bulls have their own harems of breeding females and their young, while so-called bachelor males hang out nearby like freshman boys at a fraternity party, hoping to entice a stray female away from the alpha bull's harem.

❷ Orcas

Orcas aren't as common as dolphins, but you can spot them off the Valdez Peninsula, Argentina, hunting seals and sea lions along the shore. Sometimes hungry orcas will chase their prey a few feet too far and beach themselves above the tide line, where they perish of dehydration.

❸ Whales

The Valdez Peninsula is also one of the best places to observe right whales, gentle giants of the ocean. Although the name right whale derives from whalers who designated it as the "right" whale to kill, the right whale is now protected by both national legislation and international agreements.

❹ Dolphins

Dolphins are easy to spot on tours, because they're curious and swim up to the boat, sometimes even surfing the bow wake. Commerson's dolphins are a common species in coastal Argentina and the Straights of Magellan. Among the world's tiniest dolphins, their white and black coloring has earned them the nickname "skunk dolphin" and prompted comparisons with their distant cousins, orcas.

IN THE AIR

Patagonia is a twitcher's paradise. Even non-bird-lovers marvel at the colorful species that squawk, flutter, and soar through Patagonia's skies.

5 Albatross

You can spot several species of albatross off the Patagonian coast, gliding on fixed wings above the waves. The albatross lives almost entirely at sea, touching down on land to breed and raise its young. Unless you're visiting Antarctica or the Falklands, your best bet for seeing an albatross is to take a cruise from Punta Arenas or Ushuaia.

6 Andean Condor

You probably won't see a condor up close. They nest on high-altitude rock ledges and spend their days soaring in circles on high thermals, scanning mountain slopes and plains for carrion. With a wing span of up to 10 feet, however, the king of the Andean skies is impressive even when viewed from a distance. Condors live longer than almost any other bird. Some could qualify for Social Security.

7 Magellanic Woodpecker

You can hear the distinctive rat-tat of this enormous woodpecker in nothofagus forests of Chilean Patagonia and parts of Argentina. Males have a bright red head and a black body, while females are almost entirely black.

8 Rhea (Nandu)

No, it's not an ostrich. The rhea is an extremely large flightless bird that roams the Patagonian steppe. Although they're not normally aggressive, males have been known to charge humans who get too close to their partner's nests.

9 Kelp Goose

As the name implies, kelp geese love kelp. In fact, kelp is the only thing they eat. The geese travel along the rocky shores of Tierra del Fuego in search of their favorite seaweed salad.

Tour Info **Bottazzi** (✉ *Complejo La Torre, Blvd. Brown at Martín Fierro,* ☎ *2965/474–110* 🌐 *www.titobottazzi.com*). **Causana Viajes** (✉ *Mathews 1395* ☎ *2965/452–769* 🌐 *www.causana.com.ar*). **Nievemar** (✉ *Av. Roca 493* ☎ *2965/455–544* 🌐 *www.nievemartours.com.ar*). **Miras del Mar** (✉ *Av. Roca 11* ☎ *2965/474–936* 🌐 *www.mirasdelmar.com*).

EXPLORING

El Doradillo. Following the coastal road 14 km (9 mi) north from Puerto Madryn brings you to this whale-watching spot. The ocean floor drops away steeply from the beach, so between the months of June and mid-December you can stand on the sand almost alongside southern right whales, usually mothers teaching their young to swim. During the rest of the year it's just a regular beach. It's a pleasant 1½ hours' bike ride from Puerto Madryn. Alternatively, taxis charge about 120 pesos for the round-trip including a 45-minute stay. *Free.*

EcoCentro. From its perch on a windswept outcrop 4 km (2½ mi) south of the town center, this museum and research center affords excellent views of Madryn's bays and desolate coastline. Inside, thoughtful, well-translated displays introduce you to the area's ocean fauna and seek to promote marine conservation. An invertebrates "touch pool" and a whale-sounds exhibit—which you reach by walking through a curtain imitating baleen plates—are especially good for kids. All the same, the exhibits are a little scanty to justify the astronomical entrance price. A slick gift shop and café are also on-site. ✉ *Julio Verne 3784* ☎ *2965/457–470* 🌐 *www.ecocentro.org.ar* *32 pesos* *Jan. and Feb., daily 5–9; Mar. and July–Sept., Wed.–Mon. 3–7; Apr.–June, Wed.–Sun. 3–7; Oct.–Dec., Wed.–Mon. 3–8.*

Museo Provincial del Hombre y el Mar (Ciencias Naturales y Oceanografía). This whimsical collection of stuffed animals, shells, skeletons, and engravings examines man's relationship with the sea. Housed in a restored 1915 building, the beautifully displayed exhibits evoke the marine myths of the Tehuelche (the area's indigenous people), imagined European sea-monsters, the ideas of 19th-century naturalists, through to modern ecology. It's more about experience than explanation, so don't worry about the scarcity of English translations, although the excellent room on orca behavior is a welcome exception. Finish by looking out over the city and surrounding steppes from the tower. ✉ *Domecq García at José Menéndez* ☎ *02965/451–139* *6 pesos* *Mar.–Nov., weekdays 9–7, weekends 3–7; Dec.–Feb., weekdays 9–8, weekends 3–8.*

Punta Loma Sea Lion Reserve. Some 600 South American sea lions lounge on the shore below a tall, crescent bluff at Punta Loma, 17 km (10½ mi) southeast of the city. Aim to visit during low tide. You can reach the reserve by car (follow signs toward Punta Ninfas); by bicycle, if the wind is not too strong; or by taxi—expect to pay about 145 pesos for the return trip including a 45-minute stay. *35 pesos* *Visit during low tide—check local paper or tourism office for tide schedule.*

WHERE TO EAT

$$ SEAFOOD **Cantina El Náutico.** Photos of visiting Argentine celebrities mingle with the marine-themed doodads that cover the walls at this firm local favorite. Run by three generations of a French Basque family, it specializes in

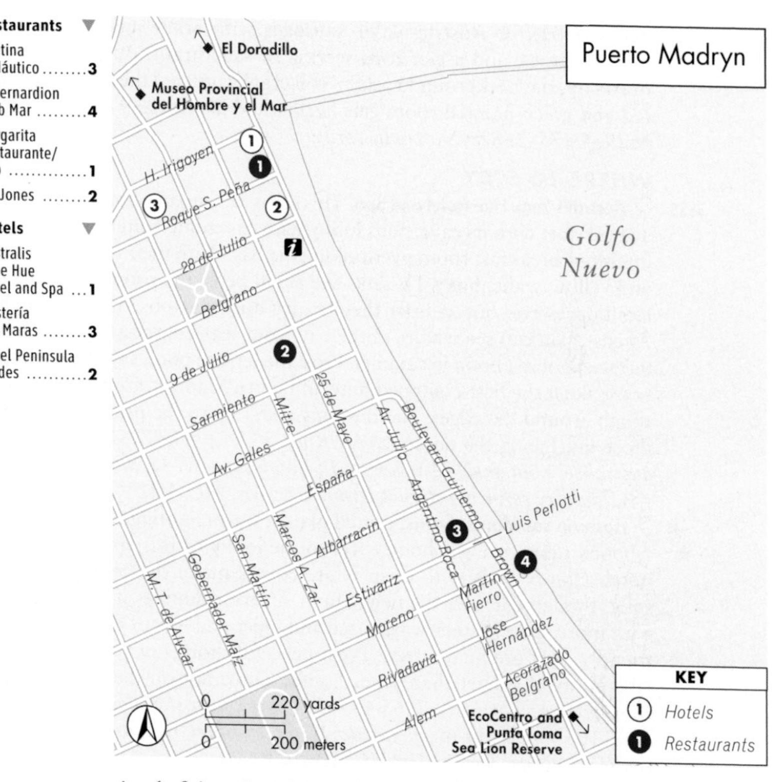

simple fish and seafood dishes and homemade pasta, all served in huge portions. ✉ *Av. Roca 790* ☎ *2965/471–404* ▭ *AE, DC, MC, V.*

$$$$ ARGENTINE ✕ **El Vernardino Club Mar.** Set right on the beach, this bright, airy restaurant has one of the most pleasant locations in Puerto Madryn. If the wind allows, bag a terrace table at lunch, the perfect setting for a big bowl of calamari or one of their imaginative salads. Candles come out at night, together with more elaborate dishes like beef in a wild mushroom and beer reduction, or fresh-caught local salmon in a creamy mussel sauce. ✉ *Blvd. Brown 860* ☎ *2965/455–633* 🌐 *www.vernardinoclubdemar.com.ar* ▭ *AE, MC, V.*

$$$$ ★ ✕ **Margarita Resto Bar.** An old shop front opens into this cheery high-ceilinged bar whose brick walls are hung with colorful carvings and mismatched light fittings. A mile-long cocktail list and great music make Margarita the most popular nocturnal hangout in town (thankfully there are pizzas and burgers to see you through the long nights). Stop by at lunch or before the party gets started, however, for a laid-back but imaginative meal of *moqueca* (fish and seafood stewed in spicy coconut milk), grilled chicken in red beer, or steak in berry sauce. ✉ *Saénz Peña 15* ☎ *2965/470–885* 🌐 *www.margaritapub.com* ▭ *No credit cards.*

$$$ CONTINENTAL ✕ **Mr. Jones.** A great range of Patagonian artisanal beers is one reason to hunker down at the worn wooden booths in this popular pub. The hearty European fare is another: fill up on Irish meat pies, goulash

and spaetzle, or Austrian-style sausages with home-made mustard, rosti potatoes, and a generous serving of sauerkraut. As the evening draws on, the background rock 'n' roll cranks up, and the already cozy red-and-green-painted room gets livelier and livelier. ✉ *9 de Julio 116* ☎ *2965/475–368* ▭ *No credit cards.*

WHERE TO STAY

$$$$ **Australis Yene Hue Hotel and Spa.** This self-styled luxury hotel gets off to a good start with its cavernous lobby with cascading water garden and luminous breakfast room overlooking the bay. With their textured gray and yellow walls, boxy TV sets, and small beds, the rooms are rather less impressive, but at least they're airy and spacious. June through August, you can see whales in the bay from seaview rooms. The small terrace pool is a boon in summer. **Pros:** the terrace pool, small gym, and spa make it the best-equipped hotel in Puerto Madryn. **Cons:** service is rough around the edges; bland rooms aren't up to the price, especially those not facing the ocean. ✉ *Av. Roca 33* ☎ *2965/471–214* ⊕ *www.australiset.com.ar* *71 rooms* *In-hotel: safe, Wi-Fi, bar, pool, gym, spa, laundry service, Internet terminal* ▭ *AE, MC, V* *CP.*

¢ ★ **Hostería Las Maras.** Sofas, potted plants, warm lighting, and polished wooden tables bring a homey feel to the lobby of this small redbrick hotel. Comfy beds with crisp white covers make the rooms just as snug, though consider the newly built superior doubles if you're after a bit more space. Either way, peace and quiet and lots of help from the friendly staff are guaranteed. **Pros:** peaceful; home-away-from-home vibe; more character than other hotels. **Cons:** not on the waterfront. ✉ *Marcos A. Zar 64* ☎ *2965/453–215* ⊕ *www.hosterialasmaras.com.ar* *10 rooms* *In-room: no a/c, Wi-Fi. In-hotel: restaurant, laundry service, Internet terminal* ▭ *MC, V* *CP.*

$$$$ **Hotel Península Valdés.** The minimal gray-and-taupe lobby and slick, wooden-walled breakfast bar are the result of the gradual renovation of this well-established hotel. The renewal process has also reached the seventh-floor rooms, which have boxy hardwood furniture and an earthy color scheme. However, they're still as cramped as the dated rooms on the other floors, with the exception of the *panoramicos*, which have bigger beds and fabulous views of the bay. **Pros:** excellent service; disabled access. **Cons:** older rooms not worth the price; gym is tiny. ✉ *Av. Roca 155* ☎ *2965/471–292* ⊕ *www.hotelpeninsula.com.ar* *76 rooms* *In-hotel: safe, restaurant, bar, gym, laundry service, Internet terminal, Wi-Fi* ▭ *AE, DC, MC, V* *BP.*

SPORTS AND THE OUTDOORS

CYCLING

Cycling is a great way to reach El Doradillo and Punta Loma. You can rent mountain bikes by the hour or the day from **Escuela Windsurf Na Praia** (✉ *Av. Almte. Brown 860* ☎ *2965/455–633* ⊕ *www.napraia.com.ar*), next to Vernadino Club Mar.

DIVING

Dive shops line Puerto Madryn's beachfront, but you'd do well to detour a block inland to talk to **Lobo Larsen** (✉ *Av. Roca 885* ☎ *2965/470–277* ⊕ *www.lobolarsen.com*). Their English-speaking dive masters offer snorkeling and introductory dives and courses to non-divers, and wreck and reef outings to certified divers. Best of all is the chance to dive or snorkel with sea lions who swim right up to you.

KAYAKING AND WINDSURFING

Escuela Windsurf Na Praia (✉ *Av. Almte. Brown 860* ☎ *2965/455–633* 🌐 *www.napraia.com.ar*) rents sea kayaks and Windsurfers, and runs guided nature-watching kayak tours to nearby bays. During their summer Sea School (🌐 *www.escueladelmar.com.ar*) local instructors work with children aged 6–14 on snorkeling, windsurfing, bait and lure fishing, basic nautical and fishing knots, and identification of local fauna, as well as offering motor and sailboat excursions. There is also a windsurfing school for adults.

PENÍNSULA VALDÉS

Fodor's Choice ★

Puerto Pirámides is 104 km (64 mi) northeast of Puerto Madryn.

The biggest attraction is the *ballena franca* (southern right whale) population, which feeds, mates, and gives birth here. The protected mammals attract some 120,000 visitors every year from June, when they first arrive, through December. Especially during the peak season of September and October, people crowd into boats at Puerto Pirámides to observe at close range as the 30- to 35-ton whales breach and blast giant V-shaped spouts of water from their blowholes.

GETTING HERE AND AROUND

About 60 km (37 mi) northeast along the coast on Ruta 2 from Puerto Madryn, the land narrows to form an isthmus. A ranger's station here marks the entrance to the Península Valdés Area Natural Protegida (Protected Natural Area), where you pay a park entry fee of 45 pesos. A further 22 km (14 mi) down the road is the newly remodeled Centro de Visitantes Istmo Ameghino (Ameghino Isthmus Visitor Center). A series of rather dry displays provide a basic introduction to the marine, coastal, and continental flora and fauna ahead of you. More exciting is the complete skeleton of a southern right whale and the views over the isthmus from the lookout tower.

From the visitor center it's another 24 km (15 mi) to the junction leading to Puerto Pirámides, 2 km (1.2 mi) to the south. By following the road 5 km (3 mi) east you reach the start of the circuit of the interconnected 32- to 64-km (20- to 40-mi) dirt roads around the peninsula.

There are different ways to explore the peninsula. If you prefer natural surroundings to cityscapes and really want to see all the area has to offer, plan on spending at least a night or two here rather than using Puerto Madryn as your base. The accommodations in Puerto Pirámides easily rival those in town, and when the tour parties leave you get the rugged, windswept coastal landscape all to yourself. Hearing whales splashing offshore at night is a particularly magical experience. By staying you also have time to do an additional whale-watching trip at sunset, and to go hiking, kayaking, or snorkeling with sea lions.

However, if your schedule is tight, consider one of the many organized day trips that operate out of Puerto Madryn. A minibus typically

Experienced divers might be lucky enough to swim near a right whale calf like the one in the foreground here.

picks you up at your hotel around 8 AM, stops briefly at the visitor center, then continues to Puerto Pirámides for whale-watching (June–December only) and lunch. During the afternoon you visit two other spots on the peninsula before returning to Puerto Madryn by about 7 PM. These tours are reasonably priced (at this writing, prices ranged from AR$240–AR$300 pesos per person) and pack a lot in. However, you spend most of the day crammed in the minibus, don't get to visit the entire peninsula, and have little time to linger at wildlife spots.

To visit the peninsula more extensively at your own pace, you need to rent a car and stay overnight. Having your own wheels also gives you the freedom to stay in the beautiful but remote lodgings at Punta Delgada and Punta Norte. Bear in mind, though, that you'll have to drive several hundred kilometers on dirt and gravel roads in varying states of repair. Stock your vehicle well with drinks, snacks, and gas (the only station is at Puerto Pirámides), and don't try to overtake the tour buses: cars are much lighter, and flipping is an unfortunately common accident here. Economy vehicle rental starts at about 280 pesos per day; the nearest place to rent from is Puerto Madryn.

If all you want to do is whale-watch, you can reach Puerto Pirámides on one of the two to three daily public bus services from Puerto Madryn run by Mar y Valle. Tickets cost 16.50 pesos each way.

For the freedom of your own car without the responsibility of driving, arrange for a remis and private driver. You can do this as a day trip from Puerto Madryn through most local tour operators (prices vary), or from Puerto Pirámides, if you're staying there, with El Gauchito. Expect to pay about 600 pesos for a full day exploring the peninsula.

Finally, you can combine some of the above approaches and get an overview of the peninsula on a tour, but then get off at Puerto Pirámides on the way back and stay overnight, do other excursions, and then return on the public bus.

ESSENTIALS

Mar y Valle (✉ *Terminal de Ómnibus, Puerto Madryn* ☎ *2965/450–600*).

Rental Cars Sigma Rent A Car (✉ *Av. Roca 27, Local 33* ☎ *2965/471–379* 🌐 *www.sigmarentacar.com*).

Visitor and Tour Info Puerto Madryn (✉ *Av. Roca 223* ☎ *2965/453–504 or 2965/456–067* 🌐 *www.madryn.gov.ar/turismo*).

Remis Tours El Gauchito (☎ *2965/495–014*).

Tour Companies Bottazzi (✉ *Complejo La Torre, Blvd. Brown at Martín Fierro,* ☎ *2965/474–110* 🌐 *www.titobottazzi.com*). **Causana Viajes** (✉ *Mathews 1395* ☎ *2965/452–769* 🌐 *www.causana.com.ar*). **Nievemar** (✉ *Av. Roca 493* ☎ *2965/455–544* 🌐 *www.nievemartours.com.ar*). **Miras del Mar** (✉ *Av. Roca 11* ☎ *2965/474–936* 🌐 *www.mirasdelmar.com*).

Visitor Info Centro de Visitantes Istmo Ameghino (Ameghino Isthmus Visitor Center) (☎ *2965/1556–5222* ⏲ *Daily 8–8*).

EXPLORING

PUERTO PIRÁMIDES

The only settlement on Península Valdés is tiny Puerto Pirámides, which transforms into Argentina's whale-watching capital between June and December. The main street, Avenida de las Ballenas, runs parallel to the shore about 200 meters inland, and is lined with pretty tin-roofed buildings among dunes and scrubby flowers. Two streets run down from it to the sea; all the whale-watching operations are clustered around the first of these, known as *la primera bajada*.

For ecological reasons, only 350 people are allowed to live here permanently, but there is a good selection of hotels and restaurants. **■ TIP→ Bring plenty of money with you, as the one ATM may be out of cash.** In addition to whale-watching and lounging around with a beer while looking out on the pyramid-shaped cliffs that gave the town its name, activities include scuba diving or snorkeling with sea lions, kayaking, sand-boarding, and mountain-biking.

PUNTAS DELGADA, CANTOR, AND NORTE

Gravel-surfaced RP2 continues 70 km (43 mi) east from Puerto Pirámides toward the edge of the peninsula. About halfway along are the **Salina Grande** and **Salina Chica**, two salt lakes you walk near. On the southeastern tip of Península Valdés lies **Punta Delgada**, marked by an old lighthouse. It now houses a luxury hotel: both the lighthouse and the surrounding beaches—home to a colony of elephant seals—are only open to hotel guests or those who dine at its restaurant.

Elephant seals also gather at **Punta Cantor,** a further 35 km (22 mi) north along the eastern coast of the island (on RP47, though it's unmarked). A well-maintained cliff-side walkway leads you from the restrooms and restaurant near the road to a viewing area above the seals. The

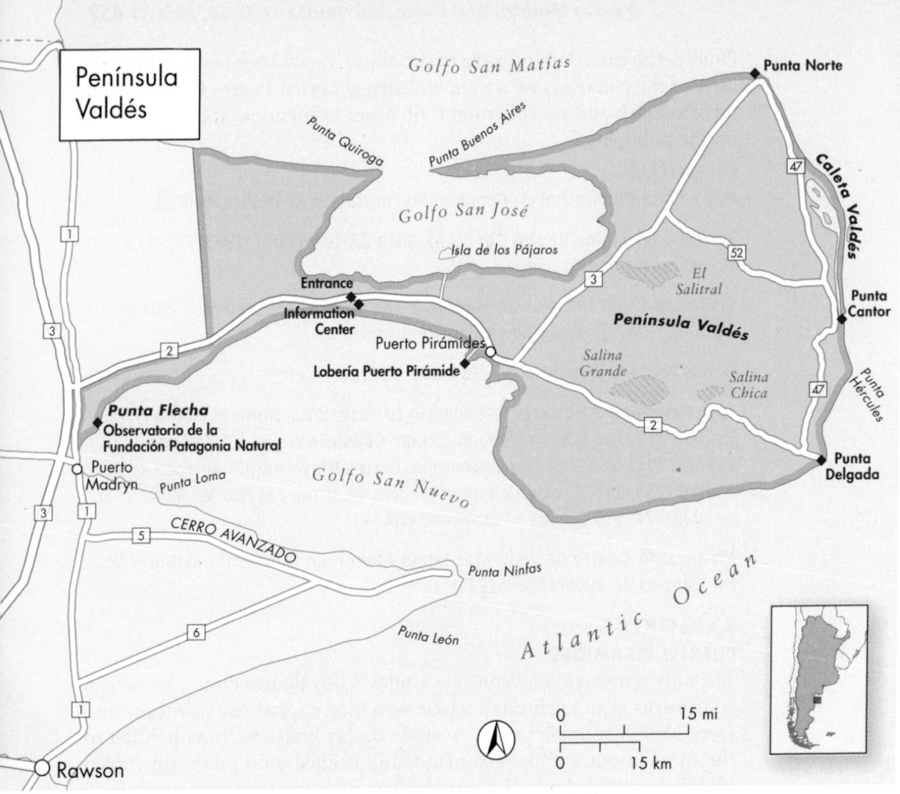

breeding season starts in August, when the males compete for beach space. Then the females arrive, form harems, give birth, and fatten up their cubs before heading out to sea in November. From Punta Cantor RP52 crosses back across the peninsula, reconnecting with RP3 to return to Puerto Pirámides. Alternatively, another 22 km (14 mi) north up the coast is **Caleta Valdés**, a long cove with turquoise waters beside which Magellanic penguins often gather.

The northeastern corner of the peninsula, **Punta Norte,** has the largest sea-lion settlement of all, and is also the best place to spot orcas in December. Magellanic penguins also roam the land from October through March. From Punta Norte RP3 is an inland shortcut that heads straight back southwest to Pirámides, passing by **El Salitral,** the largest of the peninsula's three salt-lake ecosystems.

SPORTS AND THE OUTDOORS

PUERTO PIRÁMIDES

From June to December the main attractions at Puerto Pirámides are whale-watching boat trips into the Golfo Nuevo to see southern right whales. Experienced captains pilot the boats between the huge mammals and bilingual guides tell you about their habits and habitats. Expect to use up lots of your camera memory as the graceful creatures dive, spout water, salute you with their tails, or even jump.

Most whale-watching companies operate several trips a day while the whales are in town, especially during the peak months of September and October. Standard daytime excursions last about 1¼ hours, and the price is set each year by the municipality (at this writing it was 120 pesos). Trips in smaller boats and longer tours are usually more expensive. Although no boat is allowed closer than 15 meters from the whales (the animals themselves sometimes break the rules by diving under your boat), you certainly feel closer from smaller vessels. On clear days the magical sunset tours are definitely worth paying extra for: you see the whales frolic as the sun sets over the water around them. It's best to call a day or two ahead to reserve, although many companies will fit you in if you show up on the day.

Ecological commitment is the foremost priority at **Hydrosport** (✉ *Primera Bajada* ☎ *2965/495–065* 🌐 *www.hydrosport.com.ar*), a reliable, long-running operator with three different boat sizes.

Southern Spirit (✉ *Av. de las Ballenas at Primera Bajada* ☎ *2965/15–572–551* 🌐 *www.southernspirit.com.ar*) uses large but fairly low boats that have an underwater sound-detection system so you can hear the sounds the whales make. They operate up to six trips a day and don't charge more for the one at sunset.

Although trips tend to be more expensive with **Tito Botazzi** (✉ *Primera Bajada* ☎ *2965/495–050* 🌐 *www.titobottazzi.com*), they tend to be longer than other companies' and have excellent English-speaking guides. The sunset trips are on very small boats, and include wine and cheese in Hotel Las Restingas afterward.

Kayaking in the Golfo Nuevo, nature-watching hikes, and snorkeling with sea lions are some of the adventurous activities offered by **Patagonia Explorers** (✉ *Av. de las Ballenas at Primera Bajada* ☎ *2965/15–340–619* 🌐 *www.patagoniaexplorers.com*). Guides and instructors all speak English.

Some 4 km (2½ mi) from Puerto Pirámides lies the **Lobería Puerto Pirámides,** a sea-lion colony which is also a great bird-watching spot. A signposted turnoff from the main road into town leads here, or you can follow the coastal path on foot.

WHERE TO EAT AND STAY

PUERTO PIRÁMIDES

For quick sandwiches or burgers before a whale-watching trip, try one of the snack bars that are interspersed with the tour operators on the Primera Bajada. All close at about 7 PM.

$$$$ ARGENTINE ✕ **La Estación Pub.** The coolest bar in Pirámides is also the town's best seafood restaurant. Amid the nets and nautical gear hangs a motley collection of soccer team flags, glam rock posters, and LPs. Equally eye-catching are the tables—painted tomato red, tangerine, or sea-green—and the menus, illustrated with pictures of David Bowie. As well as the requisite fish and steak dishes, offerings include a great range of pizzas and homemade pastas: try the garlicky mussel sauce. ✉ *Av. de las Ballenas s/n* ☎ *2965/495–047* 💳 *MC, V* ⊗ *Closed Tues.*

$$$ ARGENTINE ✕ **Piedra Guacha.** In the early evening a log fire and low lighting warm the wooden-paneled walls and rustic old furnishings at this resto-pub. Gore-

tex–clad whale-watchers and trekkers exchange wildlife tales over the paellas, chicken stew, or veggie stir-fries, all served in terra-cotta dishes. Settle in as plates are removed and the bar action begins. It's a five-minute walk east up the main street from the Primera Bajada. ☒ *Av. de las Ballenas s/n* ☎ *2965/15–577–897* ▭ *No credit cards* ⊙ *No lunch.*

WHERE TO STAY

$$$–$$$$ **Cabañas en el Mar.** Skip the aging A-frame cabins and try to book one of the two new apartments. Their living rooms look down the street to the ocean and include fully equipped kitchens, making them popular with families and biologists here on extended stays. The rooms are painted in soothing neutrals, and there are lots of natural fibers and materials—the bathrooms, for example, have stone walls, rough-hewn backsplashes, and rain shower heads. Each unit accommodates up to five people. **Pros:** stylish and good value, especially for groups. **Cons:** located near all the whale-watching operators, so may be noisy during the day, cabins are much less attractive than apartments. ☒ *Av. de las Ballenas s/n* ☎ *2965/495–049* ⊕ *www.piramides.net* *3 cabañas, 2 apartments* *In-room: no a/c (some), no phone, kitchen. In-hotel: laundry service* ▭ *No credit cards.*

$$$ Fodor's Choice ★ **Hostería Ecológica del Nómade.** When you're staying in a wildlife reserve, taking care of Mother Nature seems only right. But although this eco-friendly hotel uses solar panels and low-energy fittings and recycles its grey water, they haven't skimped on style. Moss- or sage-green walls offset the recycled-wood headboards, and the huge firm beds have crisp linens, natural wool throws, and lots of pillows. The wildlife documentary crews and nature-loving travelers that stay here love the homemade breads, cakes, and jams at breakfast and take gleeful advantage of the free Wi-Fi (a first in Puerto Pirámides). The young friendly staff help you organize nature-oriented expeditions all over the peninsula, including spots few tourists visit. Ask about discounts if you plan to stay for a few days. **Pros:** eco-awareness at no loss to comfort; detailed local information from staff and library of nature books; fabulous breakfasts. **Cons:** slightly removed from the restaurants on the main drag. ☒ *Av. de las Ballenas s/n* ☎ *2695/495–044* ⊕ *www.eco-hosteria.com.ar* *8 rooms* *In-room: no phone, no TV, Wi-Fi. In-hotel: Wi-Fi* ▭ *MC, V* *CP.*

$$$$ **Las Restingas.** The powder-blue clapboard facade of Puerto Pirámides's most upmarket hotel stretches along the beachfront: squint and you can see whales from the huge picture windows in the front-facing rooms and lobby lounge. Rooms are spacious and airy, if rather plain for the price. **Pros:** excellent restaurant with a deck overlooking the sea; sea (and whale) views from some rooms. **Cons:** rooms facing the village are very overpriced; tiny bathrooms. ☒ *Primera Bajada at the beach* ☎ *2965/495–101* ⊕ *www.lasrestingas.com* *12 rooms* *In-room: DVD. In-hotel: restaurant, bar, beachfront, laundry service, pool, spa, public Internet* ▭ *AE, MC, V.*

PUNTA DELGADA

$$$$ ★ **Faro Punta Delgada.** This remote complex of buildings on the tip of Península Valdés once housed a navy station, post office, and a little school, as well as the *faro* (lighthouse) that the hotel takes its name

CLOSE UP

A Bloody Hero

Look at the street signs in any Patagonian city and you're sure to spot the name General Julio Argentino Roca. (To see what he looks like, whip out your wallet: he's riding along the 100-peso note, too). But look a little closer, and you may well find stickers or stencils changing the street's name to "Pueblos Originarios" (First Peoples).

The history books celebrate Roca as the man who "civilized" Patagonia and extended Argentinean territory south, but the real story is much darker. In the late 1870s the bottom half of Argentina was still largely controlled by various indigenous peoples who resisted the European colonization of their territory. Funded by rich landowners from Buenos Aires anxious to extend their estates, war minister Roca led a series of brutal military attacks—euphemistically known as the Desert Campaigns—which led to the massacre of over a thousand Mapuche, Teheulche, and Ranquel warriors and the enslavement of countless indigenous women and children.

Despite countless attempts by indigenous rights groups to rename the streets and reprint the banknotes, for the time being, these continue to honor the man behind the massacre.

from. Punta Delgada's luxuries are simple and aristocratically old-fashioned: comfortable beds with chintz covers, a tennis court, a pleasant pub with pool and darts, board games, and utter tranquillity under starry night skies. Best of all are the guided nature walks among the sea lions and elephant seals on its private beaches and horse-riding expeditions, all included in your stay. The staff also organize private trips to other points on the peninsula. *Cordero al asador* (barbecued lamb) is the star dish at the excellent restaurant; hotel guests have it to themselves at dinner, but tour groups tend to stop by for lunch in large numbers. **Pros:** peaceful; private beaches afford great wildlife experiences; fabulous food. **Cons:** rooms don't have water views; very isolated for some; busy with tour buses at midday. ✉ *Punta Delgada, Península Valdés* ☎ *2965/458–444* 🌐 *www.puntadelgada.com* *27 rooms* *In-room: no a/c, no phone, no TV. In-hotel: restaurant, bar, tennis court, beachfront* 💳 *AE, MC, V* ⏲ *Closed Apr.–July* *BP, MAP.*

8

TRELEW, GAIMAN, AND PUNTO TOMBO

Updated by Victoria Patience

When the Welsh settlers landed on the desert-like Patagonian coast in 1865 they realized they would need to move inland to find suitable land for farming. Some 25 km (15 mi) inland, in the fertile Chubut River valley, they founded Trelew and Gaiman. Both retain Welsh traditions to this day: Trelew holds an Eisteddfod (festival of Welsh poetry, song, and dance) each October, and Gaiman is the largest Welsh settlement outside of Wales.

With almost 100,000 inhabitants, Trelew is now a large city by Patagonian standards, and its airport is the gateway to Atlantic Patagonia. Beyond the excellent dinosaur museum, however, the dusty, windswept center is of little interest to tourists. With its teahouses, rose gardens, and chapels, Gaiman retains a country-town feel. Indeed, farms and stone-fruit orchards still fill the countryside surrounding it.

On the coast 120 km (74 mi) south of Trelew lies the Punta Tombo penguin reserve, which you can easily visit on a day trip from Trelew, Gaiman, or Puerto Madryn.

TRELEW

11 km (6 mi) east of Gaiman; 250 km (155 mi) north of Camarones; 67 km (41½ mi) south of Puerto Madryn.

Trelew (pronounced Tre-*leh*-ew) is a commercial, industrial, and service hub that contains the region's main airport. Its biggest attractions are its paleontology museum and its proximity to the Punta Tombo reserve (though both can also be reached on day trips from Gaiman and Puerto Madryn). Otherwise, the city has little to recommend it: its mediocre hotels are notoriously overpriced, and aside from rental car firms, its tourism infrastructure is far less organized than Puerto Madryn's. If you come in the second half of October you can watch part of the Eisteddfod, a Welsh literary and music festival first held in Patagonia in 1875. Trelew was founded in 1886 as a result of the construction of the now-defunct Chubut railway line, which connected the Chubut River valley with the Atlantic coast. The town is named after its Welsh founder, Lewis Jones (*Tre* means "town" in Welsh, and *Lew* stands for Lewis), who fought to establish this railroad.

GETTING HERE AND AROUND

If you're driving, from the RN3 take RN25 to Avenida Fontana. The long-distance bus terminal is at Urquiza and Lewis Jones, along the Plaza Centenario. Most of what you'll visit is found in the half-dozen blocks between Plaza Centenario and Plaza Independencia, which is also where you'll find the tourist office.

ESSENTIALS

Bus Contacts Andesmar (✉ *Terminal de Ómnibus* ☎ *2965/433–535*). **Don Otto** (✉ *Terminal de Ómnibus* ☎ *2965/429–496*). **TAC** (✉ *Terminal de Ómnibus* ☎ *2965/439–207*).

Car Rental Hertz (✉ *Aeropuerto de Trelew* ☎ *2944/475–247* 🌐 *www.hertzargentina.com.ar*).

Currency Exchange Banco de la Nación (✉ *25 de Mayo 2, at Av. Fontana* ☎ *2965/449–100*).

Post Office Trelew (✉ *Av. Fontana 355*).

Visitor and Tour Info Tourist Office (✉ *Mitre 387* ☎ *2965/420–139* 🌐 *www.trelew.gov.ar*).

EXPLORING

Fodor's Choice ★ Trelew's star attraction is the **Museo Paleontológico Egidio Feruglio (MEF)**, where four hushed and darkened galleries of fossils both real and replica take you back in time. You start among the South American megafauna (giant armadillos and the like) that may have cohabited with the first humans here, then plunge back to a time before the Andes existed.

Trelew's Museo Paleontológico Egidio Feruglio, or Paleontology Museum, is bursting with oncological treasures.

Back then Patagonia was a subtropical rain forest filled with dinosaurs, including the largest creature to ever walk the earth: the 100-ton, 120-foot-long Argentinosaurus. Replicas of its massive leg bones are on display, along with countless other dino skeletons. Other highlights include a 290-million-year-old spider fossil with a 3-foot leg span and the 70-million-year-old petrified eggs of a Carnotaurus. The visit ends with a peek into the workshop where paleontologists study and preserve newly unearthed fossils. Tours in English are available—they're a good idea, as only the introductions to each room are translated. ✉ *Av. Fontana 140* ☎ *2965/432–100* 🌐 *www.mef.org.ar* 🎫 *25 pesos* ⏲ *Mar.–Sept., weekdays 10–6, weekends 9–8; Oct.–Feb., daily 9–8.*

8

Across the street from MEF is Trelew's old train station, which now contains a small museum of the town's history, the **Museo Regional Pueblo de Luis** (Trelew Regional Museum). Photos, clothing, and objects from local houses, offices, and schools form the mishmash of displays on the European influence in the region, the indigenous populations of the area, and wildlife. ✉ *Av. 9 de Julio at Av. Fontana* ☎ *2965/424–062* 🎫 *2 pesos* ⏲ *Weekdays 8–8, Sun. 2–8.*

WHERE TO EAT AND STAY

$$$ ARGENTINE ★ ✕ **Miguel Angel.** With its paneled walls, sleek black tables, and vintage photos, this stylish Italo-Argentine restaurant is the happy exception to a dining scene that's as bleak as the steppes surrounding the town. Deferential waitstaff help you pick which of their pasta specialties to go for—options include squash ravioli in wild mushroom sauce, spinach and Parma ham agnolotti, or—most indulgent of all—stuffed gnocchi. Lunching professionals come for the set menus, which often

include thick steaks and roast potatoes, and on Wednesdays they do a sushi evening. ✉ *Av. Fontana 246* ☎ *2965/430–403* 💳 *AE, MC, V* ⊙ *Closed Mon.*

$ CAFÉ ✕ **Touring Club.** Legend has it that Butch Cassidy and the Sundance Kid once stayed here—search long enough and you might find them among the old photos cluttering the walls. This cavernous old *confitería* (café) was founded in 1907, and became Chubut's first hotel in 1926. Its vintage tiles and molded ceiling don't seem to have changed much since, except that you can now use Wi-Fi from your scuffed table. The hotel's rooms are too shabby to recommend, but a toasted sandwich and a coffee or beer here is tantamount to a trip back in time. ✉ *Av. Fontana 240* ☎ *2965/433–997* 💳 *AE, DC, MC, V.*

$$$ **Hotel Libertador.** This big hotel has definitely seen better days, but because it caters to tour groups the staff speaks reasonable English. Rooms are clean, but worn around the edges—the faded bedcovers, textured wallpaper, and scuffed Formica furnishings of the standard rooms really aren't up to the price. The more recently renovated "superior" rooms are marginally better. **Pros:** on-site parking; amenable staff. **Cons:** only the superior rooms are worth the price. ✉ *Av. Rivadavía 31* ☎ *2965/420–220* 🌐 *www.hotellibertadortw.com* *90 rooms* *In-room: no a/c (some), Wi-Fi. In-hotel: restaurant, laundry service, Wi-Fi, parking (no fee)* 💳 *AE, DC, MC, V* *CP.*

$$$$ **Rayentray.** The lobby's stained carpets, scuffed paneling, and cranky old elevator don't bode well at what is supposed to be Trelew's best hotel. The rooms are only slightly better. They're furnished with a mix of old and new: aging vinyl headboards and battered closets sit alongside new armchairs and top-quality bedlinens. Like much of the hotel, the simple bathrooms are living monuments to the 1980s. **Pros:** it's a block from Plaza Independencia. **Cons:** ridiculously overpriced. ✉ *San Martín 101,* ☎ *2965/434–702* 🌐 *www.cadenarayentray.com.ar* *110 rooms* *In-room: Wi-Fi. In-hotel: restaurant, pool, laundry service* 💳 *AE, DC, MC, V* *CP.*

GAIMAN

17 km (10½ mi) west of Trelew.

The most Welsh of the Atlantic Patagonian settlements, Gaiman (pronounced *Guy*-mon) is a sleepy country town that is far more charming than nearby Trelew and Rawson. A small museum lovingly preserves the history of the Welsh colony, and many residents still speak Welsh (although day-to-day communication is now in Spanish). A connection to Wales continues with teachers, preachers, and visitors going back and forth frequently (often with copies of family trees in hand). Even the younger generation maintains an interest in the culture and language.

Perhaps the town's greatest draws are its five Welsh teahouses (*casas de té*)—Ty Gwyn, Plas-y-Coed, Ty Nain, Ty Cymraeg, and Ty Té Caerdydd. Each serves a similar set menu of tea and home-baked bread, scones, and a dazzling array of cakes made from family recipes, although the odd dulce de leche–filled concoction is testament to Argentinean cultural imperatives. Most teahouses are open daily 3–8 and charge 45–50

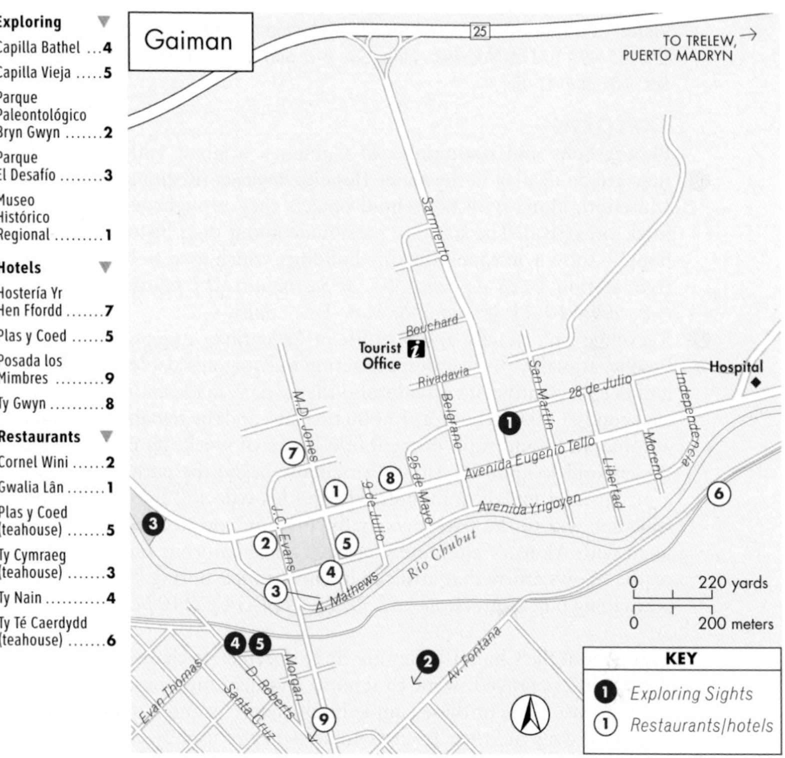

pesos per person for tea (the spreads are generous enough to replace lunch or dinner, and you can usually take away a doggy bag of any cake you don't finish). Each establishment has its own family history and atmosphere, and a there's healthy competition between them as to which is the most authentically Welsh.

GETTING HERE AND AROUND

Gaiman is easily walkable: nearly all the teahouses and other attractions are within a five-block radius of the town square at Avenue Eugenio Tello and M.D. Jones. If you don't have a car, you can access the few sites outside of town—such as the Bryn Gwyn Paleontology Park—by taking an inexpensive remis from one of the *remiserías* on the square.

Although their English isn't brilliant, the friendly young staff at the tourist office give enthusiastic advice on what to visit in Gaiman and hand out detailed maps of the town and its surroundings.

ESSENTIALS

Currency Exchange Banco del Chubut (✉ *J.C. Evans 115* ☎ *2965/491-031* 🌐 *www.bancochubut.com.ar*).

Post Office Gaiman (✉ *J.C. Evans 110*).

Visitor and Tour Info Tourist Office (*Belgrano 574, at Rivadavía 2965/491–571 Mar.–Dec., Mon.–Sat. 9–6, Sun. 11–6; Jan. and Feb., Mon.–Sat. 9–8, Sun. 11–8*).

EXPLORING

Photographs and testimonies of Gaiman's original 160 Welsh set-
1 tlers are on display in the **Museo Histórico Regional** (Regional Historical Museum), along with household objects they brought with them or made on arrival. The staff are passionate about their history, and will happily show you round the tiny building, which used to be Gaiman's train station. *28 de Julio 705, at Sarmiento 2 pesos Jan. and Feb., daily 10–11:30 and 3–6; Mar.–Dec., daily 3–6.*

3 Recycling isn't exactly a way of life in Argentina—except at **Parque El
★ Desafío,** arguably the weirdest attraction in Patagonia. Colorful, kitsch, and deeply creative, it's a sculptural theme park made entirely of recycled goods—80,000 bottles, 15,000 tin cans, and the remains of several automobiles—and took over 30,000 hours of work. Its mastermind, 90-year-old Joaquin R. Alonso, originally began the park in 1980 as a playground for his grandkids. He and his wife still live on-site and welcome you to the park personally, inviting you to stroll the paths lined with Alonso's alternately pensive and humorous musings. One reads, "Cows affirm that artificial insemination is boring." A visit here is anything but. *Av. Brown 52 2965/491–340 10 pesos Daily 3–9.*

Throughout the Chubut Valley are three dozen or so chapels where the Welsh settlers prayed, went to school, and held meetings, trials, and social events. Two of these simple brick chapels stand alongside each other just over the river from Gaiman—they're usually closed to the
5 public, but are interesting to see from the outside. The aptly named **Capilla Vieja** (Old Chapel) was built in 1880, and is used each year for the traditional Welsh Eisteddfod, when townspeople gather to celebrate—and compete with each other in—song, poetry, and dance under the chapel's wooden vaulted ceiling.

4 **Capilla Bethel**, next to Capilla Vieja, was built in 1914, and is used today by Protestants for Sunday service. To reach the chapels, walk south from the square on J. C. Evans and cross the pedestrian bridge. Locals take a shortcut by ducking through the fencing where the bridge ends and walking 100 meters to the right along the riverside. Otherwise take the first right into Morgan and follow the dirt road around several bends.

Just south of Gaiman, the green river valley gives way to arid steppes where clearly visible strata reveal over 40 million years of geological history. Some 600 acres of these badlands—many of them bursting
2 with fossils—make up the **Parque Paleontológico Bryn Gwyn** (Bryn Gwyn Paleontology Park), a branch of the Museo Paleontológico Egidio Feruglio in Trelew. Guides lead you along the fossil trail, then you're left to wander freely through the botanical gardens of native Patagonian plants. *8 km (5 mi) south of town 2965/432–100 www.mef.org.ar/mef/en/institucional/geoparque.php 8 pesos Mar.–Sept., daily 11–5; Oct.–Feb., daily 10–6.*

WHERE TO EAT

$$–$$$ ARGENTINE ✕ **Cornel Wini.** For decades the Jones family, owners of this stately redbrick corner building, ran a hotel and bar (complete with a boxing ring in the basement) here, but switched to serving steaks, pizzas, and pasta in 2007. The decision has been a success: on weekends, locals from as far afield as Puerto Madryn pack themselves round the wooden tables of the bright, high-ceilinged dining room to devour their generous *parrilladas* (mixed grills). We love the presence of Gaiman's traditional dark fruit cake in the *Postre Wini*, in combination with ice cream, nuts, whipped cream, and liqueurs. ✉ *Av. Eugenio Tello 199* ☎ *2965/491–397* ▭ *AE, MC, V.*

$$$ ARGENTINE ★ ✕ **Gwalia Lân.** Exposed brick, low lighting, wooden booths, and a traditional pub-like atmosphere make this both the warmest and the liveliest restaurant in town. Some come just for a beer—the place stays lively well into the evening—while others dine on the house specialty, homemade pastas. If you're craving sirloin, choose from the balsamic vinegar, Malbec, wild mushroom, or black-pepper sauces. ✉ *M. D. Jones 418, at Tello on the plaza* ☎ *2965/15–68–2352* ▭ *No credit cards* ⏲ *Closed Mon. No dinner Sun.*

$$$$ CAFÉ ✕ **Ty Cymraeg.** This airy redbrick teahouse opposite the Chubut River is a fairly modern construction, but photographs of the Thomas family's ancestors watch over you from the walls. An outdoor patio with tree-shaded benches lies behind it, and there's a souvenir shop off to the side. ✉ *Av. Matthews 74* ☎ *2965/491–010* 🌐 *www.gaimantea.com* ▭ *AE, DC, MC, V.*

$$$$ CAFÉ ★ ✕ **Ty Nain.** The matriarch who presides over the kitchen here, Mirna Jones, is a proud descendant of the first woman born in Gaiman. Her ivy-covered teahouse on the main square looks like a knickknack shop: it's stuffed with doodads and hung with crochet, and there are gramophones, carriage lamps, and antique radios on display above the four original chimneys, which date to 1890, although Formica paneling detracts slightly from the Old World style. ✉ *Hipólito Yrigoyen 283* ☎ *2965/491–126* ▭ *No credit cards.*

$$$$ CAFÉ ★ ✕ **Ty Té Caerdydd.** A short way out of town lies Gaiman's largest teahouse, surrounded by cypress trees, sculpted gardens, and a giant tea pot. It stands apart from its rivals culturally, too: it's run by descendents of a Spanish family, which shows in the sprawling colonial-style architecture. Otherwise you'd never know they weren't Welsh, as they do the most impressive spread of traditional cakes in town. Better yet, this was where Princess Diana took her tea during her visit to Gaiman in the early 1990s (Scotland Yard liked the security of its rural location). The cup she used, numerous photos, and other memorabilia form a shrine-like display in her honor. ✉ *Finca 202, Zona de Chacras* ☎ *2965/491–510* ▭ *AE, DC, MC, V.*

WHERE TO STAY

$ 🏨 **Hostería Yr Hen Ffordd.** Gaiman's best budget accommodation is this family-run B&B. The rooms are simple, but they're spacious and warm and have comfy beds, bright feather quilts, new bathrooms, and even free Wi-Fi (quite a find in Gaiman). The bread, scones, and jam served at breakfast are all homemade. **Pros:** great breakfasts; friendly owners give

CLOSE UP

Gaiman's Teahouses

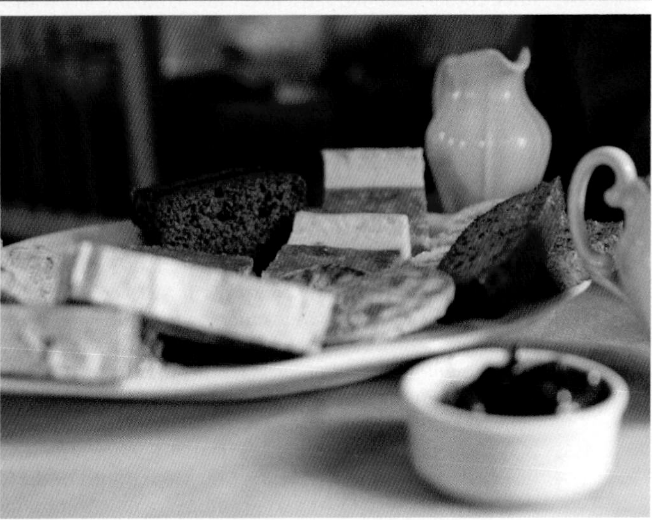

There's an Alice in Wonderland effect as you nibble various cakes and look out on the vast Atlantic Patagonian steppe (which would make anyone feel small).

Gaiman's Welsh teahouses have been famous among travelers for decades. The first teahouse, Plas y Coed, opened in 1944, and figured in Bruce Chatwin's *In Patagonia.*

Each of Gaiman's teahouses serves up its own unique family recipes for all manner of baked goodies, including *torta galesa* (a rich dried-fruit cake), seasonal fruit tarts, buns and sponges, *torta de crema* (a rich baked cream cake), as well as homemade bread, scones, and jam. The tea is always served in big china pots dressed for the occasion in deliciously kitsch hand-knitted tea cozies to ensure your brew stays warm.

Just as the recipes and tastes differ slightly from teahouse to teahouse, so do their interiors. But common to all the teahouses are tapestries and ornamental tea towels, often inscribed with Welsh words and with intricate Celtic designs around the borders. Hanging from the walls—and often for sale, too—are heart-shaped wooden spoons with intricately carved handles. Known as love spoons, they're a Welsh tradition that dates to the 16th century: a young man would carve a spoon from a single piece of wood and give it to the girl he wished to marry.

Most of Gaiman's teahouses are owned and run by descendants of the original Welsh settlers who are are happy to recount their family history if you ask about it. There's a strong sense of appreciation for how easy things are today compared to just a couple of generations ago. Ana, of Plas y Coed, whose great-grandmother was featured in Bruce Chatwin's book, told us, "Imagine making everything from scratch and running this place without refrigerators."

spot-on advice on Gaiman's sights and restaurants. **Cons:** drab carpets detract from the century-old building's charm. ✉ *Michael Jones 342* ☎ *2965/491–394* 🌐 *www.yrhenffordd.com.ar* *4 rooms* *In-room: no a/c, no phone, Wi-Fi. In-hotel: Wi-Fi* *No credit cards* *CP.*

$$ **Plas y Coed.** Gaiman's oldest teahouse has also been a bed-and-breakfast since 1997, and a stay here is rather like visiting with a favorite aunt. The rooms are simple but immaculate, and have polished wooden floors and pastel bedspreads, and there's a comfy lounge area for relaxing in. Outside the redbrick building is Gaiman's oldest rose garden: the bushes arching over the entryway to the teahouse are over 100 years old. **Pros:** an inclusive, family atmosphere. **Cons:** not much room for groups larger than six. ✉ *M. D. Jones 123* ☎ *2965/491–133* 🌐 *www.plasycoed.com.ar* *3 rooms* *In-room: no a/c, no phone, no TV. In-hotel: restaurant* *AE, MC, V* *CP.*

$$$ ★ **Posada Los Mimbres.** Wandering the nature trail alongside the Chubut River is one of the joys of staying on this working farm; picking fruit from the orchard and helping at milking time are others. Lavender and lemon fill the air in the main house, which is a century old. Its rooms have antique furnishings and chintz upholstery, while the modern annex is more like a comfortable family home. **Pros:** the option of lunch and dinner mean you don't need to go back into town for meals; most ingredients are sourced from the farm; beautiful rural setting. **Cons:** isolated from town if you don't have a vehicle. ✉ *Chacra 211* ☎ *2965/491–299* 🌐 *www.posadalosmimbres.com.ar* *6 rooms* *In-room: no a/c, no phone, no TV (some). In-hotel: restaurant, pool, bicycles* *No credit cards* *BP, AI.*

$$ ★ **Ty Gwyn.** The soaring ceilings, wooden rafters, and cobbled white walls of this cavernous teahouse make it seem like you're eating in a medieval dining hall. It was opened in 1974 by María Elena Sánchez Jones, who still directs the kitchen and runs the bed-and-breakfast. An interior garden leads to the staircase that takes you to four lovely bedrooms with wood floors, soothing mint-colored walls, heavy drapes, and dressers fashioned from antique sewing-machine tables. **Pros:** rooms overlook the river; generous breakfasts include fruit and eggs. **Cons:** cruise-ship groups arrive regularly in the high season. ✉ *Av. 9 de Julio 147* ☎ *2965/491–009* 🌐 *www.cpatagonia.com/gaiman/ty-gwyn* *4 rooms* *In-room: no phone, no TV. In-hotel: restaurant* *AE, MC, V* *BP.*

8

PUNTA TOMBO

120 km (74 mi) south of Trelew; 105 km (65 mi) north of Camarones.

Fodor's Choice ★ From the middle of September through March, up to half a million penguins live in the **Área Natural Protegido Punta Tombo** *(Punta Tombo Protected Natural Area)*, the world's largest colony of Magellanic penguins and one of the most varied seabird rookeries. From the park entrance a series of trails, boardwalks, and bridges lead you 3.5 km (2¼ mi) through the scrubby landscape where the penguins nest to the sea. The quizzical creatures seem unafraid of humans, and peer up at you from

CLOSE UP

Pandas of the Sea

You've watched the whales, seen the seals, and admired the penguins. But how about *toninas* (dolphins)? The southern coast of Argentina is home to a particularly attractive species, *Cephalorhynchus Commersonii*, whose black-and-white coloring has earned them the nickname "panda of the sea." **Toninas Adventure** (✉ *Av. Marcelino González at the docks, Puerto Rawson* ☎ *2965/498–372* 🌐 *www.enpuertorawson.com.ar/toninas* 🎫 *Boat-trip 120 pesos* ⏲ *9–6*), the only dolphin-watching enterprise in the area, operates hour-long boat trips from the port at Rawson. They guarantee sightings of their playful namesake creatures, who love to race alongside the boats in packs of three or four, regularly jumping up in perfect arcs. Puerto Rawson is on the coast 30 km (20 mi) east of Trelew, and is an easy detour on trips south to Punta Tombo or beyond. Most organized tours to Punta Tombo stop here.

under the bushes where between September and November both males and females incubate eggs, often right beside the trail. Look for the bald vertical strips on the penguins' abdomens: they pluck out feathers so the eggs can sit warm against their skin. Come December, the ground is teeming with fluffy gray young, and the adult penguins waddle back and forth from the sea to feed them. Once you reach the rocky outcrops overlooking the water you'll see how graceful and powerful these creatures (who move so comically across the land) become when they enter the water. You may also spot guanacos, seals, and Patagonian hares in the reserve, as well as cormorants and a host of other seabirds.

The last 22 km (13½ mi) of the road from Trelew is fairly bumpy gravel. If you're not driving, you can easily reach Punta Tombo on a day tour from Trelew, Gaiman, or Puerto Madryn, although note that these often give you a scant 1½ hours in the reserve. A small restaurant next to the carpark serves good lamb empanadas and also has burgers, coffee, cakes, and cold beverages. 🎫 *45 pesos* ⏲ *8–6.*

CAMARONES AND BAHÍA BUSTAMANTE

Updated by Victoria Patience

The few travelers willing to stray off RN3 to follow gravel RP1 along this stretch of Patagonia's coast will learn a new meaning of "having the place to yourself." Expect to pass next to nobody as you you travel from Puerto Madryn or Trelew to Camarones (passing Punta Tombo), and then from Camarones to Bahía Bustamante.

To some this will seem like a desolate, inhospitable landscape. Yet the land is teeming with both continental and marine wildlife, not to mention the thousands of sheep and goats populating the vast estancias along the way. To others—those who crave open, uncrowded spaces—this area will seem like a paradise. With the exception of Península Valdés, nowhere else in the region yields such a dramatic sense of endless terrain.

The village of Camarones has basic lodging and dining facilities, Punta Tombo is only for viewing wildlife, and Bahía Bustamante is a private—by reservation only—"marine estancia." Each of these stops makes for a convenient, single-day drive, although if you're an experienced road-tripper you could do the whole stretch from Trelew to Bahía Bustamante in a day. If you take RP1, expect to take at least 7 hours to do the roughly 350 km (218 mi). Via the faster but less scenic RN3, it's 258 km (160 mi) direct to Bahía Bustamante without detouring to Camarones, which should take 3–4 hours.

CAMARONES

252 km (156 mi) south of Trelew; 105 km (65 mi) south of Punta Tombo; 258 km (160 mi) north of Comodoro Rivadavía.

After driving or riding for hours along the empty coastal road (or via RP30 from Ruta 3), the tiny town of Camarones—a collection of brightly colored, tin-roofed buildings with scrollwork fascias, trim, and other curious architectural details—appears like an enchanted village. People here seem jovial and happy in their isolation. Most of the worries that plague the inhabitants of Argentina's big cities—crime, unemployment, pollution—simply don't exist here. The only controversy you may encounter is the battle between the town's two main industries, the algae farming and salmon fishing: some species of algae here are invasive, and degrade the salmon's habitat.

The one main event each year is the Fiesta Nacional del Salmón (National Salmon Festival), celebrated in early February with fishing contests and the crowning of Miss Salmoncito (Little Miss Salmon). Other than that, the main attractions are the beautiful, empty beaches south of town, and the Reserva Nartural Cabo Dos Bahías.

EXPLORING

GETTING HERE AND AROUND

Transporte El Ñandú connects Camarones to Trelew with bus service on Monday, Wednesday, and Friday, and ETAP runs services from Comodoro Rivadavía on Monday, Thursday, and Friday, returning on Tuesday, Friday, and Sunday. Rubén Catriel and Veroan provide remis services to local destinations, including Cabo Dos Bahías.

Most everything in Camarones is within four blocks of the main plaza, which slopes down to the waterfront and the *puerto*. The tourist office is open daily, provides information on lodging and dining, and runs walking tours of the town's historical buildings.

ESSENTIALS

Bus Contacts ETAP (☎ *297/489–3058* in Comodoro Rivadavía).

Transportes el Ñandú (☎ 2965/427–499 in Trelew).

Currency Exchange Banco del Chubut (✉ *San Martín 570* ☎ *297/496–3050* 🌐 *www.bancochubut.com.ar*).

Post Office Camarones (✉ *Roca 100*).

Remises Rubén Catriel (☎ 297/15–418–4077). **Veroan** (☎ 297/496–3007).

You're not the only visitor to Punta Tombo: guanaco might join you as you scope out the Magellanic penguins.

Visitor and Tour Info Camarones (✉ *Belgrano at Estrada* ☎ 297/496–3013).

Reserva Natural Cabo Dos Bahías, 28 km (17½ mi) southeast of town, is a solitude-seeking nature-lover's paradise. Chances are you'll be the only humans wandering among the penguins, sea lions, birds, seals, guanacos, rheas, and foxes.

RODS AND TANKS

Local companies **Expediciones Nauticas Patagonia Austral** (☎ *297/15–400–4844*) and **Rumbo Sur** (☎ *297/15–418–5567*) operate fishing excursions. Based in Comodoro Rivadavía, **La Naud Buceo** (☎ *2965/15–600–445* 🌐 *www.lanaud.com*) runs diving trips to Cabo Dos Bahías.

WHERE TO STAY

$$$ **Indalo Inn.** The standard block construction and stuffed animals above the television in the dining room might not seem very inspiring, but the Indalo has clean, comfortable rooms and pleasant little extras like a good wine selection and free Wi-Fi. You can stay either at the hotel or in one of six cabins right on the waterfront. **Pros:** friendly atmosphere. **Cons:** restaurant is hit-and-miss. ✉ *Av. Julio A. Roca at Sarmiento* ☎ *297/496–3004* 🌐 *www.indaloinn.com.ar* *10 rooms, 6 cabins* *In-room: no a/c (some), no phone, Wi-Fi (some). In-hotel: restaurant, Wi-Fi* 💳 *No credit cards* *CP.*

SHOPPING

Right by the tourist office on the waterfront is **Casa Rabal,** one of the most amazing places to shop in all of Patagonia. Originally built in 1901, this dry goods store has everything from locally made cheese to shoes to camping and fishing gear to drywall tools to diapers to bridles for your horse.

BAHÍA BUSTAMANTE

Fodor'sChoice ★ *89 km (55 mi) south of Camarones; 180 km (110 mi) north of Comodoro Rivadavía; 250 km (155 mi) south of Trelew.*

Spending time in Bahía Bustamante is like having your own private Península Valdés. It was founded in 1953 by Lorenzo Soriano, who searched the Patagonian coastline for seaweed to use for extracting colloids. When he found this bay filled with seaweed, he began, along with his sons, to create an entire town including a school, church, auto and boat garage, and housing for more than 400 people who worked harvesting these marine algae.

The operation slowed during the '90s, and nearly everyone moved away. In 2004, however, Lorenzo's grandson Matías returned to Bahía Bustamante and began renovating various houses and transforming the place into what he calls an "estancia marina," or marine ranch, with a special focus on ecological sensitivity, observation of marine and continental wildlife, and independence (producing all their own food and electricity). **■ TIP→ Stays are available for individuals or small groups—only 20 people at a time can stay here—by reservation only.** Aim to stay for at least two or three nights to ensure that weather conditions allow you to take advantage of all the activities included. Even if you're flying rather than road-tripping south, this makes a great stopover between Buenos Aires and El Calafate or Ushuaia (you can fly in and out of Trelew).

8

GETTING HERE AND AROUND

Getting to Bahía Bustamante is an adventure. If you're driving from Camarones, continue south along the coastal RP1 for approximately 85 km (52 mi). At the crossroads with RP28, turn left towards Punto Visser (there's also a hand-painted sign saying Bahía Bustamante). Continue for another 4 km (2½ mi), cross the small concrete bridge, and pass a sign that says Zona Alguera, Prohibido Pasar, and keep going until you reach the single-storey Administracion building. A quicker route to Bahía Bustamante from Trelew is via RN3: after about 220 km (137 mi) turn left into RP28, continue for 33 km (20 mi) to the intersection with RP1, then follow the instructions above. Alternatively, the hotel can arrange private transfers from Puerto Madryn, Trelew, or Comodoro Rivadavía. All transport within Bahía Bustamante is handled by the staff.

WHERE TO STAY

$ **Bahía Bustamante.** Each of the six guesthouses includes twin bedrooms, a living room, a bathroom, and a kitchen. There's electricity only between sunset and 11 PM. Activities include bird-watching, visits to a local petrified forest and archaeological sites, and boat excursions to the Malaspina cove where there are sea-lion colonies, plus penguin and seabird rookeries. Other options are trips to local estancias—where you might see demonstrations of old-style sheep shearing using scissors—as well as horseback riding, fishing, mountain-bike excursions, and trekking. Nearly all of the food cooked in the restaurant comes from ingredients grown at the local estancias or fished from the local waters. Bahía Bustamante currently operates between October and April, with other months available by checking in advance. Prices include all food and excursions. ✉ *RN3, Km 1676* ☎ *11/5032–8677 reservations in Buenos Aires* 🌐 *www.bahiabustamante.com* *6 houses* *In-room: no a/c, no phone, no TV (some). In-hotel: restaurant, beachfront* 💳 *AE, MC, V (only for payment in advance via e-mail)* *Closed Apr.–Aug.* *AI.*

COMODORO RIVADAVÍA

1,854 km (1,149 mi) south of Buenos Aires; 1,726 km (1,070 mi) north of Ushuaia; 945 km (586 mi) north of Río Gallegos; 397 km (246 mi) south of Rawson.

Argentina's answer to Houston, Comodoro Rivadavía is the town that oil built. Unlike Houston, however, there's not much here apart from oil drilling. Argentina's first oil discovery was made here in 1907, during a desperate search for water because of a serious drought. It was an event that led to the formation of Yacimientos Petrolíferos Fiscales (YPF), among the world's first vertically integrated oil companies. After YPF's privatization in 1995, however, thousands were laid off, bringing hard times to Comodoro's 130,000 residents.

Surrounded by barren hills and sheer cliffs off the Golfo San Jorge, Comodoro looks dramatic from a distance. Up close, it's frayed around the edges. The charmless main commercial streets, where you'll find most restaurants and bars, are San Martín and Comodoro Rivadavía.

Because visiting oil workers occupy rooms for long periods of time, there is a nearly constant shortage of hotel rooms, so never show up here without an advance reservation.

WHERE TO STAY AND EAT

$–$$ **Austral Plaza Hotel.** Comodoro's smartest hotel is actually two hotels in one: the older, larger, but more modest Austral Express, and the newer Austral Plaza, a 42-room luxury hotel with marble floors, plush towels, and spacious rooms. If you're only overnighting on your way south, consider the Express—it's almost half the price of the Plaza, but you still get amenities like free Wi-Fi and the same great breakfast. A gym and pool are currently under construction. The Austral also has one of the city's finest seafood restaurants, Tunet. **Pros:** excellent restaurant and dining room. **Cons:** gets booked up quickly; make reservations in advance. ✉ *Moreno 725* ☎ *297/447–2200* 🌐 *www.australhotel.com* *155 rooms* *In-room: no a/c (some), safe (some), Wi-Fi In-hotel: restaurant, bar, laundry service, Wi-Fi* 💳 *AE, DC, MC, V* *CP.*

$$$ SEAFOOD ✕ **Puerto Cangrejo.** The locals crowding the tables at this bustling, family-oriented restaurant are proof of its reputation as the best seafood spot in town. The best dishes are the starters: think, oyster platters, a decadently greasy bowl of calamari, or the *picada de mariscos*, a sampling of hot and cold shellfish dishes. Follow up with the *centolla* (king crab) or stuffed salmon. ✉ *Av. Costanera 1051* ☎ *297/444–4590* 💳 *AE, DC, MC, V.*

SARMIENTO AND THE BOSQUE PETRIFICADO

Updated by Victoria Patience

150 km (94 mi) west of Comodoro Rivadavía.

Built in a fertile valley formed by the Río Senguer and its two interconnected lakes, Lago Musters and Lago Colhué Huapi, the Sarmiento area is a green oasis in the middle of the hard Patagonian steppe. The town itself—home to about 13,000 people—is relatively unattractive, but a visit here gives you a taste of what is undeniably and unpretentiously the "real Patagonia." Relatively few foreign travelers come here, even though the lakes and river, petrified forest, and paleontology park are great attractions, and the rolling farmland outside of town is truly striking, with its tall windbreaks of Lombardy poplars twisting in the strong wind.

TO SPELUNK?

Unique in the region, **spelunking**, or cave exploration, is possible at the **Túnel de Sarasola**, a natural basalt tunnel 45 km (28 mi) west of Sarmiento. Agencia Santa Teresita (☎ *297/489-3238*) can arrange expeditions there.

GETTING HERE AND AROUND

There are several daily bus services between Sarmiento and Comodoro Rivadavía run by Etap and Don Otto. The latter also has services to Esquel and Bariloche. Buses arrive at the bus station at 12 de Octubre and Avenida San Martín, which runs through the center of town.

Sarmiento is only 15 blocks long and eight blocks wide, and can be walked easily, but if you get tired or would like to arrange a trip outside of town, there are various *remiserías* along Avenida San Martín.

ESSENTIALS

Bus Contacts **Don Otto** (✉ *Terminal de Ómnibus* ☎ *297/489-4749* 🌐 *www.donotto.com.ar*). **Etap** (✉ *Terminal de Ómnibus* ☎ *297/489-3058*).

Currency Exchange **Banco de la Nación** (✉ *España at Uruguay* ☎ *297/489-3127* 🌐 *www.bna.com.ar*).

Post Office **Sarmiento** (✉ *Ingeniero Coronel 317 at Sarmiento*).

Visitor and Tour Info **Sarmiento** (✉ *Pietrobelli 388* ☎ *297/489-8220* 🌐 *www.coloniasarmiento.gov.ar/turismo*).

EXPLORING

★ Sarmiento is the jumping-off point for the **Monumento Natural Bosque Petrificado Sarmiento** (Sarmiento Petrified Forest Natural Monument), about 30 km (19 mi) from Sarmiento on R26. Scattered along a vast and colorfully striated badlands are trunks of conifer and palm trees that were deposited here 75 million years ago when the area was a tropical river delta. Regardless of the time of year, bring a jacket. The wind cools you down quickly even in bright sunlight. If you don't have your own vehicle, book a remis from Sarmiento: most charge around 120 pesos for the return trip and an hour's waiting time. ✉ *30 km (19 mi) from Sarmiento on R26* ☎ *297/489-8282* 🎟 *20 pesos* 🕒 *Apr.–Oct., daily 11–6; Nov.–Mar., daily 9–7.*

8

Near Los Glaciares National Park and El Calafate, you'll find some of the most remote-feeling estancias in Argentina.

Fodor's Choice ★ **Parque Paleontológico Valle de Los Gigantes** (Valley of the Giants Paleontology Park) has life-size and scientifically accurate replicas of a dozen different dinosaurs whose fossils were discovered in the region. Guided visits in English leave directly from the tourist office every hour on the hour—arrive 10 minutes ahead to get your ticket. ✉ *200 meters from the tourist office* ☎ *297/489–8220* *8 pesos* ⏲ *Apr.–Nov., daily 11–4; Dec.–Mar., daily 10–7.*

While you're in the area, stop at **Lago Musters,** 7 km (4 mi) from Sarmiento, and **Lago Colhué Huapi,** a little farther on. At Lago Musters you can swim and there's fishing year-round.

WHERE TO STAY AND EAT

$$$–$$$$ ✕ **Rancho Grande.** This is where all the locals come to share their *parilladas*. They have excellent Patagonian lamb, plus salads and deserts, and a waitstaff that makes you feel as if you're part of the town. ✉ *Av. Estrada 419* ☎ *2974/893–513* ▭ *No credit cards.*

$$$ Fodor's Choice ★ **Hostería Labrador.** You get a taste of Patagonian country life when you stay on this working *chacra* (farm). Wife-and-husband team Ana Luisa Geritsen (who speaks Dutch and English) and Nicolás Ayling (who speaks English) welcome guests, tend the land, produce homemade fruit preserves and honey, and cook huge breakfasts for their guests. Dinner is available with advance notice. **Pros:** homey atmosphere; Nicolás can arrange local guided tours. **Cons:** far out of town—you need your own vehicle. ✉ *Ruta 20, 10 km (6 mi) from Sarmiento, 1 km (½ mi) before the Río Senguer* ☎ *2974/893–329* 🌐 *www.hosterialabrador.com.ar* *4 rooms* *In-room: no a/c, no phone, no TV* ▭ *AE, MC, V* *CP.*

$ **Los Lagos.** This small, affordable hotel has recently undergone a complete refit, including new carpets, furnishings, and bathrooms. The staff doesn't speak much English but they're friendly and helpful and there's decent on-site restaurant. **Pros:** affordable, free Wi-Fi. **Cons:** can get hot in summer. ✉ *Av. Roca at Alberdi* ☎ *2974/893–046* *20 rooms* *In-room: no a/c, no phone, Wi-Fi (some). In-hotel: restaurant, Wi-Fi* *No credit cards* *CP.*

FAIR TIME!

One of the region's best local markets, Sarmiento's arts, crafts, and food fair is held every Saturday and Sunday from 9 to 8 year-round, right across from the tourism office at Avenida Regimiento de Infantería 25 and Pietrobelli. Here you can find jams, preserves, honey, woolen garments, and other crafts produced at local *chacras*.

EL CALAFATE, EL CHALTÉN, AND PARQUE NACIONAL LOS GLACIARES

Updated by Rick Hind

The Hielo Continental (Continental ice cap) spreads its icy mantle from the Pacific Ocean across Chile and the Andes into Argentina, covering an area of 21,700 square km (8,400 square mi). Approximately 1.5 million acres of it are contained within the Parque Nacional los Glaciares (Glaciers National Park), a UNESCO World Heritage site. The park extends along the Chilean border for 350 km (217 mi), and 40% of it is covered by ice fields that branch off into 47 glaciers feeding two enormous lakes—the 15,000-year-old **Lago Argentino** (Argentine Lake, the largest body of water in Argentina and the third-largest in South America) at the park's southern end, and **Lago Viedma** (Lake Viedma) at the northern end near **Cerro Fitzroy,** which rises 11,138 feet. Plan on a minimum of two to three days to see the glaciers and enjoy El Calafate—more if you plan to visit El Chaltén or any of the other lakes. Entrance to the southern section of the park, where Perito Moreno Glacier is, costs 60 pesos.

8

EL CALAFATE

320 km (225 mi) north of Río Gallegos via R5; 253 km (157 mi) east of Río Turbio on Chilean border via R40; 213 km (123 mi) south of El Chaltén via R40.

Founded in 1927 as a frontier town, El Calafate is the base for excursions to the Parque Nacional los Glaciares, which was created in 1937 as a showcase for one of South America's most spectacular sights, the Perito Moreno Glacier. Because it's on the southern shore of Lago Argentino, the town enjoys a microclimate much milder than the rest of southern Patagonia.

To call El Calafate a boomtown would be a gross understatement. Between 2001 and 2008, the town's population exploded from 4,000 to 22,000, and it shows no signs of slowing down; at every turn you'll see new construction. As a result, the downtown has a very new sheen to it, although most buildings are constructed of wood, with a rustic aesthetic that respects the majestic natural environment. One exception is the brand-new casino in the heart of downtown, the facade of which seems to mock the face of the Perito Moreno glacier. As the paving of the road between El Calafate and the glacier nears completion, the visitors continue to flock in. These include luxury package tourists bound for the legendary Hostería Los Notros, backpackers over from Chile's Parque Nacional Torres del Paine, and *porteños* (those from Buenes Aires) in town for a long weekend—including Argentina's President Cristina Fernández de Kirchner, who owns a vacation house and two hotels down here.

GETTING HERE AND AROUND

Daily flights from Buenos Aires, Ushuaia, and Río Gallegos, and direct flights from Bariloche transport tourists to El Calafate's 21st-century glass-and-steel airport with the promise of adventure and discovery in distant mountains and glaciers. El Calafate is so popular that the flights are selling out weeks in advance, so don't plan on booking at the last minute.

Driving from Río Gallegos takes about four hours across desolate plains, enlivened by occasional sightings of a gaucho, his dogs, and a herd of sheep, and *ñandú* (rheas), shy llama-like guanacos, silver-gray foxes, and fleet-footed hares the size of small deer. **Esperanza** is the only gas, food, and bathroom stop halfway between the two towns.

Avenida del Libertador San Martín (known simply as Libertador) is El Calafate's main street, with tour offices, restaurants, and shops selling regional specialties, sportswear, camping and fishing equipment, and food.

A staircase ascends from the middle of Libertador to Avenida Julio Roca, where you'll find the bus terminal and a very busy Oficina de Turismo with a board listing available accommodations and campgrounds; you can also get brochures and maps, and there's a multilingual staff to help plan excursions. It's open daily 7 AM–10 PM. The Oficina Parques Nacionales, open weekdays 7–2, has information on the Parque Nacional los Glaciares, including the glaciers, area history, hiking trails, and flora and fauna.

TIMING

During the long summer days between December and February (when the sun sets around 10 PM), and during Easter vacation, tens of thousands of visitors come from all corners of the world and fill the hotels and restaurants. This is the area's high season, so make reservations well in advance. October, November, March, and April are less crowded and less expensive periods to visit. March through May can be rainy and cool, but it's also less windy and often quite pleasant. The only bad time to visit is winter, particularly June, July, and August, when many of the hotels and tour agencies are closed.

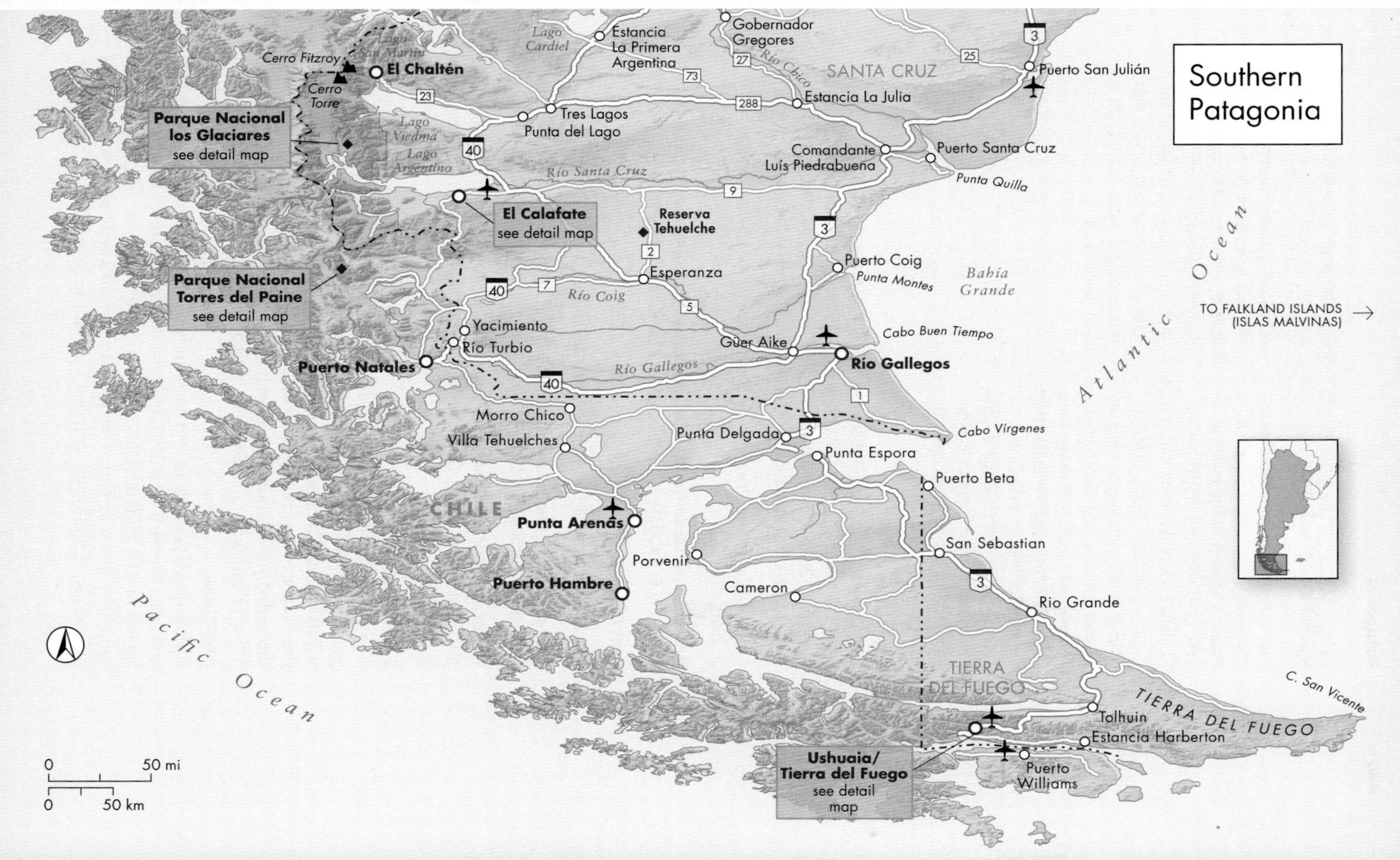

Southern Patagonia
SANTA CRUZ
CHILE
TIERRA DEL FUEGO
TIERRA DEL FUEGO
Atlantic Ocean
Pacific Ocean
TO FALKLAND ISLANDS (ISLAS MALVINAS)
Parque Nacional los Glaciares see detail map
Parque Nacional Torres del Paine see detail map
El Calafate see detail map
Ushuaia/ Tierra del Fuego see detail map
Reserva Tehuelche
Cerro Fitzroy
Cerro Torre
El Chaltén
Lago San Martín
Lago Viedma
Lago Argentino
Lago Cardiel
Estancia La Primera Argentina
Gobernador Gregores
Río Chico
Estancia La Julia
Puerto San Julián
Tres Lagos
Punta del Lago
Comandante Luís Piedrabuena
Puerto Santa Cruz
Punta Quilla
Río Santa Cruz
Esperanza
Río Coig
Puerto Coig
Punta Montes
Bahía Grande
Cabo Buen Tiempo
Yacimiento
Río Turbio
Puerto Natales
Güer Aike
Río Gallegos
Río Gallegos
Cabo Vírgenes
Morro Chico
Villa Tehuelches
Punta Delgada
Punta Espora
Puerto Beta
Punta Arenas
Porvenir
Puerto Hambre
San Sebastian
Cameron
Rio Grande
C. San Vicente
Tolhuin
Estancia Harberton
Puerto Williams
3
25
27
73
288
23
40
9
2
7
5
1
0
50 mi
0
50 km

CASH WOES

For a town that lives and dies on tourism, one of the most infuriating elements of the boom is the cash shortage that strikes El Calafate every weekend during high season. All the ATM's in town run out of money starting as early as Friday evening, and there's often no respite until midday Monday. Long queues form along the main street in front of bank branches, and tempers fray. The shortage is compounded by tour companies who offer steep discounts for cash on combined glacier, ice-trekking, and estancia tours. If credit card service goes down (not an uncommon occurrence), tensions can boil over. Apart from stocking up during the week, the only way to ensure that you won't run out is to bring all the cash you'll need.

ESSENTIALS

Bus Contacts **Bus Sur** (☎ *2966/442–765, 2902/491–631 in El Calafate*). **Cal Tur** (✉ *Terminal Ómnibus, El Calafate* ☎ *2962/491–842*). **Interlagos** (✉ *Bus terminal* ☎ *2902/491–179*). **TAQSA** (✉ *Bus terminal* ☎ *2902/491–843* 🌐 *www.taqsa.com.ar*). **Turismo Zaahj** (☎ *2902/491–631* 🌐 *www.turismozaahj.co.cl*).

Currency Exchange **Provincia de Santa Cruz** (✉ *Av. Libertador 1285* ☎ *2902/492–320*).

Medical Assistance **Hospital Distrital** (✉ *Av. Roca 1487* ☎ *2902/491–001*). **Farmacia El Calafate** (✉ *Av. Libertador 1190* ☎ *9405/491–407*).

Post Office **El Calafate** (✉ *Av. Libertador 1133*).

Remis **El Calafate** (✉ *Av. Roca* ☎ *2902/492–005*).

Rental Cars **Cristina** (✉ *Av. Libertador 1711* ☎ *2902/491–674* ✉ *crisrent@arnet.com.ar*). **Dollar Rent a Car** (✉ *Av. Libertador 1341* ☎ *2902/492–634*).

Visitor and Tour Info **Oficina de Turismo** (✉ *Av. Roca 1004* ☎ *2902/491–090* 🌐 *www.elcalafate.gov.ar*). **Oficina Parques Nacionales** (✉ *Av. Libertador 1302* ☎ *2902/491–005*).

EXPLORING

The **Glaciar Perito Moreno** lies 80 km (50 mi) away on R11, and the road has now been entirely paved. From the park entrance, the road winds through hills and forests of lenga and ñire trees, until all at once the glacier comes into full view. Descending like a long white tongue through distant mountains, it ends abruptly in a translucent azure wall 5 km (3 mi) wide and 240 feet high at the edge of frosty green Lago Argentino.

Although it's possible to rent a car and go on your own, virtually everyone visits the park on a day trip booked through one of the many travel agents in El Calafate. The most basic tours start at 80 pesos for the round trip and take you to see the glacier from a viewing area composed of a series of platforms wrapped around the point of the Península de

WORD OF MOUTH

"I was on a guided hike on top of Perito Moreno Glacier. An unforgettable experience, I was able to see unparalleled views of the Chilean Andes while climbing over ice ridges, drinking fresh glacial water, and just enjoying the natiral world as I've never seen it before." —Anna Hainze, Fodors.com member

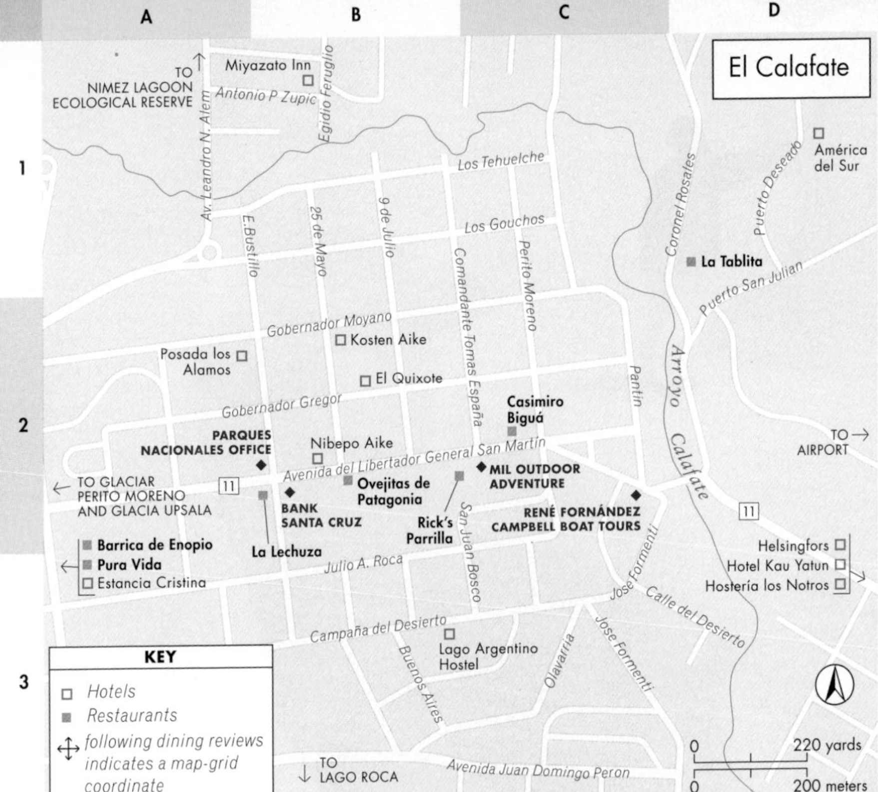

Magallanes. The platforms, which offer perhaps the most impressive view of the glacier, allow you to wander back and forth, looking across the Canal de los Tempanos (Iceberg Channel). Here you listen and wait for nature's number-one ice show—first, a cracking sound, followed by tons of ice breaking away and falling with a thunderous crash into the lake. As the glacier creeps across this narrow channel and meets the land on the other side, an ice dam sometimes builds up between the inlet of Brazo Rico on the left and the rest of the lake on the right. As the pressure on the dam increases, everyone waits for the day it will rupture again. The last time was in July 2008, when the whole thing collapsed in a series of explosions, heard as far away as El Calafate, that sent huge waves across the lake, and could be heard back in El Calafate.

In recent years, the surge in the number of visitors to Glaciar Perito Moreno has created a crowded scene that is not always conducive to reflective encounters with nature's majesty. Although the glacier remains spectacular, savvy travelers would do well to minimize time at the madhouse that the viewing area becomes at midday in high season, and instead encounter the glacier by boat or on a mini-trekking excursion. Better yet, rent a car and get an early start to beat the tour buses, or visit Perito Moreno in the off-season when a spectacular rupture is just as likely as in midsummer and you won't have to crane over other people's heads to see it.

Glaciar Upsala, the largest glacier in South America, is 55 km (35 mi) long and 10 km (6 mi) wide, and accessible only by boat. Daily cruises depart from Puerto Banderas (40 km [25 mi] west of El Calafate via R11) for the 2½-hour trip. Dodging floating icebergs (*tempanos*), some as large as a small island, the boats maneuver as close as they dare to the wall of ice that rises from the aqua-green water of Lago Argentino. The seven glaciers that feed the lake deposit their debris into the run-off, causing the water to cloud with minerals ground to fine powder by the glacier's moraine (the accumulation of earth and stones left by the glacier). Condors and black-chested buzzard eagles build their nests in the rocky cliffs above the lake. When the boat stops for lunch at Onelli Bay, don't miss the walk behind the restaurant into a wild landscape of small glaciers and milky rivers carrying chunks of ice from four glaciers into Lago Onelli. Glaciar Upsala has diminished in size in recent years, a trend many attribute to climate change.

The **Nimez Lagoon Ecological Reserve** is a marshy area on the shore of Lago Argentino just a short walk from downtown El Calafate. It's home to many species of waterfowl including black-necked swans, buff-necked ibises, southern lapwings, and flamingos. Road construction along its edge and the rabidly advancing town threaten to stifle this avian oasis, but it's still a haven for birdwatchers and a relaxing walk in the early morning or late afternoon. Strolling along footpaths among grazing horses and flocks of birds may not be as intense an experience as, say, trekking on a glacier, but a trip to the lagoon provides a good sense of the local landscape. For some reason, the gate is sometimes locked until 9 AM. If you get there early or late, go ahead and hop the fence, no one will mind. Don't forget your binoculars and a telephoto lens. ✉ *1 km (½ mi) north of downtown, just off Av. Alem* 🎫 *2 pesos.*

8

OUTDOOR ACTIVITIES

BOAT TOURS The two most popular scenic boat rides in the Parque Nacional los Glaciares are the hour-long **Safari Náutico,** in which your boat cruises a few meters away from the face of the Glaciar Perito Moreno, and the full-day **Upsala Glacier Tour,** in which you navigate around a more extensive selection of glaciers, including Upsala and Onelli, and sections of Lago Argentino that are inaccessible by land. The Safari Náutico costs 50 pesos, not including transportation from El Calafate. The first boat starts the 45-minute round trip at 10 AM and the last departs at 3:30 PM. The all day Upsala tour costs 192 pesos. **René Fernández Campbell** (✉ *Av. Libertador 867, El Calafate* ☎ *2902/491–155* 🌐 *www.fernandezcampbell.com*) is currently the only local tour operator that runs boat tours to Upsala and Onelli glaciers. Any hotel can arrange reservations.

HIKING Although it's possible to find trails along the shore of Lago Argentino and in the hills south and west of town, these hikes traverse a rather barren landscape and are not terribly interesting. The mountain peaks and forests are in the park, an hour by car from El Calafate. If you want to lace up your boots in your hotel, walk outside and hit the trail, go

SHHH!! IT'S A SECRET!!

Lago Roca is a little-visited lake located inside the National Park just south of Brazo Rico, 46 km (29 mi) from El Calafate. This area receives about five times as much annual precipitation as El Calafate, creating a relatively lush climate of green meadows by the lakeshore, where locals come to picnic and cast for trophy rainbow and lake trout. Don't miss a hike into the hills behind Lago Roca—the view of dark-blue Lago Roca backed by a pale-green inlet of Lago Argentino with the Perito Moreno glacier and jagged snowcapped peaks beyond is truly outstanding. "Shhh," said the local who suggested a visit to Lago Roca. "It's the best place in El Calafate. Don't tell everyone." Never trust a guidebook writer.

There are gorgeous campsites, simple cabins, fishing-tackle rentals, hot showers, and a basic restaurant at **Camping Lago Roca** (☎ *2902/499–500* 🌐 *www.losglaciares.com/campinglagoroca* ⏲ *Closed May–Sept.*). Make reservations in advance if visiting over the Christmas holidays; at other times the campground is seldom crowded. For more comfortable accommodations, you can arrange to stay at the Nibepo Aike Estancia at the western end of Lago Roca, about 5 km (3 mi) past the campground. The National Park entrance fee is only collected on the road to Perito Moreno Glacier or at Puerto Banderas, where cruises depart, so admission to the Lago Roca corner of the park is free.

to El Chaltén—it's a much better base than El Calafate for hikes in the National Park. Good hiking trails are accessible from the camping areas and cabins by Lago Roca, 50 km (31 mi) from El Calafate.

HORSEBACK RIDING Anything from a short day ride along Lago Argentino to a weeklong camping excursion in and around the glaciers can be arranged in El Calafate by **Gustavo Holzmann** (✉ *Av. Libertador 4315* ☎ *2902/493–278* 🌐 *www.cabalgataenpatagonia.com*) or through the tourist office.

Estancias Turísticas (tourist ranches) are ideal for a combination of horseback riding, ranch activities, and local excursions. Information on **Estancias de Santa Cruz** is in Buenos Aires at the **Provincial tourist office** (✉ *Suipacha 1120* ☎ *11/4325–3098* 🌐 *www.estanciasdesantacruz.com*). **Estancia El Galpón del Glaciar** (✉ *Ruta 11, Km 22* ☎ *2902/497–793 or 11/5217–6719* 🌐 *www.estanciaalice.com.ar*) welcomes guests overnight or for the day—for a horseback ride, bird-watching, or an afternoon program that includes a demonstration of sheep dogs working, a walk to the lake with a naturalist, sheep-shearing, and dinner in the former sheep-shearing barn served right off the *asador* by knife-wielding gauchos. **Estancia Maria Elisa** (☎ *2966/492–583* ✉ *estanciamariaelisa@cotecal.com.ar*) is an upscale choice among estancias in Santa Cruz. A good estancia to consider if you want to stay close to El Calafate is **Nibepo Aike** (✉ *50 km [31 mi] from El Calafate near Lago Roca* ☎ *2966/422–626 or 2966/436–010* 🌐 *www.nibepoaike.com.ar*). **Alta Vista** (✉ *33 km [20 mi] from El Calafate* ☎ *2902/499–902* 🌐 *www.hosteriaaltavista.com.ar*), convenient to El Calafate, is a solid choice for the standard estancia activites (horses, sheep, asados) and offers good guidance for local hikes. **Huyliche** (✉ *3 km [2 mi] from El Calafate* ☎ *2902/491–025* 🌐 *www.estancia-huyliche.netfirms.com*) is particularly close to El Calafate while still maintaining a true rustic estancia feel with outdoorsy activities, genial hospitality, and sweeping views.

★ A two-hour mini-trek on the Perito Moreno Glacier involves a transfer from El Calafate to Brazo Rico by bus and a short lake crossing to a dock and refugio, where you set off with a guide, put crampons over your shoes, and walk across a stable portion of the glacier, scaling ridges of ice, and ducking through bright-blue ice tunnels. It is one of the most unique experiences in Argentina. The entire outing lasts about five hours. Hotels arrange mini-treks through **Hielo y Aventura** (✉ *Av. Libertador 935* ☎ *2902/492–205* 🌐 *www.hieloyaventura.com*), which also organizes much longer, more difficult trips of eight hours to a week to other glaciers; you can arrange the trek directly through their office in downtown El Calafate. Mini-trekking now runs about 550 pesos for the day, but prices are marching relentlessly higher. Hielo y Aventura also runs a longer "Big Ice" trek that traverses a much more extensive area of the glacier and costs 750 pesos. If you're between the ages of 18 and 40 and want a more extreme experience, Big Ice is highly recommended.

MOUNTAIN BIKING

Mountain biking is popular along the dirt roads and mountain paths that lead to the lakes, glaciers, and ranches. Rent bikes and get information at **Alquiler de Bicicletas** (✉ *Av. Buenos Aires 173* ☎ *2902/493–806*).

LAND ROVER EXCURSIONS

If pedaling uphill sounds like too much work, check out the Land Rover expeditions offered by **MIL Outdoor Adventure.** These trips use large tour trucks to follow dirt tracks into the hills above town for stunning views of Lago Argentino. On a clear day, you can even see the peaks of Cerro Torre and Cerro Fitzroy on the horizon. MIL's Land Rovers are converted to run on vegetable oil, so environmentalists can enjoy bouncing up the trail with a clean conscience. ✉ *Av. Libertador 1029* ☎ *2902/491–446* 🌐 *www.miloutdoor.com.*

8

WHERE TO EAT

$$$ ECLECTIC

✕ **Barricas de Enopio.** The emphasis at this restaurant-bar is on the extensive wine list and great cheeses that accompany each glass. The flame grill used to barbecue *cordero* (lamb) and other Patagonian standards also doubles as a pizza oven, with thin crusts to savor. The menu also includes eclectic dishes such as pasta stuffed with venison or wild boar. The space is chic, casual, and cozy, with natural-cotton curtains and tablecloths, handmade lamps, and Tehuelche influences. This restaurant offers great value in a town where that's a rapidly diminishing commodity, but it's a bit of a walk from downtown. ✉ *Av. Libertador 1610* ☎ *2902/493–414* 🌐 *www.barricasdeenopio.com.ar (in Spanish)* 💳 *AE, MC, V* ✥ *A2.*

$$$$ ARGENTINE

✕ **Casimiro Biguá.** This restaurant and wine bar boasts a hipper-than-thou interior and an inventive menu serving such delights as Patagonian lamb with *calafate* sauce (calafate is a local wild berry). The **Casimiro Biguá Parrilla,** down the street from the main restaurant, has a similar trendy feel. You can recognize the *parrilla* by the *cordero al asador* (spit-roasted lamb) displayed in the window; your own Patagonian barbecue costs 160 pesos for two, or choose from a dozen different cuts of steak. A third branch, also on Libertador, offers Italian dishes in a less formal setting. ✉ *Av. Libertador 963* ☎ *2902/492–590* 🌐 *www.casimirobigua.com* 💳 *AE, DC, MC, V* ⊕ *C2.*

$$$ ARGENTINE ✕ **La Lechuza.** This bustling joint is known for having some of the best pizza in town. The brick oven and thin crust make for a more authentic, Italian-style taste and texture than at most spots. Their empanadas are among the best in town, pick up a few and you have the perfect pastry pick-me-up during a long day's exploring. With two other branches on the main strip, the secret is out, but stick with the original pizzeria, as the locals do. If it's not crowded, you're in the wrong one. ✉ *Av. Libertador at 1 de Mayo* ☎ *2902/491–610* 💳 *No credit cards* ⏲ *No lunch Sun.* ⊕ *B2.*

$$$ ARGENTINE Fodor's Choice ★ ✕ **La Tablita.** It's a couple of extra blocks from downtown and across a little white bridge, but this *parrilla* is where the locals go for a special night out. You can watch your food as it's cooking: Patagonian lamb and beef ribs roast gaucho-style on frames hanging over a circular asador, and an enormous grill along the back wall is full of steaks, chorizos, and *morcilla* (blood sausage) being cooked to perfection. The whole place is filled with a warm, delicious glow. The enormous *parrillada* for two (105 pesos) is a great way to sample it all, and the wine list is well priced and well chosen. It's slightly more expensive that other parillas in the center of town, but has a classier atmosphere that will make you want to linger for dessert, if there's room. ✉ *Coronel Rosales 28* ☎ *2902/491–065* 🌐 *www.interpatagonia.com/latablita* 💳 *AE, DC, MC, V* ⏲ *No lunch Mon.–Thurs. June and July* ⊕ *D1.*

$$$$ ARGENTINE ✕ **Pura Vida.** Bohemian music and earth tones mix with down-home cooking at this romantic, vegetarian-friendly restaurant several blocks from downtown. You'll be surrounded by funky artwork, couples whispering over candlelight, and laid-back but efficient staff as you try to decide which big-enough-to-share dish you'll order and work your way through a great dome of steaming bread on a platter with lashings of butter. Choose between soups, curries and bakes; the beef stew served inside a *calabaza* (pumpkin) is the signature dish. The cooking isn't quite up to the rest of the restaurant's charms, and the wine list is thin, but Pura Vida is more than the sum of its parts, attracting a curious blend of diners with an almost mystical allure. ✉ *Av. Libertador 1876* ☎ *2902/493–356* 💳 *V* ⊕ *A3.*

$$$ ARGENTINE ★ ✕ **Rick's Parrilla.** The lighting is too bright, the decor mixes utilitarian blandness with hokey equine touches, and the waiters are gruff. But this all-you-can-eat, *tenedor libre* restaurant has stayed incredibly popular for a reason. The bold canary yellow building on El Calafate's main street happens to be the center of the local social scene, but everyone comes here for the meat. Prime cuts, cooked expertly, run the gamut of traditional Patagonian lamb, steak, chicken breast, *morcilla* blood sausage, and even obscure offal selections for more adventurous diners. A waiter asks for your favorites, and they come in waves, all for 45 pesos per person. Salads are unspectacular, but the trio of traditional sauces that come with all Argentine *parrilla* are top notch. Try the fancier restaurants around town if bells and whistles are a must, but you

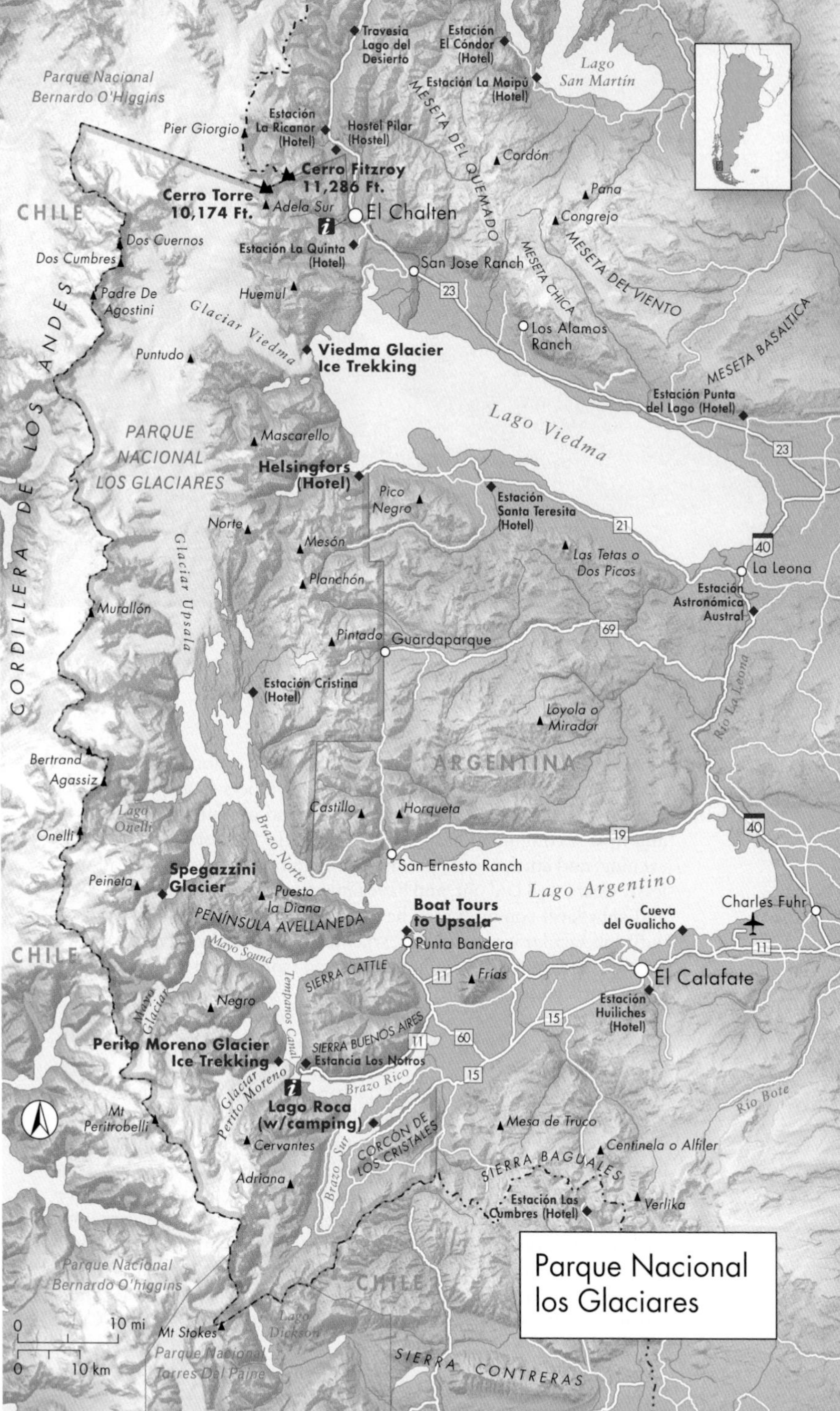
Parque Nacional los Glaciares
Parque Nacional Bernardo O'Higgins
Travesia Lago del Desierto
Estación El Cóndor (Hotel)
Lago San Martín
Estación La Maipú (Hotel)
MESETA DEL QUEMADO
Estación La Ricanor (Hotel)
Hostel Pilar (Hostel)
Pier Giorgio
Cerro Fitzroy 11,286 Ft.
Cordón
Cerro Torre 10,174 Ft.
Adela Sur
El Chalten
Pana
Congrejo
CHILE
Dos Cuernos
Dos Cumbres
Estación La Quinta (Hotel)
San Jose Ranch
MESETA CHICA
MESETA DEL VIENTO
Padre De Agostini
Huemul
23
Glaciar Viedma
Los Alamos Ranch
MESETA BASALTICA
Puntudo
Viedma Glacier Ice Trekking
CORDILLERA DE LOS ANDES
Estación Punta del Lago (Hotel)
Lago Viedma
PARQUE NACIONAL LOS GLACIARES
Mascarello
Helsingfors (Hotel)
Pico Negro
Estación Santa Teresita (Hotel)
Norte
Glaciar Upsala
Mesón
21
40
Las Tetas o Dos Picos
La Leona
Planchón
Estación Astronómica Austral
Murallón
Pintado
Guardaparque
69
Río La Leona
Estación Cristina (Hotel)
Loyola o Mirador
ARGENTINA
Bertrand
Agassiz
Lago Onelli
Onelli
Castillo
Horqueta
Brazo Norte
19
San Ernesto Ranch
Spegazzini Glacier
Peineta
Puesto la Diana
Lago Argentino
Boat Tours to Upsala
Charles Fuhr
Cueva del Gualicho
PENÍNSULA AVELLANEDA
Punta Bandera
Mayo Sound
CHILE
SIERRA CATTLE
Tempanos Canal
11
Frías
El Calafate
Estación Huiliches (Hotel)
Mayo Glaciar
Negro
15
60
SIERRA BUENOS AIRES
Perito Moreno Glacier Ice Trekking
Estancia Los Notros
Brazo Rico
Glaciar Perito Moreno
Río Bote
Lago Roca (w/camping)
Mt Peritrobelli
Mesa de Truco
Cervantes
CORCÓN DE LOS CRISTALES
Centinela o Alfiler
Brazo Sur
SIERRA BAGUALES
Adriana
Estación Las Cumbres (Hotel)
Verlika
Parque Nacional Bernardo O'higgins
CHILE
Lago Dickson
0 10 mi
0 10 km
Mt Stokes
Parque Nacional Torres Del Paine
SIERRA CONTRERAS

Great views of Cerro Fitzroy seem to wait at every bend in the trail in Parque Nacional Los Glaciares.

won't find better barbecue. ✉ *Av. Libertador 1091* ☎ *2902/492–148* ▭ *MC, V* ✥ *B2.*

WHERE TO STAY

¢–$ **América del Sur.** This hostel is regularly rated among the ten best in South America, with good reason. Staff members treat you like their new best friend, speak sparkling English and are full of useful advice and tips. A communal barbecue (for an extra 50 pesos) kicks off each evening, and attracts most guests. Dorm and private rooms are all spotlessly clean, well laid out, and have underfloor heating. The dining room and split-level common area have two-story floor-to-ceiling windows with spectacular views of Lago Argentino. Those views come at a price: a 10-minute uphill walk along a dirt road from downtown. **Pros:** great views; super-friendly staff. **Cons:** a hike from downtown. ✉ *Puerto Deseado* ☎ *2902/493–525* 🌐 *www.americahostel.com.ar* *15 rooms* *In-room: no TV. In-hotel: restaurant, bar, Wi-Fi, no elevator* ▭ *No credit cards* ✥ *D1.*

$$$$ **El Quijote.** Sun shines through picture windows onto polished slate floors in an expansive, modern lobby filled with ferns and palms—it's an incongruous but welcoming atmosphere. The quirkiness of this newly renovated and still-expanding hotel continues with a breakfast room modeled on a '50s-style U.S. diner; understated nods to Cervantes include miniature windmills and suits of armor. Rooms have carpeting, basic wooden furniture, and paper-thin walls but bathrooms are modern with large mirrors and deep, roomy baths. The lobby bar area also has a working fireplace and capacious couches. **Pros:** central location; attentive staff; large and welcoming lobby; funky dining room. **Cons:**

uncreative room decor; prices have leapt in recent years. ✉ *Gregores 1155* ☎ *2902/491–017* 🌐 *www.quijotehotel.com.ar* *119 rooms* *In-room: cable TV, digital safe. In-hotel: bar, public Wi-Fi* *AE, DC, MC, V* *Closed May to Sept.* *CP* ✣ *B2.*

$$$$ ★ **Estancia Cristina.** Boarding a catamaran for the four-hour journey across Lago Argentina, you pass a field of giant icebergs in front of the Upsala Glacier—as spectacular as Perito Moreno, minus the crowds—then disembark at Punta Bandera for a short drive up to the three guest lodges, their stark green roofs mirroring the mountain ridges beyond. Not a bad start to your stay in this remote estancia that is fast building a reputation as one of the best in the region. Fill your days with trekking, horse riding, fly fishing, bird-watching, four-wheel drive journeys to see the glacier from above, and a visit to the lovingly preserved family museum. At night, return from stargazing to the fireplace and a warming soup; in the morning you rise to jaw-dropping views of Cerro Norte. **Pros:** combines a glacier visit with a stay in a genuine estancia; gourmet packed lunches; knowledgeable guides; incredible mountain views from comfortable, well-appointed rooms. **Cons:** long boat journey to get there; chefs try too hard at dinner, pricey for a one-night stay. ✣ *Punta Bandera* *9 de Julio 69, El Calafate* ☎ *2902/491–133* 🌐 *www.estanciacristina.com* *12 rooms* *In-room: phone, safe, no TV. In-hotel: restaurant, bar, laundry service, Wi-Fi* *AE, MC, V* *Closed from May to mid-Sept.* *AI* ✣ *A3.*

$$$$ Fodor's Choice ★ **Helsingfors.** If we could recommend only one property in southern Patagonia, it would be Estancia Helsingfors, a luxurious converted ranch-house with an absolutely spectacular location in the middle of the National Park on the shore of Lago Viedma. The scenery is straight out of a *Lord of the Rings* movie and knowledgeable guides can point out dozens of species of birds; inside, a cozy fire warms the sitting room, friendly staff serve fine food and delicious house wine, and the beds are perhaps the most comfortable in Patagonia. Don't leave without visiting the jewel of Helsingfors, a breathtaking blue lake at the foot of a glacier that's a three-hour hike or horseback ride from the inn. **Pros:** unique location, wonderful staff. **Cons:** three hours by dirt road from El Calafate. ✣ *Lago Viedma, three hours by dirt road from El Calafate* *Cordoba 827, piso 11, Buenos Aires* ☎ *11/4315–1222 in Buenos Aires* 🌐 *www.helsingfors.com.ar* *8 rooms, maximum of 18 guests* *In-room: no TV. In-hotel: restaurant* *AE, MC, V* *Closed May–Sept.* ✣ *D2.*

$$$$ **Hostería los Notros.** Weathered wood buildings cling to the mountainside that overlooks the Perito Moreno Glacier as it descends into Lago Argentino. This inn is designed to exploit its unique position fronting one of the world's natural wonders, and lies 73 km (45 mi) west of El Calafate. The glacier is framed in the windows of every room. Appetizers and wine are served in full view of sunset (or moonrise) over the glacier, followed by a spectacular menu that spotlights game, including delicious venison and creative preparations of Argentine classics. The lodge offers multi-night packages, but has recently allowed guests to stay for one night. No doubt, this is property is expensive; all inclusive prices include all meals, cocktails, park entry,

8

and glacier excursions. **Pros:** unique location; totally luxurious. **Cons:** very expensive; crowds bound for Perito Moreno can detract from the secluded atmosphere. ✉ *Reservations in Buenos Aires: Arenales 1457, fl. 7* ☎ *11/4814–3934 in Buenos Aires, 2902/499–510 in El Calafate* 🌐 *www.losnotros.com* 32 rooms *In-room: no phone, no TV. In-hotel: restaurant, bar, airport shuttle, public Wi-Fi, no elevator* ▭ *AE, DC, MC, V* ⊙ *Closed June–mid-Sept.; standard rooms not available in May or Sept.* *FAP* ⊕ *D3.*

$$$$ **Hotel Kau-Yatun.** From the homemade chocolates and flower bouquets that appear in the rooms each evening to the sweeping back yard complete with swing sets for the kids, every detail of this converted ranch property is tailored to thoughtful hospitality. The property is nestled in a quiet tree-lined valley by a stream yet lies just six blocks from the main street. Guests rave about the attentive staff, the excellent food with a focus on local and organic ingredients, and the log-cabin building, which feels homier than the newer hotels in town. A full schedule of mountain biking, horseback riding, and four-wheel drive expeditions is on offer in the 17,000 hectare Estancia 25 de Mayo that starts just behind the hotel. **Pros:** great food; utmost care put into the details. **Cons:** water pressure is only adequate. ✉ *25 de Mayo* ☎ *2902/491–059* 🌐 *www.kauyatun.com* 44 rooms *In-room: room service, Wi-Fi, laundry service. In-hotel: restaurant, bar, airport shuttle, bicycles, public Wi-Fi, no elevator* ▭ *AE, MC, V* *BP* ⊕ *D3.*

Fodor's Choice ★

$$$$ **Kosten Aike.** Lined with wooden balconies, high beamed ceilings, and a slate floor, this hotel is a paragon of Andean Patagonian architecture. Tehuelche symbols feature on everything from employee uniforms to the curtains. Third floor rooms have attic ceilings that create an even cozier feel. The English speaking staff are helpful and discreet. A sunny rooftop spa, gym, and spacious Jacuzzi offer great views over town to Lago Argentino. A lobby bar and living room with fireplace, card tables, magazines, and a large TV are dangerously conducive to lounging about. **Pros:** large rooms; central location; great views from the spa; good value at this price point. **Cons:** dining room decor is uninspired. ✉ *25 de Mayo 1243, at G. Moyano* ☎ *2902/492–424, 11/4811–1314 in Buenos Aires* 🌐 *www.kostenaike.com.ar* 78 rooms, 2 suites *In-hotel: restaurant, bar, gym, 3 Internet terminals, public Wi-Fi* ▭ *AE, DC, MC, V* ⊙ *Closed May–Sept.* ⊕ *B2.*

$–$$ **Lago Argentino Hostel.** Just around the corner from the bus terminal, this chilled-out hostel is operated by the same family that runs the popular Pura Vida restaurant. Like Pura Vida, the atmosphere is cozy and eclectic, the rooms and public spaces are painted in a kaleidoscope of rustic bold primary colors. *Amor y paz* (love and peace) reads a sign in the entryway, and the friendly staff would not look out of place at a music festival. Private rooms in an annex across the street from the main building are much nicer, but more expensive, than the functional rooms in the main dorms. **Pros:** convenient location; pleasant garden. **Cons:** earplugs recommended in the open-plan dorm rooms; mattresses and pillows could be thicker. ✉ *Campaña del Desierto 1050* ☎ *2902/491–423* 🌐 *www.interpatagonia.com/lagoargentino* *In-hotel: laundry facilities, public Wi-Fi* ▭ *No credit cards* ⊕ *B3.*

"We walked from our hotel in the center of town to the Laguna Nimez Reserve. Wild horses grazed lazily amid the white wildflowers. It was a magical moment of perfect stillness. So unexpected!" —Lois Zebelman, Fodors.com member

8

$$$ **Miyazato Inn.** Jorge Miyasato and his wife Elizabeth have brought the flawless hospitality of a traditional Japanese country inn to El Calafate. Rampant construction has spread from downtown and it's encroaching on the serenity of this hotel, but it's more than made up for by Jorge's warm welcome and encyclopedic knowledge of the region. Each of the five rooms has hardwood floors, comfortable twin beds, and rice paper lampshades, and a sun-drenched dining area sits just off the lobby/lounge. The Miyasatos have two young children, and the family atmosphere makes this cozy inn a refuge of intimacy and calm. **Pros:** clean and homey; outstanding value; owners offer a human touch. **Cons:** construction and road work make for a noisy neighborhood. ✉ *Egidio Feruglio 150* ☎ *2902/491–953* 🌐 *www.interpatagonia.com/miyazatoinn* *5 rooms* *In-hotel: public Wi-Fi, no elevator* ▭ *MC, V* *CP* ✣ *B1.*

$$$ **Nibepo Aike.** This is a lovely estancia within a day-trip's distance from El Calafate in a bucolic valley overlooking Lago Roca and backed by snowcapped mountain peaks. Sheep, horses, and cows graze among purple lupine flowers, and friendly gauchos give horse-racing and sheep-shearing demonstrations. The attached restaurant serves up a truly exceptional lamb and beef barbecue. It's possible to visit Nibepo Aike by booking a day-trip at the office in downtown El Calafate, but the best way to experience this unique property is a two-night stay in comfortable rooms decorated with original antiques and ranching memorabilia. The name Nibepo is a combination of the nicknames of the original owner's three daughters—Nini, Bebe, and Porota. All-inclusive packages are available; options include ice-trekking, a cruise to the Upsala Glacier, fly-fishing, and horse riding trips where you'll ride along the shores of an emerald glacier lake. **Pros:** spectacular scenery; welcoming staff; full range of activities. **Cons:** an hour by dirt road from downtown; two night minimum stay ✉ *For reservations: Av. Libertador 1215* ☎ *For reservations: 2902/492–797* 🌐 *www.nibepoaike.com.ar* *11 rooms* *In-room: no TV. In-hotel: restaurant* ▭ *AE, MC, V* ⏲ *Closed May–Sept.* ✣ *B2.*

$$$$ **Posada los Alamos.** Surrounded by tall, leafy alamo trees and constructed of brick and dark *quebracho* (ironwood), this enormous complex incorporates a country manor house, half a dozen convention rooms, a spa, indoor swimming pool, and mini-golf course to offer all the trappings of a top-notch hotel. However, rooms are dark and sometimes musty, and there's a feeling that it has outgrown personal and attentive service. Prices halve in low season, which only adds to the sense that it's overpriced when you're most likely to visit El Calafate. **Pros:** modern and distinctive reception and public areas, beautiful gardens. **Cons:** it's easy to get lost in the maze of corridors, rooms are indifferently furnished; overly formal staff. ✉ *Moyano 1355, at Bustillo* ☎ *2902/491–144* 🌐 *www.posadalosalamos.com* *140 rooms, 4 suites* *In-hotel: restaurant, bar, spa, convention center, golf course* ▭ *AE, MC, V* *CP* ✣ *A2.*

EL CHALTÉN

222 km (138 mi) north of El Calafate (35 km [22 mi] east on R11 to R40, then north on R40 to R23 north).

Founded in 1985, El Chaltén is Argentina's newest town, and it's growing at an astounding rate. Originally just a few shacks and lodges built near the entrance to the Los Glaciares National Park, the town is starting to fill a steep-walled valley in front of Cerro Torre and Mt Fitzroy, two of the most impressive peaks in Argentina. Famous for the exploits of rock climbers who started their pilgrimage to climb some of the most difficult rock walls in the world in the 1950s, the range is now drawing hikers whose more earthbound ambitions run to dazzling mountain scenery and unscripted encounters with wildlife including condors, Patagonian parrots, red crested woodpeckers, and the *huemul*, an endangered deer species.

GETTING HERE AND AROUND

The four-hour car or bus trip to El Chaltén from El Calafate makes staying at least one night here a good idea.The only gas, food, and restroom facilities en route are at La Leona, a historically significant ranch 110 km (68 mi) from El Calafate where Butch Cassidy and the Sundance Kid once hid from the long arm of the law.

Before you cross the bridge into town over Río Fitzroy, stop at the Parque Nacional Office. It's extremely well organized and staffed by bilingual rangers who can help you plan your mountain treks and point you to accommodation and restaurants in town. It's an essential stop; orientation talks are given in coordination with arriving buses, which automatically stop here before continuing on to the bus depot.

There's only one ATM in town, and it's in high demand; because of servicing schedules, on the weekend El Chaltén runs into the same cash availability problems that El Calafate does, though on a smaller scale. ⚠ **During the week, stockpile the cash you'll need for the weekend, or bring it with you if you're arriving between mid-day Friday and mid-day Monday.**

ESSENTIALS

Visitor Info Parque Nacional Office (☎ *2962/493–004*).

EXPLORING

You don't need a guide to do the classic treks to **Cerro Torre and Cerro Fitzroy**, each about 6 to 8 hours round-trip out of El Chaltén. If your legs feel up to it the day you do the Fitzroy walk, tack on an hour of steep switchbacks to Mirador Tres Lagos, the lookout with the best views of Mt. Fitzroy and its glacial lakes. Both routes, plus the Mirador and various side trails, can be combined in a two or three day trip.

The **Laguna del Desierto** (Lake of the Desert)—a lovely lake surrounded by lush forest, complete with orchids and mossy trees—is 37 km (23 mi) north of El Chaltén on R23, a dirt road. Hotels in El Chaltén can arrange trip for about 100 pesos for the day. Locals recommend visiting Lago del Desierto on a rainy day, when more ambitious hikes are not an option and the dripping green misty forest is extra mysterious.

The **Chorillo del Salta** (Trickling Falls) is a waterfall just 4 km (2.5 mi) north of town on the road to Lago del Desierto. The falls are no Iguazu, but the area is extremely pleasant and sheltered from the wind. A short hike uphill leads to secluded river pools and sun-splashed rocks where locals enjoy picnics on their days off. If you don't feel up to a more ambitious hike, the short stroll to the falls is an excellent way to spend the better part of an afternoon. Pack a bottle of wine and a ham sandwich and enjoy the solitude.

8

WHERE TO EAT

$$$ ARGENTINE ✕ **Aonikenk.** In a dark wooden dining hall you'll share hearty steaks, warming soups and wine poured from penguin-shaped ceramic jugs, in a family restaurant that includes a hostel upstairs. It's rustic, and the food is not spectacular, but you can't beat the friendly atmosphere in what is easily El Chaltén's largest and most popular restaurant. It's also the only one that's consistently open in the off-season. ✉ *Av. M.M. de Güemes* ☎ *2962/493–070.*

$$$ ARGENTINE ★ ✕ **La Cerveceria.** While El Chaltén is still building all it needs to become a fully fledged town, it already has a successful microbrewery. The owners of this restaurant and bar pride themselves on handmade beers, with the stout or *negra* not to be missed. They call the place a "Hausbrauerei," but it's not just the hops bringing in the crowds: they also cook up delicious soups, snacks, and stew. The *locro,* a hearty traditional northern Argentine stew, is some of the best you'll find in southern Argentina. ✉ *San Martin 564* ☎ *2962/193–109* ▭ *AE, MC, V* ⊗ *Closed during off-season June–Sept.*

WHERE TO STAY

$ **Nothofagus.** A simple B&B off the main road, Nothafagus is named after the southern beech tree, and the lodge has a rough-hewn, woody feel with exposed beams and leaves stamped into the lampshades. Unlike in lodgings closer to the valley wall, the breakfast room offers unobstructed views of the Fitzroy spires on a clear morning. The rooms are comfortable and clean, if a bit bare. **Pros:** great views; bright and sunny breakfast room. **Cons:** staff energy too low for some; spartan bathrooms. ✉ *Hensen, at Riquelme* ☎ *2962/493–087* 🌐 *www.nothofagusbb.com.ar* *7 rooms* *In-room: no TV In-hotel: restaurant, laundry service, Internet terminal, Wi-Fi* *AE, D, DC, MC, V* *BP.*

$$$$ ★ **Posada Lunajuim.** A traditional A-frame roof keeps the lid on a funky, modern lodge filled with contemporary artwork, exposed brick masonry, and a spacious lounge and dining room complete with a roaring fireplace and a library stacked with an intriguing mix of travel books. At this writing, the friendly family that runs this fascinating place has plans to double capacity, but for now the place feels like the quirky home of your eccentric aunt—bright red doorways lead to quirky rooms that nonetheless have all the comforts you'd expect. Guests rave about the restaurant's seafood (especially the trout) and its extensive wine list. **Pros:** you could spend all day in the common areas; staff and owners are pleasantly energetic. **Cons:** not all rooms have views; baths are quite small; a little pricey compared to the rest of town. ✉ *Trevisan 45* ☎ *2962/493047* 🌐 *www.posadalunajuim.com.ar* *26 rooms* *In-room: phone, safe, Wi-Fi. In-hotel: restaurant, bar, laundry service, Internet terminal, Wi-Fi* *AE, D, DC, MC, V* *BP.*

SPORTS AND THE OUTDOORS

El Chaltén owes its existence to those who wanted a base for trekking into this corner of Los Glaciares National Park, specifically Cerros Torre and Fitzroy. It's no surprise that nearly everyone who comes here considers hiking up to those two mountains to be the main event—though the locro and microbrews at the end of the day are a plus.

HIKING Both long and short hikes on well-trodden trails lead to lakes, glaciers, and stunning viewpoints. There are two main hikes, one to the base of Cerro Fitzroy, the other to a windswept glacial lake at the base of Cerro Torre. Both hikes climb into the hills above town and excellent views start after only about an hour on either trail. The six-hour roundtrip hike to the base camp for Cerro Torre at Laguna Torre has (weather permitting) dramatic views of Torres Standhart, Adelas, Grande, and Solo.

Trails start in town and are very well marked, so if you stick to the main path there is no danger of getting lost. Just be careful of high winds and exposed rocks that can get slippery in bad weather. The eight-hour hike to the base camp for Cerro Fitzroy passes Laguna Capri and ends at Laguna de los Tres, where you can enjoy an utterly spectacular view of the granite tower. If you only have time for one ambitious hike, this is probably the best choice, though the last kilometer of trail is very steep. **TIP→ Water within the park is potable and delicious, so there's no need to start out with more than a liter or two.** At campsites in the hills above town hardy souls can pitch a tent for the night and enjoy sunset and dawn views of the mountain peaks. Ask about current camping regulations and advisories at the National Park office before setting off with a tent in your rucksack. Finally, use latrines where provided, and under no circumstance should you even think about starting a fire—a large section of forest near Cerro Torre was devastated several years ago when a foolish hiker tried to dispose of toilet paper with a match.

MOUNTAIN CLIMBING A guide is required if you want to enter the ice field, or trek on any of the glaciers in Los Glaciares National Park. **Casa de Guias** is a group of professional, multi-lingual guides who offer fully equipped multi-day treks covering all the classic routes in the national park, and longer trips exploring the ice field that can last more than a week. They even offer a taste of big wall climbing on one of the spires in the Fitzroy range. ✉ *Av. Costanera Sur, El Chaltén* ☎ *2962/493–118* 🌐 *www.casadeguias.com.ar*.

PUERTO NATALES

Updated by Rick Hind

242 km (150 mi) northwest of Punta Arenas.

The land around Puerto Natales held very little interest for Spanish explorers in search of riches. A not-so-warm welcome from the indigenous peoples encouraged them to continue up the coast, leaving only a name for the channel running through it: Seno Última Esperanza (Last Hope Sound).

The town of Puerto Natales wasn't founded until 1911. A community of fading fishing and meat-packing enterprises, with some 20,000 friendly residents, it has recently seen a large increase in tourism and is repositioning itself as a vacation town. It's now rapidly emerging as the staging center for visits to Parque Nacional Torres del Paine, Parque Nacional Bernardo O'Higgins, and other attractions, including the Perito Moreno Glacier across the border in Argentina. A lot of tourism is also generated by the scenic **Navimag cruise** that makes four-day journeys between here and Puerto Montt, to the north.

While there are fewer hotels and restaurants to choose from than in Punta Arenas, the town has added a string of hip eateries, cafés, and boutique hotels in recent years, and is starting to challenge the more staid larger city as a hub for exploring the entire region.

Serious hikers often come to this area and use Puerto Natales as their base for hiking the classic "W" or circuit treks in **Torres del Paine,** which take between four days and a week to complete. Others choose to spend a couple of nights in one of the park's luxury hotels, and take in the sights during day hikes.

If you have less time, however, it's quite possible to spend just one day touring the park, as many people do, with Puerto Natales as your starting point. In that case, rather than drive, you'll want to book a one-day Torres del Paine tour with one of the many tour operators in Natales. Most tours pick you up at your hotel between 8 and 9 AM and follow the same route, visiting several lakes and mountain vistas, seeing Lago Grey and its glacier, and stopping for lunch in Hostería Lago Grey or one of the other hotels inside the park. These tours return around sunset.

Argentina's magnificent **Perito Moreno Glacier,** near El Calafate, can be visited on a popular (but extremely long) one-day tour, leaving at the crack of dawn and returning late at night—don't forget your passport.

Picadas, or light snacks, reach a new level of delicious after an excursion in the wilds of Patagonia; a selection may include peanuts, pistacios, marinated baby onions, or a local cheese.

It's a four-hour-plus trip in each direction. (Some tours sensibly include overnights in El Calafate.) ⇨ *For some recommended tour agencies, see Chapter 2, Choosing Your Cruise and Tour, but there are many in town, and most book the same vans.*

GETTING HERE AND AROUND

Puerto Natales centers on the Plaza de Armas, a lovely, well-landscaped sanctuary. A few blocks west of the plaza on Avenida Bulnes you'll find the small Museo Historico Municipal. On a clear day, an early morning walk along Avenida Pedro Montt, which follows the shoreline of the Seno Última Esperanza (or Canal Señoret, as it's called on some maps), can be a soul-cleansing experience. The rising sun gradually casts a glow on the mountain peaks to the west.

ESSENTIALS

Bus Contacts Buses Fernández (✉ *Eleuterio Ramirez 399* ☎ *61/411-111* 🌐 *www.busesfernandez.com*).

Internet Cafés El Rincón del Tata (✉ *Arturo Prat 23* ☎ *61/413-845*). **The Net House** (✉ *Bulnes 499* ☎ *61/411-472*).

Rental Cars Avis (✉ *Eberhard 547* ☎ *61/614-388*).

Visitor and Tour Info Sernatur Puerto Natales (✉ *Av. Pedro Montt 19* ☎ *61/412-125*).

EXPLORING

A few blocks east of the waterfront overlooking Seno Última Esperanza is the not-quite-central **Plaza de Armas.** An incongruous railway engine sits prominently in the middle of the square. ✉ *Arturo Prat at Eberhard.*

Across from the Plaza de Armas is the squat little **Iglesia Parroquial.** The ornate altarpiece in this church depicts the town's founders, indigenous peoples, and the Virgin Mary all in front of the Torres del Paine.

A highlight in the small but interesting **Museo Historico Municipal** is a room filled with antique prints of Aonikenk and Kaweshkar indigenous peoples. Another room is devoted to the exploits of Hermann Eberhard, a German explorer considered the region's first settler. Check out his celebrated collapsible boat. In an adjacent room you will find some vestiges of the old Bories sheep plant, which processed over 300,000 sheep a year. ✉ *Av. Bulnes 285* ☎ *61/411–263* 🎫 *1,000 pesos* ⏲ *Weekdays 8:30–12:30 and 2:30–8, weekends 2:30–6.*

In 1896, Hermann Eberhard stumbled upon a gaping cave that extended 200 meters (650 feet) into the earth. Venturing inside, he discovered the bones and dried pieces of hide (with deep red fur) of an animal he could not identify. It was later determined that what Eberhard had discovered were the extraordinarily well-preserved remains of a prehistoric herbivorous mammal, *mylodon darwini,* about twice the height of a man, which they called a *milodón.* The discovery of a stone wall in the cave, and of neatly cut grass stalks in the animal's feces led researchers to conclude that 10,000 years ago a group of Tehuelche Indians captured this beast. The cave is at the **Monumento Natural Cueva de Milodón.** The cathedral-sized space was carved out of a solid rock wall by rising waters. It was the final destination for Bruce Chatwin in research for his book *In Patagonia*, but its dusty floor and barren walls are unspectacular, and the tacky life-size fiberglass model at the cave mouth is useful only as a reference to the size of the gigantic animal that lived here. ✉ *5 km (3 mi) off Ruta 9 signpost, 28 km (17 mi) northwest of Puerto Natales* ☎ *No phone* 🎫 *3,000 pesos* ⏲ *Summer, daily 8 AM–8 PM; winter, daily 9–6.*

8

WHERE TO EAT

$$ CHILEAN ★ ✕ **Asador Patagónico.** This bright spot in the Puerto Natales dining scene is zealous about meat. So zealous, in fact, that there's no seafood on the menu. Incredible care is taken with the excellent *lomo* and other grilled steaks, as well as the steak carpaccio starter. Though the wine list is serious, the atmosphere is less so—the place used to be a pharmacy, and much of the furniture is still labeled with the remedies (*catgut crin* anyone?) they once contained. There's good music, dim lighting, an open fire, and a friendly buzz; wear removable layers since it can get warm when the grill is cranking. ✉ *Prat 158* ☎ *61/412–197* 💳 *AE, DC, MC, V.*

¢–$ CAFÉ ✕ **Café Melissa.** Excellent espresso and mountainous burgers are the pride of this unpretentious café, which also serves pastries and cakes baked on the premises. In the heart of downtown, this is a popular meeting place for residents and visitors, and there's Internet access and decent Wi-Fi. You can impress the locals and stun fellow travelers by ordering a *Fanschop*—a mix of beer and Fanta that many Chileans apparently enjoy. The café stays open through the afternoon lull until 9 PM. ✉ *Blanco Encalada 258* ☎ *61/411–944* ▭ *No credit cards.*

NEED A BREAK?

When you've just gotten back from trekking the Torres del Paine and had your first hot shower in a week, sometimes you just want a place to relax that feels of home. El Living (🌐 *www.el-living.com*) couldn't be better named. It feels like a living room, albeit one that's sitting in a bohemian loft in SoHo. The British owners have littered their couches with fashion, rock-climbing, and gossip magazines, and they offer gluten-free vegetarian and vegan dishes at the base of a continent that rarely caters to people who don't eat meat. Homemade pumpkin, ginger, carrot, and coriander soup, kidney bean pumpkin bake, and toasted banana and honey sandwiches are typical hipster comfort food. They're also delicious, especially washed down with *jugo de frambuesa* (fresh raspberry juice). There's no pressure to eat and leave; you could find yourself whiling away the rest of your afternoon, and coming back the next morning for breakfast. You'll find it in the Plaza de Correo on Arturo Pratt, just next door to Asador Patagónico.

¢–$$ PIZZA ✕ **El Rincón del Tata.** This funky little spot is a strange, incongruous addition to the frontier feel of Puerto Natales. Fading movie posters and '60s-era magazine ads butt up against a collection of household items, from the town's early days, in the dining room. The wood-burning stove keeps you warm, and Internet access keeps you in touch. Lamb comes in all shapes and styles, including a middle-eastern kebab, rare in these parts. The *salmón à la mantequilla* (salmon baked in butter and black pepper) is also decent, but the grilled lamb with garlic sauce is the highlight. Not so much the highlight (but forgiveable) are the waiters' modish tango hats and the strange mannequins in the front window. ✉ *Arturo Prat 236* ☎ *61/614–291* ▭ *AE, DC, MC, V.*

$ SEAFOOD ✕ **Mama Rosa.** You'll watch the wind whip the Seno Última Esperanza from a comfortable lounge in front of the fireplace at this ultra-modern café. Complete with Apple Internet terminals and friendly English-speaking staff, this café has been recently converted from a seafood restaurant, and is now making the most of its corner location as part of the boutique Indigo Hotel. Marine fossils collected from the fjord, piles of *National Geographic* and *Outside* magazines, a range of herbal teas, lunch specials like crab ravioli, and delicate desserts served in gigantic portions make this the ideal place for a long lunch. Try the scrumptious carrot cake. ✉ *Ladrilleros 105* ☎ *61/413–609* 🌐 *www.indigopatagonia.com* ▭ *AE, DC, MC, V* ⊙ *Closed in winter; months vary.*

$–$$ CHILEAN ✕ **Restaurant Última Esperanza.** Named for the strait on which Puerto Natales is located, it is perhaps your last chance to try Patagonian seafood classics in a town being overrun by hip eateries. This traditional restaurant is well known for attentive, if formal service, and top-quality dishes from chefs Miguel Risco and Manuel Marín. Poached conger eel in shellfish sauce, king crab stew and *Cordero* (lamb) are specialties, delicious dishes served with plenty of flavor and little fuss. The room is big and impersonal, and for this reason alone the restaurant is perhaps losing ground to new arrivals more focused on atmosphere and comfort. ✉ *Av. Eberhard 354* ☎ *61/413–626* ▭ *AE, DC, MC, V.*

WHERE TO STAY

$–$$ **Hostal Lady Florence Dixie.** Named after an aristocratic English immigrant and tireless traveler, this long-established hotel with an alpine-inspired facade is on the town's main street. Its bright, spacious upstairs lounge is a great people-watching perch. Standard guest rooms are spartan—not much more than a bed, and a bit dark—although the "superior" rooms are bigger, brighter and have bathtubs. **Pros:** very convenient location; friendly owner; relaxed atmosphere **Cons:** not quite the boutique hotel it purports to be, rooms have a dowdy feel in a town that's rapidly modernizing. ✉ *Av. Bulnes 655* ☎ *61/411–158* 🌐 *www.chileanpatagonia.com/florence* *19 rooms* *In-room: safe. In-hotel: laundry service, public Internet, parking (free)* ▭ *AE, MC, V* *CP.*

$$$–$$$$ **Hotel CostAustralis.** Designed by a local architect, this venerable three-story hotel is one of the most distinctive buildings in Puerto Natales; its peaked, turreted roof dominates the waterfront, and it's expanding (over 40 new rooms were added in 2009 alone). The whitewashed walls of the lobby are lined with elegant leather and wicker chairs, sculptural Patagonian lenga logs, and chandeliers with freshly lit candles that stand guard on either side of the elevator. Rooms share the lobby's spare aesthetic, with wood-paneled entryways, thermo-acoustic windows, and Venetian and Czech furnishings. Some have a majestic view of the Seno Última Esperanza and the snowcapped mountain peaks beyond, a couple have their own balconies, and others have considerably less inspiring views out over the city. **Pros:** great views from bay-facing rooms; good restaurant; courteous and professional staff; startlingly low off-season rates. **Cons:** rooms are somewhat bland; endless corridors a little impersonal; candles and bleached walls in the lobby hark back to early '80s rock videos (though with the right attitude this could be a Pro). ✉ *Av. Pedro Montt 262, at Av. Bulnes* ☎ *61/412–000* 🌐 *www.hoteles-australis.com* *110 rooms, 5 suites* *In-room: safe. In-hotel: restaurant, room service, bar, laundry service, public Internet station, Wi-Fi* ▭ *AE, DC, MC, V* *BP.*

$–$$$ **Hotel Martín Gusinde.** Part of Chile's modern AustroHoteles chain, this intimate inn has retained an aura of sophistication even as it has grown to accommodate the surge in visitors to Puerto Natales. The hotel is named after an Austrian ethnologist who studied the native inhabitants of Tierra del Fuego. Rooms are decorated with wooden furniture, colorful patterned wallpaper, and thick, dark green drapes. New rooms have space-age massage shower cubicles, but no bath. The exposed beams in the peak-roofed restaurant hint at the region's frontier heritage but match the rest of the building's understated tone. In low

8

season, prices drop by almost two-thirds. **Pros:** atmosphere is urbane. **Cons:** staff language barrier; seedy casino neighbor; absence of baths in this style of hotel is a mystery. ✉ *Carlos Bories 278* ☎ *61/412–770* 🌐 *www.hotelmartingusinde.com* *20 rooms* *In-room: safe. In-hotel: restaurant, room service, bar, public Internet* 💳 *AE, MC, V* *CP.*

$$$$ ★ **Indigo Patagonia Hotel & Spa.** Chilean architect Sebastian Irarrazabel was given free rein by a multi-national trio of owners to redesign this building along a nautical theme. A maze of gangplanks, ramps and staircases shoot out across cavernous open spaces, minimalist wood panels line walls and ceilings, and water burbles down a waterfall that borders the central walkway. Rooms in this completely renovated hotel have amazing views down the Canal Señoret, stretching as far as the Mt. Balmaceda glacier and the Paine Grande. Blankets are made of hand-woven wool, copper shower heads are comically large, but only the suites have ultra-stylish stand-alone baths. With three high powered open-air Jacuzzis, a sauna, and massage benches with a view, the rooftop spa is a treat for the senses. Downstairs, common spaces are filled with plush couches and hammock chairs. English is spoken well, as exhibited in the Friday-night shows about Torres del Paine. Ask for one of the corner rooms—they have windows along two walls. **Pros:** steeped in ultramodern luxury; at the forefront of Puerto Natales's efforts to attract the hip young traveler market. **Cons:** so ultramodern it might be cloying if it's not your aesthetic; standard rooms do not have bathtubs (though the showers are excellent). ✉ *Ladrilleros 105* ☎ *61/413–609* 🌐 *www.indigopatagonia.com* *23 rooms, 6 suites* *In-room: no TV. In-hotel: restaurant, bar, laundry service, spa, Wi-Fi* 💳 *AE, DC, MC, V.*

WHERE TO STAY JUST OUTSIDE TOWN

Recently, several lodges have been constructed on a bluff overlooking the Seno Última Esperanza, about a mile outside of town. The views at these hotels are spectacular—broad panoramas with unforgettable sunsets. It's too far to walk to town comfortably (about 20 minutes), but there is dependable taxi service for 1,000 pesos.

$$$ **Altiplanico Sur.** This is the Patagonian representative of the Altiplanico line of thoughtfully designed eco-hotels. Nature takes center stage. The hotel blends so seamlessly with its surroundings, it's almost subterranean. Natural materials cover the exterior, with roofs that are overgrown with grass and flowers; it looks like the hotel is cascading down the hillside, with only its windows peeking out from a green bank. If you are looking for TV, Wi-Fi, and other technological accoutrements, choose a different hotel. Clean, comfortable, and well-designed rooms in a minimalist style all have great views of the Última Esperanza Sound. Slate floors, sheepskin bedcovers and modern bathrooms give a chic tweak to the worthiness of the public spaces. The dining area is bright and open. Staff do their best to help, but sometimes language proves a barrier. **Pros:** couldn't be closer to nature; stellar views of the fjords and mountains, even from a low vantage point. **Cons:** staff speaks little or no English; long walk into town and there's no shuttle bus. ✉ *Ruta 9*

Hostería Pehoe, Pehoe Lake, Torres del Paine National Park

Norte, Km 1.5, Huerto 282 ☎ *61/412–525* 🌐 *www.altiplanico.cl* ⇨ *22 rooms* ♿ *In-room: no TV, safe. In-hotel: restaurant* ▭ *AE, MC, V.*

$$$$ Fodor's Choice ★ **Remota.** For most guests, the Remota experience begins with the safari-esque transfer from Punta Arenas Airport, during which the driver stops to point out animals and other items of interest. On arrival you meet what seems like the entire staff, check into your ultramodern room, have a drink from a top-shelf open bar, and run off to the open-air Jacuzzis and impossibly serene infinity pool. The hotel is the paragon of style, deliberately designed (by the same architect as Explora) in a way that blocks out everything but the exquisite vistas. The various wings are connected by enclosed walkways; the lawns in between have been strewn with monoliths, reminiscent of a Japanese rock garden. Inside, the *lenga* walls and ceilings are left natural and deliberately unfinished, and a daybed relaxation area is the best vantage point for floor-to-ceiling views of the fjord and the mountains behind. All meals and your choice of 25 different styles of excursion are included in the price. Every morning a guide proposes a wide range of activities, demanding various levels of exertion, so you are sure to find something to suit your speed. Equipment is supplied and includes everything from Zodiacs to mountain-climbing gear to bikes, and easels for Patagonian landscape painting. Horseback riding with local gauchos is a hard activity to pass up. The guides are helpful, patient, demonstrate an infectious love for the outdoors, and know how to crack a joke. **Pros:** after a few days the staff feels like family; restaurant uses the freshest locally-sourced ingredients; becoming more flexible about minimum length of stay. **Cons:** all-inclusiveness discourages sampling local restaurants; views not as good as those from hotels inside Torres Del Paine National

Park. ✉ *Ruta 9 Norte, Km 1.5, Huerto 279* ☎ *61/414–040* 🌐 *www.remota.cl* *72 rooms* *In-room: no phone, no TV, safe. In-hotel: spa, pool, bicycles, restaurant, bar* ▭ *AE, MC, V* *AI.*

$$ **Weskar Patagonian Lodge.** Weskar stands for "hill" in the language of the indigenous Kaweskar, to whom owner Juan José Pantoja, a marine biologist, pays homage in creating and maintaining this lodge. High on a ridge overlooking the Última Esperanza fjord, the wooden building is surrounded by parkland and has fabulous views from the terrace. Rustic fireplaces and several different lounge nooks are ideal when coming back from the windy and cold outdoors. The hotel also boasts a bar and restaurant with a (somewhat overpriced) standard lunch and dinner menu. As with several other hotels in Puerto Natales, the lodge has added rooms in the last year. All are simply decorated in log cabin style but warm and welcoming with locally woven blankets—and almost all have stunning lake views, something that's not guaranteed in neighboring hotels. Staff members are unremittingly helpful and keep the grounds spotless. The three-night program includes day tours to Torres Del Paine and a sailing trip on the Ultima Esperanza sound. **Pros:** great views from your room; helpful staff. **Cons:** restaurant a little overpriced; from the dining room you can really hear the wind when it's howling; bathrooms are pokey. ✉ *Ruta 9 Norte, Km 1 / Puerto Natales* ☎ *61/414–168* 🌐 *www.weskar.cl* *21 rooms, 2 suites* *In-room: no phone, no TV, safe. In-hotel: restaurant, bar, bicycles, public Internet, laundry service.*

PARQUE NACIONAL TORRES DEL PAINE

Fodor's Choice ★ *80 km (50 mi) northwest of Puerto Natales.*

A raging inferno broke out in the Parque Nacional Torres del Paine on February 17, 2005, when a Czech trekker's gas camp stove was accidentally knocked over. At the time, he was camped in an unauthorized campsite in an area intended for grazing. The park's famous winds fanned the flames for more than a month, as 800 firefighters from Chile and Argentina tried to rein it in. According to reports by CONAF the fire consumed 13,880 hectares, equivalent to 7% of the park. The tourist later apologized in an interview with *El Mercurio* newspaper, was fined $200 by authorities, and donated another $1,000 to the restoration fund. "What happened changed my life . . . I'll never forget the flames. I would like to express my most profound regret to the Chilean people for the damage caused." The Czech government has also taken responsibility for its citizen's mistake by donating 1 million dollars and recently planting 120,000 lenga trees. The main rehabilitation project is due for completion in 2010. CONAF asks that visitors respect the camping zones and the indications of park staff. The institution posts a series of recommendations for camping, and on how to prevent future disasters, on its Web page.

About 12 million years ago, lava flows pushed up through the thick sedimentary crust that covered the southwestern coast of South America, cooling to form a granite mass. Glaciers then swept through the region, grinding away all but the twisted ash-gray spire, the "towers"

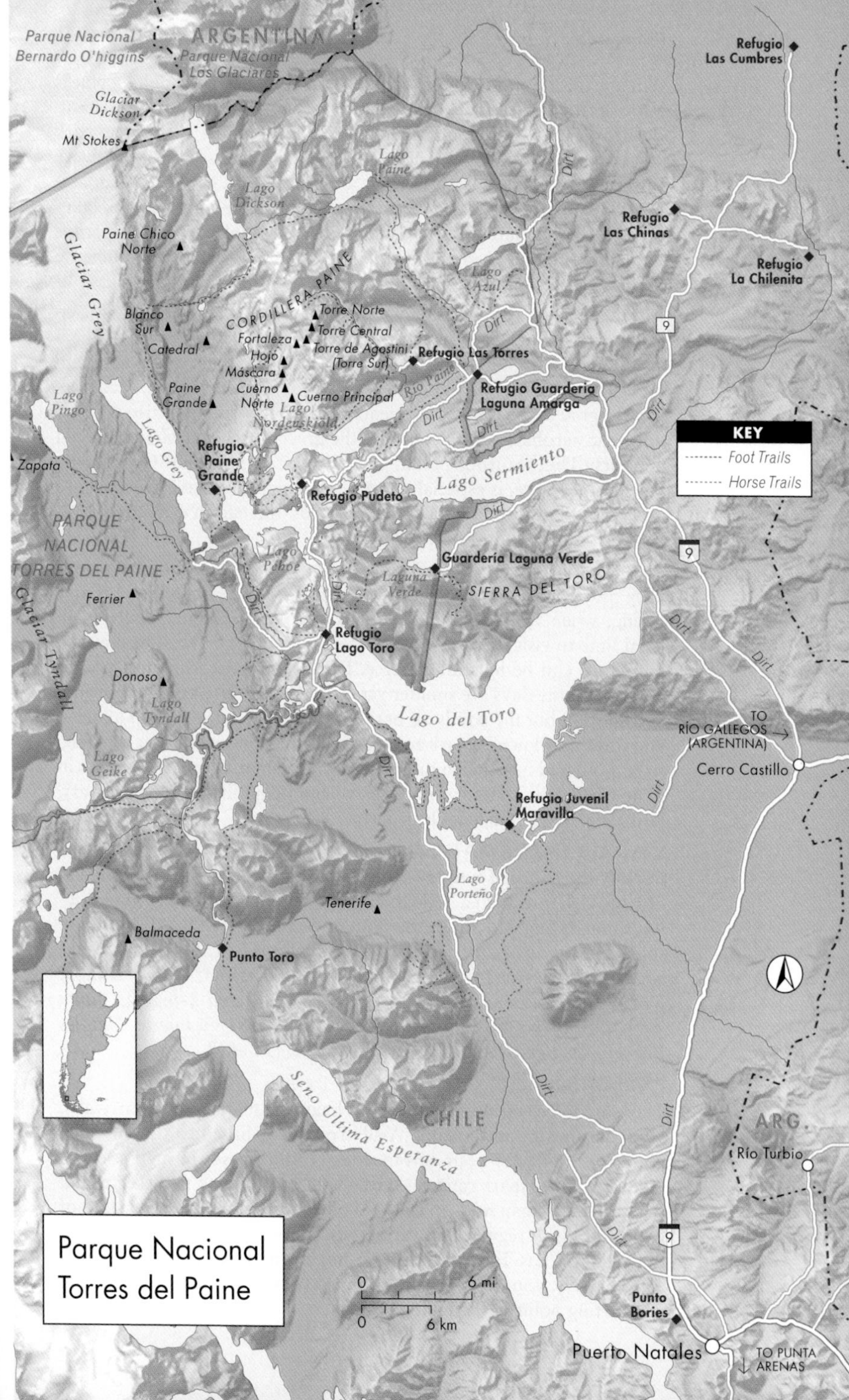

Parque Nacional Torres del Paine
KEY
Foot Trails
Horse Trails
Parque Nacional Bernardo O'higgins
ARGENTINA
Parque Nacional Los Glaciares
Glaciar Dickson
Mt Stokes
Lago Paine
Lago Dickson
Refugio Las Cumbres
Refugio Las Chinas
Refugio La Chilenita
Paine Chico Norte
Glaciar Grey
CORDILLERA PAINE
Lago Azul
Blanco Sur
Catedral
Torre Norte
Torre Central
Fortaleza
Torre de Agostini (Torre Sur)
Hojo
Máscara
Cuerno Norte
Cuerno Principal
Refugio Las Torres
Río Paine
Refugio Guardería Laguna Amarga
Paine Grande
Lago Pingo
Lago Grey
Lago Nordenskjöld
Refugio Paine Grande
Zapata
Lago Sermiento
Refugio Pudeto
PARQUE NACIONAL TORRES DEL PAINE
Lago Pehoe
Guardería Laguna Verde
Laguna Verde
SIERRA DEL TORO
Ferrier
Glaciar Tyndall
Refugio Lago Toro
Donoso
Lago Tyndall
Lago del Toro
Lago Geike
TO RÍO GALLEGOS (ARGENTINA)
Cerro Castillo
Refugio Juvenil Maravilla
Lago Porteño
Tenerife
Balmaceda
Punto Toro
Seno Ultima Esperanza
CHILE
ARG.
Río Turbio
Punto Bories
Puerto Natales
TO PUNTA ARENAS
Dirt
9
0
6 mi
6 km

of Paine (pronounced "pie-nay"; it's the old Tehuelche word for "blue") rise over the landscape to create one of the world's most beautiful natural phenomena, now the Parque Nacional Torres del Paine. The park was established in 1959. Snow and rock formations dazzle at every turn of road, and the sunset views are spectacular. The 2,420-square-km (934-square-mi) park's most astonishing attractions are its lakes of turquoise, aquamarine, and emerald green waters; and the Cuernos del Paine ("Paine Horns"), the geological showpiece of the immense granite massif.

Another draw is the park's unusual wildlife. Creatures like the guanaco (a larger, woollier version of the llama) and the *ñandú* (a rhea, like a small ostrich) abound. They are acclimated to visitors, and don't seem to be bothered by approaching cars and people with cameras. Predators like the gray fox make less-frequent appearances. You may also spot the dramatic aerobatics of falcons and the graceful soaring of endangered condors. The beautiful puma, celebrated in a National Geographic video filmed here, is especially elusive, but sightings have grown more common. Pumas follow the guanaco herds and eat an estimated 40% of their young, so don't dress as one.

The vast majority of visitors come during the summer months of January and February, which means the trails can get congested. Early spring, when wildflowers add flashes of color to the meadows, is an ideal time to visit because the crowds have not yet arrived. In summer, the winds can be incredibly fierce. During the wintertime of June to September, the days are sunnier yet colder (averaging around freezing) and shorter, but the winds all but disappear. The park is open all year, and trails are almost always accessible. Storms can hit without warning, so be prepared for sudden rain or snow. The sight of the Paine peaks in clear weather is stunning; if you have any flexibility in your itinerary, visit the park on the first clear day.

VISITOR INFORMATION

CONAF, the national forestry service, has an office at the northern end of Lago del Toro with a scale model of the park, and numerous exhibits (some in English) about the flora and fauna. ✉ *CONAF station in southern section of the park past Hotel Explora* ☎ *61/247–845* 🌐 *www.conaf.cl* 🎫 *Summer 15,000 pesos, winter 5,000 pesos* ⏲ *Ranger station: Nov.–Feb., daily 8–8; Mar.–Oct., daily 8–12:30 and 2–6:30* ✉ *Punta Arenas Branch, Av. Bulnes 0309* ☎ *61/238–581* ✉ *Puerto Natales Branch, Av. Bernardo O'Higgins 584* ☎ *61/411–438.*

EXPLORING THE PARK

There are three entrances to the park: Laguna Amarga (all bus arrivals), Lago Sarmiento, and Laguna Azul. You are required to sign in when you arrive, and pay your entrance fee (15,000 pesos in high season). *Guardaparques* (park rangers) staff six stations around the reserve, and can provide a map and up-to-the-day information about the state of various trails. A regular minivan service connects Laguna Amarga with the Hosteria Las Torres, 7 km (4½ mi) to the west, for 1,000 pesos. Alternatively, you can walk approximately two hours before reaching the starting point of the hiking circuits.

Although considerable walking is necessary to take full advantage of Parque Nacional Torres del Paine, you need not be a hard-core trekker. Many people choose to hike the **"W" route,** which takes four days, but others prefer to stay in one of the comfortable lodges and hit the trails in the morning or afternoon. **Glaciar Grey,** with its fragmented icebergs, makes a rewarding and easy hike; equally rewarding is the spectacular boat or kayak ride across the lake, past icebergs, and up to the glacier, which leaves from Hostería Lago Grey *(⇨ below)*. Another great excursion is the 900-meter (3,000-foot) ascent to the sensational views from **Mirador Las Torres,** four hours one way from Hostería Las Torres *(⇨ below)*. Even if you're not staying at the Hostería, you can arrange a morning drop-off there, and a late-afternoon pickup, so that you can see the Mirador while still keeping your base in Puerto Natales or elsewhere in the park; alternatively, you can drive to the Hostería and park there for the day.

If you do the "W," you'll begin (or end, if you reverse the route) at Laguna Amarga and continue to Mirador Las Torres and Los Cuernos, then continue along a breathtaking path up Valle Frances to its awe-inspiring and fiendishly windy lookout (hold on to your hat!) and finally Lago Grey. The W runs for 100 kilometers, but always follows clearly marked paths, with gradual climbs and descents at relatively low altitude. The challenge comes from the weather. Winds whip up to 90 MPH, a clear sky can suddenly darken with storm clouds, producing rain, hail or snow in a matter of minutes. An even more ambitious route is the "Circuito," which essentially leads around the entire park and takes from a week to 10 days. Along the way, some people sleep at the dozen or so humble *refugios* (shelters) evenly spaced along the trail, and many others bring their own tents.

EN ROUTE

For anyone seriously contemplating trekking the W or the full Circuit around Torres Del Paine, the **Erratic Rock** hostel in Puerto Natales offers a free seminar on how best to make the journey. Rustyn Mesdag, the hostel's Oregonian co-owner is a rambunctious, opinionated guide who gives the not-to-be-missed "Three O'clock Talk" describing all the routes, tips, and tricks you need to complete one of South America's most challenging treks. His hour-long presentation to a room full of eager hikers starts promptly at 3 PM every day of the high season, and is full of advice on camping, equipment, food and provisions, including the latest reports on weather and trail conditions inside the park. It's a great introduction to possible trekking partners, as CONAF doesn't allow you to complete the walk on your own. The irrepressible Mr. Mesdag also publishes the ubiquitous Black Sheep newspaper in English. ✉ *Baquedano 719* ☎ *61/414–317* 🌐 *www.erraticrock.com.*

Driving is an easier way to enjoy the park: a new road cuts the distance to Puerto Natales from a meandering 140 km (87 mi) to a more direct 80 km (50 mi). Inside the national park, more than 100 km (62 mi) of roads leading to the most popular sites are safe and well maintained, though unpaved. **■ TIP→ If you stick to the road, you won't need a 4WD.**

You can also hire horses from the Hosteria Las Torres and trek to the Torres, the Cuernos, or along the shore of Lago Nordenskjold (which

8

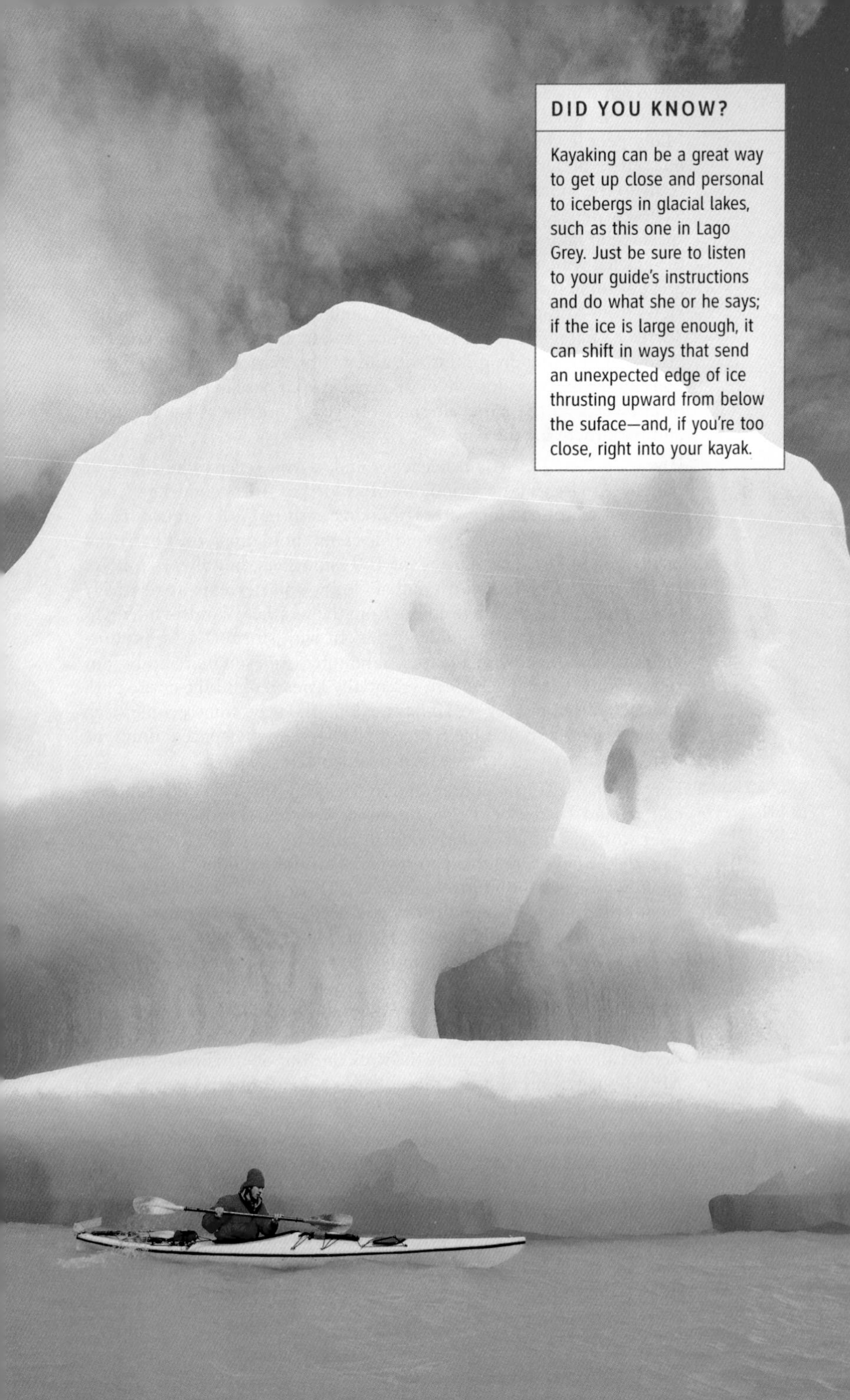

DID YOU KNOW?

Kayaking can be a great way to get up close and personal to icebergs in glacial lakes, such as this one in Lago Grey. Just be sure to listen to your guide's instructions and do what she or he says; if the ice is large enough, it can shift in ways that send an unexpected edge of ice thrusting upward from below the suface—and, if you're too close, right into your kayak.

offers the finest views in the park, as the lake's waters reflect the chiseled massif). The hotel offers tours demanding various levels of expertise (prices start at 25,000 pesos). Alternatively, many Puerto Natales–based operators offer multi-day horseback tours. Water transport is also available, with numerous tour operators offering sailboat, kayak, and inflatable Zodiac speedboat options along the Río Serrano (prices start around 50,000 pesos for the Zodiac trips) towards the Paine massif and the southern ice field. Additionally, the Hostería Lago Grey operates the *Grey II*, a large catamaran making a three-hour return trip twice daily to Glaciar Grey, at 10 AM and 3 PM; as well as dinghy runs down the Pingo and Grey rivers. Another boat runs between Refugio Pudeto and Refugio Lago Pehoé.

WHERE TO STAY

$$$$ **Hostería Lago Grey.** The panoramic view from the restaurant and bar, past the lake dappled with floating icebergs to the glacier beyond, is worth the journey here. That doesn't change the fact that this older hotel is almost scandalously overpriced and not very attractive; rooms are plain, dark and only a few have a view (at the same price as the others, so make sure you ask for one). But all rooms are comfortable and have small baths in decent bathrooms. There's a TV with DVD player in the lounge. The view—and it's one you're not likely to forget—can be enjoyed through the picture windows in the dining room. The hotel operates its own sightseeing vessel, the *Grey II*, for close-up tours to Glaciar Grey. **Pros:** great views and comfortable seating in the well-stocked bar; location; heated bathroom floors. **Cons:** thin walls in summer camp cottages; staggering price; staff speaks very little English. ✉ *Lago Grey* ☎ *61/410–172* 🌐 *www.lagogrey.com* *30 rooms* *In-room: no TV, safe, phone. In-hotel: restaurant, bar, laundry service* ▭ *AE, DC, MC, V* 🍴 *BP.*

$$$–$$$$ **Hosteria Pehoé.** Cross a 100-foot footbridge to get to this hotel on its own island with a volcanic black-sand beach in the middle of glistening Lake Pehoé, across from the beautiful Torres del Paine mountain peaks. Upon seeing the setting, non-guests are often tempted to cancel other reservations. Unfortunately, rooms at Pehoé—built in 1970 as the first hotel in the park—are dark, poorly furnished, windowless, and face an interior lawn. In the new wing, the higher the room number the better the quality. However, it's a delight to walk over the footbridge, have a drink at the ski-lodge–like bar, and take in the spectacular scenery. **Pros:** views are jaw-dropping. **Cons:** far from attractive grounds; miserably appointed rooms; Draconian cancellations policy. ✉ *Lago Pehoé* ☎ *61/411–390* 🌐 *www.pehoe.com* *40 rooms* *In-room: no phone, no TV. In-hotel: restaurant, bar, laundry service* ▭ *AE, DC, MC, V* 🍴 *CP.*

$$$ **Hosteria Tyndall.** A boat ferries you from the end of the road the few minutes around the meandering bends of the Serrano River to this wooden lodge, often surrounded by flocks of snow geese and other wild birds. The simple rooms in the main building are small but cute and spotless, with attractive wood paneling. The hallways have dramatic, colonial era light fittings, which can be seen as either broodingly romantic or just not doing their job; the lodge itself can be noisy—a problem

solved by renting a log cottage (at $242 a night they're great value for groups of four). There's also a much more basic refugio with dorm-style rooms that are very cheap. Owner Christian Bore is a wildlife enthusiast and bird-watcher; ask him for a tour of the grassy plain looking out toward the central cluster of snowy peaks. Or go fishing—the kitchen staff will cook your catch for free. The prix-fixe lunch costs $14, dinner $25. **Pros:** cheaper lodging and dining options than other places in the park; great views to Los Cuernos (the Horns) on a clear day. **Cons:** hallways are poorly lit; the lodge itself can get noisy. ✉ *Ladrilleros 256, Lago Tyndall* ☎ *61/614–682* 🌐 *www.hosteriatyndall.com* *24 rooms, 6 cottages* *In-room: no phone, no TV. In-hotel: restaurant, bar, laundry service* *AE, DC, MC, V* *BP, AI.*

$$$$ Fodor's Choice ★ **Hotel Explora–Salto Chico.** Next to a gently babbling waterfall on the southeast corner of Lago Pehoé, this lodge is one of the most luxurious—and most expensive—in Chile. The shimmering lake outside is offset by tiny rocky islets, and although there may be some debate about the aesthetics of the hotel's low-slung minimalist exterior, the interior is impeccable; it's Scandinavian in style, with local woods used for ceilings, floors, and furniture. Pressed Patagonian wildflowers and frontier photographs of indigenous people line the hallways. A dozen full-time guides tailor all-inclusive park outings to guests' interests. They're all fluent in English; some are expats, and they ferry you around in a fleet of imposing-looking vans. A four-night minimum stay is required, for which you'll pay a minimum of US$5,320 for two people, including airport transfers, three meals a day, drinks, and excursions. Rooms with better views, including one of the mountains from your bath, go up to almost double that. Yet, as a testament to the value, the place consistently sells out even during the winter. **Pros:** the grande dame of Patagonian hospitality and perhaps the best hotel in all South America; heart-stopping views from the center of the national park. **Cons:** a bank breaker; not a stunning building from the outside. ✉ *Lago Pehoé, Parque Nacional Torres Del Paine* *Américo Vespucio Sur 80, Piso 5, Santiago* ☎ *2/206–6060 in Santiago, 2/395–2580 in Lake Pehoe* 🌐 *www.explora.com* *44 rooms, 6 suites* *In-room: no TV. In-hotel: restaurant, bar, pool, gym, laundry service, airport shuttle, public Internet* *AE, DC, MC, V* *AI.*

$$$$ **Hotel Río Serrano.** What used to be a fairly humble posada has just completed a successful transformation into a grand hotel. Double doors swing open automatically (if a little uncertainly) to a crisp welcome from English-speaking staff. But the main draw is the views from rooms on the third floor, taking in the whole Torres Del Paine mountain range, with the Serrano River and a wind-stunted forest in the foreground. These spectacular vistas are worth the significant added expense, especially if you can snag a room with a balcony. The restaurant is a cavernous dining hall, serving local seafood and barbecued lamb. As with the downstairs lounge and bar area that face the peak, high, wide windows ensure you don't miss sunset over the mountains. A five-hole golf course and extensive conference rooms reveal the hotel's ambitions but guests have reported more than the usual teething problems, especially with excursions organized as part of all-inclusive tour packages that start

at US$1,500 per person for three nights. **Pros:** eager staff, impressive public areas, a stunning location with all-encompassing views. **Cons:** it's enormous, so guided tours can be a bit chaotic when the hotel's near capacity; at this writing, still ironing out the kinks; rooms are tight on space. ✉ *Lago Toro* ☎ *61/410–684 for reservations (Puerto Natales)* 🌐 *www.hotelrioserrano.cl* *99 rooms* *In-room: no TV, minibar. In-hotel: restaurant, bar, 5-hole golf course, mountain bikes, conference and seminar rooms* *AE, DC, MC, V* *BP, AI.*

$$$$ ★ **Las Torres Patagonia.** Owned by one of the earliest families to settle in what became the park, Las Torres has a long history, and is the closest hotel to the main trails into the heart of the Torres Del Paine massif. Originally an estancia, then a popular hosteria, the facility recently upgraded to a three-night-minimum, all-food-and-excursion-inclusive resort, in the style of Remota and Explora. An extensive lobby bar and restaurant area have a metropolitan feel that belies the hotel's traditional exterior. Stretched across several vast fields, the location is perfect if you want to day-hike to Mirador Torres, one of the park's highlights. The path starts at the front door, and you'll pass a range of weather-beaten hikers finishing weeklong treks. Don't forget to check out the informative mini-museum with the stuffed ñandú. **Pros:** friendly and efficient; homey atmosphere; couldn't be closer to the mountains. **Cons:** not cheap and prices keep rising; may be closer to the mountains, but the views are more sweeping at Explora or Rio Serrano. ✉ *Lago Amarga* ☎ *61/360–364* 🌐 *www.lastorres.com* *57 rooms* *In-room: no TV. In-hotel: restaurant, bar, spa* *AE, MC, V.*

USHUAIA AND TIERRA DEL FUEGO

Updated by Rick Hind

Tierra del Fuego, a more or less triangular island separated from the southernmost tip of the South American mainland by the twists and bends of the Estrecho de Magallanes, is indeed a world unto itself. The vast plains on its northern reaches are dotted with trees bent low by the savage winds that frequently lash the coast. The mountains that rise in the south are equally forbidding, traversed by huge glaciers slowly making their way to the sea.

The first European to set foot on this island was Spanish explorer Hernando de Magallanes, who sailed here in 1520. The smoke that he saw coming from the fires lighted by the native peoples prompted him to call it Tierra del Humo (Land of Smoke). King Charles V of Spain, disliking that name, rechristened it Tierra del Fuego, or Land of Fire.

Tierra del Fuego is split in half. The island's northernmost tip, well within Chilean territory, is its closest point to the continent. The only town of any size here is Porvenir. Its southern extremity, part of Argentina, points out into the Atlantic toward the Falkland Islands. Here you'll find Ushuaia, the main destination, on the shores of the Canal Beagle. Farther south is Cape Horn, the southernmost point of land before Antarctica (still a good 500 mi across the brutal Drake Passage).

USHUAIA

230 km (143 mi) south of Río Grande; 596 km (370 mi) south of Río Gallegos; 914 km (567 mi) south of El Calafate; 3,580 km (2,212 mi) south of Buenos Aires.

At 55 degrees latitude south, Ushuaia (pronounced oo-swy-ah; the Argentines don't pronounce the "h") is closer to the South Pole than to Argentina's northern border with Bolivia. It is the capital and tourism base for Tierra del Fuego, the island at the southernmost tip of Argentina.

Although its stark physical beauty is striking, Tierra del Fuego's historical allure is based more on its mythical past than on rugged reality. The island was inhabited for 6,000 years by Yámana, Haush, Selk'nam, and Alakaluf Indians. But in 1902, Argentina, eager to populate Patagonia to bolster its territorial claims, moved to initiate an Ushuaian penal colony, establishing the permanent settlement of its most southern territories and, by implication, everything in between.

When the prison closed in 1947, Ushuaia had a population of about 3,000, made up mainly of former inmates and prison staff. Today, the Indians of Darwin's "missing link" theory are long gone—wiped out by diseases brought by settlers, and by indifference to their plight—and the

60,000 residents of Ushuaia are hitching their star to tourism. The city rightly (if perhaps too loudly) promotes itself as the southernmost city in the world (Puerto Williams, a few miles south on the Chilean side of the Beagle Channel, is a small town). Ushuaia feels like a frontier boomtown, at heart still a rugged, weather-beaten fishing village, but exhibiting the frayed edges of a city that quadrupled in size in the '70s and '80s. Unpaved portions of R3, the last stretch of the Pan-American Highway, which connects Alaska to Tierra del Fuego, are finally being paved. The summer months—December through March—draw 120,000 visitors, and dozens of cruise ships. The city is trying to extend those visits with events like March's Marathon at the End of the World.

A terrific trail winds through the town up to the Martial Glacier, where a ski-lift can help cut down a steep kilometer of your journey. The chaotic and contradictory urban landscape includes a handful of luxury hotels amid the concrete of public housing projects. Scores of "sled houses" (wooden shacks) sit precariously on upright piers, ready for speedy displacement to a different site. But there are also many small, picturesque homes with tiny, carefully tended gardens. Many of the newer homes are built in a Swiss-chalet style, reinforcing the idea that this is a town into which tourism has breathed new life. At the same time, the weather-worn pastel colors that dominate the town's landscape remind you that Ushuaia was once just a tiny fishing village, populated by criminals, snuggled at the end of the Earth.

As you stand on the banks of the Canal Beagle (Beagle Channel) near Ushuaia, the spirit of the farthest corner of the world takes hold. What stands out is the light: at sundown the landscape is cast in a subdued, sensual tone; everything feels closer, softer, and more human in dimension despite the vastness of the setting. The snowcapped mountains reflect the setting sun back onto a stream rolling into the channel, as nearby peaks echo their image—on a windless day—in the still waters.

Above the city, the last mountains of the Andean Cordillera rise, and just south and west of Ushuaia they finally vanish into the often stormy sea. Snow whitens the peaks well into summer. Nature is the principal attraction here, with trekking, fishing, horseback riding, and sailing among the most rewarding activities, especially in the Parque Nacional Tierra del Fuego (Tierra del Fuego National Park).

As Ushuaia converts to a tourism-based economy, the city is seeking ways to utilize its 3,000 hotel rooms in the lonely winter season. Though most international tourists stay home to enjoy their own summer, the adventurous have the place to themselves for snowmobiling, dog sledding, and skiing at Cerro Castor.

GETTING HERE AND AROUND

Arriving by air is the preferred option. Ushuaia's Aeropuerto Internacional Malvinas Argentinas (✉ *Peninsula de Ushuaia* ☎ *2901/431–232*) is 5 km (3 mi) from town, and is served daily by flights to/from Buenos Aires, Río Gallegos, El Calafate, Trelew, and Comodoro Rivadavía. There are also flights to Santiago via Punta Arenas in Chile. A taxi into town costs about 7 pesos.

Arriving by road on the RN3 involves Argentinean and Chilean immigrations/customs, a ferry crossing, and a lot of time. Buses to/from Punta Arenas make the trip five days a week in summer, four in winter. Daily buses to Rio Gallegos leave in the pre-dawn hours, and multiple border crossings for an all-day journey. Check prices on the 55-minute flight, which can be much better value. There is no central bus terminal, just three separate companies.

There is no regular passenger transport (besides cruises) by sea.

ESSENTIALS

Bus Services Tecni-Austral (✉ *Roca 157* ☎ *2901/431–408*). **Trans los Carlos** (✉ *Av. San Martín 880* ☎ *2901/22337*).

Postal Services Ushuaia Post Office (✉ *Belgrano 96*).

Visitor Information Tierra del Fuego Tourism Institute (✉ *Maipú 505* ☎ *2901/421–423*). **Ushuaia Tourist Office** (✉ *Av. San Martín 674* ☎ *2901/432–000* 🌐 *www.e-ushuaia.com*).

EXPLORING

The **Antigua Casa Beben** (Old Beben House) is one of Ushuaia's original houses, and long served as the city's social center. Built between 1911 and 1913 by Fortunato Beben, it's said he ordered the house through a Swiss catalog. In the 1980s the Beben family donated the house to the city to avoid demolition. It was moved to its current location along the coast and restored, and is now a cultural center with art exhibits. ✉ *Maipú at Pluschow* ☎ *No phone* 🎫 *Free* 🕑 *Tues.–Fri. 10–8, weekends 4–8.*

Fodor's Choice ★ Part of the original penal colony, the Presidio building was built to hold political prisoners, murderous estancia owners, street orphans, and a variety of Buenos Aires's most violent criminals. Some even claim that singer Carlos Gardel landed in one of the cells for the petty crimes of his misspent youth. In its day it held 600 inmates in 380 cells. Today it's on the grounds of Ushuaia's naval base and holds the **Museo Marítimo** (Maritime Museum), which starts with exhibits on the canoe-making skills of the region's indigenous peoples, tracks the navigational history of Tierra del Fuego and Cape Horn, and the Antarctic, and even has a display on other great jails of the world. You can enter cell blocks and read about the grisly crimes of the prisoners who lived in them and measure yourself against their eerie life-size plaster effigies. Of the five wings spreading out from the main guard house, one has been transformed into an art gallery and another has been kept untouched, and unheated. Bone chattering cold and bleak, bare walls powerfully evoke the desolation of a long sentence at the tip of the continent. Well-presented tours (in Spanish only) are conducted at 11:30 AM and 6:30 PM daily. ✉ *Gobernador Paz at Yaganes* ☎ *2901/437–481* 🎫 *50 pesos (valid for 2 days)* 🕑 *Daily 10–8.*

At the **Museo del Fin del Mundo** (End of the World Museum), you can see a large taxidermied condor and other native birds, indigenous artifacts, maritime instruments, a reconstruction of an old Patagonian general store and such seafaring-related objects as an impressive mermaid figurehead taken from the bowsprit of a galleon. There are also

Crab really is king in Tierra del Fuego; king crab, or *centolla*, is delicious and readily available.

photographs and histories of El Presidio's original inmates, such as Simon Radowitzky, a Russian immigrant anarchist who received a life sentence for killing an Argentine police colonel. The museum is in the 1905 residence of a Fuegonian governor. The home was later converted into a bank, and some of the exhibits are showcased in the former vault. ✉ *Maipú 173, at Rivadavía* ☎ *2901/421–863* 🎫 *10 pesos* ⏲ *Oct.–Mar., daily 9–8; Apr.–Sept., daily noon–7.*

Tierra del Fuego was the last land mass in the world to be inhabited—it was not until 9,000 BC that the ancestors of those native coastal inhabitants, the Yamana, arrived. The **Museo Yamana** chronicles their lifestyle and history. The group was decimated in the late 19th century, mostly by European diseases. The bicentenary of Charles Darwin's birth passed with great fanfare in 2009, but his attitudes towards the indigenous people, dismissing them as "miserable, degraded savages" in *The Voyage of the Beagle*, are belied here by descriptions of the Yamana's incredible resourcefulness in surviving a bitter climate. Photographs and good English placards depict the Yamana's powerful, stocky build and bold body-paint; their use of seal fat to stay warm, their methods of carrying fire wherever they went, even in small canoes; and their way of hunting cormorants, which were killed with a bite through the neck. ✉ *Rivadavía 56* ☎ *2901/422–874* 🌐 *www.tierradelfuego.org.ar/mundoyamana* 🎫 *5 pesos* ⏲ *Daily 10–8.*

The **Tren del Fin del Mundo** (End of the World Train) is heavily promoted but a bit of a letdown. Purported to take you inside the Parque Nacional Tierra del Fuego, 12 km (7½ mi) away from town, you have to drive to get there, and it leaves visitors a long way short of the most spectacular scenery in the national park. The touristy 40-minute train ride's gimmick is a simulation of the trip El Presidio prisoners were forced to take into the forest to chop wood; but unlike them, you'll also get a good presentation of Ushuaia's history (in Spanish and English). The train departs daily at 9:30 AM, noon, and 3 PM in summer, and just once a day, at 10 AM, in winter. One common way to do the trip is to hire a *remis* (car service) that will drop you at the station for a one-way train ride and pick you up at the other end, then drive you around the Parque Nacional for two or three hours of sightseeing (which is far more scenic than the train ride itself). ✉ *Ruta 3, Km 3042* ☎ *2901/431–600* 🌐 *www.trendelfindelmundo.com.ar* 💴 *95 pesos first-class ticket, 50 pesos tourist-class ticket, 20 pesos national park entrance fee (no park fee in winter).*

Several tour operators run trips along the **Canal Beagle,** on which you can get a startling close-up view of sea mammals and birds on **Isla de los Lobos, Isla de los Pájaros,** and near **Les Eclaireurs Lighthouse.** There are catamarans that make three-hour trips, generally leaving from the Tourist Pier at 3 PM, and motorboats and sailboats that leave twice a day, once at 9:30 AM and once at 3 PM (trips depend on weather; few trips go in winter). Prices range start at 120 pesos; and some include hikes on the islands. Check with the tourist office for the latest details; you can also book through any of the local travel agencies.

OFF THE BEATEN PATH

Although there are a number of boat tours through the Canal Beagle, or around the bays to the Tierra del Fuego National Park, one offers an experience that will put you in the shoes of the earliest explorers to visit the far south. The operators of **Tres Marias Excursions** (🌐 *www.tresmariasweb.com* ☎ *2901/436–416*) offer a half-day sailing trip to Island H, an outcrop in the middle of the channel, with cormorant colonies, families of snow geese, seaweed stands and a weather station that records the howling winds blowing in from the misnamed Pacific Ocean. The guides are skillful sailors and storytellers. On a gusty day you'll marvel at the hardiness of the Yamana people who survived frigid winters wearing little or no clothing, by setting fires behind natural and manmade windbreaks. You'll find the same plant and moss species that grow in the high Andes; they thrive here at sea level, because the conditions kill off less hardy, temperate species. On the way back you visit a sea lion colony, but won't soon forget arriving in Ushuaia under full sail as the late sun hits the mountains. At 180 pesos it's only a little more expensive, and a lot more adventurous, than the motorized alternatives touting for business at the dock.

One good excursion in the area is to **Lago Escondido** (Hidden Lake) and **Lago Fagnano** (Fagnano Lake). The Pan-American Highway out of Ushuaia goes through deciduous beech forests and past beavers' dams, peat bogs, and glaciers. The lakes have campsites and fishing and are good spots for a picnic or a hike. This can be done on your own or as a seven-hour trip, including lunch, booked through the local travel agencies (75 pesos without lunch, 95 pesos with lunch).

One recommended operator, offering a comfortable bus, a bilingual guide, and lunch at Las Cotorras, is **All Patagonia** (✉ *Juana Fadul 26* ☎ *2901/433–622*).

A rougher, more unconventional tour of the lake area goes to **Monte Olivia,** the tallest mountain along the Canal Beagle, rising 4,455 feet above sea level. You also pass the **Five Brothers Mountains** and go through the **Garibaldi Pass,** which begins at the Rancho Hambre, climbs into the mountain range, and ends with a spectacular view of Lago Escondido. From here you continue on to Lago Fagnano through the countryside past sawmills and lumber yards. To do this tour in a four-wheel-drive truck with an excellent bilingual guide, contact **Canal Fun** (✉ *9 de Julio 118* ☎ *2901/437–395 or 2901/435–777* 🌐 *www.canalfun.com*); you'll drive *through* Lago Fagnano (about 3 feet of water at this point) to a secluded cabin on the shore and have a delicious *asado,* complete with wine and dessert. In winter they can also organize tailor-made dog sledding and cross-country skiing trips.

Estancia Harberton (Harberton Ranch) consists of 50,000 acres of coastal marshland and wooded hillsides. The property was a late-19th-century gift from the Argentine government to Reverend Thomas Bridges, who authored a Yamana–English dictionary and is considered the patriarch of Tierra del Fuego. His son Lucas wrote *The Uttermost Part of the Earth*, a memoir about his frontier childhood. Today the ranch is managed by Bridges's great-grandson, Thomas Goodall, and his American wife, Natalie, a scientist and author who has cooperated with the National Geographic Society on conservation projects and operates the impressive marine mammal museum, **Museo Acatushun** (🌐 *www.acatushun.com* 🎫 *5 pesos*). Most people visit as part of organized tours, but you'll be welcome if you arrive alone. They serve up a tasty tea in their home, the oldest building on the island. For safety reasons, exploration of the ranch can only be done on guided tours (45–90 minutes). Lodging is available, either in the Old Shepherd's House (US$120 per person with breakfast) or the Old Cook's House (US$90 per person with breakfast). Additionally, you can arrange a three-course lunch at the ranch by calling two days ahead for a reservation. Most tours reach the estancia by boat, offering a rare opportunity to explore the **Isla Martillo** penguin colony, and a sea-lion refuge on **Isla de los Lobos** (Island of the Wolves) along the way. ✉ *85 km (53 mi) east of Ushuaia* ☎ *2901/422–742* 🌐 *www.estanciaharberton.com* 🎫 *15 pesos* ⏲ *Oct. 15–Apr. 15, by tour only, daily 10–7, last tour 5:30.*

★ If you've never butted heads with a glacier, and especially if you won't be covering El Calafate on your trip, then you should check out **Glaciar Martial,** in the mountain range just above Ushuaia. Named after Frenchman Luís F. Martial, a 19th-century scientist who wandered this way aboard the warship *Romanche* to observe the passing of planet Venus, the glacier is reached via a panoramic *aerosilla* (ski lift). Take the Camino al Glaciar (Glacier Road) 7 km (4 mi) out of town until it ends (this route is also served by the local tour companies). Even if you don't plan to hike to see the glacier, it's a great pleasure to ride the 15-minute lift, which is open daily 10–5, weather permitting (it's often closed from mid-May until August) and costs 25 pesos. If you're afraid of heights, you can instead enjoy a small nature trail here, and a teahouse. You can return on the lift, or continue on to the beginning of a 1-km (½-mi) trail that winds its way over lichen and shale straight up the mountain. After a steep, strenuous 90-minute hike, you can cool your heels in one of the many gurgling, icy rivulets that cascade down water-worn shale shoots or enjoy a picnic while you wait for sunset (you can walk all the way down if you want to linger until after the *aerosilla* closes). When the sun drops behind the glacier's jagged crown of peaks, brilliant rays beam over the mountain's crest, spilling a halo of gold-flecked light on the glacier, valley, and channel below. Moments like these are why this land is so magical. Note that temperatures drop dramatically after sunset, so come prepared with warm clothing.

WHERE TO EAT

$$ ARGENTINE

✕ **Arco Iris.** This restaurant in the center of town is painted an unpromising hot pink but it's one of the finest and most popular of the good-value *tenedor libre* (all-you-can-eat) parrillas on the main strip—nobody orders à la carte. Skip the Italian buffet and Chinese offerings and fill up instead on the spit-roasted Patagonian lamb, grilled meats, and delicious *morcilla* (blood sausage). It's all you can eat for 43 pesos. Sit by the interior window towards the back where you see the *parrillero* artfully coordinate the flames and spits, and ask him to load your plate with the choicest cuts. ✉ *Av. San Martín 96* ☎ *2901/431–306* ▭ *AE, DC, MC, V* ✣ *B2.*

$$$ ARGENTINE ★

✕ **Bodegón Fueguino.** A mustard-yellow pioneer house that lights up the main street, this traditional eatery is driven by its ebullient owner Sergio Otero, a constant presence bustling around the bench seating, making suggestions and revving up his staff. Sample the *picada* plate (king crab rolls, Roma-style calamari, marinated rabbit) over an artisanal Beagle Beer—the dark version is the perfect balm on a cold windy day. Lamb dominates the mains, and the emphasis is on hearty rather than fashionable. Tables filled with locals and visitors make for a boisterous atmosphere. Don't worry about the no reservations policy as you won't have to wait long. ✉ *San Martin 859* ☎ *2901/431–972* 🌐 *www.tierradehumos.com* ✍ *No reservations* ▭ *AE, MC, V* ⏲ *Closed Christmas, New Years, May Day* ✣ *B2.*

$$$–$$$$ ARGENTINE Fodor's Choice ★

✕ **Chez Manu.** *Herbes de provence* in the greeting room, a tank of lively king crabs in the dining room: French chef Manu Herbin gives local seafood a French touch that both diversifies the Argentine gastronomy and creates some of Ushuaia's most memorable meals. Perched a couple of miles above town across the street from the Hotel Glaciar, the restaurant has stunning views of the Beagle Channel. The first-rate wine list includes Patagonian selections, while all dishes are created entirely with ingredients from Tierra del Fuego. Don't miss the baby scallops with a fondue of pulses, or the *centolla* (king crab) au gratin. ✉ *Camino Luís Martial 2135* ☎ *2901/432–253* 🌐 *www.chezmanu.com* ▭ *AE, MC, V* ⏲ *Apr.–Sept: Closed Mon.* ✣ *A1.*

$$$$ ARGENTINE SEAFOOD ★

✕ **Kaupé.** The white picket fence, manicured lawns, and planter boxes play up the fact that this out-of-the-way restaurant used to be a family home. Inside, polished wooden floors, picture windows, and tables covered in wine glasses offer a sophisticated dining experience with an intimate touch. The star ingredient is *centolla* (king crab), best presented as chowder with spinach. This resto is on a steep ridge above town and offers spectacular views, and they're only a little bit spoiled by the radio antenna sticking up from the empty plot next door. Still, it's seafood served with panache and warmth in a dining room that belies the status quo of the kitschy restaurants near the waterfront. But it can be hard to find; even taxi drivers get lost in the warren of streets above town. ✉ *Roca 470,* ☎ *2901/422–704* 🌐 *www.kaupe.com.ar* *Reservations essential* 💳 *AE, V* ⏲ *Closed Sun.* ✥ *C1.*

$$–$$$ ARGENTINE ✕ **La Cabaña Casa de Té.** This impeccably maintained riverside cottage is nestled in a verdant stand of lenga trees, overlooks the Beagle Channel, and provides a warm, cozy spot for tea or snacks before or after a hike to the Martial Glacier (it's conveniently located at the end of the Martial road that leads up from Ushuaia, tucked in behind the ski lift). Breakfast with all the trimmings costs 55 pesos, fondues are a specialty at lunchtime, and at 8 PM the menu shifts to pricier dinner fare with dishes like salmon in wine sauce. ✉ *Camino Luís Martial 3560* ☎ *2901/434–699* 💳 *AE, DC, MC, V* ⏲ *Closed Mon.* ✥ *A1.*

$$ ARGENTINE ✕ **Ramos Generales.** Entering this café on the waterfront puts you in mind of a general store from the earliest frontier years of Ushuaia. As you walk from room to room admiring the relics (like the hand-cranked Victrola phonograph), the hubbub around the bar reminds you that a warehouse like this was not just a store to pick up supplies; it was also a place for isolated pioneers to socialize and gather all the latest news from the port. Burgers and picada platters are uninspiring; choose fresh baked bread or scrumptious lemon croissants instead, and try the *submarino*—a mug of hot milk in which you plunge a bar of dark chocolate (goes well with a panini). ✉ *Maípu 749* ☎ *2901/424–317* 🌐 *www.ramosgeneralesushuaia.com* 💳 *AE, MC, V* ⏲ *Closed Mon.* ✥ *C2.*

$$–$$$ ARGENTINE ✕ **Volver.** A giant king crab sign beckons you into this red tin walled restaurant, although the maritime bric-a-brac hanging from the ceiling can be a little distracting. The name means "return" and it succeeds in getting repeat visits on the strength of its seafood. Newspapers from the 1930s line the walls in this century-old home; the service is friendly and relaxed. The culinary highlight is the *centolla* (king crab), which comes served with a choice of five different sauces. This is among the best places to try Tierra del Fuego's signature dish. ✉ *Maipú 37* ☎ *2901/423–977* 💳 *AE, DC, MC, V* ⏲ *No lunch May–Aug.* ✥ *B3.*

WHERE TO STAY

Choosing a place to stay depends in part on whether you want to spend the night in town, several miles west towards the national park, or uphill in the hotels above town. Las Hayas Resort, Hotel Glaciar, Cumbres de Martial, and Los Yámanas have stunning views, but require a taxi ride or the various complimentary shuttle services to reach Ushuaia.

$$$$ ★ **Cumbres de Martial.** This charming complex of cabins and bungalows, painted a deep berry purple, is high above Ushuaia in the woods at the base of the ski lift to the Martial glacier. Each spacious room has an extremely comfortable bed and a small wooden deck with terrific views down to the Beagle Channel. The *cabañas* are beautiful self-contained log cabins with floor-to-ceiling windows, a new Jacuzzi, and

8

Can't beat the view in Ushuaia, the world's southernmost city.

a spectacular fireplace in the living room. A new spa is housed in its own cottage, the Cabanas de Taza de Té café is also on the premises, and a small nature trail takes you through the lenga trees along the Martial River. There is, however, no complimentary shuttle service to town, so you'll need to take a 10- to 15-peso taxi to access Ushuaia. **Pros:** easy access to the glacier and nature trails; stunning views of the Beagle Channel; romantic cabins. **Cons:** you need to cab it to and from town; few restaurant options within walking distance. ✉ *Camino Luís Martial 3560* ☎ *2901/424–779* 🌐 *www.cumbresdelmartial.com.ar* ⇨ *6 rooms, 4 cabins* ♿ *In-room: safe. In-hotel: restaurant, bar, laundry service, airport shuttle* 💳 *AE, DC, MC, V* ⊗ *Closed Apr. and May* 🍽 *BP* ⊕ *A1.*

$$$$ **Hostería Patagonia Jarké.** Jarké means "spark" in a local native language, and this B&B is a bright, electric addition to Ushuaia. The three-story lodge cantilevers down a hillside on a dead-end street in the heart of town. The building's an amalgam of alpine and Victorian styles on the outside; inside, a spacious contemporary design incorporates a glass-roofed lobby, several living rooms each with great views of the waterfront, and a sunny breakfast room. Rooms have a warm color scheme, polished wood floors, peaked-roof ceilings, artisanal soaps, woven floor mats, bidets, Jacuzzi tubs, and decent views, although the windows are a little small. **Pros:** feels like home. **Cons:** steep walk home; recent jump in prices has made it less-than-stellar value; can't compete with the views from the larger hotels further uphill. ✉ *Sarmiento 310* ☎ *2901/437–245* 🌐 *www.hosteriapatagoniaj.com* ⇨ *15 rooms* ♿ *In-room: safe. In-hotel: bar, laundry service, public Wi-Fi* 💳 *AE, DC, MC, V* 🍽 *BP* ⊕ *D1.*

$$$$ **Hotel del Glaciar.** Just above the Las Hayas hotel in the Martial Mountains, this hotel has commanding views of Ushuaia and the

Beagle Channel. The rooms are bright, clean, and very comfortable but sparsely decorated. After a long day in the woods, you can curl up on the long sofa that encloses the fire pit just off the main foyer, or wander over to the cozy wood-paneled bar for a drink. Shuttle buses leave for the town center every two hours. **Pros:** old-style colonial atmosphere sets it apart from the modern behemoths on the mountain; all rooms have great views, either to the mountains behind or (for slightly more money) to the Beagle Channel. **Cons:** feels very big; staff not the friendliest in town; some of the wood panels on the outer walls are starting to show their age; late check-in (4 PM) and early check-out (10 AM). ✉ *Camino Glaciar Martial 2355, Km 3.5* ☎ *2901/430–640* 🌐 *www.hoteldelglaciar.com* *119 rooms, 4 suites* *In-room: safe, hairdryer n-hotel: restaurant, bar, laundry service, airport shuttle, public Internet, minibar* ▭ *AE, DC, MC, V* *CP* ✥ *B1.*

$$$$ ★ **Hotel Fueguino.** A gleaming ultramodern edifice in downtown Ushuaia, the Fueguino boasts all the amenities: a conference center; a gym with the latest fitness machines; a spa; shuttle service; outgoing, professional, multilingual staff; and what might be the best Wi-Fi signal in town. Rooms feature custom Italian wood furnishings, leather accents, frosted glass, blackout blinds, and brushed stainless steel in the bathrooms. The Fueguino name is branded on every trinket you can think of, from bathrobes to shoe mitts. Beds with padded headboards and California king-size mattresses are as firm as it gets. Downstairs the Komenk restaurant serves Mediterranean cuisine with Patagonian influences. A junior suite is worth the upgrade. In the winter, the hotel basement hosts international cross-country ski teams from the northern hemisphere training in their offseason. **Pros:** ultramodern excess. **Cons:** shambolic huts overrun with barking dogs just over the road; everything in the lobby is silver. ✉ *Gobernador Deloqui 1282* ☎ *2901/424–894* 🌐 *www.fueguinohotel.com* *50 rooms, 3 suites* *In-room: digital safe, minibar. In-hotel: spa, gym, room service, public Internet, Wi-Fi, restaurant, bar* ▭ *AE, MC, V* ✥ *B2.*

$$$ **Hotel Los Yámanas.** This cozy hotel 4 km (2½ mi) from the center of town is named after the local tribe and offers a rustic mountain aesthetic. Some rooms have stunning views over the Beagle Channel, and all have wrought-iron bed frames, and are furnished with simple good taste. The expansive lobby, second-floor restaurant, games room with billiards, and sauna are just as welcoming. Never overlook the virtues of a 100-peso per hour massage. **Pros:** top-notch gym. **Cons:** questionable taste in lobby decoration. ✉ *Los Ñires 1850, Km 3* ☎ *2901/445–960* 🌐 *www.hotelyamanas.com.ar* *39 rooms, 2 suites* *In-room: safe. In-hotel: restaurant, bar, gym, pool, laundry service, public Wi-Fi, minibar* ▭ *AE, DC, MC, V* *CP* ✥ *A3.*

$$$$ Fodor's Choice ★ **Hotel y Resort Las Hayas.** Las Hayas is in the wooded foothills of the Andes, overlooking the town and channel below. Ask for a *canal* view and, since the rooms are all decorated differently and idiosyncratically, sample a variety before settling in. All feature Portuguese linen, solid oak furnishings, and the Las Hayas trademark: crisp white fabric-padded walls, covered in bright one-color floral prints. A suspended glass bridge connects the hotel to a spectacular health spa, which

includes a heated pool, Jacuzzi, and even a squash court. The wonderful five-star restaurant Le Martial prepares an excellent version of *mollejas de cordero* (lamb sweetbreads) with scallops, and boasts the best wine list in town. Frequent shuttle buses take you into town. **Pros:** good restaurant; charming staff and managers have dazzling English. **Cons:** decor doesn't suit everyone; wall prints can be distracting. ✉ *Camino Luís Martial 1650, Km 3* ☎ *2901/430–710, 11/4393–4750 in Buenos Aires* 🌐 *www.lashayashotel.com* *85 rooms, 7 suites* *In-room: safe. In-hotel: restaurant, bar, pool, gym, spa, laundry service, airport shuttle* *AE, DC, MC, V* *CP* *A1.*

$$$$ ★ **La Tierra de Leyendas.** The Land of Legends is a honeymooners' delight; it sweeps up awards and is one of South America's hidden gems. The secret's out, but this adorable B&B run by Sebastian and Maria still bears their personal touch down to the family photos on the walls. The hotel is in the Estancia Río Pipo, on a wind-battered hill 4 km (2½ mi) west of town, in an area once inhabited by canoeist nomads, but it's now being encroached on by the expanding city. The five bedrooms—with names such as La Coqueta and La Mision—boast large windows facing the Beagle Channel or the snow-capped Andes, with soft, luxurious beds and charming photos of old shipwrecks; a cozy living room offers a book exchange, board games, video library, and glass display tables with antique arrows, bones, and currency. The restaurant has a top-notch gourmet menu—offering such exotic fare as *conejo a la cazadora* (stuffed Fuegian rabbit) or seafood au gratin—prepared by the owner. **Pros:** an extraordinarily quaint find for western Ushuaia; enthusiastic, personal and attentive service. **Cons:** the street name is no joke, it's insanely windy; the immediate surroundings are a bit barren; need to book a month or more in advance. ✉ *Tierra de Vientos 2448* ☎ *2901/443–565* 🌐 *www.tierradeleyendas.com.ar* *5 rooms* *In-room: DVD, safe. In-hotel: laundry service, public Wi-Fi* *AE, MC, V* *A3.*

$$$ **Los Acebos.** The new offering from the owners of Las Hayas (just around the corner on the winding mountain road), Los Acebos is a modern hotel on a forested ridge with a commanding view over the Beagle Channel. Spacious and super clean rooms feature the same iconoclastic decor as Las Hayas, including the trademark fabric-padded walls, only this time with a '60s-style color scheme. The restaurant serves international dishes in a chic dining room with sensational views. Staff are relaxed and personable, especially with the large number of well-heeled Argentine families who base themselves here, close to the nearby ski slopes. A garrulous barman presides over one of the hippest watering holes in town. Guests can imbibe by the lounge fireplace or in the game room. **Pros:** great price for spacious and super clean rooms; expansive views of the channel from the restaurant; staff good with children. **Cons:** a tad out of the way for a spa-less facility. ✉ *Luis F. Martial 1911, Ushuaia* ☎ *2901/430–710 or 11/4393–4750 (reservations from Buenos Aires office)* 🌐 *www.losacebos.com.ar* *56 rooms, 4 suites* *In-room: safe, minibar. In-hotel: restaurant, room service, public Internet, spa, gym, laundry, parking* *AE, MC, V* *A1.*

$$$$ **Los Cauquenes Resort & Spa.** This resort hotel is more of a gated campus, with a series of buildings and cabanas right on the shore of the Beagle Channel about 8 km (5 mi) west of town. Privileged beach access and sparse development in the Barrio Bahía Cauquén means a nature hike starts right outside your room. Request one with a canal view on a higher floor, as many of the ground-floor rooms are partially underground. Rooms can get uncomfortably hot, and noise goes through the walls. Aside from the rooms, the spa, gym, and sauna are high quality, offering Thai, shiatsu, and Swedish massage, a full menu of body treatments, mud baths, and even a caviar face mask. The heated pool that flows from inside to out is spectacular, a rare treat in this part of the world. On the relatively cheap menu of the restaurant Reinamora you will find the standard Patagonian lamb, rainbow trout, and a delicious king crab served with berries. **Pros:** luxurious spa offers comprehensive range of treatments and massages; specials on romantic getaways. **Cons:** no air-conditioning in rooms; thin walls can make for noisy nights. ✉ *De la Ermita 3462Barrio Bahía Cauquén, Ushuaia* ☎ *2901/441–300* 🌐 *www.loscauquenesushuaia.com.ar* *49 rooms, 5 suites, 13 cabanas* *In-room: safe, minibar. In-hotel: gym, pool, sauna, restaurant, bar, public Wi-Fi, parking* ▭ *AE, MC, V* ✣ *C1.*

NIGHTLIFE

Ushuaia has a lively nightlife in summer, with its casino, discos, and intimate cafés all close to each other. The biggest and most popular pub **El Náutico** attracts a young crowd with disco and techno music (✉ *Maipú 1210* ☎ *2901/430–415* 🌐 *www.nauticodiscopub.com*). **Bar Ideal** (✉ *San Martín 393* ☎ *2901/437–860* 🌐 *www.elbarideal.com*) is a more cozy and historic bar and café. **Kaitek Lounge Bar** (✉ *Antartida Argentina 239* ☎ *2901/431–723*) is a place to eat until 2 AM, and to dance to pop music until 6 AM. **Tante Sara** (✉ *San Martín 701* ☎ *2901/433–710* 🌐 *cafebartantesara.com.ar*) is a popular café-bar with a casual, old-world feel, in the heart of town, where locals kick back with a book or a beer (they pour Beagle, the local artisanal brew). During the day it's one of the few eateries to defy the 3–6 PM siesta.

Cine Packewaia (✉ *Cpto. Naval A. Bernadi* ☎ *2901/435–060* 🌐 *www.cinepackewaia.com*) is a huge corrugated iron barn that looks like an aircraft hangar, right next to the Presidio and Maritime Museum. It shows first run Hollywood movies three times a night, including a midnight screening.

SHOPPING

★ **Boutique del Libro–Antartida y Patagonia.** Part of a bookstore chain, this branch specializes in Patagonian and polar exploration. Along with dozens of maps and picture books, postcards, and posters, it offers adventure classics detailing every Southern expedition from Darwin's Voyage of the Beagle to Ernest Shackleton's incredible journeys of Antarctic survival. While books in English are hard to come by in the rest of Argentina, here you're spoiled for choice, and the Antarctica trip logbooks on sale at the counter might inspire you to extend your travel further south. ✉ *25 de Mayo 62* ☎ *2901/432–117* 🌐 *www.antartidaypatagonia.com.ar.*

8

Laguna Negra. If you can't get to South America's chocolate capital Bariloche, you'll find some of the best sweets in Argentina at this boutique/café in the center of town. Planks of homemade chocolate include coconut crunches, fudges, and brittles, along with Tierra del Fuego's best selection of artisanal beers, chutneys, and spices. In the small coffee shop at the back, drop a glorious slab of dark chocolate into a mug of piping hot milk—one of the best *submarinos* in town. Locals pop in for a quick cup of hot chocolate at all hours, even as other cafés close for the lull between 3 and 8 in the evening. If you get hooked, there's another branch on the main street of El Calafate. ✉ *San Martin 513* ☎ *02901/431–144* 🌐 *www.lagunanegra.com.ar* ⏲ *10–9.*

PARQUE NACIONAL TIERRA DEL FUEGO

★ The pristine park, 21 km (13 mi) west of Ushuaia, offers a chance to wander through peat bogs, stumble upon hidden lakes, trek through native *canelo, lenga,* and wild cherry forests, and experience the wonders of wind-whipped Tierra del Fuego's rich flora and fauna. Everywhere, lichens line the trunks of the ubiquitous lenga trees, and "chinese lantern" parasites hang from the branches.

Everywhere, too, you'll see the results of government folly, *castoreros* (beaver dams) and lodges. Fifty beaver couples were first brought in from Canada in 1948 so that they would breed and create a fur industry. In the years since, without any predators, the beaver population has exploded to plague proportions (more than 100,000) and now represents a major threat to the forests, as the dams flood the roots of the trees; you can see their effects on parched dead trees on the lake's edge. Believe it or not, the government used to pay hunters a bounty for each beaver they killed (they had to show a tail and head as proof). To make matters worse, the government, after creating the beaver problem, introduced weasels to kill the beavers, but the weasels killed birds instead; they then introduced foxes to kill the beavers and weasels, but they also killed the birds. With eradication efforts failing, some tour operators have accepted them as a permanent presence and now offer beaver viewing trips.

Visits to the park, which is tucked up against the Chilean border, are commonly arranged through tour companies. Trips range from bus tours to horseback riding to more adventurous excursions, such as canoe trips across Lapataia Bay.

Transportes Kaupen (☎ *2901/434–015*) is one of several private bus companies that travel through the park making several stops; you can get off the bus, explore the park, and then wait for the next bus to come by or trek to the next stop (the service only operates in summer). Yet one more option is to drive to the park on R3 (take it until it ends and you see the famous sign indicating the end of the Pan-American Highway, which starts 17,848 km [11,065 mi] away in Alaska, and ends here). If you don't have a car, you can also hire a private *remis* to spend a few hours driving through the park, including the Pan-American terminus, and perhaps also combining the excursion with the Tren del Fin del Mundo. Trail and camping information is available at the park-entrance

The banner tree, or *Tuta complementaria*, is whipped by Patagonian winds from the time it's a mere shoot; the result has a banner-like effect, hence the name.

ranger station or at the Ushuaia tourist office. At the park entrance is a gleaming new restaurant and teahouse set amidst the hills, **Patagonia Mia** (✉ *Ruta 3, Entrada Parque Nacional* ☎ *2901/1560–2757* 🌐 *www.patagoniamia.com*); it's a great place to stop for tea or coffee, or a full meal of roast lamb or Fuegian seafood. A nice excursion in the park is by boat from lovely **Bahía Ensenada** to **Isla Redonda,** a wildlife refuge where you can follow a footpath to the western side and see a wonderful view of the Canal Beagle. This is included on some of the day tours; it's harder to arrange on your own, but you can contact the tourist office to try. While on Isla Redonda you can send a postcard and get your passport stamped at the world's southernmost post office. You can also see the Ensenada bay and island (from afar) from a point on the shore that is reachable by car.

Other highlights of the park include the spectacular mountain-ringed lake, **Lago Roca,** as well as **Laguna Verde,** a lagoon whose green color comes from algae at its bottom. Much of the park is closed from roughly June through September, when the descent to Bahía Ensenada is blocked by up to 6 feet of snow. Even in May and October, chains for your car are a good idea. No hotels are within the park—the only one burned down in the 1980s, and you can see its carcass as you drive by—but there are three simple camping areas around Lago Roca. Tours to the park are run by **All Patagonia** (✉ *Juana Fadul 26* ☎ *2901/433–622* or *2901/430–725*).

OUTDOOR ACTIVITIES

FISHING The rivers of Tierra del Fuego are home to trophy-size freshwater trout—including browns, rainbows, and brooks. Both fly- and spin-casting are available. The fishing season runs November–April; license fees range from 75 pesos a day to 350 pesos for a month for non-residents. Fishing expeditions are organized by the following companies. Founded in 1959, the **Asociación de Caza y Pesca** (✉ *Av. Maipú 822* ☎ *2901/423–168*) is the principal hunting and fishing organization in the city. **Rumbo Sur** (✉ *Av. San Martín 350* ☎ *2901/421–139* 🌐 *www.rumbosur.com.ar*) is the city's oldest travel agency and can assist in setting up fishing trips. **Wind Fly** (✉ *Av. 25 de Mayo 143* ☎ *2901/431–713 or 2901/1544–9116* 🌐 *www.windflyushuaia.com.ar*) is dedicated exclusively to fishing, and offers classes, arranges trips, and rents equipment.

MOUNTAIN BIKING A mountain bike is an excellent mode of transport in Ushuaia, giving you the freedom to roam without the rental-car price tag. Good mountain bikes normally cost about 5 pesos an hour or 15 pesos–20 pesos for a full day. Bikes can be rented at the base of the glacier, at the **Refugio de Montaña** (✉ *Base Glaciar Martial* ☎ *2901/1556–8587*), or at **DTT Cycles** (✉ *Av. San Martín 903* ☎ *2901/434–939*). Guided bicycle tours (including rides through the national park), for about 50 pesos a day, are organized by **All Patagonia** (✉ *Fadul 26* ☎ *2901/430–725*). **Rumbo Sur** (✉ *San Martín 350* ☎ *2901/421–139* 🌐 *www.rumbosur.com.ar*) is the city's biggest travel agency and can arrange trips. **Tolkeyén Patagonia** (✉ *San Martín 1267* ☎ *2901/437–073*) rents bikes and arranges trips.

SCENIC FLIGHTS The gorgeous scenery and island topography of the area is readily appreciated on a Cessna tour. **Aeroclub Ushuaia** (✉ *Antiguo Aeropuerto* ☎ *2901/421–717* 🌐 *www.aeroclubushuaia.org.ar*) offers half-hour and hour-long trips.The half-hour flight (US$70, or 266 pesos, per passenger; US$90, or 342 pesos, for one passenger alone) with a local pilot takes you over Ushuaia, Tierra del Fuego National Park and the Beagle Channel with views of area glaciers, waterfalls, and snowcapped islands south to Cape Horn. A 60-minute flight (US$120, or 457 pesos, per passenger; US$150, or 571 pesos, for one passenger alone) crosses the Andes to the Escondida and Fagnano lakes.

Heli-Ushuaia (✉ *Antiguo Aeropuerto* ☎ *2901/444–444* 🌐 *www.heliushuaia.com.ar*) offers 15-minute flights over the city for a minimum of two people for US$120 each and hour-long trips if you've got money to burn.

SKIING Ushuaia is the cross-country skiing (*esqui de fondo* in Spanish) center of South America, thanks to enthusiastic **Club Andino** (✉ *Fadul 50* ☎ *2901/422–335*) members who took to the sport in the 1980s and made the forested hills of a high valley about 20 minutes from town a favorite destination for skiers. It's a magnet for international ski teams who come from Europe to train in the northern summer. **Hostería Tierra Mayor** (☎ *2901/423–240*), **Hostería Los Cotorras** (☎ *2901/499–300*), and **Haruwen** (☎ *2901/424–058*) are three places where you can ride in dog-pulled sleds, rent skis, go cross-country skiing, get lessons, and eat; contact the Ushuaia tourist office for more information.

Glacier Martial Ski Lodge (☎ *2901/243–3712*), open year-round, Tuesday–Sunday 10–7, functions as a cross-country ski center from June to October. Skis can also be rented in town, as can snowmobiles.

For downhill (or *alpino*) skiers, Club Andino has bulldozed a couple of short, flat runs directly above Ushuaia. The newest downhill ski area, **Cerro Castor** (☎ *2901/422–244* 🌐 *www.cerrocastor.com*), is 26 km (17 mi) northeast of Ushuaia on R3, and has 19 trails and four high-speed ski lifts. More than half the trails are at the beginner level, six are intermediate, and three are expert trails, but none of this terrain is very challenging for an experienced skier. You can rent skis and snowboards and take ski lessons. **Transportes Kaupen** *(⇨ above)* and other local bus companies run service back and forth from town.

WHERE TO STAY

Dotting the perimeter of the park are five free campgrounds, none of which has much more than a spot to pitch a tent and a fire pit. Call the **park office** (☎ *2901/421–315*) or consult the ranger station at the park entrance for more information. **Camping Lago Roca** (✉ *South on R3 for 20 km [12 mi]* ☎ *No phone*), within the park, charges 8 pesos per person per day and has bathrooms, hot showers, and a small market. Of all the campgrounds, **La Pista del Andino** (✉ *Av. Alem 2873* ☎ *2901/435–890*) is the only one within the city limits. Outside of town, **Camping Río Pipo** (☎ *2901/435–796*) is the closest to Ushuaia (it's 18 km [11 mi] away).

EN ROUTE

If you're in Ushuaia in the days leading up to New Year's Eve, drop in on **La Pista del Andino** campsite, on the edge of town. You'll be dwarfed by a mad mix of four wheel drives, enormous customized German trucks, and worn-out bicycles with beaten panniers. It's a tradition among overland explorers to spend Christmas and New Year in the southern most city in the world. Their routes zigzag across South America and are often painted on the sides of their vehicles—which have been known to be equipped with everything from rooftop tents to a satellite dish. Travelers share stories of crossing places like Siberia or northern Africa, and if you're lucky you'll encounter some who've ridden, driven, or pedaled the Pan-American Highway all the way from Alaska down to Ushuaia, a 17,000-mi journey that takes years to complete.

Tour Operators

Outfitter	Telephone	Web site	Activities Offered	Regions Covered
Abercrombie & Kent	630/954-2944 or 800/5540-7016	www.abercrombiekent.com	Bicycling, Coastal and Lake Cruises, Cultural Tours, Hiking, Horseback Riding, Natural History,	Antarctica, Argentine Patagonia, Chilean Patagonia, Lake District, Tierra del Fuego
Adventure Center	510/654-1879 or 800/227-8747	www.adventurecenter.com	Bicycling, Coastal and Lake Cruises, Cultural Tours, Hiking, Horseback Riding, Natural History,	Antarctica, Argentine Patagonia, Chilean Patagonia, Lake District, Tierra del Fuego
Adventure Life	406/541-2677 or 800/344-6118	www.adventure-life.com	Bicycling, Coastal and Lake Cruises, Cultural Tours, Hiking, Horseback Riding, Natural History, Rafting, Kayaking,	Antarctica, Argentine Patagonia, Chilean Patagonia, Lake District, Tierra del Fuego
Alpine Ascents International	206/378-1927	www.AlpineAscents.com	Hiking, Climbing, Mountaineering	Lake District, Antarctica
Andes Adventures	310/395-5265 or 800/289-9470	www.andesadventures.com	Hiking,	Argentine Patagonia, Chilean Patagonia, Tierra del Fuego
Australian & Amazonian Adventures	512/443-5393 or 800/232-5658	www.amazonadventures.com	Bicycling, Coastal and Lake Cruises, Cultural Tours, Hiking, Horseback Riding, Natural History, Rafting, Kayaking,	Argentine Patagonia, Atlantic Coast, Chilean Patagonia, Argentina, Tierra del Fuego
Big Five Tours & Expeditions	772/287-7995 or 800/244-3483	www.bigfive.com	Bicycling, Coastal and Lake Cruises, Cultural Tours, Hiking, Horseback Riding, Natural History,	Argentine Patagonia, Chilean Patagonia, Tierra del Fuego
BikeHike Adventures	604/731-2442 or 888/805-0061	www.bikehike.com	Bicycling, Hiking, Natural History, Rafting	Argentine Patagonia, Los Glaciares National Park, Torres del Paine National Park
Boojum Expeditions	406/587-0125 or 800/287-0125	www.boojum.com	Horseback Riding	Argentine Patagonia
Country Walkers	802/244-1387	www.countrywalkers.com	Hiking,	Argentine Patagonia
Earth River Expeditions	845/626-2665	www.earthriver.com	Rafting, Kayaking	Chilean Patagonia
ElderTreks	416/588-5000 or 800/741-7956	www.eldertreks.com	Hiking	Argentine Patagonia, Chilean Patagonia, Tierra del Fuego
Equitours	307/455-3363 or 800/545-0019	www.equitours.com	Horseback Riding	Argentine Patagonia, Chilean Patagonia, Cordoba

Tour Operators

Outfitter	Telephone	Web site	Activities Offered	Regions Covered
Experience Plus!	970/484-8489 or 800/685-4565	www.ExperiencePlus.com	Bicycling	Lake District
Explora	866/750-6699	www.explora.com	Cultural Tours, Hiking, Natural History	Argentine Patagonia, Chilean Patagonia
Fishing International	707/542-4242 or 800/950-4242	www.fishinginternational.com	Fishing	Argentine Patagonia, Lake District
FishQuest	706/896-1403 or 888/891-3474	www.fishquest.com	Fishing	Argentine Patagonia, Chilean Patagonia, Lake District
Fly Fishing And	406/425-9452	www.flyfishingand.com	Fishing	Argentine Patagonia, Lake District
G.A.P. Adventures	416/260-0999 or 800/708-7761	www.gapadventures.com	Bicycling, Coastal and Lake Cruises, Cultural Tours, Hiking, Horseback Riding, Natural History	Antarctica, Argentine Patagonia, Chilean Patagonia, Lake District, Tierra del Fuego
Geographic Expeditions	415/922-0448 or 800/777-8183	www.geoex.com	Cultural Tours, Hiking, Natural History,	Argentine Patagonia, Chilean Patagonia, Tierra del Fuego
Global Adventure Guide	800/732-0861	www.globaladventureguide.com	Bicycling	Argentine Patagonia, Chilean Patagonia, Lake District
Global Vision	888/653-6028	www.gvi.co.uk	Kayaking, Mountaineering	Chilean Patagonia
Hidden Trails	604/323-1141	www.hiddentrails.com	Horseback Riding	Argentine Patagonia, Chilean Patagonia
Inca	510/420-1550	www.inca1.com	Cultural Tours, Coastal and Lake Cruises, Hiking, Natural History	Argentine Patagonia, Antarctica
International Expeditions	205/428-1700 or 800/633-4734	www.ietravel.com	Cultural Tours, Coastal and Lake Cruises, Hiking, Natural History,	Antarctica, Chilean Patagonia
Jack Trout	530/926-4540	www.jacktrout.com	Fishing	Argentine Patagonia, Chilean Patagonia
Joseph Van Os Photo Safaris	206/463-5383	www.photosafaris.com	Photo Safaris	Argentine Patagonia, Antarctica, Chilean Patagonia
Journeys International	734/665-4407 or 800/255-8735	www.journeys-intl.com	Birdwatching, Coastal and Lake Cruises, Cultural, Natural History	Argentine Patagonia, Lake District, Tierra del Fuego
Kaiyote Tours	970/556-6103	www.kaiyotetours.com	Birdwatching	Atlantic Coast

Tour Operators

Outfitter	Telephone	Web site	Activities Offered	Regions Covered
KE Adventure Travel	303/321-0085 or 800/497-9675	www.kladventure.com	Hiking, Natural History, Mountaineering, Skiing	Antarctica, Argentine Patagonia, Chilean Patagonia, Lake District, Tierra del Fuego
Ladatco Tours	800/327-6162	www.ladatco.com	Bicycling, Coastal and Lake Cruises, Cultural Tours, Hiking, Horseback Riding, Natural History	Argentine Patagonia, Chilean Patagonia, Lake District, Tierra del Fuego
Lindblad Expeditions	212/765-7740 or 800/397-3348	www.expeditions.com	Coastal and Lake Cruises, Photo Safaris	Antarctica
Liz Caskey Culinary & Wine Experiences	56/2-933-5206 or 904/687-0340	www.lizcaskey.com	Cultural Tours	Argentine Patagonia, Chilean Patagonia
Mountain Madness	206/937-8389 or 800/328-5925	www.mountainmadness.com	Mountaineering, Trekking	Antarctica, Northwest Argentina
Mountain Travel Sobek	510/594-6000 or 888/687-6235	www.mtsobek.com	Cultural Tours, Hiking, Horseback Riding, Natural History	Argentine Patagonia, Chilean Patagonia, Lake District, Tierra del Fuego
Myths and Mountains	775/832-5454 or 800/670-6984	www.mythsandmountains.com	Cultural Tours, Natural History, Hiking	Argentine Patagonia, Chilean Patagonia, Lake District, Tierra del Fuego
Nature Expeditions International	954/693-8852 or 800/869-0639	www.naturexp.com	Cultural Tours, Hiking, Horseback Riding, Natural History, Rafting, Kayaking	Argentine Patagonia, Lake District
Off the Beaten Path	800/445-2995	www.offthebeatenpath.com	Cultural, Fly Fishing, Hiking, Natural History	Argentine Patagonia, Lake District
PanAmerican Travel Services	800/364-4359	www.panamtours.com	Bicycling, Coastal and Lake Cruises, Cultural Tours, Hiking, Horseback Riding, Natural History	Antarctica Argentine Patagonia, Chilean Patagonia, Lake District, Tierra del Fuego
Patagonia Travel Company	29/44-15-584-784	www.patagoniatravelco.com	Bicycling, Canoeing, Kayaking, Rafting, Hiking, Horseback Riding, Mountaineering, Natural History	Argentine Patagonia, Los Glaciares National Park, Tierra del Fuego
PowderQuest Tours	206/203-6065 or 888/565-7158	www.powderquest.com	Skiing	Argentine Patagonia, Chilean Patagonia, Lake District

Tour Operators

Outfitter	Telephone	Web site	Activities Offered	Regions Covered
Quark Expeditions	203/656-0499 or 800/356-5699	www.quarkexpeditions.com	Coastal and Lake Cruises, Natural History	Antarctica
Rod & Reel Adventures	541/349-0777 or 800/356-6982	www.rodreeladventures.com	Fishing	Chilean Patagonia, Tierra del Fuego
Snoventures	775/586-9133	www.snoventures.com	Skiing	Argentine Patagonia, Chilean Patagonia, Lake District
Southwind Adventures	303/972-0701 or 800/377-9463	www.southwindadventures.com	Coastal and Lake Cruises, Cultural Tours, Hiking, Horseback Riding, Natural History	Argentine Patagonia, Chilean Patagonia, Lake District
The World Outdoors	303/413-0938 or 800/488-8483	www.theworldoutdoors.com	Hiking, Natural History,	Argentine Patagonia, Chilean Patagonia, Lake District
Tours International	800/247-7965	www.toursinternational.com	Cultural Tours, Hiking, Mountaineering, Natural History, Skiing	Antarctica, Argentine Patagonia, Chilean Patagonia, Lake District, Tierra del Fuego
Travcoa	949/476-2800	www.travcoa.com	Cultural Tours, Hiking, Natural History	Antarctica, Argentine Patagonia
Victor Emanuel Nature Tours	512/328-5221 or 800/328-8368	www.ventbird.com	Birdwatching	Antarctica, Argentine Patagonia, Chilean Patagonia, Lake District, Tierra del Fuego
Wilderness Travel	510/558-2488 or 800/368-2794	www.wildernesstravel.com	Cultural Tours, Natural History, Hiking, Coastal and Lake Cruises	Antarctica, Argentine Patagonia, Chilean Patagonia, Tierra del Fuego
Wildland Adventures	206/365-0686 or 800/345-4453	www.wildland.com	Cultural Tours, Natural History, Hiking, Coastal and Lake Cruises	Argentine Patagonia, Chilean Patagonia
Wild Wings	0117/965-333	www.wildwings.co.uk	Birdwatching	Antarctica
WINGS	520/320-9868 or 888/293-6443	www.wingsbirds.com	Birdwatching	Argentine Patagonia, Lake District, Tierra del Fuego
World Expeditions	415/989-2212 or 888/464-8735	www.worldexpeditions.com	Cultural Tours, Natural History, Hiking, Mountaineering,	Argentine Patagonia, Lake District, Tierra del Fuego
Zegrahm & Eco Expeditions	206/285-4000 or 800/628-8747	www.zeco.com	Coastal and Lake Cruises, Natural History	Antarctica

MENU GUIDE

With so much meat on the menu, it's good to know how to order it: *jugoso* (juicy) means medium rare, *vuelta y vuelta* (flipped back and forth) means rare, and *vivo por adentro* (alive inside) is barely warm in the middle. Argentineans like their meat *bien cocido* (well cooked).

aceite de olivo: olive oil

alfajores: Argentine cookies, usually made with dulce de leche

arroz: rice

bife de lomo: filet mignon

bife de chorizo: like a New York strip steak, but double the size

budín de pan: Argentine version of bread pudding

cabrito: roasted kid

cafecito: espresso

centolla: King crab, a Patagonian specialty

chorizo: thick, spicy pork-and-beef sausages, usually served with bread (*choripan*)

churros: baton-shaped donuts for dipping in hot chocolate

ciervo: venison

chivito: kid

cordero: lamb

cortado: coffee "cut" with a drop of milk

dulce de leche: a sweet caramel concoction made from milk

ensalada de fruta: fruit salad (sometimes fresh, sometimes canned)

estofado: beef stew

facturas: small pastries

huevos: eggs

humitas: steamed cornhusks wrapped around cornmeal and cheese

lechón: roast suckling pig

licuado: milk shake

locro: slow-cooked stew made with hominy, beans, meat, and vegetables

medialuna: croissant

mejillones: mussels

milanesa: breaded meat cutlet, usually veal, pounded thin and fried

milanesa a la napolitana: breaded meat cutlet with melted mozzarella and tomato sauce

mollejas: sweetbreads; the thymus glands, usually of the cow

morcilla: blood sausage

pejerrey: a kind of mackerel

provoleta: grilled provolone sprinkled with olive oil and oregano

salchichas: long, thin sausages

tenedor libre: all-you-can-eat meat and salad bar

Travel Smart Argentina

WORD OF MOUTH

"We weren't planning on not using the subway, but we ended up either walking or taking taxis everywhere. [. . .] Also, note that the driving is absolutely crazy in BA. Those white stripes to delineate the lanes are apparently merely a suggestion and keep in mind the pedestrian NEVER has the right of way!!!"

—jgg

www.fodors.com/community

GETTING HERE AND AROUND

Argentina measures around 3,650 km (2,268 mi) from tip to tail, and many of its attractions are hundreds of miles apart. Carefully planning how you get around will save lots of time and money.

Buenos Aires lies about two-thirds of the way up Argentina's eastern side, on the banks of the Río de la Plata. It's the country's capital and its main transport hub. A well-developed network of long-distance buses connects it with cities all over Argentina; buses also operate between many cities without passing through Buenos Aires.

TRAVEL TIMES FROM BUENOS AIRES	BY AIR	BY BUS
To		
San Antonio de Areco	n/a	2 hours
Atlantic Coast	1 hour	5–6 hours
Córdoba	1¼ hours	9–11 hours
Mendoza	1¾ hours	12–14 hours
Puerto Iguazú	1¾ hours	16–19 hours
Salta	2¼ hours	18–21 hours
Bariloche	2¼ hours	21–23 hours
El Calafate	3¼ hours	40 hours

Three of the country's main draws are around 1,000 km (621 mi) from Buenos Aires as the crow flies: Puerto Iguazú, the base for exploring Iguazú Falls, in northeastern Misiones Province; Salta, the gateway to the Andean Northwest; and Mendoza, in the wine region, near the Chilean border. Slightly farther, this time southwest of Buenos Aires, is Bariloche, the hub for the Lake District of northern Patagonia. The hub of southern Patagonia is El Calafate, close to the Perito Moreno glacier, a whopping 2,068 km (1,285 mi) southwest of Buenos Aires.

Flying within the country makes sense given these huge distances. That said, domestic flights are expensive, and at this writing flight delays of two to six hours are regular occurrences. As a result, many visitors opt for the more reliable overnight sleeper buses for trips of up to 1,000 km (621 mi; around 12 hours).

BY AIR

TO ARGENTINA

There are direct daily services between Buenos Aires and several North American cities, with New York and Miami being primary departure points. Many airlines fly to Buenos Aires via Santiago de Chile or São Paulo in Brazil, which adds only a little to your trip time.

Aerolíneas Argentinas, the flagship airline, operates direct flights between Buenos Aires and Miami. Since its renationalization in 2008, Aerolíneas's reputation for chronic delays has greatly improved.

Chilean airline LAN is the Aerolíneas's biggest local competition. LAN flies direct to JFK, Miami, and Los Angeles, usually via Santiago de Chile or Lima. There are direct flights from Los Angeles and Atlanta on Delta. American has nonstop service from JFK, Miami, and Dallas. United flies from JFK via Washington, D.C. Continental connects Buenos Aires with Houston (and from there to Dallas) and Newark.

Flying times to Buenos Aires are 11–12 hours from New York, 9 hours from Miami, 10½ hours from Dallas or Houston, and 13 hours from Los Angeles, via Santiago de Chile.

WITHIN ARGENTINA

Most domestic flights operate from Buenos Aires, so to fly from the extreme south of the country to the extreme north, you often have to change planes here.

Aerolíneas Argentinas and its partner Austral operate flights from Buenos Aires to more Argentine cities than any other airline, including daily services (often more than one) to Puerto Iguazú, Salta, Mendoza, Córdoba, Bariloche, Ushuaia, and El Calafate. LAN also flies to these cities.

AIR PASSES

If you're flying into Argentina on Aerolíneas Argentinas, you're eligible for their South American pass, which enables you to also visit Brazil, Chile, Colombia, Paraguay, Peru, Uruguay, and Venezuela. The price is based on your total mileage: 1,900 mi cost $319, for example.

If you plan to take at least three flights within Argentina or South America in general, the OneWorld Alliance's (of which LAN Chile is a member) Visit South America pass can save money. Flights are categorized by mileage; most segments (both domestic and international) range from $119 to $359. The catch is that most domestic routes only operate from Buenos Aires, so you always have to return there. Visiting Iguazú and Calafate from Buenos Aires would cost $690, for example.

Airline Contacts Aerolíneas Argentinas (*www.aerolineas.com.ar*). **American Airlines** (*www.aa.com*). **Continental Airlines** (*www.continental.com*). **Delta Airlines** (*www.delta.com*). **LAN** (*www.lan.com*). **United Airlines** (*www.united.com*).

Airlines and Airports Airline and Airport Links.com (*www.airlineandairportlinks.com*).

Airline Security Issues Transportation Security Administration (*www.tsa.gov*).

Air Passes South American Pass (*Aerolíneas Argentinas, 800/333-0276 www.aerolineas.com.ar*). **Visit South America Pass** (*OneWorld Alliance LAN: 866/435-9526 www.oneworld.com*).

AIRPORTS

Airports in Argentina are mostly small, well maintained, and easy to get around. Security at most isn't as stringent as it is in the States—computers stay in cases, shoes stay on your feet, and there are no random searches.

BUENOS AIRES

Buenos Aires's Aeropuerto Internacional de Ezeiza Ministro Pistarini (EZE)—known as Ezeiza—is 35 km (22 mi) southwest of and a 45-minute drive from city center. It's served by a variety of international airlines, along with domestic airlines running international routes.

Aerolíneas Argentinas and its partner Austral operate out of the older Terminal B. All other airlines are based at Terminal A, a pleasant, glass-sided building. A covered walkway connects the two terminals. Each terminal has a few small snack bars, a small range of shops, a public phone center with Internet services, and a tourist information booth. The ATM, 24-hour luggage storage, and car-rental agencies are in Terminal A.

⚠ **Avoid changing money in the luggage reclaim area. By far the best exchange rates are at the small Banco de la Nación in the Terminal A arrivals area; it's open round the clock.**

Most domestic flights operate out of Aeroparque Jorge Newbery (AEP). It's next to the Río de la Plata in northeast Palermo, about 8 km (5 mi) north of the city center. Both it and Ezeiza are run by the private company Aeropuertos Argentinos 2000.

ELSEWHERE IN ARGENTINA

Several other airports in Argentina are technically international, but only because they have a few flights to neighboring countries; most flights are domestic.

Aeropuerto Internacional de Puerto Iguazú (IGR) is close to Iguazú Falls; it's 20 km (12 mi) from Puerto Iguazú and 10 km (6 mi) from the park entrance. The northwest is served by Salta's Aeropuerto Internacional Martín Miguel de Güemes (SLA), called Aeropuerto de Salta, 7 km (4½ mi) west of the city of Salta.

The airport for the wine region and western Argentina is Aeropuerto Internacional de Mendoza Francisco Gabrieli (MDZ), also known as El Plumerillo. It's 10 km (6 mi) north of Mendoza. Northern

Patagonia's hub is Bariloche, 13 km (8 mi) west of which is the Aeropuerto Internacional San Carlos de Bariloche Teniente Luis Candelaria (BRC), known as the Aeropuerto de Bariloche. The gateway to southern Patagonia is Aeropuerto Internacional de El Calafate Comandante Armando Tola (ECA), 18 km (11 mi) east of El Calafate itself.

Airport Information Aeropuertos Argentinos 2000 (*www.aa2000.com.ar*). **Aeroparque Jorge Newbery** (*Buenos Aires 11/5480–6111 www.aa2000.com.ar*). **Aeropuerto Internacional de Ezeiza Ministro Pistarini** (*www.aa2000.com.ar*).

BY BOAT

There are frequent ferry services across the Río de la Plata between Buenos Aires and the Uruguayan cities of Colonia and Montevideo. Both Buquebus and Colonia Express run fast catamarans to Colonia, which take an hour or less. Full-price round-trip tickets with each company cost 304 pesos and 198 pesos, respectively, but there are substantial off-peak and mid-week discounts if you book online. The two companies also sell packages that include bus tickets to La Paloma, Montevideo, and Punta del Este on services direct from Colonia's ferry terminal. You can order tickets by phone or online. Buquebus leaves from a terminal at the northern end of Puerto Madero. The Colonia Express terminal is on Avenida Pedro de Mendoza (the extension of Av. Huergo) at 20 de Septiembre, south of Puerto Madero. It's best reached by taxi.

Contacts Buquebus (*11/4316–6500 www.buquebus.com*). **Colonia Express** (*11/4313–5100 in Buenos Aires, 52/29676 in Colonia www.coloniaexpress.com*).

BY BUS

Frequent, comfortable, and dependable long-distance buses connect Buenos Aires with cities all over Argentina and with neighboring countries. Bus travel can be substantially cheaper than flying, and far less prone to delays. Both locals and visitors often choose overnight sleeper services for trips up to 12 hours long.

Most bus companies have online timetables; some allow you to buy tickets online or by phone. Web sites also list *puntos de venta* (sales offices)—in many cases you don't need to go to the terminal to buy tickets, though you can usually buy them there right up until departure time. Be prepared to pay cash. During January, February, and July, buy your ticket as far in advance as possible—a week or more, at least—and arrive at the terminal extra early.

Most long-distance buses depart from Buenos Aires's Terminal de Omnibus de Retiro, which is often referred to as the Terminal de Retiro or simply Retiro. Ramps and stairs from the street lead you to a huge concourse where buses leave from more than 60 numbered platforms. There are restrooms, restaurants, public phones, lockers, news kiosks, and a tourist office on this floor.

You buy tickets from the *boleterías* (ticket offices) on the upper level; there are also two ATMs here. Each company has its own booth; they're arranged in zones according to the destinations served, which makes price comparisons easy. The terminal's excellent Web site lists bus companies by destination, including their phone number and ticket booth location. (*See individual chapters for information about local bus stations.*) Keep your wits about you in the terminal: pickpockets and bag-snatchers often prey on distracted travelers.

All long-distance buses have toilets, air-conditioning, videos, and snacks. The most basic service is *semi-cama,* which has minimally reclineable seats and often takes a little longer than more luxurious services. It's worth paying the little extra for *coche cama,* sometimes called *ejecutivo,* where you get large, business-class-style seats and, sometimes, pillows and blankets. The best rides of all are on the fully reclineable seats of *cama suite* services, which are often contained in their own little booth. Bus attendants and free drinks are other perks.

On services between nearby towns, you can usually choose between regular buses (*común*) and air-conditioned or heated services with reclining seats (*diferencial*). The companies that run local services rarely have Web sites—you buy tickets direct from the bus station.

Contact Terminal de Ómnibus Retiro (✉ *Av. Antártida Argentina at Av. Ramos Mejía, Retiro, Buenos Aires* ☎ *11/4310–0700* 🌐 *www.tebasa.com.ar*).

BY CAR

Argentina's long highways and fabulous scenery make it a great place for road trips. However, if you're only going to be staying in Buenos Aires and other big cities, renting a car isn't particularly useful; stick with a *remis* (hired car) or taxi; remises can be hired to take you around the countryside, too.

GASOLINE

There are plenty of gas stations, called *estaciones de servicio*, in and near most towns and along major highways. Most are open 24 hours and usually include full service, convenience stores, snack bars, and sometimes ATMs. In rural areas, stations have small shops and toilets, but are few and far between and have reduced hours.

On long trips, fill your tank whenever you can, even if you've still got gas left, as the next station could be a long way away (signs at stations often tell you how far). Attendants always pump the gas and don't expect a tip, though most locals add a few pesos for a full tank. Credit cards aren't always accepted—look for signs saying *tarjetas de crédito suspendidas* (no credit cards).

The major service stations are YPF, Shell, Petrobras, and Esso. Locals say that YPF gas is the highest quality. It also tends to be the cheapest. Prices are often higher in the north of Argentina. South of an imaginary line between Bariloche and Puerto Madryn, gas is heavily subsidized and costs roughly half what it does elsewhere. There are three grades of unleaded fuels, as well as diesel and biodiesel. GNC is compressed natural gas, an alternative fuel. Stations with GNC signs may sell only this, or both this and regular gas.

PARKING

On-street parking is limited in big cities. Some have meter systems or tickets that you buy from kiosks and display on the dashboard. In meter-free spots there's often an informal "caretaker" who guides you into your spot and charges 2–5 pesos to watch your car, which you pay when you leave. Although nothing will happen if you don't pay, most locals see not doing so as very mean.

Car theft is common, so many agencies insist that you park in a guarded lot. Many hotels have their own lots, and there are plenty in major cities: look for a circular blue sign with a white E (for *estacionamiento* [parking]). In downtown Buenos Aires, expect to pay 7–8 pesos per hour, or 28 pesos for 12 hours. Rates are much lower elsewhere. Illegally parked cars are towed only from restricted parking areas in city centers. Getting your car back is a bureaucratic nightmare and costs around 200 pesos.

ROAD CONDITIONS

City streets are notorious for potholes, uneven surfaces, and poorly marked lanes and turnoffs. Many major cities have a one-way system whereby parallel streets run in opposite directions: never going the wrong way along a street is one of the few rules that Argentines abide by. Where there are no traffic lights at an intersection, you give way to drivers coming from the right, but have priority over those coming from the left.

Two kinds of roads connect major cities: *autopistas* (two- or three-lane freeways) and *rutas* (single- or dual-carriageways) or *rutas nacionales* (main "national routes," usually indicated with an "RN" before the route number). Both types of roads are subject to regular tolls. Autopistas are well maintained, but the state of rutas varies hugely. In more remote locations, even rutas that look like major highways on maps may be narrow roads with no central division. Always travel with a map, as signposts for turnoffs are scarce.

Night driving can be hazardous: some highways and routes are poorly lighted, routes sometimes cut through the center of towns, cattle often get onto the roads, and in rural areas *rastreros* (old farm trucks) seldom have all their lights working. Outside of the city of Buenos Aires, be especially watchful at traffic lights, as crossing on red lights at night is common practice. Beware of *guardaganados* (cattle guards). They're often raised so that your car flies into the air if speeding. For highway-condition reports, updated daily, and basic routes in Spanish, contact La Dirección Nacional de Vialidad.

A useful road-trip Web site is ⊕ *www.ruta0.com*, which calculates distances and tolls between places and offers several route options. There are basic maps and some highway-condition reports (in Spanish) on the Web site of the Dirección Nacional de Vialidad (National Highway Authority).

Information **Dirección Nacional de Vialidad** (☎ *11/4343–8520* ⊕ *www.vialidad.gov.ar*).

ROADSIDE EMERGENCIES

All rental car agencies have an emergency help line in case of breakdowns or accidents—some services take longer than others to arrive. The best roadside assistance is usually that of the Automóvil Club Argentina (ACA), which sends mechanics and tow trucks to members traveling anywhere in the country. If you have an accident on the highway, stay by your vehicle until the police arrive, which could take a while, depending on where you are. If your car is stolen, you should report it to the closest police station.

Contacts **American Automobile Association** (*AAA* ☎ *800/564–6222* ⊕ *www.aaa.com*). **Automóvil Club Argentino** (*ACA* ☎ *11/4808–4000*, emergencies *800/777–2894* ⊕ *www.aca.org.ar*). **Police** (☎ *101*).

RULES OF THE ROAD

You drive on the right in Argentina, like in the United States. Seat belts are required by law for front-seat passengers. You must use your car lights on highways at all times. The use of cellular phones while driving is forbidden, and turning left on two-way avenues is prohibited unless there's a left-turn signal; likewise, there are no right turns on red. Traffic lights turn yellow before they turn red, but also before turning green, which is interpreted by drivers as an extra margin to get through the intersection, so take precautions.

The legal blood-alcohol limit is 500 mg of alcohol per liter of blood, but in practice breathalyzing is common only along the highways of the Atlantic coast during January and February. In towns and cities, a 40-KPH (25-MPH) speed limit applies on streets and a 60-KPH (37-MPH) limit is in effect on avenues. On *autopistas* (freeways) the limit is 130 KPH (80 MPH), and on *rutas* (highways) it ranges between 100 KPH (62 MPH) and 120 KPH (75 MPH). On smaller roads and highways out of town it's 80 KPH (50 MPH). However, locals take speed-limit signs, the ban on driving with cell phones, and drunk driving lightly, so drive very defensively indeed.

Police tend to be forgiving of foreigners' driving faults and often waive tickets and fines when they see your passport. If you do get a traffic ticket, don't argue. Most tickets aren't payable on the spot, but some police officers offer "reduced" on-the-spot fines in lieu of a ticket: it's bribery and you'd do best to insist on receiving the proper ticket.

In Buenos Aires, buses and taxis (which cruise slowly on the right-hand side to pick up passengers) often drive as though they have priority, and it's good to defer to them for your own safety. If you experience a small accident, jot down the other driver's information and supply your own, then go to the nearest police station in the area to file a report. Contact your rental agency immediately.

Paved highways run from Argentina to the Chilean, Bolivian, Paraguayan, and Brazilian borders. If you do cross the border by land you'll be required to present your passport, documentation of car ownership, and insurance paperwork at immigration and customs checkpoints. It's also common for cars and bags to be searched for contraband, such as food, livestock, and drugs.

RENTAL CARS

Daily rates range from 190 pesos to 400 pesos, depending on the type of car and the distance you plan to travel. This generally includes tax and 200 free km (125 free mi) daily. Note that most cars have manual transmissions, so if you need an automatic, request one in advance.

Reputable firms don't rent to drivers under 21, and drivers under 23 often have to pay a daily surcharge of 10–15 pesos. Children's car seats are not compulsory, but are available for about 15 pesos per day. Some agencies charge a 10% surcharge for picking up a car from the airport.

Collision damage waiver (CDW) is mandatory and is usually included in standard rental prices. However, you're still responsible for a deductible fee—a maximum amount that you'll have to pay if damage occurs. The amount of this deductible is generally around 3,000 pesos for a car, and can be much higher for a four-wheel-drive vehicle. You can reduce the figure substantially by paying an insurance premium (usually 30–60 pesos per day); some companies have lower deductibles than others.

In general, you cannot cross the border in a rental car. Many rental companies don't insure you on unpaved roads. Discuss your itinerary with the agent to be certain you're always covered.

Rental Agencies Alamo (☎ *810/999–25266, 11/4322–3320 in Buenos Aires* 🌐 *www.alamo.com*). **Avis** (☎ *810/9991–2847, 11/4326–5542 in Buenos Aires* 🌐 *www.avis.com*). **Budget** (☎ *810/444–2834, 11/4311–4555 in Buenos Aires* 🌐 *www.budget.com*). **Dollar** (☎ *800/555–3655, 11/4315–8800 in Buenos Aires* 🌐 *www.dollar.com.ar*). **Hertz** (☎ *810/222–43789, 11/4816–8001 in Buenos Aires* 🌐 *www.hertz.com*). **Localiza** (☎ *800/999–2999, 11/4121–5611 in Buenos Aires* 🌐 *www.localiza.com*).

ESSENTIALS

ACCOMMODATIONS

Booming visitor numbers have sparked the construction of dozens of properties, and healthy competition is keeping prices reasonable and quality high. There's variety, too.

Nearly all hotels include breakfast in the room price, but not all include the 21% tax in their quoted rates. Prices are also linked to municipality-run rating systems, which are based on a checklist of amenities (often outdated) rather than detailed evaluation. You can get wildly different things for your money, so do your homework. In destinations popular with locals, room prices soar in high season (usually January, February, and July), and some establishments won't take bookings for less than seven days. In the off-season the same places can be a steal.

APARTMENT AND HOUSE RENTALS

There are hundreds of furnished rentals available by the day, week, or month in Buenos Aires and other cities. Reputable local reservations services ApartmentsBA.com, ByT Argentina, and Buenos Aires Habitat have large online databases.

When choosing your rental, remember that air-conditioning is a must between December and March. Always check exact street locations on a map, as listings sometimes exaggerate a property's proximity to particular neighborhoods, landmarks, or subway stations. Likewise, apartments are often more worn than they appear in gleaming Web site photos.

Most online apartment agencies act as intermediaries between you and the owner: an English-speaking representative meets you at the apartment, you sign a contract, pay the owner, and are given the keys. You pay for your entire stay up front, and usually have to pay a deposit equivalent to a week's rent, which is returned when you leave. Note that though you give a credit card number to secure your reservation, actual payment is nearly always in cash only. Read cancellation policies carefully: many agencies don't refund if you're not happy with your apartment choice.

Local Rental Agents ApartmentsBA.com (☎ *11/5254–0100* 🌐 *www.apartmentsba.com*). **ByT Argentina** (☎ *11/4876–5000* 🌐 *www.bytargentina.com*). **Buenos Aires Habitat** (☎ *305/735–2223 in U.S., 11/4815–8662 in Buenos Aires* 🌐 *www.buenosaireshabitat.com*).

ESTANCIAS

You get a taste of Argentine country life—including home-cooked meals and horseback riding—when you stay at a ranch. Estancias Travel and Estancias Argentinas are two good booking services, but you often get better rates if you call the estancia direct.

When booking, ask specifically about what activities and drinks are included in rates, and bear in mind that many establishments only accept cash payments. Be sure to factor in travel times and costs when planning your stay: remoter locations may only be reachable by private transport, often at a hefty cost.

Estancia Reservations Estancias Argentinas (☎ *11/4343–2366* 🌐 *www.estanciasargentinas.com*). **Estancias Travel** (☎ *11/4315–8084* 🌐 *www.estanciastravel.com*).

COMMUNICATIONS

INTERNET

Inexpensive Internet access is widely available in Buenos Aires. Top-end hotels tend to have high-speed in-room data ports, while budget establishments often have free Wi-Fi. Many hotels have a PC in the lobby for guests to use.

If you're traveling without a laptop, look for a *ciber* (Internet café) or *locutorios* (telephone and Internet centers). Expect to pay between 3 and 6 pesos per hour to surf the Web. Broadband connections are common.

In Buenos Aires many bars and restaurants have free Wi-Fi—look out for stickers on their windows. In general, these are open networks and you don't need to ask for a password to use them. You can also find Wi-Fi in many hotel lobbies, libraries, business and event centers, some airports, and in public spaces—piggybacking is common practice.

Contact Cybercafes (*www.cybercafes.com*) lists over 4,000 Internet cafés worldwide.

PHONES

The country code for Argentina is 54. To call landlines in Argentina from the United States, dial the international access code (011) followed by the country code (54), the two- to four-digit area code without the initial 0, then the five- to nine-digit phone number. For example, to call the Buenos Aires number 011/4123–4567, you would dial 011–54–11–4123–4567.

Any number that is prefixed by a 15 is a cell phone number. To call cell phones from the United States, dial the international access code (011) followed by the country code (54), Argentina's cell-phone code (9), the area code without the initial 0, then the seven- or eight-digit cell phone number without the initial 15. For example, to call the Buenos Aires cell phone (011) 15/5123–4567, you would dial 011–54–9–11–5123–4567.

CALLING WITHIN ARGENTINA

Argentina's phone service is run by the duopoly of Telecom and Telefónica. Telecom does the northern half of Argentina (including the northern half of the city of Buenos Aires) and Telefónica does the south. However, both companies operate public phones and phone centers throughout Argentina, called *locutorios* or *telecentros*.

Service is efficient, and direct dialing—both long-distance and international—is universal. You can make local and long-distance calls from your hotel (usually with a surcharge) and from any public phone or locutorio. Public phones aren't abundant, and are often broken; all accept coins. Phone cards can be used from both public and private phones by calling a free access number and entering the card code number.

At locutorios, ask the receptionist for *una cabina* (a booth), make as many local, long-distance, or international calls as you like (a small LCD display tracks how much you've spent), then pay as you leave. There's no charge if you don't get through. Note that many locutorios don't allow you to call free numbers, so you can't use prepaid calling cards from them.

All of Argentina's area codes are prefixed with a 0, which you need to include when dialing another area within Argentina. You don't need to dial the area code to call a local number. Confusingly, area codes and phone numbers don't all have the same number of digits. The area code for Buenos Aires is 011, and phone numbers have 8 digits. Area codes for the rest of the country have three or four digits, and start with 02 (the southern provinces) or 03 (the northern provinces); phone numbers have six or seven digits.

For local directory assistance (in Spanish), dial 110. Local calls cost 23¢ for two minutes at peak time (weekdays 8–8 and Saturday 8–1) or four minutes the rest of the time. Long-distance calls cost 57¢ per *ficha* (unit)—the farther the distance, the less time each unit lasts. For example, 57¢ lasts about two minutes to places less than 55 km (35 mi) away, but only half a minute to somewhere more than 250 km (155 mi) away.

To make international calls from Argentina, dial 00, then the country code, area code, and number. The country code for the United States is 1.

CALLING CARDS

You can use prepaid calling cards (*tarjetas prepagas*) to make local and international calls from public phones, but not locutorios. All cards come with a scratch-off panel, which reveals a PIN. You dial a free access number, the PIN, and the number you wish to call.

Many *kioscos* (convenience stores) and small supermarkets sell a variety of prepaid calling cards from different companies: specify it's for *llamadas internacionales* (international calls), and compare each card's per-minute rates to the country you want to call. Many cost as little as 9¢ per minute for calls to the United States. Telecom and Telefónica also sell prepaid 5-, 10-, and 20-peso calling cards from kioscos and locutorios. They're called Tarjeta Países and GeoDestino, respectively. Calls to the United States cost 19¢ per minute using both.

Calling Card Information Telecom (☎ *0800/555–0030* 🌐 *www.telecom.com.ar*). **Telefónica** (☎ *0800/333–9000* 🌐 *www.telefonica.com.ar*).

MOBILE PHONES

All cell phones are GSM 850/1900 Mhz. If you have an unlocked dual-band GSM phone from North America and intend to call local numbers, buy a prepaid Argentinian SIM card on arrival—rates will be cheaper than using your U.S. network or than renting a phone. Alternatively, you can buy a basic pay-as-you-go handset and SIM card (*tarjeta SIM*) for around 180 pesos.

Cell numbers here use a local area code, then the cell phone prefix (15), then a seven- or eight-digit number. To call a cell in the same area as you, dial 15 and the number. To call a cell in a different area, dial the area code, including the initial 0, then 15, then the number.

Local cell charges depend on things like the company and time of day, but most cost between 50¢ and 90¢ per minute. If you call from a pay phone, the recipient is charged.

There are three main mobile phone companies in Argentina: Movistar (owned by Telefónica), Claro, and Personal. Their prices are similar, but Claro is said to have better coverage, Movistar has the most users, and Personal is the least popular service, so cards can be harder to find. You pay only for outgoing calls, which cost between 50¢ and 1 peso a minute. You can buy an SIM card from any of the companies' outlets. Top up credit by purchasing pay-as-you-go cards (*tarjetas de celular*), available from kioscos, locutorios, supermarkets, and gas stations or by *carga virtual* (virtual top-ups) at locutorios, where sales clerks add credit to your line while you wait. Cellular phones can be rented at the airport from Phonerental. A basic handset is free for the first week and costs 20 pesos a week thereafter. Outgoing local calls cost 72¢, but you pay 60¢ per minute to receive both local and international calls.

Contacts Cellular Abroad (☎ *800/287–5072* 🌐 *www.cellularabroad.com*). **Claro** (🌐 *www.claro.com.ar*). **Mobal** (☎ *888/888–9162* 🌐 *www.mobalrental.com*). **Movistar** (🌐 *www.movistar.com.ar*). **Personal** (🌐 *www.personal.com.ar*). **Phonerental** (☎ *11/4311–2933* 🌐 *www.phonerental.com.ar*). **Planet Fone** (☎ *888/988–4777* 🌐 *www.planetfone.com*).

CUSTOMS AND DUTIES

Customs uses a random inspection system that requires you to push a button at the inspection bay—if a green light comes on, you walk through; if a red light appears, your bags are X-rayed (and very occasionally opened). In practice, many officials wave foreigners through. Officially, you can bring up to 2 liters of alcohol, 400 cigarettes, and 50 cigars into the country duty-free. That said, Argentina's international airports have duty-free shops after you land, and officials never take alcohol and tobacco purchased there into account. Personal clothing and effects are admitted duty-free, provided they have been used, as are personal jewelry and professional equipment. Fishing gear and skis present no problems.

If you enter the country by bus from Bolivia, Brazil, or Paraguay, you, your bags, and the vehicle may be subject to lengthy searches by officials looking for drugs and smuggled goods.

Argentina has strict regulations designed to prevent the illicit trafficking of antiques, fossils, and other items of cultural and historical importance. For more information, contact the Dirección Nacional de Patrimonio y Museos (National Heritage and Museums Board).

Information in Argentina Dirección Nacional de Patrimonio y Museos (☎ *11/4381-6656* 🌐 *www.cultura.gov.ar*).

U.S. Information U.S. Customs and Border Protection (🌐 *www.cbp.gov*).

ELECTRICITY

The electrical current is 220 volts, 50 cycles alternating current (AC), so most North American appliances can't be used without a transformer. Older wall outlets take Continental-type plugs, with two round prongs, whereas newer buildings take plugs with three flat, angled prongs or two flat prongs set at a "v" angle.

Brief power outages (and surges when the power comes back) are fairly regular occurrences, so it's a good idea to use a surge-protector with your laptop.

EMERGENCIES

In a medical emergency, taking a taxi to the nearest hospital—drivers usually know where to go—can be quicker than waiting for an ambulance. If you do call an ambulance, it will take you to the nearest hospital—possibly a public one that may well look run-down; don't worry, though, as the care will be excellent. Alternatively, you can call a private hospital directly.

For theft, wallet loss, small road accidents, and minor emergencies, contact the nearest police station. Expect all dealings with the police to be a lengthy, bureaucratic business—it's probably only worth bothering if you need the report for insurance claims.

American Embassy American Embassy (✉ *Av. Colombia 4300, Palermo, Buenos Aires* ☎ *11/5777-4354, 11/5777-4873 after hours* 🌐 *argentina.usembassy.gov*).

General Contacts Ambulance and Medical (☎ *107*). **Fire** (☎ *100*). **Police** (☎ *101*). **All Buenos Aires Emergency Services** (☎ *911*).

HEALTH

MEDICAL CONCERNS

No vaccinations are required for travel to Argentina. However, the Centers for Disease Control (CDC) recommend vaccinations against hepatitis A and B and typhoid for all travelers. A yellow fever vaccine is also advisable if you're traveling to Iguazú. Each year there are cases of cholera in northern Argentina, mostly in the indigenous communities near the Bolivian border; your best protection is to avoid eating raw seafood.

Malaria is a threat only in low-lying rural areas near the borders of Bolivia and Paraguay. In 2009, outbreaks of dengue fever (another mosquito-borne disease) were widespread in northern Argentina, especially in Misiones province (where Iguazú Falls is). Some cases were reported as far south as Buenos Aires. The best preventive measure against both dengue and malaria is to cover your arms and legs, use a good mosquito repellent containing DEET, and stay inside at dusk.

American trypanosomiasis, or Chagas' disease, is present in remote rural areas. The CDC recommends chloroquine as a preventive antimalarial for adults and infants in Argentina. To be effective, the weekly doses must start a week before you travel and continue four weeks after your return. There is no preventive medication for dengue or Chagas'. Children traveling to Argentina should have current inoculations against measles, mumps, rubella, and polio.

In most urban areas in Argentina, including Buenos Aires, people drink tap water and eat uncooked fruits and vegetables.

LOCAL DO'S AND TABOOS

CUSTOMS OF THE COUNTRY

Welcoming and helpful, Argentinians are a pleasure to travel among. City dwellers here have more in common with, say, the Spanish or Italians, than other Latin Americans. However, although cultural differences between here and North America are small, they're still palpable.

Outside Buenos Aires, siestas are still sacrosanct: most shops and museums close between 1 and 4 PM. Argentines are usually fashionably late for all social events—don't be offended if someone keeps you waiting over half an hour for a lunch or dinner date. However, tardiness is frowned upon in the business world.

Fiercely animated discussions are a national pastime, and locals relish probing controversial issues like politics and religion, as well as soccer and their friends' personal lives. Political correctness isn't a valued trait, and just about everything and everyone—except mothers—is a potential target for playful mockery. Locals are often disparaging about their country's shortcomings, but Argentina-bashing is a privilege reserved for Argentinians. That said, some anti-American feeling—both serious and jokey—permeates most of society. You'll earn more friends by taking it in your stride.

GREETINGS

Argentinians have no qualms about getting physical, and the way they greet each other reflects this. One kiss on the right cheek is the customary greeting between both male and female friends. Women also greet strangers in this way, although men—especially older men—often shake hands the first time they meet someone. Other than that, handshaking is seen as very cold and formal.

When you leave a party it's normal to say good-bye to everyone in the room (or, if you're in a restaurant, to everyone at your table), which means kissing everyone once again. Unlike other Latin Americans, porteños use the formal "you" form, *usted,* only with people much older than they or in very formal situations, and the casual greeting *¡Hola!* often replaces *buen día, buenas tardes,* and *buenas noches.* In small towns, formal greetings and the use of *usted* are much more widespread.

LANGUAGE

Argentina's official language is Spanish, known locally as *castellano* (rather than *español*). It differs from other varieties of Spanish in its use of *vos* (instead of *tú*) for the informal "you" form, and there are lots of small vocabulary differences, especially for everyday things like food. Porteño intonation is rather singsong, and sounds more like Italian than Mexican or peninsular Spanish. And, like Italians, porteños supplement their words with lots and lots of gesturing. Another peculiarity is pronouncing the letters "y" and "ll" as a "sh" sound.

In hotels, restaurants, and shops that cater to visitors, many people speak at least some English. All the same, attempts to speak Spanish are usually appreciated. Basic courtesies like *buen día* (good morning) or *buenas tardes* (good afternoon), and *por favor* (please) and *gracias* (thank you) are a good place to start. Even if your language skills are basic and phrasebook-bound, locals generally make an effort to understand you. If people don't know the answer to a question, such as a request for directions, they'll tell you so. ■ **TIP→ Buenos Aires's official tourism body runs a free, 24-hour tourist-assistance hotline with English-speaking operators, ☎ 0800/999–2838.**

LOCAL DO'S AND TABOOS (CONT.)

OUT ON THE TOWN

A firm nod of the head or raised eyebrow usually gets waiters' attention; "*disculpa*" (excuse me) also does the trick. You can ask your waiter for *la cuenta* (the check) or make a signing gesture in the air from afar.

Alcohol—especially wine and beer—is a big part of life in Argentina. Local women generally drink less than their foreign counterparts, but there are no taboos about this. Social events usually end in general tipsiness rather than all-out drunkenness, which is seen as a rather tasteless foreign habit.

Smoking is very common in Argentina, but anti-smoking legislation introduced in Buenos Aires in 2006 has banned smoking in all but the largest cafés and restaurants (which have to have extractor fans and designated smoking areas). Outside the city you still get smoke with your steak. Most restaurants offer no-smoking sections (*no fumadores*), but make sure to ask before you are seated. Smoking is prohibited on public transport and in government offices, banks, and cinemas.

Public displays of affection between heterosexual couples attract little attention in most parts of the country; beyond downtown Buenos Aires, same-sex couples may attract hostile reactions.

All locals make an effort to look nice—though not necessarily formal—for dinner out. Older couples get very dressed up for the theater; younger women usually put on high heels and makeup for clubbing.

If you're invited to someone's home for dinner, a bottle of good Argentinian wine is the best gift to take the hosts.

SIGHTSEEING

You can dress pretty much as you like in Buenos Aires: skimpy clothing causes no offense.

Argentinian men almost always allow women to go through doors and to board buses and elevators first, often with exaggerated ceremony. Far from finding this sexist, local women take it as a God-given right. Frustratingly, there's no local rule about standing on one side of escalators to allow people to pass you.

Despite bus drivers' best efforts, locals are often reluctant to move to the back of buses. Pregnant women, the elderly, and those with disabilities have priority on the front seats of city buses, and you should offer them your seat if these are already taken.

Children and adults selling pens, notepads, or sheets of stickers are regular fixtures on urban public transport. Some children also hand out tiny greeting cards in exchange for coins. The standard procedure is to accept the merchandise or cards as the vendor moves up the carriage, then either return the item (saying *no, gracias*) or give them money when they return.

Most Argentinians are hardened jaywalkers, but given how reckless local driving can be, you'd do well to cross at corners and wait for pedestrian lights.

However, if you're prone to tummy trouble, stick to bottled water. Take standard flu-avoidance precautions such as handwashing and cough-covering, and consider contacting your doctor for a flu shot if you're traveling during the austral winter; Argentina was hit hard by the H1N1 outbreak of 2009.

OTHER ISSUES

Apunamiento, or altitude sickness, which results in shortness of breath and headaches, may be a problem when you visit high altitudes in the Andes. To remedy any discomfort, walk slowly, eat lightly, and drink plenty of fluids (avoid alcohol). In northwestern Argentina, coca leaves are widely available (don't worry, it's totally legal). Follow the locals' example and chew a wad mixed with a dab of bicarbonate of soda on hiking trips: it does wonders for altitude problems. You can also order tea made from coca leaves (*mate de coca*), which has the same effect. If you experience an extended period of nausea, dehydration, dizziness, or severe headache or weakness while in a high-altitude area, seek medical attention. Dehydration, sunstroke, frostbite, and heatstroke are all dangers of outdoor recreation at high altitudes. Awareness and caution are the best preventive measures.

The sun is a significant health hazard, especially in southern Patagonia, where the ozone layer is said to be thinning. Stay out of the sun at midday and wear plenty of good-quality sunblock. A limited selection is available in most supermarkets and pharmacies, but if you use high SPF factors or have sensitive skin, bring your favorite brands with you. A hat and decent sunglasses are also essential.

Health Warnings National Centers for Disease Control & Prevention (🌐 *www.cdc.gov/travel*). **World Health Organization** (*WHO* 🌐 *www.who.int*).

HEALTH CARE

Argentina has free national health care that also provides foreigners with free outpatient care. Although the medical practitioners working at *hospitales públicos* (public hospitals) are first-rate, the institutions themselves are often underfunded: bed space and basic supplies are at a minimum, and except in emergencies you should consider leaving these resources for the people who really need them. World-class private clinics and hospitals are plentiful, and consultation and treatment fees are low compared to those in North America. Still, it's good to have some kind of medical insurance.

In nonemergency situations you'll be seen much quicker at a private clinic or hospital, and overnight stays are more comfortable. Many doctors at private hospitals speak at least some English. Note that only cities have hospitals; smaller towns may have a *sala de primeros auxilios* (first-aid post), but you should try to get to a hospital as quickly as possible.

MEDICAL INSURANCE AND ASSISTANCE

Consider buying trip insurance with medical-only coverage. Neither Medicare nor some private insurers cover medical expenses anywhere outside of the United States. Medical-only policies typically reimburse you for medical care (excluding that related to preexisting conditions) and hospitalization abroad, and provide for evacuation. You still have to pay the bills and await reimbursement from the insurer.

Another option is to sign up with a medical-evacuation assistance company. Membership gets you doctor referrals, emergency evacuation or repatriation, 24-hour hotlines for medical consultation, and other assistance. International SOS Assistance Emergency and AirMed International provide evacuation services and medical referrals. MedjetAssist offers medical evacuation.

Medical Assistance Companies AirMed International (🌐 *www.airmed.com*). **International SOS Assistance Emergency** (🌐 *www.intsos.com*). **MedjetAssist** (🌐 *www.medjetassist.com*).

Medical-Only Insurers International Medical Group (☎ *800/628–4664* 🌐 *www.imglobal.com*). **International SOS** (🌐 *www.internationalsos.com*). **Wallach & Company** (☎ *800/237–6615 or 540/687–3166* 🌐 *www.wallach.com*).

OVER-THE-COUNTER REMEDIES

Towns and cities have a 24-hour pharmacy system: each night there's one *farmacia de turno* (on-duty pharmacy) for prescriptions and emergency supplies.

In Argentina, *farmacias* (pharmacies) carry painkillers, first-aid supplies, contraceptives, diarrhea treatments, and a range of other over-the-counter treatments, including drugs that would require a prescription in the United States (many antibiotics, for example). Note that acetominophen—or Tylenol—is known as *paracetamol* in Spanish. If you think you'll need to have prescriptions filled while you're in Argentina, be sure to have your doctor write down the generic name of the drug, not just the brand name.

HOLIDAYS

January through March is summer holiday season for Argentines. Winter holidays fall toward the end of July and beginning of August.

Año Nuevo (New Year's Day), January 1. **Día Nacional de la Memoria por la Verdad y la Justicia** (National Memory Day for Truth and Justice; commemoration of the start of the 1976–82 dictatorship), March 24. **Día del Veterano y de los Caídos en la Guerra de Malvinas** (Malvinas Veterans' Day), April 2. **Semana Santa** (Easter Week), March or April. **Día del Trabajador** (Labor Day), May 1. **Primer Gobierno Patrio** (First National Government, Anniversary of the 1810 Revolution), May 25. **Día de la Bandera** (Flag Day), June 20. **Día de la Independencia** (Independence Day), July 9. **Paso a la Inmortalidad del General José de San Martín** (Anniversary of General José de San Martín's Death), August 17. **Día de la Diversidad Cultural Americana** (Pan-American Cultural Diversity Day, formerly European Arrival in America), October 12. **Inmaculada Concepción de María** (Immaculate Conception), December 8. **Christmas,** December 25.

MAIL

Correo Argentino, the mail service, has an office in most neighborhoods; some *locutorios* (phone centers) serve as collection points and sell stamps. Mail delivery isn't dependable: it can take 6 to 21 days for standard letters and postcards to get to the United States. Regular airmail letters cost 4 pesos for up to 20 grams.

If you want to be sure something will arrive, send it by *correo certificado* (registered mail), which costs 10.75 pesos for up to 20 grams. Postboxes are dark blue and yellow, but there are very few that are not directly outside—or even inside—post offices. Valuable items are best sent with express services like DHL, UPS, or FedEx—delivery within one to two days for a 5-kilogram (11-pound) package starts at 550 pesos.

Argentina's post-code system is based on a four-digit code. Each province has been assigned a letter (the city of Buenos Aires is "C," for instance) that goes before the number code, and each city block is identified by three letters afterward (such as ABD). In practice, however, only big cities use these complete postal codes (which look like C1234ABD; the rest of Argentina uses the basic number code (1234, for example).

Contacts Correo Argentino (🌐 *www.correoargentino.com.ar*). **DHL** (🌐 *www.dhl.com*). **Federal Express** (🌐 *www.fedex.com*). **UPS** (🌐 *www.ups.com*).

MONEY

Although prices in Argentina have been steadily rising, traveling here is still fairly cheap if you're coming from a country with a strong currency. Eating out is very good value, as are mid-range hotels.

Prices are usually significantly lower outside Buenos Aires and other large cities. Room rates at first-class hotels all over the country approach those in the United States, however.

You can plan your trip around ATMs—cash is king for day-to-day dealings. U.S. dollars can be changed at any bank and are often accepted as payment in clothing and souvenir stores and supermarkets. Note that there's a perennial shortage of change. Hundred-peso bills can be hard to get rid of, so ask for 10s, 20s, and 50s when you change money and withdraw from ATMs. Traveler's checks are useful only as a reserve.

You can usually pay by credit card in top-end restaurants, hotels, and stores; the latter sometimes charge a small surcharge for using credit cards. Even stores displaying stickers from different card companies may suddenly stop accepting them: look out for signs reading tarjetas de crédito suspendidas (credit card purchases temporarily unavailable). Outside of big cities, plastic is less widely accepted.

Visa is the most widely accepted credit card, followed closely by MasterCard. American Express is also accepted in hotels and restaurants, but Diners Club and Discover might not even be recognized. If possible, bring more than one credit card, as some establishments accept only one type. Note that throughout this guide the following abbreviations are used: **AE,** American Express; **DC,** Diners Club; **MC,** MasterCard; and **V,** Visa.

Nonchain stores often display two prices for goods: *precio de lista* (the standard price, valid if you pay by credit card) and a discounted price if you pay in *efectivo* (cash). Many travel services and even some hotels also offer cash discounts—it's always worth asking about.

ITEM	AVERAGE COST
Cup of coffee and three medialunas (croissants)	7–10 pesos
Glass of wine	15–20 pesos
Liter bottle of local beer at a bar	12–18 pesos
Steak and fries in a cheap restaurant	20–25 pesos
One-mile taxi ride in Buenos Aires	3.80 pesos
Museum admission	Free–15 pesos

Prices throughout this guide are given for adults. Substantially reduced fees are almost always available for children, students, and senior citizens.

ATMS AND BANKS

ATMs, called *cajeros automáticos,* are found all over Buenos Aires. There are two main systems. Banelco, indicated by a burgundy-color sign with white lettering, is used by Banco Francés, HSBC, Banco Galicia, Banco Santander, and Banco Patagonia. Link, recognizable by a green-and-yellow sign, is the system used by Banco Provincia and Banco de la Nación, among others. Cards on the Cirrus and Plus networks can be used on both networks.

Many banks have daily withdrawal limits of 1,000 pesos or less. Sometimes ATMs will impose unexpectedly low withdrawal limits (say, 300 pesos) on international cards—this is more common on Banelco than Link machines. You can get around it by requesting a further transaction before the machine returns your card. **■ TIP→ Breaking large bills can be tricky, so try to withdraw change (for example, 490 pesos, rather than 500).** Make withdrawals from ATMs in daylight, rather than at night.

ATM Locations Banelco (🌐 *https://w3.banelco.com.ar*). **Link** (🌐 *www.redlink.com.ar*).

CURRENCY AND EXCHANGE

Argentina's currency is the peso, which equals 100 centavos. Bills come in denominations of 100 (violet), 50 (navy blue), 20 (red), 10 (ocher), 5 (green), and 2 (blue) pesos. Coins are in denominations of 1 peso (a heavy bimetallic coin); and 50, 25, 10, and 5 centavos. U.S. dollars are widely accepted in big-city stores, supermarkets, and at hotels and top-end restaurants (usually at a slightly worse exchange rate than you'd get at a bank). You always receive change in pesos, even when you pay with U.S. dollars. Taxi drivers may accept dollars, but it's not the norm.

At this writing, the exchange rate is 3.85 pesos to the U.S. dollar. You can change dollars at most banks (between 10 AM and 3 PM), at a *casa de cambio* (money changer), or at your hotel. All currency exchange involves fees, but as a rule banks charge the least and hotels the most. You need to show your passport to complete the transaction. **TIP→ You may not be able to change currency in rural areas at all, so don't leave major cities without adequate amounts of pesos in small denominations.**

Exchange-Rate Information Oanda.com (*www.oanda.com*). **XE.com** (*www.xe.com*).

PACKING

Argentinean city dwellers are an appearance-conscious bunch who choose fashion over comfort any day. But though locals are stylish, they're usually fairly casual. Your nicer jeans or khakis, capri pants, skirts, and dress shorts are perfect for urban sightseeing. Combine them with stylish walking shoes or leather flats; sneakers are fine if they're out-about-town and hip (no beat-up runners). In summer many local women seem to live in nice flip-flops or sandals. With the exception of truly posh establishments, a dirty look is usually the only punishment restaurants give the underdressed; refusing entry is almost unheard of. A jacket and tie or stylish dress are necessary only if you plan on some seriously fine dining.

In most smaller towns and villages, dress is more practical and sometimes more conservative. Wherever you go in the country, take good-quality sunglasses, sunblock, and a cap or hat: the sun can be strong. A good insect repellent is useful in Buenos Aires in the summer and invaluable in Iguazú year-round.

Temperatures rarely drop below freezing in the northern half of Argentina, including Buenos Aires, but a heavier coat or jacket is still a must in winter. Temperatures drop dramatically at night in the high-altitude towns of the northwest, so bring a jacket even in summer. Proper cold-weather gear is essential for visiting southern Patagonia year-round.

Pharmacies in major cities stock a good range of toiletries, including some international brands, and hygiene products (note that only no-applicator tampons are available, however). Pharmacies, supermarkets, and kiosks sell condoms (*preservativos*), and oral contraceptive pills are available over the counter.

Toilet paper is rare in public restrooms, but you can buy pocket packs of tissues (known as pañuelos descartables or by their brand name, *Carilinas*) in kiosks. Antibacterial wipes and alcohol gel, available in pharmacies, can make bathroom trips more pleasant in remote areas.

PASSPORTS

As of January 2010, Argentina has started charging a reciprocal entry fee for citizens of countries that charge Argentineans for visas. This includes U.S. citizens, who must pay $131 on entering Argentina and be carrying a passport valid for at least six months. The good news is that you only need pay the fee once every ten years and you can re-enter the country as many times as you like during that period for stays of up to 90 days—you'll receive a tourist visa stamp on your passport each time you arrive. If you need to stay longer, you can apply for a 90-day extension (*prórroga*) at the Dirección Nacional de

Migraciones (National Directorate for Migrations). The process takes a morning and costs about 200 pesos. Alternatively, you can exit the country (by taking a boat trip to Uruguay from Buenos Aires, or crossing into Brazil near Iguazú, for example); upon reentering Argentina, your passport will be stamped allowing an additional 90 days. Overstaying your tourist visa is illegal, and incurs a fine of $50, payable upon departure at the airport. If you do overstay your visa, plan to arrive at the airport several hours in advance of your flight so that you have ample time to take care of the fine. You should carry your passport or other photo ID with you at all times.

Officially, children visiting Argentina with only one parent do not need a signed and notarized permission-to-travel letter from the other parent to visit Argentina. However, as Argentine citizens *are* required to have such documentation, it's worth carrying a letter just in case laws change or border officials get confused. Single Parent Travel is a useful online resource that provides advice and downloadable sample permission letters.

For information on passport and visa requirements to visit the Brazilian side of Iguazú Falls, see the Planner pages at the start of Chapter 3, Side Trips from Buenos Aires.

Contacts Dirección Nacional de Migraciones (*Av. Antártida Argentina 1355, Buenos Aires* ☎ *11/4317–0237* *www.migraciones.gov.ar*). **Embassy of Argentina** (*www.embassyofargentina.us*). **Single Parent Travel** (*www.singleparenttravel.net*).

U.S. Passport Information U.S. Department of State (☎ *877/487–2778* *travel.state.gov/passport*).

SAFETY

CRIME

Attitude is essential: strive to look aware and purposeful at all times. Don't wear any jewelry you're not willing to lose. Even imitation jewelry and small items can attract attention and are best left behind. Keep a very firm hold of purses and cameras when out and about, and keep them on your lap in restaurants, not dangling off the back of your chair.

Always remain alert for pickpockets. Try to keep your cash and credit cards in different places, so that if one gets stolen you can fall back on the other. Tickets and other valuables are best left in hotel safes. Avoid carrying large sums of money around, but always keep enough to have something to hand over if you do get mugged. Another time-honored tactic is to keep a dummy wallet (an old one containing an expired credit card and a small amount of cash) in your pocket, with your real cash in an inside or vest pocket: if your "wallet" gets stolen you have little to lose.

It bears repeating to any female headed to Argentina for the first time: women can expect pointed looks, the occasional *piropo* (a flirtatious remark, usually alluding to some physical aspect), and some advances. These catcalls rarely escalate into actual physical harassment—the best reaction is to make like local girls and ignore it; reply only if you're really confident with Spanish curse words. Going to a bar alone will be seen as an open invitation for attention. If you're heading out for the night, it's wise to take a taxi.

In Buenos Aires there's a notable police presence in areas popular with tourists, such as San Telmo and Palermo, which seems to deter potential pickpockets and hustlers. However, Argentinians have little faith in their police forces: many officers are corrupt and involved in protection rackets or dealing in stolen goods. At best, the police are well meaning but under-equipped, so don't count on them to come to your rescue in a difficult situation. Reporting crimes is usually ineffectual, and is worth the time it takes only if you need the report for insurance.

The most important advice we can give you is to not put up a struggle in the unlikely event of being mugged or robbed. Nearly all physical attacks on tourists are the direct result of their resisting would-be pickpockets or muggers. Comply with demands, hand over your stuff, and try to get the situation over with as quickly as possible—then let your travel insurance take care of it.

PROTESTS

Argentines like to speak their minds, and there has been a huge increase in strikes and street protests since the economic crisis of 2001–02. Protesters frequently block streets and squares in downtown Buenos Aires, causing major traffic jams. Some are protesting government policies, others may be showing support for these. Either way, trigger-happy local police have historically proved themselves more of a worry than the demonstrators, but though protests are usually peaceful, exercise caution if you happen across one.

SCAMS

Beware scams such as a kindly passer-by offering to help you clean the mustard/ketchup/cream that has somehow appeared on your clothes: while your attention is occupied, an accomplice picks your pocket or snatches your bag.

Taxi drivers in big cities are usually honest, but occasionally they decide to take people for a ride, literally. All official cabs have meters, so make sure this is turned on. Some scam artists have hidden switches that make the meter tick over more quickly, but simply driving a circuitous route is a more common ploy. It helps to have an idea where you're going and how long it will take. Local lore says that, if hailing taxis on the street, those with lights on top (usually labeled RADIO TAXI) are more trustworthy. Late at night, try to call for a cab—all hotels and restaurants, no matter how cheap, have a number and will usually call for you.

When asking for price quotes when shopping in touristy areas, always confirm whether the price is in dollars or pesos. Some salespeople, especially street vendors, have found that they can take advantage of confused tourists by charging dollars for goods that are actually priced in pesos. If you're in doubt about that beautiful leather coat, don't be shy about asking if the number on the tag is in pesos or dollars.

Advisories and Other Information Transportation Security Administration (*TSA* *www.tsa.gov*). **U.S. Department of State** (*www.travel.state.gov*).

TAXES

Argentina has international and domestic departure taxes of $29 and $15.50, respectively. Both are usually included in your ticket price, but are otherwise payable by credit card or in cash at booths in airports in pesos, dollars, or euros. Hotel rooms carry a 21% tax. Cheaper hotels and hostels tend to include this in their quoted rates; more expensive hotels add it to your bill.

Argentina has 21% V.A.T. (known as IVA) on most consumer goods and services. The tax is usually included in the price of goods and noted on your receipt. You can get nearly all the IVA back on locally manufactured goods if you spend more than 70 pesos at stores displaying a duty-free sign. You're given a Global Refund check to the value of the IVA, which you get stamped by customs at the airport, and can then cash in at the clearly signed tax refund booths. Allow an extra hour to get this done.

Tax refunds Global Refund (*11/5238–1970* *www.globalrefund.com*).

TIME

Most of Argentina is three hours behind G.M.T., or three hours ahead of U.S. Central Standard Time. The exception is San Luis province, which is four hours behind G.M.T. Although Argentina does not currently observe daylight saving, it has in the past, so double-check time differences when you travel.

Time-Zone Information **Timeanddate.com** (🌐 *www.timeanddate.com/worldclock*).

TIPPING

Propinas (tips) are a question of rewarding good service rather than an obligation. Restaurant bills—even those that have a *cubierto* (bread and service charge)—don't include gratuities; locals usually add 10%. Bellhops and maids expect tips only in the very expensive hotels, where a tip in dollars is appreciated. You can also give a small tip (10% or less) to tour guides. Porteños round off taxi fares, though some cabbies who frequent hotels popular with tourists seem to expect more. Tipping is a nice gesture with beauty and barbershop personnel—5%–10% is fine.

TIPPING GUIDELINES FOR ARGENTINA	
Bellhop at top-end hotels	$1–$5 per bag, depending on the level of the hotel
Hotel maid at top-end hotels	1$–$3 a day (either daily or at the end of your stay, in cash)
Hotel room-service waiter	$1 to $2 per delivery, even if a service charge has been added
Taxi driver	10%, or round up the fare to the next full peso amount
Tour guide	10% of the cost of the tour if service was good
Waiter	10%–15%, depending on service
Restroom attendants	Small change, such as 50¢ or 1 peso.

TRIP INSURANCE

Comprehensive trip insurance is valuable if you're booking a very expensive or complicated trip (particularly to an isolated region) or if you're booking far in advance. Comprehensive policies typically cover trip-cancellation and interruption, letting you cancel or cut your trip short because of a personal emergency, illness, or, in some cases, acts of terrorism in your destination. Such policies also cover evacuation and medical care. (For trips abroad you should at least have medical-only coverage; for more information, ⇨ *see Medical Insurance & Assistance under Health, above*). Some also cover you for trip delays because of bad weather or mechanical problems as well as for lost or delayed baggage.

Another type of coverage to look for is financial default—that is, when your trip is disrupted because a tour operator, airline, or cruise line goes out of business. Generally you must buy this when you book your trip or shortly thereafter, and it's available to you only if your operator isn't on a list of excluded companies.

Always read the fine print of your policy to make sure that you are covered for the risks that are of most concern to you. Compare several policies to make sure you're getting the best price and range of coverage available.

Insurance Comparison Sites **Insure My Trip.com** (☎ *800/487–4722* 🌐 *www.insuremytrip.com*). **Square Mouth.com** (☎ *800/240–0369 or 727/490–5803* 🌐 *www.squaremouth.com*).

Comprehensive Travel Insurers **Access America** (☎ *866/729–6021* 🌐 *www.accessamerica.com*). **AIG Travel Guard** (☎ *800/826–4919* 🌐 *www.travelguard.com*). **CSA Travel Protection** (☎ *800/873–9855* 🌐 *www.csatravelprotection.com*). **HTH Worldwide** (☎ *610/254–8700* 🌐 *www.hthworldwide.com*). **Travelex Insurance** (☎ *888/228–9792* 🌐 *www.travelex-insurance.com*). **Travel Insured International** (☎ *800/243–3174* 🌐 *www.travelinsured.com*).

VISITOR INFORMATION

All major cities and most smaller tourist destinations have tourist offices that can provide information on accommodation and sightseeing and maps. The quality of these varies according to local funding, but employees are usually friendly and helpful. The city of Buenos Aires has tourist information booths around the city and an excellent Web site. Each Argentine province also operates a tourist office in Buenos Aires, usually called the *Casa de [Province Name] en Buenos Aires*. The government umbrella organization for all regional and city-based tourist offices is the *Secretaría de Turismo* (Secretariat of Tourism). Their no-frills Web site has links and addresses to these offices, and lots of other practical information.

Limited tourist information is also available at Argentina's embassy and consulates in the United States.

Contacts Argentina (Official Web Portal) (🌐 *www.argentina.ar*). **Argentine Secretariat of Tourism** (☎ *800/555–0016 in Argentina* 🌐 *www.turismo.gov.ar*). **Dirección de Turismo del Gobierno de la Ciudad de Buenos Aires (Turismo Buenos Aires)** (☎ *0800/999–2838 in Argentina* 🌐 *www.bue.gov.ar*). **Embassy of Argentina** (🌐 *www.embassyofargentina.us*).

ONLINE RESOURCES

The like-minded travelers on Fodors.com are eager to answer questions and swap travel tales. The regional information and downloadable maps on slick government-run Argentina Travel Web site are a great pre-trip planning resource. Its sister site, Argentina.ar has excellent general information on different aspects of Argentine culture, studying and investing in the country, and helpful travel tips. Welcome Argentina has good overviews of Argentina's different regions.

The Web site of the *Buenos Aires Herald*, the city's English-language daily, gives a conservative take on major local news stories. Brief but often amusing commentaries on local news and cultural events are at The Argentine Post. The Web site of English-language monthly newspaper *The Argentimes* has traveler-oriented news and cultural information. *What's Up Buenos Aires is* a slick bilingual guide, run by American expats, to contemporary culture and partying in the city.

The Museo Nacional de Bellas Artes contains the world's biggest collection of Argentine art, and has lots of background on Argentine artists. Festival de Tango, the official tango site of the Buenos Aires city government, has lots of practical information and listings of classes and events. Todo Tango is an excellent bilingual tango site with tango lyrics, history, and free downloads.

Bilingual Wines of Argentina is overflowing with information about Argentina's best tipple. Mate Argentino has everything you wanted to know about mate (a type of tea) but were afraid to ask, but in Spanish only. Saltshaker, American food writer Dan Perlman's blog, is packed with insight on local cooking, restaurants, and ingredients.

All About Argentina Argentina (Official Web Portal) (🌐 *www.argentina.ar*). **Argentine Secretariat of Tourism** (🌐 *www.turismo.gov.ar*). **Argentina Travel** (🌐 *www.argentina.travel*). **Embassy of Argentina** (🌐 *www.embassyofargentina.us*). **Fodors.com** (🌐 *www.fodors.com/forums*). **Welcome Argentina** (🌐 *www.welcomeargentina.com.ar*).

Culture and Entertainment Festival de Tango (🌐 *www.festivaldetango.gob.ar*). **Museo Nacional de Bellas Artes** (🌐 *www.mnba.org.ar*). **Todo Tango** (🌐 *www.todotango.com.ar*). **What's Up Buenos Aires** (🌐 *www.whatsupbuenosaires.com*).

Food and Drink Argentine Wines (🌐 *www.argentinewines.com*). **Mate Argentino** (🌐 *www.mateargentino.com*). **Saltshaker** (🌐 *www.saltshaker.net*). **Wines of Argentina** (🌐 *www.winesofargentina.org*).

Media The Argentine Post (🌐 *www.argentinepost.com*). **The Argentimes** (🌐 *www.theargentimes.com*). **Buenos Aires Herald** (🌐 *www.buenosairesherald.com*).

INDEX

A

B

Photo Credits: 1, Ignacio Alvarez/age fotostock. 2, Sara Nixon, fodors.com member. 5, ARCO/P. Wegner/age fotostock. **Chapter 1: Experience Argentina:** 8-9, Andrew Mirhej, fodors.com member. 10 (top), jd_miller, fodors.com member. 10 (center), M. Scanel, fodors.com member. 10 (bottom), Andrew Mirhej, fodors.com member. 14, Tony Morrison/South American Pictures. 15 (left), Jacynth Roode/iStockphoto. 15 (right), berhbs, fodors.com member. 16 (left), pdqu2, fodors.com member. 16 (top center), Tokyo Tanenhaus/Flickr. 16 (bottom center), feserc/Flickr. 16 (right), fortes/Flickr. 17 (left), iStockphoto. 17 (top center), Clive Ellston, fodors.com member. 17 (bottom center), rm/Shutterstock. 17 (right), iladm/Shutterstock. 18, Andy Christodolo/Cephas Picture Library/Alamy. 19, Popperphoto/Alamy. 20, Brand X Pictures. 21 (left), AFP PHOTO/ALI BURAFI/Newscom. 21 (right), Juanderlust, fodors.com member. 22, Diego_3336/Flickr. 24, Galina Barskaya/Shutterstock. 26, Pablo Caridad/iStockphoto. 28, MIMOHE/Shutterstock. 29 (left), Image Asset Management/age fotostock. 29 (right), José Francisco Ruiz/age fotostock. 30 (left), Eduardo M. Rivero/age fotostock. 30 (bottom right), Jordi Camí/age fotostock. 31 (right), Apeiron-Photo/Alamy. 32 (left and top right), A.H.C./age fotostock. 32 (bottom right), Pictorial Press Ltd/Alamy. 33 (top left), wikipedia.org. 33 (bottom left), Roger Bamber/Alamy. 33 (top right), Tramonto/age fotostock. 33 (bottom right), Griffiths911/wikipedia.org. 34 (left), Christopher Pillitz/Alamy. 34 (top right), AFP Photos/Newscom. 34 (bottom right), DYN/Getty Images/Newscom. 35 (top), Roberto Fiadone/wikipedia.org. 35 (bottom left), wikipedia.org. 36, Flickr. **Chapter 2: Buenos Aires:** 37, Dan Leffel/age fotostock. 38, Christine Yuan, fodors.com member. 39 (top), EL UNIVERSAL/Newscom. 39 (bottom), Seamus, fodors.com member. 42, caron malecki, fodors.com member. 45, lilap/Flickr. 46, blmurch/Flickr. 50-51, iStockphoto. 55, James Wong, fodors.com member. 57, Alvaro Leiva/age fotostock. 61, Dan DeLuca/wikipedia.org. 64, caron malecki, fodors.com member. 66, giulio andreini/age fotostock. 71, wabauer, fodors.com member. 73, Beth/Queen/ZUMA Press/Newscom. 74-75, Jose Fuste Raga/age fotostock. 76, Wim Wiskerke/Alamy 80, Church of emacs/wikipedia.org. 85, Martin Byrne, fodors.com member. 92, GUY Christian/age fotostock. 97 (top), The Leading Hotels of the World. 97 (bottom left), Hyatt Hotels & Resorts. 97 (bottom right), Moreno Buenos Aires. 100, Christopher Pillitz/Alamy. 104, 2litros > raimundo illanes/Flickr. 107, Ernesto Ríos Lanz/age fotostock. 108, wikipedia.org. 109, eyalos.com/Shutterstock. 110 (top), *Picture Contact/Alamy*. 110 (2nd from top), *Christina Wilson/Alamy*. 110 (3rd from top), *Michel Friang/Alamy*. 110 (bottom), *Jason Howe/South American Pictures*. 111 (top), Archivo General de la Nación/wikipedia.org. 111 (bottom), Danita Delimont/Alamy. 112, christina wilson/Alamy. 116, Pablo Abuliak. 121, Jon Hicks/Alamy. **Chapter 3: Side Trips:** 123, David Lyons/Alamy. 124, Dario Diament/Shutterstock. 125 (top), Woodward Chile/Flickr. 125 (bottom), Carla Antonini/Wikimedia Commons. 126, brianmka/Flickr. 128, Heather Scott, fodors.com member. 129, Pablodda/Flickr. 131, Alberto/Flickr. 138, Juergen Richter/age fotostock. 150-151, *Jeremy Hoare/Alamy*. 152, *Chris Sharp/South American Pictures*. 153, *Pablo D. Flores*. 154, *Jeremy Hoare/Alamy*. 155, *SuperStock*. 156 (top), *Hughes/age fotostock*. 156 (bottom), *Johannes Odland/Shutterstock*. 161, sbassi/Flickr. 166, ricald/Flickr. 172, Pablodda/Flickr. 179, Ken Welsh/age fotostock. 180, Gerad Coles/iStockphoto. 181, Sue Cunningham Photographic/Alamy. 182-83, Fritz Poelking/age fotostock. 182 (inset), Albasmalko/wikipedia.org. 183 (inset), flavia bottazzini/iStockphoto. 184, travelstock44/Alamy. 185, vittorio sciosia/age fotostock. **Chapter 4: Córdoba and Environs:** 191, longhorndave/Flickr. 192 (left), iStockphoto. 192 (right), Avodrocc/Flickr.

193, Analia Valeria Urani/Shutterstock. 196, thoron/Shutterstock. 197 (top), Dario Alpern/wikipedia.org. 197 (bottom), Claudio Elias/wikipedia.org. 198, Beatrice Murch/Flickr. 202, Reinhard Kliem/age fotostock. 205, Nacho Calonge/age fotostock. 212, ARCO/Therin-Weise/age fotostock. 217, Emiliano Rodriguez/Alamy. 220, David/wikipedia.org. 227, Emiliano Rodriguez/Alamy. **Chapter 5: The Northwest:** 231, Fabian von Poser/age fotostock. 232, JOSE ALBERTO TEJO/Shutterstock. 233 (top), Colman Lerner Gerardo/Shutterstock. 233 (bottom), Alicia Nijdam/Flickr. 235, Javier Vidal Postigo/Flickr. 236, Ignacio Alvarez/age fotostock. 237 (top), B. Hennings, Nürnberg, Germany/wikipedia.org. 237 (bottom), Alicia Nijdam/wikipedia.org. 238, Heeb Christian/age fotostock. 239 (top), Jorge Pedro Barradas de Casais/Shutterstock. 239 (bottom), irina bazhanova/iStockphoto. 240, Guerretto/Flickr. 243, Ignacio Alvarez/age fotostock. 248-49, Wolfgang Herzog/age fotostock. 250, WYSOCKI Pawel/age fotostock. 251 (top), Walter Bibikow/age fotostock. 251 (bottom), borderlys/Flickr. 252-53, ARCO/Therin-Weise/age fotostock. 254 (top), Clive Ellston, fodors.com member. 254 (bottom), Joris Van Ostaeyen/iStockphoto. 255 (top), Lee Torrens/Shutterstock. 255 (bottom), Humawaka/wikipedia.org. 256, Ignacio Alvarez/age fotostock. 258, Clive Ellston, fodors.com member. 263, Angel Manzano/age fotostock. 268, Nacho Calonge/age fotostock. 273, ARCO/Stengert, N/age fotostock. 278, GM Photo Images/Alamy. 283, Heeb Christian/age fotostock. 290, JTB Photo/age fotostock. 297, Ignacio Alvarez/age fotostock. 300, Heeb Christian/age fotostock. 303, Ignacio Alvarez/age fotostock. **Chapter 6: Wine Regions:** 305, David Noton Photography/Alamy. 306, CASA DEL VISITANTE Familia Zuccardi, Mendoza. 307 (top), iStockphoto. 307 (bottom), dubonnet, fodors.com member. 310, Jason Maehl/Shutterstock. 311 (top), José Carlos Pires Pereira/iStockphoto. 311 (bottom), fainmen/Flickr. 312, CASA DEL VISITANTE Familia Zuccardi, Mendoza. 318, Heeb Christian/age fotostock. 324-25, Cephas Picture Library/Alamy. 328, Yadid Levy/age fotostock. 333, Luc./Flickr. 338-39, Bon Appetit/Alamy. 338 (bottom), Dizzy/Alamy. 340 (top), Douglas Peebles/Stock Connection/Aurora Photos. 340 (2nd from top), Clay McLachlan/Aurora Photos. 340 (3rd from top), WinePix/Alamy. 340 (bottom), Karen Ward/South American Pictures. 341 (top), Pablo Abuliak. 341 (2nd from top), John and Brenda Davenport, fodors.com member. 341 (3rd from top), Pablo Abuliak. 341 (bottom), matetic.com. 343 (top), Pablo Abuliak. 343 (center), CASA DEL VISITANTE Familia Zuccardi, Mendoza. 343 (bottom), Mark Surman/Flickr. 344, Tony Morrison/South American Pictures. 355, Pablo Abuliak. 365, Andre Charland from Canada/wikipedia.org. 372, Jason Maehl/Shutterstock. **Chapter 7: The Lake District:** 377, Arco Images GmbH/Alamy. 378 (top), rm/Shutterstock. 378 (center), Sam Chadwick/Shutterstock. 378 (bottom), Rafael Franceschini/Shutterstock. 379 (top), ricardo.martins/Flickr. 379 (bottom), JOSE ALBERTO TEJO/Shutterstock. 382, FLPA/Krystyna Szuleck/age fotostock. 383 (top), Greg Cooper/iStockphoto. 383 (bottom), wikipedia.org. 384, HappyTrvlr, fodors.com member. 385 (top), Josh Roe, fodors.com member. 385 (bottom), ArielMartin/Shutterstock. 386, Alfonsitomaria/wikipedia.org, 393, Yadid Levy/age fotostock. 396, Walter Bibikow/age fotostock. 402-03, hdcaplan, fodors.com member. 406-07, Diana Proemm/age fotostock. 408, Karl Weatherly/age fotostock. 410, David Kleyn/Alamy. 415, Jason Friend/Alamy. 420, Walter Bibikow/age fotostock. 424, Heeb Christian/age fotostock. 429, ImageState/Alamy. **Chapter 8: Patagonia:** 431, R. Matina/age fotostock. 432, David Thyberg/Shutterstock. 433 (top), Gerad Coles/iStockphoto. 433 (bottom), Pablo H Caridad/Shutterstock. 436, A Maywald/age fotostock. 437 (top), Eduardo Rivero/Shutterstock. 437 (bottom), Pablo H Caridad/Shutterstock. 438, Karen Coleman, fodors.com member. 443, Gareth McCormack/Alamy. 444, WYSOCKI Pawel/age fotostock. 445, Gareth McCormack/Alamy. 446, Colin Monteath/age fotostock. 447, Galen Rowell/Mountain Light/Alamy. 448 (top), Jan Baks/Alamy. 448 (bottom), Heeb Christian/age fotostock. 449, Peter Essick/Aurora Photos. 450 (left), Laura Hart/Shutterstock. 450 (top center), Michael S. Nolan/age fotostock. 450 (top right), jan.kneschke/Flickr. 450 (bottom right), ARCO/P. Wegner/age fotostock. 451 (top left), Danita Delimont/Alamy. 451 (bottom left), Derek Dammann/iStockphoto. 451 (bottom center), iStockphoto. 451 (top right), David R. Frazier Photolibrary, Inc./Alamy. 451 (bottom right), David Ryan/Alamy. 456, Michael S. Nolan/age fotostock. 463, Juan Carlos Muñoz/age fotostock. 468, paul bridgewater - www.londonmusicphotographer.com/Flickr. 472, Heeb Christian/age fotostock. 476, Raymond Forbes/age fotostock. 481, Anna Hainze, fodors.com member. 488, Tony West/Alamy. 491, Lois Zebelman, fodors.com member. 496, Michele Molinari/Alamy. 501, José Fuste Raga/age fotostock. 506, Marco Simoni/age fotostock. 513, Colin Monteath/age fotostock. 518, Dave Houser/age fotostock. 523, Danny Aeberhard/South American Pictures.

NOTES

NOTES

ABOUT OUR WRITERS

Eddy Ancinas, one of the authors of the first edition of *Fodor's Argentina,* updated the Wine Regions and Lake District chapters for this edition. She met an Argentine ski racer at the 1960 Winter Olympics; after they married, they lived in Bariloche, Argentina. Since then, Eddy has returned frequently to write about travel in Argentina, Peru, and Chile, and to lead ski and horseback trips.

Brian Byrnes (www.brianbyrnes.com), who updated the Buenos Aires Where to Eat and Where to Stay sections, lives in that city, where he reports in print, on air, and online for media outlets like CBS News, *Newsweek* magazine, CNN, *The Hollywood Reporter,* Fodors.com, and others. He first arrived in Argentina in 2001 to update the Patagonia chapter of *Fodor's Argentina,* and has worked on every edition of the guide since. He's married to a *porteña* and has a young son, to whom he is teaching the ways of the Argentine *asado* (barbecue).

Northwest chapter updater **Andy Footner**, who also worked on the After Dark section in Buenos Aires, completed a degree in philosophy at Leeds, gained office experience in London, started a record company in Sofia, Bulgaria, and edited *Time Out Istanbul* magazine in Turkey and a guidebook in Rio de Janeiro. He came to South America with his Patagonian wife, with whom he produced a documentary about a woman's gym in Iraq. They're now living in Buenos Aires, writing stories from the country and the continent, and dreaming up new projects.

Nicholas Gill (www.nicholas-gill.com), who updated the Adventure Vacations chapter, is a food and travel writer and photographer based in both Lima, Peru, and New York City. He has authored and contributed to numerous guidebooks on Latin America, and his work appears in publications such as *Islands, World Hum*, *The Columbus Dispatch,* and *Sherman's Travel.*

Rick Hind updated the Southern Patagonia portion of our Patagonia chapter. Two years ago he left behind reporting cyclones and crocodiles in Darwin for Australia's public broadcaster and moved with his partner Anna to Lima. He's led hiking groups in the Peruvian Alps, rafted down the wild Apurimac River, trekked through the flooded forests of the Amazon, and popped the question in Mendoza, the South American city that most resembles Alice Springs.

Although **Victoria Patience** grew up in Hong Kong, crowded buses and cranky old cars have taken her thousands of miles through Latin America over the last decade. Buenos Aires—first the city, then the province—has been her home for nine years. This served her well during her work on the Buenos Aires Exploring and Shopping sections, as well as on the Experience Argentina, Side Trips from Buenos Aires, and Travel Smart chapters. She also updated our Atlantic Patagonia sections. Victoria's first degree was in Hispanic Studies at the University of London, and her ongoing fascination with Latin American literature and culture came in handy when she penned the features "The Dance of Buenos Aires," "The Cowboy's at the World's End," "A Passionate History," and "Iguazú Falls." She's a freelance contributor to many Fodor's guidebooks and also runs her own translation company, www.nativawordcraft.com.